CANADA
BUSINESS

WORLD TRADE PRESS
PUBLICATIONS

General References

Importers Manual USA
Exporting to the USA
World Trade Almanac
A Basic Guide to Exporting
Dictionary of International Trade
Services: the Export of the 21st Century
Global Road Warrior

Country Business Guides

ARGENTINA Business   KOREA Business
AUSTRALIA Business   MEXICO Business
CANADA Business   PHILIPPINES Business
CHINA Business   SINGAPORE Business
HONG KONG Business   TAIWAN Business
JAPAN Business   USA Business

Passport to the World Series (Business Culture)

Passport CHINA   Passport KOREA
Passport FRANCE   Passport MEXICO
Passport GERMANY   Passport PHILIPPINES
Passport HONG KONG   Passport SPAIN
Passport INDIA   Passport TAIWAN
Passport INDONESIA   Passport THAILAND
Passport ISRAEL   Passport UNITED KINGDOM
Passport ITALY   Passport USA
Passport JAPAN   Passport VIETNAM

CD-ROMs

Importers Manual USA CD-ROM
Exporting to the USA CD-ROM
World Trade Almanac CD-ROM

CANADA BUSINESS

The Portable Encyclopedia For Doing Business With Canada

Janet Whittle Joe Reif
Alexandra Woznick Karla Shippey, J.D.
James L. Nolan, Ph.D. Edward G. Hinkelman

Molly Thurmond, J.D.   Christopher Mahon   David L. Gold
Kristin Schwaighart   Peter Levy   Kathy Johnson
Andrew Grzeskowiak   Maria Sundeen

International Monetary Fund
Ernst & Young • International Chamber of Commerce
Colliers International • CIGNA Property and Casualty
Reed Publishing (USA) Inc. • Magellan Geographix
Statistics Canada

WORLD TRADE PRESS

Resources for International Trade

1505 Fifth Avenue
San Rafael, California 94901
USA

Published by World Trade Press
1505 Fifth Avenue
San Rafael, CA 94901, USA
Tel: (415) 454-9934
Fax: (415) 453-7980
USA Orderline: (800) 833-8586
E-mail: WorldPress@aol.com

Cover and book design: Brad Greene and Peter G. Jones
Illustrations: Eli Africa
Maps: Magellan^{sm} Geographix
Desktop design and publishing: Peter G. Jones and Joe Reif
Charts and graphs: Joe Reif

Copyright © 1997 by Edward G. Hinkelman. All rights reserved.
No part of this book may be reproduced, transmitted, stored in a retrieval system, or copied in any manner whatsoever without prior written permission of the copyright holder, except in the case of brief quotations embodied in articles and reviews with full credit given to this publication. For information contact the publisher.

The name *World Trade Press* and the representation of the world map imprinted on an open book appearing in this publication are trademarks and the property of Edward G. Hinkelman.

Permission to reprint copyrighted materials has been given to *World Trade Press* as follows: Excerpts from *1995 Worldwide Corporate Tax Guide* and *1994 Worldwide Personal Tax Guide*, copyright © 1995, 1994 by Ernst & Young, reprinted with permission of Ernst & Young. Excerpts from "Canada Law Digest," *Martindale-Hubbell International Law Digest*, copyright © 1995, by Reed Publishing (USA) Inc., reproduced in abridged version with permission of Reed Publishing (USA) Inc. Canadian exchange requirements from *Exchange Arrangements and Exchange Restrictions Annual Report 1994*, copyright © 1994 International Monetary Fund, reprinted with permission of the IMF. Excerpts from *CIGNA Ports of the World* (15th ed.), copyright © 1994 CIGNA Property and Casualty Co., reprinted with permission from CIGNA Property and Casualty Companies.

Library of Congress Cataloging-in-Publication Data

Canada Business: the portable encyclopedia for doing business with
    Canada / Janet Whittle... [et al.].
p. cm. – (World Trade Press country business guides)
Includes bibliographical references and index.
ISBN 1-885073-13-5 (trade paper)
1. Canada–Economic conditions–1991- 2. Canada–Economic policy.
3. Investments, Foreign–Government policy–Canada.
4. International business enterprises –Canada. 5. Business law-
-Canada. I. Whittle, Janet, 1971- . II. Series.
HC115.C1984 1997
330.971.–DC20

Printed in the United States of America

ACKNOWLEDGMENTS

We owe many leaders in the international business community a debt of gratitude. Hundreds of trade and reference experts have brought this book to life. We are indebted to numerous international business consultants; reference librarians; travel advisors; consulate, embassy, and trade mission officers; bank officers; attorneys; global shippers and insurers; and multinational investment brokers who answered our incessant inquiries and volunteered facts, figures, and expert opinions. To all these many individuals, named and unnamed, we extend our thanks.

This publication would not have been possible without the professional talents of many researchers, authors, and editors. Special acknowledgment goes to Research Services at Statistics Canada in Vancouver, BC for supplying current statistical information and a wide range of materials on the Canadian economy, business, industries, and investment. A special thanks also to Michel Perrotte at Info Expo for his help with the Trade Fair information.

We relied heavily on the reference librarians and resources available at the libraries of the University of California at Berkeley, San Francisco Public Library, San Rafael Public Library, Marin County Civic Center Library, and Marin County Law Library. Of particular note, reference librarian Gail Lockman at the San Rafael Public Library has always been a most willing accomplice in research.

Molly Thurmond, J.D. researched and wrote several chapters for this book, including currency and foreign exchange, foreign trade, labor, and trade agreements. Legal author Kristin Schwaighart provided the information on business law and business entities and formation in Canada. Andrew Grzeskowiak clarifies and explains the various requirements and procedures involved in Canadian importing and exporting, while Christopher Mahon delves into Canadian industries and opportunities. Investment manager David Gold (Transamerica Investment Services, Los Angeles) analyzed oceans of data on Canadian foreign investment requirements and financial institutions to come up with the practical basics.

Peter Levy compiled information on Canadian travel and business culture. Author Maria Sundeen sifted through the seemingly straightforward, but sometimes complex, elements of Canadian markets. The special research and analytical skills of Kathy Johnson were essential to compiling the trade fair materials.

For reprint permissions, we found helpful allies in Cassie Arnold (Ernst & Young, San Francisco office); Kenneth Young (Publications Services, International Monetary Fund); Steve Fahrbach, Doug Crawford, and Rick Wood (Magellan^{sm} Geographix); and Barry Tarneff (CIGNA Property and Casualty Co.).

DISCLAIMER

We have diligently tried to ensure the accuracy of all of the information in this publication and to present as comprehensive a reference work as space would permit. In determining the contents, we were guided by many experts in the field, extensive hours of research, and our own experience. However, we did have to make choices in coverage, because the inclusion of everything one could ever want to know about international trade would be impossible. The fluidity and fast pace of today's business world makes the task of keeping data current and accurate an extremely difficult one. This publication is intended to give you the information that you need in order to discover the information that is most useful for your particular business. As you contact the resources within this book, you will no doubt learn of new and exciting business opportunities and of additional international trading requirements that have arisen even within the short time since we published this edition. If errors are found, we will strive to correct them in preparing future editions. The publishers take no responsibility for inaccurate or incomplete information that may have been submitted to them in the course of research for this publication. The facts published are the result of those inquiries, and no warranty as to their accuracy is given.

Contents

Chapter 1	Canada at a Glance	1
Chapter 2	Economy	7
Chapter 3	Current Issues	19
Chapter 4	Opportunities	27
Chapter 5	Foreign Investment	43
Chapter 6	Foreign Trade	51
Chapter 7	Trade Agreements	63
Chapter 8	Import Policy & Procedures	73
Chapter 9	Export Policy & Procedures	85
Chapter 10	Industry Reviews	97
Chapter 11	Trade Fairs	111
Chapter 12	Business Travel	137
Chapter 13	Business Culture	153
Chapter 14	Demographics	163
Chapter 15	Marketing	169
Chapter 16	Business Entities & Formation	183
Chapter 17	Labor	195
Chapter 18	Business Law	207
Chapter 19	Financial Institutions	223
Chapter 20	Currency & Foreign Exchange	235
Chapter 21	International Payments	239
Chapter 22	Taxation	255
Chapter 23	Transportation & Communications	267
Chapter 24	Important Addresses	285
	Index	301

Canada at a Glance

In a Nutshell The Canadian economy is the seventh-largest among the western industrialized nations. There has been a significant and steady shift from the production of goods toward an emphasis on services. Canada has recovered from the recession of the early 1980s and the economy grew by 4.6 percent in 1994, the best performance in six years. The country still faces economic problems, however. Unemployment rates are high, exports have slowed substantially, and interest rates have risen. Nevertheless, the economy is open, competitive, and outwardly focused. The North American Free Trade Agreement should help Canada's economy grow even further.

The service sector represents more than 55 percent of the economy. The manufacturing, construction, and utility sectors follow, with a combined 30 percent share. The largest manufacturing industries include transportation equipment, pulp and paper, and wood products. The automotive industry is among Canada's strongest sector for exports. Mining and energy sectors make up about 10 percent of the economy. The agriculture sector is smaller but still important with five percent of the economy. Canada accounts for about 20 percent of the world wheat trade, is the world's leading newsprint producer, and ranks among the leaders in other forestry products, as well.

OPPORTUNITIES

For buyers: Canada offers a range of goods, from agricultural and manufacturing goods to advanced technological products.

For sellers: There is a heavy concentration of imports in the industrial sector, including machinery, transport equipment, and consumer goods. Despite its proximity and cultural similarities to the United States, Canada is a unique marketplace with its own needs and desires.

For manufacturers: Canada offers a well educated workforce, and labor at all skill levels is generally available. There are, however, higher taxes and more regulations than in many other developed nations.

For investors: Canada has long been considered a stable and open environment for foreign investment, and foreign investors receive full national treatment within the context of a developed open market economy. There is, however, a formal investment review process (Canada is one of the few OECD countries that still has such a process), and foreign investment is restricted in several sectors of the economy.

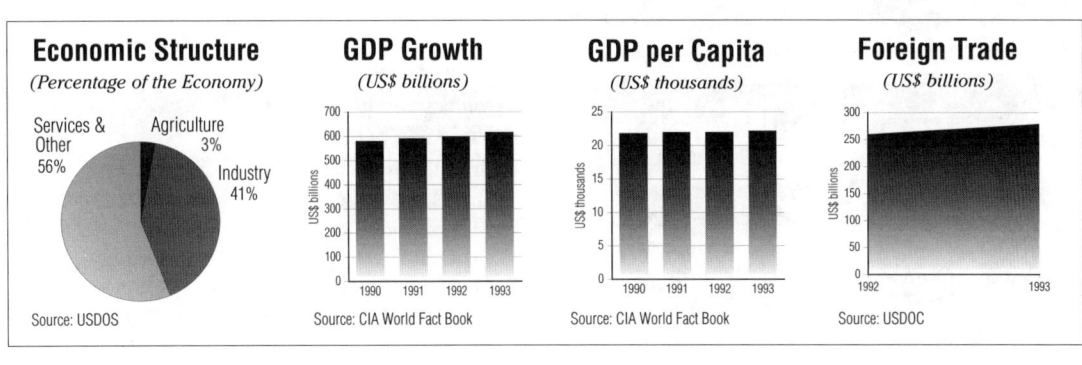

TEN REASONS FOR DOING BUSINESS IN CANADA:

1. Canada is very open to foreign investment, and for most small acquisitions and business establishments, foreign investors need only notify the Canadian government of their investment.

2. There is a trained and well-educated workforce. Canada spends an amount equal to 7 percent of its total GDP on education, and over 75 percent of students at the secondary education level go on to higher institutions (the highest percentage in the industrialized world).

3. Canada offers nearly free access to markets in the United States and Mexico because of NAFTA.

4. A broad and rich resource base is available, providing raw materials for manufacturing and massive cheap energy.

5. The 29 million citizens provide an affluent market for modern consumer products. Computers and other technological products are very popular.

6. Canada's infrastructure is modern and advanced. Railroads connect the vast north, and air services are modern and efficient. The main transportation venue is cheap water transportation throughout the Great Lakes-Saint Lawrence Seaway system.

7. Canada is one of the world's most technologically advanced countries. There are over 18 million telephones, 900 radio stations (both FM and AM), and 50 television stations throughout the country.

8. Canada is a country of enormous agricultural resources. It is the world's largest exporter of forest products and a top exporter of fish, furs, and wheat.

9. New techniques and materials make winter construction work more practical despite the cold weather.

10. Canada has become a major trading partner with the countries of Southeast Asia. Trade across the Pacific is now 65 percent greater than Atlantic trade.

Climate

Canada's climate has a full range of temperatures, from sub-polar in the north to cool in the south. The interior usually has colder and longer winters than the coasts, with temperatures well below freezing. The Pacific Coast has the warmest winters, with temperatures rarely falling below zero.

The northern territories, particularly the Yukon, have long hours of sunshine during the summer months, sometimes more than 20 hours a day. Conversely, in the winter daylight hours are very short. Despite the long summer days, permafrost and unpredictable killing frosts severely hamper extensive agriculture.

People

Languages
Official: English and French

Literacy
97 percent

Government
Executive: Queen Elizabeth II (head of state represented by a governor general), Prime Minister and Cabinet.
Legislative: Parliament (112 member Senate, 295 member House of Commons).
Judicial: Supreme Court.
Political Parties: Liberal, Bloc Quebecois, Reform, New Democratic, Progressive Conservative.

Population Distribution
More than 65% of the population still lives in the Great Lakes-St. Lawrence Lowlands, which covers less than five percent of the country.
1993 average density: 2.9 persons per sq km

Religion
Roman Catholic: 46%
Other: 28%
United Church: 16%
Anglican: 10%
source: Nations of the World

Ethnic Makeup
British origin: 40%
French origin: 27%
Other European: 20%
Other: 9%
Aboriginal Peoples of Canada: 4%
Source: Nations of the World

CANADA AT A GLANCE

Yukon
Much of the Yukon is mountainous and very cold. The yearly average temperatures are usually below the freezing mark. Because of the extreme northern position, summers are characterized by long hours of sunlight, sometimes more than 20 hours a day. Adversely, winter daylight hours are very short. Most food is imported because of the extensive frost year round.

Northwest Territories
Covering 1.3 million square miles, or one-third of Canada, the Northwest Territories contain only a little over 57,000 people. In 1992, over 135,000 square miles of land was given to the Inuit Indians, and in 1999, this land will become the self-governing Nunavut Territory.

Canada stretches from the Atlantic to Pacific Ocean, across five time zones, and is divided into ten provinces and two territories. The interior lowlands around the Hudson Bay make up about 80 percent of the land area. Canada's main rivers—the St. Lawrence, Yukon, Mackenzie, and Fraser—are among the world's 40 largest.

Saskatchewan
Saskatchewan provides more than half of Canada's wheat crop. Copper and zinc are also mined near the east-central border, and petroleum and natural-gas resources have also been developed.

Manitoba
Located near the geographic center of Canada, Manitoba links the resources of the east with the population centers in the east. Capital Winnipeg is Canada's railroad center and major exchange area for cattle and wheat.

Newfoundland
Newfoundland lies next to the Grand Banks, the world's richest fishing grounds, and has what many consider the best natural harbor in the country.

Land Area Distribution
Total Land: 9,976,140 sq km (3,851,808 sq mi)
Coastline: 243,791 km
Provinces: 10
Territories: 2
Source: Nations of the World

British Columbia
Canada's only Pacific coast province, much of the province's wealth comes from the timber that covers more than half the land area. Copper, coal, gold, lead, and zinc mining also contribute to the GDP, as well as oil refineries near Vancouver.

Alberta
Alberta is a land of contrast, with rich plains giving way to rolling foothills and the Rocky Mountains. Edmonton and Calgary are ranked among the ten largest cities in Canada. The region was once almost totally dependent on agriculture, but today also supports increasing petroleum, natural gas, and coal industries.

Ontario
Ontario has a broad industrial base and excellent public services. Toronto is Canada's largest and fastest-growing city, it is the destination for 50 percent of immigrants and most of Canada's internal migrants.

Quebec
Almost 50 percent of the population of Quebec live in the greater Montreal area. Secession has long been an issue for residents, but separation could be costly. Almost 90 percent of all exports go to the United States and Canada. To keep these markets, Quebec would have to embrace free trade. At present, it is somewhat protectionist.

Current Affairs

NAFTA

The North American Free Trade Agreement has dominated the Canadian political landscape since its inception in 1988. Canada's motives for entering into NAFTA were largely defensive—they did not want to lose out in any deal between the US and Mexico.

Many are still opposed to the free trade agreement, which eases restrictions and regulations between Canada, the United States, and Mexico. There are fears that Canadian workers will suffer from competition from Mexico. Tensions have also arisen between Canadian and US trade unions, as Canadian workers have been forced to accept more flexible US working practices. NAFTA has not ended the problems between the countries' governments either. Millions of dollars in goods cross the Canada-US border every day, most of it without any disputes, but occasionally problems arise. The US and Canada ended a long and bitter dispute recently about softwood lumber export. Canada's complaints about the effects of acid rain originating in the US northern industrial cities have fallen upon relatively deaf ears. Despite the fears and minor squabbles, however, many sectors of Canadian business, including grains, oilseeds, textiles, oil, and gas have benefited from NAFTA.

QUEBEC SECESSION

The idea of Quebec's secession has been around for some time. Agitation flared in the 1960s, as several movements tried to separate Quebec from Canada and set up a new French-speaking nation. A royal Canadian commission declared in 1965 that a partnership between the French- and English-speaking people is "vital" to Canada's existence. French was declared the official language of the province in 1974, and in 1976, a separatist party won the 1976 elections. In 1980, however, voters rejected a referendum for political independence. Quebec's leaders refused to sign Canada's constitution in 1982 because, in their words, "it lacked safeguards for French language and culture." The Supreme Court of Canada ruled in 1988 that Quebec's French-only rule violated freedom of speech.

Separatism has been a major issue in the 1990s, as well. The Meech Lake Accord, designed to satisfy French-speaking Quebec's demands for a status as a "distinct society," failed in 1990. In 1992, a parliamentary committee offered a series of constitutional reforms that reaffirmed a distinct society status for Quebec. The separatists were not appeased. In November, 1995, a referendum to separate nearly passed. Separatists, lead by the Reform Party and Bloc Quebecois, have said they will hound the Prime Minister in parliament and never let this issue go. Prime Minister Jean Chretien said he will push through parliament language recognizing Quebec as a "distinct society" for its French language and culture, and has offered to give the province a constitutional veto. Whether that does any good, however, remains to be seen.

Canada in Time

1497 John Cabot's English expedition landed in Canada, beginning European expansion.

1534 Jacques Cartier's French expedition landed in Canada.

1754-1763 The French and Indian War between Britain and France. Following the war, France was forced to give up St. Lawrence and Quebec settlements to Britain.

1775-1783 Canada becomes a refuge for British loyalists during the American War of Independence.

1846 The Oregon Treaty is drafted, confirming the present borders with the United States.

1885 The transcontinental railroad is completed.

1897 The Klondike gold rush begins.

1914-1918 Canadian troops fight in World War I.

1926 A principle of equal status with London in deciding foreign policy is accepted during the Commonwealth Conference.

1936 The Reciprocity Treaty with the United States creates increased economic links.

1939-1945 Canadian troops fight in World War II.

1949 Canada is a founder of NATO.

1968 The Quebec Party (PQ) is formed and demands complete separation from federal government.

1976 French made the official language in Quebec.

1980 Separation of Quebec fails in referendum.

1982 The United Kingdom transfers all powers relating to Canada in British law.

1984 Trudeau resigns. The Conservative Party, led by Brian Mulroney, wins the elections and gains control of the government.

1989 Discussions for the North American Free Trade Agreement (NAFTA) begin.

1988 The Supreme Court of Canada rules that Quebec's French-only rule violates freedom of speech.

1993 Charlottetown Agreement rejected in referendum. Canada, Mexico, and the United States finalize terms for NAFTA.

1993 The Liberal Party, led by Jean Chretien, regains control of the government.

1994 NAFTA takes effect.

WHAT'S INSIDE

CANADA Business is designed by businesspeople experienced in international markets to give you a head start for doing business in Canada. It will tell you how the business, legal, and social systems work, what the conditions are, who to contact, and where to get more details. **CANADA Business** is your invitation to this fascinating society and market. Welcome!

Economy surveys the financial sectors of Canadian life. A must read chapter to gain insight into the past, present, and future of the Canadian people.

Current Issues explores the events that affect the country's development, with a particular focus on what you can expect when doing business there.

Opportunities highlights the prospects in industrial, service, agricultural, and public sectors that hold potential for importers, exporters, and investors.

Foreign Investment details the ease and risk of the Canadian investment environment, including the policies, incentives, restrictions, and procedures.

Foreign Trade considers the Canadian's relative role in international trade, both in relation to domestic production and in comparison with other countries.

Trade Agreements presents the latest information on multilateral and bilateral trade arrangements, with special reference to NAFTA and GATT.

Import Policy & Procedures surveys the regulatory environment for importing and gives a nuts-and-bolts guide, from preshipment through customs.

Export Policy & Procedures views transborder shipping from the opposite side: the practice and procedure of moving goods out of Canada.

Industry Reviews outlines the competitive positions of the most prominent industries and offers industry-specific resource contacts.

Trade Fairs is a comprehensive listing of Canadian trade fairs, complete with contact information and tips on how to maximize the benefits of these events.

Business Travel is a quick reference for the information that a businessperson on the go needs to know–visas to hotels to taxis to business centers.

Business Culture offers a primer on how to adapt to local businesses and negotiating styles, improve business effectiveness, and avoid inadvertent gaffes.

Demographics supplies the basic statistical data that you will need to begin assessing the nature and demands of local Canadian markets.

Marketing outlines consumer trends, urban and rural markets, and the channels for market entry and advertising that are specific to Canada.

Business Entities & Formation discusses the requirements and registration procedures for operating a business in Canada.

Labor assembles information on the availability, capabilities, and cost of labor, as well as terms of employment and labor-management relations.

Business Law gives practical guidelines on the legal system and an abridged digest of commercial law by legal publishing authority Martindale-Hubbell.

Financial Institutions surveys the financial markets and provides a useful guide to financing and related services available to foreign businesses.

Currency & Foreign Exchange explains the exchange system and presents the Canadian annual report prepared by the International Monetary Fund.

International Payments is an illustrated, step-by-step guide to using documentary collections and letters of credit in trade with Canada.

Taxation incorporates the Ernst & Young international personal and corporate tax guides to explain the tax benefits and liabilities of doing business in Canada.

Transportation & Communications brings you current information on available ports, airports, roads, and communications throughout Canada.

Important Addresses compiles listings for government agencies, business and trade associations, financial and service firms, and other resources.

Economy

INTRODUCTION

Canada is a vast, sparsely populated nation of about 29 million people, covering 9,980,000 square kilometers and encompassing the entire land mass between the Atlantic and Pacific oceans in northern North America. It shares about 8,893 square kilometers of border with the United States (including the state of Alaska). It is also the second largest country in the world, after Russia; population density is quite low, averaging six people per square mile nationally (about 85 percent of the total population resides along the southern border). The climate can be extreme, particularly inland. The two official languages are English and French, and almost 98 percent of the population can speak either one of these languages.

By any standards, Canada is a rich country, endowed with many natural resources (energy, fisheries, minerals, agricultural cropland and timber). Although Canada is known internationally for its natural resources and primary raw materials, and is still a leading producer of wheat, wood products, and minerals, economic reliance on these natural resources has given way to a sophisticated, highly industrial, diversified economy that is also one of the world's largest exporters of manufactured equipment.

Measured in terms of GNP, it now ranks seventh in the world, with a standard of living as high as that of the United States or Europe. GDP per capita, measured in current terms, was $26,430 in 1995, according to IMF statistics.

The 1994 UN development report card ranked Canada as the world's best place to live, based on certain indices including life expectancy, standard of living, and educational attainment (the US placed eighth). Because of its great wealth, the Canadian economy has sometimes been referred to as a "solution in search of a problem," nevertheless, by the 1990s the realities of global competition, corporate restructuring, and public deficits had also set in; the coming decade portends considerable economic challenge as well as opportunities.

HISTORY OF THE ECONOMY

The Making of Quebec

Throughout the seventeenth and eighteenth centuries, Canada attracted both French and British settlers, some of them moving north from the American colonies to trade in furs or with the Indians. While the French established an early trading presence in Canadian territory, the English concentrated their settlements initially in what became the thirteen colonies of the United States. But the boundary between French and British America was never clearly demarcated, a situation which caused continuous conflict and was spurred on, to a great extent, by the history of relations between Britain and France in Europe.

Hostilities in the New World finally came to a head when, in 1756, the Seven Years War erupted in Europe between the two countries. In the colonies, this resulted in the French and Indian War, and in fact it epitomized the extent to which relations in North America were subject to events in Europe. Determined to defeat the French in the New World,

CONTENTS

Introduction	7
History of the Economy	7
Size of the Economy	9
GDP Growth	9
Inflation in Canada	10
Context of the Economy	11
Structure of the Economy, 1970 and 1996	12
Structure of the Economy	12
Elements of the Economy	15
Canadian Foreign Trade	16
Foreign Investment, 1995	17
Political Developments in Economy	18
Federal Finance	18

William Pitt, the British Minister of War, sent additional land and naval reinforcements to America. The French sent their colonies very little. One French camp after the other around the Great Lakes and Lake Champlaine along the Ohio River fell to the British, the most important being Louisbourg, which was captured in 1758 and opened up the St. Lawrence river to the British navy.

In 1759 the British sailed into the St. Lawrence with the objective of defeating the center of French command in America, Quebec City. The famous battle surrounding Quebec along the Plains of Abraham involved over 4,000 casualties on both sides in less than one day of fighting. The French army was subdued, but not captured; not until it was crushed in Montreal a year later did the final British conquest occur. The memory of "la conqueste" has continued to this day to nourish French nationalist sentiment; in the Treaty of Paris, the French relinquished all of their North American holdings east of the Mississippi, except the two small islands of St. Pierre and Miquelon, which were needed as outposts for the French fishing fleets (and remain under French designation to this day). The French also eventually relinquished to Spain all their holdings west of the Mississippi, territory which eventually came to the US through the Louisiana Purchase.

By 1774, the British acknowledged that an easy defeat of Quebec would not be not likely, and that it would be necessary to strike some sort of accord with the resilient French leaders who remained. The Quebec Act of 1774 stipulated, among other things, that French Canadians need not take an anti-Catholic oath, that French civil law could be practiced, (although criminal law would be British), and that Quebec would be governed by an appointed council, as opposed to the representative council adopted in other British colonies. The boundaries of Quebec would be extended to include much of the old French empire between the Ohio and Mississippi rivers, where the French fur traders continued to dominate the economy.

The American Revolutionary War also had important consequences for the British settlement in Canada. In the peace treaty of 1783, the British retained their holdings north of the American colonies (although Benjamin Franklin asked for Nova Scotia, Newfoundland, and the Hudson Bay territory); at the insistence of George III and Parliament, the British were able to maintain a presence in Halifax and Quebec against the northern expansion of the Americans as well as a refuge for loyalists from the thirteen colonies.

The British conceded the entire Ohio country, that great region west of the Appalachian mountains between the Mississippi and Ohio rivers, even though it was still controlled by them and traditionally dependent on Canada. This accession was to have great consequences for the development of the economy of Canada. Unable to move through the Great Lakes region or through the south, Canada's contacts with the far western territories instead had to move along the region north of Lake Superior. To do this, the first transcontinental railway was built, joining the large distances between east and west in Canada together.

Settlement in Canada was also greatly impacted by the Revolutionary War. After the peace treaty, over 40,000 loyalists, mainly from the eastern seaboard, landed in Nova Scotia, tripling the population there. Others came into Quebec north of the St. Lawrence, Lake Erie and Lake Ontario, creating for the first time a large English-speaking minority in that province, and who preferred British political and legal traditions.

With this mixed population, London saw the need to divide Quebec into two separate provinces; the Canada Act of 1791 created upper Canada (later Ontario) and lower Canada (present-day Quebec). English common law and freehold land tenure were established in upper Canada, and Quebec was allowed to retain its French civil law. That decision angered many of the English-speaking merchants in Montreal, who controlled much of the economic life in the province. The basics of provincial structure, both economically and politically, had been born: Canada was divided as distinct British colonies which had no strong links to each other. Separated by geography, language, and customs, each had its own governor or lieutenant governor, and an elected assembly.

Modernization

The second World War greatly altered the demography and the economy of Canada. The end of the war brought a wave of immigration, as thousands of people from Europe sought security and a better life, helping to double the country's population from 11.5 million in 1941, to 25 million in 1985. European immigrants tended to settle in cities, helping to urbanize the country along with the native Canadians who were moving off their farms.

The war changed Canada's economy in several ways: the country had accumulated far more wealth, it had become far more industrialized, and it emerged as one of the world's major trading nations. The war also fostered a strong symbiotic relationship between the economies of Canada and the US, and, as had been occurring since World War I, periodic rounds of American foreign investment. 1945 brought another round of American capital investment into the country. For about twenty years, the Canadian government did very little to monitor this investment; however in the 1960s, the country woke up to find that much of their economy and natural resources were foreign-owned. It remains much the same today.

SIZE OF THE ECONOMY

Gross Domestic Product

Canada is the world's seventh largest economy. In absolute terms, the Canadian economy's GDP has grown from $57.5 billion dollars in 1965, to $780 billion in 1995. (US GDP was, in comparison, about $7.6 trillion in 1995). Measured in US dollars, total output for the economy was $549 billion in 1994, and $575 billion in 1995. GDP as measured at factor cost in 1986 prices, increased from $259 billion in 1970 to $528 billion in 1994, or a real change of about 104 percent.

The biggest real increases in output in terms of dollar value were in the service producing industries, which increased almost 126 percent between 1970 and 1994–from $155 billion to $349 billion (measured in constant 1986 dollars). In contrast, the goods producing industries increased 71 percent. The contribution of the service industries to total GDP also increased from 59.6 percent to 66.1 percent between 1970 and 1994, much in line with services growth in the US and other G-7 countries.

Recent Trends

After an average growth rate of about 2.9 percent in the late 1980's, the Canadian economy slid into a fairly sharp recession, lingering through 1993/1994. GDP grew 2.4 percent in 1993, 4.1 percent in 1994, and dropped to 0.8 percent in 1995. In 1995, tighter monetary policy in the United States (to slow inflation) spilled over into Canada, raising interest rates and weakening demand. The recovery which began in 1994 was largely fueled by an increase in exports, and to a lesser extent, by an increase in foreign investment. Much of this growth in trade resulted from the strong decline in the real exchange rate since 1991–now averaging in the 70–75 cent range per one US dollar.

Inflation Following the global recession of the 1970s and early eighties, Canada's economy experienced strong inflationary pressures, running into the double digits (10.1 percent in 1980, 12.5 percent in 1981 and 12.4 percent in 1982).

Despite some anti-inflationary actions taken (primarily higher interest rates), the annual average inflation rate remained between 4–5 percent throughout the 1980s, until 1991, when it rose to 5.6 percent. In 1992, inflation dropped to 1.5 percent annually, in 1993, 1.8 percent, and in 1994, it dropped to 0.2 percent annually.

Inflation was also up slightly in 1995, to 2.2 percent, due in part to a surge in food prices resulting from poor US weather, higher gasoline prices because of a federal tax increase, and the end of the dampening effect of reductions in tobacco taxes and a drop in Quebec's provincial sales tax, which all served to moderate CPI changes in 1994. Inflation is forecast to remain low, around 2.0 percent, in 1996/1997.

Interest Rates Interest rates remained high throughout the early 1980s and, after a brief drop in 1986, also rose sharply between 1987 and 1990. Rates dropped substantially during 1992. The prime lending rate, which is what banks charge their most credit-worthy customers, eased to an average of 7.5 percent during the year, while five-year mortgage rates dipped below 10 percent for the first time since the early 1970s. This steady decrease during the past decade indicates the possibility of a long

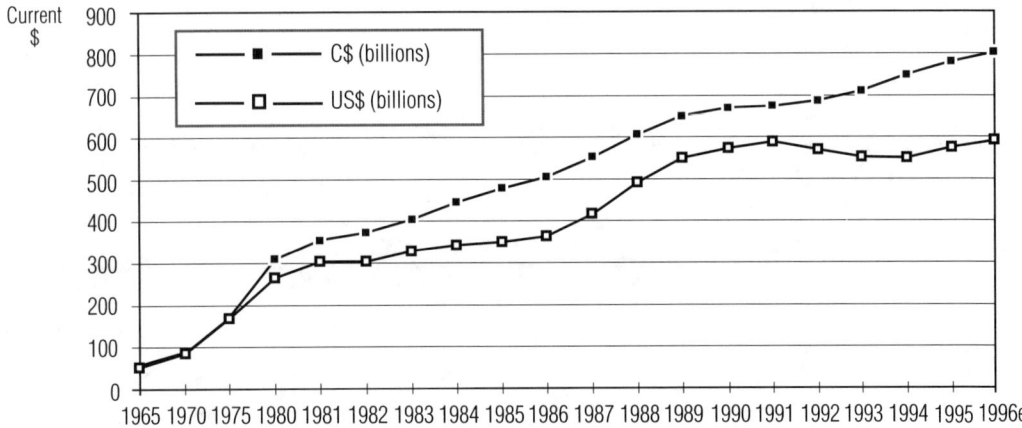

Note: US figures based on IMF yearly average exchange rate.
Sources: International Monetary Fund, International Financial Statistics Yearbook, 1995; Statistics Canada

term decrease in inflationary pressure. Rates rose again, but not dramatically, in 1994. The prime rate was 7.0 percent in March, 1996. Over the past several years, the government has encountered some criticism for supposedly maintaining rates that are too constrictive, therefore causing the currency exchange rate to remain artificially low as a way of stimulating exports (the exchange rate had appreciated for five straight years, before its reversal in 1992).

Unemployment has been a nagging problem for Canada throughout the 1990s, exceeding 10 percent in every year since 1991. Unemployment averaged 11.3 percent in 1992, and 11.2 percent in 1993. In late 1994, unemployment fell below the 1.5 million mark for the first time in three years, and the unemployment rate dropped into the single digits, to 9.6 percent (it averaged 10.4 percent for the entire year, however). Unemployment finally dropped to about 9.6 percent by September, 1995, and currently hovers around 9.4 percent. These rates are still quite high by historical standards; some analysts believe that the Canadian economy has undergone a permanent structural adjustment towards this higher rate for a variety of reasons.

Canada's economic picture is expected to be moderately "brighter" in the years ahead; and improved from the early '90s. However, very conservative fiscal policy at all levels, in an effort to control the deficit, will likely work to dampen demand and growth. Most estimates for growth fall within the 2.5-3.0 percent range for 1996 and 1997.

Standard of Living In 1994, the UN ranked Canada as the number one country to live in, based on its assessment of human development indicators such as income, education and life expectancy. Its progressive tax structure and the large amount of social transfer payments work to redistribute wealth. However, disadvantaged groups—like the Inuit and other indigenous tribes, which make up about 2 percent of the population—have struggled with much lower standards of living.

GDP per capita was $26,430 in 1995, above that of several other G-7 countries, including Japan and France, and just behind the United States. Between 1991 and 1994, however, real wage growth stagnated or fell slightly, and per capita GDP and real personal disposable income have fallen off commensurably. Between 1993 and 1994, per capita GDP dropped 1.7 percent.

Canada has 69 universities and 203 other higher education institutions. Over 75 percent of secondary school students go on to higher education–the highest proportion in the developed world. In addition, 93 percent complete secondary level schooling. This is reflected in the fact that Canada spends about 7 percent of its GDP on education, the highest percentage in the industrialized world. And, Canada spends almost one-half of its GDP on social welfare programs, either directly or through transfers to the provinces.

According to the Corporate Resources Group in Geneva, in 1994 four Canadian cities ranked in the top ten worldwide for medical and health considerations. Vancouver ranked no. 1, Montreal and Calgary 5 and 6, and Toronto, 9. (Only one US city, San Francisco, ranked in the top ten.) An international comparison of health spending for 1992 placed Canada at 10.1 percent of GDP, the US at 14 percent, the UK at 7.1 percent, and Japan at 6.9 percent. Although Canada

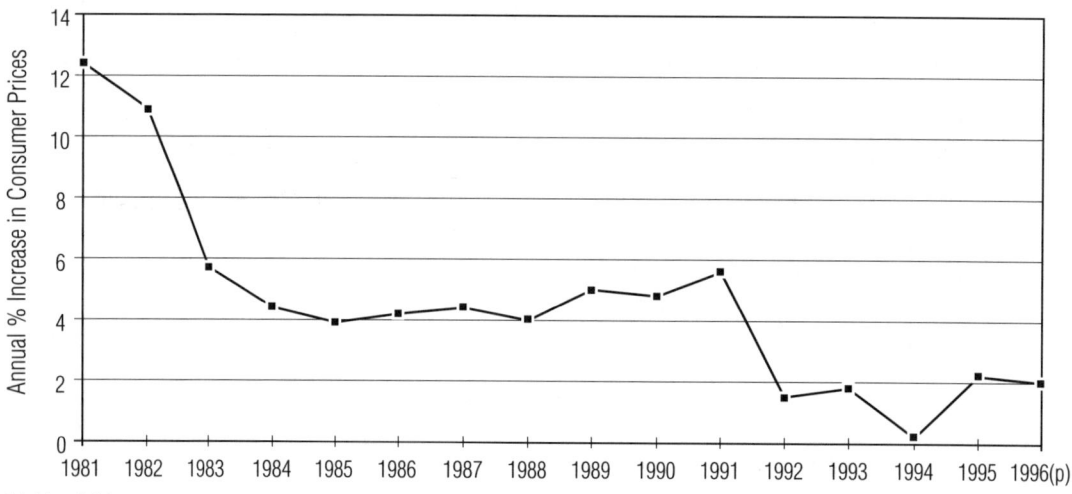

Note: (p) = projected

Source: Statistics Canada; USDOC

spends no more per capita on health care than many other developed countries, their socialized system providing "universal access" is widely regarded as the world's best. Life expectancy in Canada is two years longer than in the US, and infant mortality rate is 24 percent lower. Heart disease is also 20 percent lower. Spending cuts, medical wages, rising equipment costs and more expensive treatments, and an aging populace have all put pressure on the national health care system, and in 1995, for the first time ever, some provinces required new immigrants to wait three months upon entry to receive free initial care. Free access for foreign students and temporary residents was also halted. Socialism has not eradicated poverty, but it has helped to alleviate it—one of the basic tenets of Canadian federalism is the uniformity of standards for social services across the country. 12 percent of families lived below the poverty line in 1990, compared with 25 percent in 1969. The responsibility for social services has sometimes been a source of contention between the federal government and the provinces.

CONTEXT OF THE ECONOMY

For quite a while, natural resources and agriculture were the basic pillars of the Canadian economy. In the 19th century, Canada secured large amounts of capital investment from abroad, and imported mostly manufactured goods, paying for them with exports of raw materials and grain. Gradually, the service and manufacturing sectors began to overtake the resource and primary agricultural sectors; this has been most evident over the last fifteen years. In 1980, the resource sector accounted for 46 percent of the weighting of the stock exchange in Toronto; by 1987 this weight had decreased to just 26 percent. Because of its small population, Canada must trade heavily to maintain its standard of living; in fact, 50 percent of its GNP is generated by trade (as compared to about ten to twenty percent in other OECD countries.) This historic dependency on trade has also made Canada very dependent on the vagaries of world economic cycles.

Economic Dependence The past twenty five years saw the birth of two forms of nationalism in Canada, the first being economic, with worries over the degree of foreign ownership in the economy (this has more often than not, however, been mitigated by the realities of the positive economic impact of such investment). Economic nationalism has also been evident in the provinces' reaction to the widening scope of federal powers in Ottawa, as much as from the degree of foreign control of assets in their territories. Second, there has been a form of political nationalism within certain provinces, most evident in Quebec, that seems to be coming to full throttle in the years ahead.

The Role of the State Canada also has a long history of state intervention in private enterprise, operating many of Canada's largest corporations such as Petro-Canada and CN Railway (until privatization in 1995), and Ontario Hydro (scheduled to privatize in 1996). These nationalized industries–known as crown corporations–hold a large percentage of Canadian assets, in many different sectors: transportation, agriculture, energy, culture, and banking and finance. In fact, five banks (the Royal Bank of Canada, the Bank of Montreal, the Canadian Imperial Bank of Commerce, the Bank of Nova Scotia and the Toronto Dominion Bank) control over 80 percent of all the assets of the top 12 banks in Canada; of the top 25 financial institutions, nine are controlled by the federal or provincial governments.

Some crown corporations make a profit; others are subsidized. Privatization is gaining ground in Canada, and given the budget deficit and concerns over the level of federal spending, this should continue under Liberal Party rule into 1998 (Brian Mulroney was the first prime minister to begin to privatize by selling off Air Canada and the telecommunications giant, Teleglobe Canada).

The federal government also engages in substantial income redistribution through taxation. Due to the much stronger social welfare system, which includes unemployment compensation, free child care and medical care, free education, subsidized housing, pay-equity laws, and the state-run Canada Pension Plan (which also may be privatized), social expenditures and transfers of payment for social programs in the provinces account for almost half of all government expenditures in Canada. Federal government regulation also significantly impacts foreign investment, especially in certain sectors.

The late 1980s saw a substantial increase in the public debt (these budgetary deficits were partly attributable to the higher interest rates). By 1993, Canada's debt as a percentage of GDP had risen to almost 60 percent, and simply servicing the debt cost over $41 billion dollars, or 26 percent of total federal government expenditures. The political urgency of the situation has not been ignored by the Liberal Party's Chretien Administration, and the 1995/1996 budget, announced in February of 1995, aimed to secure a reduction in the deficit from 6 percent to 3 percent of GDP over a two-year period. The most recent budget proposed in March, 1996 by Finance Minister Paul Martin, steers much the same course, and aims to reduce the deficit to 2 percent of GDP by 1998.

US-Canada Relations It is impossible to discuss the Canadian economy in detail without taking into account the level of mutual interdependence with its neighbor to the south, the United States. The political and economic ties between the two make each other their own best ally, although often times, Canada has accused its much stronger (if not larger) neighbor that it is too frequently taken for granted. For the US, Canada is a very appropriate neighbor, with a similar language, business institutions and free markets, and democratic tradition. Political ties are close: Ronald Reagan, on his first foreign trip, went to Canada; the free trader Brian Mulroney, after he was elected prime minister in 1984, went to Washington in his first week in office. The two countries share the longest undefended border in the world, and are close allies in NATO and NORAD. The two are also each others' biggest trading partners by far, with 80 percent of Canadian exports heading south, and 20 percent of US exports going to Canada (this amounts to 70 percent of all of Canada's imports). America's trade with Canada is almost twice the size of its trade with Japan, and America sells more of its products to the province of Ontario than to either Japan or Western Europe. The two countries are also each others' most preferred area for foreign investment.

And yet for Canada, the relationship can be frustrating. The US, with an economy ten times the size, and a population ten times as large, has often behaved like a giant who unknowingly tramples on the economic needs of its neighbor. Because the two economies are so interlinked, Canada is very vulnerable to recessionary trends and the financial markets in the US, and takes longer to pull out of them once in. In the 1970s and early 1980s, Canada implemented certain domestic policies and legal restraints designed to increase self-reliance and reduce its dependence on the US; the harsher reality of this latest bout with economic nationalism set in fairly quickly, and after the elections of 1984, PM Mulroney charted a more conciliatory course.

STRUCTURE OF THE ECONOMY

Primary Sectors

Agriculture, forestry, fishing and together contributed about 2.8 percent to Canada's GDP in 1994. The number of workers in agriculture declined about 10,200 between 1990 and 1995, to a total of 430,500.

Nevertheless, agriculture is an important sector in Canada, accounting for over ten percent of exports, and Canada remains one of the world's premier exporters of wheat (second only to the US).

Principal crops harvested in Canada are wheat, barley, and cereals, and major buyers are Russia, the EEC, and China. Ironically, Canada is a large importer of many other kinds of foods, including fruit, vegetables, sugar and tobacco. Agricultural production increased by an average of 2.4 percent annually in 1980-1990, but declined by 0.3 percent in 1991 and 3.0 percent in 1992. It increased an estimated 0.7 percent in 1993. In 1995, Canada exported about $13.4 billion in agricultural products. Yet the size of this figure and their direct contribution to GDP understates somewhat the importance the primary sectors have for the entire economy: Canada's raw materials and energy resources are the basic materials for many manufactured products including paper, food and beverages, and petroleum products. About 47 percent of exports are either raw or semi-processed materials, one of the highest percentages of any developed country. As with other sectors, the state has an active role in agriculture: marketing boards and policies such as the Western Grain Stabilization and Agricultural Stabilization Acts have regulated and, to an extent, subsidized prices.

Canada's earliest European settlers came to fish

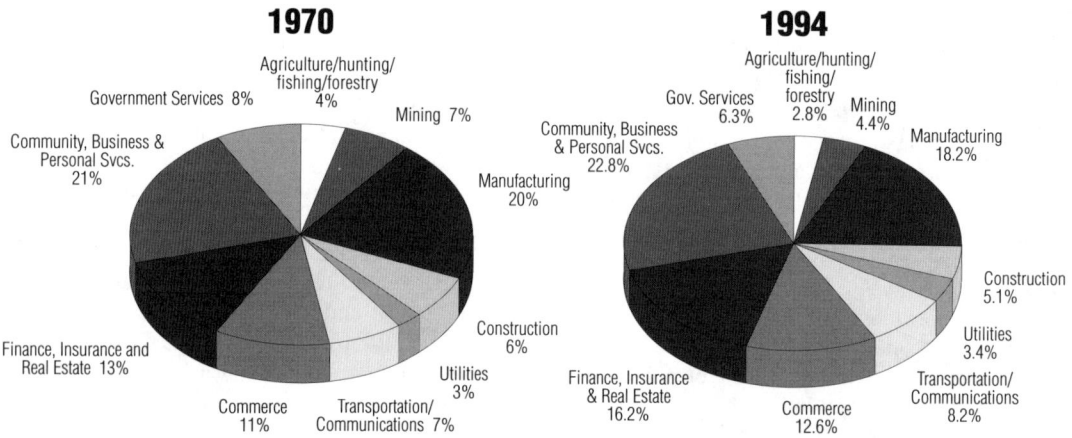

Structure of the Economy

Note: Figures based on constant 1986 dollars.
Source: Canada Business Facts 1995

its waters; they soon established contact with the Indians and began to trade in furs. Today Canada remains one of the leading producers of fish and fish products, exporting close to 80 percent of total production. The US takes about one-third of this. Canadian fishing grounds extend 200 miles off the Canadian coasts, and there are about 900 fishing plants which employ over 100,000 people. Much of this industry is located in the Maritime provinces– Nova Scotia, Halifax, and Newfoundland, as well as the west coast. In Newfoundland, about 15 percent of the population is still employed in fishing or fish processing. In 1989, Newfoundland's dependence on fishing brought it into head on conflict with France, since the French claimed the right to fish in the gulf of St. Lawrence due to French ownership of the two small islands, St. Pierre and Miquelon, located sixteen miles from Newfoundland. The dispute was not resolved until 1993.

Over-fishing and dwindling stocks have become a large problem in recent years, as yields are declining, especially for cod, herring and salmon. In 1992, the total catch had dropped almost 375 thousand metric tons, or 24 percent, from just two years prior.

The crisis is particularly severe with salmon. About 4,400 vessels and 9,000 fishermen are active in commercial salmon fishing on Canada's west coast, but dwindling stocks and high-tech fishing methods have meant there are too many boats competing for scarce fish. Total landed value of commercially caught salmon averaged more than $200 million annually between 1991 and 1994, but preliminary estimates indicate 1995 landed values fell by about 40 percent.

The severity of the situation caused the Canadian government, in April of 1996, to announce plans to halve its Pacific salmon fishing fleet. The government has announced that it will spend about $80 million to compensate boat owners who voluntarily surrender their licenses. The decision comes at a time when Canada and the US are attempting to resolve their long standing dispute over Pacific salmon fishing.

The two have been battling over how to divide the dwindling catch in the Pacific Northwest, and attempts to negotiate settlements have failed. In 1994, Canada decided to levy a $1,500 transit fee on American fishing boats traversing British Columbia's Inside Passage, a 750-mile strait between Vancouver Island and the coast. The US has responded by demanding that Canada return the fees. Tensions also increased when, in the summer of 1995, Alaska rejected catch limits, and Canada was forced to unilaterally impose drastic catch reductions as a conservation measure.

The fur trade dominated the Canadian economy from the early 1600s to the late 1700s, and even today, the sale of fur pelts continues to rise annually. Canada produced about 2 million pelts in 1992. Unlike fishing, the fur trade directed European settlers towards the interior and north of the continent. It was also an enterprise conducted by huge trading monopolies, such as the Hudson Bay Co. Partly as a result of this, Canadians did not develop the aversion to monopolistic behavior that has played such a large role in business formation and private enterprise in the United States; as mentioned earlier, evidence of this can be seen in the state-run "crown corporations" in Canada that supply many of the infrastructural and energy services that have only recently begun to be privatized.

Unlike fur, timber helped settle western Canada. Timber also stimulated some agriculture, since the land once cleared was used for planting. Timber also indirectly contributed to the development of many different kinds of manufacturing, since the logs had to be processed, transported and ultimately, built into finished products such as furniture and ships. It also created the market for many kinds of metal tools to work the lumber.

Today, Canada is one of the preeminent exporters of lumber and one of the world's largest producers, with about 15 percent of total world production. This industry employs about 300,000 people, concentrated mostly in British Columbia, Thunder Bay, and St. John's. In 1993, Canada exported about $9.2 billion in softwood lumber, $6.6 billion of newsprint paper, and $4.6 billion of wood and other pulp. This accounted for about 11.5 percent of total exports, and represented an increase of $2.6 billion from the preceding year. In 1994, Canada exported $31.16 billion of forestry products, and in 1995, almost $39.3 billion, which represented 15.4 percent of total trade.

In April, 1996 Canada and the US finally settled a long standing trade dispute regarding the export of softwood lumber, which the US claimed Canada was selling at below market prices. The five year agreement limits the amount of softwood lumber Canada can sell to the US to about 9 percent less than 1995 levels. In turn, the US agrees not to launch any new trade actions against Canadian lumber exporters.

Canada has not been able to reach agreement with the United States on pollutants from manufacturing plants in the US, a factor which is causing substantial acid rain damage to Canadian forests. In 1986, a joint US-Canadian commission recommended a $5 billion program which was never funded. Canada then proceeded with a program designed to reduce 40 percent of acid rain from domestic sources by the year 2000. In March, 1991, the US and Canadian governments signed an agreement by which the US was to contribute to pollution-reduction measures, however the issue is still a large source of contention.

Industry

Industry (manufacturing, construction, utilities and mining) provided about 31.1 percent of GDP in 1994, and employed about 3.5 million workers. Mining provided 4.4 percent of GDP in 1994, but employed only 1.3 percent of the labor force in 1992. In 1991, Canada was the world's largest producer of zinc and asbestos, and the second largest producer of nickel, potash and uranium. Gold, silver, iron, copper, cobalt and lead are also mined. Alberta, British Columbia, Quebec and Saskatchewan are the major mining regions; the Northwest Territories and the Yukon also produce minerals. In the 1980s, federal control over mineral resources was, to a large extent, granted to the provinces.

Manufacturing contributed 18.2 percent of GDP in 1994, and employed about 15.1 percent of workers. The most important sectors in 1993, as measured by value of output (excluding petroleum) were transport equipment, food products, machinery, paper and allied products, chemicals, and primary metals. The share of manufacturing products in world trade has increased from 57 percent to 73 percent between 1983 and 1993, with some of the largest increases in machinery, telecommunications, autos, and chemicals. Canada has and is well-positioned to take advantage of this growth in the ensuing decade.

Much of Canadian durables manufacturing is concentrated in Ontario and Quebec, and there is a high concentration of ownership, especially in certain industries (such as food processing and brewing). It has been suggested that historically, this high concentration has contributed to lower labor productivity among Canadian workers than other industrialized countries. During the recession of 1989-92, over one-fifth of Canadian manufacturing jobs were consolidated.

There are signs that this restructuring has changed productivity: Labor productivity in manufacturing increased 2.3 percent between 1993 and 1994, but only about 1.1 percent annually between 1986 and 1993. Canada produces and assembles a large portion of vehicle parts and components, and reexports a portion back into the United States. In 1993, the value of automobile exports/reexports was $46.5 billion, or about 26 percent of total export trade. Auto production is concentrated in Ontario and Quebec, in cities close to the US border. A significant portion of US direct investment in Canada is in the transport industry; in fact, three of the largest ten corporations in Canada (by rank in sales) are subsidiaries of the US auto giants GM, Chrysler, and Ford.

Energy

Canada is one of the few western countries with the ability to be energy sufficient in oil and gas. The two energy sources together supply about 60 percent of Canada's energy needs. Coal supplies about ten percent of energy needs, and the country is a net exporter. The energy sector directly employs about 150,000 people. The oil and gas industry is present in the western provinces, including Alberta and Saskatchewan, with very large deposits also present in the Arctic and off the coasts of Newfoundland and Nova Scotia.

Canada is the world's eighth largest oil producer, and the largest source of petroleum products to the US. Canada also exports a considerable amount of national gas into the United States. Hydroelectricity provides about 70 percent of the electricity supply; Canada is an important supplier of electricity to the United States, especially in the northeastern US. Ontario Hydro, Canada's seventh largest company with over $8 billion in sales, is a major supplier to New York and Michigan.

In 1947, the discovery of oil in Alberta brought on large levels of foreign investment in the exploration and development of energy reserves. Foreign control of key resources has been an ongoing concern in Canada; one that has sparked legislation in energy and minerals. Under Pierre Trudeau, the government passed the National Energy Policy of 1980, a series of acts which, through grants, tax write-offs and various incentives, favored Canadian-owned or controlled companies. The act was contentious from the start; the basic tenet being to "Canadianize" the country's own energy resources. In 1980, at the peak of Canada's lucrative production of oil and gas, the Canadian government designed the act to take control of at least 40 percent of its oil industry by the 1990s. From the standpoint of foreign investment, it operated retroactively to confiscate some foreign oil companies' profits, lowering the book value of the companies and therefore making them prime targets for buy-outs (by Canadians). In addition, the NEP contained a back-in clause which required the transfer of up to 25 percent of the value of an oil or gas well after a find had been made on federal land, to then state-owned oil company, Petro-Canada. In one respect, the NEP was successful–it did increase domestic ownership in the oil and gas industry. However, the timing of the policy could not have been worse. In the years leading up to the NEP, oil and gas prices had risen steadily; in the early 1980s, they declined substantially on world markets. Canadian companies found they had created serious debt problems for themselves by buying up foreign companies; these lower prices, combined with foreign investors' fear, caused drilling and exploring to completely dry up. The resulting bust severely hit Alberta's economy.

The conservative Mulroney government moved quickly to dismantle the program, and also to sign an accord with Saskatchewan, Alberta, and British Columbia allowing the provinces the freedom to develop their own resources. The discriminatory tax treatment between foreign and domestic investors was also abolished. Today, the NEP is effectively dead, and Canadian ownership in the oil industry has declined from 42.1 percent in 1985 to about 35 percent today.

Services

The fastest growing sector in Canada overall is the services sector, including wholesale and retail trade, finance, transportation and communications, recreation and tourism. About two-thirds of the Canadian work force is employed in services, or about 9.8 million people in 1995. The fastest growing area was finance, insurance, and real estate (FIRS), which increased from 12.8 percent of GDP in 1970 to 16.2 percent in 1994. FIRS also attracts the highest level of foreign investment: in 1994, the stock of direct foreign investment in this area was $29.2 billion, about one-fifth of the total. FIRS also saw the largest level of new investment year over year, about $3 billion, between 1994 and 1995.

Tourism is also an important Canadian industry, with annual revenues of US$20 billion, employing about one in ten workers. About thirteen million Americans visit Canada annually; this figure has been helped in recent years by the low Canadian dollar.

ELEMENTS OF THE ECONOMY

Labor

Canada's sophisticated educational system and level of technology supports a productive, efficient labor force throughout the country. As mentioned earlier, although unemployment has finally fallen into the single digits in Canada, real wages have suffered from restructuring and lower wage growth. The industrial restructuring that has occurred since 1989 has improved competitiveness but impacted job creation. One interesting aspect to the 1993-1994 recovery was the turnaround in the goods-producing sector. This sector suffered particularly heavy job losses and restructuring in 1992 and 1993, yet in 1994 it became the major source for employment growth. Services, which had accounted for most of the employment growth in 1993, accounted for about two-thirds in 1994; the rate of job growth in the goods producing sector succeeded services for only the second time in the past decade.

The unemployment rate in Canada has stabilized at around 9.5 percent, relatively high for a developed economy in recovery. There is some evidence that the type of corporate restructuring that occurred between 1989 and 1994 has helped move the equilibrium unemployment rate out along a continuum. A strong aspect of the last two recoveries, namely 1988-1989 and 1993-1994, was the relatively high rate of real spending on business investment in capital goods. Firms seem to be using more capital, proportionately, in their production processes, and the cost of this capital has declined somewhat relative to labor. The dramatic decline in the real cost of computers and computer-based technologies in factory production seems to have contributed substantially to this shift. Computers accounted for about 3 percent of the total expenditures on machinery and equipment in 1981, and by 1988, this share had increased to 14 percent. By 1993, this percentage had increased even further to 37 percent.

Canada has a long tradition of trade unionism and almost a third of all workers are unionized, compared with one-fifth in the US. Union membership is still increasing in Canada, however, the labor force has grown at a faster rate, and this has resulted in a decline in the proportion of union members in labor from 31.2 percent in 1978 to 29.2 percent in 1994. With a total membership of 2.5 million, the largest central labor party is the Canadian Labour Congress (CLC). The CLC accounts for approximately 61 percent of all unionized workers. The next two largest central bodies, the Confederation of National Trade Unions (CNTU), with a membership of 260,000, and the Canadian Federation of Labour, with 200,000 members, account for 6.3 percent and 4.9 percent of total union membership, respectively.

Several large strikes impacted the country in the early 1990s but in 1993, work stoppages reached a 50-year low. Work stoppages in 1994 were up only marginally. Job security, was, in fact, labor's number one priority in 1994 and is expected to remain the preeminent concern in 1995.

Trade and Investment

Trade Dependence Canada is highly dependent on foreign trade to maintain its standard of living: in 1995, the total value of merchandise foreign trade (exports and imports taken together) were worth 61 percent of Canada's GDP, more than any other G-7 nation. Three quarters of the country's output of natural resources is exported, as is more than one-half of its manufacturing output. However, about 23 percent of Canada's exports are now agricultural or forestry-related, as compared with almost 40 percent in 1965. This is a reflection of the relative increase in service and manufactured exports in recent years as a percentage of the total. The value of merchandise trade grew from $222.7 billion in 1988 to $352.5 billion in 1995, or up 59 percent. As mentioned, a large part of the recovery which began in 1994 was due to an increase in exports, particularly to the US. Likewise, total goods and services trade for Canada to all countries (merchandise and non-merchandise), went from

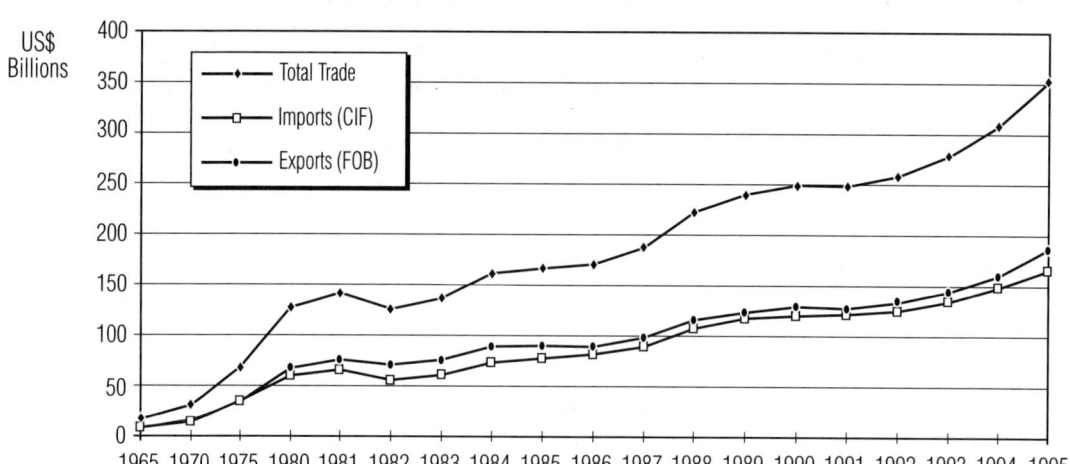

Source: IMF, International Financial Statistics Yearbook 1995; Statistics Canada

$405.9 billion to $458.7 billion between 1994 and 1995–that's an increase of 13 percent for the year.

Total trade, merchandise and non-merchandise, with the US went from $294.8 billion to $329.5 billion between 1994 and 1995, or up $34.7 billion. Merchandise exports to the US increased from $103.9 billion in 1992, to $148 billion at year-end 1995. US merchandise imports into Canada also grew from $79.3 billion in 1992 to $124 billion at year-end 1995. NAFTA certainly has had its impact: between 1994 and 1995, relative trade with the US went up 19.3 percent; trade with Canada's next leading partners, Japan and the UK, decreased 1.3 percent and 1.4 percent, respectively. Export trade with the US tends to be concentrated in certain groups, including motor vehicles, mineral fuels (petroleum and natural gas), machinery, wood products, and paper products.

Canada's merchandise trade balance has run in US$20.8 billion dollars, up substantially from US$11.2 billion dollars in 1994 (reflective of NAFTA and the low Canadian dollar). As a net importer of services, Canada has typically run a fairly large current accounts deficit; this is a function of its being a large importer of services, and the substantial income and dividend transfer payments made from direct investment and foreign subsidiaries operating inside Canada. In addition, the increasing amount of external debt has required debt service payments to be transferred outside the country.

Of the current accounts deficit—about $12 billion in 1995—over $4.1 billion was with the United States.

The fundamental mechanism for Canada's participation in the world trading system is the GATT (General Agreement on Tariffs and Trade), which Canada signed in 1948. GATT grants tariff concessions and reciprocal most favored nation trading status to all participating countries. Canada's major export trading partners for exports were, in 1995, the US, the UK, Germany, Japan, France, and the Netherlands. Major import partners for that year were the US, Germany, Japan, Mexico, the UK, France, and China.

NAFTA Takes Off Since the signing of NAFTA, US-Canadian trade has been increasing at breakneck speed, and is expected to double by the year 2000. But free trade agreements between the two countries are hardly new. After World War II Canada and the US entered into several sectorial free trade agreements, the most notable being the 1965 Automotive Trade Agreement, which was in part responsible for the extremely large volume of automotive trade now undertaken between the two countries (one-third of Canadian exports to the US are automotive). In 1985, the issue of a comprehensive free trade agreement took center stage under prime minister Brian Mulroney. With some Liberal party and union opposition, Mulroney negotiated and signed the treaty in early 1988. The debate that followed for parliamentary approval was intense, sparking a nationalist battle (Canadians have long worried that their culture and natural resources, and national identity, could be compromised by free trade, and the FTA proved to be the pivotal issue in the 1988 elections). The pact finally took effect in 1989.

In 1991, the US opened negotiations with Mexico for a bilateral agreement and Canada, not to be left out, joined forces. Before his election in 1993 Jean Chretien insisted on renegotiating portions of NAFTA, which the US and Mexican congresses had already ratified. He sought changes in dumping, energy and subsidies, but in the end, the other two countries conceded very little. NAFTA was ratified in December, 1993, and took effect in January 1994. All US tariff rates that were established under the FTA, have been incorporated into NAFTA, with phase-in periods varying for different goods.

Since the advent of NAFTA, Canadian trade with Mexico has risen from less than $1 billion to $6 billion. NAFTA creates the largest regional common market on the globe: 363 million consumers. The first year for NAFTA was marked by substantial trade and investment expansion but also some policy considerations and the resolution of some lingering technical disputes. Trade representatives from the three countries launched working groups devoted to the environment and labor. US and Canadian ministers have also spent much of 1994 and 1995 resolving some long-standing disputes over certain commodities and services (including lumber, wheat and dairy products, fish, and advertising).

In Canada, foreign investment (as with trade) has been acknowledged as an economic necessity, but not always the most welcome one: No other G-7 or developed country has such a high degree of asset ownership in foreign hands, (especially concentrated in the US); this has rankled elements of Canadian nationalism from the very start. From the early 19th century on, investment capital (much of it British) poured into Canada to build railroads, canals, and to develop the mining and lumber industries. After World War I, the US replaced Britain as the major source for foreign capital.

By the 1970s, foreign asset ownership in manufacturing was 58 percent; it was particularly high in certain industries: oil and gas, 60 percent; 70 percent in transportation; and 38 percent in mining. (In contrast, foreign investment in the US controlled only about 2 percent of American industry at the same time). At about this time, concerns over foreign asset ownership and net foreign debt led to the creation of the Foreign Investment Review Agency by the nationalistic Trudeau government. The focus of the FIRA was to control foreign investment by screening proposals made by foreigners, particularly Americans. In essence, the application had to prove that the foreign presence in Canada would be of substantial benefit to the Canadian economy by providing jobs, purchasing intermediate goods, or investing in infrastructure.

These criteria did not apply to Canadian companies, and a double standard was created. The adverse impact of FIRA was felt fairly quickly, however, and in 1984, the conservative Mulroney government replaced it with the Investment Canada Act. Offices of the Ministry of International Trade and Industry Canada review major foreign investments to determine if they are likely to be of net benefit to Canada, but it also actively promotes investment in Canada by both Canadians and non-Canadians alike. Canada screens only those direct foreign takeovers of firms with more than $5 million in assets, though the government still watches particular industries closely (culture, for example). Canada still maintains laws and policies that restrict certain types of foreign investment in sectors such as energy, publishing, telecommunications, transportation, film, music broadcasting, and cable television.

By and large, Canada seems to have capitulated to the reality that foreign investment is a critical

FOREIGN INVESTMENT, 1995

Foreign Direct Investment Into Canada		Canadian Direct Investment Abroad	
Sector	% of Total	Sector	% of Total
Food, Beverage, & Tobacco	9.5	Food, Beverage, & Tobacco	6.8
Wood & Paper	4.7	Wood & Paper	3.3
Energy	11.7	Energy	11.7
Chemicals, Chem. Products, & Textiles	10.9	Chemicals, Chem. Products, & Textiles	4.7
Minerals & Metal Products	6.1	Minerals & Metal Products	16.2
Machinery & Equipment	4.2	Machinery & Equipment	.8
Transport Equipment	10.7	Transport Equipment	2.7
Electrical & Electronic Products	7.1	Electrical & Electronic Products	5.9
Construction	6.5	Construction	3.3
Transportation/ Communication	3.0	Transportation/ Communication	13.5
Finance & Insurance	18.1	Finance & Insurance	23.7
Consumer Goods/ Services	4.6	Consumer Goods/ Services	9.7
Other	2.9	Other	.9
Total	100.0	Total	100.0

Note: Total FDI into Canada was $168.08 billion; total CDI abroad was $142.35 billion.
Source: Statistics Canada

engine for its economy's continued economic growth. The multinational integration of Canada's largest industries, including vehicles, machinery, telecommunications, and electronics, has meant the mobility of more and more capital across borders. Since 1984, total foreign investment in Canada has increased fairly rapidly–from $86 billion in 1984 to $168.1 billion in 1995, or up 95 percent. Historically, American investment has dominated the total amount of foreign investment in Canada. In 1984, the stock of US foreign direct investment in Canada was $59.7 billion out of $86 billion, or 69.4 percent. By 1995, this percentage had not changed greatly: the total stock of US investment was $113.1 billion, or 64.9 percent of $168.1 billion. The next most significant investor was Britain, with $16.5 billion in 1995. In recent years, the machinery and transport, and finance and insurance sectors have attracted the largest net flow of foreign capital inward.

In 1993, four out of the ten largest Canadian corporations were foreign-owned subsidiaries. In fact, they ranked 2, 3, 4 and 9 and were all US owned:

FEDERAL FINANCE

	Gross Revenue	Gross Expenditure	Net Debt
	(C$Millions)	(C$Millions)	(C$Millions)
1981	51,814	67,829	84,672
1985	78,055	115,039	202,104
1989	109,506	136,334	326,484
1990	120,748	148,748	354,848
1991	127,112	158,971	386,785
1992	129,170	167,141	386,785
1993	132,210	171,405	461,685
1994	129,365	171,039	503,766
1995e	136,230	175,520	543,063

e=estimated

Largest Corporations—1993 Sales

		$Millions
1.	BCE Inc.	21,777
2.	GM of Canada	21,777
3.	Ford Motor Co.	15,918
4.	Chrysler Canada	13,595
5.	George Weston	11,931
6.	Alcan Aluminum	9,329
7.	Ontario Hydro	8,363
8.	Imasco, Ltd.	7,972
9.	Imperial Oil (US)	7,809
10.	Thompson Corp.	7,545

POLITICAL DEVELOPMENTS IN ECONOMY

One of strongest political concerns impacting Canada today are the federal and provincial budget deficits. Over the last few years in particular, a great deal of debt and debt servicing has built up from the recession of the early '90s (leading to lower revenue) and the higher interest rates of the late 1980s. Per capita debt ratio is among the highest of the developed countries, and the government spends about 36 percent of revenues just servicing the debt. Ten years ago, the debt was about half the size of the economy; today, it is almost 74 percent. Clearly, managing this debt, while at the same time maintaining the basic framework of social services which Canada is known for and Canadians are used to, will be one of the strongest priorities for the Liberal Party administration over the next two years.

Government options to reduce the deficit are somewhat constrained by non-discretionary spending, however the government, under the spear of Finance Minister Paul Martin, announced in early 1996 a second "stay the course" budget designed to reduce the deficit to 2 percent of GDP by 1997-1998. Martin's targets include deficit reductions of $24.3 billion in 1996-1997 and $17 billion in 1997/1998. Key reforms on the agenda: freezing the ceiling limit of tax-free contributions to retirement savings plans; no new spending and redirected spending from cut programs; delaying funding of the Canadian Broadcasting Commission's long-promised 7.5 percent levy on certain services; and adjusting pension benefits for the old age security system to reflect gross family, not individual, income. If the deficit does manage to drop to $17 billion, and if growth can continue, then the Liberal Party will have managed a key breakthrough: debt will begin to decline as a percentage of GDP. The key to this rationale will be the maintenance of a fairly healthy rate of economic growth.

Current Issues

INTRODUCTION

With its technologically advanced, market economy and affluent and consumer-oriented society, Canada appears to closely resemble its neighbor to the south, the United States. And, indeed, in many ways it does: like the US, Canada has its political roots in English common law (with the exception of Quebec, which bases certain tenets on French civil code); it is a democracy, ruled by an elected premier and a House of Commons, (not unlike the US Congress, albeit with multiple parties); and perhaps most importantly, Canada, like the US, is an outward-looking country, an advanced democracy at work, with a strong history of supporting the NATO Alliance and US policy in many regional and global matters.

For these reasons, perhaps, the US has taken certain aspects of its relationship with Canada for granted over the past decade or so, namely its political stability and economic accessibility. During the 1980s, Canada averaged a real GDP growth rate of about 3-4 percent, one of the highest rates among the OECD nations. With its skilled and educated labor force, modernized plant and equipment, and abundant natural resources, Canada holds out excellent prospects for continued future economic growth. The US stands ready to benefit from this, especially as regards international trade: The total value of merchandise trade between the two countries in 1994 was about $243 billion, more than between any two other countries in the world. The US is the destination for more than 80 percent of Canada's exports, and Canada provides the US with over 17 percent of its imports, including major amounts of wood and wood products, grain and other agricultural products, newsprint, crude petroleum and natural gas, and motor vehicle parts and components. In conjunction with the CFTA and NAFTA, trade increased $70 billion between the two countries, or 35 percent, between 1989 and 1994.

But today, as the year 2000 approaches, it is increasingly obvious that Canada is undergoing a major political transition, one which has its roots not only in the issue of Quebec separatism but also in issues that tackle the core of what Canada has always been known to stand for. With unprecedented budget deficits at the provincial and federal levels, under attack is the Canadian government's continued ability to provide an advanced level of social services to its entire populace (especially in the areas of education and health-care). For a nation that was, just two years ago, rated No. 1 in the world in the United Nations human development index, these issues strike close to the collective identity of the Canadian people. As with other nations in the developed world, the most recent economic recovery has been largely "jobless" in nature, and many Canadians are deeply worried about their quality of life. This was evidenced strongly in the most recent national poll undertaken in January, 1996 by Maclean's magazine: in twelve years, never have the pollsters' conclusions on data regarding the "mood of the country" been so mixed.

CANADA'S POLITICAL LEGACY

Canada is a constitutional monarchy with a federal and parliamentary system, and a strong tradition of human rights (the 1982 Charter of Rights guarantees basic rights in many areas). It is composed of ten provinces, two territories, and a federal government, elected for a term not to exceed five years. Canada's federal Parliament consists of an elected House of Commons and an

---

CONTENTS
Introduction 19
Canada's Political Legacy 19
Diversity and Unity:
　A National Debate 20
Quebec Separatism 21
Facing the Deficit 24

appointed Senate. The prime minister is official leader of the majority party in power in the House, and is head of the Cabinet.

Queen Elizabeth II, as official Queen of Canada, appoints a governor general (currently Romeo LeBlanc) for a five-year term, generally on the advice of the prime minister. Each province is governed by a premier and a single, elected legislative chamber. A lieutenant governor appointed by the governor general represents the Crown in each province.

Recent Political History

The Liberal party, under the leadership of Pierre Trudeau, held power in Ottawa throughout most of the 1970s, and was reelected again in 1980. Popular support for Trudeau and his brand of socialism waned in the 1980s as the country was impacted by a major economic recession, and the popularity of Brian Mulroney, head of the Progressive Conservative party (PC), began to rise. In 1984 under popular pressure, Trudeau resigned, and his Liberal successor, John Turner, called for general elections. In September of 1984, Mulroney's party gained a strong majority and he then became prime minister.

Mulroney's tenure as Canada's prime minister was a rocky one, characterized by frequent cabinet changes and resignations, and by criticism from the Liberals and New Democrats of the government's handling of the negotiations surrounding a new US-Canadian free trade agreement (CFTA). Unlike his predecessors, Mulroney was decidedly free trade and pro-American; this rankled some members of Parliament. The opposing political parties viewed Mulroney as being overly acquiescent to US trade interests, with possible damage to Canadian economic self-reliance.

After a great deal of public debate, the Canada-US free trade agreement was approved in August, 1988 by the House of Commons. In November, the PC party was reelected, and full legislative ratification of the trade agreement finally followed in December, 1988.

In February, 1990, the Canadian government opened trade negotiations with Mexico. These discussions were soon joined by the US, and in December, 1993, Canada, the US and Mexico finalized terms for the North American Free Trade Agreement, which created a free trade zone encompassing the whole of North America. That treaty came into force on January 1, 1994.

In September, 1990 the Senate refused to support Liberal legislation that would implement a controversial Goods and Services Tax (GST). This prompted Mulroney to exercise a constitutional provision to create eight additional seats in the Senate and fill them with PC appointees in an attempt to push the GST through. The tax finally passed in January 1991; however, by that time Mulroney's government had lost much of its popular support.

The current Liberal Party government, led by prime minister Jean Chretien, won 178 of the 295 seats in the House of Commons when elections were held in October, 1993. The most recent elections, held March 25, 1996, changed the House very little, still giving the Liberal party a strong majority. The Liberals now hold 177 seats, and the main opposition party is the Bloc Quebecois party, which holds 53 seats (gaining one seat in the last election) in the House and Senate, closely followed by the Reform party, a western-based conservative party with 52 seats (the other parties–the New Democratic and Progressive Conservative–hold less than nine seats each).

DIVERSITY AND UNITY— A NATIONAL DEBATE

Canada the confederacy is attempting to cope with the increasing "dissimilarities" of its people, including a growing sense of economic regionalism and self-destiny in certain provinces (especially British Columbia and the west), and a greater political need (either perceived or real) amongst both the provinces as well as different groups for the desirability and feasibility of "self-rule."

At the heart of the national debate on the nature of unity are several key issues: Quebec's desire to preserve and strengthen its distinctive culture; the western provinces' desire for more control over their economies and natural resources, especially energy and timber; industrialized central Canada, which is concerned with economic development; the Atlantic provinces, who are facing the painful economic decline of their fisheries industries, and have resisted federal claims to the natural resources off their shores. In addition to these provincial concerns, there is also the desire of the indigenous peoples of Canada for greater self-rule.

The Indians and Inuits

One minority of special importance to the Canada are the native Inuit and Indian populations, which account for about 2 percent of the total population. When the first Europeans came to settle Canada, there were already about 200,000 native people speaking a huge variety of dialects. Today there are about 510,000 Indians registered under the Indian Act of Canada. In 1970, the government adopted a policy of assimiliation of the Indians; but this has backfired to a great extent, and the reservation's populations are remaining stable.

Not only do the Inuit and Indian reservations occupy a large amount of land, but the tribes have a special relationship, both by treaty and legislation, with the rest of Canada. About half of all the Indians, primarily those in the Prairie provinces, receive payments from treaties established earlier with the British government, and many tribes are laying claim to public lands. The question of land treaty claims came to the forefront of Canadian politics in 1990, and was in fact, part of the issue surrounding the failure of a referendum on Quebec–the Meech Lake Accord. In Manitoba, the Cree Indian representative singlehandedly prevented the legislative assembly from approving the accord because it lacked a specific clause on native rights.

In Quebec, at the same time, Mohawk Indians protested the building of a development on what they claimed were ancestral lands. Ottawa agreed to buy the land and turn it over to the tribe, but in July, 1990, Mohawk militants stormed the bridge in Montreal connecting the city with the southern shore of the St. Lawrence. Throughout Canada Indians voiced their support of the incident by blocking roads and rail lines, and conducting public demonstrations.

The Canadian government is now attempting to settle hundreds of land claims made by indigenous peoples, but the legal and political issues are immense. In October, 1992, the government approved an historic land claim in the eastern Arctic for the Inuit, the Nunavut Political Accord. The accord maps out an entire region in the Northwest Territories which will be under control of the Inuit, to be established by 1999. Nunavut will cover over 2.2 million square kilometers, and the indigenous government will operate much as the territorial governments do today.

In British Columbia, where some 49 indigenous tribes have been negotiating for land treaties, the New Democratic government has set a target of 5 percent of the province's territory to be transferred to Indian ownership. Total compensation for the transfers could reach $4.5 billion, taken mostly from federal funds. In February of 1996, a hard-won agreement was finally reached with the Nisga tribe, given them ownership of 1,930 square kilometers in the Nassy Valley, along with an annual share in British Columbia's fishing industry and cash compensation. The treaty process has been controversial, with militant Indians on the one side and white hardliners on the other, fearful that any concessions could lead to a form of "reverse racism" with Indians being granted special rights on their homelands.

QUEBEC SEPARATISM

The issue of national identity and unity is not only tied to Canada's ethnic populace, but to provincial self-rule as well. At the heart of the debate is the constitutional crisis inherent in Quebec separatism. In the past, the Canadian government has responded to the question of national unity by attempting to reform the Canadian constitution to reflect the changing dynamics of the provincial political systems. If these issues are not met head on, and some sort of lasting political consensus is not achieved, the continued viability of Canada's confederacy will come more and more under question, and the results could surprise everyone, even its placated neighbor to the south.

In the province of Quebec, where four-fifths of the population speaks French as a first language, and which "officially" maintains its own cultural identity with a set of laws governing language and culture, the question of political self-determination has indeed overcome all other issues in Canadian politics today to become the overriding political concern of the last decade.

Quebecers have considered themselves a separate culture since the late 1700s, when war between the British and French in Europe spilled over into conflict in the American territories. However, the basis of the modern-day conflict evolved in 1982, when Britain approved a transfer of legislative power from its own parliament to the Canadian central government and the provinces. Following two years of negotiations, all the provinces except Quebec had accepted these new constitutional provisions, which included a charter of rights and a formula for constitutional amendment (with the amendments needing support of at least seven provinces, and representing more than 50 percent of the population for approval). To this day, Quebec has refused to agree to this system of constitutional reform, insisting on holding its own veto power.

The 1980s and early 1990s were marked by several legislative attempts by the federal government to devise a compromise which Quebec would adhere to–all unsuccessful. The failure to appease the Quebec separatists–specifically the June, 1990 failure to ratify the Meech Lake Accord amending the constitution to allow for provincial veto power, and the October, 1992 rejection by voters of another constitutional amendment, the Charlottetown Agreement–have proved that consensus on this question will be agonizingly difficult.

Meech Lake and Charlottestown

Following the return to power of the Liberal party in Quebec province in 1985, the federal government adopted another set of new initiatives designed to include Quebec in its constitutional reform. In April, 1987 Mulroney and the provincial premiers met at Meech Lake, Quebec, with the aim of negotiating a constitutional provision acceptable to Quebec. The resulting agreement, the Meech Lake Accord, was finally approved in June. The

Meech Lake Accord defined Quebec as a "distinct society" within the Canadian confederacy, and in addition, granted all the provinces substantial new powers in the areas of federal parliamentary reform, judicial appointments, and the creation of new provinces. The Accord was required to be ratified not later than June 1990, by the federal parliament and all the provincial legislatures.

Opposition to the Meech Lake arrangements first originated in Newfoundland, on the grounds that it granted too much political influence to Quebec, and failed to provide Inuit and other indigenous minorities with the same level of constitutional treatment as the francophones. In March, 1990 the Newfoundland legislature revoked its earlier endorsement of the Accord. Following a meeting in June between Mulroney and the provincial premiers, the province of New Brunswick agreed to accept the Accord, but the provinces of Manitoba and Newfoundland upheld their opposition. Approval of the Meech Lake Accord was not completed by June, and the Quebec government, which had opposed any changes to earlier versions of the Accord, responded by refusing to participate in any future provincial conferences, and by appointing its own internal commission to make recommendations regarding the province's political future.

In May, 1990 seven Progressive Conservative members of the House of Commons, led by Lucien Bouchard (a former member of Mulroney's Cabinet) formed a new party, the Bloc Quebecois (BQ), with the stated objective of obtaining a "sovereign Quebec." The BQ soon expanded, with a few Liberal defections, to nine members.

The stalemate of the Meech Lake Accord had, in retrospect, set the tone for the continuance of the constitutional dilemma centering around separatism throughout the late eighties and until October, 1995, when the most recent referendum on separatism was held.

In late August 1992, after a number of stalemated talks throughout the spring, a new agenda of constitutional reforms, known as the Charlottetown Agreement, was finalized for submission to a national referendum. These proposals, which were endorsed by eleven of the provincial premiers as well as the leaders of the three main political parties, provided for an equal and elected Senate, a guarantee in perpetuity to Quebec of one-quarter of the seats in the federal House of Commons (regardless of future population), and also three of the nine seats on the Supreme Court of Canada. There was also to be recognition of provincial jurisdiction in cultural affairs, and increased provincial authority over certain economic and immigration policies. The inherent right to self-government of the Indian and Inuit population was also to be recognized.

Alas, substantial opposition to the Charlottetown Agreement became evident during the debates that preceded the referendum, especially among NDP and Liberal supporters (with Pierre Trudeau resurfacing to voice his denouncement). There was also substantial opposition in the western provinces. The Charlottetown proposals were ultimately defeated in a national referendum in October, 1992 by a margin of 54.4 percent to 44.6 percent, with only four of the provinces actually endorsing the amendment. Once again, federalist attempts at constitutional reform to appease the Quebecers, while at the same time attempting to preserve the essentials of unity, had failed.

The failure of the Charlottetown Agreement severely impacted the Mulroney administration's credibility, and the October, 1993 elections resulted in a wide margin of victory for the Liberals, led by the career politician, Jean Chretien. A significant realignment of the political parties was reflected in the new Parliament, with PC representation reduced to only two seats, and the Bloc Quebecois (BQ) emerging narrowly as the official opposition party, with 53 seats (including BQ leader Louis Bouchard's seat). Since this time, the BQ has articulated as its primary political agenda the achievement of full sovereignty for Quebec.

The 1995 Referendum and Its Aftermath

Tired of the country's seemingly unsolvable constitutional dilemmas, many Canadians today, especially the anglophones, focus on the nation's more pressing economic concerns. Nonetheless, the election of the sovereigntist Bloc Quebecois as Canada's official opposition party in 1993, led until just recently by the charismatic and vocal Lucien Bouchard, coupled with the election in September 1994 of the separatist Parti Quebecois as Quebec's provincial government (led by Jacques Parizeau, until he was replaced by Bouchard in March, 1996), has kept the issue of national unity and separatism growing to an unprecedented level.

Canada's latest bout with a referendum on separatism occurred in October, 1995, after a year and a half of intense lobbying on the part of Quebec leader Jacques Parizeau. Although the federal government, spearheaded by Chretien's Liberal majority, has maintained that the majority of the Quebec population still feels ambivalent towards succession, in December 1994, the Quebec legislature approved measures to prepare for the referendum, and Parizeau initiated a program of public forums in order to determine the terms under which the provincial electorate would be asked to approve Quebec's withdrawal from federal Canada.

This most recent referendum, held in Quebec in October, 1995, was clearly the most contentious yet, and its very narrow defeat (50.56 percent to 49.44 percent), has been perceived as a major indicator of the inevitability of some form of separation soon. For perhaps the first time, the rest of English-speaking Canada has had to come to grips with the possibility of a huge national change. Undoubtedly, the narrow margin of this defeat was to a very large extent achieved by the BQ leader in Ottawa, Louis Bouchard. Since 1993, Bouchard's platform has focused not on constitutional amendment—which the federalists, other provinces, and other parties have to varying degrees been amenable too—but on nothing short of sovereign separation. Bouchard's form of separatism focuses on Quebec as an absolutely culturally and linguistically distinct society, one that cannot be satisfied with constitutional concessions or even special treatment by Ottawa or the rest of the provinces. Bouchard refers to the rest of the nation as 'le Canada Anglais,' and says that even though the English-speaking Quebecers have made up their minds (with a nay vote), there is only a small minority of ambivalent French-speaking Canadians left in Quebec who could easily swing the vote in the next referendum.

For Quebecers, separatism is an "economically void" situation–there would seem to be no immediate economic gain from it, and indeed, such a move could put substantial strain on the province's budgetary decisions. But to the francophone, such realities are, well, mere formalities. Quebec francophones view themselves as a "society distinct from the rest."

The Federalist Response

It is hard to believe such an extreme change in Canada's political situation could be made based on a simple majority vote, and the federalists, for their part, have quickly come up with an agenda to nullify Quebec's power to succeed based on simple majority. In February, 1996, a new master plan on unity was presented to the government by a cabinet committee on national unity, spearheaded by Treasury Board president Marcel Masse. The first part concentrates on the economic redistribution of powers between Ottawa and the provinces, further defining the monetary responsibilities in which Ottawa can excel. The second part proposes a new hardline stance that would see the federal government refuse to honor future referendum results on separation unless a strong provincial consensus is made clear–and unless far more than 50 percent of the population votes to separate. In effect, this would give the federalists veto power over a successful Quebec referendum. These proposals will be taken up this spring.

The Chretien government, in an effort to mobilize its current unity strategy, (which includes the reorganization of the Quebec legislature), recently appointed a new Intergovernmental Unity minister, Stephane Dion (recently confirmed to the Parliament on March 25), to bolster support amongst the provinces. The reaction on the part of other provincial premiers has been mixed. There is a concern shared amongst the provinces that Quebec and the federal government are willing to allow changes to the constitution that by authorizing a "distinct society," would, by implication, confer special status to certain parts of the country, and thereby recognize different levels of citizenship. Whether Dion (himself a Quebecer) or anybody else, for that matter, can garner provincial consensus on the theoretical issues remains in question.

The former BQ leader Bouchard has returned to Quebec to take the throne as head of Parti Quebecois, after Jacques Parizeau's resignation in late January, 1996. (Parizeau was forced to resign after the referendum for blaming the defeat on Quebec's English 'minorities.' Even to the culturally distinct francophones, it seems, this bordered on racism.) Though Bouchard promises not to immediately press the separatism issue amongst vote weary Quebecers, it is very much on his agenda to reorganize and regroup. Bouchard's most pressing near-term concern will be to reconcile Quebec's budget deficit, which looms at $1 billion this year (out of $42.4 billion). Still, he has promised not to raise taxes, and his authority on the leadership of such issues is without question: a tax hike that had been scheduled by the outgoing finance cabinet ministers of Jacques Parizeau was swiftly struck down by the new premier before he had even officially arrived back in Quebec.

Bouchard's program for the near future remains vague, but he has dropped a few hints: bolster government coffers through deep spending cuts, embark on a privatization campaign for some of the provincially owned corporations. Quebec Finance Minister Bernard Landry has said the province's dim financial situation may force the Parti Quebecois government to introduce user fees on a variety of services, including highways. But Landry has also said he hoped Quebec, which now has a projected budget total deficit of $3.9 billion, can avoid the harsh cutbacks that have occurred in Ontario and Alberta.

The State of It All

Whatever Bouchard's eventual strategy, it seems clear that Ottawa is gearing up for the next round in the national unity battle. After the exceedingly narrow defeat in October of 1995, the unity issue seems to now cloud the entire federal agenda: from impending budgets to cabinet choices. This concern was articulated in January in a speech by Bank of Montreal chairman Mathew Barrett warning that Quebec separatism could cost Canada up to $200 billion in lost production. Along with other options, Barrett proposed a constituent assembly to fashion a new model for Canada. Voices from other elements of the Canadian business community are urging a cohesive agenda on unity.

Along the same lines, the Reform party in January came up with an agenda sketching 20 proposals for a new confederation, including a massive redistribution of powers from Ottawa to the provinces. Reform also proposed 20 "realities of succession"–among them, splitting the national debt between Quebec and the rest of Canada, and establishing a connecting land bridge between Ontario and the Martimes-that would, in effect, be used as a bargaining chip against Quebec should it decide to break away.

More and more, there is decreasing evidence that the "distinct-society, veto-power, incremental changes to federalism" approach can hold water. To some, Canada may be on its way to becoming an alliance of regions largely self-determining under the umbrella of a "superstructure government," one responsible for monetary policy, trade, defense and treaties, and not much else.

FACING THE DEFICIT

Even with the aftermath of federalism's near loss in the Quebec referendum, many of the average Canadian's concerns are now focused around the economic. Despite the generally healthy rate of economic growth in Canada these past four years, the private sector is also facing a laggingly high unemployment rate (over 9.5 percent) and plenty of job restructuring. Of major concern also: ongoing cuts in many of Canada's major social programs: welfare and unemployment insurance, and the future of the Canada Pension Plan. Most Canadians overwhelmingly approve of the need for deficit reduction- 66 percent, according to the Maclean poll, but, as with most things political, no one wants the pain.

Since October of 1993, the new Liberal government, headed by the bulldoggy Jean Chretien, has set out to implement an economic austerity program, one focusing on massive spending cutbacks in many social programs, reductions in defense expenditures, and the implementation of NAFTA. Chretien, an avowed federalist, has also worked hard to devise a federal unity strategy that the rest of Canada can swallow.

The crisis is such that the national debt is still rising at $100 million a day after interest charges, and the total debt to GDP ratio of 103 percent is now the second highest in the industrialized world.

In Ottawa, speculation in the spring of 1996 is ongoing as to how federal economic policy under the Liberal party and Jean Chretien, should proceed. Chretien, a strong federalist, is also a fundamental pragmatist who has shown himself capable of dealing with the most pressing issues.

In March 1996, Canada released its next two-year budget plan, which will target a two percent deficit to gross domestic product ratio for the fiscal year 1997-98–its lowest in 23 years. Spearheaded by finance minister Paul Martin, the budget calls for the deficit to decline 26 percent this year to $24.3 billion (or US $17.7 billion). The corner stones of Martin's budget: further cuts in social programs, reducing foreign aid and defense spending, a phase-out of a dairy-industry subsidy and revenue generation through privatization.

The provinces are also facing their own economic woes, as provincial budgets are also staggering under enormous debt. When Ralph Klein became Alberta's premier in December, 1992, the budget deficit stood at $3.4 billion. Klein soon introduced a Deficit Elimination Act, binding the government to balance the books by 1997. The most recent budget featured a projected deficit of $506 million– a reduction of 85 percent over three years. But the fiscal success has come at an enormous price, with over 4,500 Alberta civil servants loosing their jobs, hospitals closing, reduced services, and rising health care premiums.

Since 1989, Ontario's debt has ballooned from 15 percent to 35 percent, and the government has responded with fiscal austerity. Tory leader Mike Harris rose to power in last summer's elections on a program of "common sense revolution." In its initial cuts last July, the Harris government trimmed about $2 billion from the province's deficit of almost $11 billion, and is planning another $6 billion in cuts over the next three years. This has largely been accomplished through the province's welfare rolls.

In addition to Ontario and Quebec, in Newfoundland, newly elected premier Brian Tobin is faced with an $8 billion debt, a budget deficit of $200 million in the coming year, and unemployed workers dropping off the rolls of federal income support. Hardest hit has the been the fisheries industry. Any pending federal employment insurance reforms are sure to impact the many seasonal workers in Newfoundland's economy.

In an attempt to shore up revenues without the need for tax increases, the federal government has undergone a large round of privatizations. The fall of 1995 saw two of the largest; first on the list was the national icon, Canadian National (CN) railway, also planned is the government's remaining 70 percent stake in Petro-Canada, an oil and gas firm. The CN deal was estimated to yield about $2 billion (or $1.5 billion in US), much of this from foreign investors. Unlike other privatization schemes (such as those in Britain), the political desire for this in Canada is half-hearted; it is motivated more importantly by the overwhelming need for cash.

At the provincial level, privatization is gaining steam. Alberta has sold its telephone company, Saskatchewan has spun off big potash and uranium production mines. Still, the two biggest provinces, Ontario and Quebec, have thus far been reluctant to take on any privatization schemes.

Labor Rises from the Ashes

In spite of Martin's and other governmental official assurances, Canadian workers are beginning to react to these changes. After many years of low profile activity, Canadian workers are once again "hitting the streets." Analysts are predicting that strikes and lockouts will climb in 1996, from the lowest levels in almost half a century, as unions and public workers protest stagnant wages, government cutbacks, and continued layoffs amid historically high corporate profits.

In Ontario, Canada's richest and most populated province, organized labour is locking horns with the Harris government and the province's business community. Thousands of government workers were off the job in March in Ontario's first ever civil service strike against government plans to cut between 13,000 to 27,000 jobs from an 81,000 payroll.

Chretien, ever the realist, has just reshuffled his cabinet. His biggest surprise: bringing in two francophone Quebecers-the constitutional expert Dion, (the newly appointed unity minister), and international trade analyst Pierre Pettigrew. In a recent speech approved by Chretien in advance, Dion articulated the government's desires for an "intelligent decentralization," and cited Switzerland, one of the most decentralized federations in the world, as a possible model. Also recently brought in: David Dingwall, the new health minister, whose mandate will be to reduce Ottawa's involvement in health care. According to Chretien, the results of the latest election, with Liberal victory for five of the six seats (except for the sole BQ seat in northern Quebec), were a signal of the populace's confidence in its Liberal government. Be that as it may, Chretien's mandate, in the coming years, must prove its worth.

Opportunities

CONTENTS

Importing from Canada 27
Agricultural Machinery 27
Chemicals 28
Electronic Components 28
Energy, Oil, and Natural Gas 28
Food and Beverages 28
Forestry Products 29
Minerals 29
Motor Vehicles and Parts 29
Telecommunication Products 29
Textiles and Apparel 30
Exporting to Canada 30
Agricultural and Food Products 30
Aircrafts and Parts 31
Boating Equipment 31
Building Products 31
Computers and Computer Software 31
Electronic Products 32
Furniture and Office Supplies 32
Office Supplies 33
Health Products 33
Household Appliances and Products 34
Industrial Machinery 35
Plastics and Chemicals 35
Pollution Control Equipment 35
Telecommunication Products 36
Textiles and Apparel 36
Toys and Sporting Goods 37
Vehicles and Parts 37
Opportunities for Growth 38
Computers and Computer Software 38
Environmental Protection Industry 38
Film and Television 38
Franchising 39
Home Improvement 39
Manufacturing 39
Services 39
Telecommunications 39
Public Procurement 40
Opportunities 40
Procurement Procedures 41
NAFTA 41
Financing 41

IMPORTING FROM CANADA

Canada's emergence from the economic recession of the 1990s was in part led by a strong demand for its export products. As international demand grew, Canadian manufacturing production increased to meet that demand. Its manufacturing capability is, in part, based on the wealth of natural resources the country possesses—in agriculture, forestry, and minerals—and in the sophisticated, highly educated quality of its workforce. Many of its strongest exports are related to these strengths, as well as to the manufacturing sophistication of Canadian industry. Canada is also competing more and more on an international level with emerging industrial nations, and the demand for its products has been influenced by a reduction in tariffs based on the NAFTA and GATT agreements.

AGRICULTURAL MACHINERY

The Canadian agriculture equipment industry produces all types of machinery including combine harvesters, seeding and tillage equipment, hay handling and harvesting equipment, and grain handling and storage equipment. The industry is composed of full-line firms that market a complete line of farm equipment and short-line firms which produce a variety of agricultural implements and attachments.

Throughout the last three years, Canada's domestic production of field agriculture equipment has been driven by its export market. In fact, real growth in domestic production of field agriculture equipment has almost exactly equaled the growth in Canadian exports of this equipment. Devaluation of the Canadian currency has made Canadian exports relatively less expensive in the international market. Industry sources expect Canadian production to remain high during the period of 1995 to 1997, with real growth predicted at between 10 and 12 percent annually. Canadian domestic production of field agriculture equipment experienced real growth of 55.8 percent, from US$228.4 million in 1992 to US$337.3 million in 1993. Between 1993 and 1994, Canadian production experienced further real growth of 11.4 percent (with the total value of production at US$355.8 million) by the end of 1994.

Some Hot Items:
- balers
- combine harvester-threshers
- harrows
- harvesting machinery
- haying machines
- machinery for soil preparation or cultivation
- manure spreaders and fertilizer distributors
- mechanical sprayers
- plows
- seeders, planters, and transplanters
- threshing machine

CHEMICALS

Exports from Canada have recently been favored by increased international demand and, in some cases, by Canadian producers concentrating on becoming world-class competitors in niche markets. In 1994, sales for Canadian chemical producers increased by 16.8 percent. Exports rose by 11 percent. Free trade agreements with the US and Mexico have opened markets and company restructuring during the late 1980s and early 1990s has made the Canadian chemical industry more competitive and productive.

Some Hot Items:
- fertilizers
- inorganic chemicals
- paint and coatings
- pesticides
- petrochemicals
- plastics
- specialty and fine chemicals

ELECTRONIC COMPONENTS

The Canadian electronic components market experienced only a minor slump during the early 1990s due to the prolonged economic malaise and declining military spending of the post-Cold War era. The recent end to the recession coupled with the purchasing potential of emerging markets, such as China and India, should result in a considerable increase in sales of Canadian electronic components during the forecast period of 1994 to 1996. The combination of stronger domestic and foreign demand will help the Canadian switches and relays market reach its highest rates of productivity and growth since 1990. Capacity levels will also become less strained due to the growing trend toward buyer-vendor partnerships and just-in-time inventory systems.

Some Hot Items:
- switches
- relays
- semiconductors

ENERGY, OIL, AND NATURAL GAS

Canada is a major producer of hydroelectricity, oil, and gas. It is a net exporter of energy (primarily gas and electricity). Canada's exports and imports of oil are currently in approximate balance. Crude petroleum is the largest single component of Canada's minerals output. Canada annually produces more than 500 million barrels of oil and about 5.5 trillion cubic feet of natural gas. In 1991, its coal production amounted to 71.1 million tons and was valued at US$1.66 billion. Canada's coal resources amount to only about 2 percent of total world resources, but it exports 50 percent of its production and was, in 1991, the fourth largest coal exporting nation.

Some Hot Items:
- coal
- hydroelectric power
- natural gas
- oil

FOOD AND BEVERAGES

Canada is a world leader in the export of food products. Canada produces vast amounts of wheat, and accounts for about 20 percent of the world trade of this commodity. The prairies of Ontario and Saskatchewan are especially suited for the cultivation of field crops. Federal and provincial departments of agriculture work together with farmers to manage production and prices, and although food imports have risen sharply in recent years, Canada remains a net food exporter.

Two of the world's prime fishing areas are located off the Canadian coast—one is in the Atlantic Ocean off the coast of Newfoundland, and includes the Gulf of St. Lawrence, and the other is in the waters off the coast and in the bays and rivers of British Columbia. Salmon is the most valuable export in the Canadian fishing industry.

Some Hot Items:
- barley
- beverages and spirits
- cereals
- fresh fruit
- halibut

- herring
- lake trout
- livestock
- pickerel
- salmon
- vegetables
- wheat
- whitefish

- molybdenum
- nickel
- platinum
- potash
- silver
- uranium
- zinc

FORESTRY PRODUCTS

The country is a world leader in exporting wood and paper products. Forest covers about half of Canada's total land area. Forestry products exports, including pulp and paper, represent 15 percent of Canada's total export trade. Nearly two-thirds is exported to the US. Canada is the world's leading producer of newsprint, accounting for 40 percent of the global output. Almost 75 percent of Canada's total newsprint production is exported to the US. After experiencing difficult times during recent years, the Canadian forest industry is now undergoing a positive turnaround and is positioning itself to export a great deal of goods to world markets. Prices for wood products are increasing and markets worldwide are growing.

Some Hot Items:

- lumber
- newsprint
- printing and writing papers
- woodpulp

MINERALS

Canada ranks first in the world in mineral exports and third in mineral production after the US and the states of the former Soviet Union. It is the world's largest producer of zinc, potash, uranium, and nickel, and is among the world's largest producers in many other minerals. Every region has significant mineral resources. Since the 1970s, the minerals industry has been focusing on increasing productivity. Industry manufacturers have been investing in new and more efficient production technologies and closing expensive facilities. Although Canada is already a major world exporter of minerals, there are still large deposits of minerals it has not yet developed or has only recently begun to develop.

Some Hot Items:

- aluminum
- cobalt
- copper
- gold
- iron
- lead

MOTOR VEHICLES AND PARTS

Motor vehicles and parts account for one of the leading export categories in the Canadian economy. Much of these exports are tied to demand in the US, and products are manufactured in cooperation with a number of US automobile firms. Canada is an attractive place to assemble vehicles because of a cost-advantage (including lower health-care costs), and the more depreciated value of the Canadian dollar.

Some Hot Items:

- air bags
- anti-lock brake systems
- electronic components
- emission control equipment
- fuel injection
- internal combustion engines
- parts and accessories of bodies
- passenger and utility vehicles
- radiators
- transmission for motor vehicles

TELECOMMUNICATION PRODUCTS

The three major strengths of the Canadian telecommunications industry are its technology base, the strength of Northern Telecom, the major provider, and the sophisticated and advanced domestic Canadian market. Canada has one of the greatest levels of telephone service in the world. For many years, the charters of the domestic telephone companies included a government of Canada provision to ensure basic telephone service for all Canadians, regardless of geographic location. Overall telecommunications market growth is anticipated to average approximately 4 percent annually from 1993 to 1996. Total local production in 1994 of telecommunications products amounted to US$3.25 billion. Exports were valued at US$1.4 billion.

Some Hot Items:

- cellular phones
- central switching equipment
- data communication systems
- fiber-optic cables, connectors, and related transmission equipment
- voice processing equipment and systems

TEXTILES AND APPAREL

In 1992, an estimated 200 Canadian companies were engaged in exporting textiles and apparel. The industry's success in export markets is attributed to its growing reputation for fashion and quality products, and increased access to the large US market, resulting from the US-Canadian Free Trade Agreement (FTA) and, later, the North American Free Trade Agreement (NAFTA). Approximately 90 percent of total Canadian exports are destined for the US. Canadian companies are also adopting more structured exporting strategies such as establishing sales offices in targeted markets, and increasing niche marketing and advertising. To remain competitive, many Canadian manufacturers have recently specialized local operations and transferred remaining production to foreign subsidiaries or contract operations in low-cost producing countries such as China, Hong Kong, South Korea, and Taiwan. Canadian manufacturers continue to make adjustments and respond to global competition by investing in new technology, reducing the cost of production, and improving customer service.

Some Hot Items:

- carpets and other floor coverings
- child and infant clothing
- fur products
- men and boys' clothing
- sportswear
- synthetic fibers
- women's and girls' clothing
- wool and cotton fabrics
- yarn

EXPORTING TO CANADA

Canada is an affluent, industrialized country that depends on imports to maintain its high style of living and improve the productivity of its industrial and manufacturing base. Both individual and corporate consumers, therefore, import a wide range of products. As the Canadian economy moves to one with more high-tech manufacturing and develops its services sector, consumers have begun to import a wide range of basic manufactured products from the emerging industrial economies. The NAFTA and GATT agreements, as well as deregulation of the telecommunications sector, will continue to open the Canadian market to a wide variety of products.

AGRICULTURAL AND FOOD PRODUCTS

Canada imports a wide variety of agricultural and food products. Canadians are choosing food products based on new studies that link diet with health. Fruits and vegetables are becoming more popular; red meat is becoming less popular, though pork and beef are still bought in considerable quantities. Also, Canadian immigration over the last decade has tended to be dominated by persons whose traditional dietary habits include large amounts of fresh vegetables. In Canadian retail grocery stores, more space is devoted to fresh produce than to any other food sector.

Other sectors of the food market besides meat and vegetable staples are also growing. Canada has recently begun to import a large amount of baked goods; in the 1990s the number of imports of baked goods exceeded the number of exports. Ale is a popular liquid. Consumption of ale, beer and stout was 68 liters per person in 1993, compared with milk at 51 liters for two percent, 10 liters for one percent and six liters for skim milk. Strong growth is forecasted for snack and convenience foods.

In addition to food for human consumption, Canada also imports animal feed and pet food. The Canadian market for prepared animal feeds (livestock, poultry, horses, and fish) and feed supplements showed steady annual growth through the early 1990s, and the trend is expected to continue. Imports are expected to capture an increasing share of the market over the next few years. The total market for pet food in Canada doubled during the 1980s and has continued strong growth through the early 1990s.

Some Hot Items:

- ale and beer
- animal feeds
- bananas
- beef
- breads
- breakfast cereal
- cat and dog food
- chicken and pork
- cookies
- crackers
- fresh fruits and vegetables
- fresh or frozen fruit and vegetable juices
- lettuce
- pies
- snack foods
- rice
- dairy goods

AIRCRAFTS AND PARTS

Total imports into Canada of avionics and airport ground equipment satisfied approximately 30 percent of domestic Canadian demand during the period 1990 through 1992. Total imports of these goods into Canada increased by nearly 40 percent from 1990 to 1991 (from US$213.9 million to US$314.6 million), and then decreased slightly to US$306.9 million in 1992. Industry and government leaders anticipated that annual increases in imports for this subsector would average between 1.5 and 2.5 percent from 1993 to 1995, the same growth expected for the total market.

The Canadian government plays an active role in supporting the industry through procurement. The Department of National Defense plans to increase the amount allocated in the annual budget to purchase new equipment from 22 percent to 26 percent during the period 1993 through 1998. Defense sales comprise 30 percent of total sector sales. Canada represents the fifth largest import market for these products in the world.

Some Hot Items:
- engine components
- gas turbines
- helicopter parts
- navigational instruments and appliances
- radar apparatus
- radio navigational aids
- propellers
- turbojet and turbopropeller engines and parts

BOATING EQUIPMENT

Imports of boating equipment and accessories into Canada, which dominate the market, reached US$297.9 million in 1991 and grew to US$316.8 million in 1992, representing growth of more than 8 percent. Industry experts predict imports will grow by an average annual real rate of 5 percent over the 1993 to 1995 period.

Statistics show that the total value of imports of boating equipment and accessories is greater than that of the total Canadian market demand. This can be explained by the fact that Canadian manufacturers export a significant percentage of their own production, into which they have incorporated most boating equipment and accessory imports into Canada.

While there are manufacturers of boats in Canada, local production of boating equipment and accessories is mainly limited to some navigational equipment and several accessory lines. For instance, nearly all life jackets sold in Canada are Canadian-made since standards in Canada differ from those in the United States. Canadian-manufactured trailers also dominate the domestic market. Other locally produced lines include cordage, rope, sun shades, and awnings. However, marine hardware manufactured in Canada does not have a significant domestic market share. Furthermore, no marine engines are manufactured in Canada.

Some Hot Items:
- centrifugal pumps
- direction finding compass
- outboard motors
- radar apparatus

BUILDING PRODUCTS

In 1995, the total market size for building products was US$5.8 billion. Imports were valued at US$2.9 billion. Canada produced US$9.9 billion worth of goods and exported US$7 billion worth. Canadian demand for building products is influenced largely by the level of building construction in the residential, industrial, commercial, and institutional sectors. Although new building projects have been sluggish, Canadian demographics indicate that increased expenditures on housing during the 1995 to 1997 period will be directed more toward renovations than to new home construction, and it is this renovations segment of the market that represents the greatest potential for a variety of new building products in Canada. Opportunities in the Canadian building products market include home renovation products, materials which support energy conservation, and environmentally-friendly products containing reduced volatile organic compounds and solvents.

Some Hot Items:
- caulking compounds
- fiberglass or composite roofing shingles
- hardwood flooring
- planking
- vinyl windows

COMPUTERS AND COMPUTER SOFTWARE

The Canadian computer software market was estimated to be US$1.4 billion in 1994, and is forecasted to grow at an average annual real rate of between 12 and 15 percent from 1995 to 1997. Although the impact of the recession still affects some Canadian companies, many are beginning to recover. With this recovery, companies are expected to increase their capital outlay for advanced computer technologies, and therefore, demand for computer software is forecast to increase in the coming years. Supporting this growth will be the increased proliferation of computer technologies in non-business markets, such as the home consumer market, the educational market, the entertainment and in-house publishing industries, and the reference and information markets. Increasing demand for multimedia capability and applications will also substantially increase the demand for highly sophisticated software packages. Local area network (LAN) software sales have been expanding rapidly, with annual growth rates of 20 to 25 percent during the last three years.

The Canadian personal computer market is expected to generate revenues of US$1.9 billion in 1995, an increase of 20.6 percent over 1994, making it the most significant year in the Canadian personal computer industry (total unit shipments were estimated to reach 1,727,000). Small and medium-sized businesses account for the largest personal computer market in Canada. Demand for powerful portable computers based on Intel-compatible technologies will continue to remain strong, while demand for mainframes and mid-range computers will continue to decline.

The total market size for computer hardware in peripherals in 1995 was US$4.5 billion. Local production was valued at US$3.1 billion. Canadian exports were worth US$2.9 billion and imports were worth US$4.3 billion. Canada represents the fifth largest import market in the world for computer products. It is a sophisticated market and most of the market demand for computer hardware is supplied by imports.

Some Hot Items:
- CD-ROM software
- computer-aided design and engineering
- computer-based training software
- educational services software
- graphics software
- LAN software sales
- modems
- multimedia applications
- laptop computers
- notebook computers
- personal computers
- telecommunications software

ELECTRONIC PRODUCTS

The Canadian electronic components sector is a broad market comprising switches, relays, diodes, transistors, and various other electronic devices. The integral nature of electronic components is illustrated by the spectrum of end-user industries and applications. Medical equipment, automobiles and automotive parts, consumer goods, and military equipment are only a few of the products and applications which utilize electronic components. With the recession over, and strong growth projected in the telecommunications and information technology sectors (approximately 10 to 12 percent annually), the electronic components industry should see similar strong growth. Imports account for a significant and increasing share of the Canadian switches and relays market. In 1993, at a value of US$906.3 million, the Canadian switches and relays import market grew by a real rate of 5.1 percent from 1992 levels of US$943.5 million. This trend was largely the result of the inability of smaller Canadian firms to achieve the necessary economies of scale and scope to compete with larger foreign multinationals and their domestic subsidiaries.

Some Hot Items:
- diodes
- integrated circuits
- liquid crystal devices for instruments
- printed circuits
- relays
- semiconductors
- switches
- transistors
- transformers

FURNITURE AND OFFICE SUPPLIES

Despite the slump in total demand, imports of household furniture are expected to grow in the 3 to 5 percent range (real terms) during the next several years, with pent-up demand likely to create a boom market for exporters before the end of the decade. Opportunities exist for exporters of household wooden furniture, metal ready-to-assemble products, and especially compact casegood furniture (both are characterized by high quality craftsmanship or low retail cost), as the domestic Canadian market continues to rely less and less on domestic production.

In 1991, total imports of household furniture into Canada were valued at US$630.2 million, increasing by a real rate of 10.4 percent to US$717.4 million in 1992, followed by a slight real decrease of 2.6 percent to US$639.2 million in 1993. In 1991, 1992, and 1993, imports respectively accounted for 38 percent, 40 percent and 38.3 percent of total market demand for household furniture in Canada. Real growth rates in Canadian imports are projected to be 3 to 5 percent during the 1994 to 1996 period, as the economy in general and furniture market demand in particular recover their pre-recessionary strength.

There is an interest in ergonomic furnishings—furnishings that are designed to fit the places who use them in order to reduce injuries and increase comfort. The aging and health-conscious population is creating new markets for bedding.

Canadian household furniture demand is regionally distributed as follows: Ontario represents 46 percent of total domestic demand, followed by Quebec with 40 percent, Western Canada (including the provinces of British Columbia, Alberta, Saskatchewan and Manitoba) with 13 percent, and Atlantic Canada (including the provinces of Newfoundland, Nova Scotia, New Brunswick, and Prince Edward Island) with 1 percent. More than one-third of domestic demand for household furniture is concentrated in Canada's three largest cities: Toronto (13 percent), Montreal (13 percent), and Vancouver (6 percent).

Some Hot Items:

- bedroom sets
- bookcases
- bureaus
- car seats
- computer workstations
- dining room sets
- ergonomic home and office furnishings
- home entertainment systems for stereos, videos and TV units
- kitchen furniture
- mattresses
- metal furniture
- office desks and chairs
- ottomans
- ready-to-assemble furniture
- recliners
- sofas and sofas with matching chairs

OFFICE SUPPLIES

The 1992 Canadian market demand for office consumable products was valued at US$1.42 billion and was projected to grow at an annual real rate of 1.5 percent from 1993 to 1995. The portion of the total market demand satisfied by imports grew from 12.9 percent in 1990 to 16.8 percent in 1992. Canadian imports of office consumables were generally expected to exceed projected increases in Canadian market demand from 1993 to 1995. Industry experts also predicted an increase in imports of writing instruments of about 2 to 4 percent per annum, in real terms, for the period 1993 to 1995. German and Japanese firms will supply a third or more of this expected increase in imports of writing instruments. Imports of paper clips, fasteners, letter corners and staples from east Asia, especially China, Taiwan and Thailand, will rise dramatically through 1995. A 13 percent real annual increase in imports of paper clips, letter corners, fasteners and staples was projected from 1993-1995. Imports of office paper products were expected to increase by 2 percent per year in real terms in 1995.

Some Hot Items:

- fasteners and fittings for binders
- office paper
- paper clips
- staples
- vinyl and plastic products
- writing instruments.

HEALTH PRODUCTS

Despite Canada's relatively small population of 29 million, the country has one of the world's strongest markets for medical equipment. Canada's comprehensive public health care system is responsible for generating the strong demand for medical devices, 80 percent of which is satisfied through imports. Even though cost restrictive measures and changes in health care legislation may temper demand over the next few years, the Canadian medical system will increasingly seek technologically advanced equipment to produce efficient and cost-saving health services.

Canada's universal public health care system is partially responsible for the demand for a broad range of products, ranging from simple wound dressings to the most sophisticated electronic imaging devices. Although Canadian demand for medical equipment and supplies reached an estimated value of US$1.3 billion in 1993, recent and ongoing changes in public health care legislation have resulted in the implementation of cost reduction measures that will somewhat slow future demand. However, technologically advanced equipment and products which can provide improved cost and service efficiency will continue to be in strong demand by the Canadian health care network of public hospitals and clinics. Industry experts, therefore, forecast growth for the 1994 to 1996 period to continue at an average annual real rate of between 2 and 3 percent. Despite health care budget cutbacks, Canada's universal public health care system will continue to generate a steady demand for medical products because Canadians are accustomed to high-quality health care. Canadians will continue to seek public health care at a level that contributes to Canada's quality of life, ranked as the second highest in the world by a recent United Nations study. Investment in new equipment always increases in direct proportion to the amount of funding given hospitals by the provincial governments. The greatest growth opportunities occur when new hospitals and clinics are built.

Because of the increasing costs of full-service hospital care, there has recently been a growth in the purchase of home-care health equipment. During the 1995 to 1997 period, a surge in the demand for home care and mobility equipment is expected in Canada. Several factors will affect demand, three of which will be primary: (1) the reform of Canada's health care system; (2) the rapid design integration of technological improvements in health care equipment; and, (3) Canada's aging population with its growing number of seniors in need of care and autonomy. As a result, experts forecast annual real growth in demand for home care and mobility equipment will average between 15 and 20 percent during the next three years. The cost of providing home health care in Canada, however, remains very small compared to the total amount spent by institutions to deliver health care. In fact, current estimates indicate that Canada's cost of providing home health care is approximately US$1 billion, or about only 2 percent of the US$50 billion tab for institutionally provided health care. Since domestic production satisfies only a fraction of Canadian demand for home care and mobility equipment, Canada relies heavily on imports. In fact, since 1992, imports have supplied between 84 and 85 percent of annual market demand for these products.

Canada is renowned for its publicly funded universal health care system. However, this system does not include the direct public financing of dental care. During the 1980's, only 12 to 15 percent of expenditures incurred through professional dental care in Canada were paid by public sources. This percentage is expected to decrease dramatically throughout the 1990's. In 1992, Canadians disbursed approximately US$3 billion to obtain professional dental care from approximately 25,000 licensed professionals.

Some Hot Items:

- bathroom safety equipment: transfer and bath benches, safety rails and grab bars, raised toilet seats
- complete patient monitoring systems
- daily care equipment: blood pressure monitors, bed care equipment, commodes, dialysis pumps, insulin kits, massagers, patient seating, respiratory pumps, stethoscopes, thermometers, transcutaneous nerve stimulators (TENS), ultrasound therapy equipment
- dialysis equipment, parts, and accessories
- electrocardiographs
- electro-diagnostic apparatus
- electro-therapeutic equipment
- in-house mobility equipment: elevators, ramps, stair-aids and related in-house mobility equipment
- medical and surgical disposable supplies: bougies, cannulae, catheters, and drains
- monitors and recorders
- safely packaged and ready-to-use disposable products, such as dressings and suture kits
- self-mobility equipment: canes, crutches, orthopedic appliances, scooters, walkers, lightweight and motorized wheelchairs and accessories
- ultrasonic scanning equipment
- x-ray and radiation equipment market for medical, dental, and veterinary use

HOUSEHOLD APPLIANCES AND PRODUCTS

The 1993 total market for Canadian household consumer goods was valued at US$2.77 billion. Total imports were valued at US$1.69 billion. Although Canadian demand for household consumer goods was negatively affected in 1992, as the economy improved in 1993, consumer spending increased. This was evidenced by the fact that personal disposable income rose 1.4 percent during 1993. As consumer confidence and spending continue to rise, sales of household consumer goods in Canada will lead to increased opportunities for foreign-made products. The latest statistics indicate Canadian retail sales for household consumer goods rose by a real rate of 7.7 percent in 1993. Other contributing factors include growth in Canadian housing starts during the next few years, increased average household income, and continued reduction of tariffs.

Some trends—the predilection for Canadians to stay at home more, the increasing age of the population, a greater awareness of the need for clean air and water in the home environment—are all increasing opportunities for the sales of household goods and appliances. Current sales are at 5,500 units but industry analysts estimate a total market of 90,000 units. Awnings can be used on the growing number of outdoor wooden decks and help decrease the cost of air conditioning by placing the outside over glass windows.

Some Hot Items:

- air and water treatment systems: heaters, filters, humidifiers, air cleaners, water purifiers
- awnings
- hand-held tools
- interior doors used in home renovation projects
- kitchen appliances: blenders, food processors, specialty coffee makers, vegetable and rice steamers
- nonpowered lawn and garden equipment: spades and shovels, forks, mattocks, picks, hoes and rakes, hewing tools, one-handed secateurs, hedge shears, two-handed pruning shears, scarifiers, weeders, seeders, planters and manure spreaders.
- plumbing products: bathtubs, faucets, shower stalls, toilets

INDUSTRIAL MACHINERY

Predictions indicated that Canadian pulp and paper companies invested almost US$3 billion in 1994 (in capital spending), about one-quarter of which was spent on equipment to help mills reduce effluent. Companies supplying the pulp and paper industry with production equipment or with equipment to reduce effluent have opportunities in the Canadian market. There has been an increase in demand for certain agricultural and meat processing equipment. The Canadian market for meat and poultry processing equipment was US$25.5 million in 1991. Canada imported 91 percent or US$23.2 million worth of meat and poultry processing equipment to satisfy domestic demand in that year.

Commercial refrigeration equipment used in the food industry and in food storage applications will probably experience the strongest growth in market demand during the forecast period of 1995 to 1997. Centrifugal chillers, retail refrigeration units, and cold storage units used in warehousing and transportation refrigeration units have the most market potential since many will need to be replaced or retrofitted to allow for the use of alternative refrigerants. Desiccant systems, used mainly for applications requiring low levels of humidity (such as supermarket refrigeration systems, refrigerator and freezer display cases, compressors, heat exchangers, cooling systems, machines that recycle CFCs, and parts to retrofit existing machines), are also expected to experience good sales growth.

The oil and gas industry continues to expand in Canada, especially in Alberta, and companies need to be supplied with more and more equipment. Canada continues to rely on imports of plastics processing machinery for more than 50 percent of its demand. In fact, in 1993, imports accounted for nearly 60 percent of demand, and were valued at US$239.7 million. This represented real growth of nearly 30 percent over 1992 imports which were valued at US$204.7 million.

Some Hot Items:

- agricultural equipment
- agricultural or horticultural mechanical sprayers
- harrows (excluding discs, scarifiers, cultivators, hoes)
- seeders, planters and transplanters
- haying machines other than mowers
- straw or fodder balers, including pick-up balers
- combine harvester-threshers
- commercial refrigeration equipment
- compressors
- combined refrigerator/freezer
- individual refrigerator and freezer chests
- refrigerated display counters
- electrical power systems equipment
- electrical inductors
- gas turbine engines
- switches
- transformers
- meat processing equipment
- machinery for slaughtering, skinning, eviscerating and slicing
- oil and gas field equipment
- container tanks
- drilling rigs
- pumps and valves
- plastic processing equipment
- automation auxiliary equipment
- chillers for all processes
- granulators
- injection molding machines
- process control systems for extrusion, injection and blow molding equipment
- recycling and low energy machinery
- pulp and paper production equipment

PLASTICS AND CHEMICALS

Canada has been increasing its imports of plastic products. The Canadian plastics industry is very receptive to imported products in the auto, pipe fitting, packaging, and transportation sectors. Projected annual market growth through 1996 is 5.2 percent, in real terms. In 1995, total imports of plastic materials and resins amounted to US$2.1 billion in a market of US$2.5 billion. Canada exported US$1.7 billion worth of the products.

Canadian imports of chemicals and chemical products in 1993 were US$8.3 billion, satisfying 41 percent of total Canadian market demand. Growth in Canadian imports of soap and cleaning products has been steady in the recent past. Real growth of 15.8 percent was recorded in 1991, and 18.8 percent in 1992, with the total dollar value of Canadian imports increasing more than 30 percent since December 1990—from US$175.3 million to US$252.5 million. In 1992, imports of soap and cleaning products supplied 14.5 percent of the Canadian market.

Some Hot Items:

- herbicides
- inorganic chemicals
- organic chemicals
- plastic materials
- resins
- soap

POLLUTION CONTROL EQUIPMENT

Steady revenue growth is projected in the three primary subsectors of the pollution control equipment market during the next three years. Growth for the air, water and soil pollution control equipment subsectors has averaged 2.5 percent annually. Public concern and strong federal and provincial environmental legislation, enforced with severe fines and penalties, has created a growing demand for pollution control equipment. Canadian firms are allocating substantial funds to purchase pollution control equipment in order to modernize operations and increase efficiency, while complying with legislative requirements. Demand will also be affected by the determination of many corporations to capitalize on the employment of environmental practices to enhance public image. The principal Canadian end-users are the pulp and paper, chemical, metallurgy, and textile industries.

Some Hot Items:
- air pollution control equipment
- analytic equipment
- filters
- hazardous waste disposal equipment
- solid waste recycling systems
- water and wastewater processing systems

TELECOMMUNICATION PRODUCTS

Canada is the fourth largest import market in world for telecommunications equipment. The Canadian telecommunications equipment market is sophisticated and dynamic. Despite the world-class quality of equipment manufactured by Canadian companies such as Northern Telecom, Mitel and Newbridge, the consumer and corporate segments of the market remain receptive to imports. While the recession has decreased the demand for telecommunications equipment, the convergence of telecommunications technologies, information technology, and the cable industry should present niche markets for importers. Deregulation of telecommunications services, an increase in joint ventures between Canadian and foreign equipment and service carriers, and advances in telecommunications technology will continue to provide market opportunities for exporters.

Emerging technologies with an expected high degree of market penetration in the future include: applications using asynchronous terminal mode (ATM) technology, integrated services digital network (ISDN) technology, wireless technologies, and advanced remote communications using satellite technology. Canadians will purchase large amounts of fiber-optic cable. One of the most pressing issues before government regulatory bodies recently has been the decision of whether to allow telephone companies to carry cable television signals and vice versa. The outcome of this will have a huge impact on the Canadian telecommunications market for years to come. Industry experts predict that if telephone and cable television companies are allowed to compete for household access, virtually all existing coaxial cable will be replaced with fiber-optic cable, substantially increasing demand.

Although Canada exports 90 percent of the telephones it produces, 95 percent of its own domestic market is met by imports. In 1993, Canadian production of cellular telephones was US$70.6 million. Imports were worth US$109 million.

A new market area developing in the Canadian power line sector is the use of optical ground wire (OGW). This product is gaining favor with power utilities because it enables the simultaneous transmission of data and power. OGW is used with power poles and offers significant savings when compared to the separate cost of two projects requiring underground fiber-optic cable installation and above ground copper wire installation.

Some Hot Items:
- cellular telephones
- cordless handset telephones
- data communication systems
- optical fibers, optical fiber bundles and cables
- optical ground wire
- parts for telephonic switching apparatus
- terminal apparatus for carrier-current line systems
- voice processing equipment and systems

TEXTILES AND APPAREL

Apparel During the early 1990s, the recession contributed to the slow growth rate of the Canadian apparel industry. Recent positive Canadian economic indicators, such as a 1.4 percent rise in personal disposable income along with a 7.7 percent rise in retail sales are expected to lead to increased Canadian consumer spending on apparel. Canadian consumers will remain price-sensitive, seeking quality items at fair prices. The key to success in the Canadian apparel market during the forecast period of 1995 to 1997 is to adapt to this trend. Although there is tremendous competition from third-country suppliers, all. suppliers of low-priced quality goods have excellent opportunities to penetrate the Canadian apparel market.

Some Hot Items:
- mens' and boys' trousers, shirts, outerwear and sportswear
- pullovers
- t-shirts and other vests
- women's and girls' casual wear, dress wear, and sleepwear

Textiles The growth in market demand for textiles in Canada was modest during the early

FREE TRADE ZONES AND WAREHOUSES

With the exception of one special trade zone at the Sydport Industrial Park in Cape Breton, Nova Scotia, Canada has no free ports or free trade zones. At present, there are no federal or provincial laws specifically governing the establishment and operation of such zones. Warehouses under private ownership have been established for the storage and deposit of all imports received by various transportation modes, pending customs examination and clearance.

There are, however, certain benefits granted to importers of goods into Canada. Goods imported into Canada may be entered into customs bonded warehouses without the payment of duty but must be cleared either for export or Canadian consumption within two years. Additional periods are provided for certain goods by regulation. Customs examinations may be made and customs duties may be paid at customs ports on the border or, if goods are intended for inland destinations, they may be forwarded in bonded carriers to the port city nearest the destination at which point customs examination may be made and duties and taxes paid. Goods taken from bonded warehouses for consumption are dutiable at rates of the customs tariff then in effect, and the value for duty purposes is the value at the time of entry for warehousing. Goods exported from bonded warehouses to third countries are subject to Canadian export regulations. Repacking and sorting can be carried out in customs bonded warehouses with the permission of Canada Customs, but assembly or other industrial activity is prohibited.

1990s due to the recession. This trend is expected to continue in the short-term future. Canadian imports of textiles are expected to increase by 2 to 4 percent annually during the 1995 to 1997 period. Successful export sales to Canada depend on competitive pricing and high quality products.

Some Hot Items:

- carpets of wool or fine animal hair knotted
- denim fabrics of cotton
- knitted or crocheted fabrics, both cotton or man-made fibers
- plain weave cotton fabrics, printed
- woven fabrics of textured polyester filaments, printed

TOYS AND SPORTING GOODS

Sporting Goods Canada represents the seventh largest import market for sporting goods in the world. The Canadian market demand for sporting goods equipment is extremely sensitive to changes in economic conditions, personal disposable income, and life-styles. As a result of the economic recession in Canada, growth in overall demand was slower than would have otherwise been expected through 1993. However, as the Canadian economy emerges from the recession, growth is expected to be strong. The trend in Canada towards personal fitness has had a major impact on the demand for sporting goods products. Canadians' have a growing concern for product safety and performance standards in their sporting goods equipment; suppliers should emphasize these features in their marketing strategies.

Some Hot Items:

- aluminum hockey sticks
- archery equipment
- baseball and softball bats
- bicycles and other cycles
- fishing equipment
- general physical exercise and gymnasium athletics articles and equipment
- golf balls, clubs, and other golf equipment
- in-line roller skates
- ski equipment
- tennis balls

Toys and Games Imports of educational toys and games into Canada typically satisfy nearly all domestic demand. In addition to this, a substantial amount of imported parts are manufactured into finished goods in Canada, and reexported back to other countries. In 1991, imports were valued at US$218.4 million, increasing to an estimated US$272.9 million in 1992. From 1993 to 1995, imports were forecasted to grow at an average annual real rate of approximately five percent.

Some Hot Items:

- construction sets
- educational toys
- puzzles
- video games

VEHICLES AND PARTS

There are good opportunities for manufacturers and exporters of automotive parts and accessories in the Canadian market. Market surveys predict 7 to

9 percent real growth through 1998. Technological advances, changing distribution channels, and improvements in quality and value are the major factors influencing the demand for automotive products. In addition to auto parts needed for the assembly of new automobiles, there is a great number of older cars on the road that will need replacement parts. Canada's strong aftermarket parts market will continue to provide opportunities for exporters. The Canadian trucking industry has recently begun to boom and there is a shortage of equipment in the industry, translating into opportunities for exporters.

Some Hot Items:
- air bags
- alternate fuel conversions
- anti-lock brake systems
- climate control equipment
- drive axles
- electronics
- emission control
- fuel efficient computerized engines
- fuel injection
- parts and accessories of bodies, not elsewhere specified
- radiators
- ride control
- safety seat belts
- trailers and highway tractors
- transmission for motor vehicles
- wheels
- wind deflectors

OPPORTUNITIES FOR GROWTH

COMPUTERS AND COMPUTER SOFTWARE

Use of computer peripherals and software will continue to expand in Canada as businesses increase their investment in equipment and more individuals join the ever-growing roster of the millions buying personal computer products. Currently more than 2.3 million households, representing 23 percent of all Canadian homes, have personal computers. Major personal computer manufacturers believe that the home computer market is still in its infancy and are restructuring their businesses to compete aggressively. Some companies have created new divisions dedicated exclusively to the new consumer market. Some industry analysts predict that half of all Canadian households will own computers by 1998. Areas that will see significant growth include: data communications; voice equipment; software and services; and single-user systems.

ENVIRONMENTAL PROTECTION INDUSTRY

The Canadian environmental protection market for goods and services is estimated now to be at US$8 billion and growth is expected to be ten percent annually, which will double the size of the market by the year 2000.

The Canadian environmental industry is comprised of 4500 small and medium-sized enterprises which provide technologies, processes, products and services which address environmental problems. Although the industry is less than a decade old, firms employ approximately 150,000 people. About two-thirds of environmental industry firms provide services ranging from hazardous waste transportation, storage and treatment to environmental engineering, energy conservation, and water, soil and air quality testing. The other third of the firms are in manufacturing, which covers a broad range of products from clean process technologies and portable site remediation equipment to environmentally responsible consumer goods. The manufacturing component has yearly revenues of about US$4.7 billion. The size of firms within the industry varies from one-person consulting firms to large multinational corporations but is generally comprised of small and medium-sized enterprises, most employing fewer than 50 people.

The growth in Canada's environmental industry is the result of a number of factors which include: an evolving regulatory framework, the rapid growth in international markets for environmental goods and services, growing awareness by industry and government of the many benefits of improved environmental performance such as increased levels of efficiency, and increased public demand for environmentally responsible consumers. Need is growing in Canada itself and the ability for Canada to export its environmental goods and services is also growing.

FILM AND TELEVISION

A market-depreciated Canadian dollar has stimulated an increase in movie and television filming in Canada. Expenditures on filming grew 47 percent in 1994 and were expected to show strong growth in 1995 and 1996. More than US$880 million was spent on movie and TV production in Canada in 1994, up 47 percent from US$596 million in 1993. Industry sources estimate that nearly US$5 million was spent on new equipment in 1994, excluding cameras, which accounted for another US$1.46 million. The growth in filming and related equipment purchases was unusually strong in 1994 due to the weak Canadian dollar which drew more US movie and television productions to Canada. Canadian production companies are optimistic about continued strong growth, since they do not expect the Canadian dollar to recover to above 80–82 cents per US$1.00—a figure they cited as a psychological cost barrier for US producers—before 1996.

FRANCHISING

Franchised businesses of all varieties have enjoyed exceptional growth and success in Canada over the past decade. Franchising is an increasingly attractive method of doing business in Canada, in part because no federal regulations currently exist that specifically restrict franchise activities. Alberta is the only province to have established franchising legislation which stipulates that the franchise must be registered with the provincial securities commission. A large proportion of franchise units are restaurants, non-food retail, convenience and food establishments, automotive products and services, and business services. The steady growth in the Canadian market for franchises is expected to continue. According to the Canadian Franchise Association, the best franchising prospects are for fast food type operations. Do-it-yourself franchises are also expected to do well throughout the remainder of the decade, as are franchises which focus on housekeeping and lawncare chores.

HOME IMPROVEMENT

According to a recent Canadian article in a home center magazine, the 1990s are quickly becoming the decade of home renovation as improving economic conditions and a continued recovery in the housing market, along with changing consumer tastes and aging housing stock, boost interest in home renovation projects. Since 1991, home renovation spending has either topped or equalled spending on new residential construction, a trend that continued into 1995. As Canadian consumers continue to be optimistic about their present and future economic prospects, this represents good news for US manufacturers of home renovation supplies.

A recent Canadian mortgage and housing corporation survey revealed that nearly half of Canadian homeowners are planning a variety of home renovation projects. Total renovation spending is expected to reach US$14.7 billion in 1995. Spending on new construction rose 2.1 percent in 1994 and was expected to rise five percent in 1995, reaching US$12.8 billion. The biggest increase in renovation spending will be in the area of alterations and improvements–a category that makes up three-quarters of the renovation market. Consumer spending in this area will jump by 7 to 8 percent in 1995 as consumers have more money for discretionary items. Spending in the smaller part of the market (which includes repairs and maintenance) was up 5 to 6 percent per year in 1994 and 1995.

MANUFACTURING

Canada is recovering from the long-lasting recession of the early 1990s and growth in manufacturing is evidence of this. The strongest growth is seen in the following sectors: automobiles, office machinery, certain consumer goods, and natural gas. Moderate growth is seen in the areas of lumber, industrial machinery, tobacco, pulpwood, and tractors. The Canadian economy is closely tied to the US economy. Approximately 75 percent of Canada's exports are shipped to the US, and approximately 70 percent of its imports arrive from the US. As the US recovered from its own recession, and was able to import more goods from Canada, growth in the Canadian manufacturing sector was stimulated. In addition to that, however, is the intensified interest manufacturers have taken in boosting their productivity. As cost of production decreased and productivity improved, and as the country pulled out of the recession, profits grew.

SERVICES

In 1992, 41 percent of Canada's GDP was produced by the services sector. Services are expected to grow in relative terms, with particular emphasis on tourism, transportation and storage, retail trade (motor vehicles and discount store sales), and wholesale trade (machinery and equipment sales).

TELECOMMUNICATIONS

The Canadian telecommunications equipment market is sophisticated and dynamic. Although it remains dominated by such world-class Canadian companies as Northern Telecom, Mitel and Newbridge, the consumer and corporate segments of the industry are open to continual change and growth. Deregulation of telecommunications services, an increase in joint ventures between Canadian and foreign equipment and service carriers, and advances in telecommunications technology will continue to provide market opportunities for business people in the field. Emerging technologies with an expected high degree of market penetration in the future include: applications using asynchronous terminal mode (ATM) technology, integrated services digital network (ISDN) technology, wireless technologies, and advanced remote communications using satellite technology. As with other areas of the industrial and technological world, the Canadian telecommunications industry will respond to technological innovation, new consumer tastes and buying power, and replacement of existing systems. While the recession has temporarily decreased the demand for telecommunications equipment, the convergence of telecommunications technologies, information technology, and the cable industry, should all create new areas of growth.

PUBLIC PROCUREMENT

OPPORTUNITIES

As the largest purchaser in the country, Canada's federal government buys many kinds of goods and services, including military vehicles, scientific equipment, food, and construction and engineering services. In the 1993-94 fiscal year, Ottawa had 847 suppliers with contracts worth US$730,000 ($1 million) or more, for a total of US$5.04 billion ($6.9 billion) out of total government spending of US$5.92 billion ($8.1 billion). Government spending is most active in the following sectors: motor vehicles, defense equipment, airport and ground support equipment, medical supplies and equipment, infrastructure development projects, and computer and information services. Services constitute one of the fastest growing areas of government procurement.

Two lists that summarize the opportunities for public procurement appear immediately below. The first is a list of specific goods and services purchased by the Canadian government. The second is a list of current government projects, for which goods and services will be purchased.

Goods and Services Purchased by the Canadian Government

- advertising services
- aircraft and aircraft parts
- airport and ground support equipment
- architectural services
- automotive parts
- automotive vehicles used by Canadian postal service and other government departments
- building construction machinery, equipment, and materials
- computers and computer peripherals
- computer software
- engineering services
- fiber optic cables
- medical supplies and equipment
- military communication systems
- road construction machinery, equipment, and materials
- security services
- telecommunications goods and services
  waste water treatment equipment

Current Government Projects

The federal government has recently begun or announced a number of public projects for which goods and services will need to be purchased. They include the creation of the Canada Infrastructure Works (CIW) program, the primary objective of which is the upgrading of Canada's physical infrastructure in local communities. Funding for the CIW program will include federal government contributions of approximately US$1.5 billion, which will be matched by an additional US$3 billion from provincial and municipal governments, for a total of approximately US$4.5 billion. The CIW program will be administered by the federal regional agency responsible for each province and provincial government departments.

Other notable major projects currently underway in Canada include: the Grand Baleine hydroelectric project in the province of Quebec valued at US$10 billion over ten years; a national fiber optic data network (CANARIE), to be tendered in three phases, with a total value of approximately US$1 billion; a Department of Defense tactical command control and communications system with an estimated value of over US$600 million; the Hibernia off-shore oil platform east of Newfoundland; the Prince Edward Island fixed-link bridge; and the Vancouver Airport privatization.

In addition to these, other specific projects were in the planning and preliminary development stage or in the construction stage as of late 1995. A brief summary of the projects, with the estimated total cost (if available), is as follows:

1. A national communications network—an information superhighway—will be put in place for eastern Canada: Nova Scotia, Newfoundland, New Brunswick, and Prince Edward Island.
2. A highway between New Brunswick and Nova Scotia is under consideration. Provincial governments are now requesting financing from the federal government (US$292 million).
3. Studies are underway for a Red Cross blood products plant in Halifax. The project's development is dependent on the outcome of an inquiry on the safety of Canadian Red Cross blood bank procedures (US$109 million).

4. The province of Quebec plans to build a sewage treatment plant in Laval (US$95 million).
5. Ontario is developing a Highway 407 project across Northern Toronto. The winning bidder has been chosen and will design, build, and operate this toll highway. Construction has begun and will proceed in stages (US$880 million).
6. Toronto is expanding its Metro Convention Centre. Ground was broken on November 17, 1994 (US$132 million).
7. Toronto plans to build an International Trade Centre at the Canadian National Exhibition grounds. Although this project has received government approval, the financial package is still under negotiation (US$182 million).
8. Toronto has proposed to build a new basketball stadium (US$73 million).
9. A contract for the widening of the Queen Elizabeth Way Highway near St. Catharines, Ontario will soon be awarded (US$256 million).
10. Approximately 3.6 km of new tracks for a light rail transit system will be laid in Toronto. Construction began in 1992 and will be completed in 1997. The general contract has been awarded, however other smaller subcontracts will go to tender (US$102 million).
11. A number of subway extension projects are currently underway in Toronto and will be completed between 1996 and 2001, depending on the project (US$1.523 billion).
12. A new casino will be built in Windsor, Ontario (US$273 million).
13. A pipeline expansion project is currently under construction in the provinces of Manitoba, Saskatchewan, and Alberta (US$292 million).
14. The University of British Columbia at Vancouver is developing a long-term expansion program, which will proceed in stages (US$365 million).
15. Proposals have been made to build a new sewage treatment plant in Vancouver (US$511 million).
16. A Vancouver Island Highway is in the proposal stage. Construction is expected to begin during the next two years (US$730 million).

PROCUREMENT PROCEDURES

Most foreign firms successful in Canadian public procurement projects have done so via joint ventures with Canadian firms and/or have brought with them special skills or innovative technology. Tight Canadian profit margins, readily available skilled Canadian labor, and a plethora of large regional firms all contribute to a highly competitive business environment for bidders. The specialty market may represent the best opportunities for market penetration by foreign firms. Projects directed to energy, environment, waste management, and transportation are typically open to some form of foreign participation through services or equipment sales. Timing is critical. Firms must be prepared to prequalify for bid lists and must have current information on pending projects. One of the best ways to obtain current information on Canadian construction projects is to subscribe to Daily Commercial News and Construction Record, which can be purchased by contacting the *Daily Commercial News and Construction Record*. This publication, issued in a newspaper format, describes projects across Canada by region and by sector. See "Useful Addresses" for contact information.

Canadian products will often be favored, especially if they offer similar features at a similar cost to those from other countries. This is especially true for any government procurement, local or federal, not covered under either the General Agreement on Tariffs and Trade (GATT) or the North American Free Trade Agreement (NAFTA) rules. Moreover, many government tenders require that a regional benefit component be taken into account. Nevertheless, competition in Canada is generally fair, and foreign firms that can offer technical, cost, or feature advantages over locally produced goods, can do as well in the Canadian market as they might be able to do in their domestic markets.

NAFTA

NAFTA and the Canadian Free Trade Agreement increased the opportunities for public procurement among the signers of the treaties (US, Mexico, and Canada). Restrictions were lifted on providing the Canadian government with both goods and services. NAFTA parties must also remove citizenship requirements affecting the licensing and practice of professionals within two years of the entry into force of the Agreement. If a state or province fails to remove citizenship requirements within the allotted time frame, the other countries have the right to maintain equivalent restrictions in their own countries.

FINANCING

Over the next decade, Canada faces an estimated capital investment bill totaling billions of dollars, which will be needed to complete a variety of infrastructure projects such as roads, airports, sewers, and subways. In a search of new methods to finance these initiatives, governments at all levels in Canada are seeking private sector partners with increasing frequency. Canadian public sector investment, as a share of GDP, has declined from an average of 4.3 percent in the 1960s to 2.7 percent in the 1990s. Considering the growing public sector debt, federal, provincial, and municipal governments appear ready to embrace this new partnering concept by necessity, as much as by choice. Public-private partnering in Canada is in its developmental stage in comparison with most other developed economies. It was not until 1993 that the nation's public sector showed a real and broad commitment to private-public partnering as a viable option for infrastructure development.

To address these issues, the Canadian Minister of Public Works and Government Services opened the Secretariat for Federal-Private Sector Infrastructure Partnering in April 1994. The purpose of the Secretariat is to review private-sector partnering proposals for major infrastructure projects in areas such as the environment, technology, energy, and transportation. Also, the Canada Mortgage and Housing Corporation (CMHC), an independent government agency concerned with all aspects of housing in Canada, is attempting to provide housing for low to moderate income homeowners through public-private partnering initiatives.

USEFUL ADDRESSES

Government of Canada

Secretariat for Federal-Private Sector Infrastructure Partnering
Real Property Headquarters
Sir Charles Tupper Building, 7th Floor
2250 Riverside Drive
Ottawa, ON K1A 0M2
Tel: [1] (613) 736-3105
Fax: [1] (613) 736-2201

Canadian Centre for Public-Private Partnerships and Housing
700 Montreal Road
Ottawa, ON K1A 0P7
Tel: [1] (613) 748-4074
Fax: [1] (613) 748-2400

Private Organizations

The Canadian Council for Public-Private Partnerships
Box 48, Suite 4700
Toronto Dominion Bank Tower
Toronto, ON M5K 1E6
Tel: [1] (416) 601-8333
Fax: [1] (416) 868-0673

Publications

Daily Commercial News and Construction Record
280 Yorkland Blvd.
North York, ON M2J 4Z6
PH. 416-494-4990, FX. 416-756-2767

Canadata/Southam Construction & Information Group
1450 Don Mills Rd.
Don Mills, ON M3B 2X7
Tel: 1-800-387-0273

Foreign Investment

INVESTMENT CLIMATE AND TRENDS

The phenomenon of globalization (cross-border spread of products, production factors, firms, and markets) has permeated the domestic economy of Canada. It has changed the origin of foreign capital, the type of foreign capital invested, as well as the economic sectors to which the investment flows. In fact, this trend has actually built up Canadian residents' assets abroad to levels not seen in the past at a rate generally faster than that of foreign investment into Canada. Direct foreign investment (DFI) into Canada has increased as well, expanding at a continuous, moderate rate since the early 1950s and doubling in each of the following decades.

Several developments in the evolution of the Canadian economy have impacted foreign investment. First, Canada's dependency on the United States has diminished significantly as sources of foreign capital have become more diversified. With this diversification has come a higher net inflow of investment funds. Second, the image of Canada as a trader/natural resource provider dependent upon the resource extraction and production of lumber, wheat, and minerals has diminished as manufactured goods such as telecommunications equipment, computers, and vehicles have diversified and strengthened the country's economic base. The economic base diversification has also contributed to investor type and amount of investment. Third, the country's rapid growth rates over the past 15 years makes it one of the fastest growing and expanding free market economies in the industrialized world, has contributed to a more than doubling of cross-border flows of direct foreign investment since 1984. Before the mid-1980s, the gross cross-border inflows of foreign direct investment averaged C$5 billion per year. In comparison, that figure increased to over C$9.5 billion per year in the second half of that decade.

Canada's growth rate has been a compelling factor attracting foreign investment, but what is driving that growth and enhanced productivity, has been the main impetus for investment decision making. It was foreign and domestic equipment during the decade of the 1980s which turned the tide for Canada. As such, Canada was ranked in the top five (out of 23) industrialized nations in terms of its attractiveness as an investment location.

To help ensure an attractive climate for domestic and foreign investment, the Canadian government has been active in making changes to encourage investment. Some of these changes have included modifications to tax rates on manufacturing and processing profits, liberalizing certain capital cost allowances on productive equipment, and other tax reform measures improving direct investment returns. Other changes include the deregulation of the transportation, energy, telecommunications and financial sectors; the privatization of dozens of formerly government-owned corporations; and reforms to employment, competition, and bankruptcy laws. All of these factors have interacted to some degree or another to improve Canada's business and investment environment. In addition, increased protection for intellectual property, tax reform for global shipping and trading entities in Canada, and amendments to federal

> ## CONTENTS
> Investment Climate and Trends 43
> Leading Foreign Investors 44
> *Economic Development Programs* 44
> Investment Policy and Changes 45
> *Availability of Loans and Credit* 45
> Real Estate: Commercial and
>   Industrial Space 47
> Investment Incentives 49
> Regulatory Agencies and Investment
>   Assistance 50

> **ECONOMIC DEVELOPMENT PROGRAMS**
>
> Foreign investors may gain assistance through various government or quasi- government entities. Little or no formal economic development programs exist in the traditional sense in Canada, but the following groups may facilitate investment flows, joint ventures, and other business formations.
>
> **The Department of Foreign Affairs and International Trade (DFAIT)** encourages international investment in Canada. It also helps domestic entities locate the investment they need by working closely with investment counselors and other commercial officers at Canadian embassies and consulates abroad. In addition, the department also interacts with other federal government departments, with provincial and municipal authorities, and with business organizations.
>
> **The Investment Development Program (IDP)** falls under the jurisdiction of the federal government through DFAIT. This group actively promotes investments that take the form of joint ventures, strategic partnerships and new plants and equipment. While helping Canadian companies search for foreign sources of investment and technology, the IDP also assists foreign investors already interested in the domestic market as well as those yet to consider Canada. The IDP also targets specific economic sectors, particularly technology-intensive ones. Here, the IDP works closely with governments as well as the private sector.
>
> **The Doing Business in Canada Association (DBIC)** is a non-profit organization which assists foreign and Canadian-based companies in doing business in Canada. This group focuses on educating companies about the unique attributes of the Canadian marketplace by conducting seminars and a free matching service for companies targeting Canadians by aligning them with service organizations.

policies on foreign investment in the country's oil and gas sector have encouraged investment and development greatly in the early 1990s.

As mentioned, the nations enhanced productivity, through its economic restructuring in the 1980s and early 1990s, has substantially increased its competitive profile in the global investment arena. This main theme underlies the regional economic disparities evident across Canada. The focal point of this growth was in the provinces of Ontario and Quebec which have recently experienced heavy demand for its manufactured goods. The Atlantic region, the Prairie region, and British Columbia have benefited less so from the capital investment boom and more from a surge in world commodity prices (lumber, oil and gas, minerals) as their economies remain focused primarily on natural resource production. This imbalance should mediate, however, as foreign and direct investment gravitate towards these areas in the future

LEADING FOREIGN INVESTORS

Size of Foreign Investment

Total direct foreign investment in Canada in 1995 amounted to approximately C$15.4 billion, breaking the previous record of over C$10.7 billion in 1987. As noted, direct investment flows have been increasing steadily over the past decade and have been particularly large the past several years due to global economic expansion and liberalized foreign investment policies of the Canadian government. Totals have averaged nearly C$5 billion the past 10 years with trends following global expansion/contraction patterns. For instance, direct investment inflows ballooned in the mid-late 1980s, fell sharply during the recession of 1990-1991, and have increased steadily since then.

As such, the foreign direct investment balance (stock) in Canada has steadily increased as well. Currently, the balance stands at over C$170 billion, an all time high. Just five years earlier the balance was at C$131 billion and ten years prior was approximately C$90 billion, nearly doubling over the past decade. Much of this is attributable to gross domestic economic and productivity gains, foreign investment policy liberalization under the 1985 Investment Canada Act, and increased globalization of the worlds economy over the past decade.

Origin of Foreign Investment

The US has been for decades and continues to be the largest foreign investor in Canada, accounting for more than 70 percent ($115 billion) of the nation's cumulative foreign investment stock. Its geographic proximity, economic size, historical ties, and special investment arrangements such as those under NAFTA, providing special trading and investment status upon US entities has bolstered this position. There hardly exists a large American industrial or service firm without significant operations of one sort or another in Canada today. A distant second is Canada's cousin, the UK, with an approximate 10 percent ($16.5 billion) share of the cumulative foreign investment stock. On an annualized basis, the US has steadily increased its position, adding C$5, C$7, C$10 billion each year over the past three years (1993-1995) while the UK's position has remained much as it was in the beginning of the decade due in most part to slow growth in Great Britain during that period.

Other significant cumulative direct foreign investment positions in 1995 included Japan (C$6.7 billion), France (C$5.3 billion), Germany (C$5.0 billion), the Netherlands (C$4.3 billion), and Switzerland (C$3.4 billion). On a regional basis, after North America (C$115 billion), Europe led with over C$40 billion, followed by Asia/Oceania (C$12 billion) and the Pacific Rim (C$11.8 billion). The most significant growth in foreign investment position over the past decade for those previously mentioned was from France and Japan with a tripling of their positions over the term.

Sectors of Foreign Investment

Financial services (banking/finance/insurance), energy (oil and gas/coal), chemicals and chemical products, transportation equipment, and food/beverages/tobacco are the nation's leading direct foreign investment industry groups today. Leading the sectors is the financial services industry with over C$32 billion in current DFI, primarily in commercial lending, leasing, and insurance services. Second are large scale project investments in the energy sector (i.e. oil and gas production) amounting to approximately C$25 billion in DFI. Following is the nearly C$20 billion in chemicals and chemical products sector, C$19 billion in transportation equipment including aviation, trucking, and automobiles, and the consumer perishable segment (food/beverage/tobacco) with total DFI of nearly C$15 billion. Other important sectors rounding out the top ten in order of magnitude include minerals/metal products, wood and paper, electrical products, construction, other consumer goods and services, machinery and equipment, and transportation and communications products and services.

INVESTMENT POLICY AND CHANGES

Canada has long been considered a stable and remunerative environment for foreign investment, and its economic success has been largely made possible by a continuous inflow of foreign capital. Since the passage of the liberal Investment Canada Act in 1985, Canadian policy on foreign investment has been modified by recognizing that investment is a critical factor to overall economic growth, employment, and technological advancement. At the same time, the new policy maintained control over large acquisitions in Canada by non-Canadians and imposed the requirement that these transactions be of a net benefit to Canada. The Act provides the basic legal framework for direct foreign investment in Canada, foreign investment in specific sectors may be covered by special legislation (i.e. the Finance Department controls activities in financial services and the Telecommunications Act governs activities in broadcasting).

Definition

Foreign investment, either direct or portfolio, is broadly defined as those holdings in Canadian equity investments in the form of capital goods, patents, financial assets, for example, which have a substantial interest owned by a non-Canadian. Foreign investment transactions are governed under the Investment Canada Act of 1985 (ICA or Act) which repealed the prior governing instrument, the Foreign Investment Review Act of 1973-74. These

---

AVAILABILITY OF LOANS AND CREDIT

Canadian corporate finance, particularly for long-term facilities, has traditionally been dependent on the seven major domestic commercial bank lenders, the domestic capital market, and external funding sources such as parent companies, and the global capital market. Short-term funding is readily available due to a deep and liquid domestic money market. Commercial loans and credit from a variety of financial institutions such as the major commercial banks, provincial/regional banks, insurance companies, securities dealers, and commercial finance companies are readily available to qualified investors.

With the recent stock market boom, equity financing is a more readily available source for business funding than ever before. Foreign entities may list their existing shares on the Toronto Stock Exchange (or any of the major regional exchanges) or raise new funds with new issues there. Many forms of international stock exchange treaties exist among Canada and most other developed nations' equities markets. For some, participating in this form of financing may prove to be a beneficial way of financing their Canadian business operations.

transactions are dealt with in various ways under the act with certain transactions exempt from both review and notice requirements of the statute. Transactions involving investments by non-Canadians in new Canadian businesses or non-reviewable acquisitions by non-Canadians of Canadian businesses are notifiable only, unless *cultural heritage or national identity* exception applies, in which case there is reserve power to review transactions. Finally, there are transactions which are subject to full review under the ICA and which must pass a net benefit to Canada test.

Under the Act, a "Canadian" means:
- A Canadian citizen.
- A permanent resident within meaning of the Immigration Act of 1976 who has been a resident in Canada for not more than one year after their initial application to apply for Canadian citizenship.
- A Canadian government, federal, provincial, or local, or an agency thereof.
- An entity that is Canadian-controlled.

A non-Canadian is an individual, government or agency thereof or entity that is not Canadian. An entity is defined as a corporation, partnership, trust or joint venture.

A Canadian business means a business carried on in Canada that has:
- A place of business in Canada.
- An individual or individuals in Canada who are employed or self-employed in connection with a business.
- Assets in Canada used in carrying on business.

A new Canadian business, in relation to non-Canadian, is a business that is not already being carried on in Canada by non-Canadians and that, at the time of its establishment is:
- Unrelated to any other business being carried on in Canada by that non-Canadian.
- Is related to another business being carried on in Canada by that non-Canadian but falls within prescribed specific types of business activities that, in the opinion of the federal cabinet, is related to Canada's cultural heritage or national identity.

Investment Authorization and Procedures

Investments requiring only notification are all new Canadian businesses (regardless of size), all direct acquisitions of Canadian business with assets under C$5 million, and most indirect acquisitions of Canadian businesses with assets under C$50 million. Indirect acquisitions of Canadian businesses whose assets represent more than half of the assets involved in the total international transaction are subject to the C$5 million threshold which applies to all other indirect acquisitions.

Investments requiring review are all direct acquisitions of Canadian businesses with assets greater than or equal to C$5 million, all indirect acquisitions of Canadian businesses with assets of C$50 million or more, and indirect acquisitions of Canadian businesses with assets between C$5 million and C$50 million which represent more than half of the value of the total international transaction. In addition, and as previously mentioned, specific acquisitions of new businesses in designated types of business activities related to Canada's cultural heritage or national identity, which would normally only be notifiable, could be reviewed if the Cabinet determines that such review is in the public interest. In practice, virtually all foreign investment in the cultural sector is reviewed

Under amendments to the ICA related to NAFTA, the foregoing threshold for review of direct transactions involving NAFTA investors (US and Mexico) acquiring or divesting control of Canadian businesses is C$150 million, calculated in constant 1992 dollars. Indirect investments involving NAFTA investors acquiring or divesting are not reviewable. These amendments do not apply, however, in respect to acquiring control of Canadian businesses engaged in the production of uranium, providing any financial service, providing any transportation service or which is a cultural business.

Non-Canadians must file notice with the Agency created under the Act regarding all non-reviewable transactions or establishment of new Canadian businesses prior to implementation or within 30 days thereafter. Once notice has been filed, the agency is required to issue a receipt bearing a certified date to the foreign investor. The receipt must advise the investor either that the investment proposal is unconditionally non-reviewable or that the proposal will not be reviewed so land as the agency does not subsequently issue notice of review within 21 days of the date certified under the receipt.

Reviewable acquisitions are subject to a new test of net benefit to Canada rather than a significant benefit to Canada test under the prior legislation. The minister has final say as to whether the reviewable investment is likely to be of net benefit to Canada under the Act. Foreign investors must file an application with the agency containing information prescribed by the regulation. Generally a favorable decision must be received before the investment is implemented. Investments may be consummated prior to acceptance on the basis that the delay in processing would cause hardship to the investor or would jeopardize operation of Canadian business(es), where the investment is indirect (portfolio), or where the government determines that is must review the investment in the business.

The agency is required to issue a receipt to the

REAL ESTATE: COMMERCIAL AND INDUSTRIAL SPACE

Foreign investors seeking land for development, industrial/warehouse space for lease, office space for lease, or residential housing for rent/ownership will have little problem fulfilling their needs in Canada. As is available in most major nations, Canada has real estate consultants, real estate brokers, and real estate developers to service any and all property needs.

When investigating potential commercial/industrial sites, foreign entities can contact local municipal offices to gain access to economic development officials who may be able to provide information regarding zoning, by-laws, and permit issuance. As is true most elsewhere, public incentives play a role here. Canadian municipalities compete with each other to attract business, and as such, incentives often include: infrastructure improvements, property tax abatement, regulatory flexibility, tax credits, subsidized training, utility rate incentives, public financing and grants, and employee relocation assistance.

Leasing office space, whether in the central business district of Toronto or a suburban site near Vancouver, is more feasible than ever due to the on-going slump in office properties across North America. Lease rates and terms have come down from their highs of the late 1980s and good deals are to be had for the savvy lessee.

Several provincial restrictions exist regarding foreign ownership of Canadian realty. For example, in British Columbia, the Land Act stipulates that only Canadian citizens are entitled to a grant of a land estate from the government. The Alberta government prevents foreign citizens or non-permanent residents from acquiring an interest in private, agricultural or recreational land within the boundaries of a city, town, or mines and minerals except under certain defined circumstances. The Saskatchewan Farm Security Act ensures that Saskatchewan residents and corporations engaged in the business of farming will own the majority of provincial agricultural lands. In Manitoba, farm land is also reserved for existing and future Manitoba residents.

Ontario has no restrictions concerning property acquisitions, but Ontario may set higher tax rates for those without permanent residence in Canada or Canadian citizenship. Quebec preserves all agricultural land like those provinces noted above. New Brunswick, Nova Scotia, and Newfoundland have no legislative restrictions on ownership but foreign purchases of realty outside the boundaries of a city or town must be registered with the Foreign Land Registry office. In addition, Prince Edward Island seeks to protect its primary resource industries (farming, forestry, fishing, and tourism) by prohibiting non-residents from acquiring more than five acres, or shore frontage or more than 165 feet without provincial government permission.

Average Lease Prices for Real Estate (for September, 1995)

	Montreal	Toronto	Vancouver
Quoted Downtown Rent	$22.07	$28.69	$22.07
Quoted Suburban Rent	$14.71	$13.98	$18.39
Base Annual Rent for 100-200k sf Distribution Facility	$2.30	$2.76	$2.96
Base Annual Rent for 20-40k sf Warehouse	$2.76	$2.94	$3.31
Undeveloped Industrial Land Purchase Price - High	$3.68	$5.06	$13.24
Undeveloped Industrial Land Purchase Price - Low	$1.47	$2.20	$2.21
Annual Base Retail Rent	$40.46	n/a	$66.21
Residential - Monthly Rent, High	n/a	$1,839	$1,287
Residential - Monthly Rent, Low	n/a	$1,103	$736
Residential - Purchase Price, High	n/a	$1,103	$736
Residential - Purchase Price, Low	n/a	$147,124	$165,514

Note: All figures are in US dollars per square foot.
Source: Colliers Jardine, Canada

applicant once the application has been filed. Incomplete applications require the agency to send a deficiency notification to the applicant within 15 days of receipt. If the agency fails to respond in that time period, the application is deemed to be complete as of the date it was received. Within 45 days after a completed application has been received, the minister must notify the investor that the investment is likely to be of net benefit to Canada, or that the minister is unable to complete his review, in which case the minister has an additional 30 days to complete the review, unless the applicant agrees to a longer period, or the minister is not satisfied that the investment is likely to be of net benefit to Canada. If time limits have been elapsed, the minister is deemed to be satisfied that the investment is likely to be of net benefit to Canada.

Factors regarding the assessment of whether an investment is likely to be of net benefit to Canada are as follows:

- The investment's effect on the level and nature of economic activity in Canada, including its effect on employment, resource processing, utilization of parts, components and services produced in Canada and on exports from Canada.
- The degree and significance of the participation by Canadians in the Canadian business of new Canadian business and in any industry or industries in Canada of which the entity forms or would form part of.
- The effect of the investment on the productivity, industrial efficiency, technological development, product innovation and product variety in Canada.
- The effect of the investment on competition within any industry or industries in Canada.
- The compatibility of the investment with national, industrial, economic and cultural policies, taking into consideration policy objectives enunciated by the government or legislature of any province likely to be significantly affected by the investment and,
- The contribution of the investment to Canada's ability to compete in global markets.

If an investment is related to Canada's cultural heritage or national identity, it is reviewable if the federal cabinet, where it considers it in the public interest, on recommendation of the minister, issues an order for review within 21 days after receipt of the notice of the investment. To date, the only types of investments which have been prescribed by regulation as related to Canada's cultural heritage or national identity have dealt largely with the publishing, film, and music industries.

Reserved, Restricted, and Unrestricted Investment Activities

As previously implied, most sectors are open to foreign investment. However, there are several sectors where foreign investment is limited or prohibited. In addition, there are several sectors where private investment is not permitted at all. Here, several sectors are subject to special investment rules.

Canadian's concern that their own cultural identity will be overwhelmed by US cultural influences has resulted in restrictions on foreign investment in this sector and several subsectors:

Book Publishing and Distribution Since 1985, foreign investment in this sector has been governed by the Baie Comeau policy. Prior to 1992, under this policy, direct foreign acquisitions of Canadian-owned firms here was forbidden, and new foreign investment was limited to a minority position, and foreign investors who acquired Canadian firms in the sector through an indirect acquisition were required to divest the operation to Canadian ownership within two years. Recently, indirectly acquired Canadian firms in the sector do not have to be spun-off to Canadian ownership. In addition, the new policy permits foreign ownership if the firm is in financial distress and no Canadian buyers can be found.

Newspapers and Periodicals All investments in this sector are reviewable by Investment Canada. In 1993, the government ruled that any new foreign magazine title published in Canada would be reviewable as a new investment.

Television and Radio Broadcasting Licenses are not granted or renewed to firms that do not have at least 80 percent Canadian control.

Sound Recording All investments are reviewable.

Film and Video All investments are reviewable and new investments are subject to performance requirements.

Commercial Aviation Foreigners are limited to 25 percent ownership stake of Canadian airlines.

Energy and Mining Foreigners cannot bid on leases on federal lands and can't be majority owners of uranium mines.

Telecommunications Under the new Telecommunications Act, foreign ownership of Type I carriers (owners/operators of transmission facilities) is limited to 20 percent. Ownership and control rules are more flexible for holding companies that wish to invest in Canadian carriers, because of the often international nature of their operations and sources of capital. Under these rules, 2/3 of the holding company's equity must be owned and controlled by Canadians.

Fishing Foreigners can own 49 percent of companies holding Canadian fishing licenses.

Health Services Hospitals are a part of the

public health system. Private hospitals are not eligible to receive public health funds and are therefor not a viable investment alternative.

Real Estate Prince Edward Island and Saskatchewan limit real estate sales to out-of-province parties.

Special Programs and Considerations

US foreign investment in Canada is subject to the ICA, but NAFTA further defines the investment relationship between the two nations and adopts the principle of national treatment. The relationship and conduct assumed between the two is to ensure that future regulation of Canadian investors in the US and of US investors in Canada results in equal treatment among and within each country. Either government may regulate or restrict ongoing business operations in their respective countries provided there is no discrimination. These requirements are prospective as well (i.e. they apply to future changes in laws and regulations). Existing laws are grandfathered, except under limited circumstances. In addition, both governments are free to tax foreign owned entities on a different basis than domestic firms, provided this does not result in arbitrary or unjustifiable discrimination, and to exempt the sale of government-owned corporations from any national treatment obligations.

NAFTA also deals more specifically with the financial services sector such as eliminating discriminatory asset and capital restrictions on US bank subsidiaries in Canada. The legislation also exempts US firms and investors from the federal 10/25 rule such that they will be treated the same as Canadians. The rule continues to prevent any single non-US, non-resident from acquiring more than 10 percent of the shares, and all such non-residents in the aggregate from acquiring more than 25 percent of the share of federally regulated, Canadian-controlled financial institutions. Both the 10 percent and the 25 percent limitation were eliminated for US investors as regards acquisitions of federally-chartered non-bank financial institutions. The 10 percent limitation on any individual shareholder will continue to apply to investments in Canadian banks.

In addition, NAFTA includes provisions that enhance the ability of US investors to enforce their rights through international arbitration, prohibit a broader range of performance requirements, including forced technology transfer, and expand coverage of the investment chapter to include portfolio and intangible investments as well as direct investment.

Patents in Canada are governed by the Patent Act which allows for patenting of processes as well as products. A "first to file" system governs the system with an absolute novelty requirement. Patents run for 20 years from the filing date. Canada provides for foreign patent protection of treaty signatories under the Patent Cooperation Treaty of 1990. Under copyrights, Canada is a member of the World Intellectual Property Organization and generally enforces most copyright codes and laws as exist in all other major industrialized economies.

INVESTMENT INCENTIVES

A variety of incentives are available from federal and provincial governments in Canada. None of the federal incentives are specifically aimed at promoting or discouraging direct foreign investment in Canada. The incentives are designed to accomplish broader policy goals, such as research and development, investment in machinery, and equipment, and promotion of regional economies. The programs are available to a qualified investor who agrees to abide by the rules and regulations of the specific program.

Provincial incentives are more investor-specific and are naturally conditioned on applying the funds within the applicable province. These incentives may also be restricted to firms established in the province or who agree to establish in the province. Incentives of all types may be in the form of grants, loans, loan guarantees, venture capital, subsidies or tax credits. Incentives are not generally oriented towards export promotion.

A range of tax incentives to corporations conducting research and development are available to firms in Canada, Canadian subsidiaries of non-Canadian based firms and non-Canadian corporations that have contracted R&D to a Canadian R&D firm. In addition, some particular incentives include:

- A federal investment tax credit for 20 percent to 35 percent of all current capital expenditures
- Both non-incremental and incremental R&D expenditures qualify for the federal investment tax credit.
- Investment tax credits are fully refundable in cash, within limits, to qualifying entities, provided the tax credits are not used to offset taxes payable
- Ontario offers an additional deduction, the super allowance for incremental R&D expenditures when calculating Ontario taxable income and
- Quebec offers a wide range of provincial incentives, including a subsidy for R&D wages, additional deductions in calculating Quebec taxable income, and the option to flow through some of these provincial incentives to prospective investors.

REGULATORY AGENCIES AND INVESTMENT ASSISTANCE

The following lists official and quasi-official entities which foreign investors must or may deal with to research or gain approval for investments or get assistance for investment in Canada.

Department of Foreign Affairs & Trade
125 Sussex Drive
Ottawa, Ontario K1A 0G2
Tel: (613) 996-9134
Fax: (613) 996-9709

Citizenship & Immigration Canada
140 Promenade du portage
Hull, Quebec K1A 1L1
Tel: (819) 994-0535
Fax: (819) 953-9339

Revenue Canada (Taxation)
88 Metcalfe Street
Ottawa, Ontario K1A 0L8
Tel: (613) 957-0274
Fax: (613) 941-0914

Canadian Manufacturers Association
75 International Blvd.
Etobicoke, Ontario M9W 6O9
Tel: (416) 798-9000
Fax: (416) 798-8050

Business Council on National Issues
90 Sparks Street
Ottawa, Ontario K1P 5B4
Tel: (613) 238-3727
Fax: (613) 236-8679

Department of Finance Canada
140 O'Connor Street
Ottawa, Ontario K1A 0G5
Tel: (613) 992-1573
Fax: (613) 996-8404

Industry Canada (Corporate & Consumer Affairs)
50 Victoria Street
Hull, Quebec K1A 0C9
Tel: (819) 997-2938

Canadian Chamber of Commerce
55 Metcalfe Street
Ottawa, Ontario K1P 6N4
Tel: (613) 238-4000
Fax: (613) 238-7643

Conference Board of Canada
255 Smyth Road
Ottawa, Ontario K1H 8M7
Tel: (613) 526-3580
Fax: (613) 526-4857

C.D. Howe Institute
125 Adelaide Street
Toronto, Ontario M5C 1L7
Tel: (416) 865-1904
Fax: (416) 865-1866

Other important agencies include the Bureau of Competition, Environment Canada, provincial securities commissions, and the federal and provincial labor relations boards.

Foreign Trade

SIGNIFICANCE OF FOREIGN TRADE

Canada relies heavily on foreign trade for its economic well being. In fact, few nations in the world have a greater stake in international trade than Canada. It is the seventh largest exporter and eighth largest importer in world. Despite its modest population of less than 30 million, it leads the world's largest economies in terms of total trade as a share of Gross Domestic Product (GDP); imports and exports together account for 59 percent of Canada's GDP. (Compare this with 16.3 percent of GDP for the US, 15.2 percent for Japan, 40 percent for China, 46.2 percent for France, and 76.9 percent for Taiwan, which exists primarily as a conduit for international trade). In relative, or per capita, terms, Canada is far more heavily involved in foreign trade than are any of its trade partners: for example, with a population 11 times the size of Canada's the US exports only three times as much.

Canada's entire economy is involved to a large extent in foreign trade. It relies heavily on both imports and exports to fuel its domestic economy, although both imports and exports are dominated by trade in merchandise. Three quarters of the country's output of natural resources is exported, as is more than half of its manufacturing production. Although trade in services has seen tremendous growth over the past few years only a relatively small proportion of this sector is traded internationally. Most services and direct foreign investment contribute to Canada's foreign trade account in the form of imports.

Direct foreign investment in Canada has long played a pivotal role in the development of many Canadian industries and it remains an important source of capital, technology, expertise and innovation in the Canadian economy. However, this has not all been positive. The high degree of foreign ownership of Canadian business has also been problematic, drawing profits away from the country. Overall, about 40 percent of the country's industry is owned by non-Canadians, led by the Americans. However, over the past few years, Canadian firms have become increasingly involved in making direct investment abroad.

While Canada has traditionally relied to an extremely large extent on trade with the US, it has in the past few years actively sought out more comprehensive trading links with other nations—particularly those in the fast-growing Asia-Pacific region. It has been an active supporter of both the North American Free Trade Agreement (NAFTA) and the Asia-Pacific Economic Cooperation agreement (APEC), and has been a vocal proponent of the Summit of the Americas, which seeks to create a massive, hemispheric free trade bloc consisting of over 44 nations. Over the next few years Canada's trade with Asia is expected to grow faster than its trade with Europe or the US, although it will undoubtedly remain heavily reliant on its bilateral link with the US.

CONTENTS

Significance of Foreign Trade 51
Trade Policy 51
Trade by Commodity Grouping, 1994-1995 53
Size and Balance of Trade 53
Reliance on the United States 55
Effect of NAFTA 55
Exports 56
Top Ten Commodity Exports, 1995 56
Top Ten Commodity Imports, 1995 57
Imports 58
Top Products by Partner (In Millions) 60
Canada's Leading Trade Partners 61
Trade Partners 61

TRADE POLICY

Canada officially pursues an active policy of increasing and expanding trade links with partners all over the world. It especially seeks to establish greater trade levels, in both imports and exports, with the nations of Southeast Asia. An emphasis on seeking new markets beyond the US (which has traditionally been by far its largest trade partner) is becoming a priority of the Canadian government. It has especially targeted South Korea as a potentially lucrative trade partner. Unlike Japan or China, South Korea is a compatible and like-sized economy; it also maintains a large trade surplus with Canada, which Canada would like to see reduced.

Canada is also seeking to expand NAFTA, and encourages the application of emerging healthy, free economies such as Chile. Already, Canadian direct foreign investment in Latin America accounts for about 6 percent of its total direct foreign investment, and an expanded NAFTA would encourage further flows of direct foreign investment to the region.

In addition to seeking new trade partners, Canada is also concentrating on expanding its exports beyond the traditional lumber, raw natural resources, and agricultural products with which it is usually associated.

It has also undertaken to unilaterally reduce or eliminate many of the protectionist tariffs and quotas applied in several industries. It well recognizes that if, with its relatively sparse population, it is to effectively compete as an economic power, it must do so internationally. Its domestic economy alone could never support its disproportionately high ranking among the world's top trading nations.

Nonetheless, the government continues to pursue a schizophrenic hands-on hands-off policy toward the economy. While liberalization policies have substantially reduced or eliminated many tariffs and quotas, several remain in place. Labor and industry alike cry for more. This has resulted in a somewhat erratic policy regarding foreign trade. In short, Canadians seem uncertain as to how best to take advantage of the steady integration of their economy into the larger world. They welcome the export boom resulting from their relatively weak currency with respect to the US dollar, but they fear the invasion of American enterprises in certain sectors, particularly retail. They enthusiastically invest abroad, especially in the hot Asian and Latin American markets, but their foreign investment regime still creates substantial barriers to foreign investment in many sectors.

NAFTA

The implementation of NAFTA in 1994 saw yet more of the expansion in trade with the US that had begun in 1989 with the Free Trade Agreement (FTA) between the two countries. More significantly, NAFTA opened up long-closed doors to Mexico's markets—and opened Canada's relatively free markets to competition from low-cost Mexican producers.

NAFTA's early years were marked by vigorous trade and investment expansion, but also some friction as the countries moved toward implementing NAFTA-related institutions and resolving startup difficulties. Although 95 percent of the trade between Canada and the US is conducted without dispute, US and Canadian negotiators sought to resolve long-standing disputes over commodities such as lumber, wheat, and dairy products, and well as new differences over proposed Canadian restrictions on US broadcasters and magazines. Mexico's peso crisis resulted in the country being unable to implement or continue many of its NAFTA-mandated reforms, although it struggles to maintain its commitments under the agreement.

Overall, trade between Canada and the US continued its steady growth over the past several years, albeit at a slightly faster clip, while Canada's trade with Mexico accelerated sharply. Canada found that many of Mexico's markets were well suited to Canadian products and marketing methods, and that many Mexican industries needed Canadian capital investment and technical expertise. The tremendous rate of growth in trade between the two countries is expected to slow somewhat, although overall trade volumes between the two should continue to grow.

Investment

Although long a restricted and highly regulated destination for foreign investment, Canada has, in the past decade, become one of the most open and welcoming environments for foreign direct investment to be found anywhere in the world. Canada now welcomes foreign investment and the federal government and most provincial governments maintain a number of programs and services aimed at attracting foreign investment, particularly in technology and knowledge-intensive industries.

The 1985 Investment Canada Act requires proposed acquisitions over certain threshold levels by foreign investors to be reviewed by the federal government to ensure "net benefit to Canada," although there are several exemptions from this requirement. In 1995 the Act was amended and liberalized. The threshold levels for review of acquisitions of Canadian companies by NAFTA and World Trade Organization (WTO) countries was raised: acquisitions of C$160 million or more are relievable by the Canadian government; acquisitions of less than C$160 million need only be notified to the Canadian government.

Only a few sectors are subject to lower threshold levels for review, including: financial services, transportation, cultural sectors, and uranium. Foreign investments in these sectors are reviewable if they are more than C$5 million if direct investment and C$50 million if the investment is indirect (direct investment includes ownership of businesses with real property, equipment, proprietary technology and employees, while indirect investment includes such things as holdings of foreign currency, bonds and stocks).

Canada's liberalized foreign investment policy has resulted in a significant increase in the levels of foreign investment in the country and foreign direct investment has made a major contribution to Canada's industrial development, high standard of living and its steadily increasing ties to the US and other foreign markets.

Of continuing concern to the government, however, is the fact that foreign direct investment in Canada greatly exceeds the value of Canadian direct investment abroad. Canada has an overall net international indebtedness of over C$340 billion, about 42 percent of GDP (Canadian investment abroad in 1994 totaled C$295,902 million while total foreign investment in Canada totaled C$637,581 million). This is high by industrial country standards, but it is expected to decline as Canada's public sector and current account deficits shrink, and as the value of Canadian foreign investment abroad continues to increase.

Limitations Although Canada adheres to a remarkably liberal and open foreign trade regime, some barriers do remain. Each province maintains its own testing facilities, inspection agencies and certification bodies and some of the standards are more stringent than those mandated under GATT—and even some addressed by NAFTA. In addition, government procurement policies of many of the provinces openly favor local suppliers, and foreign sellers sometimes find it difficult to obtain federal government contracts as well.

The primary obstacles to foreign trade, however, are in the service industries, where Canada maintains strict citizenship and licensing requirements, and in its strict prohibitions regarding its "cultural industries." Protection of its cultural industries is an extremely sensitive and longstanding policy objective of the Canadian government, and it insists that these industries are exempted from most of its trade agreements and other liberalization measures.

SIZE AND BALANCE OF TRADE

Total Size

Despite a population of less than 30 million, Canada supplies about 4 percent of the world's merchandise exports and purchases only a slightly smaller share of its imports. It is one of the world's major trading countries. In comparison, the US,

TRADE BY COMMODITY GROUPING, 1994-1995 (C$ Billions)

Exports	1994	1995	% Change
Agriculture & Fishing	17.72	19.74	.11.4
Energy Products	21.31	23.36	9.6
Forestry Products	31.16	39.24	25.9
Industrial Goods	39.46	48.32	22.5
Mach. & Equip.	43.02	52.35	21.7
Automotive Parts	57.92	63.14	9
Other Consumer Goods	5.85	7.11	21.5
Special Transactions	9.42	10.44	10.8
Total	**217.85**	**253.54**	**16.4**

Imports	1994	1994	% Change
Agriculture & Fishing	12.58	13.37	6.3
Energy Products	7.15	8.11	13.4
Forestry Products	1.81	2.04	12.7
Industrial Goods	38.74	44.96	16.1
Mach. & Equip.	65.58	75.61	15.3
Automotive Parts	48.32	50.38	4.3
Other Consumer Goods	23.52	25.57	8.7
Special Transactions	4.88	5.49	12.5
Total	**202.58**	**225.53**	**11.3**

with a population 11 times the size of Canada's, provides 12.6 percent of the world's exports (only three times as much as Canada), and purchases 15.9 percent of its imports; Japan sells 9.8 percent and purchases 6.3 percent; Britain sells five percent and purchases 5.5 percent; and France sells 5.7 percent and purchases 5.3 percent.

With the exception of recessionary 1991, Canadian merchandise trade has grown substantially each year since the late 1980s. Canada's merchandise exports have shown phenomenal growth in recent years, increasing by 21 percent in 1994, to C$219 billion dollars. Merchandise imports totalled C$202 billion, up 17.7 percent over the year before. In 1995 the figures had grown to nearly C$230 billion and C$211 billion respectively—a much slower rate of increase, but growing nonetheless. Canada's merchandise trade surplus in 1994 was its highest in almost a decade, reaching C$17 billion, before reducing somewhat in 1995.

Canada consistently runs a surplus in its merchandise trade. In 1984, the surplus reached a high of almost C$20 billion, but over the past five years it has run at an average of about C$10 billion.

The consistent merchandise trade surplus, however, is not enough to offset weaknesses and continuing deficits in other export sectors, primarily the service industry. Although services have shown steady, and increasingly significant, growth, the trade in services remains limited to a few industries—primarily banking, insurance, education, and communications. The government seems to recognize that in order to sustain high growth rates in foreign trade (both exports and imports), Canada will have to further broaden its trade base to include more reliance on services and investment income. To this end, it has begun to pursue policies to free trade in both of these sectors.

Trade in merchandise remains the mainstay of Canada's foreign trade, especially as it has made much progress in recent years toward moving away from a dependency on resource exports such as lumber, wheat and minerals. Manufactured goods increasingly dominate Canada's leading exports, and high technology goods have shown phenomenal growth in the past few years. At the same time, exports of natural resource products have decreased in importance, though not in actual volumes. Overall, trade in merchandise has grown by more than 50 percent since 1990.

Balance of Trade

Canada's exports of merchandise traditionally and consistently outpace merchandise imports. In 1994 merchandise exports totalled C$217,854 million, and merchandise imports were C$202,807 million. In 1995 the numbers had grown to C$533,536 million and C$225,251 million respectively. The gap is widening: in 1994 exports outpaced imports by 7.4 percent, and in 1995 the difference was 12.5 percent. This healthy showing comes primarily from Canada's trade with Asia (excluding Japan), where exports increased by 31.4 percent from 1994 to 1995, and imports increased by a meager 3.7 percent. In 1994 the value of exports to Asia (excluding Japan) was only 72 percent that of imports from the region; in 1995 the value had grown to 99 percent of import values.

Canada runs a consistent merchandise trade surplus with its two major partners, the US and Japan. In 1994 Canada's merchandise trade surplus with the US was C$26,256 million; by the end of 1995 it had grown to C$32,923 million. Trade with Japan showed a similar pattern: the surplus at the end of 1994 was C$1,093 million, which had grown to C$3,018 by December 1995. In both cases, much of the surplus came from large increases in exports of forestry and industrial goods.

Although Canada also runs trade surpluses with some of its smaller trading partners, it usually registers deficits in its merchandise trade with the European Union (EU), and other OECD countries. Trade with the EU has shown a shift in Canada's favor lately, with the merchandise trade deficit first growing by smaller increments each year, and most recently actually declining—from C$4,539 million in 1994 to C$3,892 million in 1995. Trade deficits with smaller countries, including those in Southeast Asia upon which Canada is focusing its attentions, has shown a significant reduction as exports skyrocketed in 1995.

The continuing strength of the Japanese yen, coupled with the growing strength of other Asian currencies and the relative weakness of the Canadian dollar, have made such growth possible. Canada's diverse population bringing strong cultural links with the Asia-Pacific region, and its abundant resources, take advantage of the rapidly growing and increasingly affluent Asian markets. While it welcomes imports from this region, it has focused its energies on building export relationships, and the rapid growth in exports to these countries reflects those efforts.

Canada's total imports have always outpaced exports and will continue to do so for some time to come. In 1994 total exports from Canada were US$194.8 million, while imports were US$211.1 million. In 1995 the relative value of exports improved somewhat—to US$223.6 million compared with US$235.1 million in imports—and they are expected to remain strong relative to imports throughout 1996—exports are projected to reach about US$234.8 million and imports about US$246.9 million. Again, this reflects Canada's strengthening export performance and its increasing emphasis on exports in services and investment.

Sectors

Canada's strongest trade sector, by far, is in merchandise. Canada consistently runs a substantial, and for the most part increasing, trade surplus in merchandise. This surplus, however, is not enough to make up for the consistent trade deficit in other sectors. Although Canada has focused on increasing its exports of services—with good result; the gap has narrowed significantly—it remains a net importer of these profitable industries.

The composition of Canada's trade has shifted considerably in the past several years as lumber and minerals have declined in importance, and manufactured, finished and high-technology products have come to represent a much bigger proportion of both exports and imports. Automotive products and machinery equipment, especially, have become more prominent in Canada's export catalog; together representing almost 45 percent of Canada's exports.

In general, manufacturing and knowledge-intensive products are boosting exports in many sectors, including agricultural (with the growth of processed food products); forestry (newsprint has become a large export); chemicals (Canada has seen a big rise in sales of fertilizer); and industrial goods and materials (fabricated textiles have become popular exports, especially to the Asia-Pacific region).

Canada has also witnessed changes in the structure of its imports. Cross-border trade with the US has resulted in automotive equipment and supplies becoming not only one of the biggest exports but the one of the largest import categories as well. Together with machinery and equipment, it accounts for 56 percent of merchandise exports.

Canada's imports of consumer goods substantially exceeds its exports of these products. This is primarily due to large imports of apparel, footwear, sporting goods, toys, and various other consumer end-products which Canada still does not manufacture domestically in large quantities.

RELIANCE ON THE UNITED STATES

Canada and the US enjoy the most extensive trade relationship between any two countries in the world. But the US dwarfs Canada, both in terms of its population (the population of the US is 11 times greater than that of Canada) and GDP, thus creating disparity in the partnership. Canada's economy is heavily influenced by political and economic events in the US, both positive and negative. Since World War II recessions in Canada and the US have been very closely synchronized. Downturns have begun, on average, within one month of each other in both countries and have ended at about the same time. However, since the early 1990s, when Canada began to consciously reduce its dependence on US markets, the synchronized recessions have not been so noticeable. Despite the 1990-91 recession in the US Canadian exports grew steadily. While natural resource products and, to a lesser extent, automotive products remain sensitive to changes in American demand, the last decade has seen a rapid shift in Canada's exports away from these traditional commodities to other products which are not so sensitive to falls in demand during recession—such as machinery and equipment. Although Canada has striven to reduce its reliance on the US, its economy and foreign trade remain heavily reliant on the US economy and its ability and willingness to purchase Canadian goods. The FTA and NAFTA have served to strengthen the already deep and wide-ranging cross-border trade between the two countries.

Further strengthening the ties between the two countries is the fact that Canadians are quite partial to American products, even as they grumble about US domination. Surprisingly, they have become even more receptive to US goods since NAFTA's inception, but this is not entirely a matter of free choice. The fall of trade barriers permits US multinationals to stop making a broad range of products within Canada for sale only in that market. Now they can employ Canadian plants to turn out products for broader markets and drop items that either are not cost efficient or can find a market only in Canada (which will remain quite small for the foreseeable future).

Although 95 percent of the trade between the two countries is conducted without dispute, there are a few significant areas in which bilateral differences seriously threaten to undermine a positive trading relationship. These include issues on salmon, steel, beer, and culture. The most significant bilateral trade disputes are over agricultural products, wheat, and lumber—the traditional mainstays of Canada's export catalog.

EFFECT OF NAFTA

The Free Trade Agreement (FTA) between Canada and the US, which took effect in 1989, has been responsible for a good portion of the increase in bilateral trade between the two countries. Between 1988 and 1993 Canadian imports from the US increased by 26 percent, while exports to the US increased by 39 percent. Trade between the two countries, and between Canada and Mexico as well, has grown even further with the implementation of the NAFTA in 1993. The most significant increases have come in those sectors which Canadian and US tariffs fell, rather than in the non-liberalized industries.

With the implementation of NAFTA in 1993, which incorporated virtually all the current provisions of the FTA and extended them to Mexico, market reforms and the need for modern technology in Mexico have resulted in increased opportunities for both Canadian and US companies. Total Canada-Mexico bilateral trade grew by 14 percent in 1994, faster than the rate of growth in Canada's trade with the rest of the world. More significantly, Canada's direct foreign investment in Mexico increased by almost 100 percent in 1994. NAFTA resulted in the immediate elimination of duties on about one half of Canadian exports to Mexico in terms of value, as well as the launch of progressive reductions in remaining tariffs over the next couple of years.

Canada would like expand NAFTA to other countries in the Western Hemisphere. For most of Latin America, North America is already their main export market, and as these economies grow so will opportunities for Canadian sellers and investors.

EXPORTS

Canada has in the past few years pursued an aggressive policy of export growth. It has taken measures to expand its export base away from lumber and raw minerals and into production and high technology goods. It has also actively courted new trading partners, in Asia and elsewhere, in an effort to reduce its heavy reliance on US markets. It has, to a large degree, been successful. Exports have boomed, and continue to grow at a faster pace than imports.

Composition of Exports

The composition of Canada's export catalog has changed drastically in the past decade. In 1985, wheat accounted for nearly 20 percent of Canada's export earnings, and raw minerals such as crude petroleum, natural gas, and coal made up another 62 percent. The past few years have seen a much more diversified accounting, primarily the result of substantially decreased wheat exports and an increase in the volumes of manufactured goods which are exported. In 1995, automotive products made up 24 percent of Canada's export revenues, and other machinery and equipment accounted for another 20 percent. Industrial goods and materials followed with 18 percent of merchandise exports, and forestry products, energy products, and agricultural and fishing products lagged behind with 15, nine and 7.5 percent respectively.

Vehicle manufactures are by far the most important export product Canada offers: passenger automobiles provide nearly 15 percent of export revenues, motor vehicle parts another 6.3 percent, and trucks yet another 5.4 percent. Other important exports include high-technology office equipment such as fax machines, computers, and telecommunications equipment (11.2 percent), and lumber and wood products (10 percent).

Canada is expected to further diversify by continuing to make good use of its natural resources by manufacturing them into processed products, such as newsprint (lumber), pharmaceuticals (chemicals), fertilizers (chemicals), and processed foods (wheat).

Lumber, Wheat and Minerals

Canada has historically been known as a provider of lumber, wheat and minerals. Indeed, much of Canada's early economic history was depicted in the staples theory of economic development—a dependency on resource exports starting with fur, then lumber and wheat, and subsequently, minerals. However, although these products clearly drove Canada's trade development, they have become less and less relevant in recent decades. Although they remain important underpinnings of Canada's international trade, manufactured goods increasingly dominate Canada's exports.

Lumber Canada is one of the world's major exporters of lumber, although lumber and related products make up only about 15 percent of Canada's total export revenues. It is not without problems, however. Canada and the US are involved in a long-

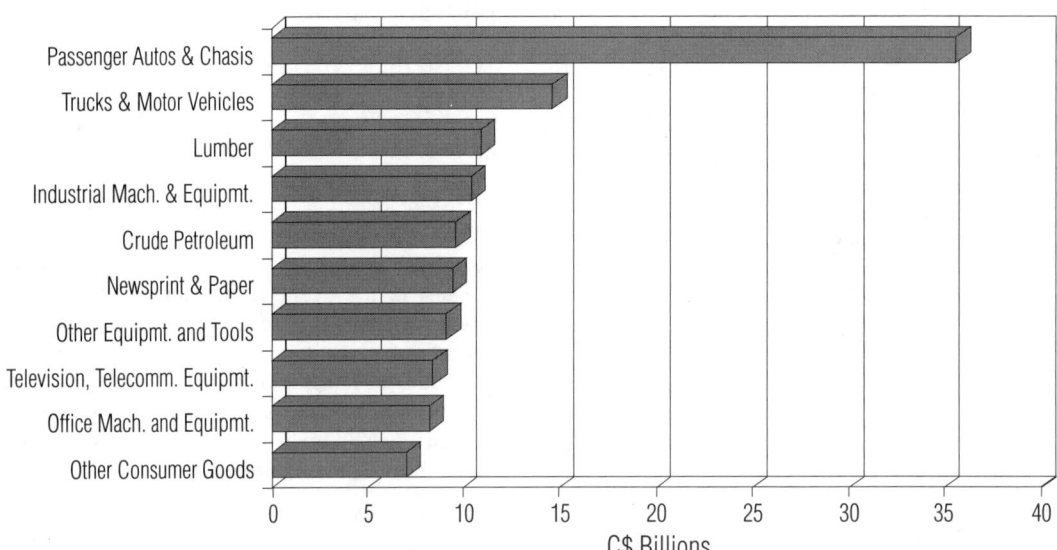

Other 1995 exports: C$139.5 billion.
Total 1995 exports: C$ 263.5 billion.
Source: Statistics Canada

running trade dispute involving Canadian subsidies to its lumber industry and export restrictions on lumber. The US charges that Canada's policies amount to market-distorting countervailing duties that are prohibited under the FTA/NAFTA. The conflict has dragged on for over a decade, and there is still no indication that a final resolution is near.

However, under continued heavy pressure from the US lumber industry, Canada, in April 1996, agreed to limit its softwood lumber shipments to the US. The two countries agreed to a pact under which Canada is expected to reduce its softwood exports by about 9 percent, or 1.5 billion board feet, a year for the next five years. The agreement sets a duty-free quota on Canadian softwood exports to the US, and the Canadian government has agreed to impose a stiff export tax on lumber shipments that surpass this limit. As part of the agreement, the US agreed not to commence any new trade action against Canada during this period. While the US lumber industry lauded the pact as providing much needed relief, the only real effect it is likely to have is to substantially raise the price of framing lumber in new homes in the US.

Canada sells C$10,062 million worth of lumber each year, about 4 percent of total merchandise exports. While total volumes continue to rise (lumber exports totalled C$8,279 million in 1993), the proportion of merchandise exports accounted for by lumber declines slightly each year; in 1993 exports of lumber accounted for 5.1 percent of merchandise exports.

Canada is, however, increasing its exports of processed or manufactured lumber products. In 1993 Canada exported newsprint worth C$6,109 million, or 3.8 percent of merchandise exports; by 1995 that figure had risen to C$14,260 million, over 5 percent of the total.

Wheat Although wheat remains a steady earner of export revenues its importance has declined drastically over the past few decades. As late as 1984, Canada exported C$4,709 million of wheat (27 percent of merchandise exports); one year later the figure had dropped to C$3,778 million (19 percent of merchandise exports). By 1995, Canadian wheat exports were C$3,933 million, representing only about 1.5 percent of total merchandise exports.

At least a part of the decline can be attributed to action by the US to curb Canadian wheat imports. In 1993 Canadian wheat imports into the US accelerated rapidly. In response, US farmers charged that the Canadian government's pricing structure and transportation subsidies were directly contributing to the increase in imports, a decrease in the US domestic price of wheat, and flagging US exports of wheat. This resulted in an "agreement" between Canada and the US that restricted US imports of wheat (almost all of which happen to be Canadian).

Minerals Minerals and natural resources continue to make up a large proportion of Canada's exports. Crude petroleum, natural gas and other energy products account for nearly 10 percent of merchandise exports and bring in about C$23,359 million each year. Metal ores, including iron,

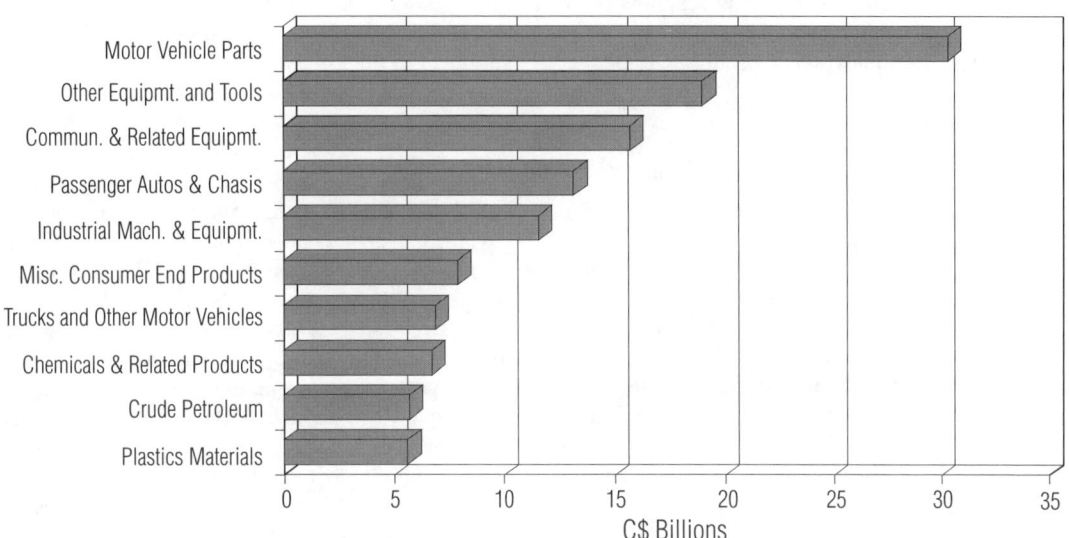

Top Ten Commodity Imports, 1995

Other 1995 imports equal C$102.9 billion
Total 1995 imports: C$ 225.5 billion.
Source: Statistics Canada

copper, nickel, and zinc, make up nearly two percent of exports, bringing yearly revenues of over C$5,000 million.

Services

Services account for more than 70 percent of Canada's domestic economic activity. Although most of these jobs are not traded internationally (Canada maintains a huge civil service sector) services are becoming an increasingly important component of global commerce. By the early 1990s, they represented about 25 percent of Canada's total international trade.

Most important to this trade are banking and securities, insurance, transportation, freight and shipping, communications, engineering, consulting, and an ever broader variety of professional services such as law, accounting, architecture, etc. Canadian companies are active competitors in the sale of all of these services internationally, and they generate billions of dollars in export earnings each year. In 1993, Canadians earned C$26.8 billion from the international sale of services, although it still recorded a net deficit in this sector, importing C$40 billion worth.

The weakest link in the foreign trade of Canadian services is travel and tourism. Receipts earned from foreigners travelling in Canada were C$9 billion, whereas Canadians spent almost C$17 billion travelling outside their country, resulting in an overall foreign travel deficit of C$8 billion.

Services exports constitute the fastest growing component of the Canada-US bilateral trade relationship. Under NAFTA, citizenship requirements affecting the licensing and practice of professionals were lifted and many laws and procedures were standardized. Thus, the Canadian service industry, especially professionals, should continue to benefit as Canadian professionals make their names in the American and Mexican markets.

Industrial and Manufactured Products

The mainstay of Canada's foreign trade catalog remains industrial and manufactured products, although the composition has changed drastically in recent years. Canada has seen a definite trend toward exporting highly processed or high-technology products in place of the simple manufactures exported a decade ago. Machinery, office and telecommunications equipment, and autos, along with chemicals and textiles, have in recent years witnessed the highest growth rates ever, and Canada is a leader in many of these areas.

Automobiles Automobiles and automotive equipment is Canada's largest export category, bringing in nearly C$65,000 million in export revenues each year. This represents almost 24 percent of total merchandise export earnings. Passenger automobiles account for over half of this amount, and much of this is exported to the US.

Under the 1965 Automobile Pact signed with the US, cross-border trade in automobiles was significantly liberalized, leading to a vast growth of production facilities in Canada. This industry continues to grow, although as the NAFTA provisions continue to take hold, the US and Mexico are expected to reclaim some of this market.

By Region

Exports to the US come primarily from Ontario, which supplies 56 percent of Canada's exports to the US. Quebec is the next largest supplier, selling 18.2 percent; followed by Alberta (10.6 percent) and British Columbia (seven percent). Saskatchewan, Manitoba, and New Brunswick each provide about 2 percent.

British Columbia supplies Japan with most of its Canadian goods, accounting for 59.2 percent of Canadian exports to Japan. Alberta is the next largest supplier, providing 13.8 percent of exports, followed by Saskatchewan (6.4 percent), and Ontario and Quebec, which each provide about 5.7 percent.

The UK gets over 40 percent of its Canadian goods from Ontario, and another 32.4 percent from Quebec. 10.3 percent come from British Columbia, and another five percent are supplied by Alberta. Nova Scotia, Manitoba and Saskatchewan supply most of the rest.

China, which is beginning to become an important export market, purchases most of its Canadian goods from Saskatchewan (27 percent) or Ontario (26.1 percent), although Alberta (16 percent) and British Columbia (14.4 percent) are also significant suppliers to the Chinese market.

IMPORTS

Canada is a net importer of services and direct foreign investment. It also imports large quantities of high-technology and telecommunications equipment, computer software, machinery, and textiles and apparel. Automotive products and machinery and equipment rank as the two biggest categories, together accounting for about 56 percent of merchandise imports. Canada's imports of consumer goods substantially exceed its exports in this sector, primarily due to extensive imports of apparel, footwear, sporting goods, toys, and various other consumer end-products which are not manufactured in large quantities domestically. US products and services account for an overwhelming share of Canada's import market, and its proportion is expected to remain strong for several years to come.

Composition of Imports

Although Canada produces a large quantity of automobiles, along with automotive parts and equipment, it is also a large importer of these products. Canada imports C$50,375 million worth of automotive products, nearly a quarter of its total merchandise imports. Motor vehicle parts represent the largest subsector in this category; imports of parts alone total C$30,264. Other machinery equipment imports constitute over 32 percent of Canada's imports, with purchases of C$75,609 million in 1995. Another large import category consists of industrial goods and materials, including metals and chemicals. This category accounts for nearly C$45,000 million, or 19.3 percent of Canadian imports. Of this, metals make up C$11,488 million, or 5 percent of total imports, and chemicals and plastics make up C$16,324 million, or 7 percent of total imports.

Products

Automotive Parts and Service Equipment By far the most important market in Canada, this sector purchased over US$4,000 million worth of automobile parts and equipment in 1995. Local production accounted for 78 percent of the total market, but this still left room for more than US$3,000 million in imports. Of this, about 85 percent comes from the US. The US is maintaining its stranglehold on the Canadian automobile import market; both total imports and imports from the US grew by 8 percent in 1995.

Apparel Apparel represents the second largest market for imports in Canada. This market is expected to grow in future years as the Canadian domestic apparel industry softens and Canadian consumers continue to seek quality items at fair prices. The Canadian apparel industry has a reputation for producing a diversified range of fashionable high-quality items, although the prices tend to be high, leaving much room for lower priced imports of good quality. The elimination of tariffs on US and Mexican-origin apparel should stimulate imports from these two countries.

The Canadian market for imported apparel, which is about 30 percent of the total apparel market, grew by three percent in 1994 and by eight percent in 1995. Of this, the US provides only about 12 percent; Mexico's share, while still insignificant, is expected to increase sharply in the next couple of years.

Electronic Components The total market value of the Canadian electronic components industry is difficult to estimate, due to its volatility and the broadness of the market. Nonetheless, it is clear that Canada imports a large quantity of all sorts of electronic components. There is a large market that imports base or semi-processed parts into Canada for additional processing and then re-exports them as highly processed components. Satellite parts and components, semi-conductors and electronic transformers represent particularly strong import markets.

The Canadian market for electronic components grew by 9 percent in 1994 and by six percent in 1995, while imports grew by 10 and 8 percent over the same period. Imports from the US in both years grew by a larger percentage than the total market; growth rates in imports from the US registered 10 and 11 percent respectively.

Computer Software The fast-growing Canadian software market is expected to continue to grow between 10 and 12 percent a year over the next few years. While local production accounts for about 80 percent of sales, there is still room for significant sales of imports. Total sales of computer software grew by 8 percent in 1994 and by 11 percent in 1995; imports of these products grew by 9 and 12 percent respectively. Imports from the US account for over 90 percent of the import market.

Services

In 1994 Canadians paid out more than C$45 billion to purchase services from foreign providers. This was far in excess of the revenues received from the sale of Canadian services to foreigners. A major reason for Canada's persistent deficit on trade in services is its travel account, which consistently runs a large deficit created by the large numbers of Canadians traveling abroad.

By Region

Ontario and Quebec are the largest purchasers of imports from most of Canada's trading partners. British Columbia and Alberta are the next largest, although Nova Scotia is a major purchaser of goods from Germany and the United Kingdom.

The US sells nearly 72 percent of its imports to Canada in Ontario. Quebec is the next largest purchaser, taking 11 percent, followed by British Columbia, with seven percent. Alberta and Manitoba together take another seven percent, with most of the remainder being sold in Saskatchewan or New Brunswick. Japanese imports are distributed in much the same proportions as those from the US.

The United Kingdom, on the other hand, sells primarily to Quebec (45 percent), followed by Ontario (40 percent). Only a small proportion of UK imports find their way to the other provinces (primarily Nova Scotia, although it only purchases 8 percent).

A large portion of imports coming from China are sold to Ontario purchasers, who buy 48.4 percent of all Chinese imports into Canada. Quebec is the next largest purchaser (28.2 percent), followed by British Columbia (20 percent).

TOP PRODUCTS BY PARTNER (IN MILLIONS)

US

Imports from Canada			Exports to Canada		
Product	C$	Percent	Product	C$	Percent
vehicles	24,907	30	vehicles	23,933	24
mineral fuels and oils	9,362	11.3	machinery and parts	19,223	9.3
machinery and parts	7,452	9.0	electrical machinery	10,821	10.9
wood articles	5,339	6.4	plastics	3,861	3.9
paper and paper products	4,192	5.1	precision instruments	3,429	3.4
electrical machinery	3,820	4.6	iron or steel products	1,888	1.9

Japan

Imports from Canada			Exports to Canada		
Product	C$	Percent	Product	C$	Percent
wood products	1,229	29.2	machinery	2,477	29.9
mineral fuels and oils	601	14.3	vehicles and parts	2,173	226.3
wood pulp	425	10.1	electrical machinery	1,691	20.4
oil seed and other grains	423	10	precision instruments	534	6.5
fish	281	5.5	rubber products	185	2.2
ores, slag, and ash	168	3.9	iron and steel	157	1.9
cereals	146	3.5	photographic products	119	1.4

European Community

Imports from Canada		Exports to Canada	
Product	Percent	Product	Percent
wood and pulp	15.1	machinery and engines	18.5
machinery and engines	8.8	mineral fuels and oils	10
ores, slag, and ash	8.4	electrical machinery	8.2
paper and paperboard	7.6	vehicles and accessories	7.3
pearls and precious stones	5.9	iron and steel	4.8
electrical machinery parts	4.4	organic chemicals	4.4
oil seed and other grains	4.2	precision instruments	3.8
nickel and nickel products	3.8	aircraft and spacecraft	3.0

Mexico

Imports from Canada		Exports to Canada	
Product	Percent	Product	Percent
oil seed and other grains	16.2	vehicles	339.1
cereals	14.4	electrical machinery parts	18
vehicles and accessories	14	mechanical appliances	17.9
electrical machinery	5.3	furniture	6.7
mechanical machinery	5.3	mineral fuels and oils	3.2
dairy products	3.9	vegetables	1.7

Canada's Leading Trade Partners

Imports - 1994

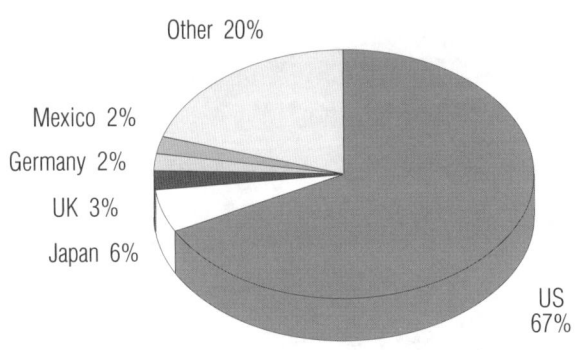

Exports - 1994

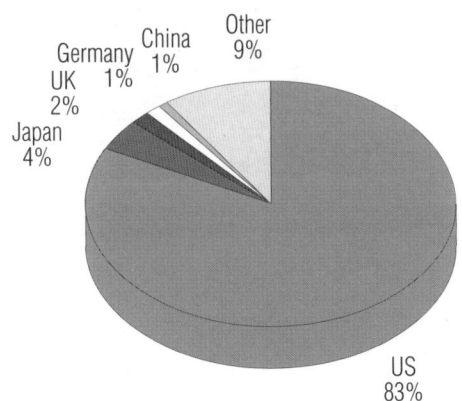

Note: Total merchandise imports in 1994 were C$202.8 billion; total merchandise exports in were C$217.9 billion.
Source: Statistics Canada

TRADE PARTNERS

The US is far and away Canada's most important trading partner, taking 81.5 percent of Canada's exports in 1994 and providing 67.6 percent of its imports. Canada's trade is, in fact, dominated by sales to and purchases from the US. In 1994 Canadian exports to the US set a new record, totalling C$175 billion, only to be broken a year later by exports of C$196 billion in 1995, an increase of 13.3 percent. Imports from the US totalled C$137 billion in 1994 and C$150 billion in 1995, an increase of slightly less than 10 percent.

Far behind the US, Japan ranks as Canada's second largest trade partner. Japan purchases 4.5 percent of Canada's exports and supplies 5.6 percent of its imports, but these figures are growing slower, if at all, as Canada continues its efforts to pursue other Asian partners. Trade with Asia (excluding Japan) continues to show steady growth. In 1994, about 4 percent of Canadian exports went to Asian markets other than Japan, up from just about 3 percent a year earlier. Imports from the same countries accounted for 7.1 percent of Canada's foreign purchases in 1993 but fell to 6.7 percent in 1994, reflecting Canada's greater emphasis on selling to this region.

Western Europe as a whole accounts for a little over 6 percent of total exports; the UK and Germany are the largest purchasers in this region although individually they account for only 1.5 percent and 1 percent respectively. Belgium/Luxembourg and France each purchase about 0.6 percent of Canada's exports. South America (with Brazil accounting for over half), South Korea, China, and Australia/New Zealand each purchase about 1 percent.

Trade figures over the past decade show well the results of Canada's sustained efforts to diversify its trading partners. In 1985 Canadian trade with South Korea was negligible, although it did substantial trade with North Korea (with whom it no longer does any significant trade). Recently, South Korea's purchases were up by over 10 percent from 1992 to 1993, and grew by another 12 percent in 1994.

Australia has also become an important trading partner. Canadian exports to Australia, while still fairly minor in overall volumes, have been climbing steadily since the 1994 agreement between the two countries opened up many heretofore closed markets.

Another burgeoning market for Canada's exports is Mexico. In 1993 Mexico purchased less than 0.5 percent of Canada's exports; in 1994 this proportion had risen to over two percent, with the share likely to keep growing as the provisions of NAFTA take effect and become entrenched in the economies of the two countries.

Trade with the Middle East, particularly Saudi Arabia, is beginning to take on significance as well. In 1985, trade with the Middle East did not even register in the statistics. While exports to Saudi Arabia are still only a fraction of Canada's total, they have climbed by a whopping 50-60 percent each year over the past three years, while imports from Saudi Arabia have stagnated at a miniscule and insignificant level.

Trade Agreements

INTRODUCTION

Canada is the world's seventh largest market economy, with a majority of its production and services in private hands. However, its population is relatively small compared to its vast size and wealth of natural resources, and it must actively pursue foreign markets in order to compete effectively in the global economy. One third of Canada's jobs and one quarter of its GDP depend on international trade. While many goods are traded freely, the federal and provincial governments remain significantly involved in the economy—especially in foreign trade. There is a broad regulatory framework regarding international trade, and the government continues to closely monitor and regulate Canada's imports.

The government has, however, since late 1984 emphasized reduction of public sector interference in the economy and strongly promoted private sector initiative and free trade. It has unilaterally undertaken to liberalize and reduce restrictions on imports, and has also joined in preferential trade arrangements with many of its trading partners. The government has in the past several years embarked on a series of trade initiatives aimed at expanding its export and investment horizons, and broadening the scope of foreign trade beyond its traditional trading partners. As a result, both imports and exports have been freed significantly. Foreign trade has flourished.

CONTENTS
Introduction 63
GATT and the WTO 64
Regional Trade Agreements 67
Bilateral Trade Agreements 70
Other Trade Agreements 71
Related Agreements 71
Emerging Trade Agreements 72
In the Future 72
Useful Addresses 72

Although there is really no such thing as free trade, Canada generally supports the idea of free trade, at least on a theoretical or ideological level. The gap between theory and practice on trade is not so much because of obstructionist intent or anti-trade bias, but rather because of the voluminous regulations of the many discrete agencies and the host of bureaucratic procedures involved in entering products into the country. Many products and commodities may actually be imported duty free and with few if any restrictions under Canada's general tariff provisions. And, through special trade agreements, Canada has also established favorable—and in some cases extremely favorable—trade conditions with specific countries and associations of countries. In many cases goods normally subject to duty may be entered duty free or at reduced rates as long as the imports satisfy the often fairly simple conditions of these programs, usually having to do with the origination of the products in the beneficiary country.

However, the importation of a number of goods into Canada remains either prohibited or restricted. These include such heavily regulated products as firearms, alcoholic beverages, foods, drugs, and live animals, to name a few. Entry of products such as these requires compliance with specific documentation, quota, licensing, and other restrictions imposed by separate regulatory agencies, in addition to the standard customs procedures acknowledged by most countries. Several items cannot be imported into Canada at all, including oleomargarine, reprints of Canadian copyrighted work, and some game birds. (Refer to the "Import Policy & Procedures" and "Export Policy & Procedures" chapters for more detailed information).

Canada participates in several important global and regional preferential trade arrangements. Trade agreements are usually based on the reciprocal extension of trade privileges between the nationals of the sovereign parties to the specific agreement. They generally serve to lower tariffs, eliminate quota restrictions, or otherwise remove protectionist barriers to cross-border trade. These agreements, coupled with Canada's generally liberal trade regime, make Canada a welcome destination for products and commodities from around the world.

Most Favored Nation Status (MFN)

Canada enjoys MFN status with most of its trading partners. MFN status represents what has come to be seen as the norm in bilateral trade relationships between countries rather than the special preferential status the name implies. Under MFN status both parties agree not to extend to any third party nation any trade preferences which are more favorable than those available under the agreement concluded between them, unless they simultaneously make the same provisions available to each other. MFN status is reciprocal, with each party agreeing to grant the status to the other. Nonetheless, MFN must be negotiated on a separate basis with each and every country, and each such agreement will include additional and specific provisions relating to national security, dispute settlement procedures, trade promotion, and various other matters.

Despite the assumption that because MFN status requires equivalent treatment no greater preferential treatment is allowed, international law and practice recognize that specific countries may make additional arrangements granting special preferences to other nations without violating MFN precepts. Such arrangements include free trade areas between two or more countries and commodity-specific and/or country-specific preferences. International canons approve such arrangements provided the agreement contains explicit rules of origin specifying limits to the benefits, and the special rate preferences are achieved by lowering internal rates among the participants rather than by raising a country's general external tariffs.

GATT AND THE WTO

GATT

The General Agreement on Tariffs and Trade (GATT) is designed to provide a standard framework for global trade by ensuring that a fair multilateral trading system exists. Founded in 1947 with 23 members, GATT has passed through 8 series of negotiations, known as rounds, each named after the city in which the opening sessions of each round were held. The most recently completed round was the Uruguay Round, begun in 1986. Initially this round was to have been completed by 1990, but was extended as the agreement became more ambitious and more difficult to conclude. The Final Agreement, consisting of more than 20,000 pages of text, was signed in December 1993 by 124 member countries, including Canada. Several other countries currently outside of GATT, including China, Russia, and Taiwan, have since applied for membership.

Effects The successful conclusion of the Uruguay Round involved new or more efficient protocols in a number of areas, including agriculture, services and intellectual property. As the provisions of the Agreement come into effect it should provide a substantial boost to international business—GATT experts estimate that the increase in international trade in agricultural and industrial products should reach $418 billion by the year 2002, and overall merchandise trade will increase by $745 billion by 2005. Canada's high quality service and production sectors are expected to benefit greatly from GATT as its liberal provisions are implemented throughout the trading world.

All international traders should benefit from either improved returns resulting from major direct savings on duties, or from increased trade volumes generated by lower trade barriers. Participation in the Agreement by several developing economies will bring better access for all to some of the fastest-growing markets in the world, particularly those in the Asia-Pacific region.

Provisions Some of the main features of the Uruguay Round Final Agreement are:
- A fundamental change from non-tariff to tariff-only protection for agriculture and several consumer industries, with substantial phased cuts in tariffs, border protections, domestic support and export subsidies;
- A bound one-third reduction in most tariffs on industrial goods, with much deeper cuts in some sectors; a framework agreement on rules for all trade in services;
- International protection and improved dispute resolution procedures for intellectual property rights (IPR). Trademarks will be protected for 7 years, patents for 20 years, and copyrights for 50 years;
- Measures to limit adverse trade effects and provide more effective international rules on subsidies, anti-dumping and countervailing rules, safeguards and standards; and
- The creation of the World Trade Organization (WTO) to integrate the outcome of negotiations in all areas of the Round, including improved settlement dispute procedures.

The Agreement also provides additional specific benefits, including the opening of the Japanese and Korean rice markets, and greater access for dairy products in a number of markets. GATT is also on record as generally promoting international free trade and opposing regional trade blocs that may lead to preferential treatment among members at the expense of nonmembers.

Customs Valuation Canada has acceded to the GATT Customs Valuation code which provides that the customs value of imported goods shall be the transaction value—the price actually paid or payable for the goods. Under the transaction value system, the value for duty is the total payment for the goods made by the buyer to the seller. The transaction value generally will be accepted by Canada Customs if the goods are sold for export to Canada and if the price paid or payable for the goods can be determined. Under the transaction value system, the value for duty of imported goods will normally be determined from data submitted by the importer. However, preparation of proper documentation by the exporter significantly contributes to expeditious entry.

Standards Canada does comply with the GATT Standards Code in general, although its standards are not specifically in compliance. Under the Standards Council of Canada, several private standards-writing organizations administer technical codes and standards for areas ranging from electrical and plumbing products to health care technology. The Canadian federal government also has numerous commodity standards to safeguard the public welfare.

Areas of Disagreement Several areas of disagreement were specifically excluded from GATT due to a failure of the major parties to reach accord, including aircraft, entertainment, financial services, shipping, steel, and telecommunications. The main antagonists over most of these issues were the US and the European Community (EC).

The World Trade Organization (WTO)

The final document in GATT included an agreement by all parties to submit to the authority of a newly created body, the WTO, which has the authority to hand down binding decisions in trade disputes. Designed along the lines of such independent international bodies as the World Bank and the International Monetary Fund (IMF), the WTO conducts trade policy negotiations among GATT signatories and is responsible for adjudicating disputes. Its main job, simply put, is to take over where GATT left off in demolishing trade barriers of all kinds, everywhere. The Uruguay Round produced some 28 agreements with provisions to establish about 20 bodies to administer them, with the WTO as the common institutional framework for the conduct of trade relations among members.

GATT and the WTO are separate organizations, and GATT is to be phased out as new business is shifted over to the WTO, though in reality the two will overlap for some time as the myriad terms of the Uruguay Round Agreement are implemented.

The WTO operates through a bureaucracy and 3-judge panels which secretly arbitrate specific disputes. Unlike GATT, which required consensus and in which the loser could simply veto an unfavorable verdict, WTO decisions may be appealed, but the final results are binding. Nations failing to conform their practice and laws to WTO rulings may have compensatory sanctions levied against them. Any signatory may withdraw from the WTO, but this is not expected to have major repercussions as the body becomes more established. The US has threatened to disclaim any verdict with which it does not agree, but to date it has submitted to WTO jurisdiction.

Generalized System of Preferences (GSP)

Under the terms of GATT, GSP programs have been set up by many industrialized nations to assist developing countries by granting selective waivers or reductions of tariffs on imports of products from developing nations. GSP programs in the US, Japan, Canada, and European Community (EC) countries promote growth in and exports from developing countries while also reducing the cost to national consumers of many imported products. More than 4,400 products from some 146 beneficiary countries are eligible for duty free entry under the GSP program. Canada's GSP program is very similar to that of the US.

General Requirements There are seven basic requirements for importing goods duty free under the GSP.

1. The product must be imported from a designated beneficiary developing country (BDC).
2. The product must be on the GSP eligible products list.
3. The product must be entirely grown, produced, or manufactured in the BDC, or it must be primarily the product of the BDC with a minimum of 35 percent of its value coming from the cost of materials and/or direct costs of processing in the BDC.
4. Proper documentation, including a certified United Nations Conference on Trade and Development (UNCTAD) Certificate of Origin Form A, must be submitted in addition to normal customs entry documentation.
5. The product must be imported directly from the BDC to Canada.
6. The importer must formally request GSP status.
7. The product must not violate the competitive needs limitations, which can be used to limit preferential treatment for specific products from particular countries.

Eligible Countries There are 117 independent countries, 26 non-independent countries and territories, and three associations of countries treated for customs purposes as single entities eligible for GSP treatment. In addition, 36 of the beneficiary countries, primarily in sub-Saharan Africa, have been designated for special treatment as least developed countries. The current definitive listing is published annually by the Canadian national government.

Eligible Products The many products eligible for GSP treatment include a wide range of manufactured and semi-manufactured products, as well as certain agricultural, fishery, and industrial products. Raw materials and similar unprocessed commodities are not generally eligible, although even basic processing qualifies many commodities as semi-manufactured.

Approximately 2,700 product categories are eligible for entry duty free under the terms of the GSP program, and these categories often include multiple individual product types, which will all be eligible. Eligibility lists are updated annually.

Country of Origin and Value-Added Requirements To be eligible for GSP, a minimum proportion of the components that contribute to the product's finished value must be grown, produced, or manufactured in the Beneficiary Developing Country (BDC). This country of origin requirement is designed to prevent the granting of preferential treatment to products which actually originate elsewhere and receive only insubstantial processing in the eligible country without substantially benefiting the BDC. An item meets the country of origin requirement if:

- It is 100 percent grown, produced, or manufactured in the BDC; or
- It is primarily a product of the BDC with at least 35 percent of its value coming from the direct costs of BDC materials and processing. This 35 percent of value stipulation constitutes the value-added requirement.

The qualifying value-added requirement enables some goods not wholly produced in the BDC to meet the country of origin requirement for eligibility. Noneligibility in this situation generally indicates that the cost of imported materials and components is greater than 65 percent. Alternatively, if goods imported into the BDC for incorporation into the final product meet the requirements for substantial transformation, their value can be added to the cost of BDC materials and processing to make up the 35 percent minimum specified. Substantial transformation usually involves operations such that the processed materials are transformed into a different product classification.

The 35 percent of value can be composed entirely of the cost of the BDC materials, of the BC processing operations, of the substantially transformed materials, or any combination of these elements. In practice, the majority of GSP imports are either wholly the product of the BDC or easily meet the 35 percent minimum with their domestic materials or processing alone. Reliance on the substantial transformation rule comes into play only in relatively rare cases.

The value-added requirement necessitates determining the actual costs of domestic materials and processing. In most cases the seller is responsible for making the determination and certifying the results on the appropriate forms. The seller must be prepared to document the costs of materials and processing to ensure that the merchandise meets the requirement. The customs department has detailed rules as to what can and cannot be included in the costs being applied to the value-added calculation. Generally, the regulations specify direct costs of processing only, so that the 35 percent figure cannot be inflated by adding overhead items to qualify a product.

Appraised Value Customs determines the appraised value–on which the 35 percent value-added requirement is calculated–only at the time of entry and does so somewhat arbitrarily. Customs will not give advance rulings on valuation as they will on pre-entry classification and rates of duty.

In general, the appraised value is either the FOB (free on board) or FAS (free alongside ship) value of the goods, which include the costs of transport from the factory to the shipping point. However, to qualify an item for GSP status, the BDC value-added portion of the appraised value must be greater than 35 percent of the item's value ex-works, or at the factory door, which excludes these additional domestic transport costs. Unless the product is one for which Customs has already established a standard value, importers should avoid situations in which the value-added figure is close to the 35 percent requirement.

Documentation In addition to the normal documentation necessary for making a Canadian Customs entry, those claiming GSP treatment must submit an UNCTAD Certificate of Origin Form A, which is also used by other nations offering GSP programs. In most cases the seller will have the responsibility for obtaining, filling out, and certifying Form A, which must also be certified by a designated official authority in the BDC.

To ensure duty free treatment, Form A should be submitted along with the usual required documentation at the time of entry. Goods may usually be entered in the absence of this document, but the importer must be prepared to submit it to Customs on demand within a specified period of time. If, when requested, it is not delivered within this period—usually 60 days—the customs department will consider the GSP duty free claim as abandoned and levy duties on the goods accordingly.

Direct Importation To be eligible for GSP status, a product must have been "imported directly" into Canada, which means the following:

- Shipped directly from the BDC to Canada; or
- If, when shipped from a BDC to Canada through another country, it does not enter into the commerce of that country, and the invoices, bills of lading, and other documents show Canada as the final destination; or
- If, when shipped through another BDCO's free trade zone, the product does not enter into the commerce of that third country, is altered only in ways that do not constitute a manufacturing process, and the importer obtains a second Country of Origin Form A from the certifying authority in the BDC maintaining the free trade zone that states what operations were performed there.

Competitive Needs Limitations The purpose of the Canadian GSP program is to make eligible products competitive in Canadian markets, but not to the point that they seriously undersell comparable Canadian goods. To protect domestic industry, an overly competitive product form a specific country loses its eligibility at least temporarily. Known as the competitive needs limitation, this requires that imports into Canada of any specific article from any single county:

- Must not represent more than 50 percent of the total imports to Canada of that article during the previous year; or
- Must not exceed an amount set annually based on a dollar value adjusted in proportion to the Canadian gross national product.
- If either of these limits is reached during the calendar year, the product from that country loses eligibility during the next year. However, in practice, the competitive needs limitations apply to relatively few products.

A country's product can regain eligibility the following year if the volume of imports of the product from the country on a non-preferential basis during the year falls below the levels established by the competitive needs limitations. However, in some cases the Canadian government may decide not to reinstate an item from a particular country because it is considered to have become competitive even without the GSP benefits.

Import Sensitivity A number of articles are ineligible for GSP treatment because they are "import sensitive;" that is, their importation is or could potentially be harmful to domestic industry. Such items have included various categories of footwear; textiles and apparel; watches; electronic products; certain glass, steel, and iron products; ball bearing; and plywood.

Import sensitive products are specifically excluded from GSP status either by the legislation or by government order. Very few items lose GSP eligibility because of import sensitivity. However, determinations of import sensitivity are subjective and decisions are usually made on a case-by-case basis.

REGIONAL TRADE AGREEMENTS

The Free Trade Agreement (FTA)

The US-Canadian Free Trade Agreement was effected in 1988 to facilitate greater trade between the two countries, standardize many policies and procedures, and reduce or eliminate tariffs and quotas on many products. As a result of the FTA, trade barriers have come down, investment rules have been liberalized, and bilateral cooperation on a wide range of issues has been expanded. The FTA laid the groundwork for the North American Free Trade Agreement (NAFTA), which enhances and expands the FTA, and extends its provisions to Mexico.

The North American Free Trade Agreement (NAFTA)

NAFTA incorporated all the provisions of the FTA, expanded many of them, added others, and included Mexico within its terms. NAFTA has created an economic bloc—consisting of Canada, the US, and Mexico —with a combined GDP greater than US$7 trillion. The agreement calls for the gradual elimination of tariff and non-tariff barriers in a variety of areas and removes numerous impediments to investment, such as performance requirements and exclusionary approval procedures. NAFTA requires the parties to adopt, maintain, and enforce rules against anticompetitive business practices. Government enterprises—federal, provincial, state, and local—will eventually be required to abide by NAFTA nondiscrimination principles when exercising their authority, including the granting of licenses.

The objectives of NAFTA are to establish a secure investment environment by applying clear rules of fair treatment of foreign investors and investments, to remove barriers to investment by eliminating or liberalizing existing restrictions, and to provide an effective means for the resolution of disputes between an investor and its host government.

Investors established in one of the three NAFTA countries are given four basic guarantees with respect to treatment by the host state: 1) non-discrimination, meaning the better of national or most favored nation treatment; 2) prohibition of performance requirements; 3) freedom to transfer earnings and other international payments associated with an investment; and 4) international law standards on expropriation and compensation. Foreign enterprises for which North America is a potential investment site may benefit from structuring their investments to take advantage of existing NAFTA protections and to anticipate the expansion of NAFTA to include Chile and other Latin American countries in future.

Rules and Principles

Competition NAFTA requires the parties to adopt, maintain, and enforce rules against anticompetitive business practices. Government enterprises—federal, state, provincial, and local—are or will be required to abide by NAFTA nondiscrimination principles when exercising their authority, including the granting of licenses. NAFTA includes specific rules on government and private monopolies, including prohibitions against discrimination. Moreover, a trilateral trade and competition committee will review laws within the framework of the principles of free trade.

Dispute Resolution The NAFTA Trilateral Trade Commission will monitor trade relations among the parties and establish bilateral or trilateral panels of private sector trade experts to resolve specific disputes. If the recommendations regarding the resolution of particular disputes are not carried out, the aggrieved nation is authorized to withdraw "equivalent trade concessions".

Government Procurement NAFTA eliminates such discriminatory practices as requiring the use of domestic purchasers or suppliers in government procurement. The agreement opens a significant portion of the government procurement market to non-discriminatory bidding, and represents the first time the government procurement of many services and construction contracts will be subject to international rules of open and competitive bidding. NAFTA does not yet extend its government procurement provisions to the state and provincial level, although the parties have agreed to extend coverage to sub-federal levels by the end of 1998.

Intellectual Property Rights NAFTA provides a high standard of protection for copyrights, patents, trademarks, trade secrets, plant breeders' rights, industrial designs, and integrated circuits (semiconductor chips). Copyright provisions provide protection for 50 years. NAFTA provides for strong enforcement, including provisions for damages, injunctive relief, and due process.

Investment NAFTA specifically reduces the need for prior government approval of foreign investments by member nationals; and provides for the elimination of various investment distortions, including the requirements that foreign investors use domestic suppliers, export a given amount of product, limit imports to a certain percentage of exports, or require the transfer of technology. NAFTA also prohibits discrimination against investors who seek to acquire, establish, or operate a business in the member countries. Under NAFTA, the members agree to eliminate screening of new foreign investments in most sectors and to limit the nature of official review in takeovers of existing enterprises. The agreement establishes procedural guidelines for the resolution of investment disputes through arbitration, including binding international arbitration. NAFTA does not cover investment in maritime concerns, government sponsored technology consortia, or research and development programs.

Market Access NAFTA covers numerous areas relevant to market access, including tariffs, quotas, and import licenses. Most significantly, the NAFTA countries have agreed to remove most import and export restrictions. Under specified circumstances each NAFTA nation may establish restrictions directly related to health, safety, and welfare as long as these are not designed as barriers to market entry. The parties have also agreed not to impose additional customs or user fees.

Rules of Origin Two explicit and strict rules of origin mechanisms are established under NAFTA: tariff-shift and value-content. Tariff-shift rules require that all non-NAFTA inputs must be transformed into a product with a different HS chapter heading or tariff item number from that under which they were admitted. A set percentage of the value of the product must be of North American origin. A de minimis rule allows NAFTA origin treatment for items containing as much as seven percent non-NAFTA content. NAFTA establishes specific rules of origin for various trade sectors. For example, light trucks and passenger vehicles ultimately will have to demonstrate 62.5 percent North American content to obtain preferential treatment. In the textiles sector, NAFTA requires that eligible garments be made from North American fabric and yarn. In order for computers to qualify under NAFTA, the motherboard (accounting for 20 to 40 percent of the value of a computer) must be manufactured in North America.

Services Services exports constitute the fastest growing component of trade between the three countries. NAFTA covers all service sectors unless specifically excluded, and applies guiding principles to services trade. A party can retain an existing law, measure, or practice that does not conform to the agreement's principles by formally lodging an exception or reservation for the measure. All federal government reservations were listed during negotiations and cannot be amended. The states and provinces are now completing their listings. NAFTA parties must also remove citizenship requirements affecting the licensing and practice of professionals. If a state or province fails to remove citizenship requirements the other countries have the right to maintain equivalent restrictions in their own countries.

Tariffs NAFTA provides for the gradual elimination of tariffs on US, Mexican, and Canadian products by the member nations based on the Harmonized Commodity Description and Coding system (HS) classification. The reduction in tariffs is occurring at different stages on a variety of products. Some tariffs were eliminated when the agreement became effective, while tariffs on other products will be removed over periods of five to 10 years. Tariffs on some sensitive products will not be completely removed for 15 years.

Technical Standards NAFTA strengthens the FTA technical standards obligations, expands coverage to include Mexico, sets up a committee on standards-related measures, establishes an Automotive Standards Council, identifies specific products for standards harmonization efforts through the creation of subcommittees on land transportation and telecommunications standards, and on labeling of textiles and apparel goods. It also affirms the rights of each party to adopt, apply, and enforce its own standards designed to promote safety and protect people, animals, plants, and the environment. However, in this case the agreement stipulates that standards-related measures must provide both national treatment and most-favored nation treatment for all members.

Canada's standards are not identical to those in the US. This does not mean that Canadian are any more or less stringent that those in the US, merely that they are different. The Canadian government is greatly concerned with protecting its citizens from faulty or unsafe products, and in delineating the precise technical specifications that are required to ensure that safety, it often uses slightly different standards. The parties to NAFTA recognize that greater standards compatibility removes structural barriers to their markets and increases the competitiveness of their manufacturers.

In the meantime, manufacturers and exporters should determine what standards are applicable to their products. If certification is required, it generally must be obtained before the goods are imported into Canada. The process can be time-consuming, and should thus be one of the first steps taken in establishing an export market in Canada. Information on which standards or organization(s) administer standards applicable to the firm's product can be obtained from the Standards Council of Canada.

Goods and Services

Agricultural Products Mexican tariffs on certain sensitive products originating in the US and Canada will be phased out over a period of up to 15 years. All US and Mexican non-tariff barriers—such as licensing—will be converted to either tariff-rate quotas or ordinary tariffs during a phase-in period.

Automobiles NAFTA is intended to liberalize and integrate the North American automotive sector by reducing barriers, increasing competitiveness, creating employment opportunities, and reducing prices paid by consumers. Mexican tariff and non-tariff restrictions on foreign sales to and participation in the Mexican market will be phased out over a 10 year period.

Energy Implementation of NAFTA immediately reduced trade and investment restrictions in many areas of the Mexican energy market. While retaining the national monopoly in the core energy production sector, it allows firms to negotiate supply contracts directly with Mexican natural gas and basic petrochemicals entities.

Environment NAFTA creates a series of mutual standards, protections, and procedures, as well as many opportunities for environmental equipment firms and services. It should in particular increase US exports of environmental control and mitigation technology to Mexico and Canada. Existing environmental accords, such as the Montreal Protocol on Substances that Deplete the Ozone Layer, have primacy over conflicting NAFTA provisions. NAFTA requires the maintenance of stringent health, safety, and environmental standards, requiring national treatment for investments.

Financial Services NAFTA provides a comprehensive approach to the regulation of providers of various financial services. The agreement contains definitive liberalization commitments and transition periods for the opening of markets. A key benefit of the agreement is that those involved in transactions in one member country will be able to use the same financial service providers for both domestic and international operations and allow foreign member operations in one country to process their financial materials in their home country. NAFTA also stipulates the need for transparency in applications procedures for the creation of financial institutions, and subjects the financial services sector to the agreement's dispute settlement mechanism.

Sanitary and Phytosanitary Measures NAFTA establishes standards for the protection of human, animal, and plant life, as well as standards for health risks due to animal pests or plant diseases, food additives, or food contaminants. While providing that each NAFTA country may establish its own sanitary and phytosanitary rules, the agreement stipulates that such regulations must be based on scientific principle and risk assessment and must be applied only to the extent necessary to meet the country's chosen level of protection. Such regulations may not be designed to restrict trade.

Services NAFTA improves access to Canada's huge market, opens Mexico's largely closed services market, and further opens the US services market to providers from the other member countries. In addition to requiring national and most favored nation treatment, NAFTA also eliminates the requirement that a service provider establish a local presence and resident status.

Telecommunications While NAFTA does not open basic telecommunications services, such as local and long-distance telephone services, it does open up services such as advanced data-processing and other enhancements.

Textiles and Apparel NAFTA covers a wide range of products, including fibers, yarns, textiles, and clothing, and it has been agreed that NAFTA has primacy over other existing textile agreements. The signatories immediately removed—or will phase out over a maximum period of 10 years—customs duties on textiles and apparel that satisfy NAFTA rules of origin. The US will initially remove import quotas on such goods produced in Mexico, and will gradually remove import quotas on other Mexican textiles and apparel that do not meet NAFTA rules of origin. Both Canada and Mexico will phase out tariffs on apparel over 10 years and tariffs on other textile products over eight years. NAFTA minimally increases most quotas on textiles and apparel by two percent per year for five years. The agreement does permit the use of unilaterally imposed tariff or quota increases, should serious damage to domestic markets result from the greater volume of imports. It provides strict rules of origin, including provisions covering yarn and fiber content, and establishes tariff rate quotas on many products.

Transportation NAFTA removes barriers to various land transport services and establishes a framework for compatible land transport technical and safety standards. Member nations' charter and tour bus operators will acquire full access to regular bus routes in the signatory countries by the end of 1996. NAFTA also allows foreign member bus and trucking firms to carry passengers and cargo throughout the bloc on a phased in schedule.

NAFTA Supplemental Agreements

Canada, the US, and Mexico agreed to supplemental accords to NAFTA on issues of labor, environmental, and import surges. These supplemental accords were designed to ensure enforcement of domestic environmental laws and workplace standards. The accords prohibit the signatories from lowering existing labor or environmental standards, although members are allowed to make such standards more stringent unless the motivation is to restrain trade. All states or provinces of the member countries remain free to enact even more stringent measures. In addition, the process of consultation, evaluation, and dispute settlement is to be opened to public comment. Access to the justice system and due process rights are to be extended to environmental and labor issues, and new administrative remedies have been added to existing formal legal procedures. The accords provide for the establishment of multilateral commissions to evaluate and settle disputes on labor and environmental issues.

Import Surges NAFTA contains several provisions safeguarding a country's industry and workforce against import surges. A bilateral safeguard mechanism permits a "snap-back" to pre-NAFTA or most-favored nation tariff rates for as long as four years if increased imports from Mexico are a substantial cause of or threaten serious injury to Canadian or US domestic industries. A global safeguard mechanism allows the imposition of tariffs or quotas on imports from Mexico or the US, or both, as part of a multilateral safeguard action when imports from either or both countries threaten or cause injury to a Canadian domestic industry. In addition, sensitive agricultural products are handled with tariff-rate quotas, under which higher most-favored nation tariffs become effective above a specified level of imports. Sensitive textile and apparel products are also covered by special provisions.

BILATERAL TRADE AGREEMENTS

Canada–Australia Trade Agreement (CANATA)

Australia and Canada are partners in a wide range of bilateral agreements, including the Canada-Australia Trade Agreement (CANATA). The CANATA provides for preferential tariffs to apply to a wide range of goods commonly traded between the two countries. Canada grants special concessions to many Australian goods and Australia grants to Canada preferences larger than to any other trading partner except New Zealand. As a result of the CANATA and the consistent efforts made by each country to increase trade, Canada's imports into Australia have grown to over US$720 each year. Exports from Australia to Canada increased from over $200 million in 1982 to nearly $1 billion in 1993.

Trade between the two partners remains relatively small, though both countries seem committed to further growth. Currently, Canada's most important exports to Australia are timber, paper and pulp, fish and machinery parts. The main imports from Australia are alumina, beef and sugar.

Canada and EC Framework Agreement

A framework agreement for non-preferential commercial and economic cooperation between the European Communities and Canada came into force in 1976. In this agreement the two sides confirmed their wish to accord each other most-favored nation treatment on an equal and reciprocal basis, and they agreed that economic cooperation should be promoted inter alia by joint ventures and increased two-way investment.

OTHER TRADE AGREEMENTS

Cairns Group

Established in 1986 by major agricultural exporting countries which do not subsidize these exports, this agreement strives to bring about reforms in international agricultural trade, including reductions in export subsidies, in barriers to access, and in internal support measures. It also represents its members' interests in GATT negotiations. Members include Argentina, Australia, Brazil, Canada, Chile, Columbia, Fiji, Hungary, Indonesia, New Zealand, Philippines, Thailand, Uruguay.

Pacific Economic Cooperation Conference (PECC)

The PECC exists to bring senior government, business and private institutional leaders together to examine key problems and issues influencing regional economic growth. It identifies regional interests in global issues as well, and generally acts to facilitate regional cooperation in specific economic sectors. It is increasingly viewed as the nucleus of a Pacific economic organization. With the establishment of a Central Fund to support stronger participation by developing countries, the organization appears poised for further institutionalization. It was especially active in formulating Pacific positions to produce substantive progress in the Uruguay round of GATT trade negotiations. Members include: The ASEAN countries (Brunei, Indonesia, Malaysia, the Philippines, Singapore, Thailand, and Vietnam), Australia, Canada, China, Japan, Korea, New Zealand, Chinese Taiwan, and the US.

Customs Cooperation Council (CCC)

Canada belongs to and adheres to policies and procedures of the CCC, a multilateral body located in Brussels through which participating countries seek to simplify and rationalize customs procedures. The CCC also examines technical aspects and related economic factors of customs systems in order to obtain harmony and uniformity, and to simplify customs formalities.

RELATED AGREEMENTS

UN Convention on the International Sale of Goods (CISG) Adopted to date by 35 countries, the CISG applies to international commercial sales of goods. It does not generally apply to services contracts, and it does not cover consumer sales, auction sales, sales of negotiable instruments or securities, or to the sale of ships, vessels, or aircraft. The CISG does, however, provide important benefits to traders negotiating international sales contracts in that it enables parties of different countries to avoid difficulties in negotiating which country's law will govern. It provides for internationally accepted substantive rules upon which contracting parties, courts, and arbitrators may rely in their business dealings.

CISG rules closely follow those of the US Uniform Commercial Code, although it differs in several important respects, including:

- **Specification of Price** A sales contract does not come into existence unless a specific price or a provision for determining price is supplied in the agreement.
- **Revocability of Offer** An offer becomes irrevocable if the offeree relies on it.
- **Terms of Acceptance** Acceptance occurs upon receipt thereof by the offeror.
- **Battle of Forms** If a written offer is modified by the offeree and then returned to the offeror, the CISG deems this to be a rejection and counter-offer.
- **Writing Requirement** The CISG does not require that any type of sales contract be reduced to writing.

The CISG also leaves questions relating to validity of contract and the rights of third-party beneficiaries to be determined by applicable domestic law.

Provisions of the CISG can be obtained in the US from the Office of the Chief Counsel for International Commerce, Tel: (202) 402-0937

Inter-American Development Bank (IDB) The IDB was founded to finance economic and social development projects and to provide technical assistance in member countries. It focuses especially on projects which address disparities in production, income and living standards, and makes loans on economically and socially useful projects which would not normally be acceptable to a bank.

Intellectual Property Rights (IPR) Canada is a party to the Paris Convention for the Protection of Literary and Artistic Works, and is a member of the World Intellectual Property Organization.

Pacific Basin Economic Council (PBEC) The PBEC is an international private-sector organization whose objectives are to strengthen the business enterprise system, to create new business relationships and to increase trade and investment through free markets and open investment policies. PBEC committees maintain close links with other business leaders, with governments at both political and departmental level, and with international institutions. Members include Australia, Canada, Chile, Fiji, Hong Kong, Japan, Republic of Korea, Mexico, New Zealand, Peru, Philippines, Taiwan, and the US.

International Chamber of Commerce (ICC) The ICC is composed of businessmen and experts from all sectors of economic life, working mainly through trade and industrial organizations and chambers of commerce from 59 countries. The ICC works closely with the United Nations and its various organizations. Its Commission of International Trade Policy campaigns against protectionism and in support of the GATT and the various agreements thereunder.

EMERGING TRADE AGREEMENTS

Asia Pacific Economic Cooperation (APEC) Founded in 1989, APEC is an informal working group of 18 Pacific Rim nations. Although no formal and legally binding agreement exists as yet, the members seem committed to forging a regional alliance of free and open trade. At their annual conference in November 1994 the members endorsed the "Bogor Declaration," which calls for "free and open trade and investment" throughout the region. The accord calls for the elimination of internal trade barriers by developed country members by 2010 and by developing country members by 2020. The group opposes protectionism and the creation of exclusionary regional trading blocs while promoting the expansion of trade. The accord also goes on record as supporting rapid implementation of the provisions of GATT; harmonization of international product testing and safety standards; simplification of customs procedures; and development of an international dispute resolution system.

Observers note that although the accord is long on generalities and short on specifics, it is remarkable that the diverse nations were able to reach a consensus on any agreement. Many of the lesser developed countries lobbied for an even longer phased and more gradual introduction for any significant provisions, and others disagreed on the implications of definitions to be used and questioned the intentions of some of the other members.

Together the APEC member countries account for 42 percent of total world trade, 52 percent of world GDP, and 38 percent of world population. Members include the ASEAN countries, Australia, Canada, Chile, Chinese Taiwan, Hong Kong, Japan, republic of Korea, Mexico, New Zealand, Papua New guinea, People's Republic of China, and the US.

Free Trade Area of the Americas (FTAA) At the "summit of the Americas" in Miami in December, 1994 all of the hemisphere's leaders except Fidel Castro agreed to set up FTAA by the year 2005. The integration of the Central American and Caribbean economies will not be easy under the best of circumstances, however. Further, the US has insisted on tying human rights and environmental issues to any discussion of trade, and this does not sit well with many Latin countries who do not wish to adhere to an agenda imposed by the US.

The OAS, which has been given the lead in creating FTAA, will concentrate on coordinating and integrating the many regional trade blocs which already exist toward creating a single free trade zone throughout the Americas.

IN THE FUTURE

Canada is actively pursuing closer trading relationships with the fast-growing Asian region. To this end, the Canadian government is considering approaching South Korea, Thailand or Malaysia—especially South Korea—in the hopes of formulating preferential trade arrangements of some type.

Like the US, Canada grows increasingly frustrated by its continuing large trade deficits with these countries, and it recognizes that trade in this region is growing at a phenomenal rate. As such there may well be a host of preferential trade agreements coming into play in the next few years.

USEFUL ADDRESSES

CAIRNS GROUP
c/o Department of Foreign Affairs and Trade
Bag 8
Queen Victoria Terrace
Canberra, ACT 2600
Australia

Canadian National Committee on Pacific Economic Cooperation
c/o the Canadian Chamber of Commerce
55 Metcalfe Street, Suite 1160
Ottawa, Ontario K1P BN4
Tel: (613) 238-4000
Fax: (613) 238-7643

Import Policy & Procedures

INTRODUCTION

Successfully importing a product or service requires identifying the market and understanding its needs. Canada is no exception. There are many similarities between Canada and the United States, but if Americans like to characterize their nation as a melting pot, Canada must be viewed as a cultural mosaic, with 10 provinces and two territories stretching between the Atlantic, Pacific and Arctic oceans. Canadians have an avid interest in overseas goods, though given the choice of a product of equal quality and price, they gravitate toward goods that are Canadian made or show some indication of Canadian content. However, the official encouragement of imports keeps the market expanding and has increased, in turn, the demand for Canadian products. One of the most important market access provisions of the Canadian Free Trade Agreement and the North American Free Trade Agreement is the elimination of tariffs on goods produced in and traded between the US and Canada; the boost these agreements give to Canada may well impact the rest of Canada's international trade.

CONTENTS

Introduction	73
Import Policies	73
Import Glossary	74
Permits and Licenses	74
Import Regulatory Policies	75
Tariffs and Import Taxes	75
Free Trade Zones/Warehouses	76
Restrictions and Prohibitions on Imports	77
NAFTA Tariff Elimination Schedule	78
Import Procedures	78
Distribution	78
Packing and Labeling	79
Tips for Exporting to Canada	80
Canada Customs	81
Useful Addresses	82

IMPORT POLICIES

Government Regulation

Commerce and industry in Canada are regulated at the federal, provincial and municipal levels of government. At the federal and provincial level, selected regulatory agencies concerned with international business are: the Department of Foreign Affairs and International Trade and Industry Canada, which administer the Investment Canada Act that regulates foreign investment; Revenue Canada, Customs and Excise, which assesses and collects duties and taxes on imported goods; the Canadian International Trade Tribunal, which investigates the question of injury to domestic industry in antidumping and countervailing duty cases. The Investment Canada Act encourages and facilitates investment within Canada from national and international businesses by providing information and assistance to potential investors. Its agencies co-operate with the Department of Industry, Science and Technology and other federal and provincial agencies as well as the private sector in Canada and abroad.

Other regulatory agencies include the Bureau of Competition, Environment Canada, Revenue Canada Taxation, provincial securities commissions, and federal and provincial labor relations boards.

In early 1994, the Canadian government announced a comprehensive review of current tariff structures, which had become considerably more complicated in recent years as a result of changes in certain trade agreements, the adoption of the harmonized system of trade and preferences, as well as changes in Canadian tariff rates resulting from competitive domestic issues. The objective of this review would be to make the tariff system simpler and streamlined and reduce the cost from a both regulatory and private point of view. A number of infrequently used and unnecessary provisions will be rescinded. Among other things, possible revisions include the elimination of British Preferential Treatment with Commonwealth countries; the reduction

IMPORT GLOSSARY

Ad valorem tariff A tariff assessed as a percentage rate on the value of the imported merchandise.

Consular visa Any one of several official endorsements by a consul of a country. A consular visa can be issued for travel, consular invoices, certificates of origin, shipping documents, and other legal documents.

Customs Broker An appointed official representative licensed to carry out customs brokerage services in Canada, who works with Canada Customs for an organization or exhibitor.

FOB value The free-on-board value of goods at a designated point, which includes the value of the goods plus all costs related to shipping—insurance, packaging, loading, transport, and other charges. FOB value at a Mexican port of entry refers to the FOB value of goods at the time they reach the Mexican port of entry.

General Agreement on Tariffs and Trade (GATT) A multilateral trade agreement aimed at expanding international trade. GATT's main goals are to liberalize world trade and place it on a secure, stable regulatory basis. GATT is the only multilateral instrument that lays down agreed-upon rules for international trade. The organization that oversees the agreement—formerly also known as GATT, but now called the World Trade Organization (WTO)—is the principal international body concerned with negotiating the reduction of trade barriers and improving international trade relations.

Harmonized System (HS) A multipurpose international goods classification system designed to be used by manufacturers, transporters, exporters, importers, customs officials, statisticians, and others in classifying goods that move in international trade under a single commodity code. The system contains approximately 5,000 headings and subheadings of goods generally organized by industry.

Legal kilo See legal weight.

Legal weight The total weight of the merchandise and its own packaging, but excluding exterior containers or packing materials. The legal weight of canned vegetables would include the vegetables and the can, but not the crate and wrappings for shipping.

North American Free Trade Agreement (NAFTA) A free trade agreement that comprises Canada, the US, and Mexico. The objectives of NAFTA are to eliminate barriers to trade, promote conditions of fair competition, increase investment opportunities, provide protection for intellectual and industrial property rights, and establish procedures for the resolution of disputes.

Organization for Economic Cooperation and Development (OECD) The primary forum for the discussion of common economic and social issues confronting the developed countries. Its fundamental objective is to achieve the highest sustainable economic growth and employment and a rising standard of living in member countries while maintaining financial stability, and thus contributing to the world economy. Members include Australia, Austria, Belgium, Luxembourg, Canada, Denmark, Finland, France, Germany, Greece, Iceland, Ireland, Italy, Japan, the Netherlands, New Zealand, Norway, Portugal, Spain, Sweden, Turkey, the UK, and the US.

---

of tariffs on the use of materials in manufacturing operations; consolidation of certain tariff schedules; deletion of provisions that legally define goods as "of a class or kind made in Canada," and update or streamline sections dealing with Canadian goods abroad. After review, the bulk of these proposed revisions will be implemented by 1998.

PERMITS AND LICENSES

There are no general licenses required for importing goods into Canada. There are, however, provisions related to a variety of prohibited, controlled and restricted goods. Certain goods require an import permit from appropriate Canadian authorities. The licensing of imports, where required, is handled mostly by the Department of External Affairs and International Trade. Permits are required for each shipment of goods under control or surveillance. These permits are valid for 30 days, and should be applied for at least 30 days prior to anticipated date of entry of goods. If the time limit expires, an extension can be requested from the

IMPORT REGULATORY POLICIES

These policies refer to legislation that may become relevant in the event of a dispute. They refer to different items and are subordinate to the Competition Act, which is the predominant policy administered by Industry Canada.

Canadian Cooperative Associations Act Regulates the powers of associations, federations and corporations with respect to all activity and transactions performed.

Competition Act This Act gives Industry Canada the power to investigate trade practices which are suspected of being anti-competitive, such as: abusing a dominant market position; mergers; refusal to deal; refusal to supply by foreigners; exclusive dealing; tied selling; and market restriction. This Act also regulates truth and accuracy in advertising.

Consumer Packaging and Labeling Act (non-food items) Imposed by both provincial and federal governments, this Act outlines packaging, labeling, sale, importation and advertising requirements for retail products. (Described more fully under Packaging and Labeling, below.)

Electricity and Gas Inspection Act Imposes specific standards for both domestic and commercial electric and natural gas meters. It also monitors the accuracy of meters used for revenue purposes.

Food and Drugs Act Helps protect consumers from injury, fraud and deceptive practices. This Act also contains labeling requirements for food, cosmetics, medical products and drugs.

Hazardous Products Act Regulates the advertising, sale and importation of hazardous products and substances.

Motor Vehicle Safety Act Regulates safety standards for all classes of motor vehicles.

National Trademark and True Labeling Act Respects the applications of a national trademark to commodities and respects the true description of commodities.

Precious Metals Marking Act Regulates identification symbols and practices for articles containing gold, silver, platinum or palladium.

Standards Council of Canada Act Established the Standards Council of Canada to foster and promote voluntary standardization in various fields.

Textile Labeling Act Enforces fabric and clothing manufacturers to disclose the weight of the fabric and to use prescribed generic names in order to make consumers aware of the weight and type(s) of fibers used in fabric or clothing.

The Bankruptcy Act Outlines all transactions, powers and responsibilities involved in the handling of bankruptcies.

Weights and Measures Act Ensures commodities are packaged with weight and price defined in metric units. Its powers complement those of the Consumer Packaging and Labeling Act.

Legal counsel is advisable to ensure import activities do not infringe on Canadian laws or regulations. For more information, contact Industry Canada, (613) 952-4782.

Special Trade Relations Bureau (see "Useful Addresses"). There are no exchange controls.

Import permits are required only for drugs, a few agricultural items, certain textile products and clothing, certain endangered species of fauna and flora, natural gas, and material and equipment for the production or use of atomic energy.

The Canadian Wheat Board is a marketing board with authority to control all imports of wheat, barley, and oats and their products by issuing import permits or licenses. Canada agreed to eliminate import licenses for these goods as soon as US support levels for them are equal to or less than those of Canada. Information relating to import licenses from countries other than the US is available from the Department of External Affairs (see "Useful Addresses").

TARIFFS AND IMPORT TAXES

The most significant factor regarding tariffs and import taxes is NAFTA. Many products shipped between the US and Canada already entered duty-free prior to the CFTA, and tariff cuts on import sensitive products, such as textiles, apparel and agricultural products, reached the halfway point on January 1, 1993. The implementation of NAFTA does not effect the scheduled elimination of tariffs on products traded between the US and Canada.

Only those items produced in a NAFTA member

country are able to benefit from preferential rates mandated by the Agreement. To ensure this, CFTA and NAFTA established specific rules of origin which prevent transshipment of goods from third countries administering CFTA/NAFTA duties. Also, products manufactured in the US or Canada using inputs imported from outside a NAFTA–member country only qualify if they meet specific rules-of-origin as specified in the NAFTA. Exporters to Canada should note that NAFTA rules-of-origin replace the rules-of-origin set out under the CFTA. Generally, the rules require that the inputs be transformed in specified ways during processing in the NAFTA–member country. Detailed information on rules-of-origin requirements or specific rulings on products may be obtained by contacting Revenue Canada, Customs and Excise.

For most other traded goods, Revenue Canada collects a seven percent value-added tax (VAT) known as the Goods and Services tax (GST) on imported goods by applying it to the duty-paid-value (customs value plus import duties). Similar to the VAT found in most European countries, the GST is imposed on most goods and services consumed in Canada. Since the GST is a VAT, manufacturers and businesses in the distribution chain pay only on the value they add to the product or service.

The final consumer bears the full cost of the tax. Unlike consumers, businesses in the production and distribution chain get tax credits for the GST they paid in the manufacture or acquisition of the product. Types of goods and services exempt from GST, in addition to exports, are basic groceries, prescribed drugs and medical services, most financial services, health and dental care services and a variety of others. In addition to the GST, each province except Alberta, the Yukon, and the Northwest Territories levies a provincial sales tax (PST). With the exception of goods bound for the province of Quebec, the PST is not collected on imports, although New Brunswick PST is collected at land crossing.

Quality Standards

Like most governments, Canada is concerned with protecting its citizens from faulty or unsafe products. Foreign manufacturers and exporters should determine what government standards are applicable to their products and receive written notification that they are in compliance prior to shipping goods to Canada. This can be a time-consuming procedure and should be one of the first steps taken in establishing an export market in Canada.

Under the aegis of the Standards Council of Canada (SCC), several private standards-writing organizations administer technical codes and standards for areas ranging from electrical and plumbing products to health care technology. These organizations include: the Canadian General Standards Association; Underwriter's Laboratories of Canada; the Canadian General Standards Board; the Canadian Gas Association.

The federal government also has commodity standards to safeguard the public welfare. The standards organizations try to avoid duplication of responsibility, but there is some overlap. Information on which standards or organizations administer standards applicable to the firm's product can be obtained from the Standards Council of Canada (see Useful Addresses).

Standards and NAFTA The basic NAFTA rule is simple: standards must not create unnecessary barriers to trade. To reduce such barriers, NAFTA applies basic principles to bilateral trade:

- testing facilities and certification bodies are treated in a nondiscriminatory manner;
- federal standards related measures will be harmonized to the greatest extent possible;
- greater openness will be provided in the regulatory process.

Greater standards compatibility removes structural barriers to the Canadian and US markets and increases the competitiveness of US and Canadian manufacturers. Significant progress toward greater compatibility between US and Canadian technical standards is taking place under the NAFTA.

FREE TRADE ZONES/WAREHOUSES

Goods may be cleared at customs ports on the border or, if intended for inland destinations, may be forwarded in bonded carriers to the port city nearest the destination at which customs examination may be made and duties and taxes paid. With the exception of two special trade zones at the Sydport Industrial Park in Cape Breton, Nova Scotia, and Stephenville, Newfoundland, Canada has no free ports or free trade zones. At present, there are no federal or provincial laws specifically governing the establishment and operation of such zones. Sufferance warehouses under private ownership have been established for the storage and deposit of all imports received by various transportation modes, pending customs examination and clearance. An entry for consumption or into a bonded warehouse must be presented to Customs within 30 days. Goods may be entered into customs bonded warehouses without the payment of duty but must be cleared either for export or Canadian consumption within two years. Additional periods are provided for certain goods by regulation. Goods taken from bonded warehouses for consumption are dutiable at rates of the customs tariff then in effect, and the value for duty purposes is the value at the time of entry for warehousing. Goods exported from bonded

UNITS OF MEASUREMENT

English	French	Symbol
gram	gramme	g
kilogram	kilogramme	kg
milliliter	millilitre	mL, ml
centimeter	centimetre	cm
meter	metre	m
square centimeter	centimetre carro	cm2
square meter	metre carro	m2
cubic centimeter	centimetre cube	cm3
cubic decimeter	decimetre cube	dm3
cubic meter	metre cube	m3

Note: Phrases such as "net," "net weight," "net contents," or "net quantity" are not necessary as part of the net quantity declaration. If such terms are used, they should appear in both English and French. The type of unit used depends on the net quantity of the product.

CHOICE OF UNITS

Measure Type	Net Quantity	Units
volumetric	Less than 100 ml	mL, ml
	1000 ml or more	L, l
weight	less than 1000	gg
	less than 1000	g
a kilogram	1000 g or more	kg
linear	less than 100 cm	cm or mm
	100 cm or more	m
area	less than 100 cm	cm
	between 100 cm and 100 dm100	dm
	1 m or more	m
cubic	less than 1000 cm	cm
	Between 1 and 1000 dm	dm
	1000 dm or more	m

warehouses to third countries are subject to Canadian export regulations. Repacking and sorting can be carried out in customs bonded warehouses with the permission of Canada Customs, but assembly or other industrial activity is prohibited.

Customs facilities are generally adequate. Many shipments are cleared at inland points designated as customs sufferance warehouses, an arrangement that relieves pressure at border points. Imported goods can be placed in bonded warehouses, generally for up to two years, thereby deferring payment of duties and taxes until the goods are withdrawn.

RESTRICTIONS AND PROHIBITIONS ON IMPORTS

The federal government is broadly opposed to the use of import controls. However, trade disputes have led it to target several imports from the US and to threaten imports from several other countries. A surge in shipping by Canadians into the US in the late 1980s, for example, resulted in the imposition of various measures in mid-1992, including special handling fees on mail orders from the US. The Export and Import Permits Act gives the government some power to impose trade restrictions, but Canada does not license imports, except as noted above.

For some agricultural items, such as butter and milk, permits are rarely issued, while others may be subject to a quota. Import restrictions apply to ice cream, ice cream novelties, ice cream mix, ice milk, yogurt, liquid forms of skim milk, and buttermilk. Other regulated goods include clothing, drug and medical devices, hazardous products, some offensive weapons and firearms, and endangered species.

Canadian restrictions prohibit consignment sales of fresh fruits and vegetables without a prearranged buyer. They also prohibit bulk produce imports without a waiver of Canadian packaging regulations.

Commercial imports of margarine, secondhand aircraft, motor vehicles, reprints of Canadian copyrighted work, and some game birds are tightly controlled or prohibited. Goods originating in certain countries such as Haiti and Iraq cannot be imported into Canada.

Where GATT Government Procurement Code or NAFTA requirements do not apply, Canadian government entities follow preferential sourcing policies favoring Canadian-based firms over foreign-based firms. In addition, Government Services Canada, the major federal procurement agency, maintains a supplier development fund to promote new Canadian sources of supply. Canada's federal and provincial crown (government-owned) corporations also follow strong "buy national" or "buy provincial" policies. Products affected include telecommunications, heavy electrical and transportation-related products.

Canada pursues an "industrial benefits policy" which is administered through a procurement review mechanism. This is intended to ensure major government procurement projects provide long-term benefits for the economic or social development of Canada beyond the immediate impact of the procurement expenditures.

Anti-Dumping Regulations Canada's anti-dumping law is designed to comply with the International Antidumping Code negotiated under the

NAFTA TARIFF ELIMINATION SCHEDULE

Eliminated January 1, 1994	Phasing Out by 1998	Out by 2003
Locomotive and rail cars	Hydraulic turbines	Other cars & coaches
Construction equipment	Air conditioners	Boats &drilling platforms
Telecommunications	Many resin	Bicycles equipment
Fertilizers	Most copper wire Most flat-rolled	stainless steel
Health & medical	Laundry soaps	Furniture equipment
Many chemicals & plastics	Wood and paper	Pharmaceuticals

auspices of the GATT. It provides for the levying of anti-dumping duties when, upon receipt of a complaint from Canadian producers, the customs authorities determine foreign goods are being sold to Canada for less than the selling price in the exporting country, and the Canadian Import Tribunal determines that the Canadian producer has been or may be materially injured.

IMPORT PROCEDURES

The Canadian government reserves the right to reduce or abolish duties and taxes on material used for manufacturing in Canada. Under normal circumstances, businesses which import to Canada must allow for the increase Canada's federal goods and services tax, provincial retail sales tax, customs duties and tariffs can impose on pricing.

DISTRIBUTION

Many international trading companies utilize sophisticated mathematical techniques to theoretically define optimal shipping point locations, but distribution in Canada tends to frustrate such analysis. Importers are better off taking a hard look at the geographic realities of the Canadian economy and recognizing the relatively small number of natural centers which can best serve a province or area nearby.

The most probable shipping centers are either the manufacturing site, when applicable, or the center of largest projected demand–frequently Toronto or Montreal. A distribution network must take into account the entire order cycle, from a day to a week or more, starting with the customer order and finishing with goods received. Once zones are established, they can be compared to potential customer service requirements to define the area in which equipment can be properly serviced from the shipping point.

For further information on Canada's warehousing and distribution facilities, contact the Canadian Association of Warehousing and Distribution Services (905) 436-8801.

Agents and Distributors Canadian government-licensed customs brokers may act as agents for importers. Customs brokers process approximately 70 percent of Canada's imports. Exporters not establishing an import operation in Canada need not be concerned with customs brokers since it is usually the importer's responsibility to arrange customs clearance. Agents represent, and act on the behalf of, another party to enter into contracts with third parties in a specific industry sector. Agents are distinct from direct employees of the principal. Principals are responsible for contracts entered into by the agent, and are also responsible for crimes committed by the agent. However, actions by an employee which are outside the scope of the employment contract may not obligate the principal.

Agency agreements may incorporate any specific references to choices of law and forum. However, sections concerning public policy are subject to Canadian jurisdiction. Without a specific choice of law provision, Canadian conflict of law rules will determine the proper law and forum. Agents are responsible for several tasks: observing the principal's instructions; remitting title on capital goods or real estate held on behalf of the principal; maintaining proper accounts; and transferring all funds due the principal in a timely and appropriate manner.

The principal is responsible for paying the agent according to their agreement, and indemnifying the agent for any losses (unless otherwise specified in the contract). Agent/principal agreements may last for any length. Indefinite-term agreements may be terminated by either party with or without just cause, though termination by the principal without just cause may allow the agent to recover indemnities for lost earnings. Agents must give principals notice before terminating agreements.

Distributors in Canada buy and sell on their own account. In most cases, they are not able to contract on behalf of the supplier. While not specifically stipulated in Canadian law, reasonable notice and remunerations should be given to a distributor when the agreement is terminated.

PACKING AND LABELING

Prepackaged products sold in Canada are subject to statutory packaging and labeling requirements, regulated by both federal and provincial governments, though the majority is done federally. Legislation protects consumers by demanding certain standards for merchandising products, articles, materials or substances.

Possibly the most overlooked factor in Canadian packaging is the fact that all messages must be printed in English and French. Exporters would be wise to keep copy short, since the French translation will require at least 20 percent of additional space. In general, Canadian companies are prepared to incorporate both languages while maintaining a visually appealing look. The three main pieces of legislation which regulate almost all product labeling and marking in Canada include: the Consumer Packaging and Labeling Act; the Weights and Measures Act; and the Agricultural Product Standards Act.

The Consumer Packaging and Labeling Act
This federal Act contains packaging, labeling, sale, importation and advertising requirements with respect to prepackaged consumer products.

Products excluded from the Act are: drugs or devices regulated by the Federal Food and Drugs Act; commercial or industrial goods produced for private use; goods produced solely for export; consumer textiles subject to the Textile Labeling Act; replacement parts for durable consumer goods not intended for display; and prepackaged artist supplies. Labels affixed to a product must include:
- **Product Identity Declaration**, which describes a product's common or generic name, or its function. The declaration must be in English and French.
- **Net Quantity Declaration**, expressed in metric units of volume, when the product is a liquid, gas, or is viscous; or in metric units of weight, when the product is solid; or by numerical count. Specifically metrically dimensioned packaging is required for foods, personal care products, and detergents. Net quantity may be expressed in other established trade terms.
- **Dealer's Name and Principal Place of Business**, where the prepackaged product was manufactured or produced for resale. In general, a name and address sufficient for postal delivery is acceptable. The declaration must be in both French and English. If the product is manufactured outside Canada but the name and address shown is within Canada, the address must be preceded by the words imported by, imported for, import par, import pour, or the geographic origin of the product may be written.

A label doesn't have to contain bilingual generic and product quantity labeling if the product is: a local product (sold in an area where either French or English is the mother tongue of less than 10 percent of the population); a test market product; a specialty product (which includes food or beverages with special religious significance, imported products not widely used in Canada and if there isn't a Canadian substitute); greeting cards; books; talking toys; or language games.

The Province of Quebec requires that all products sold there must be labeled in French and that the use of French must be given equal prominence with other languages on any packages or containers sold in Quebec stores. The Charter of the French Language requires the use of French on product labeling, warranty certificates, directions for use, public signs and written advertising. Further information on French labeling requirements is available from the Office de la Langue Francaise.

The package must not contain any false or misleading representation about the product, which includes an expression, word, figure, depiction or symbol used, arranged, or shown in such a way that it might be seen as characterizing the actual net quantity of the product, or if shown in any deceptive way. A representation is also misleading if it includes any expression, word, figure, symbol or depiction which either implies the product contains matter that is not in it, or that it does not contain any matter which is, in fact, contained in it.

The agency responsible for inspecting imports, Canada Customs, requires an indication of the country of origin, such as "Made in the US" on several classes of imported goods and on all printed matter. Goods not properly marked cannot be released from Customs until suitably marked. The goods can be marked at the importer's expense, either on Canada Customs premises or the importer's own premises under supervision of Canadian customs officials.

Environmental Labels Packaging should reflect Canadian concerns about environmental issues, such as acid rain and the need to reduce, reuse and recycle. Where possible, recycled paper and metals should be used. Packaging should also include the recycling logo, where applicable, and should display additional environmental concern by using minimal and/or biodegradable packaging. Environmental claims must be accurate and in compliance with relevant legislation. In general, environmental claims which are ambiguous, vague, incomplete, misleading, or irrelevant and that cannot be substantiated, should not be used. In all cases, environmental claims should indicate whether they are related to the product or its packaging materials. A set of guiding principles governing the use of envi-

TIPS FOR EXPORTING TO CANADA

1. Although there are few restrictions on imports, import permits are required for some goods.
2. Most imports are cleared through customs by licensed customs brokers familiar with all the requirements.
3. Certain goods are allowed duty-free into Canada under duty free remission arrangements.
4. Under the Canada-US Free Trade Agreement, goods originating in the US will ultimately be allowed to enter duty free.
5. The CFTA also allows goods ultimately entitled to enter the US duty free to incorporate inputs from third countries.
6. Exporters may take advantage of business growth in Canada by providing inputs to companies manufacturing, in Canada, goods entitled to enter the US market duty free.
7. Advice respecting import restrictions and general customs requirements can be obtained from trade commissioners.
8. Special packaging and labeling requirements exist for prepackaged consumer products exported to Canada.

ronmental labeling and advertising may be obtained from Industry Canada.

Goods produced in Canada should be promoted on the package.

Canadians like to shop Canadian; given the choice, they will tend to buy merchandise which is Canadian made. For specifics regarding product packaging, contact the Doing Business In Canada Association at 1-(800) 465-2059.

Documentation at Packing

Minimum documentation is required for commercial goods valued at less than C$1,200, provided that security is given, a full accounting is made, and taxes/duties are paid within a specified time (usually five days) after release. For shipments to Canada under C$20.00, only a standard business invoice is required. Two copies of the invoice should be attached to the outside of the package and must include: a detailed description of the goods in easy-to-understand terms, avoiding trade names or unrecognizable acronyms; and a statement of value specified in US or Canadian dollars. Shipments which qualify as "US in Origin" need not include a formal CFTA Certificate-of-Origin. The exporter may instead include the following statement directly on the invoice or attached on a separate sheet:

"I certify the goods referenced in this invoice/sales contract comply with the origin requirements specified under the US-Canada Free Trade Agreement, and that further processing or assembly in a third country has not occurred subsequent to processing or assembly in the Territory." The name, position, place, date and the signature of the exporter, manufacturer, or supplier should also appear after this statement.

A properly completed Canada Customs Invoice or its equivalent is required for all commercial shipments valued over C$1,200 exported to Canada. Three copies of this document should accompany the shipment; it is recommended to also forward a copy, under separate cover, to the importer. The information required on these documents is: the buyer and seller; price paid or payable; complete description including quantity contained in the shipment; unit of measure and quantity of goods; a transaction number (meeting customs specifications); and the number of invoice pages.

In addition to the Canada Customs Invoice, shipments must be accompanied by a completed exporter's Certificate of Origin which is required in order to obtain specialized tariff treatment under the provisions of the NAFTA. Besides these, an exporter needs the bill of lading (or air waybill or waybill) and special certificates, issuance of which depends on the type of goods being shipped and/or the request for such by the importer. Service is provided 24 hours per day at most major ports without charge.

Documentation at Shipping

Under a new system (CADEX) introduced on January 1, 1988 (and not yet generally available to all importers and brokers), the accounting can be made by computer-to-computer transmission rather than by submission of further documentation.

Mail and parcel post shipments require postal documentation in place of bills of lading. A copy of the customs invoice should be included with the shipment, and other copies (usually four) should be forwarded under separate cover to the consignee. The more accurate and detailed the customs declaration, the faster the processing and clearance can be given to mail shipments. The addressee's purchase order number and shipper's order number should be on the address label and on all copies of the invoice to identify the shipment.

Air cargo shipments require air waybills (in place of bills of lading) with the number of copies issued on requirements of the importer and of the airline used. One copy of the invoice containing all requisite data currently required by Canadian regulations should accompany the shipment and three copies sent directly to the consignee. IATA and/or ICAO regulations, and all other applicable national and/or international regulations rules governing labeling and packing of dangerous and restricted goods, as well as issuance of the special shipper's certificate required under IATA rules for such items (supplied by the airline), must be followed. ICAO rules may also require documents covering such shipments. The carrier must file a report (at the port or place of importation) on an appropriate Cargo Control Form.

Customs Clearance All goods coming into Canada must be cleared through customs at the point where they enter the country. Duties are levied at this time. These duty charges are based on an ad valorem (a percentage of the value of the item) or on a specific basis (by unit of weight or measure of quantity). In some instances a compound duty is levied.

The Customs Act states that the validation for duty is the transaction value of the goods–in other words, the selling price that appears on commercial invoices covering sales in the country of export. This price may include freight, warranty and other charges such as royalties applicable in the domestic market of the country of export. Canadian tariffs are generally higher than those of the US and the EU.

The federal government has extensive powers to reduce or abolish duties or authorize temporary remission of duties and taxes on articles used as material in Canadian manufacturing. The federal goods and services tax, excise tax and provincial retail sales taxes are also levied on imports and domestic products and services, which may add considerably to their cost.

Because tariffs are imposed by Canada's federal government, they are uniform at all points of entry. Tariffs are based on the Customs Cooperation Council Harmonized Commodity Description and Coding System for import tariff classification, which has been adopted by most major trading nations. As a result, the first six digits of the tariff classification number for any good are the same in Canada as they are in every other country whose customs tariff is based on the Harmonized System. Regardless of the type of shipment or its value, Canada Customs

CANADA CUSTOMS

Some important Canada Customs requirements to keep in mind when planning to exhibit at a convention or trade fair in Canada:

- Provide sufficient advance notice to Canada Customs, from six months to one year, when arranging your meeting or convention in Canada.
- Identify who will be responsible for processing the customs documents through the Canada. Parties who may be chosen include a customs broker, an employee of your organization, or another representative.
- Forward a letter announcing your intention to hold a meeting to the local Canada Customs office. Customs will then reply by letter, advising you of the procedures.
- Meeting and convention planners will probably find Canada's streamlined many of its customs and immigration procedures relatively easy.

requires certain documentation be presented before the goods are released to the importer.

Information to be provided at the time of accounting (which may also be the time of release) is essentially the standard information provided to any Customs authority and will include value for duty and tariff classification.

For all tariff items there are two basic rates of duty: one under the Most-Favored-Nation (MFN) Tariff, the other under the General Preferential (GPT) Tariff. Generally speaking, imports from developed countries, such as Germany and Japan, are subject to the MFN Tariff, while imports from certain developing nations, such as India, Mexico, and the Philippines are subject to the GPT Tariff. Special rates are also available for some goods originating in Australia, New Zealand and Commonwealth Caribbean countries, as well as some other countries that were or still are British Commonwealth members. Some goods from lesser-developing countries, such as Haiti, Malawi, Tanzania, and Western Samoa, are also eligible for special rates. Generally speaking, goods must be shipped directly from the country of origin to be entitled to the tariff treatment afforded that country. Under the Machinery Remission Program, certain machinery, both used and new, can be imported into Canada duty free if it can be shown there is no Canadian producer of such machinery.

Duty drawback, or the refund of duties on imported inputs incorporated into products for export, was to be eliminated under the CFTA by January 1, 1994; the same date the US agreed to eliminate customs user fees for Canadian products. The NAFTA extends this deadline to January 1, 1996. It provides duty free temporary entry of tools of the trade and professional equipment for professionals covered under the temporary entry provisions as well as allows all goods returned after repair or alteration in another NAFTA country to reenter duty free after 1998.

Payment and Credit Conditions Most business transactions are handled on an open account basis. While letters of credit are seldom used outside of specialist trades, collections against documents should be used where customer risk is significant. Credit terms should be competitive with local suppliers. Thirty to 60-day credit terms are standard, but terms are extended to 180 days for some capital goods. To offset risk, exporters for new business should utilize letter of credit terms.

As the economy emerges from the recession, recent payment problems should subside. Remittances from Canada usually pose little problems for overseas shippers. Payments are normally made within one month of due date, with exchange delays approximately two months in the case of non-US business. It is wise to run credit checks on new businesses which are vulnerable to bankruptcy in a changing economic climate. The Bankruptcy Act took effect in late 1992, making it easier for businesses to reorganize their finances rather than declare bankruptcy.

USEFUL ADDRESSES

The Standards Council of Canada
45 O'Connor Street
Suite 1200
Ottawa, Ontario
K1P 6N7
Tel: (613) 238-3222
Fax: (613) 995-4564

The Department of External Affairs
Special Trade Relations Bureau
Lester B. Pearson Building
4C-125 Sussex Drive
Ottawa, Ontario
K1A 0G2

Director
Information Directorate
Health and Welfare Canada
Brooke Claxton Building
Ottawa, Ontario
K1A 0K9
Tel: (613) 992-4575
Information Officer

Health Protection Branch
Room 164
Health and Welfare
Ottawa, Ontario
K1A 0L2
Tel: (613) 957-1748

Secretary
Canadian General Standards Board
"c/o" Supply and Services Canada
Place du Portage
Phase III
11 Laurier Street
Hull, Quebec
K1A 0S5
Tel: (613) 238-3222

Bureau de Normalisation du Quebec
50 rue Saint-Joseph est
Quebec, Quebec
G1K 3A5
Tel: (418) 643-5114

Industry, Science and Technology Canada(ISTC)
Business Service Centre
C. D. Howe Building
235 Queen Street
Ottawa, Ontario
K1A 0H5
Tel: (613) 952-4782

Foreign Commercial Service, by province:
US and Foreign Commercial Service
Place Felix Martin
455 Rene Leavesque Boulevard W.
Montreal, Quebec
H2Z 1Z2
Tel: (514) 398-0673
Fax: (514) 398-0711

US and Foreign Commercial Service
480 University Avenue
Suite 602
Toronto, Ontario
N5G 1V2
Tel: (416) 595-5414
Fax: (416) 595-5419

US and Foreign Commercial Service
Suite 1050
615 Macleod Trail SE
Calgary, Alberta
T2G 4T8
Tel: (403) 266-8962
Fax: (403) 264-6630

US and Foreign Commercial Service
1095 West Pender Street
Vancouver, British Columbia
V6E 2M6
Tel: (604) 685-4311
Fax: (604) 685-1930

Business Information Sources

Canadian Importers Association
210 Dundas Street West
#700
Toronto, Ontario
M5G 2E8
Tel: (416) 595-5333
Fax: (416) 595-8226

Canadian Manufacturers Association
75 International Boulevard
Etobicoke, Ontario
M9W 6L9
Tel: (416) 798-8000
Fax: (416) 798-8050

Canadian Chamber of Commerce
55 Metcalfe Street
#1160
Ottawa, Ontario
K1P 6N4
Tel: (613) 238-4000
Fax: (613) 238-7643

Dun & Bradstreet Canada Ltd.
5770 Hurontario Street
Mississauga, Ontario
L5R 3G5
Tel: (0\905) 568-6151
Fax: (905) 568-6197

Provincial Government Information Sources

Alberta:

Department of Economic Development
Sterling Place Building
9940-106 Street
Edmonton
T5K 2P6

British Columbia:

Ministry of Industry and Small Business Development
800 Hornby Street
No. 315
Vancouver
V6Z 2C5

Manitoba:

Manitoba Industry
Trade and Technology
155 Carlton Street
Winnipeg
R3C 3H8

New Brunswick: Department of Commerce and Development
Centennial Building
P. O. Box 6000
Fredericton
F3B 5H1

Newfoundland:

Department of Development
P. O. Box 8700
St. John's
A1B 4J6

Nova Scotia:

Department of Development
Box 519
1800 Argle Street
Halifax
B3J 2R7

Ontario:

Ministry of Industry and Trade
Hearst Block
900 Bay Street
Toronto
M7A 2E1

Prince Edward Island:

Department of Industry
Shaw Building
P. O. Box 2000
95 Rochford Street
Charlottetown
C1A 7N8

Quebec:

Ministry of Industry and Commerce
710 Place d'Youville
Quebec City
G1R 4Y4

Saskatchewan:

Department of Economic Development and Trade
919 Saskatchewan Drive
Regina
S4P 3V7

Canadian International Trade Centers
Alberta: 510 5th Street West
Suite 1100
Calgary
T20 3S2
Tel: (403) 292-6660
Fax: (403) 292-4578

British Columbia: P. O. Box 11610
900-650 West Georgia Street
Vancouver
V6B 5H8
Tel: (604) 666-0434
Fax: (604) 666-8330
Telex: 04-51191

Manitoba: P. O. Box 981
330 Portage Avenue
Winnipeg
R3C 2V2
Tel: (204) 983-8036
Fax: (204) 983-2187
Telex: 07-57624

New Brunswick: P. O. Box 1210
Assumption Place
770 Main Street
Moncton
W1C 8P9
Tel: (506) 851-6452
Fax: (506) 851-6429
Telex: 014-2200

Newfoundland: P. O. Box 8950
Atlantic Place
215 Water Street
Suite 504
St. John's
A1G 3R9
Tel: (709) 772-5511
Fax: (709) 772-5093

Nova Scotia: P. O. Box 940
Station M
1801 Hollis Street
Halifax
B3J 2V9
Tel: (902) 426-7540
Fax: (902) 426-2624
Telex: 019-22525

Ontario: Dominion Public Building
4th Floor
One Front Street West
Toronto
M5J 1A4
Tel: (416) 973-4782
Fax: (416) 954-1385

Prince Edward Island: P. O. Box 1115
Confederation Court Mall
134 Kent Street
Suite 400
Charlottetown
C1A 7M8
Tel: (902) 566-7400
Fax: (902) 566-7450
Telex: 014-44129

Quebec: P. O. Box 247
Stock Exchange Tower
800 Place Victoria
Suite 3800
Montreal
H4Z 1E8
Tel: (514) 283-3794
Fax: (514) 283-8794
Telex: 053-60768

Saskatchewan: S. H. Cohen Building
Room 401
119 4th Avenue South
Saskatoon
S7K 5X2
Tel: (306) 975-5315
Fax: (306) 975-5334
Telex: 074-2742

Export Policy & Procedures

INTRODUCTION

Exports are more than the usual engine of growth for the Canadian economy; one-third of the nation's jobs and one-quarter of its wealth depends on international trade. Merchandise exports to all countries in 1993 reached $187.3 billion, an increase of 15.2 percent from their 1992 level and the largest single increase since 1984. Three-quarters of the country's output of natural resources is now exported, as is more than half of its manufacturing production. In addition, an increasing proportion of the output of Canadian service industries is sold outside the country.

Compared with most other industrial countries, Canada remains more reliant on exports of resource-based products, particularly forest products, minerals and metals, agri-food, and energy. Even so, manufactured goods and knowledge-intensive products have become more prominent in Canada's export profile. For example, automotive products and machinery and equipment are the two leading merchandise export categories. Together with consumer goods, they represent approximately half of Canada's exports. The fastest-growing new sectors for Canadian exports include chemicals, communications equipment, computer software and specialized services. Recently, Canada has enacted a series of trade initiatives aimed at expanding export horizons. In June, 1991, negotiations began with Mexico and the US to set up the North America Free Trade Agreement (NAFTA); the agreement came into effect on January 1, 1994 and established the world's largest trading bloc. By sector, the NAFTA increases export advantages to the US and Mexico for: agriculture, the auto industry, business and professional services, textiles and apparel, and transportation.

The following section discusses Canadian export policy and the procedures for exporting from the country. This information will aid those interested in purchasing goods and services from Canadian companies, expanding current operations in Canada to serve export markets, establishing an enterprise in Canada that will supply foreign markets, or investing in an export business located in Canada.

CONTENTS

Introduction	85
Export Policies	85
Exporting Glossary	86
Export Trade Acts	87
Export Regulations and Licenses	88
Foreign Trade Zones	88
Restrictions and Prohibitions on Exports	88
Export Procedures	89
Packing and Shipping	90
Selling the Product	91
Freight Forwarders	92
After Sales Service	92
Payment for Exports	92
Financing Export Transactions	92
Useful Addresses	93

EXPORT POLICIES

Government Agencies

Production and services are predominantly privately owned and operated; however, they operate under a broad regulatory framework whereby the federal and provincial governments redistribute wealth from high-income individuals and regions to lower-income persons and provinces. However, non-privatized crown corporations still play an important role in the economy (although more privatization is occurring). As of August, 1994, roughly 40 percent of the assets of Canadian manufacturing companies were foreign-owned; of this total, about 75 percent belonged to US firms. Prices for most goods and services are

EXPORTING GLOSSARY

ad valorem Latin for, "in proportion to value." Refers to various taxes added to exports when they enter the country of destination.

advising bank A bank, operating in the exporter's country, that handles letters of credit for a foreign bank by notifying the export firm that the credit has been opened in its favor. The advising bank fully informs the exporter of the conditions of the letter of credit without necessarily bearing responsibility for payment.

balance of trade The difference between a country's total imports and exports. If exports exceed imports, a favorable balance of trade exists; if not, a trade deficit exists.

barter Trade in which merchandise is exchanged directly for other merchandise without using money. Barter is an important means of trade with countries using currency that is not readily convertible.

carnet A customs document permitting the holder to carry or send merchandise temporarily into certain foreign countries (for display, demonstration, or similar purposes) without paying duties or posting bonds.

CFR (cost and freight) A pricing term indicating that the cost of the goods and freight charges are included in the quoted price; the buyer arranges for and pays insurance.

CIF (cost, insurance, freight) A pricing term indicating that the cost of the goods, insurance and freight are included in the quoted price.

commercial invoice An itemized list of goods shipped, usually included among an exporter's collection papers.

confirmed letter of credit A letter of credit, issued by a foreign bank, the validity of which has been confirmed by a bank in another country. An exporter whose payment terms are a confirmed letter of credit is assured payment by the bank in the other country even if the foreign buyer or the foreign bank defaults (*see also* letter of credit.)

consignment Delivery of merchandise from an exporter (the consignor) to the agent (the consignee) under agreement that the agent sell the merchandise for the account of the exporter. The consignor retains title to the goods until the consignee has sold them. The consignee sells the goods for commission and remits the net proceeds to the consignor.

convertible currency A currency that can be bought and sold for other currencies at will.

countertrade The sale of goods or services that are paid for in whole or in part by the transfer of goods or services from a foreign country.

customhouse broker An individual or firm licensed to enter and clear goods through customs.

customs The authorities designated to collect duties levied by a country on imports and exports. The term also applies to procedures involved in such collection.

destination control statement Any of various statements a government requires to be displayed on export shipments and that specify the destinations for which export of the shipment has been authorized.

devaluation The official lowering of the value of one country's currency in terms of one ore more foreign currencies. For example, if the US dollar is devalued in relation to the French franc, one dollar will "buy" fewer francs than before.

distributor A foreign agent who sells for a supplier directly and maintains an inventory of the supplier's product.

drawback Articles manufactured or produced in one country with the use of imported components or raw materials and later exported are entitled to a refund of up to 99 percent of the duty charged on the imported components. The refund of duty is known as a drawback.

export broker An individual or firm that brings together buyers and sellers for a fee but does not take part in actual sales transactions.

export commission house An organization which, for a commission, acts as a purchasing agent for a foreign buyer.

export license A government document that permits the licensee to export designated goods to certain destinations. (*see also* General export license and Individually validated export license.)

export management company A private firm that serves as the export department for several producers of goods or services, either by taking title or by soliciting and transacting export business on behalf of its clients in return for a commission, salary, or retainer plus commission.

FOB "Free on board" at named port of export. A pricing term indicating the quoted price covers all expenses up to and including delivery of goods upon an overseas vessel provided by or for the buyer.

freight forwarder An independent business that handles export shipments for compensation. A freight forwarder is among the best sources of information and assistance on export regulations and documentation, shipping methods, and foreign import regulations.

irrevocable letter of credit A letter of credit in which the specified payment is guaranteed by the bank if all terms and conditions are met by the drawee.

letter of credit (L/C) A document, issued by a bank per instructions by a buyer of goods, authorizing the seller to draw a specified sum of money under specified terms, usually the receipt by the bank of certain documents within a given time.

revocable letter of credit A letter of credit that can be canceled or altered by the drawee (buyer) after it has been issued by the drawee's bank.

through bill of lading A single bill of lading converting both the domestic and international carriage of an export shipment. An air waybill, for example, is essentially a through bill of lading for air shipments. Ocean shipments, on the other hand, usually require two separate documents: an inland bill of lading for domestic carriage and an ocean bill of lading for international carriage.

---

established by the market without government involvement. The most important public industries are government services, services provided by regulated public service monopolies, most medical services, and supply-managed agricultural products (eggs, poultry and dairy products). Export-related government agencies include:

Department of Foreign Affairs and International Trade (DFAIT) Through International Trade Centres (ITCs) in Canada and its missions abroad, DFAIT implements a wide range of initiatives. DFAIT services include basic export and trade-related advice, and investment and technology development counseling. DFAIT's five geographic branches are focused on: Africa and the Middle East, Asia-Pacific, Europe, Latin America and the Caribbean, and the US. The Department also maintains a full range of on-line information services for Canadian-based companies through its InfoCentre in Ottawa (the telephone hotline is (800) 267-8376).

CanadExport DFAIT's trade newsletter is distributed to 38,500 subscribers. It is the primary publication for keeping the Canadian business community up to date about key trade matters. To receive *CanadExport*, contact: Trade Communications Division (BCT) at the Department of Foreign Affairs and International Trade (see Useful Addresses).

Access North America is designed to provide small- and medium-sized Canadian firms with the tools and counseling they need to pursue emerging opportunities in key sectors of the US and Mexico. External Affairs and International Trade Canada (EAITC), in cooperation with Industry and Science Canada (ISC), provincial trade officials and industry associations, provides Canadian companies with the information they need to trade internationally.

Export Development Corporation Helps Canadian business enter the global marketplace by providing risk management services including insurance, financing and guarantees to Canadian companies and their international customers. Tel: (613) 598-2904.

FaxLink This is a 24-hour/seven days per week interactive document retrieval system for international investors and traders who need information about Canada trade. Call from a fax machine to: (613) 944-6500. Information is available through the Department of Foreign Affairs and International Trade listed under "Useful Addresses."

EXPORT TRADE ACTS

Canada controls exports under authorization of the Export and Import Permits Act (EIPA), the Export Control List (ELC), and the Area Control List (ACL). The EIPA ensures there is an adequate supply and distribution of any article, particularly wood products, and those products produced from other natural resources. The ELC lists particular items under control and the ACL lists countries which require export permits for all goods. For further information, see "Export Regulations and Licenses," below.

Under the Western Grains Transportation Act (WGTA), the Canadian government subsidizes rail transportation of western grown wheat, barley, oats and many other agriculture commodities intended for export. In June, 1994, the government announced a proposal to phase out WGTA payments over a five-year period. Instead, the government will instead make direct income support payments to farmers.

The Free Trade Agreement eliminated subsidies on agricultural products shipped to the US through West Coast ports, but not on those shipped directly by rail or through Great Lakes ports. Under the terms of the FTA, Canada will terminate all export-based duty remission protocols by 1998. In the interim, Canada has excluded exports to the US in calculating the duty waived.

Canada's production-based duty remission program provides for the rebate of customs duties to qualifying foreign automobile firms on their imports of automobiles and original equipment automotive parts into Canada. Under the program, duty remissions are granted in proportion to the amount of "Canadian value-added" tax generated by these firms in Canada. Under the provisions of the FTA, Canada has agreed to terminate the program by 1996 and to limit application of the program to the four companies with which agreements were already in place. NAFTA does not change these provisions.

Trade Commissioners Procedural information on governmental approvals varies with each country. Canadian trade commissioners live in and work from Buenos Aires to Beijing, in over 100 countries throughout the world. As part of an extensive network of trade experts, their primary responsibility is to assist exporters in establishing sales in foreign markets. Contacting the trade commissioner in a target country is an excellent way to avoid pitfalls and seize opportunities. While unable to close a sale, be present at all negotiations, or serve as an interpreter or translator, a trade commissioner can recommend appropriate technical experts, help locate good translators, and maintain a liaison with local agents.

EXPORT REGULATIONS AND LICENSES

To support their sales, exporters may access financing and insurance services provided by the Export Development Corporation (see "Government Agencies," above). Surrendering proceeds from exports is not required and exchange receipts are freely disposable. The principal legal instrument governing export controls is the Export and Import Permits Act, which controls trade through the Export Control List and the Area Control List. The Export Control List identifies all goods controlled in order to implement intergovernmental arrangements, maintain supplies, or ensure security. It includes all items identified in the International Munitions List, the International Industrial List, and the International Atomic Energy List. Permits are required for the exportation of listed goods to all countries except, in most cases, the United States. In addition, controls are maintained over a broad range of items controlled for nonproliferation purposes (chemical, biological, and nuclear weapons and their delivery systems).

The Area Control List includes a limited number of countries to which all exports are controlled. As of 1993, the list included: Angola, Bosnia-Herzegovina, Croatia, Haiti, Libyan Arab Jamahiriya, South Africa, and the Federal Republic of Yugoslavia (formerly Serbia and Montenegro).

FOREIGN TRADE ZONES

Also called free-trade zones, goods in these ports are officially considered outside Canadian Customs territory. Merchandise may be landed, stored, displayed, used for manufacturing within the zone, and reexported without paying duties. Traders can save on costs because they can ship merchandise in one form to save costs, then alter it to reduce the duty owed before Customs entry.

Canadian special trade zone facilities are located in Sydney Harbor in Nova Scotia, and at Stephenville, Newfoundland. These facilities offer many of the standard FTZ features available worldwide, but they also operate within the regulatory framework of Canadian customs. Privately-owned bonded warehouses have been established at various points for food shipments and for the storage of imports received by truck pending customs approval and examination. Repacking and resorting is permitted in customs bonded warehouses, but sampling, assembly, or other manufacturing activity is not permitted.

RESTRICTIONS AND PROHIBITIONS ON EXPORTS

Canadian export restrictions deal primarily with the commercial fishing sector. A portion of the Pacific salmon catch must be landed in Canada before being exported. An interim agreement reached following an FTA dispute settlement permits direct export (sale at sea) of a portion of the catch by Canadian licensees. The level of direct exports, however, has been low. In February, 1994, technical changes were made in licensee requirements. A Canadian ban on reexporting unprocessed herring, aimed at Japan, also prevents Canadian processors from using US refrigeration facilities.

EXPORT PROCEDURES

Traders exporting from Canada must comply with Canadian regulations as well as the import regulations of the country where the goods will arrive. The exporter remains responsible for ensuring all statements in documents are accurate.

Methods of Exporting and Channels of Distribution

Exporters sell either directly or indirectly. Indirect selling involves an intermediary such as an export management company or an export trading company, which usually assumes responsibility for finding overseas buyers, shipping products, and getting paid. Canadian companies, particularly smaller firms inexperienced in foreign trade, will find indirect exporting advantageous since this method penetrates foreign markets without the complexities and risks of direct exporting.

Direct selling involves the Canadian producer dealing one-on-one with a foreign buyer. The advantages here include more control over exporting, a potential for higher profits, and developing closer relationships with the overseas buyer and marketplace. However, the Canadian company must spend more time, personnel, and corporate resources than with indirect export channels.

The essential factor between these two methods is the level of resources a company is willing to commit to international marketing. Other elements include the firm's size, the nature of its products, previous export expertise, and business conditions in the selected overseas markets.

Preparing Products for Export

Selecting and preparing a product for export requires understanding the product as well as the characteristics of its intended destination. Before the deal is done and the payment collected, products may have to be modified to suit buyer tastes.

Product Preparation Considerations Some key considerations include:
1. What product will your firm offer abroad?
2. What requirements will the product satisfy?
3. Should the firm modify its domestic model, or develop a new product?
4. What changes in design, color, size, brand, and packaging should the product have?
5. What specific services are needed abroad before and after the sale?
6. Can your firm offer service and repair facilities to establish a long-term, positive reputation?

Product Adaptation For success, a product may have to meet foreign government regulations, climatic conditions, buyer preferences, or standard of living. A product may have to be modified to facilitate shipment or meet engineering or design standards.

Foreign product regulations are common in international trade. Regulations can include tariffs or barriers such as product specifications. Information on regulations is available from the foreign commerce trade representatives.

Engineering and Redesign Products marketed abroad often require redesign: Electrical current, for example, often differs from country to country; phases, cycles, or voltages different from the original specifications will damage or impair the equipment.

Many kinds of equipment must be engineered in the metric system. Metric measurement, already well established in Canada, is common overseas and can be a vital selling point. Instruction or maintenance manuals should in most cases give dimensions in centimeters, weights in grams or kilos, and temperatures in degrees Celsius.

Branding, Labeling and Packaging An exporter should take the following questions into consideration:
1. Are international brand names significant when promoting a product? Or would local brands or private labels heighten local interest?
2. Can your firm print labels in official languages if required by law or practice?
3. Does the label need to include information on product content and country of origin?
4. Are weights and measures stated in local units?
5. Must each item be individually labeled?
6. Are you considering local tastes and knowledge?

A Canadian company may find building international recognition for a brand is expensive, and copyright protection is not possible or practical in all countries. The process to register a trademark, copyright, or patent may be costly and lengthy, delaying entry into the market for several years.

Installation Exporters must also consider the ease of installing the product overseas. If technical or engineering help is needed, preassembly and pretesting before shipping is a wise practice. Sending a disassembled product will save on shipping costs, but most products have to be sold fully assembled. If trained personnel are not locally available, training manuals, installation instructions and parts lists must be provided in the local language.

Warranties Often a good idea, since their initial expense is offset by long-term gains in reputation and trust. Consumer expectations vary from country to country due to levels of competitive practices, consumer activism, and quality standards. Exporters should research whether consumers expect a warranty; if not, costs can be kept lower and competition that much keener. Servicing warranties is more expensive and troublesome in foreign markets. Arranging warranty service with a local representative or distributor is usually the most reasonable course.

Servicing Consumers are concerned with the service Canadian companies provide. Service is crucial for some products, especially those which emphasize technology. Canadian exporters who rely on a foreign distributor or agent must be certain to ensure adequate service (See "After Sales Service" on page 92.).

PACKING AND SHIPPING

In packing an item for export, the shipper must allow for the demands transport puts on a package: breakage, weight, moisture and pilferage. The buyer will often specify packing requirements.

Labeling Labeling is used on export shipping containers to meet shipping regulations, ensure proper handling, conceal the identity of the contents, and help receivers identify shipments. The overseas buyer usually specifies which marks should appear on the cargo. Exporters should place the following markings on cartons:

- Shipper's mark
- Country of origin
- Weight in kilos and pounds
- Number of packages and size of cases in centimeters and inches
- International pictorial handling symbols
- Cautionary markings, such as "This Side Up," or "Use No Hooks" in at least French and English
- Port of entry
- Labels for hazardous materials.

In addition, prepackaged foods exported from Canada must satisfy these requirements:

General Requirements Information on food labels must be true, and not misleading or deceptive, and the required information must be easily read and clearly and prominently displayed (with a minimum type height of 1.6 mm [1/16 inch], based on the lower case letter "o," unless otherwise specified; and on any panel except the bottom, except for the information appearing on the principal display panel.

Foods Requiring a Label All prepackaged products require a label with the following exceptions: one bite confections; and fresh fruits or vegetables packaged in a wrapper or confining band of less than 12.7 mm (1/2 inch).

Bilingual Requirements Information on food labels must be shown in both French and English, with the following exception: the identity of the person by or for whom the prepackaged product was manufactured, produced, or packaged for resale, may be in either English or French. Information on the labels of the following may be in one official language only: shipping containers not offered for sale to consumers; products sold in a local area; official test market products; specialty foods.

Quebec has additional requirements concerning the use of French language on all products marketed within its jurisdiction.

Name and Address The name and address of the responsible party by or for whom a prepackaged product is manufactured or produced, must be declared on any label panel except the bottom, in either French or English.

List of Ingredients In general, ingredients must be listed in descending order of proportion by weight in the food. The exceptions include spices, seasonings and herbs (except salt), and food additives. The ingredient list must be shown in both English and French.

Durable Life A durable life ("best before") date is required on most packages with a durable life of less than 90 days.

Labels of Shipping Containers Labels for commercial, industrial or institutional use, are not required to be bilingual.

Instructions Export marks should be added to the standard information shown on the domestic bill of lading and should show the name of the exporting carrier and the latest permissible arrival date at the port of export. The exporter should also include instructions for the inland carrier to notify the international freight forwarder by telephone on arrival.

International shipments are increasingly made on through bills of lading under multimodal contracts. The multimodal transport operator takes responsibility for the entire shipment's movement, from factory to the final destination.

When deciding on how to move goods, the exporter may consult with a freight forwarder. Other factors to consider are shipment cost, delivery schedule, and the foreign buyer's accessibility to the shipped product. Although air carriers are more expensive, their cost may be offset by lower domestic shipping costs and faster delivery times.

Before shipping, check with the foreign buyer in case the buyer wants the goods shipped to a free trade zone or a free port, where the goods will be exempt from import duties.

Insurance Cargo insurance usually covers export shipments against loss, damage, and delay in transit. For international shipments, the carrier's liability is frequently limited by international agreements, and coverage is often different from domestic coverage. Either the buyer or seller can make arrangements for cargo insurance, depending on the terms of sale. Exporters should consult with international insurance carriers or freight forwarders for more information.

Poor weather conditions, rough handling, and other hazards to cargo make marine insurance important protection for Canadian exporters. If the

Canadian firm is responsible for insurance, it should either obtain its own policy or insure cargo under a freight forwarder's policy.

SELLING THE PRODUCT

Pricing This is often the greatest problem an exporter faces. The usual elements in making this decision include costs, market demand, and competition.

Cost Many firms new to exporting calculate product price by the cost-plus method: start with the manufacturing cost, then add administration, research and development, overhead, freight forwarding, distributor margin, customs charges, and profit. Often, however, this process produces an uncompetitive price.

A more reasonable approach is marginal cost pricing, which establishes the bottom price with the direct, out-of-pocket expenses for producing and selling products.

Besides production costs, overhead, and research and development, other costs–such as business travel, international postage, telephone calls, translation and consultant fees, freight forwarder costs and product modification–should be allocated to domestic and export products in proportion to what they yield.

Market Demand This is a crucial but fluid factor. For most consumer goods, per capita income is a reasonably good gauge of a market's ability to pay. In a lower per capita income market, simplifying the product to reduce selling price may be an answer. But these behaviors are subject to the international reputation of the firm or the product, to the market's openness to advertising or other selling techniques, and to the market's political and economic stability. Who are your primary customers? If products are designed for expatriates or the country's upper class, a high price may be profitable even if the per capita income is low.

Competition Exporters need to evaluate the competition's prices in each export market they intend to enter. A particularly attractive foreign market will demand careful estimation, often compelling the exporter to either match the going price or go below it to gain a temporary advantage. A product new to that market may command a higher price than is charged domestically.

Quotations and Pro Forma Invoices Many export transactions begin with the receipt of an inquiry from abroad, followed by a request for a quotation or a pro forma invoice. The products should be identified as new or used and quoted in Canadian dollars to reduce foreign exchange risk. A quotation describes the product, provides a unit price, sets the time of shipment, and specifies the terms of sale and payment. The description should include:

a) buyer's name and address
b) reference number and the date of inquiry;
c) listing of the requested goods and brief description; unit price
d) gross and net shipping weight, (in metric units when appropriate)
e) total cubic volume and dimensions of products when packed
f) for export, in metric units when appropriate
g) Trade discount, if applicable
h) Delivery point
i) Terms of sale
j) Terms of payment
k) Insurance and shipping costs
l) Validity period for the quotation
m) Total charges to be paid by the customer
n) Estimated shipping date to the factory or Canadian port; the latter is preferable
o) Estimated date of shipment arrival

Submitting a pro forma invoice with or instead of a quotation is a frequent request. Pro forma invoices are not requests for payment, but are essentially quotations in an invoice format. Besides the above items, a pro forma invoice should include a statement certifying the invoice is true and correct and describing the country of origin of goods.

Price quotations must explicitly state they are subject to change without notice. If a specific price is part of the sales agreement, the precise period during which the offer remains valid should be specified.

Terms of Sale The parties should agree to delivery terms, such as free on board (FOB) or free alongside ship (FAS). Confusion over terms of sale can either destroy the sale or lead to unexpected loss. The more common terms of sale can be found in the "Export Glossary" section of this chapter.

Export Controls There are no exchange controls in Canada. The licensing of exports, when required, is handled mostly by the Department of Foreign Affairs and International Trade, but other departments also issue licenses in specialized fields. Federal sales tax does not apply to exports.

After the Sale

When preparing to ship a product overseas, the exporter must ensure the merchandise is packed securely enough to arrive in good condition; labeled correctly to ensure the goods are handled properly and will arrive on time and at the correct destination; documented correctly to meet Canadian and foreign government requirements and proper collection standards; and insured against damage, loss, pilferage, and, when reasonable, delay.

FREIGHT FORWARDERS

The international freight forwarder acts as an agent for the exporter in moving cargo overseas. The freight forwarder can assist with an order by advising the exporter of the freight costs, port charges, consular fees, cost of special documentation, insurance costs, and the freight forwarder's handling fees–all of which help in preparing price quotations. The freight forwarder may also provide advice about the best packing to protect the products and can arrange to have the merchandise packed at the port or placed into containers.

When the order is ready to ship, the freight forwarder will review the letter of credit, commercial invoices, and other documents to ensure everything is in order for transport purposes.

The freight forwarder may make necessary arrangements with customs brokers, if the exporter has not already done so, to ensure the goods comply with export documentation regulations. They may also have the goods delivered to the carrier, and prepare the bill of lading or any other required documentation. After shipment, the freight forwarder will send all documents directly to the customer or to the paying bank if requested by the exporter.

PAYMENT FOR EXPORTS

Factors influencing payment method include the length of the relationship with the buyer, the buyer's financial history, and the ease of accessing various payment methods. Ranked from most to least secure for the exporter, the methods of payment are:

1. Cash in Advance Here, the shipper has no collection problems. Receipt via wire transfer allows for immediate use of the money. Payment by check, even prior to shipment, may result in collection delay. However, advance payment creates cash flow problems and increases risks for the buyer.

2. Letter of Credit Security in a bank's promise to pay the exporter is added to that of the foreign buyer when the exporter has complied with all the terms and conditions of a letter of credit.

3. Documentary Collection or Draft This is used when the buyer is uncertain the goods may not be sent if payment is made in advance. This method requires documents to be presented before payment is made. A draft, sometimes called a bill of exchange, is analogous to a foreign buyer's check and sometimes includes the risk that it will not be honored.

4. Open Account The exporter bills the trusted customer, who is expected to pay under agreed terms at a future date. This is the preferred method when the buyer is well established with a favorable payment record. Lacking documents and banking channels makes legal enforcement of claims difficult to pursue. Collection abroad is usually a costly process and receivables may be harder to finance, since drafts or other evidence of indebtedness are unavailable.

5. Credit Cards Accepted by many exporters of goods sold directly to an end user. International credit card transactions are usually placed by telephone or fax; yet these methods are open to fraudulent transactions.

6. Other Alternative Payment may include consignment sales, third country foreign currency, countertrade and barter.

FINANCING EXPORT TRANSACTIONS

Offering good payment terms is an essential part of making a sale. Exporters should understand their financing options in order to choose the one which best suits the foreign buyer as well as the Canadian seller.

AFTER SALES SERVICE

Besides quality and price, service is an essential factor in any export sales effort, especially where consumer durables are concerned. Service includes promptly delivering a product, courteous sales personnel, providing a local user or service manual, establishing ready access to a service facility, and ensuring knowledgeable, cost-effective maintenance, repair, or replacement.

Among the many options for delivering service to foreign buyers are:

- A high-cost approach, where the product is returned to the manufacturing or distribution facility in Canada for service or repair. The foreign buyer incurs a high cost and loses the use of the product for an extended period, while the seller must incur the export cost a second time to return the product.
- A joint venture or other partnership arrangement, in which the overseas partner may have service or repair capability in targeted markets. The cost of providing this service should be negotiated into the agreement.
- Using local service facilities for goods sold at retail outlets. This option requires front-end expenses to identify and train local service outlets; costs will be recouped over the long run.
- A warranty and service program, which lists authorized local warranty and service centers. This option involves administrative, training, and supervisory overhead costs.

Factors to Consider in Financing An exporter may need preshipment financing to produce or purchase the product or provide a service; or post-shipment financing of the resulting account or accounts receivable, or both. In deciding between financing methods, consider the following factors:

- The need for financing to make the sale. In some cases, payment terms the buyer considers favorable make a product more competitive. In other cases, the exporter may need financing to produce ordered goods or finance other aspects of a sale. such as promotion and selling expenses, engineering modifications, and shipping costs.
- The cost of different financing methods. Interest fees and rates vary, not only with time but by country. Their total costs and effect on price and profit should be thoroughly researched before a pro forma invoice is submitted to the foreign buyer.
- The length of time financing is required. Costs increase with time. Different financing methods are available for short, medium, and long terms.
- The risks associated with financing the transaction. Whether they actually exist or are primarily perceived by the lender, risk increases the cost to the exporter. Financing will also be more difficult to find.

Extending Credit to Foreign Buyers A useful way to decide on the appropriate credit period is to look at the usual commercial terms in the exporter's industry for internationally traded products. Usual terms range from 30 to 180 days for off-the-shelf items like consumer goods, chemicals and other industrial raw materials, agricultural commodities, and spare parts and components. Custom-made or higher-value capital equipment may warrant longer repayment periods. Exporters may have to allow for longer shipment times, since foreign buyers are usually unwilling to start the credit period before they receive the goods.

Foreign customers are often attracted by credit periods of a year or longer, but less interested in periods of up to 180 days. Most exporters absorb interest charges for short-term credit unless the foreign customer pays after the due date.

Exporters should also determine whether they incur financial liability should the foreign buyer default.

Using Commercial Banks If the exporter has a loan for domestic needs, the lender is already aware of the exporter's ability to repay and can use this awareness to extend credit for overseas ventures. When the lender wants more assurance than the transaction offers, a government guarantee program may encourage the lender to provide credit for the exporter.

A small- or medium-sized Canadian business needs to select a bank committed to dealing with companies of that size. The exporter should also determine: whether there are charges for confirming a letter of credit, processing drafts, and collecting payment; whether the bank has foreign branches or correspondent banks; whether the bank can provide buyer credit reports; whether the bank has experience with federal and provincial financing programs that support small business transactions; and what other services, such as trade leads, the bank provides.

Other Private Sources The following are other financing avenues to consider:

1) Foreign buyers, who may make down payments or progress payments as goods are completed to reduce the need for financing from other sources.

2) Suppliers who may be willing to offer terms to the exporter, such as accepting assignment of a part of the proceeds of a letter of credit or a partial transfer of a transferable letter of credit.

3) Factoring by the exporter, which is the discounting of a foreign account receivable not involving a draft. The exporter transfers title to its foreign accounts receivable to a factoring house (which specializes in financing accounts receivable) for cash as a discount from the face value.

4) Forfeiting, which is the selling, at a discount, of longer-term accounts receivable or promissory notes of the foreign buyer.

5) Confirming, a financial service in which an independent company confirms an export order in the seller's country and makes payment for the goods in the currency of that country. For the exporter, confirming means the entire export transaction from manufacture to end user can be fully coordinated and paid for over time. Confirming is common when dealing with the EU.

USEFUL ADDRESSES

Government Agencies

Canada Communication Group
45 Boulevard Sacre-Coeur
Hull, Quebec
K1A 0S9
Tel: (819) 956-4800
Fax: (819) 994-1498
[source of information on labelling and claims]

The Standards Information Service

Standards Council of Canada
Room 1210
350 Sparks Street
Ottawa, Ontario, Canada
K1K 7S8
Tel: (613) 238-3222

Director
Information Directorate
Health and Welfare Canada
Brooke Claxton Bldg.
Ottawa, Ontario, Canada
K1A 0K9
Tel: (613) 992-4575

Information Officer
Health Protection Branch
Room 164
Health and Welfare
Ottawa, Ontario, Canada
K1A 0L2
Tel: (613) 9571748

Secretary
Canadian General Standards Board
"c/o" Supply and Services Canada
Place du Portage
Phase III
11 Laurier Street
Hull, Quebec
K1A 0S5
Tel: (613) 238-3222

Bureau de Normalisation du Quebec
50 rue Saint-Joseph est,
Quebec, Quebec
G1K 3A5
Tel: (418) 643-5114

Revenue Canada, Customs and Excise
Connaught Building
Ottawa, Ontario, Canada
K1A OL5
Attn: Release and Documentation Systems
Data Control Programmes

Office of International Marketing
/223 Bureau of International Commerce
Department of Commerce
Washington DC 20230

National Philatelic Center
Canada Post Corporation
Station 1
Antigonish Nova Scotia
B2G 2R8
Canada
Tel: (800) 565-1333

Department of Foreign Affairs and International Trade
125 Sussex Drive(SKI)
Ottawa, Ontario
K1A 0G2
Tel: (613) 944-4000
Fax: (613) 996-9709

Canadian Chamber of Commerce
Head Office
55 Metcalfe
Ottawa, Ontario
K1P 6N4
Tel: (613) 238-4000

Canadian Manufacturer's Association
1 Yonge Street
14th Floor
Suite 1400
Toronto, Ontario
Tel: (416) 363-7261
Fax: (416) 363-3779

Canadian Exporters' Association
Suite 250
99 Bank Street
Ottawa, Ontario
K1P 6B9
Tel: (613) 238-8888
Fax: (613) 563-9218

Consulates General:

Calgary, Alberta–Suite 1050
615 Maclod Trail, SE
T2G 4T8
Tel: (403) 264-6630

Halifax, Nova Scotia–Suite 916
Cogswell Tower
Scotia Square
B5J 3K1
Tel: (902) 429-2480
Fax: (902) 423-6861
COM Fax: (902) 423-6861

Montreal, PQ–P. O. Box 65
Postal Station Desjardins
L5B 1G1
P. O. Box 847
Champlain, NY 12919-0847
Tel: (514) 898-9695
Fax: (514) 898-0973 (514) 898-0711

Quebec, PQ–2 Place Terraisse Dufferin
C.P. 939
G1R 4T9
P. O. Box 1547
Champlain, NY 12919-1547
Tel: (418) 693-2095
Fax: (418) 692-4640

Toronto, Ontario–360 University Avenue
M5G 1S4
P. O. Box 135
Lewiston, NY 14092-0135
Tel: (416) 595-1700
Fax: (416) 595-5419

Vancouver, British Columbia
1095 West Pender Street
V6E 2M6
P. O. Box 5002
Point Roberts, WA 98281-5002
Tel: (604) 685-4311
Fax: (604) 685-5385
COM Fax: (604) 687-6095

Government Information Sources

Industry and Science Canada
Business Service Centre
Ottawa, Canada
Tel: (613) 952-4782

Department of Regional Industrial Expansion
235 Queens Street
Ottawa, Ontario
K1A 0H5
Tel: (613) 995-5771

Department of External Affairs
125 Sussex Drive
Ottawa, Ontario
K1A 0G2
Tel: (613) 238-4000

Remission Policy Unit
Duties Relief Programs
Department of National Revenue
Ottawa, Ontario
K1A 0L5
Tel: (613) 957-8703

Canadian Regional Customs Offices
Alberta: Customs Office
Suite 720
Harry Hayes Building
220 4th Avenue SE
T2G 4X3
Tel: (403) 292-4628
Fax: (403) 292-6577

Atlantic: Customs Office
6169 Quinpool Road
Halifax, Nova Scotia
NS B3J 3G6
Tel: (902) 426-2661

Central: Customs Office
Federal Building
269 Main Street
Winnipeg, Manitoba
R3C 1B3
Tel: (204) 983-3758
Fax: (204) 983-8849

Hamilton: Customs Office
26 Arrowsmith Road
P. O. Box 2989
Hamilton, Ontario
L8N 3V8
Tel: (905) 578-8697
Fax: (905) 578-8700

Montreal: Customs Office
105 McGill
Montreal, PQ
H2Y 2E7
Tel: (514) 283-6201
Fax: (514) 283-7500

Ottawa: Customs Office
2265 Laurent Blvd.
Ottawa, Ontario
K1G 4K3
Tel: (613) 993-0534
(613) 991-0566
evenings, weekends–
Tel: (613) 998-3326
Fax: (613) 957-9080

Pacific: Customs Office
333 Dunsmuir Street
Suite 708
V6B 5R4
Tel: (604) 666-0456
Fax: (604) 666-4780

Quebec: Customs Office
130 Dalhousie Street
Quebec, PQ
G1K 7P6
Tel: (418) 648-3708
Fax: (418) 648-4504

Southwestern Ontario: Customs Office
P. O. Box 2280
Walkerville Station, Windsor, Ontario
N8Y 4R8
Tel: (519) 257-6573

Toronto: Customs Office
P. O. Box 10
Station A
2nd Floor
1 Front Street West
Toronto, Ontario
M5W 1A3
Tel: (416) 973-6413
Fax: (416) 973-3076

Industry Reviews

INTRODUCTION

Canada is an affluent, high-technology industrial society. In the 1980s, Canada registered one of the higher rates of real growth among the OECD nations (the Organization for Economic Development consists of the nations of Western Europe, North America, Japan, Australia, and New Zealand), averaging about 3.2 percent. With its great natural resources, skilled labor force, and modern capital plant, Canada has good prospects, although the country still faces high unemployment and debt.

Many Canadian industries tend to be dominated by a few enterprises that are highly concentrated geographically. In many cases, 90 percent or more of the prospective customers for an industrial product will be located near two or three cities. Canada's consumer goods market is more diffused than its industrial market. In many cases, complete coverage of the consumer market requires representation in several centers across Canada. The primary distribution centers for Eastern Canada are Toronto and/or Montreal. For Western Canada, the most appropriate distribution centers are Vancouver or Calgary.

CONTENTS

Introduction	97
Agriculture, Processed Foods, and Fishing	97
Computers and Computer Software	98
Forestry	99
Furniture	99
Health Products and Equipment	100
Household Appliances and Products	101
Industrial and Agricultural Machinery	104
Industrial Minerals, Chemicals, and Materials	105
Telecommunications	106
Textiles and Apparel	107
Toys and Sports Equipment	107
Vehicles and Vehicle Parts	108

AGRICULTURE, PROCESSED FOODS, AND FISHING

Agriculture and Processed Foods

The Canadian field crops industry exists mostly in the prairie provinces of the country, with Ontario and Saskatchewan generating almost 50 percent of the country's crop revenue. In the last several years, Canadian farmers have increased their earnings, increased their assets, limited their debts, and have begun to rapidly adapt to new technologies. High yields in 1993 and 1994 allowed farmers to sell record quantities of goods. Helped by strong grain prices, farmers from every province, with the exception of Manitoba and Newfoundland, earned more in 1994 than they did in 1993. Total farm income was estimated at US$20 billion (representing a five percent increase over 1993 farm cash receipts). During the 1995 to 1997 period, farm income is expected to range from US$16 billion to US$22 billion, as long as commodity prices remain high.

The processed foods sector has been caught between rising costs and falling prices. In addition to developing new product lines and acquiring existing product ones, companies are emphasizing service as a competitive tool. Despite difficult times, the agrifood industry in Canada, as a whole, is one of the largest industries in the country, second only to forestry in the primary sector. Others challenges include meeting the tastes and demands of a country whose market ranges from teenagers in major cities like Toronto to workers in Arctic mining camps who must survive extremely frigid conditions.

Products Canadian farmers produce a wide range of goods, including wheat, oats, barley, rye, maize (corn), buckwheat, soybeans, linseed, repassed (canola), beans, and hay. The Canadian food and beverages industry produces meat and dairy products, fresh and frozen fruits and vegetables, sugar and confectionery products, cocoa, beer, and soft drinks.

Competitive Situation Canada is one of the major food exporting countries in the world. Working in tandem with an agricultural machinery industry that can supply farmers with equipment and a government that supports the industry, Canadian agricultural workers have been able to increase production even though the number of people involved in the industry has decreased. Federal and provincial departments of agriculture guide and aid Canadian farmers in almost all aspects of production: research and development; protection of health of crops and animals; irrigation; and price regulation. And farmers have taken advantage of the latest agricultural technology to increase productivity.

The key concern for the Canadian processed foods and beverages industry is to maintain its competitive edge. It has recognized the need for better planning, better inventory control, and fewer employees. The traditional manufacturers are also up against steep price competition, as supermarkets bring their own line of products into the stores and display less name brands. Companies have recognized the need to keep the price of their products down even as the costs of production?–axes, payroll, production costs –increase. There is also the continual need to invest in technology so that the lines between farmer and ultimate consumer are shorter and the communications are more accurate.

Fishing

Canada is blessed with great natural resources for a fishing industry: it has a coastline of 18,000 miles and a network of lakes and rivers that contain more than half of the world's fresh water. The Canadian government supports the fishing industry by issuing loans to fishermen for the purchase of boats, developing the resources of both ocean and inland waters, and by expanding the domestic market. A major concern for the fishing industry is pollution, which now threatens the freshwater areas, especially in Ontario.

Products Canada produced 27,000 tons of salmon in 1994 and was projected to produce 35,000 tons of salmon in 1995. It also produces large amounts of cod, crab, small flatfishes, haddock, halibut, pollock, redfish, herring and sardine, lobsters, scallops, tuna, whitefish, lake trout, pickerel, and dried, salted, and smoked fish.

Competitive Situation Canada ranks among the world leaders in fish producers. In 1991, it was the world's third leading exporter of fish and fish products, behind the US and Norway. More than 1 billion pounds of fish are caught every year along the Atlantic coast by deep sea fishermen and those working close to shore. In the west, on the Pacific Coast, fishermen are able to harvest great quantities of salmon in the waters of British Columbia.

COMPUTERS AND COMPUTER SOFTWARE

Although US companies continue to be the dominant suppliers of computer software in the Canadian market, Canada's software industry has a strong nucleus of companies that have achieved international recognition as technical and market leaders for their products. Quebec is home to Canada's fastest growing concentration of software developers, many of which seek joint-ventures. Of the approximately 400 commercial software developers in Quebec, at least 75 percent generate export business. Eighty percent of these exports are destined for customers in the United States. Aside from the US market, Quebec's commercial software developers are now shifting their interest from European markets to the Mexican and South American markets.

A combination of smaller profit margins and a sharp decline in mainframe and mid-size systems sales caused Canada's information technology industry to grow only 1.5 percent in 1993, despite significant growth in the personal computer, networking, and software markets. Revenue from mainframe sales fell 36.8 percent in 1993, offsetting a record year for personal computer shipments and double-digit growth in revenues from routers, hubs, and voice-mail equipment. The lower Canadian dollar on international money markets also helped fuel record shipments and export sales for the Canadian manufacturer.

In 1995, total local production of computer hardware and peripherals was expected to be US$3.1 billion, with a market of US$4.5 billion. Exports were expected to be valued at US$2.87 billion, and imports were expected to be valued at US$4.3 billion. Local production of computer software was expected to be US$1.3 billion in 1995, with exports accounting for US$488 million, imports US$652 million, and a total market size of US$1.4 billion.

Products In addition to mainframe computers, Canada produces personal computers, accessories, and electronic components. Most Canadian software products are niche-oriented, with well-known applications in computer graphics and animations, advanced programming tools and languages, geographic information Systems, form processing software, and educational and computer-based training products. Also noteworthy are Canadian achievements in specialty software areas like remote sensing, telecommunications network management, expert systems for mineral processing, real-time systems design, process and industrial control, geophysical engineering and power systems analysis.

Competitive Situation Canada has traditionally excelled in software development in the education, business, science, engineering, and consumer application fields. This trend is expected to continue for CD-ROM technology. For example, Microsoft Canada, one of Canada's largest software developers, is at the forefront of CD-ROM software development. Microsoft is expected to release dozens of new consumer titles in the near future, including many on CD-ROM. Microsoft is determined to be one of the major players in the race to be the software supplier to the consumer information technology market that may dwarf the current business application software trade.

FORESTRY

The Canadian forest industry is the world's leader in exporting forestry products. Although it was hurt badly by the recession of the early 1990s, it has begun its recovery and remains one of the most important industries in Canada. Production of forestry products are particularly strong in British Columbia, where forest land covers 46 percent of the province (British Columbia holds half of the country's softwood inventory) and in Alberta, where 600 forestry-related companies operate.

The Canadian forest industry directly employed 239,000 people in 1993 and represented about 3.5 percent of the GDP. The industry indirectly generated close to one million jobs, representing 7.7 percent of the national workforce. Although the late 1980s and the first two years of the 1990s were difficult–industry job losses in 1991 and 1992 amounted to 30,900 and 7,800, respectively–conditions have begun to improve. In 1993, industry job losses slowed to 2,500. The total sales of Canadian forest products in 1993 was US$27.65 billion. This showed an increase of 13 percent from 1992 when the Canadian forest industry lost US$130 million.

Capital expenditures continued to remain plentiful during 1993, increasing to US$1.99 billion. Although pulp and newsprint capital expenditures in 1993 dropped slightly to US$1.4 billion, they still accounted for 72 percent of the total industry's capital spending. Other capital spending occurred in the paper and board mills, sawmilling sector, panelboard mills, and logging equipment.

Products The Canadian forestry industry produces lumber and panel products, wood pulp, newsprint, and other paper and board products.

Competitive Situation After experiencing difficult times during recent years, the Canadian forest industry is now undergoing a positive turnaround and is positioning itself to export a great deal of goods to world markets. Prices for wood products are increasing and markets worldwide are growing. For example, newsprint prices rose from US$440 per ton to US$550 per ton. As prices continued to rise in 1995, experts predict the industry will boom. In fact, Canadian shipments, which reached a record 29 million tons in 1994, were estimated to grow another four percent in 1995. Although the industry will still have its ups and downs, world demand for paper and cardboard is expected to double during the next 20 years. Canada, the world's largest exporter of pulp and paper products, is expected to play a big role in supplying these products. The industry has also been helped by logging restrictions in the US Pacific northwest, a weak Canadian dollar compared to the US dollar, and an end to the recession in the United States.

The market for Canadian goods, however, cannot be taken for granted. Industry leaders realize that as countries like China, Brazil, and Indonesia enter the world forestry market, Canada must do all it can to maintain its competitive edge as the world's leader in exporting forestry goods. Current goals of the industry are to maintain its competitive edge by improving management policies and labor relations and investing in new technology while, at the same time, initiating new procedures to protect the environment.

FURNITURE

The Canadian furniture industry has long been an important industry in Canada, traditionally supplying as much as 80 percent of its domestic market, but it was hit hard during the recession of the late 1980s and early 1990s (more than 400 Canadian furniture manufacturers discontinued operations during 1990–1992). Domestic Canadian production of household furniture decreased steadily between 1989 and 1991, then marginally increased between 1992 and 1993, and currently supplies approximately 60 to 65 percent of total demand. Canadian production was valued at US$1.4 billion in 1991, compared to US$1.53 billion in 1992, and US$1.56 billion in 1993.

In 1992, the Canadian household furniture industry consisted of 782 manufacturing establishments, located mainly in Quebec and Ontario, with manufacturing plants equally distributed between metropolitan areas and smaller communities. The rest of the manufacturing establishments (about 30 percent) were distributed among the provinces of Manitoba, Alberta, and British Columbia, or scattered throughout the rest of Canada. Ownership of firms in the industry is predominantly Canadian, with less than 3 percent of companies foreign-owned. The Canadian furniture industry is comprised mainly of small to medium-sized firms, and a few large manufacturers. The large firms, however–those with more than 100 employees–account for 47 percent of total shipments even though they account for only 6 percent of total manufacturing establishments.

The advantages inherent in the similarity of consumer preferences between the US and Canada, and the proximity of major market areas, have helped several large Canadian manufacturers develop markets for their products in the United States. In most cases, they have succeeded either by specializing in products targeted to specific market segments (most notably products of contemporary styling), or by focusing on products in the higher-priced market segments, in which superior design and quality are more important than price. Canadian household furniture industry experts estimate that real growth rates for domestic production during the 1994 to 1996 period will be between 1 and 2 percent.

Wooden household furniture represented the largest component of Canadian domestic production, or approximately 39 percent of the total value. Upholstered household furniture accounted for 33 percent, bed springs and mattresses 17 percent, and other miscellaneous household furniture was 11 percent of the total dollar value of shipments (which includes both domestic shipments and exports).

Products The Canadian furniture industry is comprised of the household furniture sector, which accounts for 43 percent of total furniture production; office furniture, which accounts for 24 percent; and other furniture, including many dissimilar products made for a variety of hotel, restaurant, and institutional uses, which accounts for 33 percent of furniture production. There are four primary sectors of the Canadian household furniture market: wooden household furniture, upholstered household furniture, bed springs and mattresses, and miscellaneous household furniture. Office furniture includes desks, chairs, filing cabinets, book shelves, and computer workstations.

Competitive Situation Canadian furniture manufacturers are facing increased competition. Third-country suppliers, including Malaysia, the Philippines, and Indonesia are entering the international marketplace. One of the results of NAFTA will be an increase in competition for Canadian furniture manufacturers from Mexican exports, and the GATT agreements have eliminated tariffs on furniture products. Nevertheless, Canadian manufacturers can still remain competitive internationally. Canadian manufacturers are taking a number of steps to insure a healthy future: they are increasing productivity, employing more efficient manufacturing methods, and increasing product specialization (particularly in the high-end furniture market, where they can best compete). They are also considering mergers and acquisitions and dedicating more attention to the development of new markets. While tariff and labor rates, access to raw materials, and transportation costs were formerly the critical factors in the competitiveness of furniture products, future opportunities for a comparative advantage will be established through astute marketing practices, integration of new product lines, and superior design. Manufacturers will need to focus on producing high-value products at the lowest possible cost. Canadians firms will have to pursue the gains in productivity that have been made available through the use of new technologies and advanced manufacturing systems. Research in both design and consumer markets will be very important to success in international markets.

HEALTH PRODUCTS AND EQUIPMENT

Canadian manufacturers produce items in all areas of health care products, including medical and surgical supplies, electromedical equipment, and (a growing field) home care and mobility equipment. Canada has 16 universities with medical faculties and over 85 health institutions including hospitals, clinics and rehabilitation centers equipped with product testing and developmental facilities. Each university specializes in one of six different fields of application—cardiovascular, diagnostics, orthopedics/prosthetics/orthotics, assistive devices, medical imaging, and biomaterials.

Canada has historically been one of the world's strongest markets for medical equipment, and it is renown worldwide for the quality of its national health-care. An aging population, generous research and development tax credit policies, as well as a world-class network of hospitals and universities and a comprehensive public health care system have all contributed to Canada's reputation as a leader in the medical sciences. Pressures to contain health-care costs, demographic changes, and increased health consciousness will continue to be the most notable trends in the Canadian health care industry during the coming years.

Manufacturing activity in the industry has fluctuated with the movements in the overall economy. During the recession, in 1991, domestic production of medical and surgical disposable products decreased by a real rate of 9.2 percent from US$89.7 million in 1991, to US$84.3 million in 1992. By 1993 however, the market experienced real growth of almost seven percent. Domestic production satisfied approximately one-fifth of total Canadian market demand in 1993, and this share is expected to remain at this level during the next three years.

The bulk of domestic Canadian production of medical and surgical supplies is manufactured by multinational companies, including: Johnson & Johnson (closure devices); Baxter (catheters); Smith and Nephew (dressings); Becton Dickenson (vinyl gloves); 3M (tapes), Davis & Geck (sutures); and Ingram Bell (catheters). About 70 percent of Canadian domestic production is concentrated in the province of Ontario. Production facilities located in Quebec and Alberta account for 15 and 10 percent, respectively. Producers in other provinces generate about five percent of the manufacturing activity for medical and surgical disposable supplies.

Domestic Canadian production of home care and mobility equipment, valued at US$29.8 million in 1992, grew by a real rate of slightly more than 20 percent to US$34.1 million by 1993. Canadian manufacturers of home care and mobility equipment rely on their ability to sell to large export markets, like the US and Japan, in order to remain competitive in an expanding global market. In doing so, manufacturers tend to focus on a limited number of products. As a result, although domestic production has grown substantially in recent years, it has satisfied only 15 to 16 percent of annual domestic Canadian market demand since 1992.

The production of electromedical equipment in Canada has been estimated at US$63 million in 1992. Domestic production is accounted for by a small number of manufacturers that focus on specialty market niches.

Products Any products manufactured by the Canadian health-care industry include medical and surgical supplies such as catheters, dressings, gloves, sutures, and closure devices; electromedical equipment; and home-care and mobility equipment.

Competitive Situation Although subsidiaries of multinational enterprises represent only 10 percent of medical equipment companies operating in Canada, in terms of sales volume they dominate the Canadian marketplace. The demand for health care products and equipment is so great in Canada that 80 percent of the market is provided by imports. 1994 market size was almost US$1.2 billion. Local production was US$482 million, of which US$240 million was exported. Imports amounted to US$956 million.

The Canadian network of public health-care institutions has started to reduce the scope of its activities and now increasingly focuses on the delivery of acute and intensive care as it significantly downsizes under the budgetary cuts of the past three years. As a result, new trends in health-care have emerged in Canada. These trends are currently reflected in the increasing popularity of community-based home care programs offering a comprehensive range of services which are now viewed as substitutes for institutional care services. The Canadian home-care market is, consequently, expected to grow at a real rate of about 20 percent annually over the next five years.

Due to a relatively small local market, Canadian manufacturers of electromedical equipment, for example, patient monitoring equipment, have historically established and developed their businesses through exports. Many export from 70 to 90 percent of their production, and some have acquired a reputation internationally before making inroads into the local market.

HOUSEHOLD APPLIANCES AND PRODUCTS

Canadian household appliances and products range from large items such as heating systems to medium sized items such as plumbing fixtures to small items such as steam irons. New free trade agreements, such as NAFTA, are affecting the balance of exports and imports for all items.

Air and Water Treatment Systems

As Canadian consumers spend more time at home there is a growing interest in personal comfort and health issues. More than ever, they are concerned about the air they breathe and the water they drink. Consumers want heaters that are competitively priced and have up-to-date features such as automatic shut-off. Canada endures some of the harshest winter weather conditions in North America, with temperatures ranging from zero to 40 degrees Fahrenheit. Every Canadian residential and commercial building must therefore be equipped with reliable, high-capacity heating equipment. Filters are becoming popular not only for those with allergies, but for everyone interested in the cleanest air and who have the desire to protect home electronic products from dust. Air cleaners are among the fastest selling items in the household goods market. Humidifiers add warmth to air and can save on heating costs. And water cleaners are for those who are concerned about the cleanliness of urban water supplies. Manufacturers are responding to that need with a crop of innovative products to suit every consumer taste.

Canada's only significant trading partner in this industry sector is the United States. The relationship between the US and Canadian industries, with ever-increasing industry integration, will continue as US and Canadian tariffs are decreased and completely eliminated on January 1, 1998 on most products, and as more components in Canadian products are sourced from the US. In 1993, the Canadian HVAC equipment market was valued at US$700 million, with US exports accounting for approximately 50 percent of the market. The Canadian HVAC market is projected to show marginal real growth of approximately one to three percent during the 1994 to 1996 period.

Products Manufacturers are producing a range of products such as heaters, filters, humidifiers, air cleaners, and water purifiers. The demand for such products is growing at a steady rate.

Competitive Situation Following unprecedented growth during the 1980s, the Canadian heating, ventilating and air conditioning (HVAC) industry experienced major changes resulting from the recession of 1989 to 1992, and from the import-liberalizing effects of the US-Canada Free Trade Agreement. The Canadian industry underwent consolidation and structural adjustment to achieve further economies of scale and increased competitiveness. The industry's products are also changing as consumers and governments require higher standards of energy efficiency and reduced environmental impact. New regulations are challenging and changing the industry from one whose environment has been relatively static, to one that has been compelled to acknowledge the necessity of innovation and accommodation to change.

Imports supply a significant and increasing share of Canadian heating equipment market demand. Imports have increased dramatically due in part to the Canadian Free Trade Agreement with the US, which has resulted in lower tariffs, and also due to industry consolidation in reaction to the recession and the need to streamline operations. In 1991, imports, valued at US$156.2 million, satisfied 35 percent of demand. This figure grew by a real rate of more than 25 percent the following year and, by 1993, imports satisfied nearly 60 percent of demand, when imports were valued at US$221.7 million. It is projected that Canadian heating equipment imports will increase at a real rate of between 2 to 6 percent annually during the forecast period 1994 and 1996. Imports from Germany, China, South Korea, Belgium, and Italy, with a combined market share of approximately 8 percent of total imports, have been the only significant competition for US-made heating equipment products.

As a result of the increase in imports, Canadian wholesale distributors have had to look further afield to source a variety of products. The trend towards increased awareness in air and water treatment these days, on the part of both the Canadian consumer and the retailer, relates to a variety of things. With competition so great, the deciding factor in many instances will be customer satisfaction.

Non-Powered Lawn and Garden Equipment

Total Canadian market demand for non-powered lawn and garden equipment was US$101.9 million in 1993, compared to US$83.7 million and US$81.9 million in 1992 and 1991 respectively. Industry sources have indicated that factors such as improved weather conditions coupled with the recovery of the economy contributed to the strong increase in market demand in 1993. Also, in 1993, Canadian consumers made replacement purchases which they had postponed during the 1990 to 1992 recessionary period.

In Canada, home renovations spending has been increasing significantly in recent years, especially in urban areas with high property values. Canada's aging population, Canadians' tendency to spend more time at home improving their properties, and an overall growing environmental awareness among Canadians will result in increased market demand for non-powered lawn and garden equipment. Growth in the total market demand for non-powered lawn and garden equipment is forecast to be 5 to 6 percent annually in real terms during the 1994 to 1996 period.

Canadian production of non-powered lawn and garden equipment in 1993 was valued at US$126.1 million, representing a real increase of 57 percent over 1992 production levels of US$88.3 million (which had decreased almost 4 percent in real terms over production levels of US$88.5 million in 1991). While domestic Canadian production of non-powered lawn and garden equipment satisfied approximately 25 percent of Canadian market demand in 1993, imports accounted for 75 percent.

Products Non-powered lawn and garden equipment products include the following products: spades and shovels, forks, mattocks, picks, hoes and rakes, hewing tools, one-handed secateurs, hedge shears, two-handed pruning shears, scarifiers, weeders, seeders, planters, and manure spreaders.

Competitive Situation Imports of non-powered lawn and garden equipment satisfy an increasing share of Canadian market demand. In 1991, imports represented approximately 65 percent of market demand, and were valued at US$53.2 million. By 1992, imports had grown by a real rate of almost seven percent to be valued at US$58.6 million, accounting for 70 percent of domestic Canadian demand. Growing by more than 40 percent in real terms from 1992 to 1993, imports satisfied 75 percent of total demand in 1993 and were valued at US$76.4 million. Between 1994 and 1996, imports of non-powered lawn and garden equipment are forecast to grow at an average annual real rate of between 5 and 6percent.

Plumbing Products

The Canadian plumbing industry consists of a few very large manufacturers, as well as a large number of smaller firms. The large companies are, for the most part, Canadian subsidiaries of US manufacturers. They were established in Canada many years ago to circumvent existing high import duties, and to manufacture products similar to those of their parent companies for the somewhat distinctive preferences of the Canadian market. These large companies, such as American Standard,

Crane, and Koehler, specialize in ceramic and coated metal fixtures, and supply 80 to 90 percent of the plumbing fixtures market. The smaller Canadian companies specialize in the production of less capital-intensive plumbing fixtures, including bathtubs, spas, and whirlpool bathtubs.

Between 1991 and 1992, domestic Canadian production of plumbing products grew almost 7 percent, from US$330.8 million to US$364.5 million. The industry then experienced a slight decline of approximately 2 percent in manufacturing levels, as the market decreased to US$326.3 million in 1993. This decline in Canadian production resulted from the combination of a shift in manufacturing of some Canadian subsidiaries of US firms back to the United States, and the failure of some Canadian manufacturers during Canada's recent protracted recession. In 1993, the Canadian market for plumbing products was valued at an estimated US$393 million, representing growth of slightly more than 2 percent over 1992 levels. Experts predict future real annual growth of between 4 and 5 percent during the 1994 to 1996 period.

The major Canadian markets for plumbing products are the new housing market, and the renovations market. Demand for plumbing products in the new housing market directly correlates with the number of housing starts. More than 70 percent of plumbing products used in Canadian construction are installed by contractors in new homes, as well as in major renovations of existing homes.

Products The Canadian plumbing products industry comprises manufacturers of a wide variety of products, primarily for residential housing as well as for commercial, institutional, and industrial buildings. Plumbing products are manufactured in a variety of materials including glass, steel, plastic, fiberglass, and combinations thereof, and include baths, shower-baths, wash basins, lavatory seats and covers, toilet bowls and tanks, urinals, sinks and wash basins, and faucets.

Competitive Situation The Canadian market for most types of high-volume commodity plumbing products is well supplied by domestic producers, which account for approximately 70 percent of total market sales. Price, quality, availability, and service are the predominant competitive factors in the Canadian plumbing products industry. One-third of 1993 market demand was satisfied by imports, which were valued at US$121.8 million. US plumbing products dominate the import market, representing between 75 and 80 percent of total imports in recent years. Local production of plumbing products was valued at approximately US$326.3 million, of which US$55.6 million was exported.

Imports to the Canadian market have been increasing, partly because of a decrease of tariffs. Plumbing product imports can be grouped into three basic categories: products imported into Canada by multinational manufacturers and large wholesalers to complement their locally manufactured product lines; high-style items such as European sinks and faucets; and products such as vitreous china fixtures, toilet seats, and brass valves that are produced at a lower cost in newly industrialized countries.

As a result of increased competition in the domestic market from typically larger, more sophisticated international firms, Canadian manufacturers have been forced to specialize, innovate, and develop export markets. Consequently, some Canadian manufacturers have gained an excellent reputation in foreign markets for well-designed, high quality, and innovative plumbing products. Exports of Canadian plumbing products amounted to US$55.6 million in 1993, compared to US$52.8 million and US$38.5 million in 1992 and 1991, respectively.

Portable Electric Household Appliances

The Canadian household appliance market is a combination of multinational and independent Canadian manufacturers. Many of the major firms manufacture the majority of their products outside of Canada, with a large portion of products coming from Asia (especially China) and Mexico. As a result, the Canadian market consists mainly of imports. The independent firms tend to focus on one product line like kettles or toasters. These companies' manufacturing operations may be located either in Canada or offshore.

Despite recessionary pressures, Canadian retail sales of portable appliances increased slightly in 1992 due to retailers' efforts to reduce existing inventories resulting from poor sales in previous years. Industry sources also attributed Canadian market growth in 1993 to a decline in cross-border shopping and an increase in consumer confidence. Total Canadian market growth for the 1994 to 1996 period is expected to range from 3 to 5 percent annually in real terms, although demand for certain product categories may grow at a faster rate.

The industry may also be helped by the tendency for many Canadians to choose to spend more time at home (perhaps because of the sluggish economy). Home-based businesses are on the rise and Canadians are spending more time entertaining at home. Canadians are also becoming increasingly concerned about health issues and are seeking ways to improve their eating habits while still accommodating their desire for convenience. This is demonstrated by sales of products which make it easier for Canadians to control what goes into the food they eat.

Lifestyle appliances are designed to meet the special health, convenience, space, and entertainment needs of consumer groups, as defined by their lifestyles and accompanying attitudes. These products have enjoyed high growth rates in Canada, and are expected to continue this trend during the 1994 to 1996 period.

Products The Canadian electrical household appliance industry includes a wide range of products including personal care items such as hair dryers; house cleaning items such as vacuum cleaners; apparel care items such as steam irons; and a number of kitchen appliances such as blenders, coffee makers, food processors, mixers, breadmakers, toasters, fryers, steamers, and woks.

Competitive Situation Imports have represented a significant percent of total Canadian market demand for the past three years, and are expected to grow annually through 1996. This growth rate is slightly higher than that forecasted for the total market demand. Imports from the United States and Mexico are expected to increase due to tariff reductions resulting from the implementation of the North American Free Trade Agreement (NAFTA). Asian imports are also expected to rise due to manufacturing growth in China. While most of the key players in the industry have subsidiary plants located in Canada, most manufacture at offshore plants. Factors such as improved safety features and product specialization to meet lifestyle changes lead current trends for the market in Canada. Increasingly, Canadian consumers are entertaining and spending more time at home, and are also developing healthier eating habits.

INDUSTRIAL AND AGRICULTURAL MACHINERY

Canadian manufacturers of machinery supply major Canadian industries–agriculture, energy, oil and gas exploration–with equipment. Although imports may be increasing due to lower costs in Third World economies and the tariff reductions of new free trade agreements, growth in the Canadian industries (especially agriculture and oil and gas exploration) insure a somewhat healthy base for the existing Canadian manufacturers. The Canadian industry itself is also beginning to concentrate on exporting goods in order to increase its market share.

Agricultural Equipment

The Canadian agricultural equipment and machinery industry consists of approximately 250 manufacturers. The Canadian field agriculture equipment industry consists of a wide range of establishments producing all types of machinery including combine harvesters, seeding and tillage equipment, hay handling and harvesting equipment, and grain handling and storage equipment. The industry is composed of firms that market a complete line of farm equipment and firms which produce a limited variety of agricultural implements and attachments.

In 1994, the size of the Canadian market for agricultural machinery and equipment (including parts and accessories) was estimated at US$1.73 billion. The market grew at a real rate of 27.8 percent between 1992 and 1993, and 16.3 percent between 1993 and 1994. According to industry sources, the market will continue to grow during the 1995 to 1997 forecast period at a real annual rate of between 8 and 10 percent. This growth reflects the record harvest incomes earned by Canadian farmers in 1993 and 1994, and the anticipated continuation of record setting incomes through 1997.

In 1994, Canada imported 78.7 percent, or US$1.36 billion, of its agricultural machinery and equipment requirements to satisfy domestic demand. This represented a 12 percent real increase over 1993 imports, which followed the phenomenal growth of 33.6 percent in real terms witnessed between 1992 and 1993. Canadian imports of farm equipment are expected to increase at an average annual real rate of four percent during the 1995 to 1997 period. Imports, while projected to grow through 1997, are being hindered by the low value of the Canadian dollar relative to the US dollar.

Products Manufactured products in the agricultural sector include mechanical sprayers; plows for soil preparation or cultivation; harrows; seeders, planters and transplanters; manure spreaders and fertilizer distributors; haying machines; straw or fodder balers, including pick-up balers; combine harvester-threshers; threshing machine; and harvesting machinery.

Competitive Situation The weak Canadian dollar has made Canadian-made equipment attractive to the international farm community, and, as a result, Canada has increased its export activity considerably. While Canadian production of this equipment has satisfied a relatively constant share of market demand (21.7 percent in 1992, 18.2 percent in 1993 and 21.3 percent in 1994), exports have soared. In fact, 1994 Canadian exports in this market were valued at US$689.7 million, up from US$429.1 million in 1992 and US$567.8 million in 1993. Real growth in domestic production of field agriculture equipment has equaled the growth in Canada's exports of this equipment. Canadian production is expected to remain high through 1997, with real growth predicted at between 10 and 12 percent annually.

Electrical Power Systems Equipment

Canada has the fourth largest power generating capacity in the world. Sixty-two percent of this capacity is hydro-electric power generation and 38 percent is thermal power generation, including nuclear power generation. While energy use is substantial and future growth is expected, the electrical power systems equipment market has suffered through both a cyclical downturn and the recession. However, industry analysts remain optimistic for the future.

Products Canadian manufacturers produce electrical switches, gas turbine engines, transformers and electrical inductors, and other electricity generating and distribution equipment.

Competitive Situation While Quebec and Ontario utilities continue to purchase from Canadian-based suppliers, other provincial power companies are now able to purchase their power generation equipment from abroad as they restructure and upgrade their facilities to meet future provincial power needs. The demand for equipment will continue to rise as old equipment is replaced and companies search for more efficient products. A greater demand will come from new residential and commercial building construction–something that electrical power equipment suppliers are still waiting for.

Oil and Gas Field Equipment

The estimated size of the Canadian market for oil and gas field equipment in 1993 was US$936.4 million. Projected annual growth through 1996 is 4.6 percent, in real terms. Growth in this industry can be attributed to the increasing demand for oil, coupled with increasing oil prices and technological developments for extracting and producing petroleum. Currently 200 small-to-medium-size companies make up the oil and gas field equipment industry.

Products Oil and gas field equipment products include geophysical prospecting equipment, drilling rigs and ancillary tools, pumping, cementing, well-fracturing units, dehydrators, separators, treaters and other oil field processing components, and offshore platform drilling and processing equipment.

Competitive Situation Canadian imports of oil and gas field equipment in 1993 were valued at US$262 million or 28 percent of the total Canadian market. The US share of Canada's oil and gas field equipment imports is estimated at 98 percent, with a value of US$256.8 million. The future looks bright for the Canadian oil and gas field equipment industry. The oil and gas industry continues to expand, especially in Alberta, and many companies need to be supplied with more and more equipment. State-of-the-art technology, product reliability and quality, and after-sale service will be major factors contributing to the growth of this industry.

INDUSTRIAL MINERALS, CHEMICALS, AND MATERIALS

Oil and Gas and Related Products

Canada has a large resource of fossil fuels. In 1992, natural gas production in Canada was ranked third in the world, behind Russia and the US. The value of petroleum products in that year for Canada was US$9.27 billion, and represented 54 percent of the value of all mineral production. In 1993, Alberta was the top performer in the oil and natural gas sector, with expenditures on oil and gas facilities, number of wells actually drilled, and licenses issued to drill wells all rising. Drilling contractors enjoyed banner first half drilling at rates that could rival the peak prior to the fall in oil prices in the mid 1980s. Two major natural gas pipelines serve the country. Originating in Edmonton, one pipeline extends east to Toronto and the other extends southwest to Vancouver. The natural gas pipeline network is constantly increasing.

In 1991, its coal production amounted to 71.1 million tons and was valued at US$1.66 billion. Canada's coal resources amount to only about 2 percent of the total world resources, but it exports 50 percent of its production and was, in 1991, the fourth largest coal exporting nation. The growth in the coal exporting sector is almost entirely due to the demand from Japan and South Korea.

Products Mined Canadian products in this sector include coal, natural gas, and oil.

Competitive Situation Oil and natural gas exploration continues in Canada. The most important project is the US$4 billion Hibernia oil project off the coast of Newfoundland. Construction of the Hibernia offshore oil drilling and production platform is scheduled for completion in 1997 at which time the completed platform will be towed to the Hibernia field location, approximately 315 kilometers east of St. John's, Newfoundland. The Hibernia project will then enter the production phase. Hibernia is expected to produce 150,000 barrels of oil a day for 19 years. Mobil Oil Canada and Shell Canada believe the Sable Island area near Nova Scotia may contain between two and four trillion cubic feet of natural gas and are now exploring possibilities to develop the area.

The province of Alberta is one of the most productive provinces for the oil and gas industry, with exports of oil, gas, and sulfur reaching nearly US$9 billion in 1993. In the face of depleting traditional oil reserves in the province, companies are tapping the extensive oils sands and bitumen reserves. Fifteen percent of the natural gas produced in North America is produced in Alberta. The Canadian government has also promised to help develop the ethanol industry in and around

Alberta. Hopes are to build plants that can produce 60 million liters of ethanol per year.

Plastics

Canada's plastics industry consists of 2,800 companies producing plastic materials and additives and processing them into semi-finished and finished products. Canadian plastics processing industry shipments increased by 5.6 percent to reach a market value of US$10.5 billion in 1993. Shipments were estimated to reach US$11.78 billion in 1994 and increase by an additional 10 percent in 1995. The plastics processing industry currently employs over 90,000 Canadians; this has been increasing. The three most important client industries for this sector are the packaging, construction, and automotive industries. They respectively account for 39 percent, 27 percent, and 11 percent of the resin consumption of some 2,500 Canadian plastics processors. The Canadian plastics processing industry grew rapidly during the last decade, with average annual growth of more than 10 percent. Much of the growth can be attributed to the fact that plastic compounds are replacing other materials. The use of plastics generally improves the design of products, including weight reduction and corrosion resistance, particularly in the fabrication of automotive products. Although new niches for the utilization of plastic materials continue to multiply, and international markets become more accessible, environmental concerns and consequent legislation will apply increasing pressures for change within the industry in Canada.

Products Canadian manufacturers of plastic products supply the auto, packaging, pipefitting, transportation equipment industries.

Competitive Situation Canadian imports of plastics in 1993 were valued at US$4.1 billion or 26 percent of the total market. The US share of Canada's plastic imports is estimated at 80 percent, with a value of US$3.3 billion. Growth in this industry can be attributed to the versatility of plastic, compared with more conventional materials like wood and metal, and the ease with which plastic can replace these materials. The future looks bright: Newly developed products like conductive polymers and resin blends developed with greater strength and higher resistance to heat, will be major factors in this industry's growth.

TELECOMMUNICATIONS

The Canadian telecommunications industry is composed of approximately 300 manufacturers and employs an estimated 45,500 people. The greatest concentration of employment in this industry is located in the provinces of Ontario, Quebec, and British Columbia. Three Canadian manufacturers dominate the industry and are recognized as world leaders in the field: Northern Telecom Canada Limited, Mitel Corporation, and Newbridge Networks Corporation. Northern Telecom alone accounted for over 60 percent of Canadian telecommunication sales in 1991, with domestic revenues of US$2.3 billion. The bulk of these revenues was generated by sales of digital telephone switching equipment. Canada's telecommunications equipment market, valued at US$3.6 billion in 1992, experienced average annual growth of more than 7.2 percent from 1988 to 1992. While the recession has had a significant negative impact on many segments of the market (most notably the telex and keyphone systems segments), many are experiencing significant growth. Overall telecommunications market growth is anticipated to average approximately four percent annually from 1993 to 1996.

Products Telecommunications products manufactured in Canada include cellular telephones, central switching equipment, data communication systems, voice processing equipment and systems, fiber-optic cables, connectors, and related transmission equipment.

Competitive Situation The three major strengths of the Canadian telecommunications equipment industry are its technology base, the presence of world leaders (like Northern Telecom), and the sophisticated and advanced domestic market. Canada has one of the greatest levels of telephone service in the world. For many years, the charters of the domestic telephone companies included a federal government provision to ensure basic telephone service for all Canadians, regardless of geographic location.

Despite Canada's dominant position in this worldwide industry, the domestic market is still highly receptive to telecommunications equipment imports, especially for those serving niche markets. With average annual real growth of 4 percent predicted during the 1995 to 1997 period, the Canadian telecommunications product market should present many opportunities for manufacturers offering niche products. In 1994, Canada imported US$2 billion worth of telecommunication products. It exported US$1.4 billion and produced US$3.25 billion worth of products.

The competitive landscape of the Canadian telecommunications equipment market is changing. For example, the 45-year-old preferred supplier agreement between the largest purchaser and supplier of telecommunications equipment was recently eliminated, opening the market to increased competition. Also, the domestic Canadian telecommunications market has been subjected to an extensive overhaul by its managing

TEXTILES AND APPAREL

In 1992, the Canadian apparel industry was comprised of 1,700 establishments employing 87,000 people. Although the industry is located in all provinces, it is especially important in Quebec and Ontario which respectively account for 54 percent and 31 percent of total Canadian industry employment.

The Canadian clothing market in general has enjoyed continued growth. In 1994, retail sales reached US$11.47 billion, up a healthy 4.1 percent from the previous year which saw only a 0.2 percent growth. This growth was due to a decline in cross-border shopping, an improved economy, a cool 1994 spring, and the arrival of several US retailers in Canada.

Products Canadian manufacturers produces all kinds of textiles and apparel, including wool and cotton fabrics, yarn, synthetic fibers, carpets and other floor coverings, sportswear, men and boys' clothing, women's and girls' clothing, child and infant clothing, and fur products.

Competitive Situation The Canadian domestic manufacturers have for some years been threatened by Asian importers on the low-end market and recently by US importers on the high-end market. Canadian companies can compete on price, but are simply being beat on volume and variety. Canadian consumers are demanding more choice which many domestic clothing manufacturers do not offer. The lack of Canadian marketing clout and economies of scale of the US giants invading Canada have forced several domestic clothing companies to give up their home market and concentrate on exports.

In 1992, an estimated 200 Canadian companies were engaged in exporting to some degree. The industry's success in export markets is attributed to its growing reputation for fashion and quality products, and increased access to the large US market, resulting from the Free Trade Agreement (FTA) and, later, the North American Free Trade Agreement (NAFTA). Approximately 90 percent of total Canadian exports are destined for the US. Canadian companies are also adopting more structured exporting strategies such as establishing sales offices in targeted markets, and increasing niche marketing and advertising.

According to industry sources the decline in domestic Canadian production is the result of several factors in the recessionary economy. In addition, faced with high labor and production costs in Canada, and increasing competition from low-priced imports, many Canadian manufacturers specialized local operations and transferred remaining production to foreign subsidiaries or contract operations in low-cost producing countries such as the China, Hong Kong, South Korea, and Taiwan. Additionally, the implementation of the Free Trade Agreement with the US and, later, NAFTA reduced duties on US origin products, and the relatively weak US dollar during the 1991 and 1992 period made US products more competitively priced on the Canadian market.

Despite increased competition from foreign manufacturers, Canadian domestic production accounts for 65 percent of the total market. Men's, women's and miscellaneous clothing together make up about 90 percent of clothing production, with the remaining 10 percent roughly split between children's clothing and fur garments. Canadian manufacturers continue to make adjustments and respond to global competition by investing in new technology, reducing the cost of production, improving customer service and importing products to complement their own domestic production.

TOYS AND SPORTS EQUIPMENT

Sporting Goods

Canadians are traditionally strong in producing hockey equipment and snow and ice athletic equipment. Manufacturers are currently producing hockey equipment that is of a lighter weight but equal durability as existing models. In-line skating is also growing more popular. The Canadian fitness equipment subsector has grown steadily in recent years, and has been unaffected by the slowdown in overall Canadian consumer spending as a result of the recession. Industry sources predict that the recovery of the Canadian economy from the recession and the continuing trend toward increasingly health conscious lifestyles will ensure robust future demand for fitness equipment in Canada. Growth in the industry is forecast at 10 to 12 percent annually during the 1995 to 1997 period. Market demand will be strong for sophisticated exercise units with electronic readouts and monitors, including stationary bicycles, stairclimbers and steppers, treadmills, cross-country ski machines and home gym units. Most Canadian manufacturing facilities of outdoor games equipment are located in Ontario and Quebec, and are Canadian-controlled.

The value of the Canadian market for sporting goods was estimated at US$951 million in 1994, a decline in real terms of nearly three percent from the 1993 market of US$971 million. The decline was attributed to the Canadian economic recession and high unemployment rate. The current recovery, with its accompanying increase in personal disposable income, should stimulate strong growth in demand for sporting goods in Canada during the 1995 to 1997 period. Market demand for fitness equipment should remain buoyant for the next few years as the realization of the need to be physically fit in order to maintain good health becomes increasingly important to Canadians.

Products Sporting goods produced by Canadian manufacturers include hockey equipment; in-line skating equipment; cycling exercise apparatus, equipped with and without electronic monitors; stairclimbers and steppers; mini-steppers; treadmills; rowing machines; cross-country ski exercisers; home gym units; institutional gyms; and free weights.

Competitive Situation The Canadian industry is dominated by skating and hockey equipment, and in-line roller skates. The most popular brands of Canadian hockey equipment and in-line skating equipment are recognized internationally as superior products. Approximately 67 percent of Canadian market demand for sporting goods is satisfied through imports. During the 1995 to 1997 period, total imports are forecast to grow at average annual real rates of 3 to 5 percent. Asian suppliers of low-cost equipment constitute the strongest import competition to the Canadian sporting goods equipment market.

Toys and Games

The Canadian toy and game industry, dominated by US multinational companies, has recently experienced restructuring through mergers, acquisitions, and divestitures as the multinationals have expanded their global distribution networks. This has resulted in greater ownership concentration, with production shifting to Asia. Characterized as a branch plant sector, the Canadian toys and games industry is concentrated in Ontario and Quebec. Production in Canada is mainly through licensing by US firms.

Products Canadian production of toys and games includes a wide range of skill/action games, models, hobby kits, puzzles, construction toys, toy musical instruments, and video games.

Competitive Situation Imports account for 80 percent of the Canadian US$1.04 billion market for toys and games. The market, characterized as nearly recession-proof, was expected to grow at an average annual real rate of 4.5 percent from 1993 to 1995.

VEHICLES AND VEHICLE PARTS

The Canadian automotive industry, valued at US$43 billion, employs 85,000 workers in the auto parts sector and approximately 53,000 assembly workers in Canada. During 1993 and 1994, the auto sector added about 1,000 jobs a month and the potential for growth exists as sales remain healthy.

Vehicles

Canadian production is closely tied to demand in the United States. According to industry experts, in 1994 the US market grew 8.4 percent, yet remains 1.5 million units below its peak potential. Growth in Canada, at 5.8 percent in 1994, lagged behind the US and the Canadian market was two years behind the US recovery. The bottom line is that in 1994 Canada was still at least 300,000 units below its peak potential. How far the production side of the Canadian market will grow will be determined largely by events in the US. However, what appears certain is that Canada will remain an attractive place to assemble vehicles based on cost advantages estimates, such as lower health care costs, and the market-depreciated value of the Canadian dollar.

Products Canadian manufacturers produce passenger vehicles.

Competitive Situation On the sales side, sales in the Canadian automotive industry were up in 1994 after five successive losing years. The 1994 year-end total of 1.23 million units was considerably below the record high of 1.55 million units recorded in 1988, but up 5.2 percent from 1993. Based on demographic data and the fundamental need for new vehicles in Canada, growth in sales of new automobiles in Canada is expected to continue until the market peaks in 1998. The Canadian population is growing in the range of 1.2 to 1.3 percent annually, and the number of drivers is growing at about 1.5 percent. This scenario is also based on the fact that Canadians have been putting off replacing vehicles during the past four or five years, and these vehicles will need to be replaced. The average life of a car in today's market is eight years.

Auto Parts

The Canadian automotive parts market can be divided into two subsectors: original equipment automotive parts used in the production of new vehicles, and automotive aftermarket parts and accessories used to repair and replace auto parts once the car has left the dealership. The Canadian automotive parts market was estimated at US$22.423 billion in 1993, of which imports from the United States totaled US$17.067 billion. The average annual real growth rate through 1997 is estimated at 6 to 8 percent. The best available estimates indicate that aftermarket auto parts account for approximately 15 percent of total automotive parts production in Canada while original equipment auto parts production accounts for the remaining 85 percent of parts production.

Domestic Canadian production of auto aftermarket parts was valued at about US$1.6 billion in 1993. A moderately increasing production trend is stable, despite several plant closures, and is the result of ongoing productivity improvements and the specialization (leading to optimum productivity and cost competitiveness) of the larger North American automotive firms.

Products Canadian automotive parts include air bags, anti-lock brake systems, electronic components, emission control equipment, fuel injection, parts and accessories of bodies, radiators, transmission for motor vehicles.

Competitive Situation The United States has historically been the dominant supplier of aftermarket auto parts imports into Canada. However, in recent years the US share of total imports declined due to the growing number of Japanese cars making in-roads in the Canadian market, and due to North American manufacturers' increased sourcing of components from Japan as part of their globalization strategy for their product lines. Canadian subsidiaries of US-based companies account for 90 percent of domestic production. The remaining manufacturers in Canada are mainly specialized, smaller Canadian-owned companies.

Two of the major changes facing parts producers will be accelerating technology advances and changing distribution channels. Computer controlled flexible manufacturing techniques are very expensive but are needed to produce a wider variety of products to fit all makes and models. Gaining this technological edge will be necessary to remain competitive. There is also considerable pressure, especially in the aftermarket sector, to minimize distribution costs to increase value to the retailer or installer. Manufacturers will continually seek new ways to sell directly to retailers. Consumers of automotive aftermarket products are demanding higher quality and value in the form of extended warranties, superior service, and competitive pricing.

Trade Fairs

INTRODUCTION

Canada hosts an enormous range of trade fairs and expositions that will interest anyone seeking to do business. Whether the aim is to buy Canadian goods or offer your own goods and services for sale in the Canadian market, you will almost undoubtedly find several trade fairs that suit your purposes. Canada is also a major site for international trade fairs for companies from all over the world, attracting exhibitors and buyers from many other countries as well.

The listing of trade fairs in this section is designed to acquaint you with the scope, size, frequency, and length of the events held in Canada and to give you contact information for major organizers. It is by no means comprehensive because of the vast number of trade fairs held in the Canada every year; instead, we have tried to include most of the biggest fairs held on a regular basis in Canada—many are not open to the general public. While every effort has been made to ensure that the information given is correct and complete as of press time, the scheduling of such events is in constant flux. Announced exhibitions may be canceled; dates and venues are often shifted. If you are interested in attending or exhibiting at a show listed here, we urge you to contact the organizer well in advance to confirm the venue and dates and to ascertain whether the event is appropriate for you. (See Tips for Attending a Trade Fair, following this introduction, for further suggestions on selecting, attending, and exhibiting at trade fairs.) When you are deciding whether to participate in a trade fair—as an exhibitor or as an attendee—the information in this chapter will give a significant head start.

Virtually every area of commerce from agriculture to the latest in high-tech is represented in Canadian shows. The trade show listings in the following pages contain information gathered from a number of different sources. These sources include official Canadian government agencies, convention bureaus, and trade show organizers themselves. While the editors have made every effort to verify that the entries are correct and current, it is always advisable to check with a trade show's organizer to ensure that the dates and location are firm.

The fairs taking place in Canada are distributed fairly evenly among the various urban centers. Canada continues to maintain its preeminent position among USA meeting planners booking "offshore" locations. The reasons for this popularity include the wide range of excellent destinations and facilities across the country as well as easy access, safety, cleanliness, service, and cost-effectiveness. Among

CONTENTS

Introduction	111
Exhibiting in Canada	112
Trade Fair Venues in Canada	113
For Further Information	113
Tips for Attending a Trade Fair	114
Trade Fairs in Canada	**117**
Agriculture	117
Automobiles & Motorcycles	118
Bicycles	118
Beauty Industry	118
Business & Commerce	119
Computers, Electronics, & Communications	120
Comprehensive	121
Construction	121
Fashion, Accessories & Textiles	122
Food, Beverage, & Hospitality	123
Gifts Shows	124
Health, Family, Pets, & Lifestyle	125
Home Furnishings & Improvement	126
Industry & Machinery	127
Medical & Dental	129
Professional Services	129
Recreational Hobbies	130
Resources & the Environment	131
Sports & Recreation	132
Technology	134
Transportation	135

the first-tier Canadian cities offering attractive meeting and convention facilities are Toronto, Ottawa/Hull, Montreal, and Vancouver. Second-tier cities also offering such amenities include Quebec City, Calgary, Edmonton, Winnipeg, Victoria, Halifax, Thunder Bay, Saint John, London, and Windsor. Compelling resort areas for meetings include Banff/Lake Louise, Whistler, and the Northwest

The level of sophistication in the trade show world in Canada is very high. Exhibitions range from specialized shows to large multi-industry fairs catering to a wide range of potential clienteles. This allows the prospective attendee to target the specific shows that are most likely to be of interest as well as to be able to attend the more generalized fairs to get the bigger picture. It is important for the new entrant who will be exhibiting to plan on early registration to ensure space availability.

The trade fair listings at the end of this chapter are organized first by product category, then alphabetically by name within a product category. (The product categories are provided in the table of contents.) The "Comprehensive" category represent trade shows that exhibit goods bridging several categories. When reviewing these listings, be sure to explore any related categories. The breadth of products on display at a given fair means that you may want to investigate categories that are not immediately obvious. Many exhibits include the machinery, tools, and raw materials used to produce the products associated with the central theme of a fair. Anyone interested in such items should consider a wide range of the listings.

Each listing provides the name of a trade show, recent or upcoming dates, city, specific site, frequency, and contact information; however, available data varies in its completeness. Although some shows are single events, most occur regularly, usually every two or three years, if not annually. Some events, particularly fashion shows, occur more than once a year. Certain events are repeatedly held in the same location, although some change location periodically. There are actually a number of trade fairs that alternate annually between cities. If the organizer for a particular show has changed since these listings were compiled, trade associations in your area of interest may be able to confirm the information on an upcoming show.

You will invariably discover some variations in the names of the fairs. There are many possible reasons for these variations. Larger fairs may include smaller events, associated congresses or conferences and some of the fairs may use only acronyms to identify themselves. Again, be sure to contact the show organizers for clarification as early as possible.

EXHIBITING IN CANADA

The facilities and procedures for exhibiting in Canada are world-class and thus differ little from other major exhibition centers worldwide. Any information that you receive from show organizers should be reviewed in detail to reduce possible misunderstandings which could cause problems in the future. Ask for names of exhibitors at previous shows so that you can interview them concerning any special circumstances encountered in the past and discover how best to avoid or cope with such situations. Contacting past exhibitors will also give you an opportunity to get the general flavor of a show and perhaps discover some new contacts.

The types of displays that can be used and the size, shape, and location of the space available should be confirmed with the show organizers early in the process. Such information will assist you in making decisions about what to bring from your location and what to rent at the fair site. Some exhibitors have greater success renting displays locally rather than shipping them. Another reason to look into locally rented displays is that they are more likely to be designed specifically for the size and layout of the particular exhibition space. If you do decide to bring your own display materials, make sure that you allow adequate time for everything to arrive. Canadian voltages and plugs are the same as those in the USA.

If you need help in setting up your display, be sure to communicate that clearly to the show organizers well in advance so that the necessary assistance can be arranged. Fax may be the most effective method of communicating with show organizers because it circumvents any problems associated with oral telephone communications and gives you a record of exchanges suitable for review with the organizers should any confusion arise.

For first-time exhibitors in Canada, it's a good idea to hire a customs broker to prepare documentation in advance and act as your group's designated representative when exhibit and display materials arrive in Canada. Customs brokers can provide extras such as special forms, information on which Canada Customs office you should apply to, and counselling on how your meeting or convention might be affected by Canada Customs regulations. Customs brokers can spend time with you to anticipate any needs and avert any problems. As only a few customs brokers specialize in meetings, conventions, and trade shows, you should obtain a list of customs brokers specializing in these areas by contacting the convention and visitors bureau of your host city, the facility where your event is being held or the nearest Canadian Embassy, Consulate and General or Canadian Government Trade Office. Streamlined policies and procedures now allow exhibitors to meet the Canada Customs requirements for bringing their exhibits to Canada with advice from Canada Customs Exhibitions Unit officers. A special program called "The Foreign Organizations Remission Order" is designed to meet the needs of USA organizations holding meetings or incentives in Canada. To obtain a copy of the free booklet "Welcome to Canada: Your Handy Guide to Canada Customs (For Meetings, Conventions, Trade Shows and Exhibitions)," contact the Canadian Embassy or Consulate nearest you or contact Canada Customs Exhibition Unit, PO Box 10, Stn A, One Front St. West, Toronto, ON M5W 1A3; Tel: (416) 973-8007 or Fax: (416) 973-8960.

TRADE FAIR VENUES IN CANADA

Toronto is Canada's young, dynamic, financial metropolis, recognized worldwide as a successful multicultural town with a vibrant economy and welcoming spirit for progress, culture, and new attitudes. More USA-based meetings, conventions, and exhibitions are held in Toronto than in any other foreign city in the world. Overall, the city boasts 1.5 million square feet of meeting space and more than 31,500 first-class hotel rooms. The downtown Meter Toronto Convention Centre is Canada's largest convention spot with 570,000 square feet of meeting and exhibit space, 35 meeting rooms, banquets for 7,500 and within walking distance of 13,000 first-class hotel rooms.

Picturesque Ottawa/Hull, Canada's capital area, blends languages (French and English) and cultures. The metro area shares a compact downtown area, with five short bridges across the Ottawa River linking the two communities. Ottawa's largest conference site is the Ottawa Congress Centre, featuring 70,000 square feet of meeting and exhibit space, 16 meeting rooms, and can accommodate banquets for 4,000.

Montreal is Quebec province's commercial and cultural heart, setting trends in fashion, the arts, nightlife, dining, and entertainment. The city's Place Bonaventure Exhibition Hall houses 255,000 square feet of exhibit space, 9 meeting rooms and banquet catering for 6,000. The venue is part of a downtown complex that includes the 393-room Bonaventure Hilton near to an additional 4,000 hotel rooms within a block. The Palais des Congrès de Montreal (Montreal Convention Centre) features 180,000 square feet of meeting and exhibit space, 33 meeting rooms and banquet catering facilities for 4,620. The centre is within walking distance of 11,000 hotel rooms. Fifteen minutes from downtown, the Stade Olympique with a sizeable 450,000 square feet and restaurant service for up to 53,000 boasts being the largest capacity exhibition facility in Canada.

Set in a prosperous land of rich forests and lush lifestyles, Vancouver is a magnet for new residents from Asia and eastern Canada. The city is in the midst of a building boom that will directly impinge upon future visitors. The BC Place Stadium houses 247,000 square feet of meeting and exhibit space, 10 meeting rooms and a 60,000-seat (world's largest) air-supported domed stadium. The Vancouver Trade and Convention Centre, with its distinctive sail-topped structure has 110,891 square feet of meeting and exhibit space, 21 meeting rooms and a 494-seat IMAX theater, within walking distance of 4,000 first-class hotel rooms.

Wherever your exhibition will be occurring in Canada, you will find excellent connections to and from all major international business sites. Whether you elect to travel by air, rail, water, or by road, Canadian domestic transport systems are equipped to handle the requirements. This strong infrastructure and the diversity of available venues and events creates some fantastic opportunities for doing business in Canada. Good Luck!

FOR FURTHER INFORMATION

The Canadian consulate in your home country is often the best source of information about trade fairs in this region. Each Canadian Province has its own Convention and Visitors Bureau which provides an excellent source of current information. Calendars available from these bureaus can prove invaluable for locating the current trade fairs related to your interests. The listings in this chapter include trade fairs within Canada. Your local consulate can provide the names, locations, and dates of other international shows in which the Canadian business community and government participates. Refer to the "Important Addresses" chapter for listings of embassies, consulates, and trade offices.

There are several other strategies for researching information on trade shows that can help you successfully market your product or service, or help you find suppliers in Canada. If you are interested in exporting to Canada, your country's embassy in Canada may be able to advise you about trade missions or participation in Canadian trade fairs. A number of organizations used in researching this chapter are listed in the "Useful Addresses" section at the end of this introduction. Professional associations in Canada in your area of interest are often excellent sources of information on trade fairs (refer to the "Important Addresses" chapter for listings). Basic reference materials include Exhibit Review magazine and the International Encyclopedia of Associations and Trade Fair Directory (the latter two are Gale Publications).

TIPS FOR ATTENDING A TRADE FAIR

Trade fairs can be extremely effective for making face-to-face contacts and sales or purchases, identifying suppliers, checking out competitors, and finding out how business really works in the host country. However, the cost of attending or exhibiting at such fairs can be high. To maximize the return on your investment of time, money, and energy, you should be very clear about your goals for the trip and give yourself plenty of time for advance research and preparation.

You should also be aware of the limitations of trade fairs. The products on display probably do not represent the full range of goods available on the market. In fact, some of the latest product designs may still be under wraps. While trade fairs give you an opportunity to make face-to-face contacts with many people, both exhibitors and buyers are rushed, which makes meaningful discussions and negotiations difficult.

These drawbacks can easily be minimized if you have sufficient preparation and background information. Allow several months for preparation—more if you first need to identify which fair you should attend. Even under ideal circumstances, you should begin laying the groundwork a year in advance. Don't forget that exhibiting at or attending a fair in a foreign country means more complex logistics: numerous faxes and phone calls involving you, the show operator, and local support people, plus customs and transportation delays.

Participating in international trade fairs, particularly at the outset, should be considered a means of fulfilling long-term goals. At domestic fairs, you may exhibit on a regular basis with short-term sales and marketing goals. But at a foreign fair, it is often best to participate as a way to establish your company, make contacts for the future, and learn more about a market, its consumers, and products. New exporters may not generate high sales, but they often come away with information that assists them with future marketing and product development.

Selecting an Appropriate Trade Fair

Consult the trade fair listings in this book to find some that interest you. Note the suggestions in this chapter for finding the most current calendars of upcoming fairs. Once you have identified some fairs, ask the organizers for literature, including a show prospectus, attendee list, and exhibitor list. Ask plenty of questions! Be sure not to neglect trade organizations in the host country, independent show-auditing firms, and recent attendees or exhibitors. Find out whether there are "must attend" fairs for your particular product group. Fairs that concentrate on other, but related, commodities might also be a good match. Be aware that there may be preferred seasons for trade in certain products.

Your Research Needs to Cover a Number of Points

- *Audience* Who is the intended audience? Is the fair open to the public or only to trade professionals? Are the exhibitors primarily foreigners looking for local buyers or locals looking for foreign buyers? (Many trade fairs are heavily weighted towards one or the other; others may be so oriented to local activity that they are not equipped to cater to international businesspeople.) Decide whether you are looking for an exposition of general merchandise produced in one region, a commodity-specific trade show, or both. Are you looking for a "horizontal"—one that covers a wide range of products—or a "vertical" show—one that covers those involved in the production and marketing of a narrow range of products through all stages of the process

- *Statistics* How many people attended the fair the last time it was held? What were the demographics? What volume of business was done? How many exhibitors were there? How big is the exhibition space? What was the ratio of foreign to domestic attendees and exhibitors

- *Specifics* Who are the major exhibitors? Are any particular publications or organizations associated with the fair? On what categories of products does the fair focus? Does the fair have a general theme or a changing theme? How long has the fair been in existence? How often is it held? Is it always in the same location, or does it move each time? How much does it cost to attend? Are there any separate or special programs connected with the event, and do they require additional entrance fees? What does it cost to rent space?

Before You Go
- If you have not already spoken with someone who attended the fair in the past, be sure to find someone who will give you advice, tips, and general information.
- Make your reservations and travel arrangements well in advance, and figure out how you are going to get around once you get there. Even if the fair takes place in a large city, do not assume that getting around will be easy. If the site is in a small city or a less-developed area, the transportation and accommodation systems are likely to become overburdened sooner than in metropolitan areas.
- For printed materials, pay attention to language barriers and make preparations that will help you overcome them. Assess your literature and decide what should be available in translated or bilingual editions. Have the translation work done by a seasoned professional, particularly if technical terms are used. Consider having a bilingual business card, and add the country and international dialing code information to the address and telephone number. Find out from the show organizers which countries will be represented, and prepare information in the languages of those countries as well, if necessary.
- Do you need hospitality suites and/or conference rooms
   Reserve them as soon as you can.
- Contact people you would like to meet before you go. Organize your appointments around the fair.
- Familiarize yourself with the show's hours, locations (if at multiple venues), and the schedule of events. Then prioritize.

While You Are There
- Wear businesslike clothes that are comfortable. Find out what the norm is for the area and the season.
- Immediately after each contact, write down as much information as you can. Do not depend on remembering it. Several companies now make inexpensive portable business card scanners with optical character recognition (OCR) software to read the information into a contact management program.
- Qualify your prospects before launching into a full presentation. Are you dealing with the right person
   Ask open-ended questions to find out his or her true interests.
- Consider arriving a day early to get fully oriented, confirm appointments, and rest up.
- It is common sense: make sure you take breaks, even if you have to schedule them. You'll end up having far more energy and being more effective.

After the Fair
- Within a week after the fair, write letters to new contacts and follow up on requests for literature. If you have press releases and questionnaires, send them out quickly as well. Even better, send these leads back to your office while you are still at the fair so that your new contacts receive literature on their return home.
- Write a report evaluating your experiences while they are still fresh in your mind. Even if you don't have to prepare a formal report, spend some time organizing your thoughts on paper for future reference. Aim to quantify the results. Did you meet your goals? Why or why not? What would you do differently? What unforeseen costs or problems arose?
- With your new contacts and your experiences in mind, start preparing for your next trade fair.

If You Are Selling
- Familiarize yourself with import regulations for products that you wish to exhibit at the fair.
- Set specific goals for sales leads, developing product awareness, selling and positioning current customers, and gathering industry information. For example, target the numbers of contacts made, orders written, leads converted into sales, visitors at presentations, brochures or samples distributed, customers entertained, and seminars attended. You can also set goals for total revenue from sales, cost-to-return benefit ratio, amount of media coverage, and amount of competitor information obtained.

- Review your exhibitor kit. Is there a show theme that you can tie into? Pay particular attention to the show's hours and regulations, payment policies, shipping instructions and dates, telephone installation policies, security, fire regulations, and extra-cost services?

- Find out about the labor situation at the fair site. Is it unionized, and what are the regulations Will you have to hire your own workers to set up and break down the booth, or can the organizer or showcase facility provide them for you

- Gear your advertising and product demonstrations to the expected target audience. Should you stress certain aspects of your product line? Will you need brochures and banners in different languages? Even if you do not need to translate your current materials into another language, will you need to rewrite them for a different culture? Consider advertising in publications that will be distributed at the fair.

- Plan the display in your booth carefully; you will have only a few seconds to grab the viewer's attention. Secure a location in a high-traffic area—for example, near a door, a restroom, a refreshment area, or a major exhibitor. For banners use copy that is brief and effective. Focus on the product and its benefits. Place promotional materials and giveaways near the back wall so that people have to enter your area, but make sure that they do not feel trapped. If you plan to use videotapes or other multimedia, make sure that you have enough space. Remember to ascertain whether you will need special equipment or equipment designed for different electrical current. Such presentations may be better suited to hospitality suites, because in exhibition halls lights are bright and noise levels high.

- Attend to the details. Order office supplies and printed materials that you will need for the booth. Have all your paperwork—order forms, business cards, exhibitor kit and contract, copies of advance orders and checks, travel documents, and so on—in order and at hand. If you ordered a telephone line, obtain your own host-country-compatible telephone or arrange to rent one. Draw up a schedule for staffing the booth.

- Plan and rehearse your sales pitch in advance, preferably in a space similar to the size of your booth.

- *Don't:* sit, read, smoke, eat, or drink in the booth; badmouth your competitors or complain about the show; ignore prospects while chatting with colleagues; stand with your back to the aisle or lean on booth furniture.

- If you plan to return to the next show, reserve space while you are still on-site.

If You Are Buying

- Familiarize yourself with customs regulations on the products that you seek to purchase and import into your own country or elsewhere. Be sure to get such information on any and all products in which you might be interested.

- Set specific goals for supplier leads and for gathering industry information. For example, target the numbers of contacts made, leads converted to purchases, seminars and presentations attended, and booths visited. Other goals might be a cost-to-return benefit ratio, an amount of competitor information gathered, or a percentage of projected purchases actually made.

- List all the products that you seek to purchase, their specifications, and the quantities you plan to purchase.

- Know the retail and wholesale market prices for the goods in your home country and in the country where you will be buying. List the highest price you can afford to pay for each item and still get a worthwhile return.

- List the established and probable suppliers for each product or product line that you plan to import. Include addresses and telephone numbers and note your source for the information. Before you go, contact suppliers to confirm who will attend and to make appointments.

TRADE FAIRS IN CANADA

Trade Fair	Location & Date (s)	Contact
AGRICULTURE		
Pacific National Exhibition Attendance: 1,100,000 Exhibitors: 700 Consumer-oriented agricultural fair	Vancouver Pacific National Exhibition Annual August 17–September 2, 1996	Pacific National Exhibition Exhibition Park Box 69020 Vancouver, BC V5K 4W3 Tel: (604) 253-2311 Fax: (604) 251-7726
Royal Agricultural Winter Fair Attendance: 330,000 Exhibitors: 4,000 Exhibit space: 758,000 sq. ft. International horse show, agri-products and winter gardens	Toronto Exhibition Place Annual November 5–16, 1996	Royal Agricultural Winter Fair Exhibition Place Toronto, ON M6K 3C3 Tel: (416) 393-6400 Fax: (416) 393-6488
Western Canadian Crop Productions Show Attendance: 7,500 Exhibitors: 190 Exhibit space: 140,000 sq. ft.	Yarmouth, NS Yarmouth Exhibition Grounds Every 2 years April 1997	Saskatoon Prairieland Exhibition Corp. PO Box 6010 Saskatoon, SK S7K 4E4 Tel: (306) 931-7149 Fax: (306) 931-7886
Eastern Canadian Fisheries Exposition Attendance: 6,400 Exhibitors: 130 Exhibit space: 30,000 sq. ft. Commercial fishing processing and harvesting equipment and machinery	Yarmouth, NS Yarmouth Exhibition Grounds Every 2 years April 1997	Master Promotions Ltd PO Box 565 Saint John, NB E2L 3Z8 Tel: (506) 658-0018 Fax: (506) 658-0750
Canadian International Farm Equipment Show Attendance: 50,000 Exhibitors: 600 Exhibit space: 380,000 sq. ft.	Mississauga, International Centre Annual February 4–7, 1997 February 3–6, 1998	Dawn Morris Productions Inc. 1434 Chemong Road, RR 1, #3 Peterborough, ON K9J 6X2 Tel: (705) 741-2536 Fax: (905) 741-2539
Canadian Western Agribition Attendance: 150,000 Exhibitors: 550 Exhibit space: 190,000 sq. ft. Livestock, rodeo, agricultural products and services	Regina Exhibition Park, SK Annual November 23–29, 1996	Canadian Western Agribition Canada Centre Bldg. Box 3535 Regina, SK S4P 3J8 Tel: (306) 565-0565 Fax: (306) 757-9963?E-mail: agribition@sask.sk.ca
SIMA – Salon international de la machine agricole / International Salon of Farm Machinery Attendance: 32,000 Exhibitors: 300 Exhibit space: 350,000 sq. ft.	Montreal Stade Olympique Every 2 years March 20–23, 1996	Productions Jacqueline Vézina inc. 926 Saint-Maurice, #300 Montreal, PQ H3C 1L7 Tel: (514) 861-8241 Fax: (514) 861-8246
Poultry Industry Conference and Exhibition Attendance: 5,000 Exhibitors: 155 Exhibit space: 40,000 sq. ft.	London, ON Western Fairgrounds Annual April 9–10, 1997	Western Fair Association PO Box 4550 London, ON N5W 5K3 Tel: (519) 438-7203 Fax: (519) 679-3124

CANADA Business

Trade Fair	Location & Date (s)	Contact

AUTOMOBILES & MOTORCYCLES

Canadian International Auto Show
Attendance: 250,000
Exhibitors: 125
Exhibit space: 400,000 sq. ft.
Automobiles and trucks

Metro Toronto Convention Centre and Skydome
Annual
February 14–23, 1997

Toronto Automobile Dealers Association
85 Renfrew
Markham, ON L3R 0N9
Tel: (905) 940-2800, 6232
Fax: (905) 940-2804

Canadian International Automotive Show
Attendance: 30,000
Exhibitors: 300
Exhibit space: 85,000 sq. ft.

Alternates between Mississauga and Montreal
Every 2 years
International Centre, Mississauga
April 26–28, 1998

Automotive Industry Association (AIA)
1272 Wellington St.
Ottawa, ON K1Y 3A7
Tel: (613) 728-5821 Fax: (613) 728-6021

Salon international de l'auto de Montreal/Montreal International Auto Show
Attendance: 256,571
Exhibitors: 100
Exhibit space: 355,000 sq. ft.

Montreal
Stade Olympique
Annual
January 10–20, 1997

Corporation des concessionnaires d'automobiles de Montreal inc.
2335 rue Guénette
Saint-Laurent, PQ H4R 2E9
Tel: (514) 331-6571 Fax: (514) 331-2045

Performance World Custom Car Show
Attendance: 50,000
Exhibitors: 250
Exhibit space: 250,000 sq. ft.

Mississauga
International Centre
Annual
March 1997

Mississauga
International Centre
Annual
March 1997

BICYCLES

Toronto International Spring Bike Show
Attendance: 22,000
Exhibitors: 100
Exhibit space: 150,000 sq. ft.
Motorcycles and related products

Mississauga
International Centre
Annual
April 1997

Bar Hodgson Productions Inc.
8780 Baldwin St., RR 1
Ashburn, ON L0B 1A0
Tel: (905) 427-4201 Fax: (905) 655-3812

BEAUTY INDUSTRY

International Beauty Show (Toronto)
Attendance: 7,000
Exhibitors: 165
Hairdressing, beauty and cosmetics

Toronto
Sheraton Centre
Annual
September 1996

Advanstar Communications Expositions
7500 Old Oak Blvd.
Cleveland, OH 44130, USA
Tel: [1] (216) 826-2825 Fax: [1] (216) 826-2801

Congrès d'esthetique
Attendance: 2,000
Exhibitors: 50
Exhibit space: 45,000 sq. ft.
Hairdressing techniques and products

Montreal
Place Bonaventure
September 8–9, 1996

A.M.D.E.C. International Inc. (Association des manufacturiers et distributeurs en esthetique et cosmétique)
4999 rue Sainte-Catherine Ouest, #260
Westmount, PQ H3Z 1T3
Tel: (514) 489-7248 Fax: (514) 489-6183

International Beauty Show (Toronto)
Attendance: 7,000
Exhibitors: 165
Hairdressing, beauty and cosmetics

Toronto
Sheraton Centre
Annual
September 1996

Advanstar Communications Expositions
7500 Old Oak Blvd.
Cleveland, OH 44130, USA
Tel: [1] (216) 826-2825 Fax: [1] (216) 826-2801

Trade Fair	Location & Date (s)	Contact
British Columbia Beauty Convention (Vancouver) Attendance: 3,500 Exhibitors: 50 Exhibit space: 80,000 sq. ft. Professional beauty products	Vancouver Trade and Convention Centre Annual September 22–23, 1996	Allied Beauty Association 2 Sheppard Ave. East, #1001, Box 42 Willowdale, ON M2N 5Y7 Tel: (416) 225-2359 Fax: (416) 223-3610
Quebec grand salon de la coiffure (Montreal) Attendance: 10,500 Exhibitors: 100 Exhibit space: 30,000 sq. ft. Professional beauty products for beauticians and hairdressers	Montreal Place Bonaventure Annual March 2–3, 1997	Allied Beauty Association 2 Sheppard Ave. East, #1001, Box 42 Willowdale, ON M2N 5Y7 Tel: (416) 225-2359 Fax: (416) 223-3610

BUSINESS & COMMERCE

Trade Fair	Location & Date (s)	Contact
The Entrepreneur Expo (Toronto) Attendance: 10,000 Exhibitors: 70 Exhibit space: 35,000 sq. ft. Products and information about starting a business	Toronto Exhibition Place Annual June 1996 (This expo also takes place in Calgary, Edmonton and Vancouver)	SC Promotions Inc. 6890 South Tucson Way, #112 Englewood, CO 80112, USA Tel: [1] (303) 799-9700 Fax: [1] (303) 792-9800
Canada's Merchandise Expo and World Clearance Show Attendance: 5,000 Exhibitors: 250 Exhibit space: 30,000 sq. ft. Surplus merchandise liquidation from wholesalers and distributors	Canada's Merchandise Expo and World Clearance Show Attendance: 5,000 Exhibitors: 250 Exhibit space: 30,000 sq. ft. Surplus merchandise liquidation from wholesalers and distributors	Reed Exhibition Companies Inc. (Toronto) 3761 Victoria Park Ave., #1 Scarborough, ON M1W 3S2 Tel: (416) 491-7565 Fax: (416) 491-5088
World Trade'96 Attendance: 7,000 Exhibitors: 250 Exhibit space: 40,000 sq. ft. Hardware, toys, chemicals and medical products	Toronto Congress Centre Annual October 1996	Canadian International Trade Association 2 Carlton St., #611 Toronto, ON M5B 1J3 Tel: (416) 351-9728 Fax: (416) 351-9911
Salon international de la franchise et des réseaux d'affaires Attendance: 5,000 Exhibitors: 100 Exhibit space: 8,000 sq. ft. Franchising and business networking	Montreal Place Bonaventure Annual October 18–20, 1996	Groupe promexpo inc. 801 rue Sherbrooke Est, 10e étage Montreal, PQ H2L 1K7 Tel: (514) 527-9221 Fax: (514) 527-8449
Business to Business Exposition Attendance: 15,000 Exhibitors: 200 Exhibit space: 67,000 sq. ft. New sources of supply, products, services, industy and business opportunities	Metro Toronto Convention Centre Annual April 1997	Corporate Events Management Inc. 1 Toronto St., #803 Toronto, ON M5C 2V6 Tel: (416) 869-0141 Fax: (416) 869-1660
Salon international le monde des affaires (Montreal)/ Business World Exhibition (Montreal) Attendance: 30,800 Exhibitors: 500 Exhibition space: 220,000 sq. ft.	Place Bonaventure Annual October 1–3, 1996	Martin International Communications U.P. Inc. 500 Place d'Armes, #2910 Montreal, PQ H2Y 2W2 Tel: (514) 288-3931 Fax: (514) 288-0641

CANADA Business

Trade Fair	Location & Date (s)	Contact
Salon international le monde des affaires (Quebec)/Business World Exhibition (Quebec City) Attendance: 25,000 Exhibitors: 70 Exhibit space: 50,000 sq. ft.	Congress Centre Annual January 23–26, 1997	Martin International Communications U.P. Inc. 500 Place d'Armes, #2910 Montreal, PQ H2Y 2W2 Tel: (514) 288-3931 Fax: (514) 288-0641
Canadian Real Estate Association Annual Conference and Exposition Attendance: 2,500 Exhibitors: 100 Exhibit space: 30,000 sq. ft.	Quebec City Parc de l'Exposition de Quebec Annual September 28–October 2, 1996	Canadian Real Estate Association Place de Ville, Tower A 320 Queen St., #2100 Ottawa, ON K1R 5A3 Tel: (613) 237-7111 Fax: (613) 234-2567
Cash and Treasury Management Conference Attendance: 1,300 Exhibitors: 70 Exhibit space: 25,000 sq. ft.?	Toronto Westin Harbour Castle Annual September 29–October 2, 1996	Treasury Management Association of Canada (TMAC) 8 King St. East, #1010 Toronto, ON M5C 1B5 Tel: (416) 367-8501 ext. 5 Fax: (416) 367-3240 E-mail: tmac@inforamp.net
Toronto Franchise and Business Opportunities Expo (Fall/Spring) Attendance: 6,500 Exhibitors: 100	Mississauga International Centre 2 times a year November 1–3, 1996 April 1997	Prestige Promotions PO Box 135 Etobicoke, ON M9C 4V2 Tel: (905) 238-3320 Fax: (905) 277-3397

COMPUTERS, ELECTRONICS & COMMUNICATIONS

Trade Fair	Location & Date (s)	Contact
LAN Expo Attendance: 50,000 Exhibitors: 450 Exhibit space: 160,000 sq. ft. Manufacturers and suppliers of computer network products	Metro Toronto Convention Centre and Skydome Annual July 10–12, 1996	Softbank Comdex Inc. 300 First Ave., #300 Needham, MA 02194, USA Tel: [1] (617) 433-1552 Fax: [1] (617) 449-3434 E-mail: lonergan@comdex.com
Central Canada Exhibition Attendance: 650,000 Exhibitors: 400 Exhibit space: 576,000 sq. ft. High tech general retail and international market exhibition	Ottawa Lansdowne Park Annual August 15–25, 1996	Central Canada Exhibition Association Coliseum Bldg. 1015 Bank St. Ottawa, ON K1S 3W7 Tel: (613) 237-7222 Fax: (613) 230-1748
Client Server Solution, E Mail World and Internet Expo Attendance: 10,000 Exhibitors: 100	Metro Toronto Convention Centre Annual October 1–3, 1996	Digital Consulting Inc. 204 Andover St. Andover, MA 01810, USA Tel: [1] (508) 470-3870 Fax: [1] (508) 470-0526 E-mail: dciconf1@aol.com
COMDEX/Pacrim'97 Attendance: 20,000 Exhibitors: 300 Exhibit space: 45,000 sq. ft. Computer products trade fair	Vancouver Trade and Convention Centre Annual January 1997	Softbank Comdex Inc. 300 First Ave., #300 Needham, MA 02194, USA Tel: [1] (617) 433-1552 Fax: [1] (617) 449-3434 E-mail: lonergan@comdex.com
COMDEX Canada Attendance: 45,000 Exhibitors: 550 Exhibit space: 200,000 sq. ft. Computers and information technology	Metro Toronto Convention Centre and Skydome Annual July 10–12, 1996	Softbank Comdex Inc. 300 First Ave., #300 Needham, MA, 02194, USA Tel: [1] (617) 433-1552 Fax: [1] (617) 449-3434 E-mail: lonergan@comdex.com

Trade Fair	Location & Date (s)	Contact
Softbank Comdex Inc. 300 First Ave., #300 Needham, MA, 02194, USA Tel: [1] (617) 433-1552 Fax: [1] (617) 449-3434 E-mail: lonergan@comdex.com	Frequent, alternating between Toronto (Exhibition Place) and Mississauga (International Centre) Toronto: September 12–15, 1996; February 13–16, 1997; September 11–14, 1997 Mississauga: November 29–December 1, 1996; April 18–20, 1997; November 20–30, 1997	Showfest Productions Inc. 60 St. Clair Ave. West, #5 Toronto, ON M4V 1M7 Tel: (416) 925-4533 Fax: (416) 925-7701
NetCon – Networking and Connectivity Attendance: 7,000 Exhibitors: 150	Metro Toronto Convention Centre Annual September 10–12, 1996	Plesman Expositions and Conferences Inc. 2005 Sheppard Ave. East, 4th Fl. Willowdale, ON M2J 5B1 Tel: (416) 497-9562 ext. 381 Fax: (416) 497-9427 E-mail: events@plesman.com

COMPREHENSIVE

Canadian National Exhibition Attendance: 1,800,000 Exhibitors: 1,000 Educational and service industries, arts, crafts and sciences, and hobbies	Toronto Exhibition Place Annual August 16–September 2, 1996	CNE Association Exhibition Place Toronto, ON M6K 3C3 Tel: (416) 393-6076 Fax: (416) 393-6371

CONSTRUCTION

Construct Canada Attendance: 16,000 Exhibitors: 600 Exhibit space: 200,000 sq. ft. Construction materials, systems and techniques	Metro Toronto Convention Centre Annual December 4–6, 1996	York Expositions 1 Toronto St., #803 Toronto, ON M5C 2V6 Tel: (416) 869-1156 Fax: (416) 869-1660
Ideas '97 – Industry Directed Educational Action Seminars and Shows Attendance: 7,000 Exhibitors: 200 Exhibit space: 340,000 sq. ft.	Mississauga International Centre Annual February 1997	Ideas Seminars and Shows Inc. PO Box 400, Victoria Stn Westmount, PQ H3Z 2V8 Tel: (514) 488-4332 Fax: (514) 489-5505
Expolectric 97 Attendance: 5,000 Exhibitors: 200 Exhibit space: 32,000 sq. ft. National electrical industry exhibition	Expolectric 97 Attendance: 5,000 Exhibitors: 200 Exhibit space: 32,000 sq. ft. National electrical industry exhibition	Corporation des maîtres életriciens du Quebec (CMEQ) 5925 boul Décarie, #100 Montreal, PQ H3W 3C9 Tel: (514) 738-2184 Fax: (514) 738-2192
Computer Integrated Design & Construction Attendance: 15,000 Exhibitors: 750 Exhibit space: 40,000 sq. ft.	Metro Toronto Convention Centre Annual December 4–6, 1996	York Expositions 1 Toronto St., #803 Toronto, ON M5C 2V6 Tel: (416) 869-1156 Fax: (416) 869-1660
Buildex (Vancouver) Attendance: 3,100 Exhibitors: 170 Exhibition space: 60,000 sq. ft.	Vancouver Trade and Convention Center Annual February 1997	R.K. Communications 1755 West Broadway, #306 Vancouver, BC V6J 4S5 Tel: (604) 739-2112 Fax: (604) 739-2124
Buildtech (Ottawa) Attendance: 4,500 Exhibitors: 175 Exhibit space: 40,000 sq. ft.	Lansdowne Park Annual January 1997	National Show Group Inc. 1511 Merivale Road, #250 Nepean, ON K2G 3J3 Tel: (800) 465-0346 ext. 22 Fax: (800) 224-7693

CANADA Business

Trade Fair	Location & Date (s)	Contact
Canadian Construction Show Attendance: 9,822 Exhibitors: 130 Exhibit space: 115,000 sq. ft. Heavy equipment, machinery and materials	Mississauga International Centre Annual February 1997	Southex Exhibitions (Toronto) 1450 Don Mills Road Don Mills, ON M3B 2X7 Tel: (416) 445-6641 Fax: (416) 442-2207
Canadian Home Centre Show Attendance: 2,500 Exibits: 250 Exhibitors: 246 Exhibit space: 50,000 sq. ft. Lumber, building materials and other home center products	Mississauga International Centre November 10–12, 1996	McLean Hart 55 Harbour Square, #607 Toronto, ON M5J 2L1 Tel: (416) 362-9889 Fax: (416) 362-6811
Mecanexpo CIPHEX (Canadian Institute of Plumbing and Heating Exposition) Attendance: 8,000 Exhibitors: 200 Exhibit space: 120,000 sq. ft.	Montreal Place Bonaventure Every 2 years April 24–25, 1997	Canadian Institute of Plumbing and Heating 295 The West Mall, #330 Etobicoke, ON M9C 4Z4 Tel: (416) 695-0447 Fax: (416) 695-0450
WMX – Woodworking Machinery and Supply Expo Attendance: 5,000 Exhibitors: 220 Exhibit space: 70,000 sq. ft.	Mississauga International Centre Every 2 years October 31–November 2, 1997	Reed Exhibition Companies Inc. (Toronto) 3761 Victoria Park Ave., #1 Scarborough, ON M1W 3S2 Tel: (416) 491-7565 Fax: (416) 491-5088
CEX – Canadian Environmental Exposition Attendance: 18,000 Exhibitors: 400 Exhibit space: 100,000 sq. ft. Plumbing, heating, ventilating	Metro Toronto Convention Centre Every 2 years March 22–24, 1996	H.D. Shield and Associations Ltd. 25 Bradgate Road Don Mills, ON M3B 1J6 Tel: (416) 444-5225 Fax: (416) 444-8268
CIPHEX (Canadian Institute of Plumbing and Heating Exposition) West Show Attendance: 3,000 Exhibitors: 900 Exhibit space: 25,000 sq. ft.	Edmonton Northlands Every 2 years October 1997	Canadian Institute of Plumbing and Heating 295 The West Mall, #330 Etobicoke, ON M9C 4Z4 Tel: (416) 695-0447 Fax: (416) 695-0450
Contact Attendance: 2,000 Exhibitors: 120 Exhibit space: 35,000 sq. ft. Electrical products for industrial, commercial and residential markets	Toronto Congress Centre Annual October 16–17, 1996	Ontario Electrical League 2 Lansing Square, #1000 North York, ON M2J 4P8 Tel: (416) 495-0052 Fax: (416) 495-1804

FASHION, ACCESSORIES & TEXTILES

Trade Fair	Location & Date (s)	Contact
Expo-achats Bijouterie Attendance: 2,300 Exhibitors: 150 Exhibit space: 66,000 sq. ft. Jewellery manufacturers, wholesalers and importers	Palais des Congrès de Montreal Annual August 4–6, 1996	Corporation des bijoutiers du Quebec 7585 boul Lacordaire, #1 Saint-Léonard, PQ H1S 2A6 Tel: (514) 251-2410 Fax: (514) 251-1702
Mode Accessories (Fall/Spring) Attendance: 2,500 Exhibitors: 110 Exhibit space: 31,000 sq. ft. Fashion accessories and costume jewellery	Toronto International Plaza Hotel 2 times a year August 11–13, 1996 January 24–28, 1997	Two Plus One Group Inc. 220 Duncan Mill Road, #611 North York, ON M3B 3J5 Tel: (416) 510-0114 Fax: (416) 510-0165

Trade Fair	Location & Date (s)	Contact
Ontario Fashion Exhibitors (November) Attendance: 2,000 Exhibitors: 150 Exhibit space: 45,000 sq. ft. Ready-to-wear fashion and accessories	Toronto Exhibition Place Frequent November 10–12, 1996	Ontario Fashion Exhibitors Inc. 111 Peter St., #219 Toronto, ON M5V 2H1 Tel: (416) 596-2401 Fax: (416) 596-1808
Jewellery World Exposition Attendance: 3,000 Exhibitors: 180 Exhibit space: 130,000 sq. ft.	Metro Toronto Convention Centre Annual August 25–27, 1996	Canadian Jewellers Association PO Box 2021 20 Eglington Ave. West, #1108 Toronto, ON M4R 1K8 Tel: (416) 480-1424 ext. 229 Fax: (416) 480-2342
Salon national de la technologie du vêtement/ National Apparel Technology Show Attendance: 6,000 Exhibitors: 300 Exhibit space: 100,000 sq. ft.	Palais des Congrès de Montreal Every 3 years May 1998	P.R. Charette Inc. 35 Westland Drive Montreal Ouest, PQ H4X 1M3 Tel: (514) 489-8671 Fax: (514) 487-3230
Exposition nord-Américaine fourrure et mode Montreal/ North American Fur and Fashion Exposition Montreal Attendance: 6,000 Exhibitors: 200 Exhibit space: 200,000 sq. ft.	Montreal Place Bonaventure Annual May 1997	Conseil Canadien de la fourrure 1435 rue Saint-Alexandre, #1270 Montreal, PQ H3A 2G4 Tel: (514) 844-1945 Fax: (514) 844-8593
Luggage, Leathergoods, Handbags and Accessories Show Attendance: 3,850 Exhibitors: 150 Exhibit space: 90,000 sq. ft.	Mississauga International Centre Annual April 27–29, 1997	Pro-Sho, Inc. 33 Isabella St., #102 Toronto, ON M4Y 2P7 Tel: (416) 960-8739 Fax: (416) 960-1854

FOOD, BEVERAGE, & HOSPITALITY

Trade Fair	Location & Date (s)	Contact
Les fêtes gourmandes internationales de Montreal Attendance: 400,000 Exhibitors: 100 Exhibit space: 26,000 sq. ft. World tour food festival	Montreal Ile Notre-Dame Annual August 8–18, 1996	Productions Jacqueline Vézina Inc. 926 Saint-Maurice, #300 Montreal, PQ H3C 1L7 Tel: (514) 861-8241 Fax: (514) 861-8246
Hospitality '96 Attendance: 4,500 Exhibitors: 250 Exhibit space: 35,000 sq. ft. Food, beverages, supplies and equipment for food service trade	Winnipeg Convention Centre Annual October 28–29, 1996	Manitoba Hotel Association 155 Carlton St., #1505 Winnipeg, MB R3C 3H8 Tel: (204) 942-0671 Fax: (204) 925-2567
The Canadian Food and Beverage Show Attendance: 9,595 Exhibitors: 350 Exhibit space: 55,000 sq. ft.	Mississauga International Centre Annual February 16–18, 1997	Mississauga International Centre Annual February 16–18, 1997
Bakery Showcase Attendance: 4,000 Exhibitors: 180 Exhibit space: 85,000 sq. ft.	Mississauga International Centre Every 2 years October 27–29, 1996 November 1–3, 1998	Bakery Showcase '96 3300 Don Mills Road, #PH 3 Willowdale, ON M2J 4X7 Tel: (416) 490-7910 Fax: (416) 490-6931

Trade Fair	Location & Date (s)	Contact
Canadian Fine Food Show Attendance: 3,000 Exhibitors: 270 Exhibit space: 60,000 sq. ft.	Mississauga International Centre Annual May 26–28, 1996	Meteor Show Productions Inc. 298 Sheppard Ave. East Willowdale, ON M2N 3B1 Tel: (416) 229-2060 Fax: (416) 223-2826
Hostex - Canadian International Restaurant Hotel/Motel Show Attendance: 15,000 Exhibitors: 550 Exhibit space: 132,000 sq. ft.	Toronto Exhibition Place Annual October 6–8, 1996	Canadian Restaurant and Food Services Association 316 Bloor St. West Toronto, ON M5S 1W5 Tel: (416) 923-8416 Fax: (416) 923-1450
Grocery Showcase Canada (Toronto/Vancouver) Attendance: 8,500/3,300 Exhibitors: 350/250 Exhibit space: 61,000/32,000 sq. ft.	Metro Toronto Convention Centre Annual October 27–29, 1996 Vancouver Trade and Convention Centre Annual April 1997	Canadian Federation of Independent Grocers 2235 Sheppard Ave. East, #902 Willowdale, ON M2J 5B5 Tel: (416) 492-2325 Fax: (416) 492-2347
Salon rendez-vous hotel restaurant/Hotel and Restaurant Rendez-Vous Show Attendance: 17,000 Exhibitors: 400 Exhibit space: 90,000 sq. ft.	Montreal Place Bonaventure Annual February 9–11, 1997	Association des fournisseurs d'hôtels et restaurants inc. 2435 rue Guénette Saint-Laurent, PQ H4R 2E9 Tel: (514) 334-5161 Fax: (514) 334-1279
Ottawa Wine and Food Show Attendance: 25,000 Exhibitors: 200 Exhibit space: 60,000 sq. ft.	Ottawa Congress Centre Annual October 27–29, 1996	Player Expositions International Inc. 255 Clemow Ave. Ottawa, ON K1S 2B5 Tel: (613) 567-6408 Fax: (613) 567-2718
SSA – Super salon de l'alimentation/Super Food Show Attendance: 10,675 Exhibitors: 260 Exhibit space: 60,000 sq. ft. Food products, services and equipment	Palais des Congrès de Montreal Annual April 27–29, 1997	Association des détaillants en alimentation du Quebec inc. (ADA) 300 rue Léo-Pariseau, #1100 Montreal, PQ H2W 2M9?Tel: (514) 982-0104, 289-9669 Fax: (514) 849-3021
Toronto Wine and Cheese Show Attendance: 30,000 Exhibitors: 300 Exhibit space: 100,000 sq. ft.	Mississauga International Centre Annual March 22–24, 1996	Meteor Show Productions Inc. 298 Sheppard Ave. East Willowdale, ON M2N 3B1 Tel: (416) 229-2060 Fax: (416) 223-2826
Hospitality Trade Exposition Attendance: 5,000 Exhibitors: 250	Vancouver Trade and Convention Centre Annual November 4–5, 1996	Lemaire & Co. Event Management Box 248 1857 – 4th Ave. West Vancouver, BC V6J 1M4 Tel: (604) 730-0535 Fax: (604) 736-9116

GIFTS SHOWS

Toronto Fall Gift Show Attendance: 7,500 Exhibitors: 800 Exhibit space: 280,000 sq. ft.	Toronto Exhibition Place Annual September 16–17, 1996	Southex Exhibitions (Toronto) 1450 Don Mills Road Don Mills, ON M3B 2X7 Tel: (416) 445-6641 Fax: (416) 442-2207
One of a Kind 22th Annual Christmas Craft Show & Sale Attendance: 140,000 Exhibitors: 575 Exhibit space: 163,000 sq. ft.	Toronto Exhibition Place Annual November 28–December 8, 1996	Canadian Craft Show Ltd. 21 Grenville St. Toronto, ON M4Y 1A1 Tel: (416) 960-3680 Fax: (416) 923-5624 E-mail cancraft@astral.magic.ca

Trade Fair	Location & Date(s)	Contact
Salon du cadeu de Montreal (Printemps) Attendance: 6,500 Exhibitors: 370 Exhibit space: 120,000 sq. ft. Complete range of gift industry manufactures	Montreal Place Bonaventure 2 times a year March 1997	Southex Exhibitions (Toronto) 1450 Don Mills Road Don Mills, ON M3B 2X7 Tel: (416) 445-6641 Fax: (416) 442-2207
CGTA (Canadian Gift and Tableware Association) Show Attendance: 20,000 Exhibitors: 700 Exhibit space: 250,000 sq. ft.	Mississauga International Centre 2 times a year August 11–15, 1996 January 26–30, 1997	Canadian Gift and Tableware Association (CGTA) 265 Yorkland Blvd., #301 North York, ON M2J 1S5 Tel: (416) 497-5771 Fax: (416) 497-3448
Circle Craft Christmas Market Attendance: 40,000 Exhibitors: 210 Exhibit space: 120,000 sq. ft.	Vancouver Trade and Convention Centre Annual November 7–11, 1996	Pacific Canadian Craft Shows Ltd. 1765 – 8th Ave. West, #101 Vancouver, BC V6J 5C6 Tel: (604) 737-9050 Fax: (604) 736-2186
Vancouver Gift Show (Fall/Spring) Attendance: 7,989 Exhibitors: 410?Exhibit space: 79,000 sq. ft.	BC Place Stadium 2 times a year September 8–10, 1996 March 1997	Southex Exhibitions (Burnaby) 4285 Canada Way Burnaby, BC V5X 1H2 Tel: (604) 433-5121 Fax: (604) 433-9549

HEALTH, FAMILY, PETS, & LIFESTYLE

Trade Fair	Location & Date(s)	Contact
National Pet Industry Trade Show Attendance: 4,500 Exhibitors: 150 Exhibit space: 80,000 sq. ft.	Toronto Congress Centre Annual September 7–8, 1996	PIJAC Canada 189 boul Hymus Pointe-Claire, PQ H9R 1E9 Tel: (514) 630-7878 Fax: (514) 630-7444
Salon des Thérapies alternatives et de la vie au naturel (Montreal) Attendance: 20,000 Exhibitors: 135 Exhibit space: 35,000 sq. ft. Alternative therapies and natural products	Montreal Palais des Congrès Annual October 11–13, 1996	Salon des thérapies alternatives et de la vie au naturel 515 rue Prieur Beauport, PQ G1B 3G1 Tel: (418) 666-9898 Fax: (418) 666-2403
The Great Canadian Maturity and Travel Show (Toronto) Attendance: 42,183 Exhibitors: 150 Issues and products related to senior living	Metro Toronto Convention Centre 2 times a year October 22–23, 1996	Premier Consumer Shows (Toronto) 467 Speers Road Oakville, ON L6K 3S4 Tel: (905) 815-0017 Fax: (905) 815-0511
Canadian Pet Expo Attendance: 30,000 Exhibitors: 130 Exhibit space: 60,000 sq. ft. Consumer oriented pet products and services show	Toronto Exhibition Place Annual October 25–27, 1996	Regional Shows Inc. 100 Sandiford Drive, #41 Stouffville, ON L4A 7X5 Tel: (905) 642-2422 Fax: (905) 642-2660
Parents and Kids Show (Toronto/Vancouver) Attendance: 25,000/11,000 Exhibitors: 300/150 Exhibit space: 190,000/80,000 sq. ft.	Annual at both: Metro Toronto Convention Centre November 8–10, 1996 Vancouver Trade and Convention Centre November 15–17, 1996	Corporate Events Management Inc. 1 Toronto St., #803 Toronto, ON M5C 2V6 Tel: (416) 869-0141 Fax: (416) 869-1660

Trade Fair	Location & Date (s)	Contact
The Wellness Show Attendance: 22,000 Exhibitors: 170 Consumer health and lifestyle show	Vancouver Trade and Convention Centre Annual March 1997	New Rave Productions Inc. 6252 – 6th St. Burnaby, BC V5E 3S4 Tel: (604) 526-9356 Fax: (604) 526-9358
Canadian Natural Product Show Attendance: 1,500 Exhibitors: 200 Exhibit space: 125,000 sq. ft. Organic and natural products, homeopathy, food supplements	Canadian Natural Product Show Attendance: 1,500 Exhibitors: 200 Exhibit space: 125,000 sq. ft. Organic and natural products, homeopathy, food supplements	Canadian Health Food Association 370 Steel Case Road East, #3 Markham, ON L3R 1G2 Tel: (905) 479-6939 Fax: (905) 479-1516

HOME FURNISHINGS & IMPROVEMENT

Trade Fair	Location & Date (s)	Contact
Toronto Summer Furniture Market Attendance: 1,000 Exhibitors: 65 Exhibit space: 300,000 sq. ft.	Mississauga International Centre Annual August 11–14, 1996	Ontario Furniture Manufacturing Association PO Box 85?6900 Airport Road, #200 Mississauga, ON L4V 1E8 Tel: (905) 677-6561 Fax: (905) 677-5212
Can West Hort Show Attendance: 3,500 Exhibitors: 220 Exhibit space: 70,000 sq. ft. Wholesaler horticultural products from Canada and USA	Vancouver Trade and Convention Centre Annual September 25–26, 1996	BC Nursery Trades Association 5830 – 176A St., #101 Surrey, BC V3S 4E3 Tel: (604) 574-7772 Fax: (604) 574-7773
Fall Home Show (Toronto) Attendance: 24,000 Exhibitors: 200	Toronto Exhibition Place Annual October 3–6, 1996	Southex Exhibitions (Toronto) 1450 Don Mills Road Don Mills, ON M3B 2X7 Tel: (416) 445-6641 Fax: (416) 442-2207
Toronto International Home Furnishing Market Attendance: 10,838 Exhibitors: 300 Exhibit space: 250,000 sq. ft. Manufacturers and distributors trade show	Mississauga International Centre Annual January 11–14, 1997	Association des fabricants de meubles du Quebec inc. 1111 rue Saint-Urbain, #101 Montreal, PQ H2Z 1Y6 Tel: (514) 866-3631 Fax: (514) 871-9900
Landscape Ontario Annual Congress Attendance: 8,000 Exhibitors: 350 Exhibit space: 73,000 sq. ft.	Toronto Congress Centre Annual January 14–16, 1997	Landscape Ontario Horticultural Trade Association 7856 Fifth Line South RR #4, Stn Main Milton, ON L9T 2X8 Tel: (905) 875-1805 Fax: (905) 875-3942
BC Home and Garden Show Attendance: 80,000 Exhibitors: 450 Exhibit space: 125,000 sq. ft.	Vancouver BC Place Stadium Annual February 1997	Southex Exhibitions (Burnaby) 4285 Canada Way Burnaby, BC V5X 1H2 Tel: (604) 433-5121 Fax: (604) 433-9549
Salon national de l'habitation et salon de l'aménagement extérieur (Montreal) Attendance: 300,000 Exhibitors: 600 Exhibit space: 250,000 sq. ft. Consumer and trade related home and furnishings show	Montreal Stade Olympique Annual February 28–March 9, 1997	Groupe promexpo inc. 801 rue Sherbrooke Est, 10e étage Montreal, PQ H2L 1K7 Tel: (514) 527-9221 Fax: (514) 527-8449

Trade Fair	Location & Date (s)	Contact
Salon du meuble de Montreal/ Montreal Furniture Market Attendance: 8,000 Exhibitors: 175 Exhibit space: 100,000 sq. ft.	Montreal Place Bonaventure Annual June 14–17, 1997	Association des fabricants de meubles du Quebec inc. 1111 rue Saint-Urbain, #101 Montreal, PQ H2Z 1Y6 Tel: (514) 866-3631 Fax: (514) 871-9900
Canadian Hardware, Housewares, and Home Improvement Show Attendance: 21,579 Exhibitors: 1,527 Exhibit space: 434,000 sq. ft.	Toronto Exhibition Place Annual February 2–4, 1997	Canadian Retail Hardware Association 6800 Campobello Road Mississauga, ON L5N 2L8 Tel: (905) 821-3470 Fax: (905) 821-8946
Canada Central Canadian Pool and Spa Conference and Expo Attendance: 700 Exhibitors: 100 Exhibit space: 47,500 sq. ft.	Toronto Regal Constellation Hotel Annual December 4–5, 1996	N.S.P.I of Canada 7370 Bramalea Road, #5 Mississauga, ON L5S 1M6 Tel: (905) 676-1591 Fax: (905) 676-1598
The Western Hardware and Building Products Show Attendance: 3,000 Exhibitors: 300 Exhibit space: 60,000 sq. ft.	Vancouver Vancouver BC Place Stadium Annual October 6–7, 1996	Canadian Hardware and Housewares Manufacturers' Association 1335 Morningside Ave., #101 Scarborough, ON M1B 5M4 Tel: (416) 282-0022 Fax: (416) 282-0027
IIDEX – International Interior Design Exposition Attendance: 15,000 Exhibitors: 184 Exhibit space: 89,000 sq. ft. Furniture and furnishings, decor, floor and wall coverings	Metro Toronto Convention Centre Annual November 14–16, 1996	Metro Toronto Convention Centre Annual November 14–16, 1996
International Home Show Attendance: 100,000 Exhibitors: 500 Exhibit space: 230,000 sq. ft.	Mississauga International Centre Annual November 11–14, 1996	Showcase Marketing Ltd. 1110 Sheppard Ave. East, #410 North York, ON M2K 2W2 Tel: (416) 512-1305 Fax: (416) 512-9998

INDUSTRY & MACHINERY

Trade Fair	Location & Date (s)	Contact
Salon national de l'automation industriel (S.M.Q.)/Montreal Fabricating and Machine Tool Show (S.M.Q.) Attendance: 12,000 Exhibitors: 300 Exhibit space: 70,000 sq. ft.	Montreal Place Bonaventure Every 2 years May 14–16, 1996	Reed Exhibition Companies Inc. (Montreal) 2564 rue Bergerac Saint-Lazarre, PQ J0P 1V0 Tel: (514) 455-6688 Fax: (514) 455-1771
Plant Maintenance and Engineering Show (C.M.W.) Attendance: 16,000 Exhibitors: 620 Exhibit space: 70,000 sq. ft.	Plant Maintenance and Engineering Show (C.M.W.) Attendance: 16,000 Exhibitors: 620 Exhibit space: 70,000 sq. ft.	Reed Exhibition Companies Inc. (Toronto) 3761 Victoria Park Ave., #1 Scarborough, ON M1W 3S2 Tel: (416) 491-7565 Fax: (416) 491-5088
Plast-Ex Plastics technology, machinery, equipment and raw material suppliers	Mississauga International Centre Every 3 years May 1998	Society of Plastic Industry of Canada (SPI Canada) 1262 Don Mills Road, #104 Don Mills, ON M3B 2W7 Tel: (416) 449-3444 Fax: (416) 449-5685
Canadian Rental Mart Attendance: 2,000 Exhibitors: 120 Exhibit space: 120,000 sq. ft. Tools and equipment rental products and party goods	Mississauga International Centre Annual January 18–19, 1997	AIS Communications Ltd. 145 Thames Road West Exeter, ON N0M 1S3 Tel: (519) 235-2400 Fax: (519) 235-0798

CANADA Business

Trade Fair	Location & Date(s)	Contact
Can Clean Attendance: 3,000 Exhibitors: 125 Exhibit space: 50,000 sq. ft. Sanitation and maintenance chemicals, equipment and industrial supplies	Toronto Exhibition Place Annual April 1997	Canadian Sanitation Supply Association (CSSA) 300 Mill Road, Box G10 Etobicoke, ON M9C 4W7 Tel: (416) 620-9320 Fax: (416) 620-7199 E-mail: cssa@the-wire.com
Canadian Design Engineering Show (C.M.W.) Attendance: 5,000 Exhibition space: 70,000 sq. ft. National show dedicated to the needs of the OE market	Mississauga International Centre Every 2 years October 1–3, 1996	Reed Exhibition Companies Inc. (Toronto) 3761 Victoria Park Ave., #1 Scarborough, ON M1W 3S2 Tel: (416) 491-7565 Fax: (416) 491-5088
Canadian Machine Tool Show (C.M.W.) Attendance: 16,000 Exhibitors: 620 Exhibit space: 140,000 sq. ft.	Mississauga International Centre Every 2 years September 29–October 2, 1997	Reed Exhibition Companies Inc. (Toronto) 3761 Victoria Park Ave., #1 Scarborough, ON M1W 3S2 Tel: (416) 491-7565 Fax: (416) 491-5088
Health and Safety Conference and Trade Show Attendance: 4,000 Exhibitors: 160 Exhibit space: 48,000 sq. ft.	Toronto Regal Constellation Hotel Annual April 1997	Industrial Accident Prevention Association 250 Yonge St., 28th Fl. Toronto, ON M5B 2N4 Tel: (416) 506-8692, 8888 ext. 283 Fax: (416) 506-8880
PAC-EX – Canadian National Packaging Exposition Attendance: 13,552 Exhibitors: 612 Exhibit space: 110,000 sq. ft.	Mississauga International Centre Every 2 years September 15–17, 1997	Packaging Association of Canada 2255 Sheppard Ave. East., # E330 Willowdale, ON M2J 4Y1 Tel: (416) 490-7860 Fax: (416) 490-7844
Weld Expo Canada (C.M.W.) Attendance: 3,641 Exhibitors: 139 Exhibit space: 36,000 sq. ft. Welding equipment and related products	Mississauga International Centre Every 2 years October 1–3, 1996	Reed Exhibition Companies Inc. (Toronto) 3761 Victoria Park Ave., #1 Scarborough, ON M1W 3S2 Tel: (416) 491-7565 Fax: (416) 491-5088
Transfret 96/Transfreight 96 Attendance: 5,000 Exhibitors: 170 Exhibit space: 120,000 sq. ft. Merchandise transportation, handling and logistics	Montreal Place Bonaventure Annual September 10–12, 1996	Groupe Bomart 7493 route Transcanadienne, #103 Saint-Laurent, PQ H4T 1T3 Tel: (514) 337-9043 Fax: (514) 337-1862
Logistech '96 Attendance: 7,000 Exhibitors: 200 Exhibit space: 80,000 sq. ft. Cargo conveyors, cranes, lift trucks and warehousing	Mississauga Every 2 years September 23–25, 1996	Southex Exhibitions (Toronto) 1450 Don Mills Road Don Mills, ON M3B 2X7 Tel: (416) 445-6641 Fax: (416) 442-2207
Expoplast 96 Attendance: 4,000 Exhibitors: 150 Plastics machinery, raw materials, equipment and services	Montreal Place Bonaventure Every 3 years October 8–9, 1996	Society of Plastic Industry of Canada (SPI Canada) 1262 Don Mills Road, #104 Don Mills, ON M3B 2W7 Tel: (416) 449-3444 Fax: (416) 449-5685

Trade Fair	Location & Date (s)	Contact
Mailtech (Montreal/Toronto) Attendance: 2,500 Exhibitors: 200 Exhibit space: 30,000 sq. ft. Mailing industry products and services	Montreal Site to be announced Annual January 1997 Metro Toronto Convention Centre Annual May 1997	Montreal Site to be announced Annual January 1997 Metro Toronto Convention Centre Annual May 1997

MEDICAL & DENTAL

Trade Fair	Location & Date (s)	Contact
Visualize The Next Century Attendance: 500 Exhibitors: 35 Exhibit space: 5,000 sq. ft. High tech medical equipment and software	Edmonton Coast Terrace Inn Annual June 1–6, 1996	Canadian Association of Medical Radiation Technologists 294 Albert St., #601 Ottawa, ON K1P 6E6 Tel: (613) 234-0012 Fax: (613) 234-1097
World Congress of Pharmacy and Pharmaceutical Sciences Attendance: 2,500 Exhibitors: 100	Vancouver Trade and Convention Centre Annual August 31–September 5, 1996	Canadian Pharmaceutical Association 1785 Altavista Drive Ottawa, ON K1G 3Y6 Tel: (613) 523-7877 Fax: (613) 523-0445
Academy of Dentistry Winter Clinic Attendance: 4,000 Exhibitors: 190 Exhibit space: 25,000 sq. ft.	Academy of Dentistry Winter Clinic Attendance: 4,000 Exhibitors: 190 Exhibit space: 25,000 sq. ft.	Toronto Academy of Dentistry 170 Bloor St. West, #902 Toronto, ON M5S 1T9 Tel: (416) 967-5649 Fax: (416) 967-5081
Canadian Cardiovascular Society Annual Scientific Meeting and Exhibition Attendance: 1,800 Exhibitors: 140 Exhibit space: 50,000 sq. ft.	Palais des Congrès de Montréal Annual Oct. 28–Nov. 2, 1996 Oct. 14–18, 1997 (Vancouver) Oct. 20–24, 1998 (Ottawa)	Venue West Conference and Exhibition Services 375 Water St., #645 Vancouver, BC V6B 5C6 Tel: (604) 681-5226 Fax: (604) 681-2503 E-mail: congres@venuewest.com
Ontario Dental Association Annual Spring Meeting Attendance: 7,828 Exhibitors: 200 Exhibit space: 127,000 sq. ft.	Metro Toronto Convention Centre Annual May 1–3, 1997	Ontario Dental Association 4 New St. Toronto, ON M5R 1P6 Tel: (416) 922-3900 Fax: (416) 922-9005
Ontario Hospital Association Convention and Exhibition Attendance: 8,000 Exhibitors: 260 Exhibit space: 200,000 sq. ft.	Metro Toronto Convention Centre Annual November 4–6, 1996	Ontario Hospital Association 150 Ferrand Drive Don Mills, ON M3C 1H6 Tel: (416) 429-2661 ext. 6671 Fax: (416) 429-5651 E-mail: mbatt@oha.com

PROFESSIONAL SERVICES

Trade Fair	Location & Date (s)	Contact
Motivational Marketing Expo Attendance: 5,000 Exhibitors: 240 Exhibit space: 40,000 sq. ft. Marketing-oriented motivational products, corporate awards, business gifts	Metro Toronto Convention Centre Annual September 4–5, 1996	Metro Toronto Convention Centre Annual September 4–5, 1996
The Bottom Line Exhibition Attendance: 3,000 Exhibitors: 72 Exhibit space: 15,000 sq. ft. Accounting-related business management products and services	Metro Toronto Convention Centre Annual September 4–5, 1996	Reed Exhibition Companies Inc. (Toronto) 3761 Victoria Park Ave., #1 Scarborough, ON M1W 3S2 Tel: (416) 491-7565 Fax: (416) 491-5088

CANADA Business

Trade Fair	Location & Date(s)	Contact
Canadian Bar Association Convention and Exhibition Attendance: 3,000 Exhibitors: 100	Vancouver Trade and Convention Centre Annual August 26–29, 1996	International Trade Show Services 20 Butterick Road Toronto, ON M8W 3Z8 Tel: (416) 252-7791 Fax: (416) 252-9848
Print Pacific Attendance: 10,000 Exhibitors: 150 Exhibit space: 120,000 sq. ft. Printing and graphic equipment, 7-color printing presses	Abbotsford, BC Tradex Exhibition Centre Every 2 years October 18–20, 1996	Great West Expo 279 Midpark Way SE, #201 Calgary, AB T2X 1M2 Tel: (403) 254-9222 Fax: (403) 256-8495
Print Ontario '96 Attendance: 10,000 Exhibitors: 150 Exhibit space: 1,00,000 sq. ft. Printing, graphic arts show geared to small and medium-size printers	Toronto Exhibition Place Every 2 years November 9–11, 1996	Ontario Trade Shows Ltd 1606 Sedlescomb Drive, #8 Mississauga, ON L4X 1M6 Tel: (905) 625-7070 Fax: (905) 625-4856
The Property Management Exposition and Conference Attendance: 15,000 Exhibitors: 750 Exhibit space: 67,000 sq. ft.	Metro Toronto Convention Centre Annual December 4–6, 1996	York Expositions 1 Toronto St., #803 Toronto, ON M5C 2V6 Tel: (416) 869-1156 Fax: (416) 869-1660
The Real Estate Show Attendance: 15,000 Exhibitors: 100 Exhibit space: 30,000 sq. ft. Development, leasing and management	Metro Toronto Convention Centre Annual December 4, 1996	York Expositions 1 Toronto St., #803 Toronto, ON M5C 2V6 Tel: (416) 869-1156 Fax: (416) 869-1660
Congrès annuel de l'appo Attendance: 2,000 Exhibitors: 150 Exhibit space: 40,000 sq. ft. Advertising related manufacturers and importers of promotional objects	Palais des Congrès de Montreal Annual February 8–12, 1997	Association de la publicité par l'objet du Canada inc. 4920 boul de Maisonneuve Ouest, #305 Westmount, PQ H3Z 1N1 Tel: (514) 489-5359 Fax: (514) 489-7760
Televolution Attendance: 12,000 Exhibitors: 100 Exhibit space: 120,000 sq. ft. Marketing and telemarketing products and services	Metro Toronto Convention Centre Annual March 1997	MW Productions 88 Courcelette Road, #4 Scarborough, ON M1N 2T2 Tel: (416) 691-6526 Fax: (416) 691-6928
Graphic Trade Show Attendance: 25,000 Exhibitors: 250 Exhibit space: 120,000 sq. ft.	Mississauga International Centre Every 2 years November 1997	Southex Exhibitions (Toronto) 1450 Don Mills Road Don Mills, ON M3B 2X7 Tel: (416) 445-6641 Fax: (416) 442-2207

RECREATIONAL HOBBIES

Trade Fair	Location & Date(s)	Contact
Canadian Sewing and Needlecraft Association Trade Show Attendance: 3,000 Exhibitors: 250 Exhibit space: 60,000 sq. ft.	Toronto Congress Centre Annual April 13–15, 1996	Canadian Sewing and Needlecraft Association 501 Annette St. Toronto, ON M6P 1S1 Tel: (416) 767-7501 Fax: (416) 767-7069

Trade Fair	Location & Date (s)	Contact
Canadian Toy and Decoration Fair Attendance: 3,500 Exhibitors: 1,120 Exhibit space: 215,000 sq. ft.	Metro Toronto Convention Centre Annual January 26–29, 1997	Canadian Toy Association (CTA) PO Box 294 Kleinburg, ON L0J 1C0 Tel: (905) 893-1689 Fax: (905) 893-2392

RESOURCES & THE ENVIRONMENT

Trade Fair	Location & Date (s)	Contact
Wood Tech Canada '96 Attendance: 9,000 Exhibitors: 325 Exhibit space: 80,000 sq. ft. Forestry, logging and sawmill equipment	Vancouver BC Place Stadium Every 2 years September 25–27, 1996	Southex Exhibitions (Burnaby) 4285 Canada Way Burnaby, BC V5X 1H2 Tel: (604) 433-5121 Fax: (604) 433-9549
Natural Gas Industrial Technology Showcase (C.M.W.) Attendance: 3,641 Exhibitors: 102 Exhibit space: 29,000 sq. ft.	Mississauga International Centre Every 2 years October 1–3, 1996	Reed Exhibition Companies Inc. (Toronto) 3761 Victoria Park Ave., #1 Scarborough, ON M1W 3S2 Tel: (416) 491-7565 Fax: (416) 491-5088
Salon de l'environnement des amériques (Américana 97) Attendance: 5,000 Exhibitors: 340 Exhibit space: 100,000 sq. ft. Air, water and soil quality control, recycling and waste management	Palais des Congrès de Montreal Every 2 years March 18–21, 1997	Association Québécoise des techniques de l'environnement 911 Jean-Talon Est, #220 Montreal, PQ H2R 1V5 Tel: (415) 270-7110 Fax: (514) 270-7154
Prospectors and Developers Association of Canada International Convention and Trade Show Attendance: 4,000 Exhibitors: 210 Exhibit space: 66,000 sq. ft. Mining-related equipment and services	Toronto Royal York Hotel Annual April 1997	Prospectors and Developers Association of Canada 34 King St. East, 9th Fl. Toronto, ON M5C 2X8 Tel: (416) 362-1969 Fax: (416) 362-0101
Annual Truck Loggers Association Trade Show and Conference Attendance: 12,500 Exhibitors: 200 Exhibit space: 47,000 sq. ft.	Vancouver Trade and Convention Center Annual January 1997	Truck Loggers Association 815 West Hasting St., #725 Vancouver, BC V6C 1B4 Tel: (604) 684-4291 Fax: (604) 684-7134
CETECH – Canadian Environmental Technology Showcase (C.M.W.) Attendance: 16,000 Exhibit space: 70,000 sq. ft.	Mississauga International Centre Every 2 years October 1–3, 1996	Reed Exhibition Companies Inc. (Toronto) 3761 Victoria Park Ave., #1 Scarborough, ON M1W 3S2 Tel: (416) 491-7565 Fax: (416) 491-5088
CETECH – Canadian Environmental Technology Showcase (S.M.Q.) Attendance: 13,000 Exhibitors: 85 Exhibit space: 10,000 sq. ft.	Montreal Place Bonaventure Every 2 years May 13–15, 1997	Reed Exhibition Companies Inc. (Toronto) 3761 Victoria Park Ave., #1 Scarborough, ON M1W 3S2 Tel: (416) 491-7565 Fax: (416) 491-5088

Trade Fair	Location & Date (s)	Contact
Semaine international du papier/International Paper Week Attendance: 15,000 Exhibitors: 450 Exhibit space: 190,000 sq. ft. Pulp and paper technologies	Palais des Congrès de Montreal Annual January 1997	Canadian Pulp and Paper Association 1155 rue Metcalfe, #1900 Montreal, PQ H3B 4T6 Tel: (514) 866-6621 Fax: (514) 866-3035 E-mail: ctpacda@ibm.net
GLOBE – International Environmental Industry Trade Fair and Conference Attendance: 10,000 Exhibitors: 450 Exhibit space: 50,200 sq. ft.	Vancouver Trade and Convention Centre Every 2 years March 26–29, 1996	Globe West Productions World Trade Centre 999 Canada Place, #504 Vancouver, BC V6C 3E1 Tel: (604) 775-1994 Fax: (604) 666-8123 E-mail: info@globe.apfnet.org
Toronto Environmental Trade Show and Conference Attendance: 5,000 Exhibitors: 160 Exhibit space: 30,000 sq. ft. Environmental control and hazardous materials management	Mississauga International Centre Annual May 6–7, 1996	Canadian Exhibition Management Inc. 4936 – 87th St., #240 Edmonton, AB T6E 5W3 Tel: (403) 469-2400 Fax: (403) 469-1398
Canadian Environmental Technology Showcase (C.M.W.) Attendance: 16,000 Exhibit space: 70,000 sq. ft.	Mississauga International Centre Every 2 years October 1–3, 1996	Reed Exhibition Companies Inc. (Toronto) 3761 Victoria Park Ave., #1 Scarborough, ON M1W 3S2 Tel: (416) 491-7565 Fax: (416) 491-5088
Salon des technologies de l'environnement/Canadian Environmental Technology Showcase (S.M.Q.) Attendance: 13,000 Exhibitors: 85 Exhibit space: 10,000 sq. ft.	Montreal Place Bonaventure Every 2 years May 13–15, 1997	Reed Exhibition Companies Inc. (Montreal) 2564 rue Bergerac Saint-Lazarre, PQ J0P 1V0 Tel: (514) 455-6688 Fax: (514) 455-1771

SPORTS & RECREATION

Trade Fair	Location & Date (s)	Contact
Toronto In-water Boat Show Attendance: 10,000 Exhibitors: 120 Exhibit space: 50,000 sq. ft.	Toronto Outer Harbor Marina Annual September 13–16, 1996	National Marine Manufacturers Association 370 King St. West, #804 Toronto, ON M5V 1J9 Tel: (416) 591-6772 Fax: (416) 591-3582
Canadian Golf Merchandise Show Exhibitors: 150 Exhibit space: 100,000 sq. ft.	Mississauga International Centre October 16–18, 1996	Canadian Professional Golf Association (Ontario) 705 Progress, #101 Scarborough, ON M1H 2X1 Tel: (416) 438-0970 Fax: (416) 438-8477
BC Professional Golfer's Association Trade Show Attendance: 1,000 Exhibitors: 105 Exhibit space: 29,100 sq. ft.	Vancouver Trade and Convention Centre Annual October 28–November 1, 1996	Canadian Professional Golfer's Association (Vancouver) 12180 Horseshoe Way, #4 Richmond, BC V7A 4V5 Tel: (604) 274-7822 Fax: (604) 275-8486
Toronto International Boat Show Attendance: 100,000 Exhibitors: 400 Exhibit space: 360,000 sq. ft.	Toronto Exhibition Place Annual November 1–19, 1997	National Marine Manufacturers Association 370 King St. West, #804 Toronto, ON M5V 1J9 Tel: (416) 591-6772 Fax: (416) 591-3582

Trade Fair	Location & Date (s)	Contact
Exposition de ski surf des neiges et plein air Attendance: 3,000 Exhibitors: 170 Exhibit space: 238,000 sq. ft. Ski industry, snow boards and related products and services	Montreal Place Bonaventure Annual February 23–26, 1997	Association nationale de l'industrie du ski 8250 boul Décarie, #340 Montreal, PQ H4P 2P5 Tel: (514) 737-1672 Fax: (514) 737-0724
The Toronto International Bicycle Show Attendance: 20,000 Exhibitors: 100 Exhibit space: 110,000 sq. ft.	Toronto Exhibition Place Annual March 1997	Canadian Shows and Special Events Inc. 1 Yonge St., #1801 Toronto, ON M5E 1W7 Tel: (416) 363-9035 Fax: (416) 369-0515
British Columbia Great Outdoors Show Attendance: 22,500 Exhibitors: 200 Exhibit space: 94,500 sq. ft.	Vancouver Pacific National Exhibition Annual February 20–23, 1997	Canadian National Sportsmen's Shows (Burnaby) 5945 Kathleen Ave., #501 Burnaby, BC V5H 4J7 Tel: (604) 439-9119 Fax: (604) 439-0722
Exposition de l'industrie de la chasse et sports de tir/ Canadian Hunting Trade Show Attendance: 4,000 Exhibits: 150 Exhibit space: 25,000 sq. ft. Hunting and fishing	Hull, Quebec Palais des Congrès Annual February 16–18, 1997	Canadian Sporting Arms and Ammunition Association PO Box 235 Cobourg, ON K9A 4K5 Tel: (416) 373-1623 Fax: (416) 373-1706 E-mail: pywko7a@prodigy.com
Toronto Ski Show Attendance: 35,000 Exhibitors: 200 Exhibit space: 73,000 sq. ft.	Exhibition Place Annual October 17–20, 1996	Canadian National Sportsmen's Shows (Toronto) 703 Evans Ave., #202 Toronto, ON M9C 5E9 Tel: (416) 695-0311 Fax: (416) 695-0381
Toronto Sportsmen's Show Attendance: 170,000 Exhibitors: 600 Exhibit space: 236,000 sq. ft. Camping, fishing, boating, vacation exhibits and products	Exhibition Place Annual March 7–16, 1997	Exhibition Place Annual March 7–16, 1997
Salon camping, plein-air, chasse et pêche de Montreal/ Montreal Sportsmen's Show Attendance: 60,000 Exhibitors: 270 Exhibit space: 200,000 sq. ft.	Montreal Place Bonaventure Annual April 2–6, 1997	Salons nationaux des sportsmen au Canada 1155 rue Metcalfe, #1630 Montreal, PQ H3B 2V6 Tel: (514) 866-5409 Fax: (514) 866-4092
Hunting and Outdoor Show Attendance: 35,000 Exhibitors: 250 Exhibit space: 120,000 sq. ft.	Mississauga International Centre Annual September 6–8, 1996	Ontario Out of Doors Magazine 777 Bay St., 6th Fl. Toronto, ON M5W 1A7 Tel: (416) 596-5908 Fax: (416) 596-2517
The Canadian Outdoor Retailers Show Exhibitors: 200 Exhibit space: 121,000 sq. ft.	Toronto Exhibition Place Annual September 8–10, 1996	Canadian Shows and Special Events Inc. 1 Yonge St., #1801 Toronto, ON M5E 1W7 Tel: (416) 363-9035 Fax: (416) 369-0515
Vancouver Ski Show Attendance: 30,000 Exhibitors: 200 Exhibit space: 112,000 sq. ft.	Vancouver BC Place Stadium Annual October 25–27, 1996	Vancouver Ski Foundation 1367 West Broadway, #306 Vancouver, BC V6H 1G9 Tel: (604) 878-0754 Fax: (604) 878-0754

134 **CANADA** Business

Trade Fair	Location & Date (s)	Contact

TECHNOLOGY

Trade Fair	Location & Date (s)	Contact
Telecon '96 (Toronto) Attendance: 10,000 Exhibitors: 220 Exhibit space: 75,000 sq. ft. Telecommunication industrial products and services	Metro Toronto Convention Centre Annual October 8–10, 1996	International Trade Show Services 20 Butterick Road Toronto, ON M8W 3Z8 Tel: (416) 252-7791 Fax: (416) 252-9848
Imaging Canada Attendance: 3,000 Exhibitors: 100 Exhibit space: 15,000 sq. ft. Document management, micrographis and electronic imaging	Metro Toronto Convention Centre Annual October 22–23, 1996	Canadian Information and Image Management Society 86 Wilson St. Oakville, ON L6K 3G5 Tel: (905) 849-8212 Fax: (905) 338-8926
CCTA (Canadian Cable Television Association) Convention and Cablexpo Attendance: 1,600 Exhibitors: 75 Exhibit space: 40,000 sq. ft.	Metro Toronto Convention Centre Annual May 11–14, 1997	Canadian Cable Television Association 360 Albert St., #1010 Ottawa, ON K1R 7X7 Tel: (613) 232-2631 Fax: (613) 232-2137
Multimedia Attendance: 18,000 Exhibitors: 350 Merging technologies in computers, design, photography, film and video	Metro Toronto Convention Centre Annual May 22–25, 1996	Multimedia Trade Show Inc. 70 Villarboit Crescent, #7 Concord, ON L4K 4C7 Tel: (905) 660-2491 Fax: (905) 660-2492 E-mail: exhibit sales@multi-media.ca
Focus On Video Attendance: 6,500 Exhibitors: 125 Exhibit space: 80,000 sq. ft. Trade and education-oriented information and displays of new video products	Mississauga International Centre September 7–8, 1996	Promex Productions Inc. 118 Indian Road, 2nd Fl. Toronto, ON M6R 2V4 Tel: (416) 531-2121 Fax: (416) 531-2194
CCBE Broadcast Equipment Trade Show Attendance: 4,000 Exhibitors: 51 Exhibit space: 60,000 sq. ft. Radio and television broadcast equipment	Toronto Skyway Trade and Convention Centre Annual November 1996	Central Canada Broadcast Engineers (CCBE) 104 Strathcona Ave. Ottawa, ON K1S 1X6 Tel: (800) 481-4649 Fax: (800) 481-4649
VPM Direct (Fall) Attendance: 7,000 Exhibitors: 85 Exhibit space: 60,000 sq. ft. All levels of industrial broadcast for professional video producers	Mississauga International Centre 2 times a year November 19–20, 1996	VPM Publishing Ltd. 1350 Hurontario St. Mississauga, ON L5G 3H4 Tel: (905) 271-1700 Fax: (905) 271-9964
Communications Expo – Uniglobe Attendance: 10,000 Exhibitors: 200 Exhibit space: 25,000 sq. ft. Communications equipment and services	Calgary, AB Calgary Exhibition and Stampede Annual February 5–6, 1997	Uniglobe International Exhibition Ltd. 4936 – 87th St., #240 Edmonton, AB T6E 5W3 Tel: (403) 469-2400 Fax: (403) 469-1398

Trade Fair	Location & Date (s)	Contact
Travel Technology '97 Attendance: 2,000 Exhibitors: 80 Exhibit space: 20,000 sq. ft. Automation in the travel industry	Toronto International Plaza Hotel Annual March 1997	Baxter Travel Group 310 Dupont St. Toronto, ON M5R 1V9 Tel: (416) 968-7252 Fax: (416) 968-2377
The Canadian High Technology Show Attendance: 5,500 Exhibitors: 225 Exhibit space: 40,000 sq. ft. Electronics and high technology	Mississauga International Centre Annual September 17–18, 1996	Reed Exhibition Companies Inc. (Toronto) 3761 Victoria Park Ave., #1 Scarborough, ON M1W 3S2 Tel: (416) 491-7565 Fax: (416) 491-5088
Security Canada (Central/West/East) Attendance: 2,200/700/1,500 Exhibitors: 120/50/100 Exhibit space: 30,000/10,000/40,000 sq. ft. Alarm and fire monitoring systems and equipment	Annual at each location: (Central) Toronto Congress Centre October 22–24, 1996?(West) Vancouver Bayshore Westin February 1997 (East) Montreal Palais des Congrès de Montreal April 1997	CANASA – Canadian Alarm and Security Association 610 Alden, #201 Markham, ON L3R 9Z1 Tel: (905) 513-0622 Fax: (905) 513-0624

TRANSPORTATION

Trade Fair	Location & Date (s)	Contact
Expocam 96 Attendance: 10,000 Exhibitors: 200 Exhibit space: 80,000 sq. ft Truck parts and accessories, tires and trailers	Montreal Place Bonaventure Every 2 years October 23–25, 1996	Southex Exhibitions (Toronto) 1450 Don Mills Road Don Mills, ON M3B 2X7 Tel: (416) 445-6641 Fax: (416) 442-2207
Trans-Expo '96?Attendance: 1,200 Exhibitors: 115 Exhibit space: 60,000 sq. ft. Public transportation products, services and technology	Vancouver Trade and Convention Centre Annual November 19, 1996	Canadian Urban Transit Association and Canadian Bus Association 55 York St., #901 Toronto, ON M5J 1R7 Tel: (416) 365-9800 Fax: (416) 365-1295 E-mail: cutaactu@ican.ca
Canadian Business Aircraft Association Convention and Trade Show Attendance: 800 Exhibitors: 60 Exhibition space: 20,000 sq. ft.	Ottawa Congress Centre Annual June 4–6, 1996	Canadian Business Aircraft Association 50 O'Connor St., #1317 Ottawa, ON K1P 6L2 Tel: (613) 236-5611 Fax: (613) 236-2361
Truckcan Attendance: 13,000 Exhibitors: 262 Exhibit space: 89,000 sq. ft. Truck equipment, parts & services	Mississauga International Centre Every 2 years October 31–November 2, 1996	Southex Exhibitions (Toronto) 1450 Don Mills Road Don Mills, ON M3B 2X7 Tel: (416) 445-6641 Fax: (416) 442-2207

Business Travel

INTRODUCTION

Combining sophisticated metropolitan cities with expansive wilderness and barren planes, Canada provides international businesspeople with unique problems and opportunities. Thankfully, this immense country is readily accessible to businesspeople, with generally excellent transportation, accommodations, communications, dining, entertainment, shopping, public health standards and medical services.

Those familiar with business travel in the United States with find travel arrangements in Canadian cities to be both convenient and comfortable. In many regions, government sponsored offices are set up to aid travelers in making hotel accommodations; most local residents, from your hotel's concierge to passers by on the street, are genuinely helpful with restaurant recommendations or directions.

NATIONAL TRAVEL OFFICES WORLDWIDE

Canadian Embassies, consulates and travel offices can provide you with a range of travel information, including information on visas, business convention assistance as well as guides to hotels, restaurants and entertainment. They are generally very courteous and efficient. Most offices are opened business hours and are closed on Canadian national holidays.

United States

Atlanta 400 South Omni International, Atlanta, GA 30303, USA; [1] (404) 577-7445.

Boston Three Copley Place, Suite 400, Boston, MA 02116, USA; [1] (617) 536-1731.

Buffalo One Marine Midland Center, Suite 3550, Buffalo, NY 14203, USA; [1] (716) 852-1345.

Chicago 310 South Michigan Avenue, Chicago, IL 60604, USA; [1] (312) 616-1860.

Cleveland 55 Public Square, 10th Fl., Cleveland, OH 44113, USA; [1] (216) 771-1687.

Dallas St. Paul Tower, 17th fl., 750 St. Paul St. Dallas, TX 75201, USA; [1] (214) 922-9815.

Detroit 1900 First Federal Bldg., 1001 Woodward Ave., Detroit, MI 48226, USA; [1] (313) 963-8636.

Los Angeles 510 W. Sixth St., Los Angeles, CA 90014, USA; [1] (213)622-4292.

Minneapolis 15 South 5th Street, 12th Floor, Minneapolis, MN 55402, USA; [1] (612) 332-4314.

New York 1251 Avenue of the Americas, Room 1035, New York, NY 10020, USA; [1] (212) 596-1600.

CONTENTS

Introduction	137
National Travel Offices Worldwide	137
Visa and Passport Requirements	138
Business Visas	138
Immigrants	138
Air Travel Times	139
Work Permits	139
Immunization	139
Climate	139
Business Attire	140
Airlines	140
Time Changes	140
Customs Entry	140
Foreign Exchange (Personal)	141
Tipping	141
Access to Cities From Airports	141
Accommodations	142
Cuisine	145
Local Customs Overview	146
Domestic Transportation	147
Business Hours	148
Communications	149
Staying Safe and Healthy	150
Holidays	151
Emergency Information	151
Departure Procedures	151
Useful Telephone Numbers	152
Best Travel Information	152

Philadelphia 3 Parkway, Suite 1620, Philadelphia PA 19102, USA [1] (215) 567-1709.
San Francisco One Maritime Plaza, Suite 1160 San Francisco, CA 94111, USA [1] (415) 981-8541.
Seattle 412 Plaza 600, Sixth and Stewart, Seattle, WA 98101, USA; [1] (206) 443-1777.

Europe

Denmark Embassy, Kr Bernikowsgrade 1, 1105 Copenhagen K; Tel: [45] 33-12-22-99.
France Embassy, 35 Avenue Montagne, 75008 Paris; Tel: [33] 1-44-43-29-00.
Germany Government Trade Office, Immermannstrasse 65D, 4000 Dusseldorf 1.
Ireland Embassy, 65 St. Steven's Green, Dublin 2; Tel: [353] (1) 3-478-1988.
Italy Embassy, via G B de Rossi 27, 00161 Rome; Tel: [39] (6) 44598-1.
Netherlands Embassy, Sophialaan 7, 2514 JP The Hague; Tel: [31] (70) 361-4111.
Spain Embassy, Edificio Goya, Calle Nunez de Balboa 35, Madrid; Tel: [34] (1) 430-4300.
Sweden Embassy, Tegelbacken 4 (7th Floor), Stockholm; Tel: [46] (8) 613-9900.
Switzerland Embassy, Kirchenfeldstrasse 88, 3005 Berne; Tel: [41] (31) 352-63-81.
UK Canada House Trafalgar Square, Cockspur St., London; SW1Y 5BJ. Tel: [44] (171) 258-6600.

Australia-Asia

Australia High Commission, Commonwealth Ave, Canberra ACT 2600; Tel: [61] (6) 273-3844.
Canadian Consulate General, 111 Harrington St., Level 5, Quay West, Sydney, New South Wales 2000; Tel: [61] (2) 9-364-3000; Visa Immigration Office Tel: [61] (2) 9-364-3050.
Consulate of Canada, 11th Floor, National Mutual Centre, 111 George's Terrace, Perth, Western Australia 6000 Tel: [61] (9) 321-1151.
Japan Embassy, 3-38 Akasaka 7-Chome, Minato-ku, Tokyo 107; Tel: [81] (3) 3408-2101/8.
New Zealand High Commission, 61 Molesworth St., Thorndon, Wellington; Tel: [64] (4) 473-9577.
Taiwan Trade Office, 13th Floor, 365 FU SING North Road, Taipei 10483.

VISA AND PASSPORT REQUIREMENTS

Business travelers from nearly all Western countries do not need to obtain a visa to enter Canada. Those coming from developing or third world countries, Eastern European nations as well as communist countries will need to arrange for a visa as will citizens of Portugal and South Africa.

Passports are required for visitors of all nations other than the United States. Permanent residents of the United States should carry their Alien Registration Card.

If you are intending to stay in Canada for more than six months, you must register with the Canadian authorities. If your stay is extended beyond six months while already in Canada, you must apply for appropriate permission at an immigration office.

Anyone who is not a Canadian citizen or permanent resident of Canada must have an employment authorization before being admitted to Canada to take employment, regardless of the duration.

BUSINESS VISAS

A business visa may be required if you intend a prolonged stay in Canada. Restrictions regarding business visas vary widely between nations. It is recommended to consult with the consulate or embassy in your city for current and specific information.

For US businesspeople, the CFTA facilitates the movement of US and Canadian business persons across each country's borders through streamlined procedures. The streamlined border-crossing procedures assure that qualified persons will be permitted entry on a temporary basis. Business persons applying under any of the four categories (Professional, Trader/Investor, Business Visitor, and Intra-Company Transferee) must be US citizens. At the time of entry a verbal declaration of citizenship may be sufficient. In those cases where business travelers are required to show proof of citizenship, a passport, citizenship certificate, or a birth certificate is acceptable. Business persons and dependents also must meet other admission requirements of the Canadian Immigration Act.

The temporary entry of business related material (printed material, commercial samples, blueprints, charts, audio- visual material, and play back or projection equipment) may be subject to the full rate of duty and tax, a portion thereof, or may be duty and tax-free. The amount of duty and tax payable depends on the length of the visit, the items entered, and the end use. If the goods are eligible for free entry, a refundable security deposit —in the form of cash or bond—may be required by Canada Customs.

IMMIGRANTS

Canada operates an immigration program designed to attract experienced businesspeople who will create jobs and boost the local economy. There are three categories of business immigrants:

Entrepreneurs This includes experienced businesspeople who are interested in buying or staring a business in which they will have an active and ongoing managerial role. This business must create jobs for one or more Canadians or permanent residents, other than the principal applicant and the applicant's dependents.

Investors Investors must have a proven track record in business and a new worth of at least C$500,000 (Canadian) acquired through the immigrant's own endeavors. The minimum amount of investment required varies from C$150,000 to C$250,000, depending on the province in which the funds are invested.

Self Employed These immigrants establish a business in Canada that employs only themselves. The business must contribute to the economic or cultural life of Canada and includes farmers, sports personalities, artists and owners of small community businesses. Potential entrepreneurial immigrants are encouraged to visit Canada before or shortly after they make their immigration application, so that they can meet with counselors of the federal and/or provincial industrial and trade departments to discuss their proposed business. The immigration procedure involves the submission of an application form and usually a meeting with the visa department to review the application.

WORK PERMITS

Visitors other than landed immigrants wishing to take up temporary employment during their stay in Canada must obtain a work permit, issued for a period of three moths. Only the perspective employer may apply for the permit and it is usually granted only if the employer states that no available, suitably qualified Canadian citizen can be found.

IMMUNIZATION

Canada does not require visitors to have any immunizations in order to enter the country. Travelers need shots for cholera and yellow fever if you are coming from an endemic area or have been in contact with these diseases.

CLIMATE

Canada's vast size makes any generalization about climate difficult. Much of the north is uninhabitable because of the Arctic climate and permanently frozen ground. For this reason, most of the population lives within 100 miles of the US border.

Canada has four distinct seasons throughout the country, although they arrive at different times. Latitude is the single largest determinant, as traveling just a few hours north by car can bring dramatic temperature drops. Overall, the southern portions of British Columbia and Ontario offer the longest summers and the shortest winters. In general, the weather moves from west to east, carried by prevailing westerly winds coming from the northwest Canadian Arctic. The four cities on which this chapter focuses are representative of their surrounding regions. Temperature ranges given are the average daily lows and highs.

AIR TRAVEL TIMES

Because distances are so great in Canada, few businesspeople drive or take trains from one city to another. Note that the direction one is traveling in can make a difference in flight time. In general, east-to-west flights take longer than west-to-east because of prevailing jet stream currents. It is also important to consider how many time zones you are crossing and in what direction. For example, a flight from Vancouver to Montreal that leaves at 8 am Vancouver time arrives in Montreal at 3:30 pm, so it effectively takes an entire day to fly from the west coast to the east coast. On the other hand, an 8 am flight from Montreal to Vancouver lands at 10:30 am local time.

Travel Times

Toronto nonstop to:

Vancouver	4 hours, 50 minutes
Los Angeles	5 hours
Chicago	1 hour, 40 minutes
New York	1 hour, 15 minutes
London	6 hours, 35 minutes

Montreal nonstop to:

Vancouver	5 hours, 10 minutes
LA	5 hours, 40 minutes
Chicago	2 hour, 5 minutes
NY	1 hour, 10 minutes
London	6 hours, 35 minutes

Montreal

Winter begins in Montreal by November and until March or April it remains quite cold. Average January temperatures are between -5° and -13° C. In summer months it is mild and quite pleasant with July and August temperature frequently ranging from 24° to 16°C.

Ottawa

The climate in Ottawa is similar to Montreal. Average temperatures in the winter range from -7° to -16°C. Average summer temperatures are between 27° and 15°C.

Toronto

Average January temperatures are between -1° and -8°C. Average summer temperate in July and August are between 26° and 14°C.

Vancouver

Warm and fairly dry in summer but mild, cloudy and wet in winter.

Vancouver is wetter than the rest of Canada. Average January temperatures are between 6° and 1°C. August temperatures range from 21° to 13°C.

Daily and extended weather forecasts are readily available from radio and television stations and newspapers. In summer, hotels, restaurants, theaters, cinemas and stores are air conditioned. In winter, all private and public buildings, railway stations and bus terminals are heated, and all main highways are cleared of snow. Although days in summer can be warm, evenings may be cool and business travelers should bring medium and heavier-weight apparel in addition to summer clothing. The temperature is reported in degrees Celsius.

BUSINESS ATTIRE

The clothing that Canadian businesspeople wear depends on the industry and region of the country. Businesspeople of both sexes in the big cities of the East and Midwest tend to dress conservatively in dark colors. Canadian men tend to dress in a manner more fashion conscious than their counterparts in the US Double breast Italian cut suits are often the norm and ties tend to follow a more European tradition. Casual dress is more common as you move further West; business in Calgary is frequently conducted in jeans and a cowboy hat. Foreign businesspeople trying to make a good impression are advised to dress a little more conservatively than the people with whom you will be dealing.

AIRLINES

Air Canada and Canadian Airlines are the two national airlines of Canada. The international airlines have at least one route to at least one city in Canada and many flights to the far East stop in or originate from Vancouver. If a direct flight from your point of origin is not available, Canada's international airports can be reached from the major cities in the US The largest International airports are located in Vancouver, Toronto, and Montreal with others available in Edmonton, Calgary, Regina, Winnipeg, Ottawa, Halifax, and Gander. For airlines' phone numbers, see the Important Addresses chapter.

TIME CHANGES

Canada spans six time zones with a difference from coast to coast of 5 1/2 hours. Newfoundland, the furthest city to the East is unusual because it is only 1/2 hour earlier than the adjacent Atlantic (ATL) zone. The cities of Montreal, Ottawa and Toronto as well as the Province of Quebec and the eastern 3/4 of Ontario are in the Eastern (EST) time zone. The Central (CST) time zone includes part of Ontario, all of the Province of Manitoba and the eastern half of Saskatchewan. Mountain (MST) time includes the western half of Saskatchewan and all of Alberta. Vancouver and all of British Columbia are in the Pacific (PST) time zone.

Clocks are advanced one hour for daylight savings time from the first Sunday in April until the last Sunday in October. The Province of Saskatchewan remains on Standard time all year.

City or Region	Hours from GMT
Newfoundland	-3 1/2
Atlantic	-4
Eastern	-5
Central	-6
Mountain	-7
Pacific	-8

When you are within a Canadian time zone, you can determine what time it is in any city listed here by adding the number shown to the Canadian time. If it is daylight savings time in the Canadian city you are calling from, subtract one from the number shown.

	ATL	EST	CST	MST	PST
Auckland	+16	+17	+18	+19	+20
Bangkok	+11	+12	+13	+14	+15
Beijing	+12	+13	+14	+15	+16
Frankfurt	+5	+6	+7	+8	+9
Hong Kong	+12	+13	+14	+15	+16
Jakarta	+11	+12	+13	+14	+15
Kuala Lampur	+12	+13	+14	+15	+16
London	+4	+5	+6	+7	+8
Manila	+12	+13	+14	+15	+16
Seoul	+14	+15	+16	+17	+18
Singapore	+12	+13	+14	+15	+16
Sydney	+14	+15	+16	+17	+18
Taipei	+12	+13	+14	+15	+16
Tokyo	+13	+14	+15	+16	+17

CUSTOMS ENTRY

The following import allowances are permitted without taxation:

1. 200 cigarettes and 50 cigars, and 11 cg. (2.2 lb) tobacco;
2. 1 bottle 1.14 liter (40 imp. oz.) of liquor or 24 x 355 mL (12 oz) bottles or cans (8.5 liters) of beer or ale per person (18 years of age entering Alberta, Manitoba, Quebec, 19 years of age in all other provinces and territories)
3. Small amount of perfume for personal use;
4. Gifts free of duty to the value of C$60 per gift.

Meat or meat products, fruits, plants and seeds are prohibited, as are illegal drugs. All firearms must be declared to Canada Customs at the first point of entry. In some cases, Customs officials will store your firearm until your departure. Customs officials will seize undeclared firearms and criminal charges may be laid.

Personal goods may be temporarily imported into Canada by visitors for their own use without payment of duties or taxes. These goods must be taken out of Canada at the end of the visit, with the exception of consumable items and recreational equipment for which a seasonal permit has been obtained. Some items may require a refundable security deposit to ensure the item leaves the country with the visitor.

Business travelers should declare any business related items they are bringing into Canada with them, such as laptop computers. Filing out customs forms comprehensively will help avoid possible hassles at departure.

FOREIGN EXCHANGE (PERSONAL)

The Canadian currency is the Canadian dollar (C$) and is based on a decimal system. Currency is issued in both coin and paper form. Paper currency is issued in C$2, C$5, C$10, C$20, C$50, C$100, C$500, and C$1,000 denominations. Coin currency is issued in .01, .05, .10, .25, .50 and C$1. For general use it is best to use denominations of C$20 and under.

Currency can be exchanged at any financial institution, bank, trust company, credit union, or exchange booth at airports or border crossings. Automatic Teller Machines (ATMs) are located outside many banks and financial institutions and a variety of retail centers. ATMs provide 24-hour access to money with the use of a bank card or credit card and a personal identification number (PIN). ATM access is available for card holders who are part of one of the following systems: Plus, Interac, Cirrus, Circuit, and Global Access.

To avoid paying high exchange rates, Canadian currency should be used when traveling in Canada. Many businesses will accept American dollars (or Japanese Yen in Vancouver and the Western ski regions) and the exchange rate will be posted on or near the cash register. These rates are virtually always less favorable than a bank or exchange office.

Travelers checks can be purchased at all major banks and are recommended. Travelers checks are accepted at most banks, restaurants, hotels and many business establishments. The six major Canadian banks are: The Royal Bank of Canada, The Canadian Imperial Bank of Commerce, The Bank of Montreal, The Bank of Nova Scotia, The Toronto-Dominion Bank and The National Bank. These banks have branches across Canada and representation worldwide.

Most major credit cards and principal bank cards are honored in Canada. However visitors should check with their own bank before leaving home.

TIPPING

Tips or service charges are not usually added to a bill in Canada. In general a tip of 10-15 percent of the total amount is given. This applies to waiters, hairdressers and taxi drivers. Bellhops, doormen, and redcaps (porters) at hotels, airports, and railway stations are generally tipped C$1 per item of luggage.

ACCESS TO CITIES FROM AIRPORTS

Toronto

Arriving by air into Toronto lands you Pearson International Airport, which is also referred to as "Malton" (after the once small town where it was built), or simply as "the Toronto airport." The 32 km (18 mi) trip can take over an hour during morning and afternoon rush hours. Typically a taxi or limo to a downtown hotel costs C$30 or more. Airport taxis have fixed rates to different parts of the city and these rates are generally non-negotiable. When heading from the city to the airport, it is sometimes possible to negotiate a lower fixed rate.

Many airport and downtown hotels offer free buses to and from the airport and you should inquire at your hotel if they offer this service. If not, a commercial company offers airport bus service to and from several downtown hotels. The bus operates every 30 minutes from 6 am to midnight daily and costs approximately C$11. For the budget conscious, Grey Coach [Tel: (416) 393-7911] offers bus service to three subway stops in the southwest and north-central areas of the city and costs about C$7.

Montreal

Montreal is served by two airports: domestic and most US flights arrive into Dorval International, 22 km (14 mi) west of the city. Non-US international flights arrive into Mirabel International, 54 km (34 mi) northwest of the city.

Dorval Airport is approximately 20 to 30 minutes by car from downtown Montreal. This trip by taxi averages about C$25. A taxi from Mirabel Airport to the city center will cost roughly C$50-60. Expect this same price for a trip between the two airports. It is best to have Canadian currency to pay taxis as the exchange rate for US dollars is at the discretion of the driver.

Autobus Connaisseur (Tel: (514) 934-1222) offers a much more affordable option into the city from Mirabel. Van service drops passengers next to Gare Central and the Voyageur bus station. The fare is C$14 and service runs every hour from 4 am until noon and 8 pm until 2 am, and every half hour between 12:30 and 7:30. Bus service between Mirabel and Dorval is also available for C$12, every hour from 9:20 am until 11:20 am and 8:20 pm until 11:20 pm. Between 11:40 am and 8 pm busses runs every 20 minutes.

Ottawa

Ottawa International Airport is 18 km from downtown. By car is it approximately a 20 minute trip and taxi service will cost between C$20–25. An airport shuttle takes passengers to all of the major downtown hotels and operate every half hour from 6 am until midnight at a fare of C$9. City bus service also transports passengers into the city for C$1.60 off peak and C$2.10 during peak hours (3–5 pm).

Vancouver

Vancouver International Airport is on an island approximately 14 km (9 mi) south of downtown. By car the drive from the airport to downtown is 20-45 minutes, depending on the time of day. Taxi fare from the airport to downtown is about C$25. Limousine service from Airlimo [Tel: (604) 273-1331] costs about C$30. The Airport Express (Tel: (604) 261-2299) offers bus service from the domestic arrivals level of the terminal every 15 minutes in summer and every 30 minutes in winter. It stops at all of the major hotels and the central bus station. Service operates from 5:30 am until 12:30 am. The fare is C$8.25 one-way and C$14 round trip. Many Airport hotels offer free shuttle serve to and from the airport.

ACCOMMODATIONS

There is a variety of accommodation available, including motels, hotel apartments and luxury hotels. Motels are typically situated along major highways and through-ways. They provide a comfortable room as well as food services, televisions in the rooms and often a swimming pool. Hotel apartments are located in most major cities. They provide a bedroom, kitchen, living-room and cleaning service, and can be rented for a period as short as a day and as long as a year. Luxury hotels are generally located in the city-center and offer greater elegance as well as more services at a higher cost. Modern luxury hotels frequently offer health club facilities including swimming pools and whirlpools as well as fine dining and bars in the hotel. Many also offer room service and in some cases business services such as available fax machines and computers.

In larger cities, advanced reservations should be always made through a travel agent to keep confusion and extra costs to a minimum. Reservations are also recommended for all major resorts. Further reservations can be made in Canada by using services provided by major hotel chains or with the tourism bureau of the particular province.

Canada's vast array of hotel and motel rooms is paralleled by an equally vast range of prices. You can pay as little as C$30 a night for a basic motel room, as much as C$3,000 for a night in a major hotel's most luxurious suite, and several prices in between. If you must have access to a wide range of business services and you need to impress the businesspeople you are meeting, a first class hotel is the place to stay. If, however, all you need is a place to sleep and wash up, choose a moderately priced hotel or motel.

The rates quoted here are generally the lowest possible rates for a single or double occupancy (some hotels charge the same for single and double) room on a weekday. Room rates can vary considerably depending on the day of the week and time of the year. Moreover, when business is good, rates go up; when business is slow, rates come down. Advertised rates are often subject to change without notice. Province and local taxes on hotel accommodations can also add significantly to the bill and are not always included in the rate quote.

Because such a wide range of lodging is available, visitors may want to look well beyond the limited sample of hotels listed here. The easiest way to travel in Canada is to have your travel agent do most of the work for you. If you want to save as much money as possible with the least amount of confusion, ask your agent for a package that includes airfare and hotel, or airfare, hotel and car rental.

Note: Telephone numbers beginning with (800) are toll-free numbers and can only be accessed from within North America.

MONTREAL

Top-end

Hotel Vogue 1425 rue de la Montagne, H3G 1Z3; Downtown. Each of the 148 rooms feature multi-line phones, fax machines and Jacuzzis. The hotel also offers a restaurant, an elegant bar and an exercise room. Rates start at C$180. Tel: (514) 285-5555 or (800) 465-6654; Fax: (514) 849-8903.

Bonaventure Hilton International 1 Place Bonaventure, H5A 1E4; Downtown. 393 rooms with three restaurants, a nightclub and a rooftop garden, 24 hour room service and a health club featuring a sauna and heated pool. Rates start at C$175. Tel: (514) 878-2332 or (800) 445-8667; Fax: (514) 878-1442.

Le Centre Sheraton 1201 boulevard Rene-Levesque O, H3B 2L7; Downtown. 824 Rooms and 40 suites offering two restaurants, twobars, unisex beauty parlor and a health club with whirlpool, sauna and indoor pool. Rates start at C$165. Tel: (514) 878-2000 or (800) 325-3535; Fax: (514) 878-3958.

Expensive

Hotel Radisson des Gouverneurs de Montreal 777 rue University, H3C 3Z7; Downtown. Located central to the stock exchange, this fine hotel is a favorite of convention attendees. Offering all the standard health club facilities including an indoor heated pool. It is best known for its bar with nightly live jazz and revolving restaurant. Rates start at C$125. Tel: (514) 879-1370 or (800) 333-3333; Fax: (514) 879-1761.

Chateau Versailles 1659 rue Sherbrooke O, H3H 1E3; Downtown. Four converted mansions make up this small and charming hotel. Rooms include a full bath, TV and air-conditioning. An additional annex of the hotel across the street houses an excellent restaurant. Rates start at C$109. Tel: (514)933-3611 or (800) 361-3664; Fax (514) 933-7102.

Best Western Europa Centre-ville 1240, rue Drummond H3G 1V7; Downtown. Centrally located with two restaurants, bar and rooftop terrace. Health club features large whirlpool and fitness room and available message. Rates start at C$95 Tel: (514) 861-4089 or (800) 361-3000; Fax: (514) 861-4089.

Moderate

Lord Berri 1199 rue Berri, H2L 4C6; Located adjacent to the University of Quebec at Montreal, Lord Berri offers 154 rooms with in-room movies, a restaurant and gift shop. Conveniently located to the restaurant and night life of rue St.-Denis. Rates start at C$85. Tel: (514) 845-9236 or (800) 363-0363; fax (514) 849-9855.

Quality Hotel par Journey's End 3440, avenue du Parc, H2X 2H5; Facility offers a lounge and restaurant as well as an in door garage and convenience store. Guest services include available fax machine and cable satellite TV. Rooms start at C$79 Tel: (514) 849-1413 or (800) 228-5151; Fax: (514) 849-6564.

Hotel Travelodge Montreal Centre 50, boul. Rene-Levesque O, H2Z 1A2; Clean and modest offering rooms with air conditioning with cable TV. Also on the premises are a gift shop and restaurant. Rates start at C$62. Tel: (514) 874-9090 or (800) 578-7878; Fax: (514) 874-0907.

OTTAWA

The Ottawa Ministry of Economic Development, Trade and Tourism (MEDTT) offers assistance with information and reservations at area hotels. The following discounted rates are based on reservation made through the MEDTT. For reservations and information, they can be reached throughout North America at (800) 668-2746 or internationally at (416) 314-0944.

Top-end

Westin Hotel Ottawa 11 Colonel By Drive, K1N 9H4; Downtown. Modern facility with two restaurants, lounge, health club with indoor heated pool, sauna, whirlpool and available massage and squash courts. Connects to Rideau Mall and overlooks Rideau Canal. Rates start at C$165. Tel: (613) 560-7000 or (800) 228-3000; Fax: (613) 234-5396.

Chateau Laurier Hotel 1 Rideau Street, K1N 8S7; Downtown. On Rideau canal next door to Parliament Building. This castle like hotel offers three fine restaurants and an elegant lounge. Also a health club with a heated indoor pool and sauna. Rates start at C$149. Tel; (613) 241-1414; Fax (613) 562-7030.

Minto Place Suite Hotel 433 Laurier Avenue, K1R 7Y1; Within walking distance of the Sparks Street Mall, one and two bedroom suites include full kitchen and laundry facilities. Also available is a lounge, sauna, indoor pool, whirlpool and indoor parking. Rates start at C$109. Tel: (613) 232-2200 or (800) 267-3377; Fax: (613) 232-6962.

Expensive

Novotel Ottawa Hotel, 33 Nicholas St., K1N 9M7; Downtown location features a restaurant, bar, indoor pool, sauna, whirlpool, sun terrace, fitness and conference facilities. Rates start at C$100. Tel: (613) 230-3033 or 800-668-6835; Fax: (613) 230-7865.

Cartier Place Hotel, 180 Cooper St., K2P 2L5; Downtown. Offers a restaurant, bar, indoor pool, sauna, whirlpool, and conference facilities. Most units offer kitchenette suites. Rates start at C$89. Tel: (613) 236-5000 or 800 236-8399; Fax: (613) 238-3842.

Citadel Ottawa Hotel and Conference Centre, 101 Lyon St. K1R 5T9; Centrally located and offering a restaurant, bar, conference rooms, indoor pool, sauna and fitness facilities. Rates start at C$85. Tel: (613) 237-3600 or (800) 567-3600; Fax: (613) 237-2351

Moderate

Townhouse Motor Hotel 319 Rideau St. K1N 5Y4; Downtown location offers a breakfast room, coffee shop, bar and conference room. Rates start at C$59. Tel: (613) 789-5555; Fax: (613) 789-6196.

Comfort Inn Journey's End East 1252 Michael Street, K1J 7T1; Located three miles Southeast of downtown, rooms have air-conditioning and cable TV, restaurant nearby. Rates start at C$61. Tel: (613) 744-2900 or (800) 221-2222; Fax: 613 746-0836.

Quality Hotel Journey's End Downtown 290 Rideau Street, K1N 5Y3; Located one mile from downtown. Rooms have air-conditioning and cable TV, restaurant on the premises. Rates start from C$74. Tel: (613) 789-7511 or (800) 221-2222; Fax: (613) 789-2434

TORONTO

The Metro Toronto Convention and Visitors Association (MTCVA) offers assistance with information and reservations at area hotels and facilities. The following discounted rates are based on reservation made through the MTCVA. They can be reached throughout North America at (800) 363-1990 or internationally at (416) 203-2500.

Top-end

Four Seasons Hotel 21 Avenue Rd., M5R 2G1; Toronto's most luxurious hotel is located in the heart of the fashionable Yorkville district, within walking distance of the finest museums, galleries and boutiques. The facility includes a swimming pool, spa and fitness center, two restaurants and two lounges. Rates start at C$185. Tel: (416) 964-0411 or (800) 268-6282; Fax: (416) 964-2301.

Sky Dome Hotel 1 Blue Jays Way, M5V 1J4. Part of the Toronto Skydome Stadium, 70 of the 346 rooms actually overlook the playing field. Convenient to shopping, dining and night life and featuring a health club with a pool, Jacuzzi and sauna. The facility houses the Sky Club bar and two restaurants including the Hard Rock Cafe. Rates for standard rooms (without field view) start at C$129. Tel: (416) 341-7100; Fax: (416) 341 5091.

Westin Harbour Castle 1 Harbour Square, M5J1A6; Located on the water, a 10 minute walk to downtown with a free shuttle every 20 minutes. Services include two restaurants including a revolving restaurant on 35th floor and three separate lounges. Also available is a health club with indoor heated pool, whirlpool, sauna, steam room, message, squash and tennis courts. Kids club activity center also on the premises. Rates start at C$109. Tel: (416) 869-1600; Fax: (416) 869-0573.

Expensive

Crown Plaza Toronto Centre 225 Front St. W., M5V 2X3; In the heart of the entertainment district, connected to the Convention Centre, Skydome, CN Tower and CBC Broadcast Centre. Deluxe rooms offer two telephones with voice messaging and teleconferencing, mini-bar, TV and movies. Also available are a pool, spa and fitness center, restaurant and bar. Rates start at C$109. Tel: (416) 597-1400 or (800) 227-6963; Fax: (416) 597-8128.

Delta Chelsea Inn 33 Gerrard St. W., M5G 1Z4; Toronto's largest hotel located in the heart of downtown, steps away from the Eaton Centre, the city's central business and theater district. Pool, spa and fitness center, three restaurants and four lounges on site. Rates start at C$104. Tel: (416) 595-1975 or (800) 243-5733; Fax: (416) 585-4393.

Holiday Inn on King 370 King St. W., M5V 1J9; Full service hotel located in the heart of the theater and entertainment district. Pool, spa/fitness center, three restaurants and two lounges on site. Rates start at C$99. Tel: (416) 599-4000 or (800) 263-6364; Fax: (416) 599-8889.

Moderate

Clarion Hotel Essex Park 300 Jarvis Street, M5B 2C5; Located downtown, each room has cable TV and a refrigerator. Also available is an exercise room, an indoor pool, room service, restaurant and lounge. Rates start at C$75. Tel: (416) 977-4823 or (800) 221-2222; Fax: (416) 977-4830.

Quality Hotel Journey's End Midtown 280 Bloor Street West, M5S 1V8; In the city within a mile from the center of town. Restaurant and meeting rooms are available. Rates start at C$69. Tel: (416) 968-0010 or (800) 221-2222; Fax: (416) 968-7765.

Comfort Hotel Downtown 15 Charles Street East, M4Y 1S1; Downtown. Rooms have air conditioning and cable TV. Also available is guest laundry and restaurant. Rates start at C$62. Tel: (416) 924-1222 or (800) 221-2222; Fax: (416) 927-1369.

VANCOUVER

Super Natural British Columbia (SNBC) offers assistance with information and reservations for area hotels. The following discounted rates are based on reservation made through the SNBC. They can be reached throughout North America at (800) 663-6000 or internationally at (604) 683-2000.

Top-end

Pan Pacific Hotel 300-999 Canada Place Way, V6C 3B5; Downtown. 506 rooms with a spectacular setting at the Canada Place, on Vancouver's waterfront; harbor and mountain views, in-room movies, saunas, pool, health club, valet parking, 24 hour room service, lounge, restaurants, shops. Rates start at C$175. Tel: (604) 662-8111 or (800) 937-1515; Fax: (604) 685-8690.

Four Seasons Hotel 791 West Georgia St. V6C 2T4; Downtown. 385 luxury rooms above the Pacific Center Mall, indoor and outdoor pools, valet parking, whirlpool, exercise facilities, restaurants, garden lounge. Rates start at C$295. Tel: (604) 689-9333 or (800) 332-3442; Fax: (604) 844-6744

Hotel Vancouver 900 West Georgia St. V6C 2W6; Central. This restored hotel offers a heath club with pool, Jacuzzi and sauna. Also two restaurants, a bar and a roof lounge. Rates start at C$190. Tel: (604) 684-3131 or (800) 441-1414; Fax: (604) 662-1929.

Wedgewood Hotel 845 Hornby St. V6Z 1V1; Downtown. 93 rooms in a small and elegant European-style hotel; rooms and suites, air conditioned, maid service twice a day, valet parking, breakfast room, 24 hour room service, banquet facilities, piano lounge, Italian restaurant with live entertain-

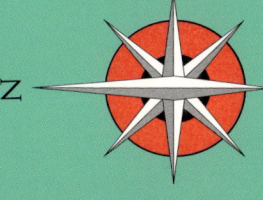

Montréal

Legend:
- Parks
- Tourist Information (T)
- Post Office
- Hospital
- Highways
- Railway
- Metro

Points of Interest:
11. Bank of Montréal
9. Bus Terminal
14. City Hall
7. Convention Hall
16. Marché Bonsecours
3. Mary Queen of the World Cathedral
5. Montréal Stock Exchange
1. Musée des Beaux Arts
13. Old Court House
8. Palais du Commerce
12. Place de la Justice
6. Place des Arts
15. Place Jacques-Cartier
4. Railway Station
2. Windsor Station
10. World Trade Centre

Hotels:
- H5 Holiday Inn
- H4 Queen Elizabeth Hotel
- H1 Ritz Carlton Hotel
- H3 Sheraton Hotel
- H2 Westin Mont-Royal

ment, health club. Rates start at C$190. Tel: (604) 689-7777 or 800 663-0666; Fax: (604) 688-3074.

Expensive

Hyatt Regency Vancouver 655 Burrard V6C 2R7. This modern downtown hotel offers a health club featuring exercise facilities, heated outdoor pool and a sauna. Also featuring indoor parking, restaurants, a lounge and rooftop meeting rooms. Rates start at C$130. Tel: (604) 683-1234 or 800 233-1234; Fax: (604) 689-3707.

Wall Centre Garden Hotel 1088 Burrard St V6Z 2R9 This elegant downtown hotel features a fitness center with Jacuzzi, sauna and indoor pool. Also offering a restaurant, bar and 24 hour room service. Rates start at C$165. Tel: (604) 331-1000 or (800) 663-9255; Fax (604) 893-7200.

Metropolitan Hotel Vancouver 645 Howe St., V6C 2Y9. Downtown. 181 doubles, 16 suites with a restaurant, bar, squash and racquetball courts, lap pool, weight room, sauna, whirlpool and massage. Rates start at C$185. Tel: (604) 687-1122 or (800) 877-113; Fax: (604) 643-7267

Moderate

Days Inn Vancouver Downtown 921 West Pender Street, V6C 1M2. Located in city center within walking distance to shopping, theaters and the convention center. Offers in-room movies, a restaurant and lounge. Rates start at C$110. Tel: (604) 681-4335 or 800 325-2525; Fax: (604) 681-7808.

Holiday Inn Downtown 1110 Howe St., V6Z 1R2; Downtown. Hotel and tower suites with or without kitchens. All offer a sauna, indoor pool, restaurants, lounge, health club and bakery. Rates start at C$145. Tel: (800) 684-2151; Fax (604) 684-4736.

Burrard Motor Inn 1100 Burrard St., V6Z 1Y7; Downtown. Lounge and restaurant at the location, some units include a kitchen. Rates start at C$69. Tel: (604) 681-2331 or (800) 663-0366; Fax (604) 681-9753.

CUISINE

Canadian cuisine combines local cooking methods and products. Beef and salmon dishes are national favorites. In British Columbia, favorites include: fish and seafood dishes, five varieties of salmon, oysters, fresh halibut, Pacific prawns, Dungeness crab, and fresh fruits (particularly apples). Ontario's cheddar cheese is world renowned. The province is a major producer of vegetables, such as corn and tomatoes, fowl, including turkey and chicken, freshwater fish, and apples and grapes. Ontario's Niagara region is well known for its wines. Quebec has a distinctive style of cuisine dating back to the days of New France when settlers adapted traditional French recipes to Canadian ingredients. Habitant pea soup, pork and veal, as well as many recipes featuring maple syrup products are local favorites. The Atlantic provinces are famous for their fish and vegetable dishes. Restigouche salmon, salt and freshwater fish, scallops and lobsters are popular favorites. New Brunswick fiddleheads and Prince Edward Island and New Brunswick potatoes are staples in this region. In addition to the typical Canadian cuisine a wide variety of international dishes are offered in specialized restaurants from coast to coast. Italian, French, Chinese, Japanese, German, Ukrainian, Hungarian, Mexican, Middle Eastern and Indo-Pakistani foods are among the more popular foods offered.

OTTAWA

Courtyard Restaurant French. Just five minutes from the Parliament Building and one of Ottawa's finest French restaurants. Elegant ambiance and outstanding cuisine make this a favorite of locals and visitors alike. Located at 21 George Street. Reservations required. Dress: Jacket required. Tel: (519) 565-2611. Expensive. Credit cards accepted.

Flippers Seafood Features at this seafood restaurant change with the fresh fish available. Replete with marine artifacts and model ships. Located at 823 Bank Street, 2nd Floor. Reservations advised. Dress: Jacket required. Tel: (613) 232-2703. Expensive. Credit cards accepted.

MONTREAL

Montreal is a city that takes dining seriously. The variety and quality of Montreal's restaurants is extraordinary. In warmer months, dinners may have dinner at one restaurant, then stroll through the city streets before enjoying coffee and dessert or night cap at another. A dinner for two at one of Montreal's finer restaurants would likely cost at least C$100. Wine selection will of course influence this price. There is, however, an abundance of moderately priced restaurants throughout many of the city's neighborhoods.

Les Mignardises French. Considered by many to be the finest and certainly the most expensive restaurant in town, this fine dining establishment holds just 20 tables. Located at 2035-37 rue St-Denis. Reservations required. Dress is casual but neat. Tel: (514) 842-1151. Expensive. Credit cards accepted.

Zen Offering fine Chinese with some Thai, Malaysian and Indonesian dishes, Zen is an excellent choice for delicate Asian fare. Located in the basement of Le Westin Mount-Royal, 1050 Sherbrooke St. W. Reservations are advised. Dress is casual but neat. Tel: (514) 499-0801. Expensive. Credit cards accepted.

Bocca d'Oro Italian Excellent for a variety of pasta dishes, the comfortable atmosphere and friendly service makes Bocca d'Oro feel like an authentic trattoria. Located at 1448 rue St-Mathieu. Reservations are advised. Dress is casual but neat. Tel: (514) 933-8414. Moderate. Credit cards accepted. Closed Sundays.

Wilensky's Light Lunch Delicatessen. A city institution since 1932, they are most famous for their Italian-American salami on a kaiser roll blanketed in mustard. Their grilled sandwiches are also quite tasty and the fast and friendly service is equally renown. Located at 34 Fairmount O. No reservations. Dress is casual. Tel: (514) 271-0247. Very moderate. No credit cards. No liquor license. Closed weekends.

VANCOUVER

The distinct influence of Asian culture in Vancouver is widely showcased in the city's dining. That is not to suggest that a gastronomical experience in Vancouver is limited; excellent cuisine from around the world is abundantly available. A dinner for two at one of Vancouver's finer restaurants would likely cost at least C$100. Wine selection will of course influence this price.

Chartwell Continental. With decor suiting an upper-class British club, the flagship dining room of the Four Season's Hotel is a popular place to conduct business lunches and dinners. 791 W. Georgia St. Reservations advised. Jacket advised. Tel: (604) 844-6715. Expensive. Credit cards accepted. Closed for weekend lunch.

Kirin Mandarin Restaurant Featuring northern Chinese cuisine in a lavishly decorated setting, Kirin is just two blocks from many of the major downtown hotels. Located at 1166 Alberni St. Reservations advised. Dress: causal but neat. Tel: (604) 682-8833. Moderate. Credit cards accepted.

Le Gavroche French. Charming turn of the century house featuring classic French cooking. Tables by the front windows offer exquisite mountain and water views. Located at 1616 Alberni St. Reservations advised. Dress: jacket and tie advised. Tel: (604) 685-3924. Expensive. Credit cards accepted. Closed lunch, Sun., and holidays.

Tojo's Japanese. One of Vancouver's best loved sushi restaurants, Tojo presides over this intimate establishment. Also serving a full menu of traditional Japanese fare. Located at 777 W. Broadway, No. 202. Weekend reservations advised. Dress: casual but neat. Tel: (604) 872-8050. Moderate to expensive. Credit cards accepted. Closed lunch and Sundays.

TORONTO

Toronto's restaurant scene continues to actively evolve. The haute cuisine has been replaced by a diversity of new ethnic fare and neighborhoods such as Little Italy, Little India and three separate China towns all help organize the city's offerings. In the finer restaurants, dinner for two would likely cost at least C$100. Wine selection will of course influence this price.

Centro Italian. Considered by many to be one of Toronto's finest restaurants, every detail is carefully attended to. The menu features specialties from a variety of Italian regions. Located at 2472 Yonge St. Reservations required. Dress: jacket advised. Tel: (416) 483-2211. Expensive. Credit cards accepted. Closed Sundays.

North 44 Mixed menu. Elegant and distinctive decor is matched by exquisite cuisine from a variety of cultures. Located at 2537 Yonge St. Reservations advised. Dress: casual but neat. Tel: (416) 487-4897. Moderate to expensive. Credit cards accepted. Closed Sunday dinner.

Jose's Seafood Frequented by the international art set, this sensuosly decorated two story restaurant offers a delightful array of tasty seafood. Located at 202 Davenport Rd. Reservations required. Dress: casual but neat. Tel: (416) 925-1903. Moderate to expensive. Credit cards accepted. Closed Sat. lunch, Sun.

Auberge du Pommier French country. The comfortable setting and impeccable cuisine are well worth the 20 minute cab ride from the city center.

Located at 4150 Yonge St. Reservations advised. Dress: Jacket advised. Tel: (416) 222-2220. Expensive. Credit cards accepted. Closed Sat. lunch, Sun.

LOCAL CUSTOMS OVERVIEW

Residents of Canada are less formal and ceremonial in business situations than people of other cultures. However, politeness and consideration in Canada are largely the same as they are elsewhere, with some significant variations. In general, Canadian citizens are tolerant of foreign ways, to a point.

Because there are many similarities, it is tempting to consider Canadian businesspeople as if they were Americans on a higher latitude. While the differences between the two cultures are subtle, they are also distinct. Canadians are proud of their culture. Be mindful to not make comments that assume Canadians are like Americans.

Treat a woman on your level of authority or expertise as your equal, the same as you would treat a man. Despite continuing discrimination in the workplace, the status of women in Canadian business has increased in the last 20 years and continues to slowly improve. Businesswomen in Canada do not take kindly to demonstrations of machismo. They do not expect and do not want to be regarded either as special or as unimportant. You have been granted a meeting with them because they are the people you need to meet, not because they are ornaments. Nor should you feel that you are somehow being insulted by being referred to a woman. Open a door for someone as a gesture of politeness, not as a concession to the person's gender. If a Canadian businesswoman is taking you to lunch, allow her to pay the check just as you would allow a male host. Any attempt to categorize her by gender is dangerous, and sexually suggestive remarks will generate a cold response, if not a hostile retort. You are there to do business, not jeopardize your chances by offending your Canadian counterpart.

You should also treat members of other races in the increasingly multiracial and multi-ethnic Canadian business society as equals. Again, discrimination continues among Canadian residents, but as a society Canada has committed itself to equality. Canada is among the world's most cosmopolitan cultures, home to people from every country on earth. Tolerance is not merely appropriate, it is essential.

Be on time for your appointments. If you cannot make your appointment on time, call ahead to advise your host, who can reschedule you and do something else with the time. If you are late, your meeting may be canceled, and you will have to reschedule.

The handshake is the universal greeting, used by both men and women, whether on first introduction or in subsequent meetings. In some places, a handshake commits one's honor to the business relationship that begins at that point.

Business cards are not as significant in Canada as they are elsewhere, especially in Asia. You may offer your card and it will be accepted, but do not expect the recipient to pay much attention to it or necessarily to receive one in return. Usually, you will be asked for your card only if the recipient expects to contact you at a later time.

Canadian businesspeople begin their negotiations from a point of middle ground. Rather than initially requesting much more than they actually want and negotiating to an agreeable compromise, Canadians will begin by establishing common ground. It is hoped that this act of forthrightness will be reciprocated by their negotiating counterpart. Canadians are very flexible in negotiations and hesitate to say no unless demands placed on them are clearly unreasonable.

Any meal is an opportunity to discuss business. Working breakfasts, lunches and dinners are common and unlike the European tradition, business is discussed throughout the meal.

Always ask if you can smoke before you light up. Smoking is prohibited by law on airplanes and in public places. Businesses often prohibit smoking in their buildings. Realize that it is likely that smoking will offend a nonsmoker.

Gift Giving

Gift giving is not as important in the Canada as elsewhere, and may indeed present problems. It is better not to give a gift at all than to give the wrong one, or give it to the wrong person. A gift may be looked upon as trying to gain influence in an underhanded way. Canadian laws actually prohibit government employees from receiving gifts in the course of their jobs. Business firms often keep a close watch on such gift-giving. And because it is not a normal and accepted practice, gift-giving may embarrass both the recipient, who is not equipped to reciprocate, and others who did not bring gifts.

Gift Giving Exceptions One of the best gifts to give and receive is entertainment. It can be a drink at a nice bar, a fancy dinner, tickets to a show or a sports event. However, allow your Canadian hosts to make the first offer. This is the only way you can understand what is appropriate and what is frowned upon by that particular company. Anything too costly is likely to be embarrassing and is usually refused. Gift-giving is traditional and accepted at Christmas, not only in families but also among business associates. Business-related gift-giving should generally be restricted to gifts that can be used in business: pens, calendars, planners, paperweights, and the like. Extravagance is an embarrassing mistake. Another exception might be your first meeting with a person who is very important to the success of your visit, or your final encounter after successful negotiations just before your departure. Here, the best gift is something modest (but not cheap or tasteless, such as an advertising or marketing trinket) that is unique to your home country: a local handicraft, your national beverage, or a descriptive book on your country. In these circumstances, do not expect your recipient to give you a gift immediately. Except at Christmas, reciprocation may come much later, if at all.

DOMESTIC TRANSPORTATION

Except in remote areas of the north, Canada possesses an advanced transportation system comparable to that of the United States. An extensive air network links all major and many minor traffic points with adequate connections to the United States and the rest of the world. Domestic air fares per mile are generally higher than US fares, and distances between population centers are considerably greater. Rates are lower for a round trip fare and higher when traveling first class. Nearly all major airlines offer reservations through toll-free "800" phone numbers. Travel agents can also handle travel arrangements, generally at no charge.

Canada has an extensive railway system connecting the country from sea to sea. The Canadian National Railway deals exclusively with cargo, whereas VIA Rail offers passenger service. Distances between Canadian cities can be quite large, so if time is a key issue, travelers will be better advised to arrange for air travel.

In spite of extensive public transport arrangements, Canada is as much an automobile society as is the United States. A good highway system (with somewhat less emphasis on interstate roads) exists within 200 miles of the US border and supports extensive truck, bus and automobile traffic.

Gasoline is sold in liters in Canada, and Canadian safety standards for cars are similar to those in the United States. Left-hand-drive vehicles are standard; traffic moves on the right side of the road. International highway symbols are used in Canada, and distances are in the metric (or metric and miles) system. Seat belts and infant/child seat restraints are mandatory in all Canadian provinces. Fines are imposed for non-use of seat belts and child restraints. Motorists typically drive with headlights on at all times, a measure that has been shown to increase safety. Driving while intoxicated is strictly illegal, and most states prohibit carrying open containers of alcohol in motor vehicles. City and state police are on the lookout for drunk drivers and for speeders.

To drive in Canada, you need a valid driver's license issued by a country that is a signatory to the 1949 Geneva Motoring Convention. However, it is wise to get an international license in the event that a car rental agency asks for one.

It is very easy to rent a car in Canada if you have a valid license and a major credit card. You can very often get a hotel and rental car package deal at very reasonable rates. Otherwise, any hotel will have information on car rental, as will all airports, which usually have fleets of rental cars parked near the terminals with free shuttles to take you to your car. Some agencies in some cities can even provide a car phone that you can activate with your credit card.

Speeds are marked in kilometers per hour (kph). The national speed limit on highways is generally 100 kph (62 mph). On freeways, the far left lane is intended for passing.

Your rental car or contract should contain a notice describing what to do if you have an accident or a breakdown. Accidents usually receive prompt attention from police. If your car breaks down, look for a telephone—some highways have call boxes at regular intervals. If you are on a limited access highway or freeway and there is no phone, tie a handkerchief or scarf to the radio antenna or door handle or leave your emergency flashing lights on and wait for police. It is illegal and dangerous to walk along one of these high-speed roadways. Unaccompanied women in particular should stay in the car with the doors locked until police arrive. Many national automobile associations have reciprocal arrangements with the Canadian Automobile Association (CAA) [Tel: (613) 226-7631].

Car rental agencies will try to sell you collision insurance at high rates. Before you buy this overpriced insurance, check with your own insurance company to see if you are covered for rental cars in a foreign country. If you want to drop the car off in a city different from the one you rented it in, it is likely you will have to pay an additional charge, usually at least C$50, and often much more. However, many agencies will allow you to pick cars up and drop them off at different locations within the same metropolitan area. Car rental rates average about C$50 a day, depending on availability, the size of the car, and whether or not there is unlimited mileage. Many firms offer several hundred kilometers free, or a daily rate with a kilometer charge added. There is usually an additional cost for insurance and a credit card or cash deposit is usually required. Visitors must be at least 21 years of age in order to rent a vehicle.

Taxi fares vary from city to city. However, on average, there is an immediate charge of approximately C$2.35 upon entering the taxicab and an additional C$1.25 for each additional kilometer traveled. Available cabs can be stopped in the street simply by holding out one's hand to the attention of the driver. You can also have your hotel or restaurant personnel call a taxi for you, or place the call yourself.

Public transit can be used for transportation within all major cities. Average fares start at about C$2.00 and include transfer privileges. Fares are charged at a set rate, and do not vary according to distance traveled. Exact fare is required on many city vehicles. Tickets for public transit can be purchased in advance at designated sale sites as bus drivers do not sell tickets or carry money. Transfers should be requested upon boarding the public vehicle.

BUSINESS HOURS

Most retail businesses are open from 9 am to 5:30 or 6 pm daily. Many shops have extended hours on Thursdays and Fridays, until 9 pm Some provinces allow shops to be open on Sundays from noon to 5 pm Many small neighborhood stores remain open late and on weekends, and sell groceries, some personal items and newspapers.

Government offices are generally open from 9 am until 5 pm, Monday through Friday. Banking hours are not less than 10 am to 3 pm Monday through Thursday, and 10 am to 6 pm on Friday. Many banks are open for longer periods and on

Saturdays. Commercial businesses are typically open from 9 am to 5 pm daily, except Sundays. Automated banking machines are common, and are available 24 hours a day.

COMMUNICATIONS

Communications are highly sophisticated in Canada, comparable with those of the United States. Canada is integrated with the US direct long-distance dialing system (dial 1, area code and number). All forms of communication and transmission are possible (including voice, text, data, and video), and worldwide telegraphic services are available.

Telephones

All Canadian phone numbers have a three-digit area code followed by a seven-digit local number. When calling a number within the same area code, do not dial the area code. In some cities, however, the number you want to call may be far enough away to require that you dial a "1" before the seven-digit number; you will discover this if you dial the seven numbers and you hear a recording that tells you to dial a "1" first. This type of call, while not long distance, is still a toll call, meaning that you will be charged more than the base rate, although not the full long distance rates.

Some metropolitan areas have more than one area code. Your hotel room should have a telephone book, which includes maps of area codes, or you can call Directory Assistance at "411" for numbers in the same area code, or 1 (area code) 555-1212 to obtain numbers in different area codes. For a listing of area codes across Canada, refer to the "Important Addresses" chapter.

Finding a public phone that works can be a problem in some areas: they are favorite targets of vandals, and many public phones are old and broken down. Because most Canadian pay phones accept only coins, you are advised to use your credit card or phone card for calls lasting longer than a minute if you do not want to walk around with several dollars in change weighing you down. Each pay phone usually has an instruction chart for making credit card or collect calls, or you can simply dial "0" to reach an operator.

International Calls If possible, avoid direct dialing internationally from your hotel room; hotels usually impose a substantial surcharge on such calls. Instead, call the international operator in your own country and have your call charged to your home credit or phone card—this system is called Home Country Direct or World Connect. To reach the operator, dial "00" and ask the operator how to use the system. The system is also the best alternative if your hotel does not offer international direct dialing. Call the operator and give the country code, city code, and local number you are calling. The operator will connect you.

If the surcharge does not matter to you, simply dial the international access code (011), then the country code, then the area or city code, and finally the local number. For example, to call someone in Tokyo, Japan, dial 011-81-3 then the local number. If you want operator assistance—for collect calls, person-to-person calls, or to use your calling card—the international access number is 01 rather than 011. (Note: These instructions are for AT&T long-distance service. If you wish to use another carrier, hang up and dial the appropriate access code before dialing 011 or 01.) (See "Useful Telephone Numbers" on the following page for access numbers to other long distance carriers.)

Calling the US from Canada is the same as calling long-distance within Canada. Simply dial 1, then the area code and local number.

Fax, Telegram, and Telex

Fax machines and services can be found in every city. Most large hotels offer fax services or can direct you to the nearest service. Many photocopy shops also offer fax services and are listed in the yellow pages. You can send telegrams through Western Union and electronic mail via AT&T EasyLink. Telegrams or "Teleposts" should be telephoned to CN/CP Telecommunications for transmission. The addresses and telephone numbers of a CN/CP Telecommunications office can be found in local telephone directories. In Newfoundland and Labrador, telegrams should be sent through Terra Nova Tel.

Post Office

The Canadian Postal Service picks up, sorts, and delivers a phenomenal amount of mail every day, most of it on time. The service offers overnight and two-day delivery at competitive prices, provides certified and registered mail services with proof of delivery, and generally can deliver a first class letter within two to five days anywhere in the country for 43 cents for the first ounce. Most post office branches are open from 8 am to 5 pm weekdays. In larger cities, some are open on Saturdays.

If you need a parcel or important papers delivered on the same day or overnight, you may be better off with a courier service. Canada has several large national and international courier services, plus local couriers.

Foreign-Language Media

Canada has both English and French newspapers in all of the major cities. Asian language newspapers are available in Vancouver. The larger newsstands will also carry publications in a wide variety of languages from around the world. (See the business culture section for more information on local media)

Local Services

All major Canadian cities have virtually every business service businesspeople may need, from phone to fax to copying to secretarial to delivery.

Canada has several large firms specializing in providing temporary offices for businesspeople. They can provide office space, furnishings, staff, communications systems, meeting rooms, secretarial services, phone answering, and even desktop publishing; you pay only for what you need.

Central Park Business Center, Vancouver. Tel: (604) 435-2500.

HQ Business Centers, Vancouver. Tel: (604) 443-5000.

Corporate Executive Offices, Ontario. Tel: (905) 332-1320.

Execu-Center Inc., Montreal. Tel: (514) 393-1100.

Telsec Business Centers, Montreal. Tel: (514) 393-8222.

(For assistance in other locations, contact the Executive Suite Association at (800) 237-4741.)

Housing Some firms specialize in obtaining temporary housing in apartments or condominiums for businesspeople at a cost far lower than hotels, with much greater convenience. One of the major companies offering such accommodations for Canada's Eastern cities is Global Travel Apartments; Tel: (800) 667-8483. For housing in Vancouver, contact Oakwood Corporate Housing; Tel: (800) 888-0808.

Mailing Addresses If you are going to be in one city for an extended period, you may want to engage one of the mailbox services. For a small fee, these provide a mailing address, a private box, wrapping, packing, mailing, and mail forwarding services, access to courier services such as UPS or FedEx, photocopying, notary service, fax machines, and stationery supplies. They are listed in the Yellow Pages under "Mail Boxes" or "Mail Receiving."

Translation and Interpretation Services Many such companies provide a wealth of services, which may include written translation of any language in any subject, consecutive and simultaneous oral interpreters, desktop publishing, typesetting, graphics, or audiovisual adaptations. Some perform their translation services by computer modem and fax within 24 or 48 hours. In addition, large cities have independent translation and interpretation service listed in the Yellow Pages of local phone books.

Accredited Language Services: (800) 755-5775
Ad-Ex Worldwide: (800) 223-7753
AT&T Language Line Services: (800) 752-0093
Business Translation Services: (800) 544-5721
The Language Lab: (800) 682-3126
Berlitz Translation/Interpretation Services:
Vancouver: (604) 685-9331
Toronto: (416) 924-7773
Ottawa: (613) 234-8686
Montreal: (514) 288-3111 or (514) 387-2566

Printing Major Canadian cities have printers that offer overnight service for business cards and letterhead stationery. You can find photocopiers in pharmacies and even grocery stores, as well as in the large national chains, some of which are opened 24 hours. All are listed in the Yellow Pages under "Copying" or "Printers."

Temporary Secretarial Services Most cities have many secretarial services firms that provide word and data processing, transcription, mail services, fax services, and many other office services, either in your office or in their own offices. These local firms, which you can find in the Yellow Pages of the local phone book under "Secretarial Services," are in addition to the large national firms that can also provide temporary workers in a wide variety of employment fields. These include accounting, legal, insurance, customer service, clerical, or administrative services. Look in the local yellow pages under "Employment Services" or "Employment Services—Temporary."

STAYING SAFE AND HEALTHY

Crime in Canadian cities occurs at rates far lower than many others around the world. If you avoid the more dangerous neighborhoods and take some simple precautions, your chances of becoming a victim, particularly of violent crime, are extremely low. Ask at your hotel about the safety of nearby neighborhoods. Keep to well lit streets, and try to avoid looking like a tourist—that is, confused, and preoccupied. Walk as if you know what you are doing and where you are going. Avoid the display of valuable jewelry or cameras. Women should carry their purses over their shoulders rather than in their hands and keep them close when in restaurants or walking on streets. Large sums of money and important documents should be kept in the hotel safe. Consider parking on the street instead of in a parking garage if the garage does not have a good security system.

Public drinking water in Canada is safe, and food is generally prepared under safe conditions. However, as a foreign visitor, you may experience occasional digestive upsets common to travelers everywhere in the world. Pharmacies and grocery stores are everywhere and offer everything you need for an upset stomach, headache, cold, or allergy. However, unlike in some countries, pharmacists cannot prescribe for you or sell prescription medications to you without a doctor's prescription.

Getting enough exercise is difficult when you are traveling, but Canada has many health clubs. Many hotels that cater to businesspeople now provide exercise facilities; if yours does not, the concierge or desk clerk should be able to direct you to a nearby health club, oftentimes one where guests of the hotel receive a temporary courtesy membership or discount.

Canadian hospitals and medical services are excellent. Hospitals care for non-residents of Canada may be charged at a daily rate determined by the hospital and/or province. In addition, physician fees may also be charged.

Hospital charges vary from province to province and from hospital to hospital. Daily rates may average from C$1,000 to C$3,000 per day. Traveler's health insurance is strongly recommended. Two possible options that must be purchased in advance of your trip are:

International SOS Assistance, Inc. Membership offers 24 hour world-wide assistance centers, multi-lingual medically trained personnel, pre-trip information, doctor and lawyer referrals and full-scale emergency evacuations. Tel: (800) 363-0263 or (514) 874-7674 (collect calls are accepted).

Travel Guard International Available only for Canadian and US residents only, policy includes 24 hour world-wide assistance centers, multi-lingual medically trained personnel, doctor and lawyer referrals, full-scale emergency evacuations and assistance with lost baggage and money transfers. Tel: (800) 826-1300

EMERGENCY INFORMATION

In an emergency, dial "911". This will immediately connect you to an operator who is trained and equipped to handle and coordinate emergency services including police, fire or ambulance. Do not dial this number unless you have a true, immediate emergency.

High-quality medical care is easily available nationwide. Better hotels have a doctor on call and all can direct you to a hospital or clinic. If you become ill while driving, stop at any roadside service station or store and ask for the nearest hospital; or look for roadside signs indicating directions to a hospital; or stop next to an roadside phone and call the state police.

DEPARTURE PROCEDURES

Foreign travelers are entitled to a refund for some of the tax paid on accommodations, as long as you stay less than one month in that accommodation. You can also claim a tax refund on eligible goods you take home. This program includes refunds for the Goods and Services Tax (GST) and provincial sales tax paid in the provinces of Quebec

HOLIDAYS

List of National Holidays

New Year's Day	January 1
Good Friday	Friday before Easter
Easter Monday	Mon. following Easter
Victoria Day	Monday before May 24
Canada Day	July 1
Labor Day	first Monday in Sept.
Thanksgiving Day	second Monday in Oct.
Remembrance Day	November 11
Christmas Day	December 25
Boxing Day	December 26

List of Provincial Holidays

Alberta:

Family Day	Third Monday in Feb.
Heritage Day	First Monday in Aug.

British Columbia:

British Columbia Day	First Monday in Aug.

Manitoba:

Civic Holiday	First Monday in Aug.

Newfoundland:

Commonwealth Day	Second Monday in Mar.
St. Patrick's Day	March 17
St. George's Day	April 23
Discovery Day	June 27
Memorial Day	July 7
Orangemen's Day	July 10

Ontario:

Civic Holiday	First Monday in Aug.

Quebec:

St. Jean Baptiste Day	June 24

Saskatchewan:

Civic Holiday	First Monday in Aug.

Yukon Territory:

Discovery Day	Third Monday in Aug.

Northwest Territories:

Civic Holiday	First Monday in Aug.

and Manitoba. You can apply for all three refunds using the same application form. Tax refunds are available at any participating Canada duty free shop (cash refunds up to C$500) or by completing and mailing an application to Revenue Canada.

To qualify for the refund you must not be a resident of Canada, have your original sales receipts and

USEFUL TELEPHONE NUMBERS

(Note: 800 numbers may only be used in North America)

Telephone access and operators

Domestic operator	0
Long-distance operator	00
International access code	011
Local directory assistance	411
Long dist. directory	1 (area code) 555-1212
AT&T inter. dialing info:	(800) 874-4000
AT&T inter. services info:	(800) 222-0900
AT&T access	10288
Sprint access	10333
MCI access	10222

Car rental numbers

Avis:	(800) 268-9927
Budget	(800) 268-8900
Dollar	(800) 800-4000
Hertz	(800) 263-0600
National	(800) 227-7368

Lost or stolen credit cards

Visa	(800) 336-8472
Visa Gold	(800) 847-2911
MasterCard	(800) 826-2181
Diners Club	(800) 525-9135
American Express	(800) 528-4800
Discover	(800) 347-2683

To wire money

Western Union	(800) 325-6000
or	(800) 257-4900
American Express	(800) 543-4080
Citibank	(212) 657-5161

To send telegrams from Canada

Western Union	(800) 257-4900
or	(800) 325-6000
AT&T EasyLink	(800) 242-6005
or	(416) 502-1740

Courier services

Airborne	(800) 426-2323
DHL	(800) 225-5345
FedEx	(800) 238-5355
Intrn'l Bonded Couriers	(800) 322-3067

you must spend at least C$100 Canadian for each tax you are claiming. For more information, contact Revenue Canada's Visitor Rebate Program in Canada at (800) 668-4748 or internationally at (613) 991-3346.

BEST TRAVEL INFORMATION

Travel Books

Canada 1995, The Complete Guide to Cities, Parks, and Outdoor Adventures. Fodor's Travel Staff. 1994, Fodor's Travel. ISBN 0-679-02702-5.

Canada: A Travel Survival Kit by Mark Lightbody and Tom Smallman. Fifth ed. 936pp. 1994, Lonely Planet Publications. 0-86442-216-4.

Culture Shock, Canada. Pang Guek Cheng and Robert Barlas. 256pp, 1992, Graphic Arts Publishing Company. ISBN 0-92-0641-14-8.

Frommer's Montreal and Quebec City. 1993-1994. 288pp, P-H Gen. Ref. & Travel. ISBN 0-671-84697-3.

Frommer's Vancouver and Victoria. 1993-1994. 288pp, P-H Gen. Ref. & Travel. ISBN 0-67184697-3.

World Wide Web Sites

Canadian Embassy, Washington, DC
http://www.nstn.ca/wshdc

Tourism Canada
http://info.ic.gc.ca-data/iip/tourism

British Columbia Tourism Info
http://www.tbc.gov.bc.ca/tourism/tourismhome.html

Ottawa Online Ventures
http://ottawa.microworks.ca/default.html

Dept. of Foreign Affairs & International Trade
http://www.dfait-maeci.gc.ca

Business Culture

INTRODUCTION

Believing that the culture of Canada is identical to that of the United States seems very logical. After all, Canada is a technologically modern country, and Canadians, much like people from the US, are well-educated and hard-working. Many US products are sold in Canada, and much of the Canadian population enjoys US television programs, movies, and music.

This attitude will ultimately lead to embarrassment and business failure, however. Canadians strive to be different than their neighbors to the south, and a blank assumption that they are merely "just another state" will be seen as rude and unprofessional. Also prepare for several differences between provinces, much more so than other countries. Businesses in Vancouver, BC may have some influence from the Pacific Rim, for example, and Montreal businesses may expect foreign businesspeople to speak French. Preparing for these cultural differences may not guarantee a successful trip, but it will undoubtedly keep humiliating situations to a minimum.

HISTORY AND IMMIGRATION

The history of Canada is one of constant immigration and settlement. The earliest arrivals in Canada were the Paleo-Indians, a migratory people who crossed into North America across the frozen Bering Strait from Siberia. Following the retreating glaciers of the last Ice Age, these early settlers migrated south and east and within a thousand years had occupied the entire continent. Due to the differing environmental conditions found in the various regions of Canada, there emerged among the descendants of these early migrators a group of diverse cultures. Along the west coast of Canada, the abundance of seafood allowed for the development of a sophisticated and artistic culture whose influences can still be seen in northwest Indian art today. In the plains areas of western Canada, a bison hunting culture emerged that employed primitive hunting techniques and a migratory way of life. The great lakes region of central Canada was the area of highest population density and was also the site of the only agricultural tribes in early Canada. The Eskimos of the far north lived on caribou and seals, which they hunted from small boats made of skin.

While these early inhabitants of Canada played an important role in the development of the nation, it was the European settlement, beginning in the sixteenth century, that had the most significant impact on the future of Canada.

The first Europeans to arrive in Canada were fishermen, drawn by the abundant catch found in the waters off Newfoundland's coast. While it is possible that fishing villages were established along the coast as early as the 13th century, it was not until the early 1500s that Europeans began to look inward toward the continent. The French were the first to realize the vast potential of the unexplored interior. In 1534, Jacques Cartier traversed the Gulf of St. Lawrence as far as modern Quebec City and claimed all of the surrounding territory for France. New France, as the territory became known, soon developed a lucrative fur trade with the Indians. As the market for furs in Europe increased, the British were soon drawn to Canada to try and claim a share of the spoils.

This signaled the start of an era of almost constant warfare between the French and the

---

CONTENTS
Introduction 153
History and Immigration 153
Canadian Social Values,
    Beliefs, and Behaviors 154
The National Business Style 156
Provincial Attitudes 158
Business Etiquette 160
Overseas Resources on
    Canadian Culture 161
Large versus Small Firms 162

British for control of Canada. Both countries encouraged settlers from the mother country to come to Canada as a way of bolstering their control over their own regions. The French and British armies, each aided by their own Indian allies, fought savagely in a series of wars that culminated in 1759 when the British, under General Wolfe, defeated the French and British control was extended over all of Canada. The extension of British control was followed by a large influx of immigrants from throughout the British Isles. The American Revolution, which began 15 years later, was responsible for a second large influx of British settlers from the Americas who moved north rather than joining in the American colonies' opposition to England. Known as United Empire Loyalists, these loyal British subjects settled mostly in present day Ontario and their conservative influence can still be felt there today.

Throughout the 18th and early 19th century, the demand for immigrants to Canada remained strong. The government encouraged immigration with subsidized transportation fees and the promise of free land. Canadian land agents recruited from all over Europe and America. Between 1901 and 1911, more than 1.5 million immigrants entered the country. The western half of Canada was still vastly underpopulated and hardy individuals were needed to tame the forests and till the soil. While immigrants from all over Europe were accepted, the majority of settlers came from England, Scotland, or Ireland.

The only people who were not welcome during this period of massive immigration were the Asians. In 1884, a head tax was levied on Chinese immigrants that steadily increased with time. In 1923, the Canadian Chinese Immigration Act was passed which virtually excluded Asian immigrants. After World War II, however, attitudes changed and the racially-based immigration policies were replaced.

With the completion of two intercontinental railways in the second half of the 19th century, Canada was able to open up the vast expanse of fertile prairie in the center of the country for settlement. Many Eastern Europeans were recruited to settle in this region, especially Ukrainians. Even today, there are more than one million Canadians of Ukrainian descent. On July 1, 1867, the provinces of Ontario, Quebec, New Brunswick, and Nova Scotia joined together in a confederation to form the country of Canada. The British North American Act of 1867 made the confederation legal. Other provinces and territories have since joined the confederation, the last being Newfoundland in 1949, to make up the modern country of Canada. While the creation of the confederation was the beginning of independence from Britain, Canada still remained tied to England for another 120 years. Until the passage of the Constitution Act of 1982, any changes to Canada's constitution had to be approved by the British government. After 1982, however, Canada became a fully independent nation. Although she holds no authority, the Queen of England is still Canada's Head of State, a recognition of the long ties between the two nations.

Immigration has continued at a rapid pace in Canada (more than 215,000 immigrants entered the country in 1994) but its makeup has changed dramatically. In the 1950s, for example, more than 85 percent of the immigrants to Canada were from Europe, with 30 percent from England alone. By 1989, the percentage of immigrants coming from Europe had dropped to 25 percent and the majority of immigrants (40 percent) came from Asia with a large minorities coming from Africa and Central America. Some experts say that by the turn of the century more Canadians will have origins outside North America than inside.

Another big change from the past is the destination of most immigrants. Most earlier immigrants tended to work on the land or in the mining or forestry industries. As a result, they tended to settle out in the rural areas. By contrast, almost all modern immigrants settle in the major cities, 50 percent in Toronto and Vancouver alone. A full 38 percent of Toronto's booming population is made up of people born outside of Canada. In Vancouver, which has an enormous Asian population, the figure is closer to 30 percent.

CANADIAN SOCIAL VALUES, BELIEFS, AND BEHAVIORS

Due to the enormous influence of immigration and the tendency among immigrants to Canada to retain their individual cultures, Canadian society can be said to be a mosaic of the various communities within its borders, rather than an entity of its own. There are some characteristics, however, that can be said to be general to many Canadians.

Tolerance, Diversity, Acceptance

Tolerance and respect of cultural differences is one of the most important qualities in the Canada. While there is certainly a degree of tension among the various ethnic groups that compose Canadian society, the Canadians as a whole are very accepting of different cultural values, religions, and lifestyles. While doing business in Canada, it is important for the visitor to remember that there is no one ethnic background that can be considered especially "Canadian." One major effect of this national attitude of tolerance is a relatively low degree of racism and discrimination in Canadian society.

Canadian business people expect international visitors to be polite, cordial, and knowledgeable about business. All people, regardless of gender, age, race, class, business, or income category are expected to be treated in the same professional manner. Canadian businesspeople are particularly concerned about results, profits, and fairness and they expect their foreign counterparts to be similarly oriented. When considering a deal, a Canadian person will want to know that a foreign businessperson has a history of performing and completing assignments.

Canadians will respond best if you treat them in a friendly and respectful manner. An attitude of superiority or condescension on the part of foreign negotiators is inappropriate, as is any behavior that suggests discrimination.

The Cautious Canadian

A common stereotype of Canadians is that they are overly-reserved, perhaps somewhat boring. While this is an exaggerated view at best, Canadians are overall a more cautious and conservative people than their American neighbors. Historically trapped between the demands of their two dominant cultures and the differing desires of Britain and the United States, this attitude of caution has enabled the Canadians to survive into the twentieth century.

In business, this sense of caution is illustrated by the slow and deliberate process that often accompanies major decision making. Canadians prefer to have detailed information for review and may take much longer to come to a decision than is usually expected. A product sample or demonstration can be a useful tool in influencing purchasing and partnership negotiations. Canadians are very wary of the "hard sell" and will most likely respond negatively to attempts to force them into making a quick decision. It is also quite common for Canadian businesses to appoint a committee to make major decisions as opposed to a single individual.

Canadians are generally reserved and formal in their business dealings. While this may vary to a great degree among individuals, in general Canadians prefer to conduct their business affairs in a formal and decorous manner. Emotional displays or brash or impatient behavior will most likely be looked upon with disfavor and may jeopardize a business relationship.

Provincial Attitudes

The separation of Canada into ten provinces and two territories is more than just a geographical division. Each province has its own unique flavor and Canadians tend to focus on their home province as opposed to the country as a whole. Many businesses operate only within their own home province and may be reluctant to expand beyond the surrounding geographical region. Canadians are also more likely to be interested in previous business dealings one has had in their own province than in work done in some far corner of the country.

Weather

No discussion of Canadian culture is complete without a discussion of the profound role that weather plays in Canadian life. While there are some climate differences, for most of the country, the winter months (November to March) are filled with snow and cold. Travelers to Canada in the winter should be prepared for temperatures well below freezing. Unlike people from the US who tend to dislike the cold, Canadians generally approach the winter months with a sense of optimism. Many try to take advantage of it by participating in winter sports and carnivals, which feature ice skating and enormous ice sculptures.

Education

Primary and secondary education in Canada is a provincial responsibility and the period of compulsory attendance varies from province to province. In general, primary education is from age five or six to 13 and is followed by three to five years of secondary education or "high school." Ninety-five percent of pupils attend public schools which are funded entirely with provincial and municipal monies. "Separate schools" (usually Roman Catholic) are funded by the tax dollars of those who indicate a preference and by the various provinces. There are also a small number of private and alternative schools scattered throughout Canada. French speaking students in some provinces are entitled by law to instruction in French. The popularity of these "French-only" schools is growing.

There are approximately 70 universities and more than 200 other institutions of higher learning in Canada. Canada enjoys the highest rate of postsecondary school enrollment in the world with more than 75 percent of secondary school graduates going on to some form of higher education. While a university degree is not essential for advancement in Canada, it is unusual to find someone in a high position in Canadian business who does not have some form of education beyond secondary schooling.

Virtually 100 percent of the Canadian population is literate and a large percentage are literate in both French and English.

Religion

The majority of Canadians consider themselves some form of Christian, divided mainly among Roman Catholics (4 percent) and mainline Protestant (41 percent). Canadian society is highly secularized and with the possible exception of the religiously based national holidays of Christmas and Easter, the international businessperson is likely to find transactions unaffected by religion. A visitor to Canada is rarely expected to be aware of the religion of the people with whom business is conducted and, as with most potentially charged topics, discussion of religion are best avoided.

Class

There is no formal class system in Canada and a person from a humble background has the opportunity to become a highly successful individual. In the eastern provinces of Ontario and Quebec, there are still remnants of an outdated class system that placed English speaking persons in a higher social and economic strata than French speaking ones. The government of Canada has taken strides in the last two decades to eliminate economic and social inequalities, however. As such, it is unwise to try to make assumptions about an individual's social position based on their language or ethnicity.

The international visitor is likely to conduct business primarily with members of the upper-middle and middle classes and the majority of the citizens of Canada would consider themselves in these categories. The upper middle class includes well paid executives and professionals from the public and private sectors. The middle class would include small business owners, teachers, farmers, and blue and white collar workers who own their own homes and have the disposable income to travel and buy a wide range of consumer goods.

Sleeping with the Elephant

Former Prime Minister Pierre Traded once described sharing a border with the United States as being similar to sleeping with an elephant. "No matter how friendly or even tempered is the beast, if I may call it that," he said, "one is affected by every twitch and grunt."

The relationship between Canada and the United States profoundly affects almost every aspect of Canadian society. The two nations share the longest undefended border and are the world's largest trading partners. NAFTA serves to strengthen what is for both countries their most important economic relationship. The influence of American culture is pervasive throughout Canada. Canadians watch American television and read American magazines and books.

While there are many cultural similarities between the two countries, Canadians take pride in being different and generally resent being treated or referred to as "Americans north of the border."

Canadian businesses do not appreciate being treated as simply an extension of a larger and more important US market. If a company plans to do business in both countries, an effort should be made to include the correct address prefixes ("Province" and "Postal Code" instead of the American "State" and "Zip Code") and bilingual packaging and text whenever possible. Canadians are very aware of their own marketplace and have a tendency to "Buy Canadian" whenever possible. Emphasizing the Canadian contribution to a product is always a good idea.

THE NATIONAL BUSINESS STYLE

Canadian business people are generally friendly and eager to establish positive working relationships. At the same time, they are generally eager to conduct the business at hand and usually do not desire to waste much time on niceties and formalities. In the major cities of the Eastern provinces such as Toronto and Montreal, the business pace is brisk and professional. As one moves farther out toward the West Coast, the pace generally slackens and the conduct of business is often less formal. While individual behavior varies from person to person, the style of Canadian business can still be described in general terms.

Direct Communication

Direct communication is valued in the Canadian business community at all times, regardless of the situation surrounding a discussion. This directness is associated with the English language, which is known as a "low context" language: the content of a word varies little regardless of the context in which it is spoken. Thus, "no" means "no" regardless of whether it is shouted in a boardroom or whispered at a formal dinner. Canadian businesspeople take pride in saying what they mean and they expect the same of others. As a result, some confusion can arise when a Canadian person meets with someone whose language is "high context" and whose words therefore have different meanings depending on where, when, and how they are spoken.

Business Hours

Business hours are generally 8:30 a.m. to 5:00 p.m. Monday through Friday, and many employees work on the weekends, as well. Banking hours are generally the same but the trend has been toward longer hours and weekend service. Hours for shops vary but in general they are open from 9:00 a.m. until 5:00 p.m. with some staying open longer or some (convenience and grocery stores) open 24 hours.

Negotiations

Negotiations are very much a integral part of the Canadian business process. The foreign businessperson needs to be aware that while Canadian businesspeople are generally interested in making constructive compromises that will result in a mutually beneficial agreement, they will certainly deal with a view toward their own self interest. Canadians value compromise and do not see willingness to compromise as a sign of weakness. Hard line attitudes or a total refusal to give any ground during negotiation will be interpreted as non-cooperation and may result in a break in the relationship.

Do everything possible to avoid miscommunication. This is particularly important when cultural differences exist between the parties. Canadians value honesty and will most likely sever a business relationship if they feel that the other parties to the negotiation have not been entirely forthright.

Canadians tend to make decisions cautiously and may employ a committee rather than a single representative in negotiation. They may also interrupt negotiation sessions to discuss developments among themselves. This should not be interpreted as either a sign of weakness nor incivility. Attempting to pressure Canadians into a decision or deal will most likely backfire and may permanently damage a business relationship.

If a decision can be authorized only after deliberation by all the principals over time, that requirement should be expressly stated. Such a statement is likely to find more acceptance than the action of the foreign trader who fails to follow through on a negotiated plan, claiming lack of authority.

Canadian negotiating style is usually open and direct. While negotiations are not rigidly formal, first names are not generally used and polite and reserved behavior is expected. As this varies greatly among individuals and regions, it is best to let the Canadian business people set the tone. It should be noted that Canadians are somewhat easy going and may look askance at angry or emotional outbursts during negotiation.

Working with Women

As in many countries, the prevalent attitudes toward women in the Canadian workplace were for many years somewhat patronizing. Many industries were devoid of female employees and very few high level jobs were held by women. In the last two decades, however, great strides have been made toward equality for women. It is now illegal to discriminate in hiring and promotion based on sex and legislation requiring pay equity is on the books in most Canadian provinces.

In business dealings, no deference should be paid to the gender of the Canadian businessperson. The same cultural characteristics are likely to be present, regardless of whether the person is male or female. The underlying rule is to treat a Canadian businesswoman with professional business respect—not gender based courtesy or condescension. Canadian women are protected by laws against harassment and discrimination in the workplace. Harassment may be broadly defined, and to avoid potential legal and social problems, you should never make sexually oriented comments, nor act in such a manner.

Working with Ethnic Groups

When working with one of the many ethnic groups in Canada, the most important thing to remember is to be tolerant and understanding of differences. Ethnic groups in Canada can be surprisingly unassimilated as compared to their counterparts in the United States. This should not be perceived as a lack of sophistication but rather a choice made possible by Canada's diverse and tolerant society.

Environmental Awareness

Canada is a land of natural beauty so it comes as no surprise that the Canadians are very environmentally conscious. Canadians will base purchasing decisions on environmental factors and will value goods that are recyclable and reusable over their disposable counterparts. The media is definitely helping spread the word of environmental awareness, with a number of features on the preservation of forests, the effects of acid rain, and the greenhouse effect. Many household products are being sold in environmental packaging.

Foreign businesses that show a lack of concern for the environment or deal in industries that are commonly associated with environmental degradation will be met with a cold reception by Canadians. Acid rain originating in the factories of manufacturing regions of the northern United States is a particularly sensitive environmental issue.

Language

Unofficially, Canada is a land of many languages. By law, however, Canada's languages are French and English, and just about all information, from street signs to cereal boxes, comes available in both languages. Although the languages have evolved somewhat from the French and English spoken in their native lands, they are still very similar.

Foreign businesses that intend to do business throughout the country should prepare all public materials in both French and English in order to avoid the perception of favoring one over the other. It should also be noted that in Canada, the British spelling of words is the most widely used, i.e. "colour" instead of "color," and "centre" instead of "center."

Sport

Sports are an important part of the social life in Canada. The official national sport of Canada is lacrosse, which is a modern version of an ancient Indian game played with a ball and sticks with small nets affixed to the end. The sport most visitors associate with Canada, however, is hockey. Watching hockey on television is a Saturday night tradition for many Canadians. Skiing, ice skating and tobogganing are also popular winter sports in Canada. For those who have never tried skiing or ice skating, it should be noted that these are skills that take some time to master and that attempting either without appropriate practice can be dangerous. In the summertime, swimming, tennis, and golf are popular recreational sports. Bicycling, whether for pleasure or sport, is also very popular, especially in the French speaking Quebec. Professional sports include Canadian football, which is similar to American football, baseball, soccer, and basketball. While most Canadians do not consider themselves to be as fanatical about sports as their American neighbors, (with whom they share their professional baseball, basketball, and hockey leagues), they are usually knowledgeable and willing to explain the details of a sport. Sports are also a safe topic for small talk.

Holidays

In Canada, national holidays are established by federal statute. A holiday that falls on a Saturday or a Sunday is observed the following Monday. During national holidays all government offices, banks and businesses are closed across Canada. In Quebec, most businesses are open on Victoria Day, and after 1:00 p.m. on Boxing Day.

PROVINCIAL ATTITUDES

The separation of Canada into ten provinces and two territories is more than just a geographical division. Each province has its own unique flavor and Canadians tend to focus on their home province as opposed to the country as a whole. Many businesses operate only within their own home province and may be reluctant to expand beyond the surrounding geographical region. Canadians are also more likely to be interested in previous business dealings one has had in their own province than in work done in some far corner of the country.

The Atlantic Region

Nova Scotia, New Brunswick, Newfoundland, and Prince Edward Island are Canada's Atlantic provinces. The proximity to the ocean, and especially the Great Banks fishery, off the coast of Newfoundland, has made the Atlantic provinces an important part of Canada's economic history. The first settlers in the region were French fishermen referred to as Acadians. In the 1700s, the British settled heavily in the Atlantic region and began widespread agricultural development. Some of the earliest settlers of African descent, mostly slaves from the American colonies who had jumped ship in Canadian ports or snuck aboard a Canada bound ship, also settled in New Brunswick and Nova Scotia.

The major industries in the region are fishing, farming, mining and forestry. The protection of the fishing industry and the prevention of illegal and overfishing have become hot political issues in the last decade as the fish stocks have declined. Newfoundland, traditionally dependent on fishing, has been especially hard hit by the fishing fiasco. While the province is trying to develop mining and other industries, it still has the lowest per capita income in all of Canada. The per capita income of the entire Atlantic Region makes it the poorest section of Canada.

In Prince Edward Island and New Brunswick, fruit crops and potatoes are widely grown for export. New Brunswick and Nova Scotia also have extensive forests that permit a large pulp and timber industry. The forest products industry is the most valuable manufacturing sector of the economy in New Brunswick. Most of the manufacturing in the region involves the processing of agricultural goods, timber and fish. There is also a flourishing tourist trade that attracts thousands each year to the Atlantic region to view its spectacular scenery and enjoy its beaches.

Ontario

Ontario is the richest and most economically important of all of Canada's provinces and is also the most diverse. Its capital city, Toronto, is the largest city in Canada and the business and financial center of the nation. The early settlers of Ontario were the United Empire Loyalists that fled the American Colonies at the start of the American Revolution. Staunchly British, Ontario has historically served as the main opposition of the predominantly French-speaking province of Quebec. There is, however, a large French speaking minority in Ontario, the largest in Canada outside of Quebec.

Toronto is a very multi-ethnic city, with a full 38 percent of its metropolitan population having been born outside of Canada. It has the reputation of being a clean, safe city. The crime, grafitti, and concentrated poverty that is so apparent in other large cities is not as prevalent here.

The most important sectors of Ontario's economy are its manufacturing and service industries The automobile industry is the single most important manufacturing industry in Ontario and forms one of Canada's most important exports. Mining is also very important, with Ontario mines producing more ore than any other province. Southern Ontario is an important agricultural region, producing much of the country's fruit and vegetables.

Quebec

The largest and most populous province in Canada, Quebec is home to a large French speaking population. Known as Quebecois, these descendants of the early French settlers have zealously guarded their cultural identity and to this day more than 80 percent of the residents of Quebec speak French as a first language. There is a strong independent movement among the Quebecois and many of them consider themselves part of a separate nation tied economically to the rest of Canada. In November of 1995, a public referendum on the independence of Quebec was defeated by an extremely narrow margin. In the wake of the referendum, feelings may still be strong about French-English relations in certain circumstances.

While most major businesspeople in Quebec are capable of conducting affairs in English, any attempt to use French will be highly appreciated and may go a long way toward cementing a positive relationship. In addition, any written materials and instructions should be bi-lingual. Gestures such as the use of French and the preparation of bi-lingual materials will demonstrate to the Quebecois businessperson that you consider them to be a unique and important market.

Etiquette and politeness are considered very important in Quebec. First names and informal greetings are generally not used and modes of dress are even more conservative and formal than in the rest of Canada.

Burping and other bodily noises are considered very offensive, even if apologized for. In addition, gesturing downward with the thumb is an offensive gesture and should be avoided. The natural resources of Quebec has helped the province to develop many important industries. Quebec is Canada's largest producer of pulp and paper and is a major producer of minerals.

The largest city in Quebec and second largest in all of Canada, Montreal is a major transportation hub for the region as well as the center for fashion and culture. Metropolitan Montreal is also a major manufacturing region, producing metal, chemical and wood products. Two-thirds of the people in Montreal are French-speaking, but there is a large English population in the downtown area, perhaps surprisingly so.

Prairie Provinces

Alberta, Manitoba and Saskatchewan are known as the prairie provinces. The prairies are plains that stretch across the southern part of the region. Treeless and very fertile, the region is primarily a center for grain and cattle ranching. Saskatchewan is the largest producer of wheat in Canada and Alberta leads the nation in beef cattle ranching. There is also a large energy industry devoted to tapping the region's large reserves of natural gas, coal and oil. Manitoba, known as the Land of 100,000 Lakes, is a large source of Canada's hydroelectric power. While energy and farming are very important industries in the region, there is also a large service and manufacturing sector to the local economy. The people of the prairie provinces are known for their hardiness and tolerance. Descendants of immigrants from Europe and elsewhere, the people in the prairie regions have a reputation for both hardiness and tolerance.

British Columbia

The west coast of Canada is comprised of the province of British Columbia. A mountainous and heavily forested province, British Columbia relies on its natural resources to underpin its economy. The forest industry in BC is the largest in Canada and accounts for more than half of all goods produced in the province. Salmon fishing and hydroelectric power are also extremely important resource industries in the region.

The early settlers in British Columbia were fur traders who arrived as the fur trade spread to the West in the 1800s. In the late 1800s, thousands of Chinese were brought to BC to help finish the transcontinental railroad. Many of their descendants stayed in BC and the province now has the largest Asian population of any part of Canada.

Vancouver, the largest city in BC and the third largest in Canada, provides important air and sea links to important markets in the United States and Asia.

British Columbians often jokingly refer to their province as "British California." The great distance from Ottawa and the close economic ties with the United States combine to give British Columbians a sense of isolation from their own country. A British Columbian businessperson is more likely to do business in Seattle or San Francisco than Toronto.

The Far North

The North, comprised of the province of the Yukon and the Northwest Territories, is an area of vast size and infinitesimal population. Intensely cold during the winter, the North is inhabited by a mixture of aboriginal peoples and workers in the mining and energy industries. Many of the aboriginal people in the region still make a living from their traditional hunting and trapping, but the most important industry for the native peoples is their arts and crafts that are sold throughout Canada. Thousands of people first came to the north during the Yukon Gold Rush at the end of the 1800s. A modern day gold rush is going on today with mining for gold, lead and zinc and the development of oil and gas ventures.

The weather is the predominant feature of life in the North. The sun shines all day and night during the short summer season, giving the region its name "Land of the Midnight Sun." The winters, however, are long, dark and brutally cold. The coldest temperature ever recorded in Canada was in the Yukon (-63 C).

BUSINESS ETIQUETTE

Greetings

People usually greet each other by smiling and making eye contact. Firm handshakes are given and received using the right hand. A weak handshake may convey a negative impression of uncertainty, lack of confidence or even insincerity. Most Canadians are not comfortable with the use of first names in the beginning of a business relationship, although this varies among individuals.

Greetings in a business situation are usually "Good Morning" or "Good Evening" depending on the time of day. To this you should repeat whatever greeting your host has offered. In a social situation, salutations include something along the lines of "Hi" or "Hello." Any of these greetings may be followed by a question such as "How are you?" or "How is it going?" The expected response is a brief one—such as, "Fine, thanks, and you?"—to which the first speaker says "Fine" or makes a similar short reply. These ritualized greetings are seldom designed to elicit an honest or detailed response and a literal response abut your health, mental state or business conditions will confuse the questioner.

Beyond handshakes, physical touching is not the norm and it may indicate a different type of relationship. The European tradition of kissing lightly upon the cheeks can be found on occasion in Quebec but will most likely not be employed with a foreign visitor and should not be attempted.

Most Canadians prefer to stand or sit at least an outstretched arm's length away while having conversation. Some may spontaneously touch your arm or shoulder while making conversation but most find such touching annoying or even offensive.

On the other hand, failure to make eye contact frequently on meeting and during subsequent interaction may create the impression that you are untrustworthy.

Canadians are also self effacing and do not take themselves too seriously. Conversation that may appear overly boastful or self laudatory should be avoided.

Making Conversation

After a greeting, a common question for first time acquaintances is "What do you do?" The appropriate answer is brief description of one's profession, usually with a designation that clues the other person into the responsibility of your position—such as "I own a wine import company" or "I am the director of international marketing for the ABC corporation" or "I am a patent attorney for a bio technology company."

Good topics of conversation include sports (hockey, basketball, baseball or Canadian Football), travel, jobs and hobbies.

Gestures

Gestures are used to varying degrees in Canada. They may be used freely and expansively, in a restrained manner, for emphasis, or unconsciously. Shaking the head from side to side means no, while shaking it up and down indicates agreement. Surprise may be shown by raising the eyebrows. People are beckoned by curling the index forward toward oneself while holding the palm upward. Uncertainty may be indicated by shrugging the shoulders. Holding the palm out with the palm facing forward means stop.

Many gestures that are considered rude or even obscene in other countries may be used innocently in Canada. Foreigners should not take offense to such gestures unless the person making them is from a similar background and clearly intends disrespect. As in the United States, the upturned middle finger while holding the other fingers into the hand is a gesture intended to show offense. Turning the hand over so that the thumb points downward is also a gesture that should be avoided.

Business Dress

The Canadians are stylish dressers and have an overall conservative dress code. International standards of corporate attire that are accepted in cosmopolitan cities around the world apply. Most men wear suits or sport jackets and trousers, accented with a patterned necktie. Shoes are minimally adorned and made of dark leather; dark socks are the norm. In the cosmopolitan cities of Montreal and Toronto, expensive Italian suits are very popular and business men often dress with the intent of displaying a impression of wealth and power.

Women wear skirts or suits with pants, ensembles of skirts or trousers with jackets or dresses that often coordinate with jackets.

Hem lengths vary from just above the knee to a few inches above the ankle. Most women executives wear little or no discernible makeup and style their hair simply.

Dress is less formal in manufacturing and similar firms where client contact is less important and formal dress less functional. Extremes of fashion are generally not accepted. Jewelry should be inconspicuous on both genders. Neatness is essential.

OVERSEAS RESOURCES ON CANADIAN CULTURE

Rather than relying on the often distorted or outdated view of Canadians found in literature and film, observers of Canadian business culture recommend that prospective foreign visitors to Canada prepare by reading Canadian newspapers. The national newspaper is The Globe and Mail. The national business newspaper is The Financial Post. Each major city also has at least one daily paper.

Vancouver - *The Vancouver Sun,*

Ottawa- *The Ottawa Citizen, Le Adroit*

Toronto- *The Toronto Sun, The Toronto Star*

Montreal- *The Gazette, Le Devoir, Le Journal de Montreal, La Presse*

Quebec- *Le Soleil.*

The most important Canadian business magazines are The Financial Post Magazine and Canadian Business, both published monthly. The Nation's weekly newsmagazine, Maclean's, also has a business component.

Current television news programs can also be helpful in suggesting a sense of Canadian business style, concerns, and attitudes. Canada has two national television networks, the Canadian Broadcasting Corporation (CBC) and Canadian Television (CTV). Both networks offer morning and evening news shows.

The best guidebook for doing business in Canada is *The Wall Street Journal Guides to Business Travel: USA & Canada*, New York: Fodor's Travel Publications, 1991. ISBN 0-679-02176-0. US $50 (boxed set). City-by-city guide to the major business cities of Canada and the United States with maps, information on business services available, and other tips for the business traveler. Unfortunately, it has not been updated since 1991 and can be difficult to find.

A growing amount of information about Canada is available over the Internet. Some newsgroups of interest include soc. culture.Quebec and soc.culture.canada. The Department of Foreign Affairs and International Trade (DFAIT) has a Web site at http://www.dfait-maeci.ac.ca/english/menu.htm. Canadian-based Information Systems has an address at http://www.cs.cmu.edu/Web/Unofficial. Canada Business Center's address is http://csclub.uwaterloo.ca/u/nckwan/html/, and Welcome to Industry Canada's is http://info.ic.gc.ca/ic-data/ic-eng.html.

Firms, businesspeople, and business associations that are non native but have had dealings with Canadian businesses are often good sources.

Canadian businesses operate in many countries, and their employees are sometimes amenable to meeting with those who wish to learn more about Australia and to initiate a network of referrals.

Requests to and consultation with the Canadian embassy, consulates, and other governmental agencies, specifically those regulating the business in which you are interested, can be sources on industry and regional variations from the general Canadian business style.

Home country banks with Canadian operations or Australian bank branches in your country may have services that can advise you.

For industry-specific information, trade associations and chambers of commerce in Canada are also excellent sources. Refer to the "Important Addresses" chapter for contact information on Australian publications, organizations, and bookstores.

Business Cards

In Canada, business cards are exchanged informally usually during initial contact. A well designed card is striking but understated and clearly identifies you and your company. Bilingual cards with English on one side and French on the other are a nice touch that will be noticed and remembered.

Timeliness

Business appointments and meetings begin on time. Keeping you waiting is not an accepted business practice and lateness may be viewed in an extremely negative light. Foreign business travelers should plan to arrive a few minutes early to all appointments and should contact the other parties in the case of unavoidable delay. To keep relationships smooth, regular contact should be maintained and businesspeople should take pains to avoid catching their Canadian business partners by surprise.

LARGE VERSUS SMALL FIRMS

Large Firms

Large businesses are by nature hierarchical. They tend to distribute authority across a wide range of functional, project or geographical specializations and strive for the highest return. Many of the largest firms in Canada are jointly or totally owned by American firms or are a Canadian subsidiary of a larger American firm. In this case, the corporate culture will be more American in flavor than Canadian.

The reaction times of large firms is often quite long and decisions can take several months due to the many layers of management that must be consulted.

What large lack in flexibility and responsiveness, they more than make up for with their depth in resources. Corporations are not necessarily the faceless, impersonal machines that they may seem. Each will have its own personality and culture.

Medium Firms

Generally, medium size firms in Canada are able to blend some of the stability of the larger business with the agility of the smaller one. Medium size firms are often geared toward doing business in their own geographical area (usually their province) and may lack a continental or global vision.

Small Firms

Businesses that are smaller—especially entrepreneurial ones—are generally more accommodating, more emotionally driven and quicker to act. However, due to a lack of funds and resources, smaller firms may be unable to sustain new or different programs. Small firms in Canada often have a very narrow vision that encompasses their own province and little else.

Small firms are usually more interested in growth and stability than they are in maximizing profits. Because of their small size and limited resources, small firms cannot rely on reserves and momentum to carry them along: when things go bad, they tend to go bad quickly.

Demograhics

STATISTICAL SOURCES

The statistics gathered in this section represent a variety of sources and timelines. The data may vary somewhat from source to source, but should provide the reader with a solid background on trends in Canada. Most of the sources listed below are updated annually, and the most recent available were consulted for this chapter. A number of these statistical resources are now available online. Refer to the "Important Addresses" chapter for listings of other statistical publications and sources.

Canada Business Facts 1994 and 1995, Canadian Department of Foreign Affairs and International Trade, and Statistics Canada

CIA World Factbook 1995, US Central Intelligence Agency

Demographic Year Book, New York, United Nations Statistical Office

Europa World Year Book 1995, London, England: Europa Publications, Ltd

International Marketing and Data Statistics, 1995, London, England: Euromonitor International, Inc.

National Trade Data Bank, US Dept. of Commerce, Dept. of State, and Dept. of Labor

OECD Economic Survey, Canada 1994. Paris, France: Organization for Economic Cooperation and Development

Statistical Abstract of the World 1994, New York: Gale Research Inc.

Statistical Abstract of the United States, Washington, DC: US Department of Commerce

World Economic and Social Survey, New York: United Nations

Population

AGE DISTRIBUTION

Population by Age and Sex, 1993 (thousands)

Age	Male	Female	Total
Total	14,343	14,686	29,029
0-14	3,034	2,898	5,932
15-34	4,620	4,481	9,101
34-54	4,049	4,012	8,061
55-74	2,127	2,349	4,476
75+	513	946	1,459

Source: Statistics Canada

ETHNIC ORIGIN

British	40%
French	27%
Other European	20%
Indigenous	13%

Source: CIA World Factbook, 1995

POPULATION PROJECTIONS

in millions

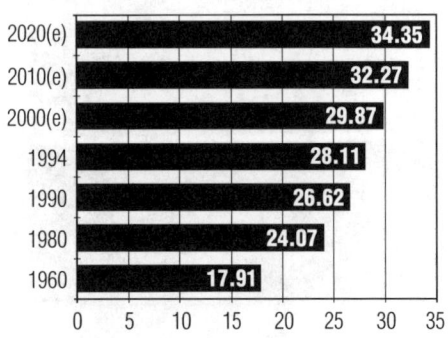

2020(e)	34.35
2010(e)	32.27
2000(e)	29.87
1994	28.11
1990	26.62
1980	24.07
1960	17.91

Source: Statistical Abstract of the World, 1994

POPULATION TRENDS

Population:	28,434,545
Population growth rate:	1.09%
Birth Rate:	13.74 births/1,000 population
Death Rate:	7.43 deaths/1,000 population
Net migration rate:	4.55 migrant(s)/1,000 population
Adult Literacy	97%
Life Expectancy at Birth:	
male:	74.93 years
female:	81.81 years
Total fertility rate:	1.83 children born/woman

Source: CIA World Factbook, 1995

URBAN VS. RURAL POPULATION

% of population	1931	1961	1991
Urban	53	70	77
Rural	47	30	23

Education

PUBLIC EDUCATION EXPENDITURES
(C$ millions)

	1980	1985	1988	1989	1990
Total educational expenditures	22,100	32,429	42,024	44,187	47,708
as a % of GNP	7.4	7.1	7.2	7.1	7.4
as a % of total govt. expenditures	17.3	12.7	15.9	15.3	15.6

Source: Statistical Abstract of the World, 1994

EDUCATION OF WORKERS

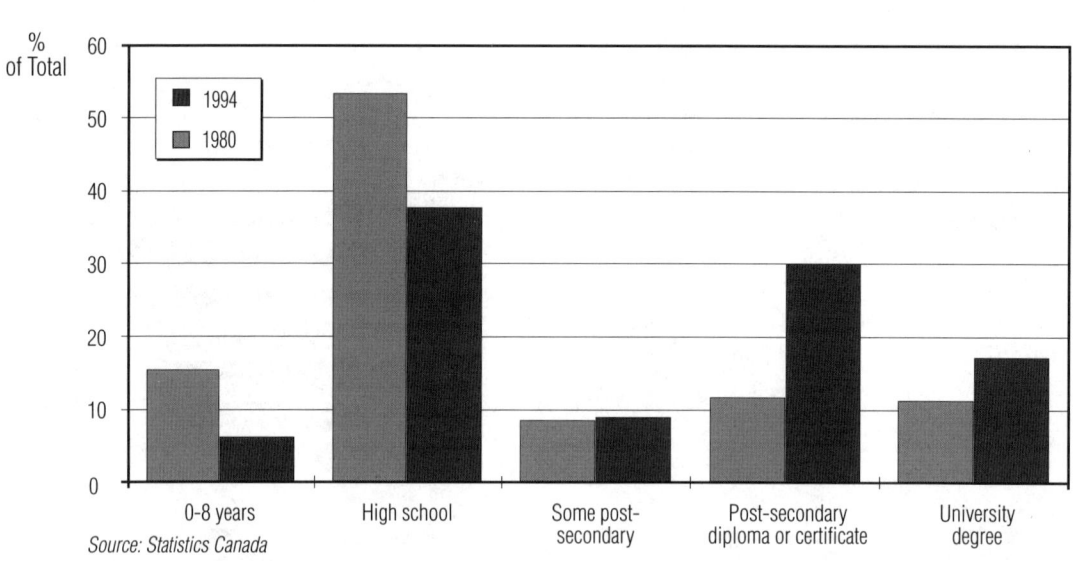

Source: Statistics Canada

Labor

LABOR TRENDS

	1993	1994	% Change
Per Capita GDP, current prices (US$)	19,092	18,769	-1.7
Labor Force, civilian (millions)	13.8	13.9	0.7
male	7.6	7.6	0.0
female	6.2	6.3	1.6
Labor Force Participation (%)	48.5	48.5	0.0
Employment, civilian (millions)	13.0	13.3	2.1
in industry	2.8	3.0	4.5
in agriculture	0.5	0.4	-5.6
in services	9.7	9.9	1.8
Unemployment Rate	11.2	10.4	-7.1
Labor Productivity in Manufacturing (1986=100)	108.6	111.1	2.3
Work Days Lost from Industrial Disputes	498.7	726.6	45.7
Hourly Compensation Costs for Workers in Manufacturing	16.97	16.33	-3.8
Unionization of Labor (%)	29.5	29.2	-1.0
Average Disposable Income per Year at Current Prices (US$)	16,874	16,801	-0.4

Source: USDOL, Foreign Labor Trends

EMPLOYED PERSONS BY MAJOR INDUSTRY

	1990	1995	% Change
Goods Industries (total)	3,809,400	3,653,100	-4.1
Service Industries (total)	9,355,700	9,852,400	5.31
Agriculture	440,700	430,500	-2.31
Other Primary Industries	297,600	295,700	-0.64
Manufacturing	2,105,000	2,060,900	-2.10
Construction	824,000	723,600	-12.18
Community, business and personal services	4,487,500	5,036,300	12.23
Trade	2,355,600	2,306,700	-2.08
Transportation, communications & other utilities	995,200	1,032,800	3.78
Public administration	869,500	809,900	-6.80
Finance, insurance, and real estate	790,300	809,200	2.39
Total	13,165,100	13,505,500	2.59

Source: Census of Canada

HEALTH CARE STATISTICS

Doctors per 1,000 (1988-1992)	Nurse-to-Doctor ratio (1988-1992)	Hospital Beds per 1,000 (1985-1990)	Health Expenditures (as a % of GDP)
2.22	4.7	16.1	9.1

Source: Statistical Abstract of the World, 1994

WAGE SETTLEMENTS (EFFECTIVE ANNUAL % OF INCOME)

	1991	1992	1993	1994
All Industries	3.6	2.1	.6	.3
Commercial	4.0	2.6	.9	1.2
Non-commercial	3.4	1.8	.5	-.2
Employees ('000)	1,346	1,318	1,417	906

Source: Canada at a Glance 1995

SELECT CONSUMER EXPENDITURES, 1993

(units '000)

	Canada	US
TVs	1,371	20,603
Washing Machines	538	5,902
Video Recorders	1,300	12,100
Stereos	1,430	7,412
Microwaves	796	6,970
In-car entertainment	2,596	26,029

Source: International Marketing and Data Statistics, 1995

TOTAL RETAIL SALES OF SELECTED GOODS, 1993

CDs (millions of units)	38.8
LPs (millions of units)	2.0
Pre-recorded cassettes (millions of units)	28.3
Toys & Games (US$ millions)	1,019.3
Recorded Music (US$ millions)	869.8

Source: International Marketing and Data Statistics, 1995

Transportation

HIGHWAYS

in kilometers

	Highways		Inland		
Total	Paved	Unpaved	Waterways	Ports (#)	Airports (#)
849,404	253,692	595,712	3,000	15	1,420*

*Usable: 1,142. With permanent surface runways: 457; w/runways over 3,659 m, 4; runways under 2,440 m, 360.

Source: CIA World Fact Book 1995

NEW REGISTRATIONS OF VEHICLES 1981-1993

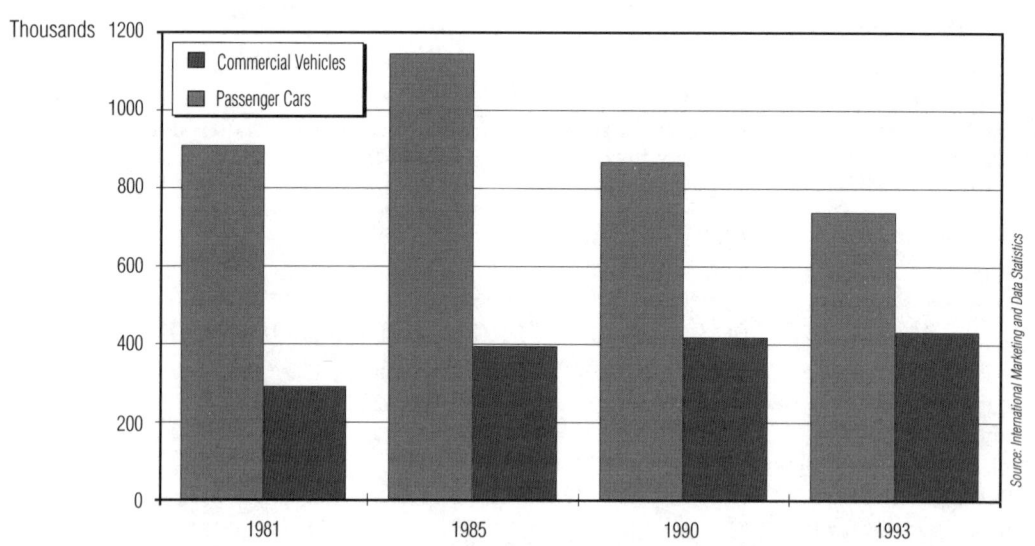

Source: International Marketing and Data Statistics

Media, Communications and Advertising

ADVERTISING BY MEDIUM
(as a Proportion of total billing)

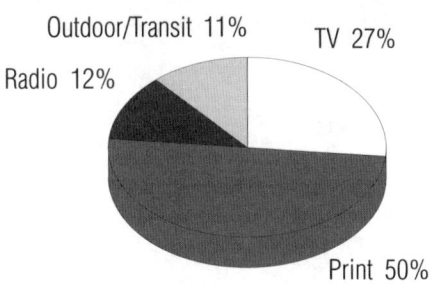

Outdoor/Transit 11%
TV 27%
Radio 12%
Print 50%

Note: Total expenditures in 1992/93 were C$8.3 billion
Source: International Marketing Data and Statistics, 1995

OWNERSHIP OF MEDIA EQUIPMENT -1992

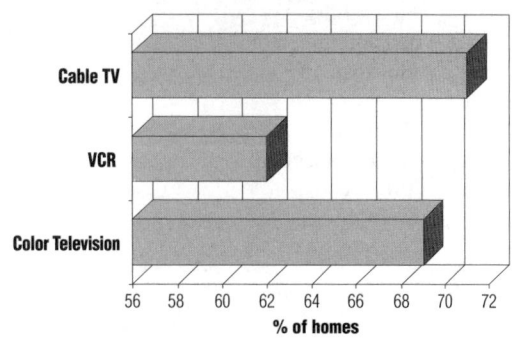

Source: International Marketing and Data Statistics 1995

CANADIAN NEWSPAPERS

Year	English	Circulation	French	Circulation	Total Circ.
1981	106	6,408,000	11	980,000	5,620,000
1991	95	4,828,000	11	987,000	5,815,000

CABLE

	1986	1991
Total Revenues ($000)	767,040	1,477,609
Number of Subscribers	6,005,000	7,286,000
Total Households w/Cable	7,686,000	9,241,000

PHONES IN USE (MILLIONS)

	Business	Residential	Total	Total per Population
1981	4,430	10,866	15,296	57%
1990	5,193	11,751	16,944	70%

Source: Canada Year Book, 1994

OVERALL EXPENDITURES IN ADVERTISING
(in millions)

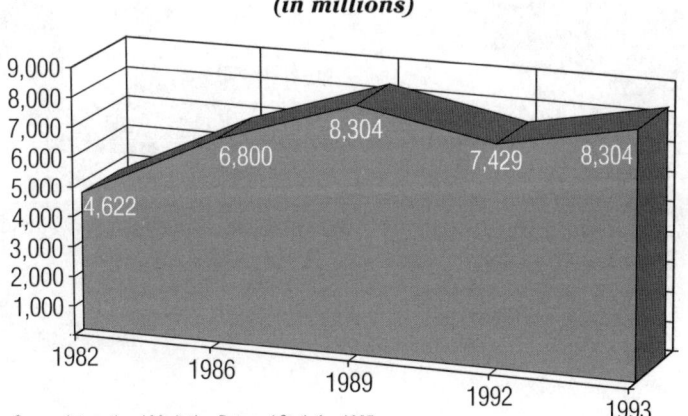

1982: 4,622
1986: 6,800
1989: 8,304
1992: 7,429
1993: 8,304

Source: International Marketing Data and Statistics 1995

TOP 10 CITIES FOR MEDICAL AND HEALTH CONSIDERATIONS

1. Vancouver
2. Geneva
3. Luxemborg
4. Stockholm
5. Montreal
6. Calgary
7. Helsinki
8. San Francisco
9. Toronto
10. Munich

Source: Corporate Resources Group, 1995

TOP 10 CITIES WITH HIGHEST QUALITY OF LIFE*

1. Geneva
2. Vancouver
3. Vienna
4. Toronto
5. Luxemborg
6. Ottawa
7. Zurich
8. Montreal
9. Dusseldorf
10. Singapore

Note: QL indicator is composite of 42 variables

POPULATION BY PROVINCE/TERRITORY

	1981	1993	1994	% Change '93/'94
Newfoundland	567,000	582,700	577,900	-.82
Prince Edward Island	122,500	133,900	135,600	1.27
Nova Scotia	847,400	932,700	935,800	.33
New Brunswick	696,400	756,700	759,100	.32
Quebec	6,438,400	7,270,400	7,308,200	.52
Ontario	8,625,100	10,872,700	11,004,800	1.21
Manitoba	1,026,200	1,126,100	1,131,800	.51
Saskatchewan	968,300	1,010,900	1,013,600	.27
Alberta	2,237,700	2,701,400	2,727,300	.96
British Columbia	2,744,500	3,627,000	3,724,100	2.68
Yukon	23,100	29,600	29,700	.34
Northwest Territories	45,700	64,300	65,400	1.71

Source: Census for Canada

Energy

ENERGY CONSUMPTION AND PRODUCTION - 1991

Consumption by type
- Nuclear 9%
- Coal 10%
- Petroleum 30%
- Natural Gas 23%
- Hydroelectric Power 28%

Production by type
- Natural Gas Liquids 5%
- Nuclear 7%
- Coal 12%
- Crude Oil 24%
- Natural Gas 29%
- Hydroelectric Power 23%

Source: Statistical Abstract of the World, 1994

Marketing

KEYS TO MARKETING IN CANADA

With some cultural and social limitations, Canadian markets are relatively accessible to foreign products and businesses, from the smaller independent operator to the large multinational. Marketing goods and services in Canada can involve selling to a local retailer, or establishing a company, or even a national network of sales, distribution, and service centers. One of the major challenges Canadian markets can present lies in the multicultural and independent nature of the Canadian provinces. Canada is often referred to as a mosaic rather than a melting pot of different cultures. Rather than a mixture of cultures, there are islands, or pockets, of individual cultural attitudes and beliefs. Marketing strategies will probably have to be adapted to work in Canada, each province with a different scheme. An additional barrier to entry is the level of competition that exists in highly developed markets, rather than the difficulties associated with getting the product into the country, as is often the case elsewhere. Significant advance planning is a necessity to successfully market in Canada.

CONTENTS

Keys to Marketing in Canada	169
Speaking Lingua Franca	170
Marketing to Diversity	171
Current Demographic and Economic Trends	172
Current Breakdown of Canadian Households	174
Where is the Market Located?	175
Canadians By Age	175
Advertising Channels	177
1994 Canadian market Expenditures (C$)	178
Exporting to Canada: Five In-House Rules	180
Useful Addresses	181

Marketing Basics

One key to successful entry into Canada is to keep initial costs as low as possible until you have established a foothold; this argues for careful test marketing. It is not necessary to spend a fortune on research to learn whether there is a market; it is easy to find that out from a variety of sources. This book is one, others include foreign embassy commercial services, the Canadian Department of Commerce, Canadian trade associations, private marketing research firms such as Nielsen Canada and Canadian Facts, and state and local economic development agencies in Canada.

Another key to success in the Canadian marketplace is to ensure timely delivery of your product. Industrial and individual customers in Canada place strong emphasis on timeliness. If promised goods are not delivered on schedule, a Canadian company is likely to seek another source of supply, and if a product is not stocked in a store, a Canadian customer will often purchase a competing item. Do not promise something that cannot be delivered, and always deliver on what has been promised.

A careful approach to marketing can often make the difference between profit and loss: This is particularly critical if a market is saturated with a product that costs all manufacturers roughly the same to produce and distribute. Development of a different product may seem wise in such a situation, but an innovative and careful marketing plan may prove to be just as workable; and, ultimately more profitable, than undertaking the costs and delay associated with new product development.

Manufacturing, agriculture, forestry, mining, tourism, and services are all well-developed markets in Canada. Indeed, the question to ask is not "Is there a market?" but "What is the best market for the product or service in Canada?" The answer to this question must be derived from an evaluation of the product or service's intended and potential uses, which in turn leads to identification

> ## SPEAKING LINGUA FRANCA
>
> Canada has two official languages, English and French, and the government provides equal right and privileges to their use in all institutions. Approximately 63 percent and 25 percent of the population speak these two languages, respectively. In addition, 13 percent can speak Italian, Chinese and German. Fifty-four percent of non-English and French speakers live in Toronto, Montreal or Vancouver.
>
> It is imperative to be aware of the differences in Canadian language. Marketing in Canada should take into account the unique combinations of language used, as both Canadian English and Canadian French employ components of French, British and American spelling. Indeed, Canadian French differs significantly from European French, just as Canadian English differs significantly from British English. The Quebec Charter of the French Language includes provisions concerning firm names, public signs and commercial advertising, product labeling, catalogs and brochures. It is highly recommended that anyone seeking to do business in or with Canada refer to the Quebec Charter and obtain a good Canadian dictionary. Showing sensitivity to Canadian linguistic particulars will demonstrate that a company understands Canadians and can meet their needs.
>
> There is quite a bit of British influence on Canadian spellings. Some of the most common differences with Canadian and American spellings include:
> - "-re" versus "-er" endings. Words such as "center" and "meter" in American would be spelled "centre" and "metre" in Canada, respectively.
> - "-our" versus "-or" endings. American words like "color" and "neighbor" would probably be spelled "colour" and "neighbour" in Canada.
>
> There are also many differences that don't fit into any category. While Canadians use the British 'cheque' rather than the American 'check', they also use curb instead of the British kerb.
>
> Marketing to French-speaking Canadians can sometimes be a very delicate matter. By law, marketing and other product material must be available in both languages. Keep in mind, however, that the French copy will normally be 20 percent longer than the English copy.

of the most likely users. To sell a product or service successfully in today's crowded and competitive Canadian consumer market, one must recognize the customers likely to use the product, determine the product attributes most likely to appeal to those customers, and tailor the merchandise, quality, packaging, and presentation accordingly. A trader's research should include:
- Evaluation and identification of the customers most likely to purchase the product (and how they will use it).
- Learning the characteristics of regional and other niche markets.
- Identifying the best marketing channels for your product, and find the right means of advertising.
- Tailoring the product to overcome obvious and hidden trade barriers.

Moreover, it is advisable to consult with a lawyer if your marketing activities include: comparative advertising; contest rules and copy; free or discount offers; price mentioning; disclaimers, testimonials, guarantees or warranties; facsimiles of currency, coinage or stamps; new names or trademarks; and product packaging. (A review of the "Industry Reviews" and "Opportunities" chapters will help identify the domestic competition and the opportunities for trading with Canadian businesses. Helpful contacts, particularly trade associations, chambers of commerce, and government agencies are listed in the "Important Addresses" chapter.)

The Canadian Market

Encompassing 3,851,808 square miles and stretching across five time zones, Canada is the world's second largest country (Russia is the largest). Still, Canada has a lower population density than virtually any other nation and almost 90 percent of the country is uninhabited. Total population is 29 million people, 85 percent of whom live within 100 miles (161 km) of the US border.

In a 1994 UN assessment of development indicators, Canada was ranked second in income, education, life expectancy and other variables; Canadian consumers tend to be very knowledgeable and sophisticated. Annually, over $200 billion in goods are traded between the US and Canada, making the two countries each other's largest trading partners. Despite this proximity to and close trading association with the US, Canadians inherit a large part of their culture from other Commonwealth countries and the francophile world, as 24 percent report French as their mother tongue. As a result, marketing to Canadians as if they were Americans can be a very costly and time consuming mistake.

Additionally, Canadians tend to be more conservative and reserved, with a definite but subtle sense of national pride. Despite the passage of NAFTA, Canadians remain skeptical of free trade and are very cognizant of the need to support domestic industries. Thus, shopping Canadian is something that is encouraged. If an international trader wants to optimize marketing success, goods should be marked as Canadian-made or indicate any Canadian content.

Sensitivity to Canadian ways is critical. That means using Canadian media, bilingual packaging and Canadian forms and warranty cards that ask for the province and Canadian postal code.

It is also important to note that Canadians are very environmentally aware: reduce, reuse and recycle are key buzzwords for consumers. Businesses, products or services that are environmentally sensitive have an advantage in the Canadian marketplace. For example, products that are ozone friendly will be better received than those that are blatantly over-packaged, non-biodegradeable or result in toxic waste. Companies that threaten, exploit or deplete those resources are met with strong opposition. Much of this is rooted in the fact that Canada is rich in natural resources. Indeed, since the early 1970s, consumer advocates, environmental groups and politicians have been active in educating Canadians about the need to preserve the country's natural resources.

Geography and Climate

As the second largest country in the world, half of Canada's land mass is the central Canadian Shield, a glacier of large rock centered on Hudson Bay. Only eight percent of Canada is suitable for cultivation. The physical geography is generally made up of three lowland zones, sparsely populated interior plains, ice-covered Arctic plains, and the Great Lakes and St. Lawrence areas, which are the most populated.

The far west geography includes the Cordillera, parallel mountain ranges which fall into Vancouver, and the Queen Charlotte Islands. To the east there are the Appalachians which run from Quebec through the Gaspe Peninsula to Newfoundland. Canada's highest point is Mount Loga, which stands 6,050 meters (19,850 feet), and Canada's main rivers (the St. Lawrence, Yukon, Mackenzie and Fraser) are among the world's forty largest. Canada is comprised of ten provinces and two territories, the Yukon and Northwest Territories, and is bound by three oceans (the Atlantic, Pacific and Arctic).

Utilizing this information along with a level of geographic knowledge will likely elicit positive responses from Canadians sensitive to their region and environment.

Canada's climate ranges from polar and sub-polar in the north to cool in the south. Winters in the interior are long and typically are made up of deep snow and temperatures well below freezing. In general, there are mild, continental weather patterns in the prairies (fairly dry inland with a monthly average temperature range of 17°C to 19°C (61°F to 66°F), to northern Arctic temperatures elsewhere. The Pacific coast tends to be mild and wet, with the warmest winters and temperatures that rarely fall below zero.

MARKETING TO DIVERSITY

With almost 90 percent of the country uninhabited, more than 61 percent of the population is clustered around the four major cities of Montreal, Toronto, Winnipeg and Vancouver. And because the total Canadian population is roughly 1/10 that of the US, marketing to Canadians is more expensive per capita than it is to most other markets. (The average population density in 1993 was three people per square kilometer, or 7.7 per square mile, with distribution ranging from 0.02 per square kilometer, or 0.045 per square mile, in the Northwest Territories, to 22.8 per square kilometer, or 59 per square mile, on Prince Edward Island.) Due to the large size and sparsely populated nature of the country, and its wide variety of climates and terrains, distribution costs are dramatically higher. All but the Maritime provinces have large areas that are virtually uninhabited, and 77 percent of all Canadians live in urban communities.

Approximately 51 percent of the population is female, with 83.5 percent of the population Canadian-born. Those of whole or partial British or Irish origin comprise 44.6 percent of the population, with people of French origin making up 31.1 percent, Germans 3.3 percent, Italians 2.8 percent, Ukranians 1.5 percent and Dutch 1.3 percent. Almost 30 percent of the population claims multiple ethnic origins. About 16 percent, or four million, of the Canadian population is classified as immigrant. In addition to family and business immigration, Canada sometimes provides asylum for persecuted refugees and has harbored more than 568,000 persons within the last decade.

American Indians make up the sixth largest ethnic group, at 1.4 percent. In 1993 there were more than 604 Indian tribes living in Canada on 2,364 reservations. In addition, there are more than 30,000 Inuits or Eskimos living in the Northwest Territories, with about half of those living in the

Canadian Arctic. In 1991 they were accorded their own autonomous state, Nunavut, which consists of part of the mainland of the Northwest Territories and several Arctic Islands, including Baffin Island.

Ethnic diversity is growing. Immigration averaged more than 118,600 for the years 1975 through 1985. By 1993 immigration jumped to more than 252,000 annually, with 53 percent from Asia, 20 percent from Europe, 8 percent from Africa, 7.5 percent from the Caribbean, 4.5 percent from South America and 2.6 percent from the US. This, coupled with Canada's shrinking birthrate, indicates the Canadian population is experiencing a marked shift in cultural dynamics. Asian immigrants are beginning to dominate, totaling nearly 40 percent in the city of Toronto and 24 percent in the province of Ontario.

Marketing and other promotional material should take these realities into account and reflect a sensitivity to the role women and minorities play in Canadian society. Examples of this include utilizing material that is not gender-specific and ensuring that a representative mix of race and gender is included.

Religion

The Canadian Bill of Rights specifically protects freedom of religion for all Canadians. There are, therefore, many thriving religious groups within the country. The Roman Catholic Church (45 percent), the United Church of Canada, the Anglican Church, the Presbyterian Church, Lutherans and Baptists represent the principal religious denominations in Canada. Unlike some countries where religion determines business, social and political conduct, product marketing in Canada should be free from religious overtones.

Education

Canadian education is taken very seriously with more than 95 percent literacy among Canadian adults. Primary and secondary education is free and compulsory, with 92 percent attendance for secondary school. In the last 25 years, university enrollment has increased 110 percent and the student-teacher ratio dropped from 23 to 15. In 1993 there were 69 universities and 203 other institutions of higher learning. Indeed, Canada has the highest proportion of educated students in the industrialized world, with more than 75 percent of secondary students going on to some form of higher education.

Government

The Canadian government is a parliamentary and federal monarchy, with the British monarch, represented by the governor-general, as formal head of state. The legislature has a 112-member Senate nominated by the provinces and the prime minister, and a 295-seat House of Commons elected from single-member constituencies for a term of up to five years. Executive power is held by a prime minister and cabinet drawn from the majority party in the House of Commons.

Canada's ten provinces have responsibility for most social services, labor matters and the civil law and maintain considerable political and social autonomy.

CURRENT DEMOGRAPHIC AND ECONOMIC TRENDS

While the fundamental characteristics of Canadian society will remain more or less fixed for some time to come, modern consumer tastes are changing at an increasingly rapid pace. A trader must stay abreast of developing trends when evaluating current customer information: anticipation of shifts in trends will help to identify current customer needs.

The Typical Canadian: Mr. and Ms. Jones

Lifestyles in Canada have become more diverse. Mass marketing of consumer products can be difficult in Canada because of the diversity among consumers. The traditional nuclear family (mother, father, and 2.2 children) is decreasing in prevalence with the rise and recognition of the nontraditional family unit. This can range from a household consisting of one person, unrelated persons, a same-sex couple and a single parent, to a childless married couple, or any combination of the above. Related to this trend is a rise in dual-earner families and in the number of women in the workforce, with the result that shopping patterns show a significant increase in the number of men and teenagers who are sharing responsibility for household buying decisions. Every new life-style offers a potential new market niche.

The Canadian nuclear family is becoming smaller, as single parents or families with both parents working have become the norm. Households are smaller and more transitory. The decline of the nuclear family, coupled with the recession years of the early 1990s, has affected markets for businesses that have relied on buyers of new homes. Many households occupy smaller spaces, including not only smaller new houses but also apartments, condominiums, townhouses, or mobile units. The needs of these households (which also tend to be more transitory) have changed in accordance with their lifestyles, creating new market opportunities, such as for adjustable and collapsible furnishings, foldaway furniture, small cars, mini-appliances, space organizers, and similar items. However, at the other end of the spectrum, the Canadian population is aging, with the median age at 33 and 21 percent of the population between

45 and 54. Those now or soon to be reaching middle age are increasing the demand for family housing that includes even more spacious floor plans that need to be filled with additional goods.

Canada Is Aging, Too

The typical Canadian is about 33 years old, married, of British descent, lives in a household with about $50,000 annual income, drives to work, works in some administrative capacity, enjoys high-tech electronic toys and has at least a high school education and some college. Canadian society is also getting older, reflecting, to a large extent, the demographics of western developed countries. The median age jumped to 33 in 1991, from 28 in 1950 to 26 in 1970.

The aging of the Canadian population is a significant consumer trend, creating immediate opportunities for marketing to the middle-aged and elderly. At the same time, competition among producers of products aimed at the younger consumers is intensifying as that market segment begins to contract. Over the next two decades, however, the younger market segment will become the dominant consumers as more than 20 percent are currently 15 years age or under. Marketers who pay attention to fluctuations in Canada's birthrates will have a clue as to the rise and fall of markets from decade to decade and can anticipate those changes within their own marketing strategies, altering their product lines to appeal to the biggest spenders as they grow older and their needs and desires change with time.

Many consumers are now turning toward reduced-fat diets, vitamin-mineral supplement plans, and alternative health food products. Funding for charities and nonprofit institutions is an area of growing concern as government reduces its support for many such programs, and product promotions in which businesses donate a percentage of the proceeds to a worthy cause are on the rise and showing favorable results. More companies are offering innovative programs such as exercise clubs, stress reduction and health seminars, ergonomic equipment testing, on-site day care, and confidential counseling to enhance the personal health and improve the quality of life for employees during the workday, in the hope of encouraging loyalty and better job performance.

Renewed Growth in the 90s

Canada is making a slow but progressive recovery from the global recession of the early 1990s. With unemployment hovering at 10 percent in mid-995, one of the higher in the developed world, the recession that hit the Canadian economy in 1989 is still lingering somewhat on the Canadian marketplace. Between 1988 and 1992, unemployment shot up two percent, forcing workers out of jobs and cutting manufacturing and production. Since then, private consumption has been growing at a steady rate of one percent and by the end of 1993, Canada's gross domestic product grew by 4.1 percent in 1994. Despite these improving numbers, retail sales are still having a difficult time moving merchandise and even economic optimists don't expect to see real improvement until at least 1997. Despite this, manufacturers and exporters of motor vehicles, office machinery, certain consumer goods and natural gas have been making significant gains. Other industries feeling this boost are industrial machinery, tobacco, lumber, pulpwood and tractors. In addition, more than 200,000 full-time jobs have been created since January 1994 in the consumer products sector alone.

Technology is transforming the manufacturing and production sectors. The services sector is the largest share of Canadian business activity, representing more than 60 percent of the economy. The manufacturing, construction and utility sectors in turn account for a 30 percent share. While Canada is a leader in the development of fiber optics, the largest manufacturing industries are: food and beverages, transportation equipment, pulp and paper, primary metals, metal fabrication, wood products, chemicals and mineral fuels. Rapid technological progress in computers and telecommunications has played an instrumental role in the development of all these sectors as Canadian manufacturers turn towards the use of advanced state-of-the art electronic, robotic, communications and information technology.

The US versus Canada: Sisters Rather than Twins

The US and Canada have a great deal in common. Despite their similarities, however many cultural, linguistic and business attitudes and beliefs differ greatly. Similarities include:
- a positive attitude toward Americans
- a free enterprise system; including free trade under NAFTA and GATT.
- a common language
- a common border
- a well-educated, affluent population

According to some, however, Canadians have at least seven traits that set them apart from the United States. They tend to be:
- more careful and finicky buyers
- more entrepreneurial, needing less assistance
- attentive to conflicts of interest
- sensitive to US and Canadian spellings
- address-aware (noting province and postal code rather than state or zip code is important)
- translation-friendly to American currency and forms of measurement (celsius, metric)
- provincially-focused

CURRENT BREAKDOWN OF CANADIAN HOUSEHOLDS

	1986	1991	Percent Increase
Total Private Households	8,991,675	10,018,265	10.2
Family	6,634,996	7,235,235	8.3
Non-Family	2,356,675	2,783,035	15.5
One Person	1,934,710	2,297,060	15.8
Two or More Persons	421,965	485,975	13.2

Source: Statistics Canada, 1991 Census of Canada

Consumer Information

Canada is heavily dependent on imports, with the US having a whopping 70 percent market share. The Canadian market, therefore, is relatively open for marketers of many primary and manufactured products.

High-tech developments have made information on consumer markets and opportunities in Canada more accessible today than ever before. Product codes, scanners, and other electronic means allow for an ongoing, up-to-the-minute tally of sales information. This data can then be utilized to study buying patterns, to help introduce the products in the most effective way and to determine quickly whether a particular ad campaign has been effective. National, regional, and local demographic data is compiled by many public agencies including Statistics Canada (Canada's Census Bureau), economic development offices, trade associations and universities. Reports can also be obtained from private data service firms, which typically tailor information to the needs specified by the client.

Many electronic (online) services carry current news, offer research sources, allow for input from subscribers, and provide for information exchange among Canadian subscribers. Also available online are databases, publication abstracts, and sometimes the entire text of specific books, periodicals, or articles. There are more than a thousand databases of raw data on potential Canadian markets that are available on CD-ROM. Additionally, federal, state, and local government agencies may have online services listing opportunities for trading with Canadian companies. For contact information, see "Useful Addresses" at the end of this chapter.

Utilizing Your Resources

Considering the avalanche of information available, the trick is knowing how to sort through it and what to do with it. The idea is to focus marketing efforts by analyzing the data in terms of the needs and preferences of potential customers and then formulating an effective sales strategy that will reach and appeal to the most likely buyers. The basic theory behind amassing information about consumer attributes is that their purchasing behavior can be predicted from an analysis of their general characteristics. Some marketers hire an information service company to generate, process, and distribute customer information about a particular market, often electronically. These companies commonly assist in developing information systems tailored to the needs of the particular marketing organization. By subscribing to such a system, a businessperson can review financial management, research, marketing, purchasing, and administrative information. Market research firms can carry this analysis a step further, performing a professional review of the data and advising the trader about markets that appear to be most lucrative. For a full package of services—market research, analysis, and advertising development and placement—an advertising company can be employed.

Regardless of whether one obtains the assistance of a professional in marketing, one should gain at least a general familiarity with, if not in-depth knowledge about, the types of customer information available and how to use it. Most of this information falls into four areas: demographics (physical and environmental attributes), psychographics (what the customer thinks and values), buying patterns (what, where, and how often the customer buys and how much is spent), and media attraction (where they most often learn about what they buy). From a review of all of this data, a trader can begin to target the market for a particular product. Keep in mind that if any part of this combination is missing, the analysis is less accurate and more likely to cause marketing and product errors. Thus, to predict who will buy a product or service, analysis of customer information should proceed as follows:

- Determine the demographic, physical and environmental characteristics of potential customers: who they are in terms of such factors as age, education, geographical environment, earned income, and family status and structure.

- Add the psychographic data revealed by the customers' preferred lifestyles to find out why they act the way the do, why they want a product or service, why they prefer one item over another, what they are likely to spend their

money buying, and what will be most likely to influence their decisions.
- Mix in buying patterns to figure out how much purchasing power the potential customers have-how often they purchase a product, how much they spend, and where they go to buy it.
- Identify the media channels that appeal most to the potential customers in order to penetrate the market most efficiently-that is, to "get the biggest bang for the buck."

This research will ideally lead to an evaluation of the product itself to determine whether it is more than likely going to fit the intended market, that is, whether the product will satisfy the current needs of the primary buyers. It should suggest whether customers might consider the product a necessity or a luxury item (which in turn would indicate whether the product will sell regardless of its packaging and whether customers will make single or repeated purchases). Another factor that should become apparent is the frequency of purchases, which will help to determine how fast the customer base will have to grow to ensure the success of the business. The marketer should also look at the product in terms of trends in the data in an effort to anticipate whether the product will have to be altered or the product line modified in order to meet the changing needs and desires of the targeted customers.

WHERE IS THE MARKET LOCATED?

After determining the primary applications of a product and its most likely customers, a marketer should review the regions of Canada and identify the areas where the major users of the product are concentrated. From agricultural valleys and forested areas to bustling commercial centers and ports, Canada holds outstanding opportunities for marketing both standard and innovative products to business and personal customers.

The trend in marketing has been away from a nationwide approach towards customized regional and local plans. In this manner, merchandise can be targeted to selected audiences, and if necessary product content, packaging, labeling, and advertising can be tailor-made to appeal to certain segments of the Canada populace. However, regional marketing of modified products costs more than national promotion of a standardized product line. Therefore, regional markets must be carefully evaluated to ensure that marketing efforts are as efficient as possible in relation to the market penetration and returns to be achieved.

In researching geographic Canadian markets, keep in mind the Canadian population ranges from urban to rural in varying extremes. Populations have typically shifted from rural to urban due to changes

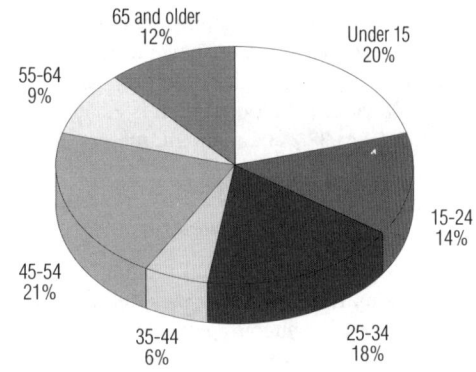

CANADIANS BY AGE

- 65 and older 12%
- Under 15 20%
- 55-64 9%
- 15-24 14%
- 45-54 21%
- 25-34 18%
- 35-44 6%

Source: 1991 Canadian Census

in market and employment needs. Interprovincial migration is generally east to west, where opportunities are expanding with Asian trade. It is important to note that the Canadian provinces are very individualistic, and have a number of barriers erected against each other's businesses. They levy their own corporate taxes, control property ownership, their own legal system and offer incentives and programs to attract investment. Knowing the particulars of each region will help a marketer make the right selection about where to start a business or introduce a product or service. The regions and cities mentioned have populations ranging from at least 100,000 to several million as Canadian urban areas tend to be concentrated with limited suburban settlement. By province, 36.9 percent live in Ontario; 25.3 percent live in Quebec; 12 percent live in British Columbia; and 9.3 percent live in Alberta. The capital, Ottawa, has a population of 920,857.

British Columbia

As the westernmost province, British Columbia has a rich resource base with a high volume of US and Pacific Rim trade. Its largest city, Vancouver (pop. 1,602,502), offers 98 miles of water portage and is the second largest port in North America. Prince Rupert is another major harbor to the Pacific and Alaska. British Columbia has 892,677 square kilometers of land area with a total population of 3,282,061 million people. Its principal industries are wood products, paper, primary metals, petroleum and coal production, aluminum extraction, fish processing, meat packing and fruit.

Alberta

Alberta is Canada's largest producer of oil and natural gas, and has a rapidly expanding forest products industry. In addition, more than 40 percent of all Canadian mineral production comes from Alberta. Principal industries include petroleum and pipelines, coal products, primary metals, metal fabrication, chemicals and petrochemicals, non-metallic mineral products, fertilizers, cement, agriculture, wood products, portable homes and trailers. With this spread of new industry, Alberta is considered by many to be the most Americanized part of Canada. Total population is 2,545,553 with a land mass of 638,233 square kilometers. Its capital is Edmonton (pop. 839,924).

Saskatchewan

Although farming and ranching remain the prime industrial base, the Saskatchewan government is actively encouraging the growth of new industry in order to diversify the economy. Principal industries include agricultural, petroleum and coal products, primary metals, non-metallic mineral products, potash refining, chemicals, cement manufacturing, meat packing and flour milling. The total population 1,001,600 over a land area of 570,113 square kilometers. The capital is Regina and the largest provincial city is Calgary (pop. 754,033).

Manitoba

Manitoba sits geographically midway between the Atlantic and Pacific coasts, making this province a natural point for transportation and accessibility to Canadian markets. The province also has its own coastal passage via the deep-sea port of Churchill on the west coast of Hudson Bay, which allows access to export markets. Primary industries include metals, clothing, petroleum, agricultural machinery, transportation equipment, inorganic fertilizers, agriculture, cement, food processing and meat packaging, chemicals and electric power. Winnipeg (pop. 652,354) is Manitoba's capital. Total land area is 547,704 square kilometers and population is 1,091,942.

Ontario

Ontario is the largest manufacturing and agricultural province and contributes more than 40 percent to Canadian GNP. Its capital and largest city, Toronto (pop. 3,893,046), is the country's business and financial center and is home to 80 percent of corporate head offices. Principal industries include transportation equipment, food processing, chemicals, electrical and electronic products, machinery, primary and fabricated metal industries. Ontario's location is its greatest advantage. Half of the consumers in North America and more than 50 percent of its industries are within one day's reach. Additionally, Thunder Bay offers a direct outlet to the Atlantic via the St. Lawrence Seaway. As Canada's most industrialized province, Ontario has an extensive transportation network and highly sophisticated telecommunications network. Additionally, the labor force is highly educated and trained.

Quebec

In recent years, the political relationship between French-speaking Quebec and the rest of the country has been a key constitutional issue. And although it is doubtful that the separatist movement will ever be a success, the uncertainty over Quebec's future has taken its toll. Combined with a series of recessions, it has been difficult for the province to attract new investment. Despite this, Quebec has developed certain high-tech industries that bode well for its future. The province is the home of the Canada's two national railroads, the Canadian National Railway and the Canadian Pacific Railway, both of which are connected to the Montreal port which can accommodate more than 3,000 ships a year. It is also home to 100 of Canada's top 500 corporations, including Air Canada, the Bank of Montreal, Bombardier and the country's telephone giant, BCE Inc., formerly Bell Canada. (It is important to note that a company must adopt a French firm name in order to be incorporated, registered or licensed in Quebec). Other principal industries include textiles, pulp and paper, automobile and aircraft manufacturing, chemicals, iron and steel, shipbuilding, aluminum extraction, appliances, oil refining and cement. Quebec is also the leading producer of low-cost hydroelectric power, while tourism is a big source of income. The French-speaking population is 80 percent and the English-speaking population is around 18 percent. Total population is 6,898,963 within 1,357,812 square kilometers. Quebec's capital is Quebec City (pop. 645,550) and its largest city is Montreal (pop. 3,127,242).

The Atlantic Maritime Provinces

New Brunswick The most important manufacturing industries in New Brunswick are forest resources and the production of food and beverages, although in recent years the industrial base has been diversifying. Saint John is a major year-round port with access to the Atlantic and transportation to eastern US and central Canadian markets. Its capital is Fredericton, with a total population is 723,900 within 71,569 square kilometers.

Newfoundland and Labrador Although Newfoundland has some of North America's oldest streets and is Canada's oldest settlements, the province is the youngest, having entered the Confederation in 1949. The province contains Newfoundland Island and Labrador on the mainland, site of the Churchill Falls power generating station. Principal industries include pulp and paper, lumber, fish processing and packing, mining, and offshore gas and oil exploration. The province is in economic transition, developing extensive resource expansion and the accompanying services and skills. With a total population of 568,474 within

371,635 square kilometers, the capital is St. John's.

Nova Scotia With a continental rather than maritime climate, Nova Scotia is the most populated of the Atlantic provinces and offers the largest workforce. Its capital, Halifax, is one of the foremost research and development centers in Canada and is one of only three centers for marine scientific activities in the Western Hemisphere. It is also Canada's biggest and busiest container port and the closest North American port to Europe. Technology-oriented industries are burgeoning here through government programs and other financial support. Other principal industries are pulp and paper, lumber, fish processing and packing, iron and steel production and fabrication, shipbuilding and shipping, oil exploration and refining. The total land area in Nova Scotia is 52,841 square kilometers and the total population is 899,942.

Prince Edward Island Moving away from dairy and fish manufacturing as primary industries, this province is actively seeking light industries that require specialized technical skills (this is aimed primarily at competitive markets such as metalworking for agricultural industries). Principal industries are agriculture, fishing, processing and packaging of seafoods and agricultural products, and tourism. The capital is Charlottetown with a total provincial population of 130,600 over 5,660 square kilometers.

Territories

Canada's northern lands consist of the giant Northwest Territories and the Yukon, which stretch across all four western provinces. Together, they account for 40 percent of Canada's total land area. Despite this fact, only about 0.3 percent of the Canadian population lives in these territories. Much of this is due to the extreme climate and limited history of exploration. More than 60 percent of the population is Inuit, as well as Dene and Metis Indians, but the population has been changing as the existing mineral and fuel deposits are being explored. Indeed, mineral production (zinc, along with oil and gas) is the prime area of development in the area. In addition, there are enormous water resources for the future development of hydroelectric power. In 1999, the Inuit will receive more than 135,135 square miles of land. This Nunavut Territory will allow the Inuit to be self-governing.

Northwest Territories The capital of the Northwest Territories is Yellowknife. It is situated over Alberta, Saskatchewan and parts of British Columbia and Manitoba, ending at Hudson Bay. The total land area is 3,246,389 square kilometers with a total population of 57,649.

Yukon Territory The Yukon Territory is the most northwestern territory in Canada. Its total population is 27,797 with a land area of 531,844 square kilometers. The capital city is Whitehorse.

ADVERTISING CHANNELS

With a larger square area and only 1/10 the population of the US, media and postage rates tend to be high on a cost-per-thousand basis, in addition to higher printing and labor costs. Mass manufacturing and marketing are not recommended for the Canadian marketplace. Factors such as small shipment locations far from the manufacturing site, high production costs, costly marketing research, and high advertising and promotional expenses combined with Canada's two languages and the coastal cultural disparities make marketing in Canada an operation that deserves detailed and focused attention. Consult the Canadian Code of Advertising Standards as well as federal and provincial legislation for specific marketing and advertising directions and recommendations. Marketing and advertising in Quebec also has very specific laws and regulations. It is recommended that a marketer wishing to do business in or with Quebec do additional research regarding rules of language, packaging and marketing.

The communications media is widespread, with an array of potential advertising options. Telecommunications, print, and broadcast media are all well developed. The traditional pathways—newspapers, magazines, radio, and television—have each splintered into numerous alternatives on both the national and local levels. Radio and television services reach approximately 99 percent of Canadian homes, with television divided up into standard broadcast, cable and satellite reception. It offers specialized sports, music, and news in addition to general network programming. Some of these feature "infomercials" (longer-format commercials designed as programming that offer more detailed explanations of productions or services. Currently, Canadian regulations prohibit infomercials between 6 a.m. and midnight. Satellite television makes many stations available from around the world to more remote areas. There are also the more familiar local, national, and foreign networks. Community access or public television is very highly prized in Canada, although these stations usually have no commercials but do announce the names of program sponsors.

Among newspapers, a customer can choose from among national, regional, and local daily newspapers; weekly and monthly news, trade, or specialty journals; community shopper papers; and papers targeted at particular occupations-such as legal, medical, real estate, or accounting-or various interest groups. Magazines are becoming increasingly specialized and narrowly targeted as well. Thus, marketers face a chal-

1994 CANADIAN MARKET EXPENDITURES (C$)

Consumer Goods	$932 million
Charitable Donations	$1,193 million
Consumer Services	$2,380 million
Business to Business	$2,547 million
Catalogue	$1,795 million
Broadcast	$240 million
Total	**$9.087 billion**

Source: Canadian Direct Marketing Association's Annual Fact Book

lenging task in deciding which medium provides the best fit for a given product; the diverse opportunities may require considerable time and study to investigate and absorb.

According to recent statistics, Canada has more than 100 daily newspapers and more than 1,000 community, campus and ethnic papers. In 1991, magazines and other trade and specialty periodicals totaled 1,503, representing an annual circulation of 521 million or a yearly average of 346,893 per publication.

Newspapers and small regional news journals tend to be the least expensive advertising channels. Television advertising tends to be the most expensive, although it generally reaches the large (though not always the most targeted) audience. Extreme variations in advertising costs are seen across the country, primarily because of regional differences in the level of media competition. In general, the more competition there is among the media companies, the lower the advertising costs (although overall high costs in urban areas affect prices for advertising there regardless of greater competition). Households in smaller population areas with fewer media options tend to be more costly to reach by advertising than those in large urban centers.

Print Media

The Canadian newspaper industry was hit hard by the nationwide recession in the early 1990s. With less disposable income to cover ever increasing personal expenditures, many customers have eliminated the purchase of some discretionary items, including newspaper subscriptions. Recovery has remained slow, with many papers showing little or no growth in circulation. Recent jumps in the cost of newsprint are also expected to hurt newspaper profits. However, the outlook for the next several years is still somewhat rosier: newspapers are expecting increases in circulation and advertising receipts as the nation's economy improves and consumer confidence returns. Although newspapers have a shrinking share of total media advertising expenditures, they are still one of the least expensive and quickest means of getting the word out to a relatively large market. Newspapers are more dependent on advertising revenues than any other medium in Canada. The trend among newspaper companies is toward regularly published special interest sections such as daily, weekly, or other periodic grouped features on real estate, entertainment, food and cooking, home improvement, or some other specialty subject. Canada has more than 100 daily newspapers and more than 1,000 community, campus and ethnic papers.

La Press is the leading French-language daily. Some newspapers with a circulation covering distinct geographic markets prepare special neighborhood sections for suburban readers. All of these developments offer marketers ways to more finely tune and target their advertising.

Much like newspapers, the Canadian periodicals industry has suffered from recession and is now slowly recovering. In an effort to pick up the pace of growth, many periodical publishers have been discounting advertising rates and making special offers to attract advertising. The total number of periodicals operating in Canada is well over 1,500, and although there are many consumer magazines, only *Maclean's* is truly national. Foreign magazines are available in many locations as well. Most magazines are sold to the public by subscription and through a wide range of single-copy outlets-newsstands, bookstores, supermarkets, and other retail stores. However, subscriptions account for nearly 80 percent of total circulation.

Though periodicals have the reputation for being a secondary advertising medium, in fact they can be extremely useful tools to focus on particular markets as well as trade and other special interest groups. Periodicals can be found for a nearly unimaginable variety of specific facets of life: finance, investment, business, consumer sales, farm, gardening, agriculture, home improvement, design, entertainment, music, medicine, real estate, outdoor recreation, sports, education, children, computers, electronics, television, technology, science, telecommunication, fashion, literature, religion, art, aviation, cars, food, or health. A number of publishers also offer special editions of their products tailored to particular age or interest groups that would otherwise not purchase subscriptions.

New technologies have allowed periodical

publishers to expand beyond the printed page into cross-media and multimedia products: fax services, electronic networks, CD-ROM databases, and videotext productions are increasing in popularity and offer immediate and interactive contact with the customer.

Television

In 1989, there were 106 television stations, 338 AM radio stations and 161 FM radio stations in addition to the Canadian Broadcasting Corporation (CBC). For that same year, radio and television broadcasting revenues increased 8 percent over the previous year, totaling $2.3 billion.

There are three national TV networks, two of which are run by the Canadian Broadcasting Corporation (CBC), with one channel in English and one in French. In large part, Canadian television is best known for its news and sports coverage. There are also many small, community private and public stations, all of which total more than 100 Canadian television stations available. It is important to note, however, that more than three-quarters of the country can receive broadcasts from the US and four networks (ABC, CBS, NBC and FOX). Thus, competition to draw and hold viewers is intense. The Canadian networks, which rely on advertising revenues to a much greater extent than does cable television, have had a financially difficult decade and have had to streamline their operations in order to produce new programs while keeping advertising rates manageable, marketers generally seem to agree that the power of television advertising is worth the price.

Cable television is also expanding in viewership. Although distribution is limited to the subscribers of a particular company, a large majority of the television viewing public prefers cable service to broadcast television's traditional antenna on the roof because the quality of reception is good in any kind of weather and most cable companies provide a wider range of channels than are readily available over the airwaves. Most cities now have cable television, which offer at least one multilingual or ethnic channel. That number is expected to increase and then level off at about 70 percent by the end of the decade. Unlike network television companies, cable companies have the advantage of earning revenue from subscriptions, not just advertising, with the result that their advertising rates are somewhat more affordable. The more important advantage to cable television is that it can appeal to niche audiences; the most common arrangement is for subscribers to take a basic set of channels and then select additional ones from any of several specific interest packages, such as a group of sports, educational, or movie stations. Thus, specific markets can be more easily targeted.

Radio

Radio in Canada is more international in orientation than radio in the US. Both radio and television facilities extend from the Atlantic to Pacific Oceans and north to the Arctic Circle. Radio Canada International, the CBC's short-wave service, broadcasts in 12 languages to Europe, Africa, Latin America, Asia, the Middle East, the South Pacific, and the US. Despite this, radio advertising accounts for the smallest percentage of overall advertising expenditures in Canada, due mostly to limited listenership and the multitude of other media. Nevertheless, the competition can be fierce for prime-time radio advertising slots, particularly during commute hours in urban centers because morning and evening "drive time" programs are very popular with listeners sitting on congested highways. In cities the airwaves offer music, foreign language, news, religious, and financial stations, while in the less populated regions the number of radio stations fall dramatically. Radio stations tend to poll the likes and dislikes of their listeners, and therefore targeted advertising on radio stations can be done relatively easily and accurately.

Other Advertising Formats

Promotions Nearly half the advertising expenditures in Canada go into promotions, which may be anything from a giveaway pen or notepad to cents-off coupons or price discounts for repeat purchases. Sales, price reductions, prizes, and frequent buyer discounts are common tools used to persuade potential customers to try a product and come back for more.

Billboards In many areas of the country, advertisers display their products on gigantic billboards, most often placed strategically along a highway or attached to the visible sides of buildings in a city center. The design and preparation of these can be costly and time-consuming. The message must be seen, understood, and remembered by a passerby within the instant it takes to drive past it. Note that some communities have banned billboards as being unaesthetic and unsafe because they can be distracting to drivers.

Marketing and Advertising Firms

Many firms offer product promotion services to assist foreign or domestic businesspersons in defining, locating, and breaking into Canada optimally. Full-service advertising agencies have dominated this area for many years both in Canada and abroad, and many work out of branch and subsidiary offices in foreign countries as well as in major cities within Canada. Because agencies have the reputation of offering the services of highly skilled personnel and providing a complete marketing

EXPORTING TO CANADA: FIVE IN-HOUSE RULES

1. Eliminate as much guesswork as possible.

You cannot successfully export to Canada by accident; you need a well-thought-out marketing plan, and you might find that use of expert consultants represents time and money well spent. It is never simply a matter of saying, "Let's sell our product in Canada." You need to know where and how you're going to market it. You need to find out whether your product needs to be changed to fit into the Canadian market or to meet government requirements. You need to figure out how you are going to find a buyer or wholesaler. You need to have some idea of your target market, how to reach that market, how much you can expect to sell, and how many different products to introduce. A plan is the best way to uncover hidden traps and costs before you get overly involved and end up in a mess. You may see an opportunity, but you need to know how to exploit it successfully.

2. Just go for it.

If your product is new to the market, there may be almost no pre-existing marketing information, and you may essentially have no choice other than just to dive in. Planning is important and should never be forgotten, but sometimes the best plan is to use a shotgun approach-just blast away and see if you hit anything. You can narrow your options later.

3. Commit to exporting.

You must explicitly commit to exporting to Canada. In light of the number of available media options and the diversity in Canadian markets, your first entry could well flop. Success in marketing in Canada may mean sticking with your desire to export, weathering the initial setbacks, adding the financial backing needed to try again, and just hanging on until you reach the critical level that allows your product to take off. International marketing consultants report that many companies invariably cut their international trade budgets when the results in the first few months are anything less than wonderful: these cuts represent premature decisions and produce unnecessary failures. The hard fact is that exports do not bring in money as quickly as domestic sales. It takes time and persistence for an international marketing effort to succeed. You have to overcome many hurdles, personal, political, cultural, and legal, to name a few. It could take a few months or a year or more to see the first glimmers of success. Be patient, keep a close but not suffocating watch on international marketing efforts, and give your venture a chance to develop.

4. Avoid an internal tug-of-war.

The complex strategies, relationship building, and legal and cultural accommodations that export marketing require will mean that support and teamwork within your own company are crucial to the success of the venture. Allowing internal conflict to continue between partners, divisions, or investors in your own company over current intentions and plans domestically and abroad will amount to creating your own obstacles to exporting success.

5. Stick with exporting even if business booms at home.

Exporting is not something to allow to surface only when domestic markets falter and then to submerge when business at home increases. It is difficult to move into exporting. All upfront investment in relationships, financial ties, and management resources that export marketing entails will require that a clear commitment be made right at the start. Any other attitude is likely to doom the venture from the beginning. It is therefore critical to decide that you are going to export and that exporting is going to be a significant part of your business.

---

package, they also charge substantial fees. However, they are meeting some price resistance as competition intensifies from public relations, information service, and database firms. (Refer to the "Important Addresses" chapter for contact information.)

Public Relations Firms

A public relations (PR) firm can help a businessperson market a product by establishing and promoting an image that will best appeal to targeted buyers. A PR firm can build a client's reputation by arranging corporate sponsorships and community betterment projects, and can spread the word about a product, help with labor relations, or even lay the groundwork for obtaining financial assistance for the client company. Sometimes a well-placed, well-timed news release is all that is needed to attract the interest of the consuming public and start a flow of orders. For this reason, PR firms are kept on retainer to polish the image of many big Canadian enterprises. This concept of boosting image recognition has also led to the trend of advertising designed to promote an image rather than a specific product.

Product Labeling and Quality Requirements

Strict laws and complex government agency regulations apply to many products marketed within Canada, particularly those sold to consumers, health care institutions, restaurants, and the like. Information on these requirements can be obtained by contacting the relevant federal regulatory agency. Similarly, state regulatory agencies should be contacted in order to learn whether additional local requirements must be met before introducing a product into a market. Those interested in importing products into Canada should note that while transparent, the requirements can be complex, stringent, and spread among numerous agencies, making compliance difficult. (Refer to the "Important Addresses" chapter for contact information on regulatory agencies.)

The overwhelming number of Canadian consumers and businesses use the metric system, unlike the US which prefers the English measures: gallons, quarts, pints, cups, and fluid ounces; miles, yards, feet, and inches; pounds and tons; and so on. Likewise, Canadian residents measure temperatures in Celsius, not Fahrenheit. Products should therefore generally be labeled with metric measures.

USEFUL ADDRESSES

Canada Advertising Rates and Media
Maclean Hunter Canadian Publishing
(416) 867-9500

The Cohen Group Inc.
(905) 886-8086

Statistics Canada
(613) 951-5072

Economic Council of Canada
(613) 993-1895

Ministry of Industry, Trade and Technology (MITI)
(416) 487-4893

Metro Toronto Board of Trade
(416) 366-6811

US Department of Commerce
Office for Canada
Room 3033
Washington, DC 20320
(202) 377-3101 or 482-3101
Fax: (202) 482-3718

Association of Canadian Venture Capital Companies
(416) 687-0159

Department of Economic Development - Ontario
City Hall
100 Queen Street West, East Tower, 20th Floor
Toronto, Ontario M5H 2N2
(416) 392-7987

Economic Development Edmonton
9797 Jasper Avenue Nw
Edmonton, Alberta T5J 1N9
(800) 661-6965

Economic, Consumer and Corporate Affairs
10025 Jasper Ave, 22nd Floor
Edmonton, Alberta T5J 3Z5
(403) 422-3935 or 422-6236

Ministry of Development, Trade and Tourism
1770 Pacific Blvd South, 2nd Floor
Vancouver, British Columbia V6B 5E7
(604) 660-3908

Department of Industry, Trade and Tourism
155 Carlton Street, 4th Floor
Winnipeg, Manitoba R3C 3H8
(204) 945-2466

Department of Development and Tourism
P.O. Box 6000 Fredericton
New Brunswick E3B 5H1
(506) 729-5600

Department of Economic Development and Tourism
Yellowknife
Northwest Territories X1A 2L9
(403) 873-7239

Department of Economic Development
P.O. Box 519
Halifax, Nova Scotia B3J 2R&
(902) 424-4211

Ministry of Consumer and Commercial Relations
Companies Br.
393 University Avenue
Toronto, Ontario M7A 2H6
(416) 596-3757

Ministry of Industry, Commerce and Trade
700 Sherbrooke Street West, 8th Floor
Montreal, Quebec H3A 1G1
(514) 982-3013

Enterprise PEI
West Royalty Industrial Park
Charlottetown, Prince Edward Island C1E 1B0
(902) 368-6324

Department of Economic Development
1919 Saskatchewan Drive
Regina, Saskatchewan S4P 3V7
(306) 787-2232

Statistics Canada
Ottawa K1A0T6
(800) 267-6677

Canada Flash Facts Hotline
(202 482-3101

Public Works and Government Services Canada (PWGSC)
c/o Canada Communications Group
45 Sacre-Coeur Blvd
Hull, Quebec K1A0S9
(819) 956-4800
Fax: (819) 994-1498

Canadian Direct Marketing Association (CDMA)
(416) 391-2362

Watts List Management (Canada File
(416) 252-7741

Canadian Franchise Association
(416) 595-5005

International Franchise Association
(202) 628-8000

FDR Canada
(203) 452-1919 or (416) 322-8200

Zed Marketing
(415) 348-8145

Cornerstone List Managers
(416) 932-9555

Essential Lists
(514) 695-8218

The Marketing Information Bureau
135 Brian Drive
North York, Ontario M2J 3Y8
(516) 333-9480 or (800) M-I-BUREAU

Target Mail
(416) 297-7359

Prospects Unlimited
(416) 581-0258

Direct Media
(203) 532-1000

Canadian Postal Primer
Group 1 Software
4200 Parliament Place, Suite 600
Lanham, MD 20706
(800) 368-5806
Fax: (301) 731-0306

Bernice Bush (Canadian Magazine Subscribers
(714) 891-3344

Northbound Direct Marketing
34 Crowfoot Place
Scarborough, Ontario M1W 2X7
(905) 873-7386
Fax: (905) 877-8262

Canadian Facts

Nielsen Canada

Professional Marketing Research Society (PMRS)

Canadian Association of Marketing Research Organizations (CAMRO)

Business Entities & Formation

FORMS OF BUSINESS ENTERPRISES

Businesses in Canada may be organized in a myriad of ways; however, the alternatives most often used are sole proprietorships, corporations, and partnerships. Investors may also enter into franchise or distributorship agreements. Each business form has its own particular attributes, and the choice of the appropriate organizational structure for carrying out business activities and investments in Canada depends on the goals of the business, the desired degree of control, the preferred tax treatment, the amount of risk, the anticipated duration of the investment, and other personal and business circumstances. (Refer to the "Taxation" chapter for discussion of tax treatment.)

This chapter provides a general overview of the available entities and how each is most advantageously used to transact business in Canada. There are no restrictions as to the form of business entity in Canada. However, foreign entities conducting business in Canada typically operate in one of three ways: foreign businesses may transact business without a formal legal presence in Canada by selling products to Canada from the foreign jurisdiction; foreign businesses may transact business through branch operations; or foreign businesses may transact business through Canadian subsidiaries. In the latter situations, the businesses are subject to notification or review procedures; further, most provinces require foreign corporations carrying on business in the province to acquire a license. The threshold business activities that constitute carrying on business vary from province to province.

CORPORATIONS

Traditionally, the most common form used by foreign businesses to undertake business operations in Canada is the corporation. Although sole proprietorships outnumber corporations in Canada, foreign investors generally prefer the corporate form because proprietorships are run by individuals and most start and stay relatively small.

Statutes The corporate statutes of most Canadian jurisdictions endow a corporation with a distinct existence separate from that of its investors. A corporation has the capacity and, in general, the rights, powers, privileges, and legal status of a natural person, permitting the corporation to own real and personal property, possess rights, incur liabilities, and transact business. The primary advantage of the corporate structure is that it limits the liability of its investors, the shareholders, to the amount invested in the corporation. Courts will only pierce or lift this corporate veil when just and necessary, based on improper conduct such as incorporating for fraudulent purposes or as a puppet for an individual. In addition, the ownership of corporate shares is readily transferable (absent transfer restrictions), and the legal continuity of the business is ensured regardless of any shareholder's death or change in management or corporate ownership. Equity shares are not assigned a par value.

CONTENTS

Forms of Business Enterprises	183
Corporations	183
Key Regulators and Registries	184
Partnerships	186
Joint Ventures	187
Branch or Representative Offices	187
Sole or Individual Proprietorships	188
Trusts	188
Franchises and Distributorships	188
Trusts	188
Registering a Business	189
Basic Authorization and Application Process	189
Ten Reminders, Recommendations, and Rules	190
Further Reading	191
Useful Addresses	191

KEY REGULATORS AND REGISTRIES

The Department of Foreign Affairs and International Trade DFAIT helps to attract foreign investment to Canada, assisting international companies seeking Canadian partners and promoting Canadian businesses as investment, commercial, and technologically advanced partners. DFAIT shares responsibility for applications for foreign investments with Industry Canada. The two agencies have established 12 international trade centers throughout the country as contact points for international investors.

Industry Canada, Business Services This branch of Industry Canada provides a host of business information, business development programs, and expertise to facilitate foreign investment in Canada.

Human Resources Development Canada This agency provides information about employment, manpower, and immigration in Canada.

Office de la Langue Francaise This agency works with companies to comply with Quebec's language laws, requiring the use of French, the official language of the province.

Federal Business Development Bank FBDB promotes and assists most types of business in Canada, focusing on small and medium-sized businesses, usually in the start-up stages, and administers loan and venture capital programs. FBDB has offices in all major cities in Canada.

In general, a company with a few thousand dollars in capital may incorporate under the same statutes as a company with millions of dollars in capital. However, larger companies with shares that are publicly issued and traded are subject to more stringent reporting and disclosure requirements than companies with shares held by just a few investors. In the latter situation, that of a private or closely held corporation, the corporate charter must restrict the number of shareholders to no more than 50, restrict the transfer of shares, and prohibit the public offering of shares, debentures, or other securities of the corporation. Legal counsel can advise foreign investors in determining whether the corporate form is the most advantageous for their purposes, and they should always be consulted

Incorporating Foreign businesses may elect to incorporate a subsidiary in Canada, or conduct business in Canada through the existing corporate structure as a branch operation (See "Branch or Representative Offices" on page 187.). If a non-resident business entity elects to incorporate a subsidiary, the entity must determine whether to incorporate under the federal Canada Business Corporations Act (CBCA) or under the corporate statutes of any province or territory. One primary advantage of incorporating at the federal level that many companies enjoy is that the corporation becomes entitled to conduct business in any province under its corporate name; although provinces may be able to charge a registration or license fee, they cannot prevent business operations under that corporate name.

In contrast, under provincial incorporation, a corporation may be precluded from conducting business under its registered name in another province if its registered name is too similar to a name previously registered in the other province. Disadvantages of federal incorporation include higher costs, longer processing time, and the federal requirement that the financial statements of private corporations with gross revenues or total assets in excess of specified thresholds (including affiliates and parent companies), must be filed annually in Ottawa and are a matter of public record. Because provincial laws also vary, caution should be exercised in determining which of the provinces and territories would be most suitable for the incorporation of a particular business. The decision to incorporate in one province or territory does not prevent a corporation from doing business in another. Before commencing business in another province, typically the corporation need only file certain documents with the proper authorities and pay the requisite fees (subject to the caveat regarding name similarity discussed above). The cost of such qualification varies from state to state, like the cost of incorporation, but overall, these costs are not unduly burdensome. Nonetheless, most provincial and territorial laws regulating the formation and operation of corporations are similar.

With respect to specific incorporation procedures, the federal government and the provincial and territorial governments have their own codified corporation laws detailing how a corporation may be organized. Typically, the appropriate governmental agency (the director at the federal level) approves the name of the company and the charter or articles of incorporation signed by the incorporators. The articles of incorporation, together with the corporate bylaws, set forth the rules and regulations by which the corporation will be governed. Thereafter, a minimum amount of capital must be paid into the corporation, and shares are issued to the owners (that is, the shareholders) of the corporation. The incorporation process is not particularly complicated or time consuming, but the federal incorporation process tends to be lengthier. Typically, a certificate of incorporation can be issued within days of the submission of the prescribed application form and accompanying documents; further, a company can incorporate with a number name pending the completion of a name search and then change the corporate name later by amendment. Incorporation can be relatively inexpensive, or it can cost substantial amounts if complex business and shareholder arrangements are needed. At the federal level, the application filing fee is C$500 and does not depend on the number of shares stated in the articles of incorporation.

Corporate existence begins as of the date stated in the certificate of incorporation. In general, persons who execute written contracts in the name of (or on behalf of) a corporation before it becomes a corporation, typically promoters and incorporators, are personally bound by the contract and entitled to its benefits unless the contract provides that the person is not bound. However, a corporation may, within a reasonable time of coming into existence, may adopt preincorporation contracts by action or conduct signifying an intent to be bound by the contract.

The corporate name must include one of the following words, expressions, or abbreviations: Limited, Limitee, Incorporated, Incorporee, Corporation, Societe par Actions de Regime federal, Société Commerciale Canadienne, Ltd., Ltee., Inc., Corp., S.A.R.F., or S.C.C. A corporation may not be incorporated with, have, carry on business under, or identify itself by a name that is (1) prescribed, prohibited, or deceptively descriptive or (2) reserved for another corporation or intended corporation. Name similarity issues, which can involve generic words, are ordinarily resolved by determining whether or not there is a likelihood of confusion; the prospect of confusion is less if the businesses are substantially different.

Shareholders In theory, shareholders hold ultimate corporate authority over policies and operational decisions, but their authority is usually exercised through a board of directors that they elect. In many corporations, shareholders are only required to approve a few major corporate actions directly. For example, the shareholders may vote on amendments to the charter or articles of incorporation, increases in the authorized capital of the corporation, the sale of substantially all of the corporation's assets, a merger with another corporation, or the voluntary dissolution of the corporation, but on little else. As long as a shareholder's only involvement is through holdings of the corporation's securities, or through independent, arm's length business transactions with the corporation (that is, dealings conducted at market prices and conditions that do not involve special considerations), the shareholder is generally not liable for any liability, act, or default of the corporation. The shareholder's sole responsibility is for fulfilling promises, if any, to contribute additional capital. However, if the shareholders properly execute a unanimous shareholder agreement (or a written declaration in the case of a sole shareholder), the shareholders assume the directors' responsibility for managing the corporation and assume the directors' liability. A Shareholder agreement can transfer as little or as much of the management authority to the shareholders, and specify the manner of exercise of the transferred authority. Shareholders may be liable for the value of any property distributed to the shareholder pursuant to the dissolution of the corporation.

Directors One or more corporate directors manage the business and affairs of the corporation, subject to any unanimous shareholder agreement. If any issued securities of a corporation are or were part of a public distribution and remain outstanding and are held by more than one person, the corporation must have at least three directors, at least two of whom are not officers or employees of the corporation or any of its affiliates. A majority of the directors of the corporation must be resident Canadians. Directors transact business by passing resolutions and serve until they resign, die, become disqualified, are removed, or their term expires. The directors may appoint a managing director (who must be a resident Canadian) or a committee of directors to manage the corporation. In most jurisdictions, the directors also appoint (and remove) corporate officers, who conduct the company's daily operations and act as agents of the corporation to the extent of their authority as set forth in the applicable statutes, articles, or bylaws.

Typically, the following corporate officers are named: (1) a president or chief executive officer; (2) one or more vice presidents; (3) a treasurer or chief financial officer; and (4) a secretary. In many companies, one or more of the top corporate officers also are members of the board of directors. Directors and officers have a fiduciary duty to the corporation and must disclose the nature and extent of any material interest in any transaction to which the corporation is or may be a party. They must act honestly and in good faith with a view to the best interests of the corporation and must exercise the care and skill of a reasonably prudent person under comparable circumstances. In the case of a breach of fiduciary duty or gross negligence in attending to their responsibilities for operating the corporation, directors and officers may be subject to personal liability to the corporation, its shareholders, or its creditors. Areas that may give rise to personal liability include: corporate governance and compliance matters, including fiscal responsibility; employee wages and withholding; environmental protection issues; taxation issues; and pension requirements. Although directors' and officers' potential liabilities are often covered by insurance, directors should remain fully informed of their responsibilities and potential liabilities under current legislation.

Bylaws The corporate bylaws constitute a set of rules that govern the procedures for shareholders' meetings, the selection of directors, the authority of directors and officers, and any other internal procedures required to be codified for the operation of the business. Shareholders and directors must usually meet at least once a year. However, shareholders or directors may take most actions, including those reserved for annual meetings, without actually holding a formal meeting in a physical location, provided they give unanimous written consent to the proposed action. Directors may by resolution make, amend, or repeal bylaws regulating the business or affairs of the corporation, subject to the articles of incorporation, the bylaws, or a unanimous shareholder agreement. The change must be presented to the shareholders at the next shareholders' meeting.

Special tax treatment applies to any dividends received by individuals from taxable Canadian corporations: this treatment recognizes any taxes already paid at the corporate level on the accumulated income that is the source of the dividend distribution. The result of this gross-up income/tax credit treatment is that the combined tax (the corporate tax on the original income and the net individual tax on the dividend) approximates the tax that would have been paid on the original income as if the individual had received it directly rather than through the corporate entity (refer to the "Taxation" chapter for a discussion of tax treatment).

The distribution of securities is regulated by the provincial governments. Typically, the corporation must file a prospectus for the approval of the appropriate provincial securities commission. A corporation that files or distributes, in any jurisdiction, a prospectus, statement of material facts, registration statement, security exchange take-over bid circular, or similar document relating to the public distribution of the corporation's securities must send a copy to the Director at the federal level.

PARTNERSHIPS

The use of partnerships, particularly limited partnerships, has become increasingly popular with foreign investors, because the transaction of business through a Canadian partnership can offer significant flexibility. A partnership arises from any agreement between two or more individuals or corporations to combine property, capital, labor, skills, or other resources to establish and carry on a profit-oriented business as co-owners with a view toward sharing profits. The existence of a partnership depends on the parties' intent; no formal documentation is required for a general partnership. Although the actions of individuals may imply the existence of a partnership, the better practice is to execute a written document, a partnership agreement, to define the rights and obligations of each partner. Under Canadian law, two types of partnerships exist: general and limited partnerships.

Provincial law governs the formation and regulation of partnerships. Because a partnership is essentially a contractual agreement, parties have a great deal of flexibility in using this form of organization and generally can adapt it in any way that best suits the particular needs of the partnership's business.

Partnerships are distinguishable from corporations in that a partnership is not a separate legal entity. However, all property contributed to or otherwise acquired by the partnership is partnership property. A registered partnership can ordinarily sue and be sued in the partnership name. Each partner agrees to share in profits and losses and, when acting in what appears to be in the normal course of partnership business, each partner is an agent of the partnership (and all the other partners). Each partner owes the partnership and the other partners a duty of loyalty and good faith. A partnership may be formed for a definite or unlimited term. However, unless the partnership agreement specifies to the contrary, the death of a partner automatically dissolves the partnership.

All partnerships should register in the province or territory where organized; unregistered partnerships cannot initiate court proceedings, but can be sued. Further, some provinces require partnerships registered in another province or territory to register with their registrar of partnerships before initiating business.

Foreign investors may find the partnership form of organization beneficial for certain types of investment (such as the acquisition of interests in real property), because, subject to certain limitations, this organizational form enables investors to apply partnership deductions or losses against other Canadian income in computing a partner's Canadian taxable income. For Canadian tax purposes, a partnership is not treated as a separate taxable entity; items of income, gain, loss, deductions, and credits flow through to the partner. The income of a partnership is allocated among the partners pursuant to the terms of the partnership agreement or, absent agreement, by applicable partnership law. (Refer to the "Taxation" chapter for discussion of tax treatment.)

General Partnerships Two or more persons may form a general partnership to transact business in common with a view toward sharing profits. Typically, each general partner is actively engaged in the conduct of the partnership business. Unless otherwise stated in the partnership agreement (that, together with any applicable provincial statute, governs the management and operation of the partnership), each partner has the same rights, obligations, and authority as every other member of the partnership. Moreover, unless specifically prohibited by the partnership agreement, any partner may enter into contracts that are binding on the partnership. The principal drawback of a general partnership is that each partner has unlimited personal liability for all the debts and obligations of the partnership, including those wrongfully incurred by another partner. General partnerships are governed by the law and registration requirements of the provinces and territories.

Limited Partnerships A limited partnership is distinguished from a general partnership in that only some of the partners have unlimited liability. In a limited partnership, at least one partner must be designated as a general partner with unlimited liability for partnership debts and obligations. The liability of the non-general partners, referred to as limited partners, is limited to the amount of each partner's contribution to the partnership as set forth in the partnership agreement. However, if a limited partner participates in the active management of the limited partnership's business, the limited partner automatically becomes a general partner and the protection of limited liability. The capital contribution of a limited partner may consist of cash or property, but usually not services. A limited partner may share in partnership profits to whatever extent is allowed in the partnership agreement. A limited partnership is a creature of statute; a partnership will only be treated as a limited partnership if the appropriate declaration is filed with the provincial or territorial registrar of partnerships.

JOINT VENTURES

The term joint venture is not specifically defined under a Canadian law. In general, a joint venture is an association of natural or corporate persons who contractually agree to combine resources in a definable enterprise for joint profit; a joint venture is not a corporation or partnership, and the entity is often formed for a specific business goal. A joint venture can be particularly useful to foreign investors planning to carry out a specific business transaction in Canada for a limited period of time. Joint ventures are often used when a project requires a pooling of skills, knowledge, or capital, that can often be better achieved through a coalition of several individuals or companies.

In general, the mutual rights and liabilities of participants in joint ventures, joint venturers, with respect to their common enterprise are equivalent to those of partners, and the principles of law applicable to partnerships also apply to the joint venture. A joint venture contract must establish a community of interest among the venturers; each venturer is both principal and agent in dealing with third parties.

Canada imposes few requirements on joint ventures although some must be approved by the government under the Investment Canada Act. Approval is based on whether or not the proposed venture is likely to be of net benefit to Canada; this net benefit evaluation relates to whether or not the venture will have a positive impact on Canadian productivity, the level of Canadian participation, product innovation and variety, technological development, and industrial efficiency. In crucial industries, joint ventures with Canadian partners may be the only method of market entry. (Refer to the "Taxation" chapter for discussion of tax treatment.)

BRANCH OR REPRESENTATIVE OFFICES

Rather than incorporating a separate subsidiary in Canada to handle business operations, a non-resident corporation may prefer to conduct business directly in Canada through a Canadian branch or division. A branch operation typically consists of an office, and employees or agents in Canada. Factors that should be analyzed in this determination include the relatively higher compliance costs of maintaining a separate corporation as opposed to a Canadian branch, corporate law considerations, provincial licensing requirements, financing and tax considerations, and Canadian market considerations. Direct investments in Canada, through either a branch or subsidiary, are subject to notification or review procedures. Commercial and tax considerations may make the use of a Canadian subsidiary preferable to a branch office.

Typically, a foreign corporation establishing a subsidiary must obtain a provincial license for each province in which it plans to conduct business operations. The procedure to obtain a provincial license includes a formal application, a certificate of status from the jurisdiction of incorporation, and the appointment of a local agent for service of process. Assuming no name conflicts, this procedure is relatively simple and straightforward; however, Quebec imposes language requirements and mandates the adoption of a French corporate name.

SOLE OR INDIVIDUAL PROPRIETORSHIPS

The typical sole or individual proprietorship is an unincorporated business owned and operated by a single individual. A sole proprietorship has no intermediate organizational structure. Ordinarily, the owner conducts business for his or her own account; the owner is actively engaged in the transaction and management of the business and is entitled to all the profits of the business. However, the owner may employ as many workers as necessary to carry out business activities. Because this business form is not recognized as a legal entity separate from its owner, the owner has unlimited personal liability for the debts, obligations, and losses of the business; a sole proprietor cannot limit the risk to a predetermined portion of the investment in the business. For this reason, a sole proprietorship is typically used in small rather than large enterprises, and is rarely seen in the context of foreign investors.

No special laws govern the formation and operation of sole proprietorships. These matters are generally governed only by the provincial and territorial laws of contract, agency, tort, and licensing usually applicable to all business operations. Accordingly, the sole proprietorship offers the individual owner a great deal of flexibility, including the ability to make and implement policy without delay or formality.

The profits of a sole proprietorship are taxed as income to the owner at the owner's tax rate. Similarly, all items of deduction, loss, and credits flow directly to the owner.

TRUSTS

Under a trust structure, the person managing the assets of the trust, the trustee, holds legal title to both real and personal property for the benefit of other persons, the beneficiaries. The trustee has the authority to manage the property, and owes a duty of honesty and loyalty and reasonable care to the beneficiaries. Absent negligence or bad faith on the part of the trustee, the beneficiaries have no real power to direct the trustee's actions.

The formation and operation of trusts are generally governed by the provincial and territorial laws of contract, agency, tort, and licensing usually applicable to all business operations. With the exception of Quebec, trust laws are similar throughout the provinces and territories.

Because of the distinction between the management and beneficial ownership of the trust assets, trusts are not typically used for active business ventures. Rather, the trust entity is ordinarily used as an investment vehicle in connection with passive investments, most commonly in the estate planning area.

FRANCHISES AND DISTRIBUTORSHIPS

Many business opportunities exist in Canada for franchises or distributorships, such as restaurants, hotels, automobile dealerships, and car rental agencies. A franchise or distributorship is not a separate form of business entity, but rather a method of doing business.

A basic distinction between a franchise and a distributorship is that a franchisor exercises more control over the method of delivering the product or service than does a distributor. In the common franchise arrangement, a company (the franchisor) typically owns a trademark, which it licenses others to use on condition that the licensee (the franchisee) will conform its business operations to the standards required by the franchisor. Adherence to the specified standards is generally required only to the extent that the products or services sold are associated with the trademark, allowing the franchisee at least some flexibility its business operations. The franchisor usually operates through a limited number of franchisees and often provides assistance to the franchisee in terms of organization, promotional activities, management training, marketing plans, and other business affairs. Because some franchise agreements can be extremely rigid and can tend to favor the franchisor, those interested in franchising should have agreements closely examined by legal counsel.

A distributorship may be set up similar to a franchise, although usually the company whose products a distributor sells exercises less control over business operations and provides less business support to its dealers. Thus, a supplier of goods or services may arrange with any number of companies to distribute those products or services. A common condition placed on an individual distributor is to sell a certain average amount of products or services within a designated time, but the methods used in fulfilling this obligation are often left to the individual distributor, particularly if the supplier does not license any trademark to the distributor. This method is particularly common in automobile and retail gasoline distribution.

Franchises can be advantageous to foreign

investors who want to invest in products with proven domestic markets and who wish to receive the type of business support ordinarily provided by a franchisor. Investors looking for greater independence may prefer a distributorship, precisely because it is subject to less governmental regulation and supplier control. Foreign businesspersons offering products or services for importation into Canada may consider establishing their own franchise or distributorship systems, although they should first conduct comprehensive market and legal research to determine the demand and feasibility of establishing a new franchise or distributorship line.

REGISTERING A BUSINESS

Competent businesspeople, both foreign and domestic, seek legal, accounting, and tax advice from professionals familiar with the provincial and federal laws, regulations, and business practices and customs when creating business plans. With this assistance, business owners may be able to structure their companies to maximize governmental compliance and business opportunities while minimizing the cost and effort of regulatory compliance.

Many federal and provincial government approvals and registrations are valid only for limited periods. Certain documents must be filed and certain fees paid on an annual or other periodic basis to keep registration in force. Investors and owners should record and make note of critical dates, such as expirations of approvals or filing deadlines, to ensure that all registrations and approvals remain current and valid. Once a business is established, its investors and operators will need to remain current on new legal and accounting developments that may impact their business plans and operations. (Refer to the "Important Addresses" chapter for partial listings of government agencies and legal and accounting firms.)

BASIC AUTHORIZATION AND APPLICATION PROCEDURES

In addition to the general procedures set forth earlier in this chapter, individuals starting a business should be mindful of the following procedures, which relate more specifically to whichever entity has been selected and may be required in the specific province in which the business is to operate.

Sole Proprietorships A sole proprietorship can be established with few formalities. It is prudent to take the following steps:
1) File public notices of registration, such as a fictitious business name or doing business as (dba) statements for the name of the enterprise, if required in connection with local licensing regulations.
2) Obtain local business licenses, if required.
3) Maintain proper financial books and records in accordance with federal and provincial tax requirements. (Independent audits are not required for the financial statements of a sole proprietorship, although financial institutions may require more formal records in connection with lending.)

Partnerships Additional decisions and steps are needed to establish a partnership than a sole proprietorship. The formation and regulation of partnerships are governed by provincial law; although these procedures vary somewhat in accordance with the partnership law of the province where the business is formed, the following steps must ordinarily be taken:
1) Determine whether to form a general or limited partnership.
2) Negotiate, prepare, and sign a written partnership agreement.
3) Register partnership in province where business is created.
4) If creating a limited partnership, comply with provincial legislation that requires the filing of an appropriate declaration of limited partnership with provincial registrar of partnerships.
5) File any statements required by provincial law to specify the partnership's address and principal place of business.
6) File public notices of registration, if required in connection with licensing regulations.
7) Obtain local business licenses.

Maintain proper financial books and records in accordance with federal and provincial tax requirements, paying particular attention to the tax consequences of any partner's distributive share of partnership income or loss that is either from Canadian sources or effectively connected with a Canadian trade or business. (Refer to the "Taxation" chapter for a discussion of tax treatment.)

Corporations Although most of the provincial laws stating the requirements for incorporation are modeled after the federal statute, the laws vary in some respects from the federal level to the provincial level (and as between provinces), making the decision of where to incorporate nearly as complicated as the decision of whether to incorporate at all. A business that is incorporated at the federal level under the CBCA may do business in any province; a business that is incorporated in one province must typically obtain a license from any other province in which the corporation will do business. (Refer to Corporations, above.) The most common steps to be taken to incorporate a business

TEN REMINDERS, RECOMMENDATIONS, AND RULES

1. Selection of the most appropriate form of business entity is one of the most important decisions facing a new enterprise. Although selection of the proper entity format cannot ensure the success of the venture, a wrong choice may contribute to a venture's failure.

2. Because the laws and regulations applicable to establishing and operating a business in Canada are spread throughout federal and provincial or territorial sources, and a certain amount of overlap exists between the federal and provincial schemes, advice from legal and accounting professionals familiar with the specific jurisdiction of interest is essential.

3. Canadian laws and regulations and their interpretations are constantly changing. Businesspeople, foreign and domestic alike, find it helpful to belong to chambers of commerce, business associations, and other organizations that monitor legislative, judicial, and economic changes and make regular reports of their findings to their members.

4. The attitude of the Canadian government toward foreign investment in Canada is generally positive and Canada does much to encourage foreign investment. Provincial, territorial, and municipal governments vary considerably in their attitudes toward foreign investment: some areas may be very supportive of foreign investment and actively solicit it, while other areas may be significantly less encouraging of foreign investment. Check the political, demographic, and economic conditions in your particular area of interest before proceeding to form a business entity.

5. If several investments or lines of business are contemplated, the creation of a holding company with separate subsidiaries for each investment or enterprise should be considered.

6. Any foreign individual or entity that conducts business in Canada is required to obtain the same necessary permissions and registrations, at the federal and provincial or territorial levels, as a Canadian person or entity before undertaking any business.

7. Foreign individuals and entities can generally own land and immovable fixtures in Canada, subject to certain limitations and reporting requirements. (Refer to the "Foreign Investment" chapter for a detailed discussion of reserved and restricted foreign investment activities.)

8. Depending on the nature of the investment and the desired business structure, tax matters may be complex; all tax considerations should be evaluated as part of the decision-making process, rather than after the fact.

9. Canada maintains a business immigration program to attract experienced business persons who will create employment opportunities and contribute to economic and technological development. Three categories of business immigrants are acknowledged: entrepreneurs, investors, and self-employed persons. Companies seeking to bring in skilled workers must obtain employment validations from Employment and Immigration Canada; companies seeking to bring in foreign nationals as senior executives or managers may do so through an intercompany transfer program. People seeking temporary employment who are not business immigrants must obtain a work permit. (Refer to the "Business Travel" chapter for a more complete discussion.)

10. Once the business entity is established, the managing participants must pay regular attention to the maintenance of business records, making and updating registrations and filings, and paying all taxes and fees required on time.

in Canada at the federal level are as follows:

1) Conduct name check; select and reserve name for ninety days.
2) Prepare and have incorporators sign articles of incorporation, pursuant to the applicable federal or provincial requirements, which typically set forth:
   a) the name of the corporation
   b) the place in Canada where the registered office is located
   c) the powers of the corporation
   d) the authorized capital structure of the corporation
   e) the classes and maximum number of shares that the corporation is authorized to issue and, if more than one class is authorized, the attributes (such as, rights, privileges, restrictions, and conditions) applicable to

the shares of each class
f) a statement identifying the nature of any restriction on the issuance, transfer, or ownership of shares
g) the number (or minimum or maximum number) of directors (at least three directors, two of whom are not employees) if the shares are publicly traded)
h) any restrictions on the business that the corporation may conduct.
3) File application for incorporation, with the articles of incorporation and any other required documents (such as the notice of registered office and the notice of initial directors) to the Director for filing, along with any required tax payments and filing fees.
4) Prepare and sign bylaws of the corporation and any other organizational documents relating to such matters as the election of corporate officers, issuance of stock, and adoption of important agreements and contracts.
5) Obtain the appropriate securities permits or exemptions from registration.
6) If corporation will conduct business in a province in which it is not incorporated, obtain a provincial license.
7) Obtain any necessary local business licenses.
8) Prepare and maintain proper books and records at registered office or other location designated by the directors, including copies of the articles of incorporation, bylaws, amendments, any unanimous shareholder agreement, minutes of meetings, director or committee resolutions, directors' and shareholders' resolutions, copies of all notices filed with the administrative body with jurisdiction over the corporation, including the notice of directors (or change of directors), securities register, and accounting records in accordance with federal and provincial business and tax requirements.
9) Call first annual meeting of shareholders within 18 months of incorporation and comply with all applicable annual filing requirements, including annual informational filings and audited financial statements.

Joint Ventures Parties who desire to unite their resources in a joint venture should proceed as follows:
1) Negotiate, prepare, and sign a written joint venture contract, which should include:
   a) the designation of the joint venture parties
   b) the contributions and obligations of each joint venturer
   c) the purpose of the joint venture
      -the term of the venture
      -the process for distribution of profits and losses.
2) Follow any other procedures for establishing either a partnership or corporate entity, as applicable.

Branch or Representative Offices A foreign businessperson may open a branch or representative office in the Canada by completing the following:
1) File requisite certificates and documents with the appropriate provincial and territorial government offices, such as: certificates of good standing indicating that the corporation exists in good standing in the country of its incorporation, together with English or French translation if needed; and statements providing administrative information about the foreign corporation.
2) Maintain proper financial books and records and make appropriate filings as required for the operation of any business.

Franchises or Distributorships Persons who desire to do business through a franchise or distributorship should take the following steps to set up that arrangement:
1) Create the form of business organization under which the franchisee or distributor will operate, most typically a sole proprietorship, partnership, or corporation.
2) In the case of a franchise, carefully review the franchisor's offering circular and other documents related to the franchise business.
3) Negotiate, prepare, and sign a franchise or distribution agreement.
4) Conduct business in accordance with the franchise requirements (if applicable) and the laws and regulations relating to the operation of any business.
5) Maintain proper financial books and records and make appropriate filings as required for the operation of any business.

FURTHER READING

The preceding discussion is provided as a basic guide for those interested in doing business in Canada. The resources described in this section contain additional information on business law, financing, investment, taxation, accounting, and procedural requirements.

Doing Business in Canada, Ernst & Young. New York: Ernst & Young International, Ltd., 1995. Also available in more than 120 other countries in which Ernst & Young maintains local offices. Provides an extensive overview of the investment environment in Canada, together with information about taxation, business organizational structures, business practices, and accounting requirements.

USEFUL ADDRESSES

Individuals or firms interested in establishing a

business in Canada should first contact the appropriate government regulatory agencies for information, forms, and guidance on the legal requirements. In addition, much useful assistance and information is available from the federal, provincial or territorial, and municipal governments; local chambers of commerce; national, regional, and special services offices of Industry Canada (IC); and private sector sources, including business associations. The following list is presented in alphabetical order.

Association of Canadian Venture Capital Companies
120 Eglinton Avenue East, Suite 1000
Toronto, Ontario
M4P 1E2
Tel: (416) 487-0519

Atlantic Canada Opportunities Agency (ACOA)
International Division
Blue Cross Centre
644 Main Street
Moncton, New Brunswick
E1C 9J8
Tel: (506) 851-2271
Fax: (506) 851-7403

Bank of Canada
234 Wellington Street
Ottawa, Ontario
K1A 0G9

Bureau of Competition Policy
Consumer & Corporate Affairs Canada
Place du Portage
50 Victoria Street, 21st Floor
Hull, Quebec
K1A 0C9

Business Council on National Issues
90 Sparks Street, Suite 806
Ottawa, Ontario
K1P 5B4

The Canadian Chamber of Commerce, Head Office
55 Metcalfe Street, Suite 1160
Ottawa, Ontario
K1P 6N4
Tel: (613) 238-4000

The Canadian Exporters' Association (CEA)
99 Bank Street, Suite 250
Ottawa, Ontario
K1P 6B9
Tel: (613) 238-8888
Fax: (613) 563-9218

The Canadian Federation of Independent Business
4141 Yonge Street
Willowdale, Ontario
M2P 2A6
Tel: (416) 222-8022
Fax: (416) 222-4337

The Canadian Franchise Association
88 University Avenue, Suite 607
Toronto, Ontario
M5J 1T6
Tel: (416) 595-5005
Fax: (416) 595-9519

The Canadian Importers' Association
210 Dundas Street West, Suite 700
Toronto, Ontario
M5G 2E8
Tel: (416) 595-5333
Fax: (416) 595-8226

The Canadian Manufacturers' Association (CMA)
1 Yonge Street, Suite 1400
Toronto, Ontario
M5E 1J9
Tel: (416) 363-7261
Fax: (416) 363-3779

Corporate and Technical Services Division
Department of Economic Development and Tourism
P.O. Box 1320
Yellowknife, Northwest Territories
X1A 2L9
Tel: (403) 873-7364
Fax: (403) 873-0101

Department of Economic Development
P.O. Box 2703
Whitehorse, Yukon
Y1A 2C6
Tel: (403) 667-5466
Fax: (403) 667-8601

Department of Economic Development and Tourism
P.O. Box 2000
Charlottetown, Prince Edward Island
C1A 7N8
Tel: (902) 368-4250
Fax: (902) 368-4224

Department of Foreign Affairs and International Trade (DFAIT)
Lester B. Pearson Building
125 Sussex Drive
Ottawa, Ontario
K1A 0G2
Tel: (613) 944-4000
Fax: (613) 996-9709

Development Services
Saskatchewan Economic Development
7th Floor, 1919 Saskatchewan Drive
Regina, Saskatchewan
S4P 3V7
Tel: (306) 787-4707
Fax: (306) 787-1620

Federal Business Development Bank (FBDB)
800 Victoria Square
P.O. Box 335
Montreal, Quebec
H4Z 1L4
Tel: (514) 283-5904
Fax: (514) 283-0617

Human Resources Development Canada
140 Promenade du Portage
Ottawa, Ontario
K1A 0J9

Industrial Promotion Branch
Nova Scotia Economic Renewal Agency
1800 Argyle Street, Suite 608
P.O. Box 519
Halifax, Nova Scotia
B3J 2R7
Tel: (902) 424-5320
Fax: (902) 424-0664

Industry Canada (IC)
Business Service Centre
1st Floor, East Tower
235 Queen Street
Ottawa, Ontario
K1A 0H5

Industry Canada (IC)
Corporations Directorate
9th Floor, Journal Tower South
365 Laurier Avenue West
Ottawa, Ontario
K1A 0C8
Tel: (613) 941-9042

Industry Canada (IC)
Patents, Trademarks, Copyrights, and Industrial Design Office
Place du Portage
Hull, Quebec
K1A 0C9

Industry Development
Department of Industry, Trade, and Tourism
410-155 Carlton Street, 4th Floor
Winnipeg, Manitoba
R3C 3H8
Tel: (204) 945-2456
Fax: (204) 957-1793

Investment Branch
Investment Office
Ministry of Employment and Investment
999 Canada Place, Suite 600
Vancouver, British Columbia
V6C 3E1
Tel: (604) 844-1828
Fax: (604) 844-1893

Investment Canada
5th Floor West
240 Sparks Street
P.O. Box 2800, Station D
Ottawa, Ontario
K1P 6A5

Investment Case Management
Ministry of Economic Development and Trade
Hearst Block, 5th Floor
900 Bay Street
Toronto, Ontario
M7A 2E1
Tel: (416) 325-6833
Fax: (416) 325-6814

Investment Services
Ministry of Industry, Commerce, Science, and Technology
770 Sherbrooke Street West, 7th Floor
Montreal, Quebec
H3A 1G1
Tel: (514) 982-3013
Fax: (514) 873-4503

Marketing and Investment Division
Department of Industry, Trade, and Technology
P.O. Box 8700
St. John's, Newfoundland
A1B 4J6
Tel: (709) 729-2781
Fax: (709) 729-59366814

National Research Council (NRC)
Building M-55
Montreal Road
Ottawa, Ontario
K1A 0R6
Tel: (613) 993-9101

Northern Ontario Development Fund (FedNor)
FedNor Head Office
302 Queen Street East
Sault-Ste. Marie, Ontario
P6A 1Z1
Tel: (705) 942-1327
Fax: (705) 942-5434

Office de la Langue Francaise
Public Relations Services
Tour Place Victoria, 16th Floor
Montreal, Quebec
H4Z 1GZ
Tel: (514) 873-6565
Fax: (514) 873-3488

Revenue Canada
Rulings Directorate
25 Nicholas Street
Albion Towers, 15th Floor
Ottawa, Ontario
K1A 0L8

Revenue Canada
Customs, Excise, and Taxation
Voice Mail Information
Ottawa, Ontario
Tel: (613) 993-0534

Standards Council of Canada
Standards Information Service
350 Sparks Street, Suite 1200
Ottawa, Ontario
K1P 6N7
Tel: (613) 238-3222

Tourism, Trade, and Investment Division
Department of Alberta Economic Development and Tourism
4th Floor, Commerce Place
10155 – 102nd Street
Edmonton, Alberta
T5J 4L6
Tel: (403) 422-6236
Fax: (403) 422-9127

Trade and Investment Branch
Department of Economic Development and Tourism
P.O. Box 6000
Fredericton, New Brunswick
E3B 5H1
Tel: (506) 444-4292
Fax: (506) 444-4277

Western Economic Diversification Canada (WED)
Suite 1500, Canada Place
9700 Jasper Avenue
Edmonton, Alberta
T5J 4H7
Tel: (403) 495-4164
Fax: (403) 495-4557

Alberta
International Trade Centre
Room 540
Canada Place
9700 Jasper Avenue
Edmonton, Alberta
T5J 4C3
Tel: (403) 495-2944
Fax: (403) 495-4507

Calgary Office
Suite 1100
510 - 5th Street S.W.
Calgary, Alberta
T2P 3S2
Tel: (403) 292-6660
Fax: (403) 292-4578

British Columbia
International Trade Centre
P.O. Box 11610
900 - 650 West Georgia Street
Vancouver, British Columbia
V6B 5H8
Tel: (604) 666-0434
Fax: (604) 666-8330

Manitoba
International Trade Centre
P.O. Box 981
330 Portage Avenue, 8th Floor
Winnipeg, Manitoba
R3C 2V2
Tel: (204) 983-6531
Fax: (204) 983-2187

New Brunswick
International Trade Centre
P.O. Box 1210
Assumption Place
770 Main Street
Moncton, New Brunswick
E1C 8P9
Tel: (506) 851-6452
Fax: (506) 851-6429

Newfoundland
International Trade Centre
P.O. Box 8950
Atlantic Place
215 Water Street
Suite 504
St. John's, Newfoundland
A1B 3R9
Tel: (709) 772-5511
Fax: (709) 772-2373

Nova Scotia
International Trade Centre
P.O. Box 940
Station M
1801 Hollis Street
Halifax, Nova Scotia
B3J 2V9
Tel: (902) 426-7540
Fax: (902) 426-2624

Ontario
International Trade Centre
Dominion Public Building
4th Floor
One Front Street West
Toronto, Ontario
M5J 1A4
Tel: (416) 973-5053
Fax: (416) 973-8161

Prince Edward Island
International Trade Centre
P.O. Box 1115
Confederation Court Mall
134 Kent Street, Suite 400
Charlottetown, Prince Edward Island
C1A 7M8
Tel: (902) 566-7400
Fax: (902) 566-7450

Quebec
International Trade Centre
5, Place Ville-Marie, Suite 800
Montreal, Quebec
H3B 2G2
Tel: (514) 496-4636
Fax: (514) 283-8794

Saskatchewan
International Trade Centre
The S.H. Cohen Building
Room 401
119 - 4th Avenue South
Saskatoon, Saskatchewan
S7K 5X2
Tel: (306) 975-5315
Fax: (306) 975-5334

Regina Office
6th Floor
1919 Saskatchewan Drive
Regina, Saskatchewan
S4P 3V7
Tel: (306) 780-6325
Fax: (306) 780-6679

Labor

THE LABOR ECONOMY

Canada's sophisticated economy supports a well-educated, highly trained, productive labor force. A lingering recession, from which Canada is only now emerging, has, since 1988, placed heavy pressure on the economy in general and on labor in particular. The past decade has been a bumpy ride: As real wages ratcheted downward, and unemployment and underemployment rose, Canada's gradually weakening dollar has made its exports more attractive, especially for its largest trading partner, the United. The current recovery, begun in 1994, has not shown many of the positive indicators that previous recoveries have. However, it is most definitely export-led, and this has created a boom in production which is just now easing some of the fears many workers have faced.

However, downsizing throughout industry remains, and this has caused workers to review their positions and reassess their goals in light of these new trends. Job security is one of the primary concerns of working age Canadians, and many are focusing on enhanced education to retain their marketability.

CONTENTS

The Labor Economy	195
Population	196
Labor Force	196
Unemployment and Underemployment	197
Comparative Unemployment	198
Human Resources	199
Canadian Unemployment Rates	199
Conditions of Employment	200
Change in Wages	201
Comparative Average Weekly Wages - 1992	202
Wages and Benefits	203
Labor Relations	204

The education system has had to scramble to keep pace with the rapid workforce changes, and to assimilate the skilled, older students returning to school, but most believe it has done a good job. There is more focus on vocational training, high technological skills, and on actual job placement as part of the educational process. Good communication skills—both written and oral—are increasingly being stressed, as Canada recognizes that much of the future lies in the service industries.

In short, Canadians reacted quickly and responded positively to recessionary conditions, and a reviving—albeit much restructured—economy is the result.

Gone for the most part are the comprehensive health and welfare benefits to which workers once considered themselves entitled. Gone are the annual pay increases and hefty year-end bonuses. In place instead are efficient and economical benefit plans, pay increases which may or may not keep pace with inflation, and bonuses tied to productivity.

Canada is also observing significant restructuring in labor-management relations. The once powerful and extremely adversarial unions have begun to coexist with management and to actively seek ways to work together to increase productivity and competitiveness throughout industry. Workers are acceding to reduced wage increases and are settling instead for more job security and broader benefits. In general, Canada's wage levels are higher than those of developing countries, but somewhat lower than those in the United States. It's benefits structure is comprehensive, and the government mandates that employers contribute generously to several benefits programs.

With the implementation of NAFTA, Canada offers an attractive production site or home office headquarters for companies looking to do business in the North American region. With its multiethnic population, highly skilled workforce, and modern facilities it lacks for almost nothing.

POPULATION

Canada is a large country with a small population. As compared with the US, whose 5,623 square miles support nearly 260 million people, Canada's 5,985 square miles are home to only 29 million. A vast majority of Canada's population reside in or near large urban areas around the provincial capitals. Less than 25 percent live in rural areas. In between, there are vast wilderness areas where small towns are few and far between, and are connected only by air or endless deserted roadways.

Canada is divided into 12 provinces and territories, with Quebec and Ontario together being the home of over half of Canada's total population. British Columbia, the next most populous province, is currently showing by far the largest yearly gains in population-much of this coming from immigrating Asians. Toronto is the largest city, housing nearly 4.5 million people, followed by Montreal, which is home to over 3 million, and Vancouver with 2 million. Nearly half of the population live in the major metropolitan areas of Toronto, Montreal, Vancouver, Ottawa-Hull, Edmonton, Calgary, Quebec, Winnipeg, Hamilton and London.

Canada's population is overwhelmingly working-aged, with nearly 50 percent of its people between the ages of 15 and 44. Another 20 percent are between 44 and 64 years. However, the fastest growing age groups are those older than 45, and this will likely put some strain on the country's generous social benefits programs in the future. The birth rate declined by 2.6 percent in 1994 to a low of 14.1 births per one thousand population. Life expectancy remains high, at 74 years for males and 81 for females.

Canada supports an extremely heterogeneous ethnic population, and this will increase in the future, since its native population growth does not keep pace with growth through immigration. Though nearly 60 percent of the people are native English speakers, and virtually everybody speaks English fluently (outside of Quebec at least), there are large and very prominent pockets of French speakers (many of them found outside French-speaking Quebec). Italian, Chinese, German and various other languages are often heard and used throughout the country. Unlike the US, which encourages immigrants to blend into the melting pot, Canada has long encouraged its immigrants to retain their ethnic traditions in order to form a rich mosaic of cultures within the country. Canada's immigration continues to significantly outpace emigration; immigration rose by 7.6 percent in 1995, while out migration fell by 4.3 percent. Immigration from Asian countries (primarily from Hong Kong and China) rose by nearly 60 percent in 1995 and looks set to maintain this pace in the near term.

Along with its multiethnic population, Canada supports a multiplicity of religions, and religious tolerance is broad and comprehensive. There is little open discrimination, and most forms of bias or discrimination are prohibited by law. Nearly every religion in the world is openly practiced in the country. Roman Catholics make up the largest religious group, with 46 percent of the religious community claiming this affiliation, followed by the United Church, with 16 percent, and the Anglicans with 10 percent. Several other religions are also well represented, and are primarily found in specific pockets throughout the country.

LABOR FORCE

In 1994, the total labor force consisted of 14.9 million people, 8.2 million of whom were male and 6.7 of whom were female. Of these, about 7.4 million males were currently employed, as were 6.1 million women.

Canada's largest employing sector is the services industry, which employs over 10 million people. Industry employs about three million, and agriculture supports only about half a million people. Employment by sector is as follows: manufacturing, 2.1 million; construction, 723,000; community, business and personal services, 5 million; trade, 2.3 million; transportation, communications and other utilities, 1 million; public administration, 810,000; finance, insurance and real estate, 809,000. The largest gains over the past five years have been in the services industries, while construction has suffered a loss of over 12 percent of its jobs over the same period.

Canada is currently experiencing strong economic growth, which is mirrored in the labor market. Overall, employment has grown by between 2 and 3 percent over the past few years. A distinctive characteristic of the current labor market is the strong turnaround in the goods-producing sector. This sector, which suffered heavy job losses in the early 1990s, saw average employment rise significantly thereafter, and has once again become a major source of employment growth. Regional distribution of employment growth is also widespread. While growth in the early 1990s was concentrated primarily in British Columbia and Ontario, more recently Alberta, Quebec and Nova Scotia have all registered sizable employment gains as well.

Canada's is a productive workforce, with productivity in manufacturing rising steadily year after year. Canada had historically been considered a relatively low-productivity center due to its developed manufacturing base and high wages, but a major restructuring over the past few years in response to the recession has already produced results. Despite falling sales, manufacturing firms worked on maximizing their excess capacity to produce more goods, achieving nearly 80 percent capacity utilization by mid-1993. At the same time, and in direct response to falling profits, they put a stranglehold on wages. The average rate of pay increase in the business sector was first chopped to 2.9 percent from a long-time average of 6.9 percent, and was then reduced further to barely 2 percent. Labor costs per unit of output continue to fall, and have fallen by nearly 3 percent since 1992.

Canadian workers that survived layoffs and saw their average salary raises slashed have been the force behind the first major pickup in labor productivity since the late 1980s. In 1992, productivity recorded an increase of 1.5 percent, and has been growing steadily since. Although this is good news, it was also fundamentally necessary. With the implementation of NAFTA it very soon became clear that the only way Canada could become a competitive exporter of manufactured goods and was to drastically improve its business operations. Canada has aggressively competed in the new free trade environment brought about by NAFTA.

UNEMPLOYMENT AND UNDEREMPLOYMENT

The unemployment rate, after falling drastically from its highs of the late 1980s to early 1990s, seems to have stabilized at about 9.5 percent. The underemployment rate, however, remains high, at about 13 to 14 percent. Workers who are seeking full-time positions, but who are able only to find work for fewer than 35 hours per week are considered underemployed.

While the national unemployment rate fell in both 1994 and 1995, the situation for the chronically unemployed (those without work for more than a year) worsened. Between 1990 and 1994, the number of unemployed in this category more than tripled, with the average duration of unemployment rising by nearly one-third. Adult men currently account for 56 percent of this group.

The national unemployment rate is forecast to remain in the mid- to upper-nine percent range. Employment gains are expected to be flat given continued private and public sector downsizing, slower export growth, weaker corporate profits, and flat to negative investment in residential and non-residential construction. Thus, job hunters are not expected to have an easier time of it anytime soon. Even government optimists don't expect to see a real improvement in unemployment until at least 1997.

Part of the problem is rooted in a vicious cycle-consumers that don't have jobs or expect to be laid off soon are reluctant to spend their money. When domestic demand is weak, as it is in Canada now, manufacturers have no reason to increase production and add new workers. And, on top of that, workers that do have jobs have been dealing with historically low wage increases for the last several years, and thus overall purchasing continues to decrease.

However, 1996 is so far proving to be a better year on the employment scene. Employment grew by 44,000 in February, continuing the generally upward trend observed over the prior six months. The number of persons unemployed was virtually unchanged as expansion of the labor force kept pace with the growth in jobs. This left the unemployment rate unchanged at 9.6 percent, it has just recently (in early 1996) dropped slightly further, to 9.4 percent.

A rising participation rate is generally viewed as an indicator of improved job opportunities, and the participation rate has risen slowly but steadily over the past several months. Both youths and adults have contributed to this gain. Gains have been fairly evenly spread between youths and adults and between full and part time employment. By sector, most employment gains of late have been seen in the services industries.

Unemployment rates remain fairly dynamic across Canada's provinces. Newfoundland has suffered the most, with unemployment rising steadily by large percentages. Underemployment, too, continues to rise as the seasonal jobs upon which many of the province's residents rely continue to diminish in both duration and pay. Manitoba and British Columbia, on the other hand, have registered vast improvements in their unemployment situation, with unemployment rates falling by 8.5 and 7.2 percent respectively over the past few months.

Foreign Workers

Canadian immigration policy recognizes the need to facilitate the entry of visitors to Canada in order to foster trade, commerce, tourism, cultural and scientific activities, as well as international goodwill. Thus, the Canadian government maintains a comprehensive business immigration program which includes both non-immigrant and immigrant status. Its laws and policies are designed to attract experienced business people and skilled individuals to the country.

Temporary Residents Normally, a non-resident applying to enter and work in Canada must obtain a work permit from the Canadian immigration authorities. The permit is generally valid for one year, and is only granted if the applicant can prove that he/she has a job offer validated by a Canada Employment Centre, which confirms that there is no Canadian available for that job. A non-refundable C$75 processing fee must accompany the application. The process is simplified when it involves a corporate transfer of executive or managerial personnel, as employment validation is generally not required. Employers should allow sufficient time for the processing of temporary work permits. Family members of the applicant may be admitted as visitors but may not work unless they also satisfy Employment and Immigration Canada's work criteria. Student authorizations under this program are fairly easy to obtain.

A temporary resident who decides to remain in Canada must follow the application procedures for permanent status.

Permanent Residents Application for permanent residency must be filed and a visa must be obtained before entering Canada. Admission to Canada may be subject to terms and conditions which may be imposed for up to six months, and it normally takes nearly a year to complete the application process. There are several basic classes of admissible immigrants, including that of "Business Immigrant."

The Business Immigration Program is to promote, encourage and facilitate the immigration of experienced businesspersons from abroad who will make a positive contribution to Canada's economic development by applying their risk capital and know-how to Canadian business ventures, which will in turn create jobs for Canadians. Applicants wishing to enter this program must first make an application through any overseas Canadian visa office. This application must be accompanied by a business plan or a summary of their business intentions. High priority is given to business applicants, although they pay an exceptionally high processing fee of C$500.

There are three basic types of business applicants:

1. Self-employed: These are persons who are willing and able to establish a business in Canada, which will employ the applicants and contribute to the economy or to cultural and artistic life in Canada.

2. Entrepreneurs: These are persons who are willing and able to establish, purchase or invest in a business which will significantly contribute to the economy and will create or maintain jobs for one or more Canadians.

3. Investors: These are persons who have a proven track record in business and have a personal net worth of C$500,000 or more. They must be willing to make an irrevocable investment of at least C$150,000 for at least three years in a project, which has been assessed by the province as being beneficial to the economy, and which will contribute to the creation or continuation of job opportunities for Canadians. (In Ontario and Quebec the minimum investment amount is C$250,000).

NAFTA NAFTA makes it easier for certain types of businesspersons to be admitted to Canada on a temporary basis. There are four immigration categories under NAFTA:

1. Business Visitors: Business visitors from the US or Mexico may be admitted at a port of entry without the requirement on an employment authorization and without the requirement of prior approvals or labor validation. Such visitors may apply for temporary entry into Canada at a port of entry upon proof of US or Mexican citizenship; documentation demonstrating that they will be

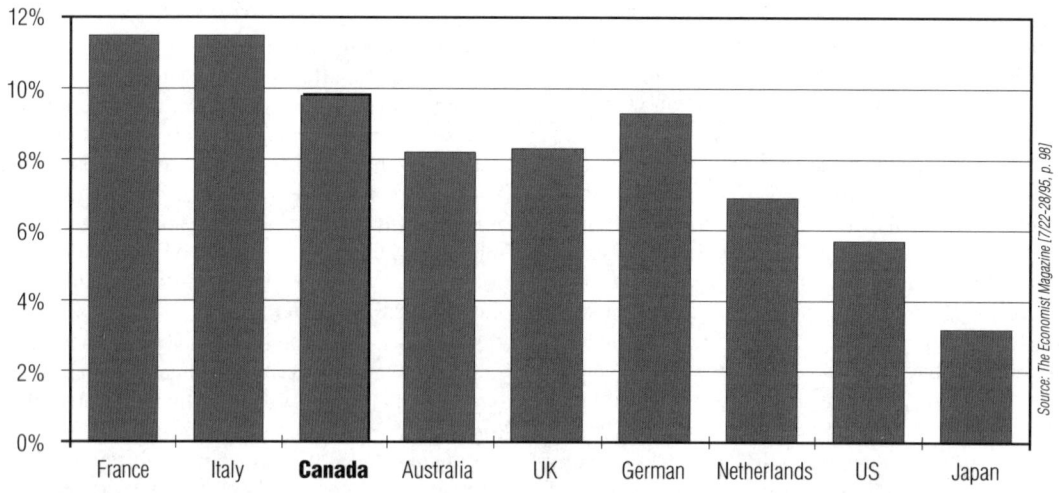

Comparative Unemployment –Mid-1995

Source: The Economist Magazine [7/22-28/95, p. 98]

engaged as a temporary business person and describing the purpose of their entry; and evidence that the business activity is international in scope and that they are not seeking to enter the local labor market. The primary source of remuneration for the proposed business activity, and the individual's place of business and actual place of an accrual of profits must be outside Canada.

2. Traders and Investors: This category facilitates temporary entry and provides employment authorizations for business people seeking to carry on substantial trade in goods and services, principally between the US, Mexico and Canada, or to those wishing to establish, develop, administer or provide advice, or key technical services to the operation of an investment to which the business person or their enterprise has committed or is in the process of committing a substantial amount of capital. Such individuals must be in a capacity that is supervisory, executive, or involves essential skills. No labor validation is required, but individuals must apply through a Canadian Consulate or Embassy, and cannot apply at the Canadian port of entry.

3. Intra Company Transfers: This category provides for the temporary entry and issuance of employment authorizations to business persons who are employed by an enterprise and who seek to enter Canada to render services to that enterprise or a subsidiary or affiliate thereof, in a capacity that is managerial, executive or involves specialized knowledge. Such an individual must also have been employed continuously by the enterprise for one year within the three year period immediately preceding the date of application for admission. No labor validation is required and individuals may apply at a port of entry.

4. Professionals: This category is designed to facilitate the temporary entry and the provision of employment authorizations to persons seeking to engage in business activities at a professional level in a profession that is set out in NAFTA. They must be able to prove their US or Mexican citizenship and have documentation demonstrating that they will be engaged in the profession indicated. Naturally, they must also be able to substantiate their qualifications as a professional in that category.

HUMAN RESOURCES

Education

Canada's educational system is one of the best in the world, providing top quality graduates who become highly trained, professional contributors to Canada's economy. Among the leading developed countries of the world, Canada is second only to the US in per capita post-secondary enrollment. Canada leads the world in terms of providing public sector support for education, with spending measured as a percentage of GDP. As a result, Canada offers one of the most highly educated workforces available anywhere. Approximately 25 percent of Canadians have graduated from post-secondary institutions, and about half of these are university graduates- and these percentages are increasing year after year. Virtually the entire population over the age of 15 can read and write.

There are over 200 community colleges and 80 universities in Canada, together servicing nearly one million students. In 1994 Canadian schools conferred 126,538 bachelor's or first professional degrees, 21,292 masters degrees, and 3,552 doctorates.

Universities offer broad incentives for students,

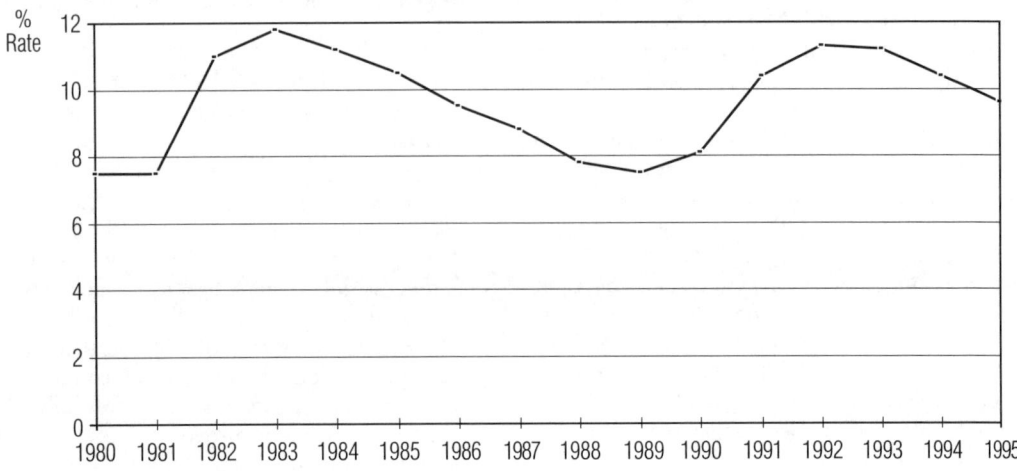

Canadian Unemployment Rates

Sources: Statistics Canada

including low-interest loans, job counseling and placement, and various educational stipends.

In response to the recent recession, and the sweeping changes in the job market as a result of both NAFTA and the trend toward automation and high-technology employment, many schools have modified their curricula to better equip their students for the new workplace. More emphasis is being placed on developing specific skills rather than on the broad, general education formerly stressed. Vocational training courses have made a comeback, and professional training programs are more narrowly focused on specific job applications. Overall, Canadian schools turn out graduates who are well-educated, motivated, and ready to perform in a productive capacity.

Women in the Workforce

Women are well-represented at all levels of business and government, and there is very little, if any, overt discrimination against them in the workplace. However, noticeable discrepancies are still found in average pay scales between men and women, and most of these cannot be accounted for by different experience levels. Women earn on average 40 percent less than men of the same age and education level. Overall, women earn an average 78 percent of what men do but only 12 percent of that gap can be explained by differences such as work experience, education or demographics, shows a recent survey by Statistics Canada.

The federal Employment Equity Act, passed in 1986, increased the representation of women in the workforce to over 45 percent, a level only slightly below the workforce availability figure of 46 percent. In all sectors except communications the representation of women increased significantly between 1990 and 1995. Womens' gains were also reflected in improvements in income. Nevertheless, the fact that many women continue to be employed in lower paying jobs means that there is still a wage gap.

Indeed, pay equity is a major concern confronting Canadian employers. Ontario in 1990 enacted legislation requiring employers with 500 or more employees to implement a pay-equity program under which employers classify all jobs, based on their mix of employees, as either female, male or gender neutral. Every female gender job must be compared with male gender jobs of equal value, and any difference in salary must be eliminated over time. Currently the federal government and federally regulated companies in Ontario are excluded from this law, but the federal government and other provinces in Canada are planning to pass some form of pay-equity legislation, making the law even more widespread.

Changes in the division of labor between the sexes are also being seen throughout Canada. In 1987, 70 percent of all female employees were working in clerical jobs. By 1993, that figure had dropped to around 65 percent, and it now hovers closer to the 62 percent mark. Women's share of middle management positions has also risen significantly in the past six years. The representation of women in senior management nearly doubled between 1988 and 1994. But there is still a long way to go to meet the current availability estimate of 25 percent. Employers must look more critically at the hiring and promotion of women into their senior ranks if they are to be fairly represented at the top of the ladder by the turn of the century.

Claims of discrimination on the basis of sex remained one of the largest group of complaints brought to the Canadian Human Rights Commission. Sexual harassment and discrimination because of pregnancy are the most common forms of sex discrimination but women also continue to be denied employment opportunities for other reasons related to their sex.

CONDITIONS OF EMPLOYMENT

With its long tradition of strong labor organization, Canada maintains some of the highest labor conditions and standards in the developed world. As in many highly unionized countries, layoffs can be complicated and costly to employers. Due to the rapid economic changes resulting from the implementation of NAFTA, as well as a sluggish economy, efforts are underway to simplify termination requirements and lower such costs to employers. The unions have largely accepted this as inevitable, but they are pressing the government to pay greater attention to the problems of economic restructuring as it affects working people. Still, there is a noticeable new camaraderie between labor and management, and a definite willingness to work together for the long term benefit of both parties.

Working Hours, Overtime, Holidays, Vacations

Workweek The determination of a standard workweek is left to each province. Most provinces define a workweek as between 44 and 48 hours. There is a strong move to reduce the standard workweek to the 40 hours generally observed in industry in an effort to create more jobs, but to date the federal government has taken no legislative action on these proposals.

Most union jobs require that overtime be paid for all hours worked in excess of certain stated maximums, and Canadians make liberal use of these overtime provisions. In an average week, Canadians work 6.4 million hours of paid overtime.

Vacations Annual paid vacations in industry are

usually two to three weeks, increasing to three, four and in some cases five weeks after a specific number of years. Workers under federal jurisdiction are entitled to a minimum two-week vacation with pay after one year of service and a third week after six years of service, plus nine statutory holidays per year. Employment vacation standards for other workers are set out in provincial legislation.

Holidays There are ten federally observed holidays and several other holidays throughout the provinces. The federal holidays are New Year's Day, January 1; Good Friday and Easter, changes from year to year; Victoria Day, May 27; Canada Day, July 1; Labor Day, September 2; Thanksgiving Day, in October, changes from year to year; Remembrance Day, November 11; Christmas, December 25; Boxing Day, December 26. In addition, there are many regional religious holidays, upon which stores and offices may be closed for business.

The provinces are free to legislate various holidays. For example, in Ontario, retail businesses must ensure that they are not open for business on the following holidays: New Year's Day, Good Friday, Victoria Day, Canada Day, Labor Day, Thanksgiving Day, Christmas Day, Boxing Day and any other proclaimed public holiday. In most of the other provinces stores may remain open, although they are usually required to pay overtime to working employees.

Sunday Closing In Canada, the law regarding Sunday closings has been the subject of ongoing controversy. The federal Lord's Day Act, which made it unlawful for any person (aside from certain states exceptions) to engage in commercial dealings or paid employment on Sunday, has been dismissed by the Supreme Court of Canada. However, there are provincial laws governing Sunday closings, and these should be investigated before establishing or acquiring a business.

Special Leave

Maternity By establishing maternity leave benefits, Canada allows mothers to stay home and care for their babies before rejoining the workforce. After a two-week waiting period, the mother receives a percentage of her income as benefits, up to a maximum, for a period of 15 weeks and her job is guaranteed, providing she was employed for 20 weeks immediately prior to her leave and she returns to work within the allotted time frame.

In addition to maternity leave, a parental leave from work may be taken by the mother or father of the baby or by a combination of both. Parental leave benefits are paid for a maximum of 10 weeks and the parent's job is guaranteed. The length of each leave varies, depending on the province and how the employer is incorporated.

Jury Duty All employers are required to grant leave to employees to serve on juries, though there is no legislation that requires them to compensate employees for loss of income while doing so. Nonetheless, almost 80 percent of the workers covered by major collective agreements are entitled to paid leave for jury duty. Not all of these employees, however, receive full pay. And in smaller organizations, the incidence of paid leave is considerably lower.

Change in Wages

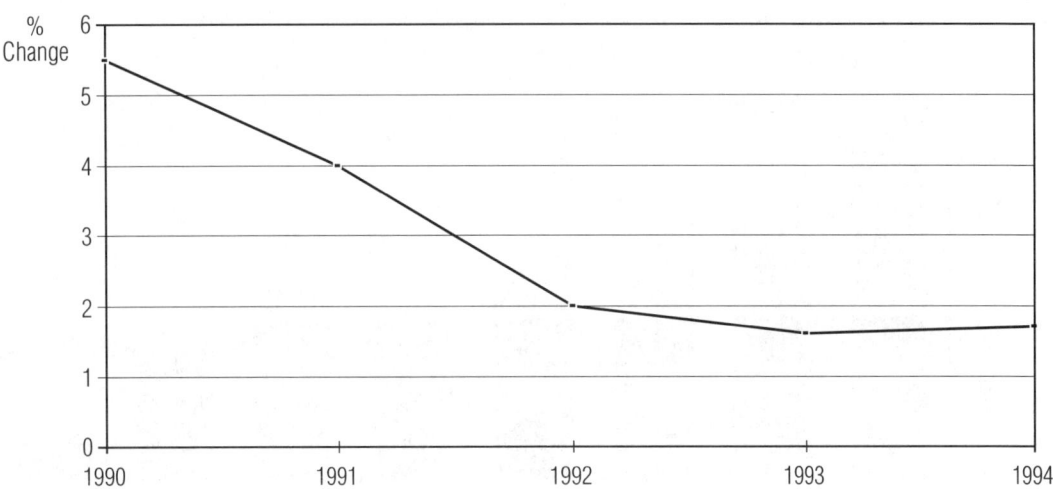

Source: Statistics Canada; Dept. of Finance

Employment of Minors

Generally, workers must be 17 years of age to work in an industry under federal jurisdiction. Provincial standards (covering over 90 percent of the national workforce) vary, but generally require parental consent for workers under 15 or 16 and prohibit young workers in dangerous or nighttime work. In all jurisdictions, a person under 16 cannot be employed in a designated trade, or, in other words, become an apprentice before that age.

Hiring Policies

In theory, and largely in practice, firms are free to hire whomever they please. Some of the employment equity legislation currently before the legislatures aims to set quotas or restrictions upon hiring policies, but these are unlikely to pass. There are many who object to a concept of employment equity that goes beyond ensuring equal opportunity for all, and legislation that appears to grant employment preferences to members of designated groups is seen by some as a form of discrimination rather than as a way to prevent discrimination.

Some collective bargaining agreements require preferential hiring policies, either based on union membership or seniority, but outside these contractual restraints, there are few actual limitations placed on employers in the hiring process.

Termination of Employment

Generally, a business has the right to arbitrarily terminate employment subject to legislated minimum notice periods or pay in lieu of such notice. Statutory termination rights tend to be minimal and are supplemented by common-law right of reasonable notice or pay in lieu thereof.

In practice, however, broad restraints are placed on an employer's ability to terminate an employee with or without cause. For instance, an employee cannot legally be terminated for complying with environmental or other laws, nor for turning in an employer who does not do so. Female employees cannot be terminated for pregnancy, nor for any other reason which may be deemed sexual harassment. Employees may not be terminated for reasonably refusing to work under hazardous conditions, or when they have reason to believe the working conditions may be hazardous. In short, employers must treat employees in a fair and nondiscriminatory or repressive manner; aside from this, they are free to hire and terminate at will.

Workplace Safety

Since the 1970s, most jurisdictions in Canada have required workplaces with more than a certain number of employees (usually 20 or more) to establish a joint health and safety committee. The functions of these committees include investigating worker complaints, undertaking inspections, and making recommendations to employers on changes in equipment and practices. These committees have usually been considered effective in reducing workplace accidents and injuries and in generally improving the safety of the workplace.

In most jurisdictions, an employee has the right to refuse to do work when he or she has reasonable cause to believe that it would be dangerous. When the employer and the employee disagree as to

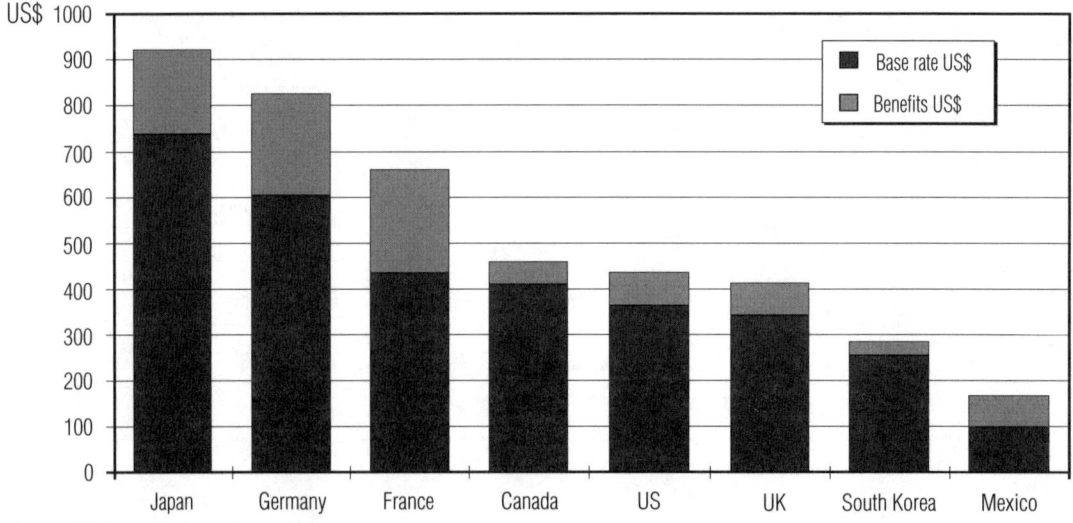

Comparative Average Weekly Wages - 1992

Source: US Department of Labor

whether or not the work is dangerous, a government safety officer is called in to investigate and rule on the question. If the officer concludes that there is no danger, the employee is required to return to work. However, as long as the employee has "reasonable cause" to refuse to work, the employee cannot be disciplined for doing so. If a dangerous condition is confirmed, the safety officer may order that it be removed or corrected. The officer's decision may be appealed by either party to the Labour Relations Board.

Workplace Hazardous Materials Information System Applicable to all of Canada, the Workplace Hazardous Materials Information System (WHMIS) regulation took effect in October 1988. It was designed and implemented in an effort to protect Canadian workers by informing them about any hazardous materials used in their workplace. This regulation stipulates that all materials listed in the federal Hazardous Products Act must be identified and labeled. Suppliers are responsible for obtaining and developing information sheets which provide engineering controls, safe work procedures and required personal protective equipment.

WAGES AND BENEFITS

Minimum Wages

The federal minimum hourly wage rate has remained at C$4.00 since 1986. This rate applies to all employees under federal jurisdiction, which includes industries such as banking, shipping, air transport, broadcasting, railways, grain elevators, and pipelines. In reality, this represents an unrealistic wage rate, and virtually all workers are paid at a higher rate than the federal minimum.

Each province sets its own minimum wage levels, and some of these set different minimum levels for different industries. The current minimum wage rates for experienced adult workers are as follows:
- Newfoundland: C$4.75
- Prince Edward Island: C$4.75
- Nova Scotia: C$5.15
- New Brunswick: C$5.00
- Quebec: C$6.00
- Ontario: C$6.85
- Manitoba: C$5.40
- Saskatchewan: C$5.35
- Alberta: C$5.00
- British Columbia: C$7.00
- Yukon Territory: C$6.72
- Northwest Territories: C$6.50

Wage and Salary Rates

Skilled labor costs in Canada compare favorably with other countries, and are in general quite a bit lower than those in the neighboring United States. While relative labor costs between countries vary with the fluctuation of exchange rates, Canada's close manufacturing links with the US ensure that Canadian wage rates remain competitive with—and on average lower than—US wages.

Employers' benefits costs, as a percentage of total compensation, are lower in Canada than in the US, due in part to the government's financial support of health care coverage. As in the US, defined benefit plans are common among major employers. Because of differences in tax treatment, however, Canada has a greater proportion of contributory defined benefit plans and has relatively fewer defined contribution plans than the United States. However, there is a very clear trend recently to force employers to pick up more of the costs of many benefits schemes, and this will undoubtedly have an impact both on wages and on benefit levels in the future.

The gap between executive and rank-and-file pay is smaller in Canada than in the US, primarily because US executives are paid significantly more than their counterparts in Canada. Executives in Canada also receive a lower proportion of their compensation in variable pay than do executives in the US. In Canada, there is a close correlation between the size of the company and the amount of compensation, the bigger the company, the higher the pay of the top executive. There is also a fairly significant—though not nearly so great—link between pay and performance of the company.

Average annual salary ranges in Canada are as follows:
- Laborers C$15,000-35,000
- Accounting clerks C$20,000-26,000
- Secretaries C$24,000-30,000
- Mechanics C$25,000-40,000
- Mid-level managers C$40,000-60,000
- Engineers C$60,000-90,000
- Senior accountants C$75,000-110,000

Benefits

Both the federal government and the individual provinces have employment statutes which cover matters such as minimum wages, payment of wages, paid vacation, record keeping, hours of work, overtime pay, public holidays, equal pay for equal work, benefit plans, pregnancy leave, notice of termination of employment, and severance pay. Many companies provide additional employee benefits, including the following: life insurance; accidental death or dismemberment insurance; prescription drugs; vision care; dental care; short and long-term disability insurance; pensions; employee education and training; bonuses; company savings plans; and profit-sharing plans.

Some of the benefits are funded by joint employee-employer contributions, but others are funded by employers only.

Unemployment Benefits Canada has several government-sponsored programs to which employers, employees or both contribute. These programs are designed to provide support for retirees and workers who are unemployed, sick or injured on the job. The Unemployment Insurance Program (UI) is intended to provide a minimum income to workers who become unemployed, but workers must demonstrate that they are unemployed. Anyone who leaves a job without just cause is no longer eligible for unemployment insurance payments. UI benefits are also paid to one of the two spouses on parental leave. Benefits are based on a proportion of the workers' salary, while employed, up to a certain limit. Although UI benefits are paid regardless of wealth or other income, the benefits must be repaid if the recipient's income exceeds certain thresholds. The program is funded by contributions from employers and employees.

Workers' Compensation Workers' compensation programs are governed and administered by the provinces. They provide basic income to workers injured in employment-related accidents, until those individuals are able to return to work or it they are no longer capable of working. Funding for these plans is supplied by employer contributions as a percentage of payroll, based on the industry's accident experience.

Health Care Provincial health-insurance programs provide unlimited basic hospital and medical care. They are financed from general revenues and, in some provinces, through payroll taxes as well.

Child Tax Benefit The child tax benefit is paid monthly, generally to the mother of the child. The amount of the payments is based on family income, as well as on the number of children under the age of 18 in the family. The payments are not taxable.

Old Age Security Pension The OAS pension, funded out of general government revenues, is a pension payable at age 65 to individuals who, after reaching the age of 18, have been resident in Canada for 40 years. A partial OAS pension is available to those who have resided in Canada for at least 10 years after reaching the age of 18, or for 20 years if benefits are payable outside Canada.

The Canada Pension Plan The Canada Pension Plan (CPP) is an earnings-related, contributory pension plan that provides all working employees with basic pension benefits for retirement. The amount of benefits is based on the amount of contributions paid into the plan on behalf of the employee. Employees and employers in provinces other than Quebec participate in this federal program. To fund the plan, most employees between the ages of 18 and 65 must contribute 2.6 percent of their earnings, up to a maximum. Employers must match their employees' contributions. Employee contributions are withheld from wages, and both employer and employee contributions must be remitted monthly by the employer to the federal government. Quebec offers a similar program, the Quebec Pension Plan (QPP), in which working residents of Quebec must participate.

Social Security Agreements Canada has entered into several social security agreements with other countries, including the United States. These agreements usually permit individuals working for foreign employers and assigned for a period of time to Canada to continue being covered by the social security system of their employer's country rather than the CPP. They also generally provide that periods of coverage under a foreign-based social security plan are counted when benefits accruing under the Canadian-based plans are determined.

LABOR RELATIONS

Unions and the Labor Movement

Except for members of the armed forces, workers in both the public and private sectors have the right to associate freely, and to exercise their rights to organize and bargain collectively. Some essential public sector employees have limited collective bargaining rights which vary from province to province. These rights are widely exercised.

Union membership has been rising generally over the past two decades except for the two more recent recessionary periods in the early 1980s and early 1990s. However, this longer-term growth rate of union membership appears to have moderated since the mid-1980s. In the late 1980s, union membership rose at a much lower rate than employment and, consequently, the unionization rate fell continuously in that period. In the early 1990s, the overall decline in non-agricultural paid employment was greater than that in union membership, resulting in a modest increase in the unionization rate. Labor force growth has been more steady than the growth in both non-agricultural employment and union membership. Thus, the continuous labor force growth at a rate above that in union membership has resulted in a longer-term decline in the proportion of union members in the labor force - from 31.2 percent in 1978 to 29.2 percent in 1994.

A unique feature of the Canadian labor scene is the coexistence of international unions (with affiliates in both the US and Canada) and national unions (comprised solely of Canadian members). Memberships in national unions represents 66.1

percent of total union membership, up from 65.8 percent in 1993. International unions have suffered a drop in both total membership and in the proportion of union members they represent.

The Canadian Union of Public Employees, with a membership of 409,800, and the National Union of Public and General Employees, with a membership of 307,600, are the two largest unions in Canada. The Canadian Autoworkers (CAW) has recently merged with several other unions to become the largest private sector union in the country. It has recently changed its name to National Automobile, Aerospace, Transportation and General Workers Union of Canada to reflect the changing face of the union from one focused on the auto industry and confined largely to Ontario and Quebec, to a diverse organization with a national presence, extending into a variety of new sectors, from railways to mining.

Labor Relations

Across Canada, labor-management alliances are emerging in unionized work sites. These arrangements come in many shapes and structures and no two are exactly alike. But all reflect a growing recognition that traditional autocratic styles of management and confrontational labor relations are not conducive to highly empowered, high performance work systems. They are also recognizing, more realistically perhaps, that in recessionary conditions, and with the long-term need to compete in the free trade environment brought on by NAFTA, Canadian employees can no longer afford to demand high wages, job protections and other forms of security in return for their agreement not to strike.

This new, friendlier attitude has already had a positive effect on Canadian labor. Nearly 70 percent of unionized companies have adopted cooperative processes to supplement traditional collective bargaining practices. These innovations, with a high degree of employee involvement, had a positive impact on such competitiveness indicators as efficiency/cycle time, productivity, and quality and customer service. Many also experienced a decrease in overall labor costs.

Strikes and Disputes

Although Canadians enjoy the right to strike, it is in some cases a qualified right—essential services must of course be maintained while the strike is in progress. In other cases, as in the recent railway dispute, it is a right that exists only as long as workers do not exercise it, at least for any length of time. As long as strikes occur only occasionally, the best approach—and the one consistent with the principle of free collective bargaining—is to encourage or require the parties to make greater efforts to resolve disputes without resort to work stoppages. This seems in fact to be the clear trend in Canada.

Over the past two years, Canada has enjoyed relative labor peace. Time lost due to major work stoppages is near a record low as low inflation and high unemployment continue to cause job insecurity and put downward pressure on wages. There were 29 major work stoppages in 1994, involving 55,013 workers, compared to 25 stoppages and 73,757 workers in 1993. A 28-day work stoppage by Newfoundland and Labrador teachers and the continuation into 1994 of a 95-day work stoppage at various Miracle Food Mart locations in Ontario accounted for over 40 percent of the total person-days not worked. Both disputes occurred during contract renegotiation centering on job security issues, and wage and other concessions.

In federal jurisdiction, back-to-work legislation was used to end an 11-day strike involving 3,500 British Columbia longshoremen. And, in March 1995, the government resorted to back-to-work legislation to halt another strike by longshoremen at West Coast ports and a strike by Canadian railway workers—which completely shut down passenger service and most freight rail service in Canada. Because the strikes were causing serious disruptions to major export industries the government moved quickly to get the workers back on the job. Another high point was the signing of a new 30-month contract between Canada Post and its largest union, the Canadian Union of Postal Workers, without even resorting to the time-honored strike threat. It was the first contract signed before the old one expired and only the third peaceful settlement in 15 years.

New attitudes on the part of both management and labor have contributed to the peaceful resolution of many collective bargaining negotiations. A milestone seems to have been the peaceful conclusion of a new contract for Canada Post, where collective bargaining had often been conflictive—and usually disruptive. Indeed, most strikes and labor disputes have occurred in the public sector, where labor-management relations have been especially conflictive.

ADDRESSES

Labor Organizations

Canadian Labour Congress (CLC)
2841 Riverside Dr.
Ottawa, Ontario, CAnada KIV 8X7
Tel: (613) 521-3400
Fax: (613) 521-4655

Confederation of National Trade Unions (Confederation des Syndieats Nationaux) (CSN)
1601, Avenue de Lorimier
Montreal, Quebec, Canada H2K 4MS

Canadian Union of Public Employees
21 Florence Street
Ottawa, Ontario, Canada K2P OW6
Tel: (613) 237-1590
Fax: (613) 237-5508

National Automobile, Aerospace, Transporations and General Workers of Canada
205 Placer Court
Willowdale, Ontario, Canada M2H 3H9
Tel: (416) 497-4110
Fax: (416) 495-6559

International Brotherhood of Teamsters
804-2540, Daniel Johnson
Laval, Quebec, Canada H7T 253
Tel: (514) 682-5521
Fax: (514) 681-2244

Laborer's International Union of North America
44 Hughson Street South
Hamilton, Ontario, Canada L8N2A7
Tel: (905) 522-7177
Fax: (905) 522-9310

There are over 900 unions in Canada. Information on each one can be found in the "Directory of Labour Organizations in Canada," available from:

The Department of Human Resources Development
Place du Portage, Phase II, 11th Floor
165 Hotel de Ville Street
Hull, Quebec, Canada K1A 052
Tel: (819) 997-1493
Fax: (819) 953-5685

Government Labor Contacts

Minister of Labour - Atlantic Canada
5151 Terminal Road, 6th Floor
P.O. Box 697
Halifax, Nova Scotia, Canada B3J 2T8
Tel: (902) 424-6647
Fax: (02) 424-0575

Minister of Skills, Training and Labour, B.C.
Parliament Buildings
Victorial, British Columbia, Canada V8V 1X4
Tel: (604) 387-1986
Fax: (604) 387-3200

Minister of Labour, Ontario
400 University Avenue, 14th Floor
Toronto, Ontario M7A 1T7
Tel: (416) 326-7600
Fax: (416) 326-1449

Minister of Labour, Quebec
200 Chemin Ste-Fay, 6th Floor
Quebec, Quebec, Canada GIR 551
Tel: (418) 643-5297
Fax: (418) 644-0003

Minister of Human Resources Development
Place du Portage, Phase IV
Hull, Quebec, Canada KIA 059
Tel: (819) 994-2482
Fax: (819) 994-0448

Business Law

THE CANADIAN LEGAL SYSTEM

INTRODUCTION

The complex national, provincial, and territorial laws of Canada are frequently subject to legislative change and differing judicial interpretations. Moreover, numerous national and provincial agencies impose rules and regulations on trade and other business activity within Canada, many of which affect foreign businesses operating in the country.

The information in this chapter is intended to summarize some of the important topics in Canadian business law. As such, it cannot convey all of the detail necessary to evaluate the issues involved in a specific proposed transaction or operation. This summary does not constitute legal advice, nor should it be relied on in lieu of legal advice from a licensed attorney. The international trade should be careful to review business activities with an attorney familiar with international transactions as well as with the laws of Canada and your own country. All current legal requirements that apply to the particular business activities should be reviewed, regardless of how tangential they seem. (Refer to the "Important Addresses" chapter for a listing of law offices in Canada.)

BASIS OF CANADIAN LEGAL SYSTEM

The Canadian legal system is based on the tradition of common law developed in Great Britain; British common law forms the basis of federal, provincial, and territorial law. The common law system differs from the civil law system (followed by most European and Latin American countries and the province of Quebec) in that the law is not only codified in statutes made by the legislature, but also evolves from court judgments interpreting statutes. Under the doctrine of stare decisis, prior court interpretations of law govern subsequent and similar cases. Review of judicial decisions is therefore an integral part of understanding Canadian law on any issue.

Quebec law is based on the French civil law system. In 1994, the new Civil Code of Quebec came into force; this code is a revision of the civil law relating to persons (including consumers and employees), contracts, property, security and guarantees, franchise agreements, and securities.

CONTENTS

The Canadian Legal System 207
Introduction 207
Basis of Canadian Legal System 207
Legal Glossary 208
Geographical Scope 209
Structure of Government and Laws 209
Laws Governing Business 209
The International Transaction:
    Basics of a One Time Sale 210
Practical Application 213
The US Foreign Corrupt Practices Act 215
Dispute Resolution 216
Related Sections 217
Law Digest 218
Aliens 218
Arbitration 218
Bankruptcy 218
Business Registration 218
Contracts and Dispute Resolution 218
Corporations 218
Environment 219
Foreign Investment 219
Foreign Trade 219
Intellectual Property Rights 220
Labor 220
Legal Briefs 221
Legal System 221
Legal System 221
Monopolies 221
Notaries Public 221
Taxation 222
Treaties 222

LEGAL GLOSSARY

acceptance An unconditional assent to an offer or one conditioned on minor changes that do not affect material terms of the offer. See counteroffer, offer.

acknowledgment The act of conferring legal authenticity on a written document, typically made by a notary public, who attests and certifies that the document is in proper legal form and that it is executed by a person identified as having authority to do so. Acknowledgment is also referred to as authentication.

agency The relationship between an agent and a principal. The agent represents and acts on behalf of the principal, who instructs and authorizes the agent to act.

arm's length Without collusion, as if between self-interested and unrelated parties operating at parity.

counteroffer A reply to an offer that materially alters the terms of the offer. Example: A seller who accepts a buyer's offer on the condition that the goods will be made of a different material has made a counteroffer. See acceptance, offer.

domicile The place where a party is living or located with no definite, present intention of moving away.

fiduciary obligation An obligation placed on a party (the fiduciary) entrusted to handle money or property for the benefit of another party. The fiduciary must act in good faith with due regard for the benefit of the other party. See good faith.

good faith A legal standard implying honesty in fact in the conduct or transaction concerned, honesty of intention, or freedom from an intention to defraud or take improper advantage, depending on the circumstances.

injunction A court order that either requires a party to take a specific action or prohibits that party from taking a specific action.

legal act An action intended to have and capable of having an effect that is specified by law, such as the creation, termination, or modification of a right accorded by law. Example: the signing of a power of attorney is a legal act because it gives lawful authority to an agent.

legal person An individual or entity recognized under law as having rights and obligations specified by law. Example: corporations and partnerships are entities recognized as legal persons.

negligence A failure to exercise reasonable care, which could result in legal liability for damages caused to others. See reasonable care.

negotiable instrument A written document transferable merely be endorsement or delivery.

offer A proposal that is made to a specific individual or entity to enter into a contract. The proposal must contain definite terms and must indicate the offeror's intent to be bound by an acceptance.

power of attorney A written document by which one individual or entity (the principal) authorizes another individual or entity (the agent) to perform stated acts on the principal's behalf. Example: a principal may execute a special power of attorney that authorizes the agent to sign a specific contract or general power of attorney that authorizes the agent to sign all contracts for the principal.

privity The concept that in order to maintain an action on any contract, a connection or relationship should exist between the plaintiff and the defendant as parties to the contract on which the action is being brought.

reasonable care The level of care that an ordinary, prudent person would exercise under the same or similar circumstances. See negligence.

statute of frauds A law that requires designated documents to be in writing in order to be enforced by a court. Example: contracting parties may orally agree to transfer ownership of real property, but a court might not enforce that contract or award damages for breach unless that contract was in writing.

tort A legal wrong committed on a party or property based on a violation of some duty to the plaintiff when that duty is imposed by law and does not arise under a contract.

warranty An affirmation of fact regarding the characteristics, safety, or suitability of a product. An express warranty is one that is explicitly stated.

GEOGRAPHICAL SCOPE

This chapter describes Canadian federal laws, which are national in scope and govern in all provinces and territories. Provinces and territories have their own laws, governing matters of primarily local concern. Therefore, the laws of particular region where business will be transacted must always be checked for differences with federal requirements. Banking and intellectual property are regulated exclusively by the federal government. Canadian securities are generally regulated by the securities administrators of the provincial and territorial governments. Canada has five stock exchanges.

STRUCTURE OF GOVERNMENT AND LAWS

Canada is a federal parliamentary state, divided into ten provinces and two territories, and is a member of the Commonwealth of Nations. Under the Constitution Act of 1982, executive power is vested in the British monarch as head of state. This executive power is exercisable by the monarch's representative, the governor-general, as her chief executive officer to carry on the government; however, this role is largely ceremonial and executive power effectively rests with the cabinet. The federal parliament includes the head of state, the prime minister; a nominated Senate appointed on a regional basis; and a House of Commons. A federal parliament may last no longer than five years.

Each province has a lieutenant-governor, an executive council, and an elected unicameral legislature similar to the House of Commons, subject to the five-year limitation. The provinces regulate their own affairs and disburse their own revenues; their jurisdiction includes civil and property rights, licenses, natural resources, provincial taxation, and other local matters. Both territories have elected legislative bodies although the federal government still has extensive authority.

Exclusive legislative jurisdiction over specific subject matters is assigned to the Dominion Parliament (federal) and the provincial legislatures. The exclusive legislative authority of the Dominion parliament extends primarily to matters of national import, including: national and international trade and commercial regulation and competition regulation; national taxation; fisheries and shipping; banking and currency; defense; bankruptcy; patents, copyrights, and trademarks; criminal law; and human rights. The Dominion Parliament has the residuary power to enact laws for peace, order, and government regarding all matters not exclusively assigned to provincial legislatures.

The exclusive legislative authority of the provincial legislatures extends to licensing, municipal institutions, incorporation of companies planning to operate within provincial borders, property rights within provincial borders, direct taxation within province borders, education, and other matters of a local or private nature within the province.

Canada has also ratified numerous bilateral and multilateral international treaties and conventions that contain provisions affecting business transactions. For example, Canada is a signatory of the North American Free Trade Agreement (NAFTA), a party to the Berne Convention on copyright law and a member of the Paris Union with regard to trademarks.

LAWS GOVERNING BUSINESS

The Investment Canada Act (ICA) was enacted in 1985 to promote domestic and international investment in Canada. Investment Canada offices were disbanded in 1994 and its responsibilities divided between the Department of Foreign Affairs and International Trade (DFAIT), responsible for investment promotion and research, and the Department of Industry, which handles notifications of new investments and approval applications for foreign investment through Industry Canada. (Refer to the "Foreign Investment" section.)

The Canada Business Corporations Act (CBCA) governs the formation and operation of corporations at the federal level. The CBCA has been revised and updated to be more responsive to business needs. Industry Canada is committed to this ongoing revision process, particularly in the areas of director residency, insider trading, corporate takeovers, and unanimous shareholder agreements.

Canada is a signatory of the North American Free Trade Agreement (NAFTA), which is changing business opportunities in Canada, Mexico, and the US by reducing restrictions on foreign service firms, mandating creation of a dispute arbitration system, and increasing protection for intellectual and industrial property rights. Canada is also a party to the Berne Convention on copyright law and a member of the Paris Union with regard to trademarks.

One of the most common legal problems faced by foreign persons doing business in Canada is understanding the split in and the overlay of government regulation at the federal and provincial or territorial levels. Obtaining timely and proper legal advice on the formal requirements for doing business in Canada can facilitate structuring businesses and transactions to avoid noncompliance problems. (Refer to "Role of Legal Counsel" section later in this chapter.)

Additional Laws In Canada, intellectual property, copyright, trademark, patent law, trade secrets, and industrial designs fall under the jurisdiction of the federal government. The federal statutes establish a

THE INTERNATIONAL TRANSACTION: BASICS OF A ONE-TIME SALE

When dealing internationally, you must consider the business practices and legal requirements of the country where the other party to your contract is located. Parties ordinarily have the freedom to agree to any contract terms that they desire, but the laws of your country or the other country may require a written contract. In some transactions, the laws may even specify all or some of the contract terms. Whether a contract term is valid in a particular country is mainly of concern in case you have to seek enforcement. Otherwise, you have fairly broad flexibility in negotiating contract provisions. However, you should always be certain to come to a definite understanding with the other party on four basic issues: the goods (quantity, type, and quality); the time of delivery; the price; and the time and means of payment.

For a small, one-time sale, an invoice or a simple contract may be acceptable. For a more involved business transaction or an ongoing relationship, a formal written contract is preferable in order to define clearly the rights, responsibilities, and remedies of all parties. Contracts that involve capital goods, high credit risks, or industrial or intellectual property rights will require special protective clauses. In preparing such contracts, it is essential to obtain legal advice from a professional who is familiar with the laws and practices of both countries involved.

For a simple, one-time deal, you need to consider at least the following clauses:

Contract Date

Specify the date when the contract is signed. This date is particularly important if payment or delivery times are fixed in reference to it, for example, "shipment within 30 days of the contract date."

Identification of Parties

Name the parties, describe their relation to each other, and designate any persons who are authorized to act for each party. The persons designated should also be the ones who sign the contract. If a person is signing on behalf of a company, you should be certain of that person's authority-request a statement or corporate resolution if you are uncertain. A company will be bound to a contract in Canada if the person signing has apparent authority.

Goods

Description Describe the type and quality of the goods. You may simply indicate a model number, or you may have to attach detailed lists, plans, drawings, or other specifications. This clause should be clear enough that both parties fully understand the specifications and have no discretion in interpreting them.

Quantity Specify the number of units, or other measure of quantity, of the goods. If the goods are measured by weight, you should specify net weight, dry weight, or drained weight. If the goods are prepackaged and are subject to weight restrictions in the end market, you may want to ensure that the seller will provide goods packaged to comply with those restrictions.

Price Indicate the price per unit or other measure, such as per pound or ton, and the extended price.

Packaging Arrangements

Set forth packaging specifications, especially for goods that could be damaged in transit. At a minimum, this provision should require the seller to package the goods in such a way as to withstand transportation. If special packaging requirements are necessary to meet consumer and product liability standards in the end market, you should specify them also.

Transportation Arrangements

Carrier Name a preferred carrier for transporting the goods. You should designate a particular carrier if, for example, a carrier offers you special pricing or is better able than others to transport the product.

Storage Specify any particular requirements for storage of the goods before or during shipment, such as security arrangements, special climate demands, and weather protection needs.

Notice Provisions Require the seller to notify the buyer when the goods are ready for delivery or pickup, particularly if the goods are perishable or fluctuate in value. If your transaction is time-sensitive, you could even provide for several notices to allow the buyer to track the goods and take steps to minimize damages if delivery is delayed.

Shipping Time State the exact date for shipping or provide for shipment within a reasonable time from the contract date. If this clause is included and the seller fails to ship on time, the buyer may claim a right to cancel the contract, even if the goods have been shipped, provided that the buyer has not yet accepted delivery.

Costs and Charges

Specify which party is to pay any additional costs and charges related to the sale.

Duties and Taxes Designate the party that will be responsible for import, export, and other fees and taxes, and for obtaining all required licenses. For example, a party may be made responsible for paying the duties, taxes, and charges imposed by that party's own country, since that party is best situated to know the legal requirements of that country.

Insurance Costs Identify the party that will pay the costs of insuring the goods in transit. This is a critical provision because the party responsible for insurance bears the risk if the goods are lost during transit. A seller is typically responsible for insurance until title to the goods passes to the buyer, at which time the buyer becomes responsible for insurance or becomes the named beneficiary under the seller's insurance policy.

Handling and Transport Specify the party that will pay shipping, handling, packaging, security, and any other costs related to transportation; these costs should be enumerated in the contract.

Terms Defined Contracts for the sale of goods most commonly use Incoterms (as defined by the International Chamber of Commerce in Paris) to assign responsibility for the risks and cost of transport. (Refer to the "International Payments" chapter for explanations of the Incoterms.)

Insurance or Risk of Loss Protection

Specify the insurance required, the beneficiary of the policy, the party who will obtain the insurance, and the date by which it must have been obtained.

Payment Provisions

In a one-time transaction, the seller will typically seek the most secure form of payment before committing to shipment, while a buyer will want the goods cleared through customs and delivered in satisfactory condition before remitting full payment. If payments cannot be made in advance, parties most often agree to use documentary credits. (Refer to the "International Payments" chapter for an explanation of documentary credits.)

Method of Payment State the means by which payment will be tendered, for example, delivery of a documentary letter of credit or documents against payment; prepayment in cash or traveler's checks; or credit for a specified number of days.

Medium of Exchange Designate the currency to be used, for example, Canadian dollars, the currency of the non-Canadian country of origin, or the currency of a third country.

Exchange Rate Specify a fixed exchange rate for the price stated in the contract. You may use this clause to lock in a specific price and ensure against fluctuating currency values.

Import Documentation

Designate the documents for exporting and importing that each party will be responsible for obtaining, completing, and presenting to customs. Shipment of the goods, and even the contract itself, may be made contingent on a party's having obtained in advance the proper licenses, inspection certificates, and other authorizations. (Refer to the chapters "Import Policies & Procedures" and "Export Policies & Procedures" for further discussion of these requirements.)

Inspection Rights

Provide that the buyer has a right to inspect goods before taking delivery to determine whether the goods meet the contract specifications. This should specify the party who will make the inspection, for example, the buyer, a third party, or a licensed inspector; the location where the inspection will occur, such as at the seller's plant, the buyer's warehouse, or a receiving dock; the time at which the inspection will occur; the presentation of a certified document of inspection, if needed; and any requirements related to the return of nonconforming goods.

Warranty Provisions

Limit or extend any implied warranties, and define any express warranties on property fitness and quality. The contract may, for example, state that the seller warrants that the goods are of merchantable quality, are fit for any purpose for which they would ordinarily be used, or are fit for a particular purpose requested by the buyer. The seller may also warrant that the goods will be of the same quality as any sample or model that the

THE INTERNATIONAL TRANSACTION: BASICS OF A ONE-TIME SALE (cont'd)

seller has furnished as representative of the goods. Finally, the seller may warrant that the goods will be packaged in a specific way or in a way that will adequately preserve and protect the goods.

Indemnity

Agree that one party will hold the other harmless from damages that arise from specific causes, such as the design or manufacture of a product.

Enforcement and Remedies

Time Is of the Essence Stipulate that timely performance of the contract is essential. In Canada, inclusion of this clause allows a party to claim breach merely because the other party fails to perform within the time prescribed in the contract. Although common in Canadian contracts, a clause of this type is considered less important in other countries.

Modification Require the parties to make all changes to the contract in advance and in a signed written modification.

Cancellation State the reasons for which either party may cancel the contract and the notice required for cancellation.

Contingencies Specify any events that must occur before a party is obligated to perform the contract. For example, you may agree that the seller has no duty to ship goods until the buyer forwards documents that secure the payment for the goods.

Governing Law Choose the law of a specific jurisdiction to control any interpretation of the contract terms. The law that you choose will usually affect where you can sue or enforce a judgment and what rules and procedures will be applied.

Choice of Forum Identify the place where a dispute may be settled, for example, the country of origin of the goods, the country of destination, or a third country that is convenient to both parties.

Arbitration Provisions Arbitration can be used as an alternative to litigation for the resolution of disputes that arise. You should agree to arbitrate only if you seriously intend to settle disputes in this way. If you agree to arbitrate but later file suit, the court is likely to uphold the arbitration clause and force you to settle your dispute as initially agreed in the contract.

An arbitration clause should specify whether arbitration is binding or nonbinding on the parties; the country where arbitration will be conducted (which should be Canada or another country that has adopted the UN Convention on Recognition and Enforcement of Foreign Awards or a similar convention); the procedure for enforcement of an award; the rules governing the arbitration, such as the UN Commission on International Trade Law Model Rules; the institute that will administer the arbitration, such as the International Chamber of Commerce (Paris); the law that will govern procedural issues or the merits of the dispute; any limitations on the selection of arbitrators (for example, a national of a disputing party may be excluded from being an arbitrator); the qualifications or expertise of the arbitrators; the language in which the arbitration will be conducted; and the availability of translations and translators if needed.

Severability Provide that individual clauses can be removed from the contract without affecting the validity of the contract as a whole. This clause is important because it provides that, if one clause is declared invalid and unenforceable for any reason, the rest of the contract remains in force.

---

system of registration and enforcement designed to protect the intellectual property rights of individuals and companies. Most enforcement of intellectual property rights is by private infringement action rather than government administrative proceedings.

If intellectual property can be classified as a trade secret or confidential information, it may be entitled to legal protection even if it cannot be protected under copyright, trademark, patent, or industrial design laws. This protection takes the form of preventing those with access to the trade secret or confidential information from using or disclosing it.

Under the Industrial Design Act, the appearance of an article, or design aspects that are intended to make the product more visually appealing can be protected. The proprietor (the designer or the person for whom the design was created) of the design must apply for registration; registration is mandatory to protect industrial designs in Canada. Registration must occur within one year of the publication of the design in Canada; registration lasts five years and is renewable.

Under the Copyright Act, literary works, original compilations (such as franchising contracts and users' guides), architectural plans, designs, and works of art, dramatic, musical, and artistic works, choreographic or cinematographic works, and computer programs (specifically forms of expression rather than ideas embodied in the programs), may be protected from infringement for the life of the author plus 50 years. A certificate of registration creates a presumption of ownership and affords the holder the sole right to produce or reproduce work, or any substantial part of the protected work, in any material form whatever. A copyright can be assigned, licensed, or transferred, or made subject to territorial limitations. Infringement, when applied to a copy of a work in which copyright subsists, means any copy, including a colorable imitation, made or imported in violation of the Copyright Act.

Under the Trade Marks Act, the right to the exclusive use of symbols, words, or pictures used to distinguish one's products or services from those of another can be protected. Trademark rights can be created through use and registration is not mandatory. However, registration ensures the exclusive right of use throughout Canada and is necessary for the owner's protection if the owner intends to license the trademark for others' use; each licensee must be registered as a user of the trademark. Registration lasts 15 years and is renewable for additional 15-year terms on payment of the applicable fee.

Under the Patent Act, patents can be obtained and enforced in Canada. The inventor must file an application with the Commissioner of Patents; registration is mandatory to obtain exclusive rights to the invention in Canada. On average, it takes three years to secure a patent from the date of filing the application. Patents are valid for 20 years.

PRACTICAL APPLICATION

Foreign Investment

Canada has significant import and export foreign trade, sophisticated capital markets, and a highly educated and well-trained work force. Foreign persons are generally treated equally with Canadian citizens under the law and, as a matter of practice, do not face significant legal problems in doing business in Canada or with Canadian companies. Foreigners have equal access with Canadians to Canadian judicial remedies. At both the federal and provincial levels, legislation permits foreign persons to enforce their rights within a particular Canadian jurisdiction. More specifically, federal and provincial legislation provides for reciprocal enforcement of judgments between Canada and the US, as well as between Canada and many other foreign jurisdictions.

Federal statutes control the amount or percentage of permissible foreign ownership in order to limit the growth of foreign-controlled businesses in some industries. Although generally opposed to import controls and licensing, the federal government may impose trade restrictions under the Export and Import Permits Act.

In general, the provincial governments do not limit or prohibit foreign investment. (Refer to "Notification and Review" section.) However, some provinces limit non-resident ownership of certain types of real estate and some provinces tax some acquisition of real estate by nonresidents.

Notification and Review Foreign investments may be subject to a notification or review process. New, non-Canadian business ventures, other than investments that might have a significant impact on the public interest, or Canada's national identity or cultural heritage (such as publishing and film and music investments), are subject to an approval measure or notification requirement, depending on the size and percentage control of the investment. Investors must inform Industry Canada of new investments within 30 days of the transaction. No additional information is required unless the investment is an acquisition of an existing business by non-Canadians and the investment exceeds certain size and percentage thresholds. In general, an investment review is mandatory when a non-Canadian acquires control of an existing business and one of the following applies: (1) the Canadian business is being acquired indirectly, through the acquisition of a non-Canadian parent, and the Canadian business assets are at least C$50,000,000; (2) the Canadian business is being acquired directly and the business' assets are at least C$5,000,000; or (3) the Canadian business is being acquired indirectly, through the acquisition of a non-Canadian parent, the Canadian assets represent more than half the total value of the deal, and the business' assets are at least C$5,000,000.

Direct and indirect investments by non-Canadians that exceed the investment review thresholds must be reviewed by Industry Canada to assess the net benefit to the nation (that is, that no detriment to Canada results from the transaction). Similarly, investments that might have a significant impact on Canada's national identity or cultural heritage are subject to review. For investments subject to the review requirement, investors must submit an application to Industry Canada before the close of the transaction, or within 30 days of the close of an indirect acquisition. The review requirements are the same as between NAFTA partners and all other foreign investors, except that the thresholds for NAFTA partners are higher. Once Industry Canada accepts an application for review, the industry minister has up to 75 days to determine whether the transaction is acceptable; if no decision is issued within 75 days, the investment is deemed approved. Industry Canada may consult with any provinces that would be significantly affected by the transaction.

Industry Canada considers the following factors when assessing the net benefit to the nation: any effect of the investment on Canada's competitiveness in world markets and within Canadian industries; the degree of Canadian participation in the business; the effect on Canadian economic activity, productivity, technology, and product innovation; and the compatibility of the acquired business' activities with the industrial, economic, and cultural policies of any interested federal, provincial, and territorial governments.

Canada imposes no exchange controls. The Canadian dollar is fully convertible and the repatriation of capital is unrestricted. Although unrestricted, the transfer of profits and dividends is subject to withholding taxes.

Investment Incentives Federal and provincial governments offer numerous incentives, primarily to promote investment and expansion in sectors with high unemployment or limited or lagging development; to encourage research and development; and to attract new technologies and capital. These incentives include tax advantages, research and development funds, and loan guarantees. In addition, some provinces have joined together to provide regional incentives, and municipal governments also offer incentives to induce companies to set up businesses in their locales.

Role of Legal Counsel Because of the diversity and overlay of federal, provincial, and territorial business and tax laws across Canada, attorneys and accountants play an important role in structuring and negotiating business transactions. A growing number of law firms, particularly in major metropolitan areas, specialize in international trade and investment. Of recent significance is the implementation of the Canada-US Free Trade Agreement (CFTA) and the passage and implementation of the North American Free Trade Agreement (NAFTA), which have created new opportunities for attorneys and law firms in Canada, Mexico, and the US by reducing restrictions on foreign service firms, mandating creation of a dispute arbitration system, and increasing protection for intellectual and industrial property rights. As a result, many Canadian, Mexican, and US attorneys and firms are establishing affiliations (partnerships or strong associations) with counterpart firms to serve on a consultant, referral, or other basis. Embassies and consulates located in Canada can be valuable sources of referrals for local attorneys experienced in international trade and business.

Canadian attorneys play a very active role in business transactions and are typically consulted on an ongoing basis by both local and foreign parties. Many Canadian corporations are likely to have either a firm on retainer or the in-house capacity to deal with legal concerns on a daily basis. Foreign investors typically consult with Canadian attorneys for a variety of business activities: for general advice on establishing a business presence; the negotiation and drafting of specific contracts; advising and dealing with regulatory agencies both during the transaction process, as well as on a continuing, ongoing basis; the exercise of due diligence before the close of a transaction; the review of transactions; expertise in negotiating a settlement; handling any litigation arising from the transaction; marketing a product or service requiring copyright, trademark, or patent protection; and experience in alternative dispute resolution to conclude disagreements. Most Canadian attorneys have some general knowledge of business law and, in larger commercial areas, many attorneys specialize in business law.

In most instances, Canadian attorneys do not advise or represent both parties to a transaction. Each province, through its law society, has rules of professional conduct dealing with and restricting an attorney's ability to advise both parties. In situations where dual representation occurs, such as when a lawyer might act for a mortgage company and one of the transacting parties, there is a duty of full disclosure of the nature of the dual representation and any potential conflicts of interest. In the event of any dispute concerning the transaction, the attorney must withdraw from representing any of the parties. Before an attorney is engaged to advise both parties to a single transaction, the attorney should obtain the express, written consent of both parties; this consent should also acknowledge the liability that, in the event of a conflict, the attorney would need to withdraw representation from all parties and could be a compellable witness for and against each party.

One of the more common sources of legal confusion encountered by foreign persons doing business in Canada is the split in jurisdiction between the federal government and the individual provincial and territorial governments concerning various legal matters. The federal government maintains

THE US FOREIGN CORRUPT PRACTICES ACT

US business owners are subject to the Foreign Corrupt Practices Act (FCPA). The stiff penalties imposed under this act may make a US business owner reluctant to deal with a foreign company if there is even a hint of corrupt practice related to the transaction. The FCPA makes it unlawful for any US citizen or firm (or any person who acts on behalf of a US citizen or firm) to use a means of US interstate commerce (examples: mail, telephone, telegram, or electronic mail) to offer, pay, transfer, promise to pay or transfer, or authorize a payment, transfer, or promise of money or anything of value to any foreign appointed or elected official, foreign political party, or candidate for a foreign political office for a corrupt purpose (that is, to influence a discretionary act or decision of the official) for the purpose of obtaining or retaining business.

It is also unlawful for a US business owner to make such an offer, promise, payment, or transfer to any person if the US business owner knows, or has reason to know, that the person will give, offer, or promise directly or indirectly all or part of the payment to a foreign government official, political party, or candidate. For purposes of the FCPA, the term "knowledge" means both "actual knowledge"—the business owner in fact knew that the offer, payment, or transfer was included in the transaction—and "implied knowledge"—the business owner should have known from the facts and circumstances of a transaction that the agent paid a bribe, but failed to carry out a reasonable investigation into the transaction. A business owner should make a reasonable investigation into the transaction, for example, if the sales representative requests a higher commission on a particular deal for no apparent reason, if the buyer is a foreign government, if the product has a military use, or if the buyer's country is one in which bribes are considered customary in business relationships.

Legal Payments

The provisions of the FCPA do not prohibit payments made to facilitate routine government action. A facilitating payment is one made in connection with an action that a foreign official must perform as part of the official's job. In comparison, a corrupt payment is made to influence an official's discretionary decision. For example, payments would not generally be considered corrupt if made to cover an official's overtime if such overtime is necessary to expedite the processing of export documentation for a legal shipment of merchandise or to cover the expense of additional crew to handle a shipment.

A person charged with violating FCPA provisions may assert as a defense that the payment was lawful under the written laws and regulations of the foreign country and therefore was not for a corrupt purpose. Alternatively, a person may contend that the payment was associated with demonstrating a product or performing a preexisting contractual obligation and therefore was not for obtaining or retaining business.

Enforcing Agencies and Penalties

Criminal Proceedings The US Department of Justice (DOJ) prosecutes criminal proceedings for FCPA violations. Firms are subject to fines of up to US$2 million. Officers, directors, employees, agents, and stockholders are subject to fines of up to US$100,000, imprisonment for up to five years, or both.

A US business owner may also be charged under other federal criminal laws. On conviction, the owner may be liable for one of the following: (1) a fine of up to US$250,000; or (2) if the owner derived pecuniary gain from the offense or caused a pecuniary loss to another person, a fine of up to twice the amount of the gross gain or loss.

Civil Proceedings Two agencies are responsible for enforcing the civil provisions of the FCPA: the DOJ handles actions against domestic concerns, and the Securities and Exchange Commission (SEC) files actions against issuers. Civil fines of up to US$100,000 may be imposed on a firm, or on any officer, director, employee, agent, or stockholder acting for a firm. In addition, the appropriate government agency may seek an injunction against a person or firm that has violated or is about to violate FCPA provisions.

Conduct that constitutes a violation of FCPA provisions may also give rise to a cause of action under the federal Racketeer-Influenced and Corrupt Organizations Act (RICO), as well as under similar state statutes if such exist in a state with jurisdiction over the US business.

Administrative Penalties A person or firm that is held to have violated any FCPA provisions may be barred from doing business with the US government. Indictment alone may result in suspension of the right to do business with the government.

exclusive control over certain legal fields, while the provinces and territories maintain control over others. In other fields, there is often a significant amount of overlap between the federal and provincial statutory schemes. It can be difficult for foreign investors to determine which regulatory authority they should be dealing with in a particular instance and, in the context of locating or structuring a business, which statutory and regulatory scheme might best suit the proposed business. Foreign investors can lessen or avoid the potential of regulatory problems by taking a proactive approach and consulting a Canadian attorney at an early stage in the proposed transaction. Timely and proper legal advice on the formal requirements for doing business in Canada and complete disclosure of all potential consequences arising out of the transaction from a regulatory perspective can facilitate structuring businesses and transactions to avoid noncompliance problems.

Attorneys licensed to practice law in foreign countries may only advise or practice in Canada after being recognized by the provincial law society in each province in which the foreign attorney proposes to practice. Each individual law society has its own rules, standards, and prerequisites that must be satisfied before a foreign attorney will be granted the status to practice in that province. Typically, foreign attorneys are permitted to act as co-counsel.

Contracts Contracts in Canada can be complex and lengthy documents, especially for trade, investment, and real estate matters. Contracts are quite integral to the Canadian business community and typically form the basis of long-term, ongoing relationships between contracting companies. Although contracts tend to be transaction specific, not every business arrangement requires detailed contracts, and greater informality is tolerated particularly with established business relationships. However, the corporate culture of some businesses requires detailed, specific contracts for all significant transactions.

The contract negotiation process is primarily a function of whether the parties have a preexisting working relationship and whether they negotiate and operate on an equal basis. Contract language should be clear, concise, and understandable to all parties. Each party should retain separate legal counsel so that the legal advice is tailored to that party's particular needs and is not potentially compromised by an attorney having a conflict of interest between the parties.

Contract law is primarily governed by provincial law. Canada and all of its provinces and territories have adopted the US Convention on Contracts for the International Sales of Goods (the Vienna Convention); these provisions apply to all contracts for the international sale of goods between countries in ratifying countries unless the parties opt out of the Convention. Canada has no federal legislation governing formation and termination of distributorships, dealerships, and franchises; these arrangements are subject to provincial legislation.

In the event of a contract breach, the first step is to attempt to negotiate some sort of resolution, such as whether the breach can be cured or compromised with or without compensation, or whether the contract will be terminated with or without compensation or damages. Ordinarily, litigation is only pursued when a negotiated settlement or alternative dispute resolution does not appear viable. Advising clients of their rights under contracts is an important role played by attorneys practicing business law in Canada.

The Role of Notaries In general, notaries perform the following functions in all provinces and territories other than the province of Quebec: swearing solemn declarations; taking affidavits for use in federal or provincial courts; witnessing the attestation or execution of any writing, deed, or instrument or of the truth of any fact or account; and certifying copies of documents. In the Province of Quebec, notaries have the authority not only to verify signatures but also to draft and file documents and provide certain legal services that are reserved to attorneys in the other provinces and territories.

The use of notaries in business depends to a great extent on the type of business being conducted and, in many Canadian provinces, attorneys also act as notaries. Typically, the requirement that a particular business document be notarized usually arises when the document is being delivered from one province or territory to another within Canada. If a particular business is making transactions only within a single province or territory, the use of notaries is rather limited.

DISPUTE RESOLUTION

Resolving disputes through lawsuits in Canada tends to be a costly, lengthy, and sometimes acrimonious proposition. Therefore, various alternative dispute resolution processes, such as arbitration and mediation services, exist throughout most provinces and territories, and are readily available in all of the larger commercial centers.

The use of mediation or arbitration in commercial disputes is typically dependent on the selection of alternate dispute resolution as set forth in the formal contracts or by the agreement of the parties. Under a typical arbitration clause, the parties to a contract agree in advance to submit any disputes to arbitration and agree on a method of selecting an arbitrator or arbitrators from an approved group of recognized authorities. Under a typical mediation clause, an expert is available during the term of the contract to assist the parties in resolving their disagreements; the expert may have been previously identified by the parties in the contract, or subsequently agreed to by the parties.

Business persons contemplating the use of alternative dispute resolution procedures should seek advice on the relative advantages and disadvantages in comparison with those of litigation. These alternative procedures are usually but not always less expensive and time-consuming than litigation. Parties seeking to rely on alternative dispute resolution procedures will need to specify in their contracts matters such as whether business operations must be suspended during a dispute, whether or not the decisions by arbitration boards or mediators will be binding, whether or not information revealed and decisions made during the process remain confidential, and whether the rules of procedure and evidence that govern in courts of law will also apply to their private dispute resolution hearings.

NAFTA provisions encourage the use of arbitration and mandates the establishment of an arbitration system to deal with NAFTA-related issues.

RELATED SECTIONS

Refer to the "Taxation" chapter for a discussion of tax issues in Canada; the "Foreign Investment" chapter for a discussion of investment regulations; the "Business Entities and Formation" chapter for a description of the business forms recognized in Canada and the applicable organizational procedures; the "Labor" chapter for employment rules and standards; and the "Trade Agreements, "Import Policy & Procedures" and "Export Policy & Procedures" chapters for discussions of the various rules involved in trade.

LAW DIGEST

ALIENS

Immigration Officers and Senior Immigration Officers are empowered to administer the Immigration Act. The Immigration and Refugee Board is empowered to hear and determine certain appeals by immigrants, refugees, persons against whom removal order has been made, and certain sponsors of immigrants.

The Minister of Employment and Immigration may be permit authorize certain persons otherwise inadmissible to enter or remain in Canada.

ARBITRATION

Canada's laws of arbitration and award are different depending on the province. Canada has adopted the United Nations Convention on the Recognition and Enforcement of Foreign Arbitral Awards. Canada also adopted in 1986 the United Nations Convention on the Model Law on Commercial Arbitration.

BANKRUPTCY

Bankruptcy laws are uniform throughout Canada and are governed by the Bankruptcy and Insolency Act. The act applies to persons, including individuals, partnerships, unincorporated associations, cooperative societies, organizations and corporations incorporated under laws of Canada or province and foreign corporations having an office in or carrying on business in Canada, except those corporations which are building societies having capital stock, banks, savings banks, loan companies, railway, companies, trust companies, and insurance companies. Persons engaged solely in farming, fishing or tillage of soil and wage earners earning less that $2,500 a year and who do not in their own account carry on business, although not subject to provisions regarding involuntary bankruptcy, may make authorized assignments.

BUSINESS REGISTRATION

The federal government and each of the provinces has the power to create corporations. A company whose operations are to be confined to one province would normally incorporate under the laws of that province. Companies which operate throughout Canada or in more than one province may be incorporated under federal laws which will reserve the right to use the corporate name throughout the country. Federally incorporated companies may be required pursuant to provincial laws to register and obtain various licenses to operate in a particular province. The same is true of corporations incorporated in one province which operate in another.

Canadian corporations may be created either by certificate of incorporation issued pursuant to Canada Business Corporations Act which contains general legislation governing corporations, or in special cases by act of parliament.

Companies whose operations are to be confined to one province should be incorporated under laws of that province. Companies which carry on business throughout country or in several provinces or in foreign countries should be incorporated under federal laws.

CONTRACTS AND DISPUTE RESOLUTION

Contracts are governed by common law principles and the Civil Code in Quebec, though some specific contractual rights may be affected by statute law. For example, sale of goods and consumer protection laws exist in most provinces which provide certain statutory or implied warranties in certain circumstances. The civil courts are the normal forum for the resolution of contractual disputes. However, the increasing cost of litigation as well as delays and backlogs in the civil courts have led to a recent trend throughout the country for parties to consider alternate dispute resolution techniques such as mediation and arbitration. Consideration is being given in some provinces to implementing mediation sessions as a required part of the litigation process to provide the parties with an opportunity to explore mediation as an alternative to litigation. An increasing number of potential litigants are viewing the alternative dispute resolution processes more favorably than the litigation process as disputes in some circumstances may be resolved more quickly and with more input and participation from the parties themselves.

CORPORATIONS

Canadian corporations may be created either by certificate of incorporation issued pursuant to Canada Business Corporation Act.

Companies whose operations are to be confined to one province should be incorporated under laws

---

This source is an abridged version of "Canada Law Digest," Martindale-Hubbell International Law Digest, 1995 edition, printed with the permission of Reed Publishing (USA) Inc. Copyright ©1995 by Reed Publishing (USA) Inc.

of that province. Companies which carry on business throughout the country or in several provinces or in foreign countries should be incorporated under federal laws. Canadian companies are entitled to carry on business throughout the country, and no province has constitutional power to impair this right by discriminatory legislation. They are, however, subject to provincial laws of general application, and may be required to obtain extra provincial corporation licences.

ENVIRONMENT

There is increasing federal regulation of all aspects of the environment, in addition to extensive provincial regulation. Jurisdiction of governments is determined according to constitutional law division of powers. Major federal statutes include the Transportation of Dangerous Goods Act and regulations applicable to all inter-provincial and trans-border shipments of regulated dangerous goods, including hazardous wastes. Labelling, shipping, registration, and notification are required. The Canadian Environmental Protection Act regulates toxic substances, including information disclosure, import and export, spill clean-up; nutrients; international air pollution; and ocean dumping. Both statutes set out extensive penalties, including director's liability. The Hazardous Products Act, c. H-3 governs importation, selling, or supplying of controlled products as defined in regulations. Labelling and information disclosure provisions; penalties include director's liability. The Canada Labour Code, has special worker information and training provisions in relation to hazardous materials.

Information on environmental protection and government restrictions is available from the Department of the Environment, Ottawa, Canada. Transportation of dangerous goods information is available from Transportation of Dangerous Goods Directorate, Transport Canada, Ottawa.

FOREIGN INVESTMENT

The Foreign Investment Review Act is as follows:

"Recognizing that increased capital and technology would benefit Canada, the purpose of this Act is to encourage investment in Canada by Canadians and non-Canadians that contributes to economic growth and employment opportunities and to provide for the review of significant investments in Canada by non-Canadians in order to ensure such benefit to Canada."

Foreign investment transactions are dealt with in various ways under the Act. Certain transactions are exempt from both review and notice requirements of Act. Those transactions which involve investments by non-Canadians in new Canadian businesses or non-reviewable acquisitions by non-Canadians of Canadian businesses are notifiable only, unless "cultural heritage or national identity" exception applies, in which case there is reserve power to review transaction. Finally, there are those transactions which are subject to full review under Act and which must pass "net benefit to Canada" test.

FOREIGN TRADE

In addition to being party to GATT, Canada has entered into trade agreements with over 50 countries. Recently concluded Uruguay Round of GATT negotiations will result in significant changes to Canada's trade regulations. These will, however, not be implemented until sometime in 1995.

North American Free Trade Agreement— NAFTA Implementation Act amends domestic Canadian legislation and provides for preferential treatment for US, Mexican and "North American" origin goods and investment. While many provisions of NAFTA are similar to the Canada-United States Free Trade Agreement (CFTA), they are not identical in all respects and new legislation must be referred to. Like CFTA, NAFTA provides for gradual elimination of tariffs on goods either immediately or (depending on category) over five or ten or 15 year periods.

Export and Import Permits Act—Pursuant to the Export and Import Permits Act, Canada controls certain imports and exports. The Canadian government has established an export control list of goods, "an export control list of countries," and "an import control list of goods." Goods and countries listed in aforementioned lists vary considerably from time to time and must be updated frequently. Under the Export and Import Permits Act, the Canadian government has established export controls over natural resources to encourage further processing in Canada, to limit the export of goods in circumstances of oversupply or depressed prices, to restrict the export of softwood lumber products, to ensure that there is adequate supply and distribution of certain goods, to give effect to intergovernmental arrangements or commitments, and to ensure that military or strategic goods are not exported to destinations representing strategic threat to Canada.

Foreign Extraterritorial Measures Act (FEMA)– permits Canadian government to limit production and disclosure of documents and to block extraterritorial application of foreign legislation or trading directives in circumstances where Canadian trading interests are adversely affected or Canadian sovereignty is infringed; and it enables Canadian government to restrict application of foreign antitrust law.

Where in the opinion of the Attorney General of

Canada, a foreign tribunal has exercised, is exercising or is proposing or likely to exercise, jurisdiction or powers of a kind or in a manner that is adversely affected or is likely to adversely affect significant Canadian interests in relation to international trade or commerce involving business carried on in whole or in part in Canada or that otherwise has infringed or is likely to infringe Canadian sovereignty, the Attorney General may by order prohibit or restrict production or disclosure of records to foreign tribunal where such documentation is in possession or in the control of a Canadian citizen or of a person resident in Canada.

INTELLECTUAL PROPERTY RIGHTS

Regulation of all intellectual property rights is within the power of the federal Parliament which has enacted several laws relating to such rights.

Copyright Act

A computer program, as defined in the Act, is included in the definition of literary work and thus is provided protection under the Act. While no registration is necessary for copyright protection under the Act, registration under the Act does confer several advantages if a dispute arises. With certain limited exceptions the term of protection offered is the life of the author plus fifty years.

Trademark Act

A registration system for trademarks in Canada has been set up under the Act. In addition to this, there is also protection available for trademarks at common law if the mark has, through use, become associated in the public mind with the owner's goods or services in a particular geographical area. Under the Act, registration lasts for fifteen years but is renewable indefinitely.

Patent Act

Patent protection can only be obtained through registration under the Act. The term of protection is twenty years from the filing date for applications filed after October 1, 1989. Generally, priority is given to the first applicant to file rather than the first to invent.

Industrial Design Act

The protection offered under the Act applies to features of shape, configuration, pattern or ornament and any combination of these features that, in a furnished article, appeal to and are judged solely by the eye. There is no protection without registration and designs registered after January 1, 1994 are valid for ten years, though maintenance fees must be paid. Designs enter the public domain once the term expires.

Patent Breeders' Rights Act

The Act provides for certain rights with regard to new plant and seed varieties. Protection is provided only to those who have registered under the Act. The term of protection is eighteen years from the date of the issue of a certificate of registration.

Integrated Circuit Topography Act

The Act provides protection for the original design of an integrated circuit topography and gives the creator exclusive rights to reproduce the topography, or any substantial part thereof, or to manufacture and integrate circuit products incorporating the topography or any substantial part thereof. Registration under the Act is necessary for protection. The term of protection is until December 31 of the tenth year after the date of first commercial exploitation, or the year of filing, whichever is earlier.

Trade Secrets and Confidential Information

No laws have been enacted in Canada which provide protection for trade secrets or confidential information. What protection is available is enforced by the courts under the common law. Protection for such information has been provided by the courts in different circumstances through the application of the principles of fiduciary duty, duty of confidentiality, the law of trusts, the law of contract, the law of property, the law of bailment, and unjust enrichment.

LABOR

Workers throughout Canada have the right to associate freely in unions and to bargain collectively. Where employment is within a federal work, undertaking, or business it comes within the federal jurisdiction and is then governed by the Canada Labor Code. Federal works, undertakings, or businesses include navigation, shipping, railways, air transportation, broadcasting, banks or other undertakings declared by parliament to be for the advantage of two or more provinces. Labor relations which do not fall within the federal jurisdiction are governed by the labor relations or trade union legislation of each of the provinces. While the legislation is similar in all the provinces there are variations from province to province. Aside from the regulation of labor relations, each of the provinces also has the power to set standards for such things as minimum wages, hours of work, holidays, and minimum requirements for notice of dismissal.

Unemployment Compensation Tax—provides for insurance against unemployment of certain classes of employed persons, with certain exceptions. Both employers and employees are required to make contributions based on weekly earnings of employees.

Employers must deduct each employee's contribution from his wages and make a contribution equal to 1.4 times employee's contribution to scheme. Employers must deduct and remit employees' premiums and remit employers' premiums together with information returned in form authorized by the Minister of Manpower and Immigration to Receiver General of Canada on or before the 15th day of month following the month in which employer paid insurable earnings to an employee.

LEGAL BRIEFS

Canadian Charter of Rights and Freedoms

In 1982 the Constitution was amended to include the Canadian Charter of Rights and Freedoms. The Charter applies to federal and provincial laws and laws inconsistent with its provisions are to the extent of inconsistency of no force or effect. A provision in the Charter allows the federal parliament or the legislative assembly of a province to avoid the provisions of the Charter if the legislation expressly declares that it shall operate notwithstanding the provisions of the Charter. The rights protected under the Charter include fundamental freedoms, such as freedom of conscience and religion and freedom of association, democratic rights of citizens, mobility rights of citizens, the right of everyone to life, liberty and security of the person, and the right of equality of individuals under the law.

Competition Act

The federal Competition Act provides criminal sanctions for restraint of trade and production and price fixing practices which fall within the Act. Misleading advertising generally, and the making of certain other representations to the public are also prescribed. Relatively wide investigative powers are provided under the Act. A competition tribunal administers the provisions of the Act.

LEGAL SYSTEM

Canada is a federation of ten provinces. The Canadian constitution, among other things, provides for the division of powers between the federal parliament and the legislative assemblies of the provinces. There are also two federal territories in Canada, the Yukon Territory and the Northwest Territories, which are entirely subject to the authority of the federal parliament and which are governed by elected councils regarding generally those matters within the jurisdiction of the provincial legislative assemblies. Included in the legislative authority of the federal Parliament pursuant to the Constitution are: authority in relation to the regulation of trade and commerce; the raising of money by any form of taxation; currency; banks and banking; bankruptcy and insolvency; patents; and copyrights. Among the powers allotted to the provincial legislative assemblies are: direct taxation within the province; municipal institutions in the province; the incorporation of companies with provincial objects; property and civil rights; and the administration of justice. In addition to statute law, the common law, based mainly on the English common law, is applied in Canada. The province of Quebec is the only province with a civil law code.

MONOPOLIES

It is indictable offense (crime) to conspire, combine, arrange or agree: (1) to limit unduly facilities for transporting, producing, manufacturing, supplying, storing, or dealing in any product, (2) to prevent, limit or lessen, unduly the manufacture or production of product, or to enhance unreasonably the price thereof, (3) to prevent, or lessen, unduly, competition in production, manufacture, the purchase, barter, sale, storage, rental, transportation or supply of product, or in the price of insurance upon persons or property, or (4) to otherwise restrain or injure competition unduly, and upon conviction, the person is liable to imprisonment for five years or fine of $10,000,000 or both.

This does not apply in respect of combinations or activities of workmen or employees for their own reasonable protection as such workmen or employees, certain contracts between or among fishermen, employers associations for collective bargaining, certain arrangements between underwriters, or arrangements between teams, clubs, and leagues, pertaining to amateur sport. In establishing that conspiracy, combination, agreement, or arrangement is in violation of Act, it is not necessary to prove that conspiracy, combination, agreement, or arrangement, if carried into effect, would or would be likely to eliminate, completely or virtually, competition in the market to which it relates or that it was the object of any or all of parties thereto to eliminate, completely or virtually, competition in that market.

NOTARIES PUBLIC

The appointment and powers of notaries are a provincial jurisdiction, and each province has its own legislation governing notaries. Notaries may administer oaths and take affidavits. Documents that must be notarized or commissioned may vary from province to province but would normally include documents relating to the registration and transfer of real property and written evidence in civil court proceedings.

TAXATION

Nonresidents pay tax on generally: their incomes from duties or offices and employments performed in Canada, their incomes from businesses carried on in Canada; their taxable capital gains from dispositions of any interest in real property in Canada, any Canadian resource property, and timber resource properties, any income allocated to retiring partner; any other capital property used in business carried on in Canada, any interest in capital stock of public corporation (i.e., corporation resident in Canada), any interest in capital stock of other than private corporation resident in Canada if during the last five years more than 2.5% issued shares belonged to, generally, nonresident persons, and interest in partnership under certain conditions, capital interest in a trust resident in Canada, unit of unit trust, unit of mutual trust under certain conditions; less allowable losses from business carried on in Canada; less applicable deductions. If a nonresident disposes of any taxable Canadian property, he is required to file notice with the Minister setting forth the name and address of proposed purchaser, description of property, estimated amount of proceeds and amount of adjusted cost base to taxpayer of property.

TREATIES

Implementing Treaties—Legislation for a treaty between Canada and a country is enacted by Parliament on the basis of division of legislative powers between parliament and provincial legislatures.

Province may not negotiate treaties directly with foreign powers since provinces of Canadian this connection have only such powers as are related to their legislative jurisdiction. Under international law only nations are recognized as international persons with authority to enter into treaties with one another.

Financial Institutions

INTRODUCTION

Canada's position in the global financial community is truly unique. It is the only developed nation harboring a distinctive, independent economic and financial system while at the same time commingling its economic and monetary policies with the world's largest industrial entity to the south. At times, Canada flourishes under this circumstance, gaining riches in lock-step with US-led economic and financial growth. At other times, however, it suffers to a relatively greater degree than its neighbor during global slowdowns. The balancing act between independent control and global pull has been a challenge to Canadian government and business leaders. In spite of these realities, Canada remains one of the world's most influential and dynamic international financial centers.

The Canadian financial sector is well-developed and diversified, offering most every financial product and service found anywhere in the world. A wide range of financial institutions exist, from large commercial banks to highly-specialized service entities which together may provide virtually any financial requirement foreign business operators may have. Investment and capital markets in equities, bonds, money market instruments, foreign exchange, futures, and commodities are highly developed and efficient, offering foreign and domestic companies a variety of ways to raise, invest, and manage funds. In addition, Canada boasts one of the finest payments systems in the world. Same-day value is given irrespective of where in Canada any bank account is located.

The Canadian financial services system has undergone a series of changes in the past few years which have served to enhance domestic competition and efficiency and to increase foreign participation. These include three main developments: a comprehensive reform of federal financial services legislation in mid-1992, the Canada-US Free Trade Agreement (CFTA) in 1989, and the North American Free Trade Agreement (NAFTA) between Canada, the US, and Mexico in 1994. The most immediate impact was felt under the 1992 federal reforms which were intended in part to expand competition within the four financial pillars in Canada: banking, loan and trust, securities, and insurance. In short, Canadian banks and foreign financial institutions (with CFTA & NAFTA) have been allowed to enter into or expand in the aforementioned sectors where they were effectively barred from before. The net effect is to bring competitive forces to bear on industries suffering from a lack of capital, technology, and management expertise.

THE BANKING SYSTEM

The Canadian banking sector dominates the nation's financial sector controlling over C$850 billion in assets and over C$1.2 trillion in assets administered and managed. Recently, Canadian banking enjoys the benefits of low inflation, moderate economic growth, and expansion of traditional bank activities and investments into complementary sectors such as insurance (Canadian banks are still prohibited from direct participation in the insurance industry, such as offering insurance products through its branches), asset management, securities, and trust services. In addition, banks own, develop, and manage land through their real property corporations and may own real estate firms.

CONTENTS

Introduction	223
The Banking System	223
Financial Glossary	224
Canadian Interest Rates	227
Non-bank Financial Institutions	227
Financial Markets	230
Further Reading	233
Useful Addresses	233

FINANCIAL GLOSSARY

asset-backed securities Debt securities issued by corporations which has as its collateral, and is repaid out of, a pool of assets previously owned by the issuer. Typically, the assets backing the debt obligation are contractual obligations of a third party, but are now owned by the investor in the asset-backed security. Assets such as residential and commercial mortgages, automobile loans, credit card receivables, and bank loans are common types of collateral pooled together under this arrangement.

asset-based lending Any type of commercial loan which hold as collateral specified assets as security for repayment of the loan. Typically, the loan is originated to initially purchase such asset(s). These may include real property such as inventory, transportation/construction equipment, or computer hardware or may be financial assets such as accounts receivable or mortgage loans.

capital adequacy A financial measurement of a financial institution's equity capital in comparison with the level of its liabilities. This ratio is used extensively, by regulators and financial managers, to measure the level of inherent solvency of a particular entity. In general, the higher the capital adequacy measure, the lower the level of default and liquidity risk to the company's bond and stock holders.

capital formation Any process which directly or indirectly adds new capital to a business or economy. Capital can be formed through new securities being issued, loan origination, or through the use of business earnings for capital investments or reinvestment. Capital formation is vital to the continued growth and stability of an economy, sector, or individual business.

commercial paper A negotiable, short-term instrument used in commerce. Types of commercial paper are bills of exchange, promissory notes, and bank checks.

convertibility Ease of exchanging one currency for that of another nation or for gold.

custodial services The management and safeguarding of securities or other negotiable instruments owned by an individual or company by a financial institution offering this service.

derivatives Financial instruments and investments whose repayment and/or underlying collateral base is comprised of related assets or third-party contracts. Types of these include index options, interest rate swaps, and asset-backed securities, among others. This market has grown tremendously over the past decade. These instruments are used in financial instrument structures and for investment hedging.

equity-linked bonds Debt securities issued by corporations which has as a repayment feature either a conversion of a part or all of the bond into common equity, or where the price or coupon of the bond is a function of the price of the issuer's equity securities.

exchange-traded A description for a financial instrument bought and sold on a designated stock, futures, or options exchange.

factoring The discounting of an account receivable in order to receive immediate payment. Factoring is used by businesses as a short-term funding vehicle and to lower the level of accounts receivable on its balance sheet.

index-linked bonds Debt securities issued by corporations whose periodic coupon payments are directly linked to the value of an assigned financial index.

letter of credit (trade) A document issued by a bank stating its commitment to pay a party (supplier/exporter/seller) a stated amount on behalf of a buyer (importer) so long as the seller meets specified terms and conditions.

liquidity (a) A company's ability to meet its financial obligations at all times. (b) The availability of liquid funds in an economy. (c) The measure of a company's short-term assets with its short-term liabilities.

monetary policy A state-controlled, economic and financial tool used to manage an economy's price level, activity, and solvency. Typically, relegated to the central bank, monetary policy is instituted through the bank's manipulation of the money supply and lending environment by various means such as changing interbank interest rates, printing new money, changing bank rules and regulations, and altering the level of the nation's reserve base.

offshore banking Refers to banking operations transacted outside the country in question. In a host country, this would refer to an ability of a foreign entity to bank at a host country's financial institution without regard to foreign nation's rules and regulations. Entities typically utilize offshore banking facilities to escape more restrictive domestic banking operations, rules, and regulations in force.

over-the-counter market A marketplace for financial securities transactions conducted away from operating exchanges. Most transactions here take place electronically as opposed to under the open-outcry system on a stock exchange.

reinsurance A practice in the insurance industry of the placing of one insurance company's risk portfolio on another's. Reinsurance is essentially the secondary market for insured risks, where the company's primary risk exposure to the public is transferred to another insurance company for the purpose of risk diversification and mitigation.

retail banking Banking functions provided to the public at large (retail market). These services include deposit taking, checking accounts, residential mortgages, and other individual products and services.

wholesale banking Banking functions provided to the business or industrial economy (wholesale market). These services include commercial lending, factoring, securities underwriting, and export financing, among others.

The banks are the nation's primary deposit taking institutions, comprising a major component of Canada's official money supply. The 1980 Bank Act established two types of banks, Schedule I and Schedule II banks. Schedule I banks (seven banks as of January 1995) are both majority Canadian-owned and widely held, with their shares traded on the major stock exchanges and no one party allowed to own more than 10 percent of its shares. Schedule II banks (55 banks as of January 1995) are almost all foreign-owned, and have the same powers a Schedule I banks.

Banking is one of the most regulated industries in Canada, with powers set out at the federal level in Bank Act legislation. In addition, the Office of the Superintendent of Financial Institutions (OSFI) monitors banks' ongoing operations for solvency and regulatory compliance. The system is also self-regulated through their industry association, the Canadian Banker's Association (CBA), which implements joint standards such as those relating to technology, consumer protection, and fraud and criminal protection.

Unique among the world's systems, Canada's 61 banks maintain over 7,700 branches providing its customers with the highest full-banking branches to population than any other industrialized nation. As such, customers enjoy an unparalleled degree of convenience, plus nationwide access to their own bank and its services. Ultimately, Canada's retail banking system combines the innovative culture of North America with Western Europe's integrated, well-regulated national markets. There exists an effective mix of aggressive competition with a cooperative style in regulatory and customer service matters among banks.

Central Bank – The Bank of Canada

The Bank of Canada, the nation's central bank since 1935, has been wholly-owned by the Ministry of Finance since 1938. It derives its powers, functions, and responsibilities from the 1985 Bank of Canada Act. The Bank of Canada Act requires the bank to "regulate credit and currency in the best interests of the economic life of the nation, to control and protect the external value of the national monetary unit and to mitigate by its influence, fluctuations in the general level of production, trade, prices and employment, so far as may be possible within the scope of monetary action." Through this charge, the Bank of Canada (BOC) has jurisdiction over the financial system of Canada. It is also responsible for maintaining internal and external monetary stability (money supply and interest rate stability) through monetary policy actions and open market operations (buying and selling short-term government securities). In addition, the BOC guarantees deposits of all authorized banking institutions, acts to preserve the international value and convertibility of the Canadian dollar, and provides banking services for the government.

The BOC is managed by a board of governors. The board is made up of the governor, the senior deputy governor and 12 directors. The board members are drawn from various regions and business sectors, and are appointed for three-year terms by the minister of finance and approved by the governor. The governor and senior deputy governor are appointed in the same way, but for seven-year terms. The deputy minister of finance sits on the board, but is not allowed to vote.

The central bank moves to improve and control credit conditions by influencing market liquidity and interest rates. Its primary tool is the day-to-day adjustments. The bank abandoned targeting M1 (basic money supply level) in 1982 and has since monitored a variety of economic and financial indicators, including credit aggregates and nominal demand to control price inflation. Policy is not to defend any particular exchange rate level for the Canadian dollar. However, the BOC periodically intervenes against the market during times of volatility.

Commercial Banks

The seven domestically-owned and the 55 foreign-controlled chartered commercial banks function as commercial and savings banks combined. They offer a complete range of retail and wholesale banking services such as checking and savings deposits, consumer loans (personal, credit card, and education) short- and medium-term commercial loans (short-term working capital, project finance, and export finance), foreign currency exchange, investment management, and investment banking products such as debt and equity financing and securities underwriting. Most of the large commercial banks have their head offices in Toronto, which took over from Montreal in the 1970's as the nation's leading financial center. The remaining banking sectors primarily playing host to regional banks are in Ottawa, Vancouver, Calgary, and Winnipeg.

With Canadian banks facing a saturated market and slow growth at home for the past decade, the major players have expanded internationally and now count themselves among the most influential in global markets. Canadian banks have close to 300 foreign branches or private banking centers and operate in over 60 countries. Canadian banks have working agreements (correspondent relationships) with thousands of other banks in all nations making trade and other transactions operate smoothly. The Bank of Montreal, the largest in Canada, is truly an international player with over one-third of its earnings coming from overseas ventures. The Canadian Imperial Bank of Commerce (CIBC) ranks second in assets size but is first in Canadian-dollar money market products and, among foreign banks, in commercial paper dealing. It also plays a dominant role in investment banking with ownership of its brokerage subsidiary Wood Gundy Inc. The Bank of Nova Scotia, Royal Bank of Canada, Toronto Dominion Bank, the National Bank of Canada, and Hong Kong Bank of Canada round out the seven Schedule I commercial banking institutions.

The major commercial banks play the dominant role in the domestic and international payment system. In their role as general financial intermediaries, the majors operate across all sectors and are engaged in virtually every type of financial transaction except those precluded or limited by statutory requirements. The seven majors are funded locally with consumer and wholesale deposits (CDs) and in the inter-bank debt market, and internationally on the global debt and money markets. Recently, a surge in foreign capital flows have been a net positive for the Canadian banks, easing the terms and rates on which they access international funds.

As mentioned, the Canadian financial sector was historically divided into the "four pillars" of banking, trust insurance, and securities activities with each sector required to stay within its own field. The 1992 revisions to the Bank Act coupled with other government regulatory changes resulted in expanded bank activities both inside and out of the financial sector. Banks now have the right to own a broader range of institutions. In addition to the right to own securities dealers granted in 1987, banks may now own trust firms and insurance companies. Banks may also set up networking arrangements with financial institutions in other sectors and distribute those institution's products and services in their bank branches to their own customers (it is still forbidden for a bank to provide auto leasing or to sell most insurance products through their branches, however). In addition, banks may provide information processing, advisory services for information management systems, and may also own, develop, and manage land through their real estate entities. Banks may own real estate firms. Finally, since banks now have the right to own "specialized financing corporations," they may undertake more broad venture capital and merchant banking activities and venture capital investing than in the past.

Foreign Banks

Until fairly recently, Canadian government policy placed limits on the ability of foreign banks allowed to operate (either directly or through Canadian-domiciled subsidiaries) in the country. Since the deregulation of the industry, foreign banks have been granted a greater ability to engage in banking and other financial services. The Bank Act permits foreign banks to engage in very restricted forms of business in Canada. Specifically, a foreign bank may not directly or indirectly undertake any banking business in Canada, or maintain a branch or automated banking machine in Canada for any purpose. The intention of the Act, however, was to require foreign banks wishing to operate in Canada to do so by establishing a Schedule II subsidiary. Here, a foreign bank or widely held non-bank financial institution (where a single person or entity may hold no more than 10 percent of the outstanding voting rights of the company's shares) may own 100 percent of a Schedule II bank.

An eligible foreign institution may have a significant interest in a Schedule II bank, if the institution controls the bank. To be an eligible foreign institution, that entity must, in the opinion of the Minister of Finance, be widely held, have sufficient financial resources, and have sound and feasible business plans and sufficient management expertise to manage a banking operation. A foreign bank may maintain properly registered representative offices in Canada. These representative offices have limited ability to carry on business in Canada other than to promote the foreign bank and its relationship with its customers. In addition, a foreign bank may establish a head office in Canada, subject to the approval of the federal cabinet. From that head office, the bank may issue directions and manage its operations for its business outside of Canada. Also, a minimum of one-half of the directors of a foreign bank subsidiary must be residents of Canada and one-third of the directors must be persons who are not affiliated with the bank. In general, the aggregate domestic assets of all non-NAFTA nation controlled foreign bank subsidiaries in Canada cannot be greater than 12 percent of the total domestic bank assets in Canada.

Although Canada's major banks have long been considered significant international players, much of the impetus for these policy changes comes from the specter of economic growth challenges facing Canada. The goal is to ensure a sound, competitive, and dynamic Canadian financial sector to effectively compete in the ever globalized services industry.

To a broader extent, the threat of foreign banks taking away domestic bank business is less of an issue than that of the desertion of big corporate borrowers to the broader domestic and international capital markets. This is already evident in the move of top Canadian corporate borrowers towards the US capital market, and away from bank term loan borrowing. This trend mirrors the one that has been occurring in global banking for over a decade. It is clear that if domestic banks are to continue to perform well, they must not only meet the challenge of new entrants into their own territory, but to move to compete strategically with the ever more complex and dynamic product offerings of the financial services industry.

Development and Other Specialized Banks

Because Canada has a large market of private funding for debt financing of projects, the role for development banks in its economy is quite limited.

CANADIAN INTEREST RATES

	Discount Rate	Treasury Bill	Prime Lending
1980	17.26	12.79	14.25
1981	14.66	17.72	19.29
1982	10.26	13.66	15.81
1983	10.04	9.31	11.17
1984	10.16	1.06	12.06
1985	9.49	9.43	10.58
1986	8.49	8.97	10.52
1987	8.66	8.15	9.52
1988	11.17	9.48	10.83
1989	12.47	12.05	13.33
1990	11.78	12.81	14.06
1991	7.67	8.73	9.94
1992	7.36	6.58	7.48
1993	4.11	4.84	5.94
1994	7.43	5.50	6.88
1995	6.07	6.34	7.75

Note: Year-end figures. The prime lending rate was 6.75% as of April 13, 1996.

Domestic and foreign commercial banks have traditionally provided project financing term debt and are usually the only source of project credit. Here, project and development loans may be originated by other lenders, but credit enhancement on the loan is provided by the larger credit providers in the form of bank guarantees and/or letters of credit.

Other Commercial Banks or Similar Institutions

Canada has a variety of regional trust companies and mortgage and loan companies that are run by credit unions. These entities primarily serve small/local businesses and like development projects. These 60 or so institutions account for only 10 percent of total banking system assets but perform vital functions and provide essential products to their constituents. Those foreign entities doing business in Canada may find that these operators have a more limited array of products and services but are a viable alternative to their larger counterparts.

NON-BANK FINANCIAL INSTITUTIONS

Specialized Commercial Financial Institutions

The remainder of Canada's financial sector assets comes under the control of non-bank commercial and consumer financial institutions. Among the most prominent business types in the commercial sector include manufacturer's captive commercial finance and leasing companies, independents, and a host of specialized operators covering sectors such as asset-based lending, equipment finance, inventory finance, and real estate finance, among others. As in the other major industrialized economies, the Canadian commercial finance sector is highly competitive and is for the most part already saturated. The dominant players in each sub-sector maintain market share mainly due to their own individual low cost of funds which, in turn, allows each to offer the most competitive rates. The following is a brief overview of the major sectors of the commercial finance industry.

The small business sector, and, to a lesser extent, corporate Canada, is the market arena for the nation's commercial finance companies. These operators provide funds on short- and medium-term basis operating in areas where borrowing needs are not met by the banks. The major forms of commercial lending for these firms are wholesale financing, factoring, lease financing, and commercial and property development loans. The major finance companies, which are owned either in whole or in part by the major trading banks, account for the majority of total industry assets.

As in other financial sectors, foreign-controlled entities dominate commercial lending. Canadian-domiciled subsidiaries of large financial firms from the United States provide the bulk of the market's products and services. The firms have the lowest cost of funds, and as such, can provide the broadest array of financial products as the lowest cost. Significant commercial finance operators include multi-line companies such as General Electric Capital Canada and Transamerica Finance Corp., and captive finance companies such as Caterpillar Financial Services Corp. and John Deere Finance Ltd., among others. These larger groups obtain their funds primarily through secured and unsecured debt issues and other borrowings of their parent companies. Significant, independent Canadian firms such as Newcourt Credit and Commcorp compete directly with their larger counterparts in the asset-based finance markets.

The equipment, inventory, transportation, real estate, and other collateralized finance markets are a mature, broad-based, and highly competitive sector of the Canadian financial services industry. Over 100 companies compete in the leasing market offering an array of lease types such as operating leases, direct finance leases, and capital leases. As interest rates declined and business activity took off in 1992, lease pricing and their accompanying implicit interest rates fell to their lowest level in years. This variable, coupled with a strong rate of economic expansion in 1994-1995, has greatly invigorated the Canadian leasing industry.

There has been little change in the number of lease market players over the years. Large lessors, primarily bank leasing subsidiaries and captive leasing companies of equipment manufacturers, dominate the vehicle and large equipment market. Smaller lessors compete directly with their larger counterparts through equipment dealer networks and direct efforts. Foreign nationals are free to enter lease and other finance-type contracts with few if any restrictions.

Specialized Consumer Financial Institutions

The bulk of consumer financial services are available from any of the major commercial and regional banking groups. In addition, mortgages, secured and unsecured personal loans, credit cards, and other consumer financial products are available from the numerous finance companies. Automobile loans and leases are available from the manufacturers' captive finance companies or from a host of bank-owned finance subsidiaries or stand-alone finance and leasing companies. Foreign operators are eligible to engage these entities for personal financial services by are more likely to find a more comprehensive mix of services from the larger commercial banking entities.

Insurance Companies

The Canadian insurance industry is comprised of diverse companies that offer a wide variety of specialized insurance products including property and casualty, automobile, liability, life and health insurance and, in some cases, financing services. While a few are privately held, most are owned by shareholders of stock companies, policy holders of mutual companies or by the government. These companies do very little business outside Canada from their Canadian-based operation. Only 2 percent of total premium volume is written outside Canada, mostly as an accommodation to Canadian policyholders. Therefore, it is argued that the Canada-US Free Trade Agreement will have little impact on the industry. On the other hand, the Canadian insurance industry is inundated with non-resident companies holding a 60 percent share of the market. Nationwide there are over 450 Canadian insurance companies licensed to offer various types of property/casualty and life insurance in Canada and nearly 200 non-resident companies licensed to operate on a branch basis.

Foreign operator entry into the insurance market is relatively straightforward. Investors desiring to incorporate a new insurance company must demonstrate that they have sufficient financial resources and that management has expertise in the insurance industry. A minimum initial capital of C$5 million is required to incorporate a federal insurance company. The Office of the Superintendent of Financial Institutions (OSFI) requires higher amounts of capital for companies that engage in riskier types of insurance, such as those carriers covering environmental risks. In general, less capital is required to incorporate a provincial insurance company.

There are no federal restrictions on foreign acquisitions of existing or new Canadian companies or on the transfer of ownership in foreign firms between non-residents, aside from the restrictions applicable under the Investment Canada Act. However, the providence of Quebec imposes stricter foreign ownership limitations than its Canadian counterparts. In the providence of Quebec no-nonresident investor may own more than 10 percent, and no non-resident group of investors can own more than 25 percent of new or existing Quebec-incorporated property/casualty and reinsurance companies. (Statistics demonstrate that this has allowed foreign insurers to dominate the Canadian insurance industry). Notwithstanding the foregoing, this relative ease of entry for foreign companies into the Canadian insurance industry has allowed non-resident companies to control the property/casualty insurance sector, collecting over 60 percent of the premiums written across Canada annually. Most of the large insurers in Canada are foreign-controlled and were established to operate only in Canada

The Canadian insurance industry, like the insurance industry worldwide, is cyclical. It is characterized by periods of intense price competition and rate cutting according to the availability of capital, which determines the industry's capacity to underwrite risk, with capital availability and insurance rates having an inverse relationship. The property/casualty insurance sector and its products have remained relatively unchanged over the past 25 years due to the characteristically inelastic demand for the product, a maturation of the sector, limited economic and population growth, and weakening consumer loyalty. In addition, property/casualty premiums in Canada have increased at an average annual rate of 10 percent between 1978 and 1989. This represents an average annual real rate of growth of only 2 percent. The industry has not reported a profit on its underwriting and therefore has become increasingly reliant on investment income and reinsurance practices. This slow pace of premium increases highlights a significant weakness for the industry. With the Canadian government proposing the expansion of business powers that would allow banks and other federal financial institutions to their own insurance subsidiaries, which would, however, prohibit deposit-taking financial services from retailing insurance through their branches. The combined impact of these proposals in uncertain.

The Canadian insurance market, like that of most of its bank and finance counterparts, is financially sound but suffers from oversaturation; just too many operators for a market of less than 30 million people. With several hundred direct insurance underwriters, the Canadian insurance industry offers most any and every type of commercial and retail insurance product. As such, there should be no rush by foreign insurers to enter this market in the near future. The top Canadian life insurers include Manufacturers Life Insurance Co., Sun Life Assurance Co. of Canada, Great-West Life Assurance Co. of Canada, and London Life Insurance Group, Inc. Major property and casualty insurers include Insurance Corp. of British Columbia, Co-operators Financial Service, Ltd., Zurich Canada, Royal Insurance Co. of Canada, and National Nederlanden P&C Group.

As in other major national insurance markets, Canadian life and property/casualty insurers are major providers of long-term funding for government, business and industry, and consumers. They are primary investors in long term corporate and government debt obligations and have large holdings in equity in real estate and company shares. In addition, Canadian insurers have holdings in most all sectors of the financial services industry in the form of wholly- or partially-owned subsidiaries. They are also very active in pension funds management. Currently, like most other mature economies, the industry is experiencing as a rash of mergers as the industry slowly consolidates to take advantage of economies of scale.

Pension Funds

Canada's retirement income system is comprised of the following components: basic income support for the elderly under the Old Age Security (OAS) system; the Canada Pension Plan (CPP) and Quebec Pension Plan (QPP): and the Private pension system, which consists of Registered Pension Plans (RPP) and Registered Retirement Saving Plans (RRSP).

The public pension sectors consist of the Old Age Security Pension (OAS), the Canada Pension Plan (CPP), and Quebec Pension Plan (QPP). The OAS pension, funded out of general government revenues, is a pension payable at age 65 to individuals who, after reaching the age of 18, have been a resident in Canada for 40 years. A partial OAS pension is available to individuals who have been resident in Canada for at least 10 years after reaching age 18, or for 20 years if benefits are payable outside Canada. The full pension is adjusted quarterly for inflation. In 1994, a full pension payment was C$387 per month. Individuals may also be eligible for guaranteed income supplements: both spouses and widow(er) age 60-64 may qualify for a spouse's allowance. If an individual's income exceeds a certain threshold, the basic pension benefits received from the OAS may have to be repaid.

The Canada Pension Plan and Quebec Pension Plan, on the other hand, is an earnings-related, compulsory contributory pension plan that provides all working employees with basic pension benefits for retirement. The amount of benefits is based on the amounts of contributions paid into the plan on behalf of the employee. For a person retiring at age 65, the maximum monthly pension, which is adjusted for inflation, is C$694.44 in 1994. To fund the plan, most employees between the ages of 18 and 65 must contribute 2.6 percent of their earnings, up to a maximum of C$806 a year in 1994. This amount is also indexed annually for inflation. Employers are required to match their employee's contributions, which are withheld from wages. The employer is compelled to remit both the employee and employer contributions to the federal government. Quebec offers a similar program, the Quebec Pension Plan (QPP), in which residents are required to participate.

For the most part, Canadians save for retirement through two types of tax-assisted plans: registered pension plans (RPPs) and registered savings plans (RRPs). The Income Tax Act assists individuals in saving for retirement by authorizing the creation and registration of RPPs and RRPs. Both plans permit deductions from income, within limits, as contributions to the plans, which are exempt from taxation. However, payments from these plans are included in the recipient's income unless they are transferred to another plan within time limits. Canada has two basic types of RPPs: defined benefit plans and money purchase plans. In a defined benefit plan, the employer or sponsor pays as a pension a flat dollar amount or a set percentage of income earned for each year of pensionable service. A money purchase plan provides whatever pension income the accumulated contributions and return on investment in the plan will buy retirement. Most plans require contributions from both the employer and the employee. A Registered Retirement Savings Plan (RRSP) is a tax shelter provided under the Income Tax Act to give tax payers an incentive to save money for retirement. Within certain limits, an individual may claim deductions for contributions to an RRSP. Because income accumulates tax-free the RRSP is a popular retirement vehicle. Funds withdrawn prior to maturity are subject to tax upon receipt and the accumulated funds are included in income and taxed, unless they are used to purchase a retirement annuity or registered retirement income fund. Exercise of these options defers receipt and taxation of the funds until they are received as retirement income. An individual is allowed to contribute the lesser of 18 percent of the individual's earned income and the RRSP limit for the year and are reduced for any benefits accruing under the individual's RPP. The maximum dollar limit on annual RRSP contribution is C$13,500 in 1994, increasing to C$15,500 in 1996. The maximum dollar limit is indexed for inflation after 1996.

Underground Financial Operations

Financing and services are relatively easy to obtain in Canada, despite economic cyclical variations in credit availability. As exists in other industrialized economies, illegal activities such as money laundering and counterfeiting do occasionally occur. In general, however, there is little in the way of an underground financial market in Canada.

FINANCIAL MARKETS

Securities Industry/Equities Markets

In finance, Canada offers a highly sophisticated and developed securities market on par with major industrialized economies. The Toronto Stock Exchange (TSE) is the most important of the five Canadian exchanges, accounting for over 70 percent of total trading volume. Founded in 1852, the TSE was incorporated in 1878 and ultimately merged with the Standard Stock and Mining Exchange in 1934. Today, the TSE enjoys major market status as a home for some of the world's largest corporations. Other prominent Canadian securities exchanges are located in Montreal, Vancouver, Winnipeg, and Alberta. While no official figure exist on the exact distribution of ownership of Canadian equities, it is estimated that the split of the dollar value of trading on the TSA is 70 percent institutional and 30 percent retail. Much of the rise of the Canadian equity market in the mid-1990's is due to the growth of the nation's 700 mutual funds, whose assets under management has more than doubled in the past few years to over C$130 billion in 1996.

The first half of the 1990's has seen several record breaking years for the TSE, as measured in market trading volume and share price appreciation. Total trading volume is currently over C$200 billion annually from the nearly 1,300 companies listed on the exchange. As Canada is a world leader in natural resource extraction and production, its most actively traded stocks are resource-based companies such as Place Dome, Lac Minerals, and Nova Corp. A close second are the Schedule I banks such as Toronto Dominion Bank and the Bank of Nova Scotia. Its 10 largest listed stocks as measured by total market capitalization are Seagram Co., BCE Inc., Northern Telecom, Thomson Corp., American Barrick Resources, Royal Bank of Canada, Imperial Oil, Canadian Pacific Ltd., Placer Dome, and Alcan Aluminum. Together these companies account for nearly a quarter of the entire Canadian national stock market capitalization. Though this may portend a high degree of concentration, it is roughly on par with the top 10 share in other G-7 nations such as Japan (20 percent), France (27 percent), and the UK (23 percent).

Canadian equities have shared in the bounty of the global "bull" stock market of the 1990's. In particular, it has been greatly influenced by strong gains in the US as the correlation with Canada is quite strong due to the two economies' close links. As such, total market capitalization has grown by nearly 50 percent since 1990 to over C$450 billion. Over the same time period, transaction volume has more than doubled. The relative health of the Canadian markets has simultaneously attracted newcomers to the exchange as well as global investors. A large number of companies were eager to take advantage of equity market strength over the past several years contributing to the markets breadth, depth, and liquidity.

The major TSE market index is the TSE 300. This index is a market float-weighted index of the largest 300 companies listed on the TSE. Two other indexes exist to measure slightly different market segments, the TSE 100 and the TSE 200. A wide range of sub-indices track the performance of individual industrial sectors.

Special mention must be made of the Vancouver Stock Exchange (VSE), known as Canada's venture capital exchange. The VSE is a haven for smaller companies seeking capital. Taking advantage of its proximity to the Pacific Rim, the VSE is establishing itself as a gateway for Asian companies into the financial markets of North America and Europe. It has been one of the most aggressive exchanges in North America pursing these countries. Those companies unable to comply with more strict listing standards of the Hong Kong Stock Exchange look to the VSE for a more advantageous place to go public. These efforts combined with a new computerized trading system may make the VSE a highly competitive player among the world's major stock exchanges.

The securities administrators of the ten provincial and two territorial governments are responsible for the regulation of securities in Canada. Each individual stock exchange is a self-regulating organization with their own by-laws and policies. Each stock exchange is a non-profit making organization. Trading in Canadian equities was conducted by market specialists in an open outcry floor-based system, or pure auction. Stocks are now traded through the computer assisted trading system (CATS), with all orders for shares being entered from office trading terminals. Settlement of equity transactions in Canada is usually on a T+5 day basis. Official trading hours on the TSE are between 9:30 am and 5:00 p.m., Monday through Friday.

There are several different categories of listing on the TSE and while the listing requirements vary, the most common financial and distribution minimum requirements are net tangible assets of C$5 million and 1 million freely-tradable shares, having an aggregate value of $2 million, held by at least 300 public shareholders each holding 100 or more shares.

Companies typically obtain a listing by filing a formal application with the TSE in conjunction with an initial public offering. A new issue prospectus is filed with one or more of the provincial/territorial government securities administrators or an exchange offering prospectus. It is also possible to obtain a listing by means of a share exchange takeover bid. In addition, a new company may be created by spinning off a portion of the business of an existing public company.

Because the US equity markets are geographically so close and have more specialized pools of capital, many Canadian companies go public in the US, with or without a Canadian listing. This option has been enhanced with the introduction of the Multi-jurisdictional Disclosure System (MJDS) which streamlines the access of established companies from Canada or the US to access the other's markets. For companies to take advantage of this system, the company must have a public float of at least US$75 million and a reporting history of at least 12 months.

Foreign issuers may be listed on Canadian exchanges subject to similar requirements of domestic counterparts. Recently, the securities administrators simplified the rules governing public offerings into Canada by large capitalization (at least C$3 billion) foreign issuers. The main features of this new policy include: allowing the same offering document used in certain countries (i.e. US, UK, and France) to be used in Canada, allowing financial disclosure prepared in accordance with UK or US generally accepted accounting principles, allowing a foreign issuer to comply with Canadian continuous disclosure requirements by observing home country reporting, and minimizing the Canadian authorities' review of the offering document if it consists of a US prospectus, a disclosure document use in connection with a US Rule 144A offering or listing particulars files the London Stock Exchange.

A large network of active broker/dealers and a group of prominent investment banks and fund managers exist to serve the needs of issuers and investors in Canadian equities. Any and all securities-related products and services are available, including trading, securities lending, custodial services, and advisory services, to name a few. Few restrictions exist as to the ownership, buying, and selling of domestic shares by foreign investors.

Debt and Money Markets

The Canadian capital markets are broad and sophisticated, providing eligible companies access to virtually any funding alternative as is available in the US, the world's largest and most dynamic capital market. The only limitations, if any, are the comparatively smaller sizes of each market sector. Recently, Canadian debt markets have benefited in the 1990's from the combination of overall economic growth, lower inflation and interest rates, and market reforms and liberalization. The combination of these factors has greatly improved the liquidity and vibrancy of their capital markets.

The short end of the Canadian capital market is deep and liquid, with vehicles such as commercial paper, intercompany loans (overnight facilities), promissory notes, and bankers acceptances providing issuing/investing alternatives in the Canadian money market. The bankers acceptance (BA) market is one of the most popular sources of short-term credit. BA's are drawn off lines of credit and are sometimes among the least expensive forms of short-term financing available from commercial banks. The commercial paper (CP) market is well developed with a total CP issuance value of over C$30 billion. Large, financially secure companies tap this market on a regular basis for working capital and for funds to smooth-out seasonal cash-flow fluctuations. Most CP issues require credit ratings from the major bond rating agencies similar to those required for US commercial paper issuers. Virtually all of the business is conducted through the offices of the money market dealers who work with a network of borrowers and lenders throughout the country and around the world.

The Canadian corporate bond market, an important source of funds for Canadian companies, is one of the world's most efficient. Total new bond issuance by Canadian corporations average nearly C$25 billion annually, with a total market size of approximately C$850 billion outstanding (including foreign pay issues). Five- and 10-year terms are most common for borrowers here, with limited players in the 30-year maturity range. An over-the-counter secondary market in corporate and government securities exists and is maintained by large, full-service investment dealers, both foreign and domestic. Major bond issuers include electric utilities such as Hydro-Quebec and Ontario Hydro, natural resource companies, bank/finance companies, and consumer product companies. A number of European and American issuers are active in Canada's bond markets. Companies such as Rabobank, General Electric Capital Corp., Household Finance, Daimler-Benz, and Ford Motor Company are among the dozens of entities that have a continuous presence in the dynamic Canadian corporate debt market.

The dynamic nature of the corporate bond market is also evident in the continuous development of new products. Floating rate notes, index-linked bonds, equity-linked debt, and asset-backed securities are among the innovations reaching into the corporate market today. Issuers often chose the Canadian debt market to target investors interested in Canadian dollar-denominated debt.

Underwriting procedures for both foreign and domestic entities are rather straightforward and can be carried out by a number of domestic underwriters and broker/dealers. There is no discriminatory treatment of foreign investors. As such, foreigners are not restricted as to the amount and type of debt they may buy, sell, or trade. Foreign entities wishing to issue debt must follow the procedures for domestic companies such as registration with the CSA's prior to issuance.

Legendary deficits have hampered the federal and provincial governments over the years and in turn, have greatly impacted the workings of the Canadian government debt market. A large level of debt relative to the other G7 countries (second only to Italy) has kept the cost of debt financing high for these entities, which have been several percentage points higher than the global benchmark US Treasury rates. However, as the economy has strengthened, budget deficits are beginning to be put under control and institutional investors are beginning to regain their faith in Canada's fundamentals. Today, the government enjoys high investment grade credit ratings which ensure continuous funding in the domestic and global marketplace. The government bond ratings vary from high investment grade for British Columbia to low investment grade for Newfoundland. The differences can add several percentage points to annual interest costs for lower rated entities versus their counterparts.

The Government of Canada issues Canadian government bonds known as Canadas. There were around C$300 billion outstanding in 1996. The provinces had approximately C$350 billion outstanding as well. Provincial governments are extremely active borrowers in international markets. Canadas generally have bullet maturities (principal is due all at once at the stated maturity date of the bond) and are issued by the Bank of Canada on behalf of the department of finance. Sixty primary dealers are active in Canadas, although less than 20 of these are likely to make markets in them.

Federal government bonds are issued in two-, five-, 10-, and 30-year maturities at regular quarterly bond auctions. All are traded over-the-counter and are not listed on any exchanges. The bond market is very liquid with trades settled through the computerized book-entry system on the Canadian Depository System or through Cedel or Euroclear.

FURTHER READING

For more detailed information on financial institutions and markets, refer to the following publications and sources:

Books & Periodicals

Doing Business in Canada
30 Wertheim Court
Richmond Hill, Ontario L4B 1B9
1-800-465-2059

Moody's Canadian Bond/Money Market Guide
Moody's Investors Service, Inc.
99 Church Street
New York, NY 10007
212-553-1653

Department of Foreign Affairs & International Trade
125 Sussex Drive
Ottawa, Ontario K1A 0G2

Canadian Banker
Canadian Bankers Association
(no address available)

Bank of Canada Review
(no address available)

USEFUL ADDRESSES

Federal Government Agencies

Bank of Canada
(no address available)

Industry Canada
235 Queen Street
Ottawa, Ontario K1A 0H5
Tel: (613) 954-2788
Fax: (613) 954-1894

Department of Finance
140 O'Connor Street
Ottawa, Ontario K1A 0G5
Tel: (613) 992-1573
Fax: (613) 996-8404

Department of Foreign Affairs and Intl. Trade
125 Sussex Drive
Ottawa, Ontario K1A 0G2
Tel: (613) 996-9134
Fax: (613) 996-9709

Major Commercial Banks

Bank of Montreal
129 rue St., Jacques ouest
Montreal, Quebec H2Y 1L6
Tel: (514) 877-7110
Fax: (514) 877-7525

Royal Bank of Canada
1 Place Ville Marie
Montreal, Quebec H3C 3A9
Tel: (514) 874-2110
Fax: (514) 874-7188

Canadian Western Bank
10303 Jasper Avenue
Edmonton, Alberta T5J 3X6
Tel: (403) 423-8888
Fax: (403) 423-8897

Bank of Nova Scotia
44 King St. West
Toronto, Ontario M5H 1H1
Tel: (416) 866-6161
Fax: (416) 866-3750

Toronto Dominion Bank
Toronto-Dominion Centre
55 King St. west
Toronto, Ontario M5K 1A2
Tel: (514) 871-2424
Fax: (514) 871-3553

National Bank of Canada
600 rue Lagauchetiere ouest
Montreal, Quebec H3B 4L2
Tel: (514) 394-4000
Fax: (514) 394-8880

Stock Exchanges

Toronto Stock Exchange
The Exchange Tower
2 First Canadian Place
Toronto, Ontario M5X 1J2
Tel: (416) 947-4700
Fax: (416) 947-4662

Vancouver Stock Exchange
Stock Exchange Tower
609 Granville Street
Vancouver. British Columbia V7Y 1H1
Tel: (604) 689-3334
Fax: (604) 688-6051

Currency & Foreign Exchange

CURRENCY

Canadian currency is similar in many respects to that of that of the US; bills are all the same size but they vary in their colors and the images imprinted on them. The government periodically changes the pattern of certain bills, and sometimes more than one version of a particular bill is in circulation. There are usually no problems using bills that have been recently changed.

The unit of currency used in Canada is the dollar (C$), which is divided into 100 cents. Bank notes come in 2, 5, 10, 20, 50, 100, 500 and 1,000 bills, but bills larger than C$20 are very rarely seen. Coins come in one-cent (penny), five-cent (nickel), 10-cent (dime), 25-cent (quarter), 50-cent (half-dollar, though this is rarely seen in general circulation), and C$1 (loonie) pieces. The "loonie" replaced the C$1 bill, which was then taken out of circulation. The "loonie" is gold-colored, 11-sided, and has a picture of the common loon swimming on it. There are no longer any C$1 bank notes.

Coins have increasingly come under attack; bankers and the public alike deem them a time-consuming nuisance, and they have definitely shown a drastic reduction in circulation. At least one bank has done away altogether with pennies and begun rounding up to the nearest nickel. Many retail establishments do the same, but do not assume that this is so. Offer pennies if you have them.

CONTENTS

Currency	235
Accessing Funds	235
Foreign Exchange Regime	236
The 20 Percent Discount	236
Payment Arrangements	237
Canadian Foreign Exchange Rates	236

ACCESSING FUNDS

Changing Money

Changing money is best done at commercial foreign exchange dealers, which are located in all major cities, and in many smaller ones as well, throughout the country. In some of the larger cities, such companies operate small exchange offices and booths along main streets. These establishments will give you the best rate, and they usually deal in several different currencies. Banks will usually exchange foreign currency, but the rates can vary and there may be hefty service fees involved. Hotels, stores, gas stations, and tourist locations will also usually exchange foreign currency, but the rates at these places will not particularly be in your favor. Personal checks are rarely accepted at any commercial enterprise.

Banks

Most banks offer a variety of currency and foreign exchange services, including transfers, wires, bank drafts, and cashiers' checks. Many foreign banks have branches throughout Canada—more that 50 foreign banks have branches in Toronto alone.

Banking hours are fairly liberal and they vary widely between regions and establishments. Many banks are open late on Thursday and Friday, and stay open all day Saturday, although most ATM services are provided 24 hours every day.

Travelers' Checks

A very efficient way to handle currency while traveling in Canada is with Canadian dollar-denominated travelers' checks. These can be purchased through VISA or American Express in many countries, and they are accepted virtually everywhere in Canada. The rationale behind purchasing travelers'

Copyright © 1995 International Monetary Fund, reproduced from Exchange Arrangements and Exchange Restrictions Annual Report 1994 with permission of the IMF; position as of December 31.

checks denominated in Canadian dollars is that many Canadian banks will not change travelers' checks denominated in foreign currency - even US dollars - and those that do charge a hefty commission. Although hotels and establishments accustomed to the tourist trade will do so, you will be left with little purchasing power elsewhere. Nearly all establishments, however, will accept Canadian dollar travelers' checks so long as proper personal identification is provided. Personal checks are rarely accepted at any commercial enterprise.

Credit Cards

Credit cards are widely used to make purchases in Canada, and they can prove essential for identification purposes, security deposits for renting cars, booking accommodations or purchasing traveling tickets. They can also be used at most banks to withdraw cash.

VISA, American Express, MasterCard, and Diners Club are honored most everywhere, but many establishments will honor the smaller cards as well.

Automated Teller Machines

Automated teller machines (ATMs) are common throughout Canada and can usually be found not only at banks, but at grocery stores, gas stations, retail stores, shopping centers, and at bus and train stations as well. With a card and personal information number (PIN), businesspeople can obtain money and perform a number of banking services.

Most Canadian ATMs feature interbank services such as Plus and Interac. Ask at your local bank whether its cards are good for use in the Canadian banking networks. Most US ATM cards can be used in Canadian ATMs.

Many Canadian ATMs will exchange foreign currency, and they often offer the best rates available and low transaction fees.

FOREIGN EXCHANGE REGIME

The Canadian dollar is very closely linked to, and dependent on, the US dollar. In general, the Canadian dollar moves in tandem with the US dollar—preceding or following by no more than a few months both rises and declines in value. Canada is the largest net foreign debtor in the G7; it is heavily reliant on foreign capital flows, which exposes the C$ to significant downside risks in the case of political or fiscal uncertainties. The Canadian dollar's volatility is somewhat determined by the strength or weakness of the Quebec separatist movement. The recent strength of Canada's currency is due in part to the separatists' loss in the 1995 referendum. In general, however, movements in the Canadian dollar are relatively sedate by international standards.

Since 1992 the Canadian dollar has hovered around C$1.35/US$1; the medium term expects the Canadian dollar to trade at about C$1.34/US$1 - C$1.38/US$1. This range reflects the anticipated firmness of the US dollar over the next few years.

THE 20 PERCENT DISCOUNT

The Canadian dollar is routinely worth about US$.75, but prices in the two countries are virtually

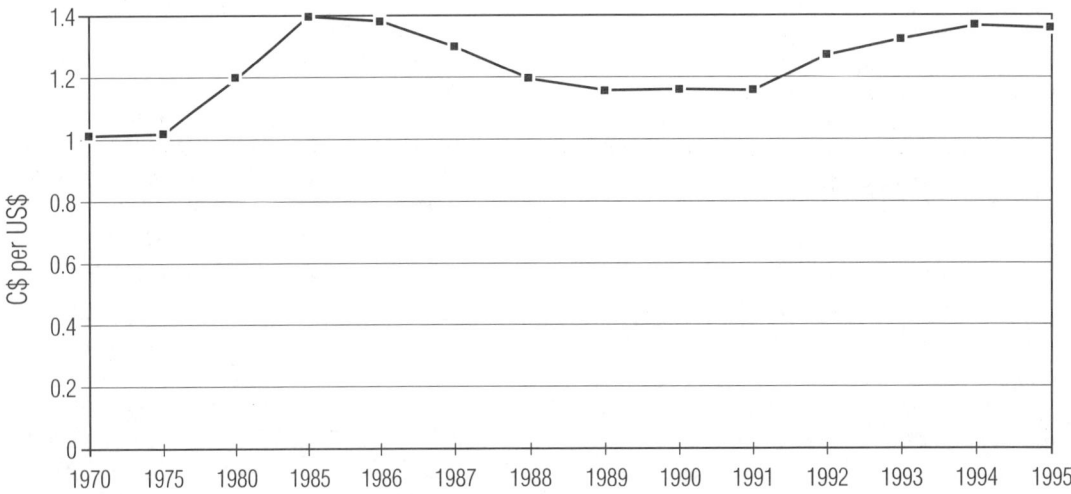

Canadian Foreign Exchange Rates

Note: The exchange rate was C$1.3628 per US$ on April 22, 1996.

Source: International Monetary Fund, International Financial Statistics Yearbook, 1995; Bank of Canada

identical. Thus, travelers with US dollars automatically obtain a 20 - 25 percent discount on all Canadian purchases - from a liter of milk to a hotel room. If you are traveling with US dollars and have not changed your currency to Canadian dollars, don't worry. Most tourist establishments will accept US currency. There is usually a sign by the cash register that reads, "US Currency 20%." Don't forget, this 20 percent is the premium the establishment will pay for your US dollars; this means that the cashier will view every US dollar as worth C$1.20. Thus, for an C$8.00 purchase, you only need to pay $6.40 in US dollars.

This discount applies fairly consistently throughout the economy. The quality of goods available is at least as good as in the US, in some cases better, and in many instances are identical to goods you pay 20 - 25 percent more for just across the border.

PAYMENT ARRANGEMENTS

Financial Markets

The financial markets in Canada are stable, mature and easily accessible. Most businesses operate through either equity or debt financing, both of which are readily available in both Canadian and US dollars. Consumer credit is also used extensively.

Canada imposes no restrictions on payment arrangements; it generally follows international standards and procedures in the execution of payments. Terms may be freely negotiated. The surrender of proceeds from exports is not required and exchange receipts are freely disposable. There are no control requirements on exchange payments for or exchange receipts from invisibles. No exchange control requirements are imposed on capital receipts or payments by residents or nonresidents.

Canada has no restrictions on the movement of funds into or out of the country. Banks, corporations, and individuals are able to deal in foreign funds or arrange payments in any currency they choose. Exchange rates are determined on the basis of supply and demand, and the Canadian dollar is fully convertible. The US dollar is the intervention currency, and movements in the Canadian dollar are closely linked to changes in value of the US currency.

Buyers and sellers can dispose of charges on export collections or letters of credit through normal banking channels, and these should be taken care of at the time of sale. Canadian buyers are generally accustomed to these charges and will accept them, but these terms should nonetheless be negotiated and clarified in advance - especially as to which currency is being used.

Bank branches are numerous, both within Canada and near its borders with the US, and these provide traders with maximum flexibility of methods of payment, as well as facilitate the settlement of accounts.

Gold

Gold may be freely purchased by residents, who may also hold and sell gold in any form. Gold originating in the US requires a permit when re-exported to any country other than the US. Importing articles that contain small amounts of gold, such as watches or jewelry, is unrestricted and free of license.

Cash

Cash is a popular payment method in Canada. Although terms vary from one industry to another and among trading channels, discounts of from 1 to 2 percent of the invoice are expected by Canadian buyers if the invoices are paid within 10 days. Some industries, particularly retail department stores, expect a discount of from 8 to 10 percent if payment is made within ten days. Canadian sellers commonly offer these discounts to foreign purchasers.

The government has undertaken a drive to move financial transactions to a cashless basis but this has been met with less than enthusiasm by the general public. Canadians prefer cash; and they like their bills crisp. Each day, Canadian banks process out of circulation thousands of torn, defaced, or simply worn out bank notes, and replace them with crisp, new bills. However, standards of fitness vary throughout the country. For instance, in Saskatchewan, people are very critical of the quality of their bank notes, while people in Ontario tend to be more tolerant.

While there are still no cashless banks in Canada, banks, retail establishments, grocery stores and service vendors have all moved toward reducing the number of cash transactions. To this end, general utility prepaid cards are becoming popular, and virtually all chartered banks in Canada offer debit cards. Grocery stores seem to be the most popular venue for this type of transaction.

International Payments

International transactions add an additional layer of risk for buyers and sellers that are familiar only with doing business domestically. Currency regulations, foreign exchange risk, political, economic, or social upheaval in the buyer's or seller's country, and different business customs may all contribute to uncertainty. Ultimately, however, the seller wants to make sure he gets paid and the buyer wants to get what he pays for. Choosing the right payment method can be the key to the transaction's feasibility and profitability.

There are four common methods of international payment, each providing the buyer and the seller with varying degrees of protection for getting paid and for guaranteeing shipment. Ranked in order of most security for the seller to most security for the buyer, they are: cash in advance, documentary letters of credit (L/C), documentary collections (D/P and D/A Terms), and open account (O/A).

Cash in Advance

In cash in advance terms the buyer simply prepays the seller prior to shipment of goods. Cash in advance terms are generally used in new relationships where transactions are small and the buyer has no choice but to prepay. These terms give maximum security to the seller but leave the buyer at great risk. Because the buyer has no guarantee that the goods will be shipped, he must have a high degree of trust in the seller's ability and willingness to follow through. The buyer must also consider the economic, political and social stability of the seller's country, as these conditions may make it impossible for the seller to ship as promised.

Documentary Letters of Credit

A letter of credit is a bank's promise to pay a seller on behalf of the buyer so long as the seller meets the terms and conditions stated in the credit. Documents are the key issue in letter of credit transactions. Banks act as intermediaries, and have nothing to do with the goods themselves.

Letters of credit are the most common form of international payment because they provide a high degree of protection for both the seller and the buyer. The buyer specifies the documentation that he requires from the seller before the bank is to make payment, and the seller is given assurance that he will receive payment after shipping his goods so long as the documentation is in order.

Documentary Collections

A documentary collection is like an international cash on delivery (COD), but with a few twists. The exporter ships goods to the importer, but forwards shipping documents (including title document) to his bank for transmission to the buyer's bank. The buyer's bank is instructed not to transfer the documents to the buyer until payment is made (Documents against Payment, D/P) or upon guarantee that payment will be made within a specified period of time (Documents against Acceptance, D/A). Once the buyer has the documentation for the shipment he is able to take possession of the goods.

D/P and D/A terms are commonly used in ongoing business relationships and provide a measure of protection for both parties. The buyer and seller, however, both assume risk in the transaction, ranging from refusal on the part of the buyer to pay for the documents, to the seller's shipping of unacceptable goods.

Open Account

This is an agreement by the buyer to pay for goods within a designated time after their shipment, usually in 30, 60, or 90 days. Open account terms give maximum security to the buyer and greatest risk to the seller. This form of payment is used only when the seller has significant trust and faith in the buyer's ability and willingness to pay once the goods have been shipped. The seller must also consider the economic, political, and social stability of the buyer's country as these conditions may make it impossible for the buyer to pay as promised.

Documentary Collections (D/P, D/A)

Documentary collections focus on the transfer of documents such as bills of lading for the transfer of ownership of goods rather than on the goods themselves. They are easier to use than letters of credit and bank service charges are generally lower.

This form of payment is excellent for buyers who wish to purchase goods without risking prepayment and without having to go through the more cumbersome letter of credit process.

Documentary collection procedures, however, entail risk for the seller, because payment is not made until after goods are shipped. In addition, the seller assumes the risk while the goods are in transit and storage until payment/acceptance take place. Banks involved in the transaction do not guarantee payments. A seller should therefore only agree to a documentary collection procedure if the transaction includes the following characteristics:

- The seller does not doubt the buyer's ability and willingness to pay for the goods;
- The buyer's country is politically, economically, and legally stable;
- There are no foreign exchange restrictions in the buyer's home country, or unless all necessary licenses for foreign exchange have already been obtained; and
- The goods to be shipped are easily marketable.

TYPES OF COLLECTIONS

The three types of documentary collections are:
- Documents against Payment (D/P)
- Documents against Acceptance (D/A)
- Collection with Acceptance (Acceptance D/P)

All of these collection procedures follow the same general step-by-step process of exchanging documents proving title to goods for either cash or a contracted promise to pay at a later time. The documents are transferred from the seller (called the remitter) to the buyer (called the drawee) via intermediary banks. When the seller ships goods, he presents documents such as the bill of lading, invoices, and certificate of origin to his representative bank (the remitting bank), which then forwards them to the buyer's bank (the collecting bank). According to the type of documentary collection, the buyer may then do one of the following:

- With Documents against Payment (D/P), the buyer may only receive the title and other documents after paying for the goods;
- With Documents against Acceptance (D/A), the buyer may receive the title and other documents after signing a time draft promising to pay at a later date; or
- With Acceptance Documents against Payment (Acceptance D/P), the buyer signs a time draft for payment at a later date. However, he may only obtain the documents after the time draft reaches maturity. In essence, the goods remain in escrow until payment has been made.

In all cases the buyer may take possession of the goods only by presenting the bill of lading to customs and shipping authorities.

In the event that the prospective buyer cannot or will not pay for the goods shipped, they remain in the legal possession of the seller; however he may be stuck with them in an unfavorable situation. Also, the seller has no legal basis to file claim against the prospective buyer. At this point the seller may:
- Have the goods returned and sell them on his domestic market; or
- Sell the goods to another buyer near where the goods are currently held.

If the seller takes no action the goods will be auctioned or otherwise disposed of by customs.

PROCEDURE

The documentary collection process has been standardized by a set of rules published by the International Chamber of Commerce (ICC). These rules are called the Uniform Rules for Collections (URC) and are contained in ICC Publication No. 322. (*See* "Further Reading" on page 253 for ICC addresses and a list of available publications.)

The following is the basic set of steps used in a documentary collection. Refer to the illustration on the following page for a graphic representation of the procedure.

① The seller (remitter, exporter) ships the goods.
② and ③ The seller forwards the agreed upon documents to his bank, the remitting bank, which in turn forwards them to the collecting bank (buyer's bank).
④ The collecting bank notifies the buyer (drawee, importer) and informs him of the conditions under which he can take possession of the documents.
⑤ To take possession of the documents, the buyer makes payment or signs a time deposit.
⑥ and ⑦ If the buyer draws the documents against payment, the collecting bank transfers payment to the remitting bank for credit to the seller's account. If the buyer draws the documents against acceptance, the collecting bank sends the acceptance to the remitting bank or retains it up to maturity. On maturity, the collecting bank collects the bill and transfers it to the remitting bank for payment to the seller.

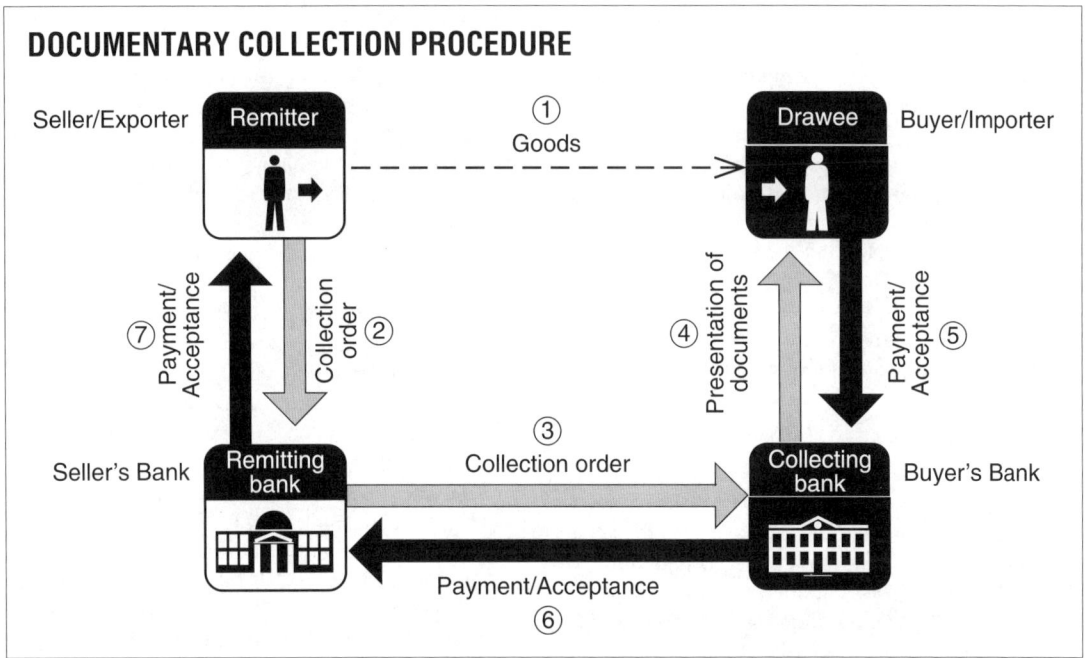

TIPS FOR BUYERS

1. The buyer is generally in a secure position because he does not assume ownership or responsibility for goods until he has paid for the documents or signed a time draft.

2. The buyer may not sample or inspect the goods before accepting and paying for the documents without authorization from the seller. However, the buyer may in advance specify a certificate of inspection as part of the required documentation package.

3. As a special favor, the collecting bank can allow the buyer to inspect the documents before payment. The collecting bank assumes responsibility for the documents until their redemption.

4. In the above case, the buyer should immediately return the entire set of documents to the collecting bank if he cannot meet the agreed payment procedure.

5. The buyer assumes no liability for goods if he refuses to take possession of the documents.

6. Partial payment in exchange for the documents is not allowed unless authorized in the collection order.

7. With documents against acceptance, the buyer may receive the goods and resell them for profit before the time draft matures, thereby using the proceeds of the sale to pay for the goods. The buyer remains responsible for payment, however, even if he cannot sell the goods.

TIPS FOR SELLERS

1. The seller assumes risk because he ships goods before receiving payment. The buyer is under no legal obligation to pay for or to accept the goods.

2. Before agreeing to a documentary collection, the seller should check on the buyer's creditworthiness and business reputation.

3. The seller should make sure the buyer's country is politically and financially stable.

4. The seller should find out what documents are required for customs clearance in the buyer's country. Customs brokers may be of help.

5. The seller should assemble the documents carefully and make sure they are in the required form and endorsed as necessary.

6. As a rule, the remitting bank will not review the documents before forwarding them to the collecting bank. This is the responsibility of the seller.

7. The goods travel and are stored at the risk of the seller until payment or acceptance.

8. If the buyer refuses acceptance or payment for the documents, the seller retains ownership. The seller may have the goods shipped back or try to sell them to another buyer in the region.

9. If the buyer takes no action, customs authorities may seize the goods and auction them off or otherwise dispose of them.

10. Because goods may be refused, the seller should only ship goods which are readily marketable to other sources.

Letters of Credit (L/C)

A letter of credit is a document issued by a bank stating its commitment to pay someone (seller/exporter/supplier) a stated amount of money on behalf of a buyer (importer) so long as the seller meets very specific terms and conditions. Letters of credit are often called documentary letters of credit because the banks handling the transaction deal in documents as opposed to goods. Letters of credit are the most common method of making international payments, because the risks of the transaction are shared by both the buyer and the seller.

STEPS IN USING AN L/C

The letter of credit process has been standardized by a set of rules published by the International Chamber of Commerce (ICC). These rules are called the Uniform Customs and Practice for Documentary Credits (UCP) and are contained in ICC Publication No. 500. (*See* "Further Reading" on page 253 for ICC addresses and list of available publications.) The following is the basic set of steps used in a letter of credit transaction. Specific letter of credit transactions follow somewhat different procedures.

- After the buyer and seller agree on the terms of a sale, the buyer arranges for his bank to open a letter of credit in favor of the seller.
- The buyer's bank (the issuing bank), prepares the letter of credit, including all of the buyer's instructions to the seller concerning shipment and required documentation.
- The buyer's bank sends the letter of credit to a correspondent bank (the advising bank), in the seller's country. The seller may request that a particular bank be the advising bank, or the domestic bank may select one of its correspondent banks in the seller's country.
- The advising bank forwards the letter of credit to the seller.
- The seller carefully reviews all conditions the buyer has stipulated in the letter of credit. If the seller cannot comply with one or more of the provisions he immediately notifies the buyer and asks that an amendment be made to the letter of credit.
- After final terms are agreed upon, the seller prepares the goods and arranges for their shipment to the appropriate port.
- The seller ships the goods, and obtains a bill of lading and other documents as required by the buyer in the letter of credit. Some of these documents may need to be obtained prior to shipment.
- The seller presents the required documents to the advising bank, indicating full compliance with the terms of the letter of credit. Required documents usually include a bill of lading, commercial invoice, certificate of origin, and possibly an inspection certificate if required by the buyer.
- The advising bank reviews the documents. If they are in order, they are forwarded to the issuing bank. If it is an irrevocable, confirmed letter of credit, the seller is guaranteed payment and may be paid immediately by the advising bank.
- Once the issuing bank receives the documents it notifies the buyer who then reviews the documents. If the documents are in order the buyer signs off, taking possession of the documents, including the bill of lading, which he then uses to take possession of the shipment.
- The issuing bank initiates payment to the advising bank, which pays the seller.

The transfer of funds from the buyer to his bank, from the buyer's bank to the seller's bank, and from the seller's bank to the seller may be handled at the same time as the exchange of documents, or under terms agreed upon in advance.

PARTIES TO A LETTER OF CREDIT TRANSACTION

Buyer/Importer — Buyer  | Seller  — Seller/Exporter/Supplier

Buyer's bank — Issuing bank 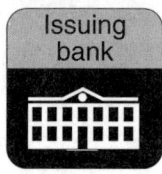 | Advising bank  — Seller's bank

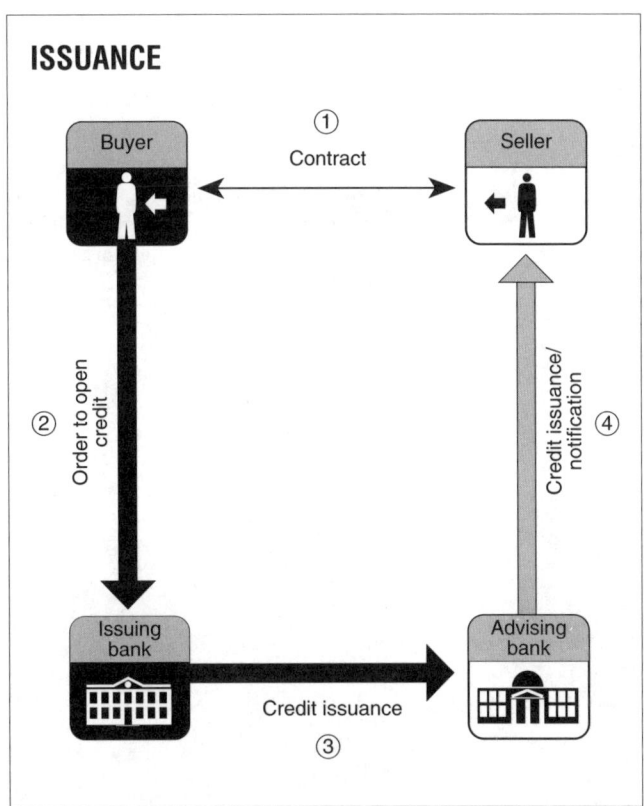

ISSUANCE OF A LETTER OF CREDIT

① Buyer and seller agree on purchase contract.
② Buyer applies for and opens a letter of credit with issuing ("buyer's") bank.
③ Issuing bank issues the letter of credit, forwarding it to advising ("seller's") bank.
④ Advising bank notifies seller of letter of credit.

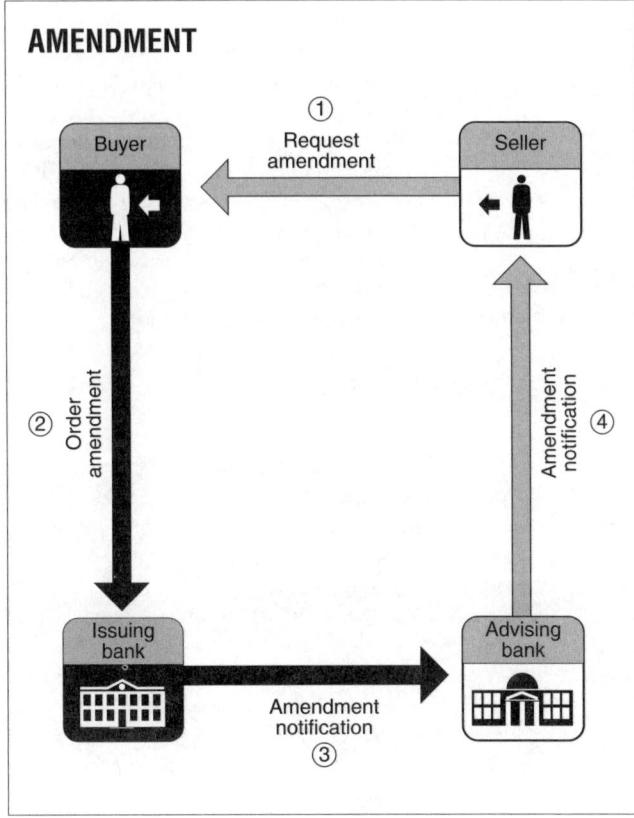

AMENDMENT OF A LETTER OF CREDIT

① Seller requests (of the buyer) a modification (amendment) of the terms of the letter of credit. Once the terms are agreed upon:
② Buyer issues order to issuing ("buyer's") bank to make an amendment to the terms of the letter of credit.
③ Issuing bank notifies advising ("seller's") bank of amendment.
④ Advising bank notifies seller of amendment.

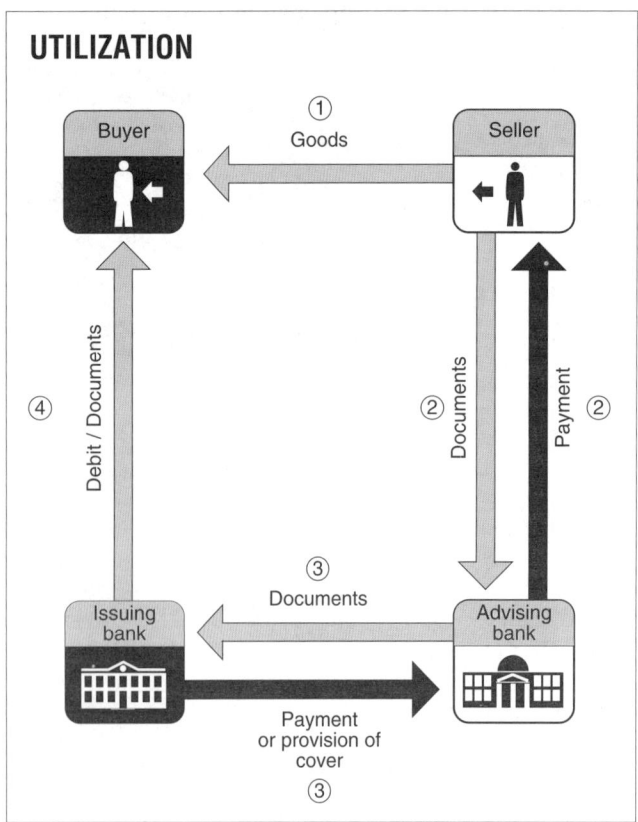

UTILIZATION OF A LETTER OF CREDIT

(Irrevocable, confirmed credit)

① Seller ships goods to buyer.
② Seller forwards all documents (as stipulated in the letter of credit) to advising bank. Once documents are reviewed and accepted, advising bank pays seller for the goods.
③ Advising bank forwards documents to issuing bank. Once documents are reviewed and accepted, issuing bank pays advising bank.
④ Issuing bank forwards documents to buyer. Seller's letter of credit, or account, is debited.

COMMON PROBLEMS IN LETTER OF CREDIT TRANSACTIONS

Most problems with letter of credit transactions have to do with the ability of the seller to fulfill obligations the buyer establishes in the original letter of credit. The seller may find the terms of the credit difficult or impossible to fulfill and either tries to do so and fails, or asks the buyer for an amendment to the letter of credit. Observers note that as many as half of all letters of credit are amended or renegotiated entirely. Since most letters of credit are irrevocable, amendments to the original letter of credit can only be made after further negotiations and agreements between the buyer and the seller. Sellers may have one or more of the following problems:

- Shipment schedule stipulated in the letter of credit cannot be met.
- Stipulations concerning freight cost are deemed unacceptable.
- Price is insufficient due to changes in exchange rates.
- Quantity of product ordered is not the expected amount.
- Description of product to be shipped is either insufficient or too detailed.
- Documents stipulated in the letter of credit are difficult or impossible to obtain.

Even when sellers accept the terms of a letter of credit, problems often arise at the stage in which banks review, or negotiate, the documents provided by the seller against the requirements specified in the letter of credit. If the documents are found not to be in accord with those specified in the letter of credit, the bank's commitment to pay is invalidated. In some cases the seller can correct the documents and present them within the time specified in the letter of credit. Or the advising bank may ask the issuing bank for authorization to accept the documents despite the discrepancies found.

Limits on Legal Obligations of Banks

It is important to note once again that banks deal in documents and not in goods. Only the wording of the credit is binding on the bank. Banks are not responsible for verifying the authenticity of the documents, nor for the quality or quantity of the goods being shipped. As long as the documents comply with the specified terms of the letter of credit, banks may accept them and initiate the payment process as stipulated in the letter of credit. Banks are free from liability for delays in sending messages caused by another party, consequences of Acts of God, or the acts of third parties whom they have instructed to carry out transactions.

TYPES OF LETTERS OF CREDIT

Basic Letters of Credit

There are two basic forms of letters of credit: the Revocable credit and the Irrevocable credit. There are also two types of Irrevocable credit: the Irrevocable credit not confirmed, and the Irrevocable confirmed credit. Each type of credit has advantages and disadvantages for the buyer and for the seller. Also note that the more the banks assume risk by guaranteeing payment, the more they will charge for providing the service.

Revocable Credit This credit can be changed or canceled by the buyer without prior notice to the seller. Because they offer little security to the seller, revocable credits are generally unacceptable to the seller and are rarely used.

Irrevocable Credit The irrevocable credit is one the issuing bank commits itself irrevocably to honor, provided the seller complies with all stipulated conditions. This credit cannot be changed or canceled without the consent of both the buyer and the seller. As a result, this type of credit is the most widely used in international trade. Irrevocable credits are more expensive because of the issuing bank's added liability in guaranteeing the credit. There are two types of irrevocable credits:

- **The irrevocable credit not confirmed by the advising bank (unconfirmed credit)** This means that the buyer's bank which issues the credit is the only party responsible for payment to the seller, and the seller's bank is obliged to pay the seller only after receiving payment from the buyer's bank. The seller's bank merely acts on behalf of the issuing bank and therefore incurs no risk.
- **The irrevocable, confirmed credit** In a confirmed credit, the advising bank adds its guarantee to pay the seller to that of the issuing bank. If the issuing bank fails to make payment the advising bank will pay. If a seller is unfamiliar with the buyer's bank which issues the letter of credit, he may insist on an irrevocable confirmed credit. These credits may be used when trade is conducted in a high risk area where there are fears of outbreak of war or social, political, or financial instability. Confirmed credits may also be used by the seller to enlist the aid of a local bank to extend financing to enable him to fill the order. A confirmed credit costs more because the bank has added liability.

Special Letters of Credit

There are numerous special letters of credit designed to meet specific needs of buyers, sellers, and intermediaries. Special letters of credit usually involve increased participation by banks, so financing and service charges are higher than those for basic letters of credit. The following is a brief description of some special letters of credit.

Standby Letter of Credit This credit is basically a payment or performance guarantee. It is used primarily in the United States because US banks are prevented by law from giving certain guarantees. Standby credits are often called non-performing letters of credit because they are only used as a backup payment method if the collection on a primary payment method is past due.

Standby letters of credit can be used, for example, to guarantee the following types of payment and performance:

- repayment of loans
- fulfillment by subcontractors
- securing the payment for goods delivered by third parties.

The beneficiary to a standby letter of credit can draw from it on demand, so the buyer assumes added risk.

Revolving Letter of Credit This credit is a commitment on the part of the issuing bank to restore the credit to the original amount after it has been used or drawn down. The number of times it can be utilized and the period of validity is stated in the credit. The credit can be cumulative or noncumulative. Cumulative means that unutilized sums can be added to the next installment whereas noncumulative means that partial amounts not utilized in time expire.

Deferred Payment Letter of Credit In this credit the buyer takes delivery of the shipped goods by accepting the documents and agreeing to pay his bank after a fixed period of time. This credit gives the buyer a grace period, and ensures that the seller gets payment on the due date.

Red Clause Letter of Credit This is used to provide the seller with some funds prior to shipment to finance production of the goods. The credit may be advanced in part or in full, and the buyer's bank finances the advance payment. The buyer, in essence, extends financing to the seller and incurs ultimate risk for all advanced credits.

Transferable Letter of Credit This allows the seller to transfer all or part of the proceeds of the letter of credit to a second beneficiary, usually the ultimate producer of the goods. This is a common financing tactic for middlemen and is used extensively in East Asia.

Back-to-Back Letter of Credit This is a new credit opened on the basis of an already existing, nontransferable credit. It is used by traders to make payment to the ultimate supplier. A trader receives a letter of credit from the buyer and then opens another letter of credit in favor of the supplier. The first letter of credit is used as collateral for the second credit. The second credit makes price adjustments from which come the trader's profit.

OPENING A LETTER OF CREDIT

The wording in a letter of credit should be simple but specific. The more detailed an L/C is, the more likely the seller will reject it as too difficult to fulfill. At the same time, the buyer will wish to define in detail what he is paying for.

Although the L/C process is designed to ensure the satisfaction of all parties to the transaction, it cannot be considered a substitute for face-to-face agreements to do business in good faith. It should therefore contain only those stipulations required from the banks involved in the documentary process.

L/Cs used in trade are usually either irrevocable unconfirmed credits or irrevocable confirmed credits. In choosing the type of L/C to open in favor of the seller, the buyer should take into consideration generally accepted payment processes in the seller's country, the value and demand for the goods to be shipped, and the reputation of the seller.

In specifying documents necessary from the seller, it is very important to demand documents that are required for customs clearance and those that reflect the agreement reached between the buyer and the seller. Required documents usually include the bill of lading, a commercial and/or consular invoice, the bill of exchange, the certificate of origin, and the insurance document. Other documents required may be copies of a cable sent to the buyer with shipping information, a confirmation from the shipping company of the state of its ship, and a confirmation from the forwarder that the goods are accompanied by a certificate of origin. Prices should be stated in the currency of the L/C, and documents should be supplied in the language of the L/C.

THE APPLICATION

The following information should be included on an application form for opening an L/C.

① **Beneficiary** The seller's company name and address should be written completely and correctly. Incomplete or incorrect information results in delays and unnecessary additional cost.

② **Amount** Is the figure a maximum amount or an approximate amount? If words like "circa," "ca.," "about," etc., are used in connection with the amount of the credit, it means that a difference as high as 10 percent upwards or downwards is permitted. In such a case, the same word should also be used in connection with the quantity.

③ **Validity Period** The validity and period for presentation of the documents following shipment of the goods should be sufficiently long to allow the exporter time to prepare the necessary documents and ship them to the bank. Under place of validity, state the domicile of either the advising bank or the issuing bank.

④ **Beneficiary's Bank** If no bank is named, the issuing bank is free to select the correspondent bank.

⑤ **Type of Payment** Availability Sight drafts, time drafts, or deferred payment may be used, as previously agreed to by the seller and buyer.

⑥ **Desired Documents** Here the buyer specifies precisely which documents he requires. To obtain effective protection against the supply of poor quality goods, for instance, he can demand the submission of analysis or quality certificates. These are generally issued by specialized inspection companies or laboratories.

⑦ **Notify Address** An address is given for notification of the imminent arrival of goods at the port or airport of destination. Damage of goods in shipment is also cause for notification. An agent representing the buyer may be used.

⑧ **Description of Goods** Here a short, precise description of the goods is given, along with quantity. If the credit amount carries the notation "ca.," the same notation should appear with the quantity.

⑨ **Confirmation Order** It may happen that the foreign beneficiary insists on having the credit confirmed by the bank in his country.

SAMPLE LETTER OF CREDIT APPLICATION

Sender American Import-Export Co., Inc. 123 Main Street San Francisco, California Our reference AB/02	**Instructions to open a Documentary Credit** San Francisco, 30th September 19.. Place / Date
Please open the following [X] irrevocable [ ] revocable documentary credit	**Domestic Bank Corporation** Documentary Credits P.O. Box 1040 San Francisco, California
Beneficiary ① Quebec Trading Company 1981 ave Collège McGill Montreal, PQ H3A 2W8 CANADA	Beneficiary's bank (if known) ④ National Bank of Canada (Banque Nationale du Canada) 600 rue de la Gauchetière ouest Montreal, PQ H3B 4L2 CANADA
Amount ② US$70,200.--	Please advise this bank [ ] by letter [X] by letter, cabling main details in advance [ ] by telex / telegram with full text of credit
Date and place of expiry ③ 25th November 19.. in San Francisco	
Partial shipments Transhipment [X] allowed [ ] not allowed [ ] allowed [X] not allowed	Terms of shipment (FOB, C & F, CIF) CIF San Francisco
Despatch from / Taking in charge at For transportation to Montreal San Francisco	Latest date of shipment Documents must be presented not later than 10th Nov. 19.. ③ 15 days after date of despatch
Beneficiary may dispose of the credit amount as follows [X] at sight upon presentation of documents ⑤ [ ] after ......days, calculated from date of	[ ] by a draft due .... drawn on [ ] you [ ] your correspondents which you / your correspondents will please accept

against surrender of the following documents ⑥
[X] invoice   (...3...copies)
Shipping document
[X] sea: bill of lading, to order, endorsed in blank
[ ] rail: dublicate waybill
[ ] air: air consignment note
[ ]
	[X] insurance policy, certificate (......copies)
	covering the following risks:
	"all risks" including war up to
	[ ] Additional documents final destination in
	                                the USA
	[X] Confirmation of the carrier that the
	    ship is not more than 15 years old
	[X] packing list (3 copies)

Notify address in bill of lading / goods addressed to American Import-Export Co., Inc. ⑦ 123 Main Street San Francisco, California	Goods insured by [ ] us [X] seller

Goods ⑧
1'000 "Record players ANC 83 as per pro forma invoice
       no. 74/1853 dd 10th September 19.."
       at US$70.20 per item	

Your correspondents to advise beneficiary [ ] adding their confirmation [X] without adding their confirmation ⑨ Payments to be debited to our... U.S. Dollars............account no 10-32679150	

NB. The applicable text is marked by [X]

American Import-Export Co., Inc.

Signature _____

For mailing please see overleaf

TIPS FOR PARTIES TO A LETTER OF CREDIT

Buyer

1. Before opening a letter of credit, the buyer should reach agreement with the seller on all particulars of payment procedures, schedules of shipment, type of goods to be sent, and documents to be supplied by the supplier.
2. When choosing the type of L/C to be used, the buyer should take into account standard payment methods in the country of the seller.
3. When opening a letter of credit, the buyer should keep the details of the purchase short and concise.
4. The buyer should be prepared to amend or renegotiate terms of the L/C with the seller. This is a common procedure in international trade. On irrevocable L/Cs, the most common type, amendments may be made only if all parties involved in the L/C agree.
5. The buyer can eliminate exchange risk involved with import credits in foreign currencies by purchasing foreign exchange on the forward markets.
6. The buyer should use a bank experienced in foreign trade as the L/C issuing bank.
7. The validation time stated on the L/C should give the seller ample time to produce the goods or to pull them out of stock.
8. The buyer should be aware that an L/C is not fail-safe. Banks are only responsible for the documents exchanged and not the goods shipped. Documents in conformity with L/C specifications cannot be rejected on grounds that the goods were not delivered as specified in the contract. The goods shipped may not in fact be the goods ordered and paid for.
9. Purchase contracts and other agreements pertaining to the sale between the buyer and seller are not the concern of the issuing bank. Only the terms of the L/C are binding on the bank.
10. Documents specified in the L/C should include those the buyer requires for customs clearance.

Seller

1. Before signing a contract, the seller should make inquiries about the buyer's creditworthiness. The seller's bank generally assists in this process.
2. The seller should confirm the good standing of the buyer's bank if the credit is unconfirmed.
3. For confirmed credit, it should be determined that the seller's local bank is willing to confirm credits from the buyer and the buyer's bank.
4. The seller should carefully review the L/C to make sure these can be met: specified schedules of shipment, type of goods to be sent, packaging, and documentation. All aspects of the L/C must be in conformance with the terms agreed upon, including the seller's address, the amount to be paid, and the prescribed transport route.
5. The seller must comply with every detail of the L/C specifications; otherwise the security given by the credit is lost.
6. The seller should ensure that the L/C is irrevocable.
7. If conditions of the credit have to be modified, the seller should contact the buyer immediately so that the buyer can instruct the issuing bank to make the necessary amendments.
8. The seller should confirm with the insurance company that it can provide the coverage specified in the credit and that insurance charges in the L/C are correct. Insurance coverage is often for CIF (cost, insurance, freight) value of the goods plus 10 percent.
9. The seller must ensure that the details of goods being sent comply with the description in the L/C and that the description on the invoice matches that on the L/C.
10. The seller should be familiar with foreign exchange limitations in the buyer's country that could hinder payment procedures.

GLOSSARY

DOCUMENTS IN INTERNATIONAL TRADE

The following is a list and description of some of the more common documents importers and exporters encounter in the course of international trade. For the importer/buyer this serves as a checklist of documents he may require of the seller/exporter in a letter of credit or documents against payment method.

bill of lading A document issued by a transportation company (such as a shipping line) to the shipper that serves as a receipt for goods shipped, a contract for delivery, and may serve as a title document. The major types are:

- **straight (nonnegotiable) bill of lading** Indicates that the shipper will deliver the goods to the consignee. The document itself does not give title to the goods. The consignee need only identify himself to claim the goods. A straight bill of lading is often used when the goods have been paid for in advance.
- **order (negotiable or "shippers order") bill of lading** This is a title document which must be in the possession of the consignee (buyer/importer) in order for him to take possession of the shipped goods. Because this bill of lading is negotiable, it is usually made out "to the order of" the consignor (seller/exporter).
- **air waybill** A bill of lading issued for air shipment of goods, which is always made out in straight non-negotiable form. It serves as a receipt for the shipper and needs to be made out to someone who can take possession of the goods upon arrival—without waiting for other documents to arrive.
- **overland/inland bill of lading** Similar to an Air Waybill, except that it covers ground or water transport.

certificate of origin A document certifying the country of origin of the goods. Because a certificate of origin is often required by customs for entry, a buyer will often stipulate in his letter of credit that a certificate of origin is a required document.

certificate of manufacture A document in which the producer of goods certifies that production has been completed and that the goods are at the disposal of the buyer.

consular invoice An invoice prepared on a special form supplied by the consul of an importing country, in the language of the importing country, and certified by a consular official of the foreign country of origin.

dock receipt A document/receipt issued by an ocean carrier when the seller/exporter is not responsible for moving the goods to their final destination, but only to a dock in the exporting country. The document/receipt indicates that the goods were, in fact, delivered and received at the specified dock.

export license A document, issued by a government agency, giving authorization to export certain commodities to specified countries.

import license A document, issued by a government agency, giving authorization to import certain commodities.

inspection certificate An affidavit signed by the seller/exporter or an independent inspection firm (as required by the buyer/importer), confirming that merchandise meets certain specifications.

insurance document A document certifying that goods are insured for shipment.

invoice/commercial invoice A document identifying the seller and buyer of goods or services, identifying numbers such as invoice number, date, shipping date, mode of transport, delivery and payment terms, and a complete listing and description of the goods or services being sold including prices, discounts, and quantities. The commercial invoice is usually used by customs to determine the true cost of goods when assessing duty.

packing list A document listing the merchandise contained in a particular box, crate, or container, plus type, dimensions, and weight of the container.

phytosanitary (plant health) inspection certificate A document certifying that an export shipment has been inspected and is free from pests and plant diseases considered harmful by the importing country.

shipper's export declaration A form prepared by a shipper/exporter indicating the value, weight, destination, and other information about an export shipment.

INCOTERMS 1990

Incoterms are a codification of international rules for the uniform interpretation of common contract clauses in export/import transactions. Incoterms were developed by the International Chamber of Commerce (ICC) in Paris, France.

CIP—carriage and insurance paid to (... named place of destination)

"Carriage and insurance paid to..." means that the seller has the same obligations as under CPT, but with the addition that the seller has to procure cargo insurance against the buyer's risk of loss of or damage to the goods during the carriage. The seller contracts for insurance and pays the insurance premium. The buyer should note that under the CIP term the seller is only required to obtain insurance on minimum coverage. The CIP term requires the seller to clear the goods for export. This term may be used for any mode of transport including multimodal transport.

CPT—carriage paid to (... named place of destination)

"Carriage paid to..." means that the seller pays the freight for the carriage of the goods to the named destination. The risk of loss of or damage to the goods, as well as any additional costs due to events occurring after the time the goods have been delivered to the carrier, is transferred from the seller to the buyer when the goods have been delivered into the custody of the carrier.

"Carrier" means any person who, in contract of carriage, undertakes to perform or to procure the performance of carriage, by rail, road, sea, air, inland waterway or by a combination of such modes. If subsequent carriers are used for the carriage to the agreed destination, the risk passes when the goods have been delivered to the first carrier. The CPT term requires the seller to clear the goods for export. This term may be used for any mode of transport including multimodal transport.

CFR—cost and freight (... named port of destination)

"Cost and Freight" means that the seller must pay the costs and freight necessary to bring the goods to the named port of destination but the risk of loss of or damage to the goods, as well as any additional costs due to events occurring after the time the goods have been delivered on board the vessel, is transferred from the seller to the buyer when the goods pass the ship's rail in the port of shipment. The CFR term requires the seller to clear the goods for export. This term can only by used for sea and inland waterway transport. When the ship's rail serves no practical purpose, such as in the case of roll-on/roll-off or container traffic, the CPT term is more appropriate to use.

CIF—cost, insurance, freight (... named port of destination)

"Cost, Insurance, Freight" means that the seller has the same obligations as under CFR but with the addition that he has to procure marine insurance against the buyer's risk of loss of or damage to the goods during the carriage. The seller contracts for insurance and pays the insurance premium.

The buyer should note that under the CIF term the seller is only required to obtain insurance on minimum coverage. The CIF term requires the seller to clear the goods for export.

This term can only be used for sea and inland waterway transport. When the ship's rail serves no practical purpose such as in the case of roll-on/roll-off or container traffic, the CIP term is more appropriate to use.

DAF—delivered at frontier (... named place)

"Delivered at Frontier" means that the seller fulfils his obligation to deliver when the goods have been made available, cleared for export, at the named point and place at the frontier, but before the customs border of the adjoining country. The term "frontier" may be used for any frontier including that of the country of export. Therefore, it is of vital importance that the frontier in question be defined precisely by always naming the point and place in the term. The term is primarily intended to be used when goods are to be carried by rail or road, but it may be used for any mode of transport.

DDP—delivered duty paid (... named place of destination)

"Delivered duty paid" means that the seller fulfils his obligation to deliver when the goods have been made available at the named place in the country of importation. The seller has to bear the risks and costs including duties, taxes and other charges of delivering the goods thereto, cleared for importation. While the EXW term represents the minimum obligation for the seller, DDP represents the maximum obligation.

This term should not be used if the seller is unable directly or indirectly to obtain the import licence. If the parties wish the buyer to clear the goods for importation and to pay the duty, the term DDU (delivered duty unpaid) should be used.

If the parties wish to exclude from the seller's obligations some of the costs payable upon importation of the goods (such as value added tax (VAT)), this should be made clear by adding words to this effect: "Delivered duty paid, VAT unpaid (... named place or destination)."

This term may be used irrespective of the mode of transport.

"ICC NO. 460 INCOTERMS 1990, Copyright © 1990 by ICC Publishing S.A. All rights reserved. Reprinted with the permission of the International Chamber of Commerce through ICC Publishing, Inc., in New York."

DDU—delivered duty unpaid (... named place of destination)
"Delivered duty unpaid" means that the seller fulfils his obligation to deliver when the goods have been made available at the named place in the country of importation. The seller has to bear the costs and risks involved in bringing the goods thereto (excluding duties, taxes and other official charges payable upon importation as well as the costs and risks of carrying out customs formalities). The buyer has to pay any additional costs and to bear any risks caused by his failure to clear the goods for import in time.

If the parties wish the seller to carry out customs formalities and bear the costs and risks resulting therefrom, this has to be made clear by adding words to this effect.

If the parties wish to include in the seller's obligations some of the costs payable upon importation of the goods (such as value added tax (VAT)), this should be made clear by adding words to this effect: "Delivered duty unpaid, VAT paid (... named place or destination)." This term may be used irrespective of the mode of transport.

DEQ—delivered ex quay (duty paid) (... named port of destination)
"Delivered Ex Quay (duty paid)" means that the seller fulfils his obligation to deliver when he has made the goods available to the buyer on the quay (wharf) at the named port of destination, cleared for importation. The seller has to bear all risks and costs including duties, taxes and other charges of delivering the goods thereto.

This term should not be used if the seller is unable directly or indirectly to obtain the import licence.

If the parties wish the buyer to clear the goods for importation and pay the duty the words "duty unpaid" should be used instead of "duty paid."

If the parties wish to exclude from the seller's obligations some of the costs payable upon importation of the goods (such as value added tax (VAT)), this should be made clear by adding words to this effect: "Delivered ex quay, VAT unpaid (... named port of destination)." This term can only be used for sea or inland waterway transport.

DES—delivered ex ship (... named port of destination)
"Delivered Ex Ship" means that the seller fulfils his obligation to deliver when the goods have been made available to the buyer on board the ship uncleared for import at the named port of destination. The seller has to bear all the costs and risks involved in bringing the goods to the named port of destination. This term can only be used for sea or inland waterway transport.

EXW—ex works (... named place)
"Ex works" means that the seller fulfils his obligation to deliver when he has made the goods available at his premises (i.e. works, factory, warehouse, etc.) to the buyer. In particular, he is not responsible for loading the goods on the vehicle provided by the buyer or for clearing the goods for export, unless otherwise agreed. The buyer bears all costs and risks involved in taking the goods from the seller's premises to the desired destination. This term thus represents the minimum obligation for the seller. This term should not be used when the buyer cannot carry out directly or indirectly the export formalities. In such circumstances, the FCA term should be used.

FAS—free alongside ship (... named port of shipment)
"Free Alongside Ship" means that the seller fulfills his obligation to deliver when the goods have been placed alongside the vessel on the quay or in lighters at the named port of shipment. This means that the buyer has to bear all costs and risks of loss of or damage to the goods from that moment. The FAS term requires the buyer to clear the goods for export. It should not be used when the buyer cannot carry out directly or indirectly the export formalities.

This term can only be used for sea or inland waterway transport.

FCA—free carrier (... named place)
"Free Carrier" means that the seller fulfills his obligation to deliver when he has handed over the goods, cleared for export, into the charge of the carrier named by the buyer at the named place or point. If no precise point is indicated by the buyer, the seller may choose within the place or range stipulated where the carrier shall take the goods into his charge. When, according to commercial practice, the seller's assistance is required in making the contract with the carrier (such as in rail or air transport) the seller may act at the buyer's risk and expense.

This term may be used for any mode of transport, including multimodal transport.

"Carrier" means any person who, in a contract of carriage, undertakes to perform or to procure the performance of carriage by rail, road, sea, air, inland waterway or by a combination of such modes. If the buyer instructs the seller to deliver the cargo to a person, e.g. a freight forwarder who is not a "carrier," the seller is deemed to have fulfilled his obligation to deliver the goods when they are in the custody of that person.

"Transport terminal" means a railway terminal, a freight station, a container terminal or yard, a multipurpose cargo terminal or any similar receiving point. "Container" includes any equipment used to unitise cargo, e.g. all types of containers and/or flats, whether ISO accepted or not, trailers, swap bodies, ro-ro equipment, igloos, and applies to all modes of transport.

FOB—free on board (... named port of shipment)
"Free On Board" means that the seller fulfills his obligation to deliver when the goods have passed over the ship's rail at the named port of shipment. This means that the buyer has to bear all costs and risks of loss of or damage to the goods from that

point. The FOB term requires the seller to clear the goods for export.

This term can only be used for sea or inland waterway transport. When the ship's rail serves no practical purpose, such as in the case of roll-on/roll-off or container traffic, the FCA term is more appropriate to use.

INTERNATIONAL PAYMENT TERMS

advice The forwarding of a letter of credit or an amendment to a letter of credit to the seller, or beneficiary of the letter of credit, by the advising bank (seller's bank).

advising bank The bank (usually the seller's bank) receiving a letter of credit from the issuing bank (the buyer's bank) and handling the transaction from the seller's side. This includes: validating the letter of credit, reviewing it for internal consistency, forwarding it to the seller, forwarding seller's documentation back to the issuing bank, and, in the case of a confirmed letter of credit, guaranteeing payment to the seller if his documents are in order and the terms of the credit are met.

amendment A change in the terms and conditions of a letter of credit, usually to meet the needs of the seller. The seller requests an amendment of the buyer who, if he agrees, instructs his bank (the issuing bank) to issue the amendment. The issuing bank informs the seller's bank (the advising bank) which then notifies the seller of the amendment. In the case of irrevocable letters of credit, amendments may only be made with the agreement of all parties to the transaction.

back-to-back letter of credit A new letter of credit opened in favor of another beneficiary on the basis of an already existing, nontransferable letter of credit.

beneficiary The entity to which credits and payments are made, usually the seller/supplier of goods.

bill of exchange A written order from one person to another to pay a specified sum of money to a designated person. The following two versions are the most common:

- **draft** A financial/legal document where one individual (the drawer) instructs another individual (the drawee) to pay a certain amount of money to a named person, usually in payment for the transfer of goods or services. Sight drafts are payable when presented. Time drafts (also called usance drafts) are payable at a future fixed (specific) date or determinable (30, 60, 90 days etc.) date. Time drafts are used as a financing tool (as with documents against acceptance D/P terms) to give the buyer time to pay for his purchase.

- **promissory note** A financial/legal document wherein one individual (the issuer) promises to pay another individual a certain amount.

collecting bank (also called the presenting bank) In a documentary collection, the bank (usually the buyer's bank) that collects payment or a time draft from the buyer to be forwarded to the remitting bank (usually the seller's bank) in exchange for shipping and other documents which enable the buyer to take possession of the goods.

confirmed letter of credit A letter of credit containing a guarantee on the part of both the issuing and advising bank of payment to the seller so long as the seller's documentation is in order and terms of the credit are met.

deferred payment letter of credit A letter of credit by which the buyer takes possession of the title documents and the goods by agreeing to pay the issuing bank at a fixed time in the future.

discrepancy The noncompliance with the terms and conditions of a letter of credit. A discrepancy may be as small as a misspelling, an inconsistency in dates or amounts, or a missing document. Some discrepancies can easily be fixed; others may lead to the eventual invalidation of the letter of credit.

D/A Abbreviation for "documents against acceptance."

D/P Abbreviation for "documents against payment."

documents against acceptance (D/A) *See* documentary collection.

documents against payment (D/P) *See* documentary collection.

documentary collection A method of effecting payment for goods whereby the seller/exporter instructs his bank to collect a certain sum from the buyer/importer in exchange for the transfer of shipping and other documentation enabling the buyer/importer to take possession of the goods. The two main types of Documentary Collection are:

- **documents against payment (D/P)** Where the bank releases the documents to the buyer/importer only against a cash payment in a prescribed currency; and

- **documents against acceptance (D/A)** Where the bank releases the documents to the buyer/importer against acceptance of a bill of exchange guaranteeing payment at a later date.

draft *See* bill of exchange.

drawee The buyer in a documentary collection.

forward foreign exchange An agreement to purchase foreign exchange (currency) at a future date at a predetermined rate of exchange. Forward foreign exchange contracts are often purchased by buyers of merchandise who wish to hedge against

foreign exchange fluctuations between the time the contract is negotiated and the time payment is made.

irrevocable credit A letter of credit that cannot be revoked or amended without prior mutual consent of the seller, the buyer, and all intermediaries.

issuance The act of the issuing bank (buyer's bank) establishing a letter of credit based on the buyer's application.

issuing bank The buyer's bank which establishes a letter of credit in favor of the seller, or beneficiary.

letter of credit A document stating commitment on the part of a bank to place an agreed upon sum of money at the disposal of a seller on behalf of a buyer under precisely defined conditions.

negotiation In a letter of credit transaction, the examination of seller's documentation by the (negotiating) bank to determine if it complies with the terms and conditions of the letter of credit.

open account The shipping of goods by a seller to the buyer prior to payment for the goods. The seller will usually specify expected payment terms of 30, 60, or 90 days from the date of shipment.

red clause letter of credit A letter of credit which makes funds available to the seller prior to shipment in order to provide him with funds for production of the goods.

remitter In a documentary collection, an alternate name given to the seller who forwards documents to the buyer through banks.

remitting bank In a documentary collection, a bank acting as an intermediary, forwarding the remitter's documents to, and payments from the collecting bank.

revocable letter of credit A letter of credit which may be revoked or amended by the issuer (buyer) without prior notice to other parties in the letter of credit process. It is rarely used.

revolving letter of credit A letter of credit which is automatically restored to its full amount after the completion of each documentary exchange. It is used when there are several shipments to be made over a specified period of time.

sight draft *See* bill of exchange.

standby letter of credit A letter of credit used as a secondary payment method in the event that the primary payment method cannot be fulfilled.

time draft *See* bill of exchange.

validity The time period for which a letter of credit is valid. After receiving notice of a letter of credit opened on his behalf, the seller/exporter must meet all the requirements of the letter of credit within the period of validity.

FURTHER READING

For more detailed information on international trade payments, refer to the following publications of the International Chamber of Commerce (ICC).

How to Order ICC Publications

ICC Publications are available from ICC National Committees and Groups, which exist in 64 countries, or from:

ICC Publishing S.A.
38, Cours Albert 1er
75008 Paris, France
Tel: [33] (1) 49-53-29-23, 49-53-29-56
Fax: [33] (1) 49-53-29-02

ICC Publishing, Inc.
156 Fifth Avenue, Suite 308
New York, NY 10010, USA
Tel: [1] (212) 206-1150
Fax: [1] (212) 633-6025

Documentary Credit Rules Publications

Uniform Customs and Practice for Documentary Credits (1993 Revision) This sixth edition from the ICC came into force on January 1, 1994. The 49 articles of the new *UCP 500* are a comprehensive and practical working aid to bankers, lawyers, importers and exporters, transport executives, educators, and those involved in international trade transactions worldwide. Also available in bilingual English-Spanish and English-Russian editions. Order ICC No. 500, 1993 edition, 60 pages, US$9.95.

UCP 500 and 400 Compared An article-by-article comparison study between the 1993 revision and the 1983 revision to the *UCP*. This study also incorporates commentaries on the rationale for rewrite of the articles. Order ICC No. 511, 1993 edition, 135 pages, US$39.95.

ICC Guide to Documentary Credit Operations, by Charles del Busto. Offers a complete explanation of the documentary credit process including: international trade considerations; a list of political, legal and economic issues; documentary requirements; roles of the issuing and advising banks; types and uses of documentary credits. Contains graphs, charts and sample documents to illustrate and highlight important points as well as a suggested checklist for documentary preparation and examination. Also available in bilingual English-Spanish edition. Order ICC No. 515, 1994 Edition, 122 pages, US$34.95.

Standard Documentary Credit Forms Source-book of forms to use with *UCP 500*. Gives precise instructions about how the revised forms should be filled out. These standard forms have been developed on the basis of the UN's layout key and this alignment with other documents in international trade makes this publication an invaluable aid to all parties to a documentary credit. Order ICC No. 516, 1994 edition, 80 pages, US$29.95.

UCP 500 and Standby Letters of Credit: Special Report, by Brooke Wunnicke, Esq. and Diane B. Wunnicke. Focuses on sections of ICC's 1993 revision to *UCP 500* that relate to standby letters of credit. A John Wiley publication, distributed by ICC Publishing, Inc. Order ICC No. 938, 1994 edition, 100 pages, US$75.00.

Documentary Credits Insight A quarterly newsletter designed to keep you on top of worldwide letter of credit developments, which impact directly on your business. Published four times a year, DCI contains analytical commentary and up-to-the-minute information from the experts who drafted *UCP 500*. DCI also offers you a country-by-country update on documentary credit developments from correspondents in more than 25 countries. Must be ordered directly through ICC Publishing S.A. in Paris. Tel: [33] (1) 49-53-29-56 Fax: [33] (1) 49-53-29-02.

Incoterms Publications

Incoterms 1990 Defines the thirteen 1990 trading terms and specifies the respective rights and obligations of buyer and seller in an international transaction. Also available in bilingual Spanish-English and Russian-English editions. Order ICC No. 460, 1990 edition, 216 pages, US$27.95.

Guide to Incoterms 1990 Contains the full text of *Incoterms 1990* plus commentary illustrating how each Incoterm is interpreted in law and everyday practice. Order ICC No. 461/90, 1991 edition, 150 pages, US$49.95.

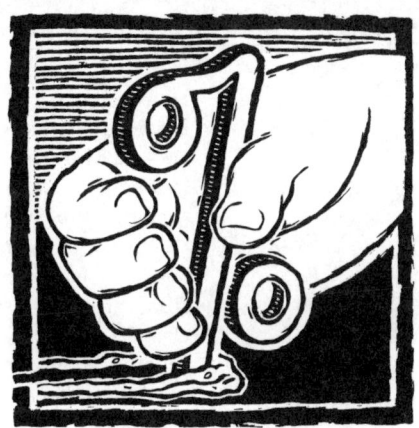

Taxation

CORPORATE TAXATION

TAXES ON CORPORATE INCOME AND GAINS

Corporate Income Tax For Canadian income tax purposes, a corporation's income generally consists of income from business or property and net taxable capital gains realized on any disposition of the corporation's capital assets.

CONTENTS

Corporate Taxation	**255**
Taxes on Corporate Income and Gains	255
Taxation At a Glance	256
Determination of Taxable Income	258
Other Significant Taxes	259
Miscellaneous Matters	259
Treaty Withholding Tax Rates	257
NAFTA Tariff Elimination Schedule	260
Personal Taxation	**261**
Income Tax - Employment	261
Federal Tax Rates	261
Taxable Income	261
Tips for Exporting to Canada	262
Taxable Income	262
Top Marginal Rate	263
Self-Employment/ Business Income	263
Directors' Fees	263
Investment Income	264
Relief for Losses	264
Capital Gains and Losses	264
Estate and Gift Taxes	265
Social Security Taxes	265
Administration	265
Nonresidents	265
Double Tax Relief/Double Tax Treaties	266

Corporations resident in Canada (whether owned by Canadians or nonresidents) are taxed on their worldwide income from all sources, including income from business or property and net taxable capital gains. Nonresident corporations are taxed only on their Canadian-source income. In general, a corporation is deemed to be resident in Canada if it is incorporated in Canada or has its central mind and management located there.

If a tax treaty exists between Canada and the country in which the taxpayer is resident, the determination of whether a nonresident is taxable in Canada may be restricted or modified, and lower rates may apply. In general, Canada's tax treaties provide that residents of the other country are subject to Canadian tax on income derived from carrying on business in Canada only if the nonresident has a Canadian permanent establishment.

Rates of Income Tax Corporations are taxed by the federal government and by one or more provinces or territories. The basic rate of federal corporate tax is 38 percent, but it is reduced to 28 percent by an abatement of 10 percentage points on a corporation's taxable income earned in a province or territory. A 4 percent surtax is imposed on the amount of federal tax. Provincial and territorial tax rates are added to the 28 percent basic rate and generally vary between 8.9 percent (subject to certain exemptions) and 17 percent of taxable income.

The federal government and the provincial and territorial governments may apply lower rates of tax to active small business earnings and earnings derived from manufacturing and processing.

Nonresident corporations carrying on business in Canada through a branch are taxable at the full corporate rate on their net business income earned in Canada. In addition, they must pay an additional

---

Note: *This chapter is reprinted from Worldwide Corporate Tax Guide, 1996 Edition and Worldwide Executive Tax Guide, 1996 Edition, copyright © Ernst & Young, and courtesy of that firm. This material should not be regarded as offering a complete explanation of Canadian taxation. Ernst & Young is a leading international professional services firm with offices in more than 125 countries, including Canada. Refer to the "Important Addresses" chapter of this book for contact information for Canadian offices associated with Ernst & Young.*

TAXATION AT A GLANCE

CORPORATE TAXATION

Corporate Income Tax Rate (%)	29.12(a)
Capital Gains Tax Rate (%)	21.8(a)(b)
Branch Tax Rate (%)	25.0(c)
Withholding Tax (%)	
Dividends (a)	25.0(d)
Interest	25.0(d)
Royalties from Patents, etc.	25.0(d)
Branch Remittance Tax	0.0
Net Operating Losses (Years)	
Carryback	3.0
Carryforward	7.0

(a) The rate is applied to income that is not eligible for the manufacturing and processing deduction or the small business deduction. It comprises a basic rate of 28% plus a 4% surtax. Additional tax is levied by the provinces and territories of Canada, and the combined federal and provincial or territorial rates vary from 38.02% to 46.12%.

(b) 75% of capital gains is subject to tax.

(c) This tax is imposed in addition to the regular corporate income tax.

(d) Final tax applicable only to nonresidents. The rate may be reduced by a tax treaty.

PERSONAL TAXATION–MAXIMUM RATES

Income Tax Rate (%)	53.19(1)
Capital Gains Tax Rate (%)	39.89(2)
Net Worth Tax Rate (%)	0.0
Estate and Gift Tax Rate (%)	0.0

(1) This is a combined rate for 1995 in Ontario, which consists of:

Federal Component	31.32%
Provincial component	21.87%
Total tax rate	53.19%
Basic federal rate	29%
Surtax on taxes payable under Part 1	3%
Extra surtax on taxes payable under Part 1 exceeding $12,500	5%
Ontario provincial tax rate as % of basic federal tax	58%
Ontario surtax on provincial tax exceeding $8,000	30%

The rate varies depending on the provincial rate. The rates take into account budget measures introduced through June 30, 1995.

(2) Seventy-five percent is included in income as taxable capital gains.

---

excess of capital gains is termed "net capital loss" and may be carried back three years and carried forward indefinitely, but may be applied only against taxable capital gains.

Proceeds in excess of cost from the disposition of capital assets are generally taxed as capital gains. For depreciable assets, tax depreciation previously claimed that is recovered on disposition is generally fully included in income.

If control of a corporation is acquired during the year by persons who did not control it at the end of the preceding year, net capital losses from any previous year and from the current year to the time of the change of control cannot be deducted in a year after the acquisition of control. Also, the carryback of capital losses to years prior to such change of control is prohibited. A flow through of net capital losses is provided for on certain amalgamations and liquidations.

If a sale of what would normally be a capital asset is regarded as a sale in the course of a taxpayer's business (such as dealers in real estate, securities or art) or as an undertaking in the nature of normal trading, the gain or loss is fully taxable or deductible as a normal trading operation.

Administration A corporation's tax year usually ends on the same date as the financial statement year-end. If a change in control occurs, the corporation is deemed to have a tax year ending immediately before the change of control.

Corporate income tax returns are required to be filed within six months following a corporation's tax year-end. A penalty is levied on returns that are filed late, equal to 5 percent of the unpaid tax at the required filing date, plus an additional 1 percent per month (not exceeding 12 months) of such unpaid tax for each month that the return remains unfiled.

Federal and provincial corporate tax installments must be made monthly during the corporation's tax year. The remaining balance of taxes owed must be paid by the end of the second month following the tax year-end (third month for Canadian-controlled private corporations carrying on an active business).

Interest is charged on late or deficient tax payments based on Revenue Canada's prescribed rate. The prescribed rate varies each quarter and is currently 11 percent. A penalty may be applied for late or deficient tax installments, equal to 50 percent of the installment interest payable for the year in excess of the greater of C$1,000 and 25 percent of the interest that would have been payable if no installments had been made.

Dividends Generally, dividends paid by one Canadian corporation to another are tax-free. However, to prevent the use of private companies to obtain significant tax deferrals on portfolio divi-

---

tax of 25 percent on after-tax income, subject to an allowance for investment in Canadian property. This branch tax may be reduced by treaty.

Capital Gains and Losses The taxable portion of capital gains and the deductible portion of capital losses are 75 percent.

The deductible portion of capital losses (other than allowable business investment losses) in

TREATY WITHHOLDING TAX RATES

The rates on the following table reflect the lower of the treaty rate and the rate under domestic tax law for dividends, interest and royalty payments from Canada to residents of various treaty countries. Exceptions or conditions may apply, depending on the terms of the particular treaty.

Recipient Residence	Div.%	Interest%(a)	Royalties%(b)(c)
Argentina	15/10	12.5/10	15/10/5/3
Australia	15	15	10
Austria	15	15	10
Bangladesh	15	15	10
Barbados	15	15	10
Belgium	15	15	10
Brazil	25/15	25/15	25/15
Cameroon	15	15	15
China	15/10	10/0	10
Côte d'Ivoire	15	15	10
Cyprus	15	15	10
Czechoslovakia	15/10	10	10
Denmark	15	15	15
Dominican Rep.	18	18	18
Egypt	15	25/15(f)	15
Estonia	15/5	10/0	10
Finland	15/10	10	10
France	15/10(o)	10/0	10/0(j)
Germany	15	15/0	10
Guyana	15	15	10
Hungary	15/10	10	10
India	25/15	15/0	25
Indonesia	15	15	15
Ireland	15/0	15	15/0
Israel	15	15	15
Italy	15	15/0	10/0
Jamaica	15	15	10
Japan	15/10	10/0	10
Kenya	25/15	15	15
Korea	15	15/0	15
Latvia	15/5	10/0	10
Luxembourg	15/10/5	15	10
Malaysia	15	15	15
Malta	15	15	10
Mexico	15/10	15	15
Morocco	15	15	10/5
Netherlands	15/10/6(h)	10/0	10/0(k)
New Zealand	15	15	15
Norway	15	15	15/10/0
Pakistan	15	15	15
Pap.New Guinea	15	10	10
Philippines	15	15	10
Poland	15	15	10
Romania	15	15	15
Russian Fed.	15/10	10	10
Singapore	15	15/0	15
South Africa	15/5	10/0	10/6(n)
Spain	15	15/0	10/0
Sri Lanka	15	15	10
Sweden	15	15/0	10/0
Switzerland	15	15/0	10/0
Tanzania	25/20	15	20
Thailand	15	15	15/5
Trin. and Tob.	15/5	10	10
Tunisia	15	15	20/15
USSR(e)	15	15/0	10/0
UK	15/10	10/0	10/0
US(g)	15/10/6	10/0(i)	10/0(i)
Zambia	15	15	15
Zimbabwe	15/10	15	10
Nontreaty countries	25	25(l)	25(m)

(a) The lower rate usually applies to government debt or government-assisted debt.

(b) The lower rate usually applies to royalties on cultural works.

(c) Withholding tax of 25% applies if the royalty relates to the use of real or immovable property, including resource property.

(d) Canada honors the Czechoslovakia treaty with respect to the Czech and Slovak Republics.

(e) At the time of writing, Canada considers the treaty with the former USSR to be in force with respect to Belarus and the Russian Federation.

(f) The higher rate applies to mortgage interest in Egypt.

(g) These are the rates under a recently ratified protocol to the treaty.

(h) The 6% rate applies to dividends paid to corporate shareholders owning a substantial shareholding in the payer. The rate is reduced to 5% for 1997 and subsequent years. Under the Netherlands treaty, a substantial shareholding is 25% of the Canadian company. Under the US treaty, it is 10% of the voting shares of the Canadian company. The 10% rate applies to dividends paid by NROs. The 15% rate applies to other dividends.

(i) The 0% rate applies to, among other items, interest payments that are exempt under Canadian domestic law.

(j) The 0% rate applies to payments for the use of, or the right to use, computer software, patents and information concerning industrial, commercial and scientific experience.

(k) The 0% rate also applies to payments for the use of, or the right to use, computer software.

(l) Interest on certain government and long-term debt obligations is exempt from withholding tax.

(m) Most copyright royalties are exempt from withholding tax.

(n) The 6% rate applies to royalties paid on copyrights, computer software, patents and certain types of information.

(o) Under a protocol to the treaty, the withholding tax on certain direct dividends will be reduced to 5% for 1997 and subsequent years.

dend income, such corporations are subject to a special 33 1\3 percent refundable tax on dividends received from portfolio investments. Additional taxes may be imposed on dividends paid on certain preference-type shares.

Dividends paid by a Canadian company to a Canadian resident individual are generally taxable, but the individual also receives a tax credit because the income has already been taxed within the corporation. A dividend from a foreign affiliate may be exempt from tax.

Foreign Tax Relief Taxpayers resident in Canada may deduct from their Canadian tax liability a credit for income or profits tax and for withholding tax paid to another country. The foreign tax credit is calculated separately for foreign business tax and foreign nonbusiness tax.

If a Canadian company receives dividends from a foreign affiliate, the normal foreign tax credits are replaced by either a complete or partial exemption for the dividend income.

DETERMINATION OF TAXABLE INCOME

General Taxable profits are computed in accordance with generally accepted accounting and commercial principles, modified by certain statutory provisions in the Canadian Income Tax Act. In general, only 50 percent of meal and entertainment expenses is deductible for income tax purposes.

Inventories For tax purposes, inventories may be valued at the lower of cost or fair market value (as per financial statements) or at fair market value. The last-in, first-out (LIFO) basis is not permitted for tax purposes, despite its acceptability for accounting purposes in certain instances. Corporations may use a different inventory valuation method for tax purposes than the one used for accounting purposes.

Provisions In general, provisions (such as warranty reserves) are not deductible for income tax purposes. Only actual expenses incurred are tax-deductible.

Depreciation and Amortization Depreciation or amortization included in financial statements is added back, and tax depreciation, generally calculated on a declining-balance basis beginning when the asset is available for use, is deducted for tax purposes. The deduction is generally reduced in the first year an asset is depreciated. Tax depreciation may be fully or partially claimed at the taxpayer's option.

The following are the depreciation rates under the declining-balance method for major categories of assets:

Asset	Rate (%)
Commercial and industrial buildings	4
Office equipment	20
Motor vehicles	30
Plant and machinery	20

Capital assets are pooled into various classes. In general, if an asset is disposed of, the balance of the assets in the class is reduced by the proceeds from the disposition. However, if the asset is the only asset in the class and if the proceeds from the disposition exceed the tax value of the class after

UNITS OF MEASUREMENT

English	French	Symbol
gram	gramme	g
kilogram	kilogramme	kg
milliliter	millilitre	mL, ml
centimeter	centimetre	cm
meter	metre	m
square centimeter	centimetre carro	cm2
square meter	metre carro	m2
cubic centimeter	centimetre cube	cm3
cubic decimeter	decimetre cube	dm3
cubic meter	metre cube	m3

Note: Phrases such as "net," "net weight," "net contents," or "net quantity" are not necessary as part of the net quantity declaration. If such terms are used, they should appear in both English and French. The type of unit used depends on the net quantity of the product.

CHOICE OF UNITS

Measure Type	Net Quantity	Units
volumetric	Less than 100 ml	mL, ml
	1000 ml or more	L, l
weight	less than 1000	gg
	less than 1000	g
a kilogram	1000 g or more	kg
linear	less than 100 cm	cm or mm
	100 cm or more	m
area	less than 100 cm	cm
	between 100 cm and 100 dm100	dm
	1 m or more	m
cubic	less than 1000 cm	cm
	Between 1 and 1000 dm	dm
	1000 dm or more	m

depreciation, the excess is recaptured and is subject to tax at the regular corporate tax rates.

Consolidated Reporting Canada does not allow consolidated tax reporting for related companies and does not provide relief for group losses.

OTHER SIGNIFICANT TAXES

The table below summarizes other significant taxes:

Nature of Tax	Rate (%)
Goods and Services Tax (GST), a value-added tax, applies to a broad range of goods and services	7
Provincial/territorial income tax, on taxable income allocated to jurisdictions in which corporations have permanent establishments	8.9 to 17
Provincial/territorial capital tax, with capital allocated in the same manner as income for the provincial/territorial income tax	Up to 0.64
Provincial payroll tax, paid by employers (varies by province)	0 to 4.5
Part VI tax on financial institutions, effectively a minimum tax deductible from income tax; applied on a nonconsolidated basis to capital in excess of C$200 million; the rate of Part VI tax on life insurance companies is slightly higher; in addition, for the period from February 28, 1995 through October 31, 1996, a temporary surcharge of 12 percent applies to the Part VI tax imposed on certain financial institutions	1.25
Large Corporations Tax, effectively a minimum tax, which may be reduced by the 4 percent corporate surcharge; applied on capital employed in Canada in excess of C$10 million	0.225
Canada Pension Plan, on pensionable earnings between C$3,500 and C$35,400 (1996 rates)	
Employer	2.8
Employee	2.8
Self-employed individual	5.6
(The Province of Quebec offers a similar plan for residents of Quebec.)	
Unemployment insurance, on insurable earnings up to a maximum of C$39,000 (1996 rates)	
Employee	2.95
Employer (1.4 times the employee rate)	4.13

MISCELLANEOUS MATTERS

Foreign-Exchange Controls Canada does not impose foreign-exchange control restrictions.

Debt-to-Equity Rules Canada imposes a thin capitalization rule restricting nonresidents from withdrawing profits through interest charges. The interest deduction is restricted if interest is paid by a Canadian resident corporation to a specified nonresident on debt exceeding three times the shareholder's equity in the corporation. A specified nonresident is a nonresident shareholder who, either alone or with other persons not at arm's length, owns 25 percent or more of the issued shares of any class of the corporation or any nonresident who deals at other than arm's length with such a shareholder.

Foreign Affiliates A nonresident corporation is considered a foreign affiliate if a Canadian corporation and related persons directly or indirectly own at least 10 percent of any class of shares of that nonresident corporation. Dividends received by a Canadian corporation from a foreign affiliate are generally received tax-free in Canada if the dividends are derived from active business profits earned in a country with which Canada has entered into a tax treaty. Dividends are taxable in Canada if they are derived from most Canadian sources, passive operations or any operations in a nontreaty country, with relief for foreign tax on such income.

Passive Income of Controlled Foreign Affiliates Any Canadian taxpayer that controls (as defined) a foreign affiliate is taxed on its share of that entity's passive investment income in the year such income is earned, regardless of whether such income is currently paid to the shareholder.

Corporate Reorganizations In general, most transactions must be recognized at fair market value. In certain specified circumstances, however, some types of corporate reorganizations may be accomplished with little or no immediate tax cost.

Antiavoidance Legislation Revenue Canada may apply an antiavoidance rule to eliminate any form of advantage resulting from one transaction or a series of transactions if a tax advantage is the primary reason for the transaction and other criteria are met.

Transfer Pricing Under Canada's transfer-pricing rules, acceptable transfer-pricing methods include comparable uncontrolled price, resale price and cost-plus. Other methods may be used if the result obtained is similar to the result that would be obtained from a normal transaction. The profit-split method is not acceptable. It is possible to reach agreements in advance with Revenue Canada.

Change of Control Considerations If control of a corporation has been acquired, the target corporation is deemed to have a year-end immediately before the change in control. A new tax year begins immediately thereafter, and the new year-end is

NAFTA TARIFF ELIMINATION SCHEDULE

Eliminated January 1, 1994	Phasing Out by 1998	Out by 2003
Locomotive and rail cars	Hydraulic turbines	Other cars & coaches
Construction equipment	Air conditioners	Boats &drilling platforms
Telecommunications	Many resin	Bicycles equipment
Fertilizers	Most copper wire Most flat-rolled	stainless steel
Health & medical	Laundry soaps	Furniture equipment
Many chemicals & plastics	Wood and paper	Pharmaceuticals

determined by the target corporation. Special rules apply to the treatment of capital losses, business losses and depreciable property.

Nonresident-Owned Investment Corporations (NROs) An NRO can sometimes be used advantageously by a nonresident as a Canadian holding company. An NRO must be a Canadian corporation, all of whose shares, bonds, debentures and funded indebtedness are owned by nonresidents. The type of income an NRO is permitted to earn is limited (principally income from securities), and no more than 10 percent of its gross revenue may be from certain sources, such as rents. As a result of a lower tax rate and the provision for a tax refund, the use of an NRO effectively results in tax that is equal to the withholding tax on dividend distributions. A corporation must elect to be taxed as an NRO.

Capital Gains Realized by Nonresidents Nonresidents are required, subject to applicable tax treaty provisions, to pay Canadian tax on their net taxable capital gains arising on the disposition of taxable Canadian property. Such property includes land situated in Canada, shares of Canadian private corporations (excluding NROs in certain cases), shares of Canadian public corporations (in limited circumstances), property used in a business carried on by the nonresident in Canada, an interest in a partnership in which more than 50 percent of the property consists of taxable Canadian property and interests in certain trusts resident in Canada. Under proposed legislation, for dispositions occurring after April 26, 1995, taxable Canadian property will include the shares of a nonresident corporation or an interest in a nonresident trust if more than 50 percent of the value of the corporation or trust is derived from Canadian real property or Canadian resource properties (as defined).

A nonresident vendor of Canadian property (other than property that qualifies as excluded property) must obtain a clearance certificate from Revenue Canada and provide acceptable security or pay tax on the disposition at the time of sale. Unless the vendor has obtained a clearance certificate, the purchaser, if he or she knows the vendor is a nonresident, must withhold and pay to the federal government up to 33 1\3 percent of the cost of the property.

PERSONAL TAXATION

INCOME TAX - EMPLOYMENT

Who Is Liable

An individual resident in Canada is taxable on his or her worldwide income. Nonresidents are taxed only on Canadian-source income.

The tax statutes do not contain a specific definition of "residence." Accordingly, the residence of an individual is determined by reference to such matters as the location of dwelling places, spouse and dependents; personal property; economic interests; and social ties. However, a statute provides that a nonresident individual who stays temporarily in Canada for 183 days or more in a calendar year is deemed to be a resident of Canada for the entire year. This provision pertains only to an individual who would otherwise be considered a nonresident and not to an individual who purposely takes up residence in Canada or to an existing resident who ceases to be a resident upon moving from Canada. Such individuals may be treated as part-year residents.

Taxable Income

Income from employment includes salaries, wages, directors' fees and most benefits received by virtue of employment. Some examples of taxable benefits are low-interest loans, the use of company-owned automobiles, subsidized or free personal living expenses and stock-option benefits. Among the few nontaxable benefits are employers' contributions to certain employer sponsored retirement savings plans, such as registered Canadian pension plans and deferred profit-sharing plans.

Income Tax Rates

Married persons are taxed separately, not jointly, on all types of income.

Federal/Provincial Taxing Authorities The federal and all provincial governments, as well as the territories, impose income taxes on resident individuals. However, only the province of Quebec collects its own individual income tax and requires a separate return to be filed. The federal government collects the provincial tax on behalf of all other provinces, which means that only one combined federal/provincial return must be filed.

The calculation of an individual's tax payable is a two-step process. An individual's federal income tax for a given year is calculated on taxable income using a single graduated rate schedule. From this amount is deducted whatever federal personal tax credits are available to the individual and the dividend tax credit. The net result is the individual's basic federal tax payable. Federal surtaxes are then applied to this amount.

Income taxes for the provinces and territories, except Quebec, are calculated by applying the appropriate provincial rate to the "basic federal tax payable" for the year.

FEDERAL TAX RATES

Canada has three tax brackets, which are partially indexed annually for inflation. The brackets for 1995 are as follows:

In addition, a surtax of 3 percent of basic federal tax is added to federal tax, and an additional surtax of 5 percent of basic federal tax in excess of $12,500 is levied.

TAXABLE INCOME

Exceeding $	Not Exceeding $	Tax on Lower Amount $	Rate on Excess %
0	29,590	0	17
29,590	59,180	5,030	26
59,180	–	12,724	29

Provincial Tax Rates–1995 In addition to federal tax, all provinces (except Quebec) collect tax currently at the following rates applied to federal tax:

Province	%
Alberta	45.5(1)(2)
British Columbia	52.5(1)
Manitoba	52.0(2)
New Brunswick	64.0(1)
Newfoundland	69.0
Nova Scotia	59.5(1)
Northwest Territories	45.0
Ontario	58.0(1)
Prince Edward Island	59.5(1)
Saskatchewan	50.0(1) (2)
Yukon	50.0
Nonresident	52.0

(1) Each of these provinces levies an additional provincial surtax on high income earners, ranging from 5% to 50% of provincial taxes payable in excess of certain threshold amounts.
(2) Each of these provinces applies an additional flat tax, ranging from 0.5% to 2.0% based on the individual's net income or taxable income.

Quebec Tax Rates - 1995 Residents of Quebec receive a federal tax abatement of 16.5 percent of basic federal tax. The province of Quebec requires a separate calculation of taxable income similar to the

TIPS FOR EXPORTING TO CANADA

1. Although there are few restrictions on imports, import permits are required for some goods.
2. Most imports are cleared through customs by licensed customs brokers familiar with all the requirements.
3. Certain goods are allowed duty-free into Canada under duty free remission arrangements.
4. Under the Canada-US Free Trade Agreement, goods originating in the US will ultimately be allowed to enter duty free.
5. The CFTA also allows goods ultimately entitled to enter the US duty free to incorporate inputs from third countries.
6. Exporters may take advantage of business growth in Canada by providing inputs to companies manufacturing, in Canada, goods entitled to enter the US market duty free.
7. Advice respecting import restrictions and general customs requirements can be obtained from trade commissioners

calculation of federal taxable income However, treatment of some items differs. For instance, the federal government provides tax credits for amounts such as tuition fees, while Quebec allows deductions for these expenses. To calculate tax payable, individuals apply a single graduated rate schedule to Quebec taxable income. Individuals then deduct available Quebec personal tax credits and the Quebec dividend tax credit to determine adjusted tax payable. Quebec then levies a provincial surtax of 5 percent on the amount of provincial tax that exceeds $5,000 and an additional 5 percent surtax on the amount of provincial tax that exceeds $10,000.

Quebec provincial tax is levied on Quebec taxable income at the rates shown below:

TAXABLE INCOME

Exceeding %	Not Exceeding %	Tax on Lower Amount $	Rate on Excess %
0	7,316	0	00.00
7,316	14,000	0	19.00
14,000	23,000	1,270	21.00
23,000	31,000	3,160	23.00
31,000	50,000	5,000	24.15
50,000	52,625	9,589	25.20
52,625	----	10,250	26.40

Minimum Income Tax To ensure that high income taxpayers pay a certain level of tax, an alternative minimum tax applies. Under its provisions, individuals are required to recalculate taxable income without deducting certain items that are otherwise deductible in the regular tax calculation. In recalculating such taxable income, a blanket $40,000 exemption is permitted. In 1995, a combined federal and provincial rate ranging from 26 percent to 31.8 percent, depending on the province of residence, is applied to alternative minimum taxable income. The individual then pays the greater of the regular tax or the minimum tax. If the minimum tax exceeds the regular tax, the excess amount may be carried forward for seven years. The carryforward amount may be used to reduce regular tax to the extent that regular tax exceeds minimum tax.

Deductible Expenses

Few deductions are allowed in computing income from employment. Among the items permitted to be deducted are employee contributions to a registered pension plan (up to a certain maximum), traveling and certain other expenses of commission salesmen, certain traveling expenses of other employees, and union or professional dues.

Employers generally must withhold income tax, government pension contributions and unemployment insurance premiums from remuneration paid to employees and remit those amounts to the taxation authorities for credit to the employees' accounts.

Interest may be claimed as a deduction in the year it is paid or when it becomes payable, depending on the practice normally followed, as long as the money was borrowed for the purpose of earning income. Other carrying costs such as investment counseling fees and accounting costs (but not tax return preparation fees) are deductible. Personal interest, such as interest on mortgages or charge accounts, is not deductible. Other deductions include contributions to registered retirement savings plans (an individual retirement income plan) and payments for alimony, moving expenses for moves within Canada and certain child care expenses.

Personal Credits and Allowances

An individual is allowed to deduct a number of personal tax credits in computing the amount of basic federal tax for the year. Personal tax credits include a basic personal credit of $1,098 for 1995, a spousal credit subject to thresholds for spousal income, a disabled dependent's credit, an age credit, a disability credit and education and tuition fee credits. An employee's Canada/Quebec pension plan contributions and unemployment insurance contributions are also eligible for credit treatment.

Charitable donations (up to 20 percent of net income) will be eligible for a tax credit of 17 percent on the first $200 and a 29 percent tax credit for donations in excess of $200. The unused portion of the donation credit may be carried forward for up to five years. Similarly, medical expenses in excess of the lesser of $1,614 or 3 percent of net income will be eligible for a tax credit equal to 17 percent of the excess. Furthermore, an individual will be eligible for a tax credit of up to $170 on the first $1,000 of qualifying pension income.

SELF-EMPLOYMENT/ BUSINESS INCOME

Who Is Liable

Every resident who carries on a business is taxable on his or her worldwide business income. Nonresidents are taxable on business income from Canadian sources.

Taxable Income and Deductible Expenses

The computation of an individual's income from a business or property is similar to that for a corporation, with business income generally computed on the accrual basis of accounting.

Interest and other carrying charges incurred to acquire business assets or investment property may generally be deducted. Limitations are placed on the deduction of automobile and home office expenses. Deductions for business meals and entertainment expenses are limited to 50 percent of actual expenditures.

Income of a partnership is allocated among the partners in accordance with the partnership agreement or, in the absence of such an agreement, governing partnership law. Deductions and credits also flow through to the individual partners. Special rules limit the amount of business or property losses that may be claimed by a limited partner of a limited partnership.

Top Marginal Rates The following table summarizes the top marginal tax rates in 1995 for an individual residing in various provinces and territories:

TOP MARGINAL RATE [1]

Province	Ordinary Income %	Dividends %[2]	Capital Gain %[3]
Alberta	46.07	31.40	34.55
British Columbia	54.16	36.57	40.62
Manitoba	50.40	36.33	37.80
New Brunswick	51.36	34.69	38.52
Newfoundland	51.33	34.66	38.50
Nova Scotia	50.30	33.97	37.73
Northwest Territories	44.37	29.96	33.28
Ontario	53.19	35.92	39.89
Prince Edward Island	50.30	33.97	37.73
Quebec	52.94	38.72	39.70
Saskatchewan	51.95	36.51	38.96
Yukon	46.55	31.43	34.91

1) The rates shown are the maximum combined federal and provincial marginal tax rates, including surtaxes and additional provincial flat taxes.
2) The rates apply to the actual amount of taxable dividends received by individuals from taxable Canadian corporations.
3) Only 75 percent of capital gains are included in taxable income. Consequently, total capital gains are effectively taxed at 75 percent of the ordinary tax rates.

DIRECTORS' FEES

Residents Directors' fees from Canada or a foreign country are taxable to a Canadian resident as employment income. Tax treaties signed by Canada generally do not allow a resident of Canada to exempt, or otherwise treat favorably, directors' fees received from a foreign (nonresident) company.

Individuals are subject to social security contributions on directors' fees in the same manner as on other employment income. It is irrelevant whether the fees are subject to social security contributions in the other country.

Nonresidents Canadian law states that a director's fee is considered to be earned where the services of the director are rendered. Thus, fees for services rendered at a specific board meeting in Canada are taxable in Canada. If the fee is related to services rendered both in and outside Canada, it may be possible to prorate the fee in proportion to the number of days that the director spent in Canada in the year. No specific guidelines for such allocations are provided, however.

Under certain tax treaties, fees are considered similar to compensation from regular employment. If the conditions exempting a nonresident from Canadian taxes on compensation from regular employment are met, the directors' fees are exempt.

INVESTMENT INCOME

Interest Interest income may be reported by the individual on the cash basis (when received), on the receivable basis (when the income is due) or on an accrual basis as it is earned during the year. Whichever method is selected, it must be applied to an investment consistently. For most investments acquired after 1989, accrued interest must be included in income annually.

The bonus or premium paid on maturity of certain investments, such as treasury bills, strip bonds or other discounted obligations, must be reported as interest income.

Dividends Special treatment is accorded dividends received by individuals from taxable Canadian corporations to recognize corporate taxes already paid on the accumulated income used as the source of funds for the dividend distribution. For these dividends, 125 percent of the actual amount received is included in income, and a credit against tax (federal and provincial combined) is allowed in an amount approximately equal to 25 percent of the cash amount of the dividend. For many Canadian-controlled private corporations and their shareholders, the result of this gross-up and dividend tax credit procedure is that the combined corporate tax on the original income and the net personal tax on the dividend is approximately equal to the tax that would have been paid on the original income had it been received directly by the individual rather than passed through the corporation.

Royalties and Rental Income Rental and royalty income are taxed as ordinary income. In computing a loss from the rental of real estate or leasing of other property, depreciation that may be claimed by an individual is generally limited to the net income determined before deducting depreciation. Therefore, the depreciation claimed by an individual cannot create or increase a rental loss.

RELIEF FOR LOSSES

In general, business losses not utilized in the year incurred may be deducted from taxable income earned in the three years preceding the year of loss or in the next seven years.

CAPITAL GAINS AND LOSSES

Seventy-five percent of the year's capital gains are included in income to the extent that amount exceeds 75 percent of capital losses for the year. This includes capital gains on real estate and personal property, regardless of whether used in a trade or business, and shares held for personal investment. Special rules apply to determine the nature of the gain or loss on the sale of depreciable property.

Capital gains on the sale of a principal residence are generally exempt from tax. Capital losses incurred on the sale of a principal residence cannot be used to reduce income for the year.

The lifetime capital gains exemption of $100,000 which applied to capital gains on most properties was eliminated in the 1994 federal budget (subject to a one time transitional election which had to be filed with the 1994 individual tax return). Gains on the sale of qualifying farm property and shares of small business corporations (see below) continue to qualify for a lifetime $500,000 exemption. However, the amount of this exemption is reduced by any amounts claimed under the now repealed general $100,000 exemption.

Qualifying Farm Property Farmers are eligible for a lifetime $500,000 exemption on the sale of qualified farm property (which includes farmland, shares of a family farm corporation or an interest in a family farm partnership). The available exemption is reduced by the amount of any exemption claimed on the disposition of any other capital property in the year or preceding years.

Shares of a Small Business Corporation Capital gains realized on the disposition of shares of a small business corporation qualify for a lifetime $500,000 capital gains exemption, provided that certain criteria are met. This exemption amount is reduced by any portion of a gain eligible for the exemptions described in the preceding paragraphs.

The use of this exemption may be restricted in a particular year because of cumulative net investment loss (CNIL) rules. Essentially, an individual's CNIL is the excess of his or her post-1987 investment expenses over investment income for those same years. To the extent an individual has a CNIL balance, the capital gains for the year eligible for the exemption are reduced.

An individual using the various capital gains exemptions may nevertheless be subject to minimum tax.

Capital Losses Capital losses, except for allowable business investment losses, not utilized in the year realized are deductible only against net capital gains realized in another year. Unused capital losses may be carried back to any of the three preceding years or carried forward indefinitely.

Allowable business investment losses (ABILs), a

special type of capital loss, are deductible against any other source of income in the year incurred. Any unused ABIL realized in a particular year is converted into a business loss and is subject to the business loss carryover rules. If a portion of the ABIL remains at the end of the seven years following the year it was realized, the loss converts back into a capital loss and may be carried forward indefinitely.

ESTATE AND GIFT TAXES

No gift tax is levied. In the year of death, the income of a deceased taxpayer includes, subject to relief provisions described below, income on an accrual basis from all sources to the date of death, including accrued capital gains and losses. Various provisions alleviate hardship caused by the taxation of income and capital gains on an accrual basis at death. Included among these provisions are the option to file a separate tax return for certain types of income and the option to have certain amounts taxed in the hands of the beneficiaries to whom they have been transferred.

SOCIAL SECURITY TAXES

In 1995, Canadian individuals are required to make government pension plan contributions up to $850.50 ($1,701 for self-employed individuals) and unemployment insurance premiums up to $1,271. Tax credits of 17 percent of the amount contributed may be taken.

The maximum monthly Canada/Quebec pension plan benefits for 1995 are:

Retirement $713.19
Disability $854.74

The maximum amounts are paid to a person at age 65. The pension amount is reduced if a person retires before reaching age 65.

Canadian resident individuals or employers may have to contribute to health care plans operated by the provinces. Most hospital bills and physicians' fees, including those for drugs and dental care in some provinces, are covered by these plans.

To provide relief from double social security taxes and assure benefit coverage, Canada has concluded a number of totalization agreements. The agreements usually apply for a maximum of two to five years. Canada has concluded totalization agreements with the following countries:

Antigua and Barbuda	Australia
Austria	Barbados
Belgium	Cyprus
Denmark	Dominica
Finland	France
Germany	Greece
Guernsey	Iceland
Ireland	Italy
Jamaica	Jersey
Luxembourg	Malta
Netherlands	Norway
Portugal	Saint Kitts-Nevis
Saint Lucia	Spain
Sweden	United States

ADMINISTRATION

Individuals are required to file tax returns if they have tax payable or if they are specifically requested to do so by the taxation authorities. In addition, because of the capital gains exemption rules, all individuals with capital gains or losses are required to file income tax returns regardless of whether tax is owed for the year.

Income tax returns generally must be filed on or before April 30 of the year following the taxation year. Individuals may be required to make quarterly installment payments if the difference between tax payable and the amount withheld at source for these individuals is greater than $2,000 (for Quebec residents, $1,200 of federal tax payable, after federal withholding) in both the current year and either of the two preceding years. The amount of the quarterly installments is based on the lesser of the liability as calculated by Revenue Canada on installment notices sent to the individual, the liability for the preceding year, or that projected for the current year, after deduction of withholdings for the current year. Any unpaid income taxes are due when the return is filed. Penalties are levied if a return is not filed on time, and interest is charged on unpaid taxes

NONRESIDENTS

Full Taxation

Nonresident individuals generally must file Canadian income tax returns if they earn employment or business income (including resource income) in Canada or if they have capital gains from dispositions of "taxable Canadian property," which includes the following property:

a) Real estate in Canada;
b) Property used in carrying on business in Canada;
c) Shares of a company resident in Canada other than a public corporation;
d) Shares of a public company resident in Canada if the nonresident alone or with related persons held at least 25 percentof the shares of any class within the preceding five years;
e) A capital interest in a trust resident in Canada;
f) An interest in a partnership having at least 50 percent of its value represented by the items listed above or resource properties (generally oil, gas and mineral rights). (There are currently proposals that would significantly expand the

look-through rule, effective after April 26, 1995 so that it would apply to shares of the capital stock of most non-Canadian corporations and interests in a trust (other than a mutual fund trust) if the 50 percent threshold was contravened.)

Canada's double tax treaties may modify or exempt nonresidents from these tax provisions.

Withholding Taxes on Other Income

Nonresidents with other sources of income from Canada are generally subject to a withholding tax of 25 percent of gross income received. Examples of income subject to withholding tax are rental income, royalties, interest, dividends, trust income, pensions and alimony. The payer must withhold and remit the appropriate amount of tax and file the required returns.

Interest payments on most government and some corporate bonds are exempt from withholding taxes. Specifically, no tax is required to be withheld on interest paid by a corporation resident in Canada to an arm's length nonresident if:

a) The indebtedness has been issued after June 23, 1975;
b) The Canadian corporation is not obliged to pay more than 25 percent of the principal amount of the indebtedness within five years from the date of issue; and
c) The interest owing on the bond is not related to the Canadian corporation's revenue, cash flow or profits.

The exemption applies even if the debt is convertible into shares, provided that the shares cannot be redeemed or canceled within five years after the issue of the debt.

Interest paid to nonresidents on foreign currency deposits at financial institutions is also exempt from withholding tax.

Canada's double tax treaties generally reduce withholding taxes on most types of passive income paid to nonresidents to 15 percent or less. Withholding taxes are generally a final tax, and tax returns are not required to be filed for this income.

DOUBLE TAX RELIEF/DOUBLE TAX TREATIES

Foreign Tax Relief

If an individual has received foreign-source income that has been subject to foreign tax, foreign tax credit relief is provided to reduce the effects of double taxation. The foreign tax credit is computed on a country-by-country basis and may be taken only to the extent of Canadian tax on the net foreign income from the particular country. Separate foreign tax credits are computed for business income and nonbusiness income. The nonbusiness foreign tax credit allowed on income from property, other than real property, is further limited to 15 percent of gross foreign income from property.

To the extent that foreign taxes paid on foreign non-business income have not been credited against Canadian federal tax, the individual may deduct the excess amount in computing income from property. The individual also has the option of deducting from property income any foreign nonbusiness income taxes paid rather than applying the amount for foreign tax credit purposes. Unused foreign business tax credits may be carried back three years and forward seven years. Unused foreign nonbusiness tax credits are not eligible for carryover.

Provincial foreign tax credit relief is also provided. The provincial credit is generally limited to the lesser of the provincial taxes on the income and the excess of any foreign taxes paid over the amount of the taxes allowed as a credit and deduction for federal income tax purposes.

Double Tax Treaties

Canada has negotiated treaties for the avoidance of double taxation and the prevention of fiscal evasion with most of the major industrialized nations and many of the less-developed nations. All treaties negotiated subsequent to 1971 generally follow the provisions of the model treaty developed by the Organization for Economic Cooperation and Development (OECD). Many treaties currently in force were negotiated prior to 1972 and may vary significantly from the OECD model treaty.

Double taxation treaties have been concluded with the following countries:

Argentina	Australia	Austria
Bangladesh	Barbados	Belgium
Brazil	Cameroon	China
Cyprus	Czech Rep.	Denmark
Dominican Rep.	Egypt	Finland
France	Germany	Guyana
Hungary	India	Indonesia
Ireland	Israel	Italy
Ivory Coast	Jamaica	Japan
Kenya	Korea	Liberia
Luxembourg	Malaysia	Malta
Mexico	Morocco	Netherlands
New Zealand	Norway	Pakistan
Papua New Guinea	Philippines	Poland
Romania	Singapore	Slovak Rep.
Spain	Sri Lanka	Sweden
Switzerland	Thailand	Trin and Tob
Tunisia	UK	US
USSR(1)	Zambia	Zimbabwe

1) Canada honors the USSR treaty with the republics of the Commonwealth of Independent States (CIS). It does not honor the treaty with Georgia or the Baltic States (Estonia, Latvia and Lithuania) because they are not part of the CIS.

Transportation & Communication

INTRODUCTION

Importers have an embarrassment of riches when choosing entry points into Canada for their goods; railways, roads and airports are internationally accessible by the dozens. Transport Canada, the government's overseeing agency, issued a budget late in 1994 which addresses passenger as well as freight issues, calling for an overhaul of transportation policy and streamlined regulations. These new policies are intended to save over C$1 billion by 1997/1998, and should bring market discipline to all transport services. Eventually, Transport Canada will come close to putting itself out of business. Instead of owning, operating and subsidizing large parts of the transportation infrastructure, it will focus on policy development and standards enforcement.

Some critics have suggested Canada's transportation system is overbuilt. For example, 94 percent of air passengers use only 26 of the more than 60 airports with international routes; 84 percent of rail traffic rolls on only 33 percent of the rail lines; and 80 percent of marine traffic passes through only 30 of the 300 public ports. Nevertheless, trucking, air and rail traffic are booming, and the entire transport system will be restructured to become more cost-effective by the end of the century.

Canada and the US are each other's top trading partners, with goods and services moving between the two countries under the rubric of the North American Free Trade Agreement (NAFTA), which took effect on January 1, 1994. Shippers are carefully examining the agreement to determine how best to take advantage of the lower tariff rates NAFTA offers. Software developers are introducing packages designed to help brokers and forwarders fill out the new, more complicated forms and to eventually automate the customs process. NAFTA has increased trade, but it has also introduced additional complexities in transportation than the previous bilateral Canadian Free Trade Agreement had.

Through the 1970s and mid-1980s, Canada was a world leader in telecommunications; the divestiture of AT&T then threw open the doors to a decade of often bewildering competition. Since 1992, Canada has adjusted to the multiple carrier environment with regulation aimed at increasing access and reducing costs. Equal access to long distance is country-wide, as is fax/modem availability. The government has set up a national advisory council to formulate and implement its "Information Superhighway" strategy, access to which is being sought by both telephone and other communications companies. Home workers who telecommute are a growing population, as are cellular phone users, and manufacturers of computer and communications hardware are enjoying a booming business.

CONTENTS

Introduction	267
Air Transportation	267
Transportation Glossary	268
Top Canadian Airports	270
Water Transport	271
Overland Transport	272
Top Canadian Ports – 1993	272
Top Ten Ports of Entry	273
Communications	275
Information Technology Revenue Growth	276

AIR TRANSPORTATION

Geography can be an obstacle as well as an opportunity. Canada's large size presents the challenge of efficiently delivering goods to remote markets. In many communities, the airport is the most accessible means to the rest of Canada and the world. Canada operates 68 major airports and nearly 150 smaller, regional air facilities; there are over 500 private strips and fields as well, though these generally have no commercial use.

TRANSPORTATION GLOSSARY

bill of lading A document issued by a carrier to a shipper, signed by the captain, agent, or owner of a vessel, furnishing written evidence regarding receipt of the goods (cargo), the conditions on which transportation is made (contract of carriage), and the engagement to deliver goods at the prescribed port of destination to the lawful holder of the bill of lading. A bill of lading is, therefore, both a receipt for merchandise and a contract to deliver it as freight.

bulk cargo Cargo that consists entirely of one commodity and is usually shipped without packaging. Examples of bulk cargo are grain, ore, and oil.

charter A charter party or charter agreement is a lease or agreement to hire an airplane, vessel, or other means of conveyance to transport goods on a designated voyage to one or more locations.

consolidation The combining of less than a container load (LCL) of cargo from a number of shippers at a centrally located point of origin by a freight consolidator, and transporting them as a single shipment to a destination point. Consolidation of cargo often results in reduced shipping rates.

containerization The practice or technique of using a boxlike device (container) in which a number of packages are stored, protected, and handled as a single unit in transit. Advantages of containerization include: less handling of cargo, more protection against pilferage, less exposure to the elements, and reduced cost of shipping.

customs broker An individual or firm licensed by a government to act for importers or exporters in handling the sequence of customs formalities and other details critical to the legal and speedy exporting and importing of goods.

freight forwarder A person engaged in the business of assembling, collection, consolidating, shipping and distributing less-than-containerload or less-than-truckload freight. Also, a person acting as agent in the transshipping of freight to or from foreign countries and the clearing of freight through customs, including full preparation of documents, arranging for shipping, warehousing, delivery and export clearance.

Incoterms 1990 A codification of international rules for the uniform interpretation of common contract clauses in export/import transactions. Developed by the International Chamber of Commerce (ICC) Paris.

intermodal transport The coordinated transport of freight, especially in connection with relatively long-haul movements using any combination of freight forwarders, piggyback, containerization, air-freight, ocean freight, assemblers, and/or motor carriers.

reefer container A controlled temperature shipping container, usually refrigerated.

roll-on, roll-off (Ro-Ro) A broad category of ships designed to load and discharge cargo which rolls on wheels. Broadly interpreted, this may include train ships, trailer ships, auto, truck and trailer ferries, and ships designed to carry military vehicles.

unitization The practice or technique of consolidating many small pieces of freight into a single unit for easier handling.

Warsaw Convention The informal name for The Convention for the Unification of Certain Rules Relating to International Carriage by Air, signed in Warsaw in 1929. An international multilateral treaty which regulates, in a uniform manner, the conditions of international transportation by air. Among other things it establishes the international liability of air carriers and establishes the limits for loss, damage, and delay.

waybill A document prepared by a transportation line at the point of a shipment, showing the point of origin, destination, route, consignor, consignee, description of shipment and amount charged for the transportation service, and forwarded with the shipment, or direct by mail, to the agent at the transfer point or waybill destination.

Definitions in this glossary are excerpted from the Dictionary of International Trade, *World Trade Press, copyright © 1994.*

After sluggish traffic in the late 1980s and early 1990s, Canada is experiencing resurgent interest in air transport which should continue to increase since the bilateral, "open skies" agreement was reached with the US in the spring of 1995. Under this agreement's provisions, international carriers using Canadian airports face an interesting choice: if they don't use their landing slots in two years, they lose them. On the cargo side, Canadian carriers can start flying to US cities immediately, while US operators have immediate access to all Canadian cities except for Toronto, Montreal and Vancouver; though that restriction will be lifted by June, 1996. US carriers and Air Canada, the major carrier for cargo and passengers, are responding by inaugurating dozens of daily nonstop flights on new routes between US and Canadian cities. Air Canada is shedding its image as a crown corporation. It's new identity is that of a lean, fully privatized enterprise with new services and alliances, and a new fleet of aircraft. This agreement has proven to be an immediate success, raising the volume of air traffic passengers between the two countries by 1.15 million in just under a year. It is also expected to lead to a 50 percent increase in traffic by the year 2000.

Transport Canada is committed to providing low-cost, efficient transportation; the planned changes should revolutionize Canada's air infrastructure. The most radical proposed changes include commercializing the air navigation system in the form of a non-profit corporation and offering regional, local, and small airports with scheduled passenger traffic to provincial and local governments, airport commissions, and other interests. This shift to local management should lower costs and raise efficiency.

Airports

The largest airport for cargo operations is the Lester B. Pearson International Airport outside Toronto. Approximately 40 percent of all Canadian cargo traffic passes through Pearson on its way to 60 nations. Its cargo volume outpaces its west coast rival, Vancouver International.

Vancouver serves as Canada's business connection to Asian markets. Its average yearly cargo volume is 130,000 metric tons. International cargo has placed Vancouver International among the 100 busiest airports in the world. Current construction projects include adding two cargo terminals and 70,800 square meters of warehouse space. The airport is also building a new terminal with 15 wide-body gates, increased customs inspection stations and 120 customer check-in counters. A parallel runway will increase Vancouver's current annual aircraft movement capacity by approximately 150,000 planes. Just finished is a 65 meter control tower which will make Vancouver the first airport in Canada to use a category-III instrument landing system.

Shipments and passengers moving into or out of eastern Canada via Quebec may choose between Mirabel or Dorval international airports in Montreal. Aircraft weighing under 17 metric tons can unload at Dorval, but anything larger must move to the principal cargo airport of Mirabel.

Air Carriers

Canada's aviation industry is primarily made up of two major airlines, Air Canada and Canadian Airlines International (other smaller carriers are described below). Fully privatized, Air Canada ships cargo to 21 foreign countries; Canadian Airlines serves 17. Canadian Airlines' cargo operations, Canadian Air Cargo, moved 555 freight ton-kilometers in 1992, making it the 28th-largest cargo carrier in the world. In addition to a domestic cargo service, the airline offers a guaranteed priority service and express overnight, door-to-door delivery. It operates regularly scheduled connections between Canada and destinations in Japan, Southeast Asia, the US and South America, including links to New Zealand, Hong Kong, Mexico City, Paris, Australia, Sao Paulo and Milan.

The following list of the country's air carriers, including a description of the cities they serve and a statement, when applicable, of their status as of 1995:

- Air Alliance: A Quebec-based regional carrier, 75 percent owned by Air Canada, serves 12 destinations in Canada, plus Boston and New York.
- Air Alma: This Quebec carrier serves Montreal and three other Canadian cities.
- Air Atlantic: Based in Newfoundland and feeding Canadian Airlines International, this company may require considerable help to stay in operation.
- Air BC: The Air Canada Connector serves 26 destinations in western Canada, plus Seattle and Portland.
- Air Canada: The largest Canadian carrier, experiencing considerable growth in recent years. New routes include Seoul, Osaka and Hong Kong, with a total of six Pacific routes. This airline offers the most luxurious air travel in the country, including sleeper seats, personal televisions, satellite telephone and fax service by combining first and business class into "premium business class."
- Air Club: A new charter carrier, based in Toronto.
- Air Creebec: Headquartered in Val d'Or, Quebec, Air Creebec serves several points with a fleet of ten craft.
- Air Inuit: This Montreal-based carrier includes a dozen various-sized planes.

- Air Manitoba: Out of Winnipeg, this line flies six craft to nine points.
- Air Nova: A subsidiary of Air Canada, this five-year-old line flies to the Atlantic Maritime provinces, Quebec, Ottawa, Boston and New York.
- Air Ontario: Serving 13 destinations in Canada and to Baltimore, Cleveland and Hartford, recently adding Columbus and Indianapolis. Seventy-five percent owned by Air Canada.
- Air Transit: This charter service has a fleet of nine craft to a wide variety of destinations.
- Athabaska: Based in Prince Albert, this carrier flied to eight cities.
- Bearskin: Thirty-two aircraft fly out of Ontario to an expanding network.
- Calm Air: One of six Canadian partners, this Manitoba-based carrier serves cities in Manitoba and the Northwest Territories.
- Canadian Airlines: Parent PWA Corporation, which is in the process of changing its name to Canadian Airlines Corporation, is utilizing a large cash injection from American Airlines to financially restructure and increase profitability. CAI partner American plans to share 64 flights a day.
- Canadian Regional: The Canadian Airlines International subsidiary flies throughout the western half of Canada and to several US points with a fleet of 39.
- Central Mountain Air: This British Columbia-based carrier filed for protection from creditors in June, 1994, but continues to fly to 12 destinations.
- First Air: Based in Carp, Ontario, this is one of Canada's larger carriers.
- Harbour Air: From Richmond, British Columbia, Harbour flies to several cities in western Canada.
- Helijet: This helicopter airline flies five aircraft between Vancouver and Victoria.
- Inter-Canadien: A Montreal-based Canadian partner flies nine craft to 24 destinations.
- Jetall: This Ontario carrier operates scheduled freight service to 23 points in Canada and the US.
- Kenn Borek Air: From Calgary, this carrier flies to several northern points.
- Labrador Airways: This carrier has 15 craft of various sizes and flies out of Goose Bay.
- NorOntair: Based in Sault Ste. Marie, this Ontario carrier holds a marketing agreement with Air Ontario and flies six craft.
- NWT Air: This firm is based in Yellowknife and flies four craft.
- Pacific Coastal: Seven craft fly to four points out of Vancouver.

TOP CANADIAN AIRPORTS
(with total aircraft movements in thousands)

Airports	1993*	% Change
Lester B. Pearson Int'l	178,700	2
Vancouver Int'l	166,565	2
Calgary Int'l	119,055	4
Montreal/Dorval	108,200	6
St. Hubert	101,881	7
Boundary Bay	100,502	26
Victoria Int'l	99,296	17
Toronto/Buttonville	87,014	2
Ottawa Int'l	86,636	6
Winnipeg	80,976	3
Abbotsford	80,643	26
Quebec	77,035	8
Edmonton	67,777	7
Hamilton City	66,281	8
Springbank	62,775	13
Halifax Int'l	161,962	6
St. Honore	60,668	16
Toronto Island	57,875	2
London	55,309	12
Villeneuve	53,142	6
St. Andrews	50,633	9
Saskatoon	48,421	20
Yellowknife	44,180	26
North Bay	43,053	23
Moncton	37,451	13

*through July 1995

Source: Statistics Canada

- Perimeter: Based in Winnipeg, this carrier flies 21 craft to several small cities.
- Provincial: The Newfoundland carrier's fleet includes 17 craft with scheduled service to 13 cities.
- Trans Capital: A new charter service, launched in the summer of 1994.

---

*Port facility information in this section is excerpted from Ports of the World (15th ed.), copyright © 1994 CIGNA Property and Casualty Co., reprinted with permission from CIGNA Property and Casualty Companies.

WATER TRANSPORT

Coastlines on the oceans, as well as connections to the US across the Great Lakes, have made shipping an important mode of reaching Canadian markets. Reflecting US and Canadian trade interdependence, Canadian ports move the largest proportion of their tonnage either to or from their southern neighbor. Although NAFTA has increased road and rail traffic, most Canadian shipping moves east-west through Canada, Europe and Asia.

Ports *

Vancouver, British Columbia In the third quarter of 1993, Vancouver moved 6.3 million metric tons of cargo, nearly 98 percent of which was international. Vancouver handles an average of 3,000 foreign vessels from more than 40 nations every year. During the 1993 third-quarter period, the port surpassed the tonnage of its closest competitor, the Port of Sept-Iles in Quebec, by more than three million metric tons.

Bulk commodities, such as coal and grain, make up over three-quarters of the tonnage moving through Vancouver. In 1992, the port ranked just below Houston and Hampton Roads as the third-busiest bulk port in Canada and the United States. Since it focuses on bulk shipments, the port is trying to improve its container-handling ability to capture more of the shipments moving through Seattle and Tacoma. It is finishing a new container terminal to double its container-handling ability, which will total approximately one million TEUs a year when complete in the fall of 1996.

Transportation Service—Truck, rail and barge.

Cargo Storage—Port area has sufficient covered and open storage facilities.

Special Cranes—Heavy lift capacity, 300 tons (floating crane). Container, seven to 60 ton capacity.

Air Cargo—Vancouver International Airport: 16 km. outside the city.

Cargo Handling—Containerized, bulk and general cargo can all be handled adequately through Vancouver. Coal and grain are among Vancouver's principal imports.

General—Temperatures range from -4 C to 32 C, and annual rainfall is roughly 110 cms. Vancouver Port Corporation has launched a development program entitled Port 2010, a 20-year plan designed to meet the future challenges of trade.

Montreal, Quebec

Transportation Service—Truck and rail.

Cargo Storage—Excellent open areas and shed facilities at port.

Special Cranes—Heavy lift capacity is 258 tons. Container cranes are available.

Air Cargo—Dorval International and Mirabel Airports serve this major transportation hub.

Cargo Handling—This multinational port boasts five full-scale container terminals, three dry bulk terminals, berths for handling liquid bulk, and two grain elevators. Over the last decade, Montreal, Canada's top container port, has handled an average of more than 21 million tons of highly diversified cargo annually. Special ramps are available to accommodate Ro-Ro cargo.

General—This year-round port experiences a wide range of climactic conditions with temperatures ranging from -33 C to 36 C. Annual rainfall averages 95 cms.

Quebec, Quebec

Transportation Service—Truck and rail.

Cargo Storage—Open: Storage is ample. Covered: 59,125 sq. m. including three insulated/heated sheds.

Special Cranes—Heavy lift capacity, 440 tons. Also, 5 bulk loading towers are available for ore and bulk cargo.

Air Cargo—Ancienne Lorette Airport: 19 km. Provides cargo connections to Eastern Canada.

Cargo Handling—All cargo can be handled through Quebec; however, the majority of traffic through the port is handled by Quebec's eight tanker berths, ore and bulk terminals and Ro-Ro offloading points.

General—Winters are very cold, summers warm; annual rainfall is roughly 100 cms. Quebec enjoys a 12-month navigation season.

Halifax, Nova Scotia

Transportation Service—Truck and rail.

Cargo Storage—Covered: 61,450 sq. m. with over 71,000 sq. m. of open storage.

Special Cranes—Seven gantry cranes, as well as floating cranes and mobile heavy lift cranes to 270 ton capacity.

Air Cargo—Halifax International Airport: 35 km.

Cargo Handling—Containerized and general cargo are handled by existing port equipment. Halifax's principal imports include crude oil, automobiles and refined petroleum. Special handling goes through the port's 9 tanker berths and numerous Ro-Ro offloading points.

General—Halifax is an all-weather port, free of ice in the winter. Both container terminals have undergone extensions to berthing facilities.

Saint John, New Brunswick

Transportation Service—Truck and rail.

Cargo Storage—Adequate covered and open storage facilities available.

Special Cranes—Heavy lift capacity, 300 tons. Container, three with 40 ton capacity.

Air Cargo—St. John Airport: approximately eight kilometers.

Cargo Handling—Containerized, bulk and general cargo can all be adequately handled by existing port equipment. One grain elevator, five tanker terminal berths and Ro-Ro offloading points are available for specialized cargo.

General—St. John serves as the eastern terminus of Trans Canadian Highway, which runs from Newfoundland, and inland transportation routing is fairly good. Heavy snowfall and high winds exist from January through April.

Great Lakes marine shipping is carried out primarily by Canada's principal lake ports: Hamilton, Toronto, Windsor and Thunder Bay. The lakes are connected to the Atlantic Ocean through the St. Lawrence Seaway, a 3,500 km.-long water passage operational only eight months of the year due to winter freezing.

Hamilton, Ontario

Transportation Service—Truck and rail.

Cargo Storage—Covered: 59,272 sq. m. Open: Tanks storage for oils, open spaces for coal, sand and similar bulk commodities.

Special Cranes—Heavy lift capacity is 200 tons. Container, one with 68 ton capacity.

Air Cargo—Toronto International Airport: 48 km. east; Hamilton Airport: 16 km., provides cargo connections to Ottawa and Montreal.

Cargo Handling—Containerized, bulk and general cargo are adequately handled by existing port equipment. Among Hamilton's principal imports are machinery, motor vehicles and parts, petroleum and steel.

General—This port is open from April to December. Temperatures range from -8 C to 30 C, and annual rainfall is 90 cms.

Toronto, Ontario

Transportation Service—Truck and rail.

Cargo Storage—Covered: 320,000 sq. m. Ample open storage area available.

Special Cranes—Heavy lift, one fixed crane with 300 ton capacity. Various container cranes are available.

Air Cargo—Toronto International Airport, a major cargo facility: 35 km.

Cargo Handling—All normal cargo traffic can be handled. Toronto has ore and bulk cargo facilities, tanker terminal and Ro-Ro platforms for specialized cargo handling.

General—Winter lows can reach -20 C and summers are warm. Annual rainfall is 80 cms.

Windsor, Ontario

Transportation Service—Truck and rail.

Cargo Storage—Covered: 1,113,000 sq. m. (86,000 sq. m. open storage area).

Special Cranes—Two mobile, 110 and 125 ton capacity.

Cargo Handling—Aggregate loads, grain, lumber, steel, and salt.

TOP CANADIAN PORTS – 1993
(Hundreds of Tons)

Port		% Change 93/92
Vancouver	14,123	0
Sept Iles Pte. Noire	6,999	9
Montreal	5,544	14
Saint John	4,526	1
Hamilton	3,961	11
Quebec/Levis	3,719	15
Thunder Bay	3,705	21
Halifax	3,600	4
Nanticoke	2,576	16

Source: Statistics Canada

Thunder Bay, Ontario

Transportation Service—Truck and rail.

Cargo Storage—Adequate open areas.

Special Cranes—Various container cranes are available.

Cargo Handling—All-weather covered conveyers with 1,500,000 ton storage loading rate up to 8,000 tons per hour. Cargoes include petroleum, grain, coal, potash and general cargoes.

Shipping Firms

Although Canadian ports are open to foreign steamship lines, three domestic firms handle much of the country's national trade. CAST offers sailing services between Montreal; Zeebrugge, Belgium; and Felixstowe, UK. It also runs a North America/Mediterranean service between Montreal and Naples, Livorno and Genoa, Italy. Canada Maritime Agency runs container services calling at Montreal, Felixstowe, Hamburg, Antwerp, and Le Havre. Its Mediterranean rotation stops at Livorno, Genoa, Valencia, Cadiz and Lisbon. Canada Steamship Line is active in the translake trade, and also calls at US, European and Mexican ports. All three lines are based in Montreal, Quebec.

OVERLAND TRANSPORT

Canada's infrastructure for intermodal transport offers many choices, with sometimes too little emphasis in the past for maintaining its millions of kilometers of railways and roads. Highway investment shows Canada ranking behind the UK, Germany, the US, Australia, Italy and Spain in terms of expenditures per 1,000 km of highways; yet most of the C$400 billion US annual export volume goes to Canada by truck. Therefore, Transport Canada has made reorganization in these sectors a top priority.

Railways retain a romantic patina for most Canadians, evoking shining steel bands pinned with a golden spike lining the countryside. As far as it goes, this picture is accurate, but it fails to address falling profits and outmoded attitudes towards the economic reality of modern day transport.

Canadians are rising to these serious challenges. Overland modes are being linked in new ways; computer information on rail and truck trade between the US and Canada will soon be available to the public on disk from the US Department of Transportation. The customs clearance between these countries and Mexico is moving toward complete automation. Even the transportation players in North American commerce are moving into changing roles: operators, coordinators, and operator/coordinators. Operators are asset-based companies that have made significant investments in providing the infrastructure to transport and warehouse North American trade. Coordinators tend to be non-asset-based companies functioning as middlemen in branch offices throughout North America. Operator/coordinators combine asset-based operations with services purchased from operators. Traders who ship overland can be certain of two things: they have many carrier choices, and the current infrastructure will radically change by the close of the century.

Trucking NAFTA at first generated more heat than light, but one of the chief transportation sectors to alter as a result was the trucking industry. The current infrastructure lends itself more readily to increased truck transport than air carriers, and trucking is the most responsive and pervasive part of the transportation system; almost 80 percent of all money spent on freight transported on the North American continent is earned by trucking firms. The primary market here is US/Canada traffic, since most Atlantic to Pacific shipping is handled by rail. Canadian regulatory regimes present an advantage over those of its southern neighbor, permitting larger and heavier vehicles and a route system which enables an eight-axle, 30 metric ton truck to travel from coast to coast.

Another set of possibilities provides for alternative ownership. While NAFTA permits foreign ownership of trucking companies, that portion of the Act doesn't go into effect until 1997; since most trade links were already formed, NAFTA opens future opportunities.

The curve of trucking commerce does not lead unfailingly upward. Ever since the mid-1980s, Canada has experienced precipitous drops in labor and equipment. A driver shortage has begun to grow over since 1993, with turnover rates hovering between 100 and 125 percent. Ontario needs at least 2,000 drivers to reach maximum transport capacity by the end of 1996. There's a one-year waiting period for trailers and nearly eighteen months for highway tractors. These statistics do not reinforce the feeling that trucking can provide levels of service and performance shippers currently demand, although that can be seen as good news for investors in Canadian trucking; Canadian truckers now carry 80 percent of Ontario-US trade, a complete reversal since the late 1980s.

The problems described above are being addressed. Washington DC has responded with a Driver Training & Development Alliance forum in 1995 which attracted nearly 200 managers and executives from all segments of the US and Canadian trucking community. This meeting was designed to lay the groundwork for developing industry practices in driver selection, training, and development. The forum was the first time the trucking industry put aside its rivalries and partisan attitudes to address this threat to its future. Continued efforts like these are not only logical but hopeful.

With nearly 70 points of entry along the 6,400 km. Canada/US border for trucks, the dominant concern within the industry is to move goods fastest at the lowest cost. The table "Top Ten Ports of Entry" contains city names unfamiliar to most Canadians and Americans, but access creates its own demands. Buffalo, around 160 km. south of Toronto, is connected by bridge to Fort Erie, Ontario. A nearby span between Lewiston, New York, and Niagara Falls, Ontario, also figures into the Buffalo total.

TOP TEN PORTS OF ENTRY

Number of Trucks	Port Shipments
Buffalo, NY	1,217,092*
Detroit, MI	876,376
Port Huron, MI	479,499
Champlain, NY	367,256
Blaine, WA	264,691
Alexandria Bay, NY	146,200
Pembina, ND	145,086*
Highgate Springs, VT	113,698
Sweetgrass, MT	100,649*
Derby Line, VT	69,831*

* includes rail shipments

Source: US Customs Service

Detroit has both a tunnel and a bridge which link it to Windsor, Ontario. Port Huron, nearly 100 km. north of Detroit, is heavily industrialized and companies from each country operate plants in the other's territory. Champlain, New York, is where Interstate 87 joins Quebec's route 10, right on the heavily traveled New York-Montreal corridor.

The crossing at Blaine, Washington, funnels traffic between the Pacific Northwest and Canada's western provinces. North of Syracuse, New York, the 1000 Islands Bridge over the St. Lawrence River near Alexandria Bay carries truck traffic from the Middle Atlantic states destined for Toronto and central Ontario. Pembina (an Ojibwa Indian word for summer berry) sits in the northeast corner of North Dakota, 250 km. north of Fargo, where I-29 connects to Saskatchewan's main route into Winnipeg, 120 km. north—the hub of Central Canada.

Highgate Springs and Derby Line, Vermont, are New England gateways to the Atlantic provinces of Canada and to Quebec. Sweetgrass, Montana, sits at the north end of Interstate 15, directly south of Calgary and Edmonton, with Salt Lake, Denver and Houston to the south. Sweetgrass also is a checkpoint for traffic headed towards eastern cities such as Chicago, and from the Alaska Highway, which ends at Edmonton.

The table above also implies unprecedented levels of cooperation between the historically opposed trucking and railroad lines. The two industries, faced with expanding revenue possibilities, are increasingly treating each other as partners. Motor carriers offering service between the US and Canada, either direct or through cross-border partnerships, include Celadon Trucking Services; Central Transport; Challenger Motor Freight; Contract Freighters; J. B. Hunt Transport, Inc.; Schneider National Inc.; and Yellow Freight System.

Railroads For over a century, Canada's railroad system has often acted as the glue which has held the country's provinces together, but recent demand has begun to strain rail capacity. The railroads possess sufficient north-south track for the near term; what's needed is retooling for greater efficiency. CP Rail System (formerly Canadian Pacific Railway) was responsible for westward expansion across the nation, and today it and the Canadian National Railways (CN) form the backbone of transcontinental cargo transportation in Canada. Both lines are based in Montreal.

CP Rail System, the third-largest North American railway network, operates lines through eight Canadian provinces with connections in 19 US states. Linked to Soo Line Railroad and the Delaware and Hudson Railroad, CP's system reaches as far south as Louisville, Kentucky and Kansas City, Missouri. It also has connections to Washington, DC, Philadelphia, New York, Boston and Buffalo. Nearly 70 percent of CP's cargo is made up of bulk commodities, primarily grain and coal, but also fertilizers and chemicals. Other commodities moving aboard CP trains include forest products, manufactured goods, and automobile parts and equipment. Its intermodal operations offer doublestack service from Vancouver to Montreal via Chicago and Toronto. Doublestack trains also run between Saint Johns, Boston, New York, Baltimore, Philadelphia and interior Canada.

While CP Rail Systems is Canada's major privately owned railroad, the other large railroad is Canadian National Railway, the largest federally-owned company. In addition to its east-west network across Canada, CN developed connections through interline arrangements with other North American rail lines, including Burlington Northern and CSX Intermodal, to provide seamless service into the US and Mexico. It operates a direct rail link in Chicago, with additional freight exchange points with US rail lines in Detroit. CN also offers doublestack service across Canada and into the US.

To improve its services, CN is implementing a C$2 billion, five-year spending plan to replace older sections of track, widen tunnels and replace bridges to accommodate doublestack trains, add new rail equipment, and update intermodal facilities. In April, 1995, CN opened the mile-long St. Clair River tunnel. The C$140 million project drew heated opposition from CP, which uses a different gateway into the US. The border cities of Detroit and Windsor, Ontario, wanted the tunnel built near them, but President Clinton deemed the tunnel as being "in the national interest." The tunnel will lower transit time by 25 percent between Toronto and Chicago, improving on-time delivery from 65 to 90 percent and putting the railway on a competitive basis with truck prices and service levels.

CN is shifting its focus from the icons of long steel rails and powerful engines to providing reliable and economical transportation. Privatization, a thorny issue as Canadians lose their affection for big government, drives these reforms.

Perhaps the most promising sign of much-needed change in this sector is the reestablishment of short line rails. Since 1986, eight new railways have been created, saving more than 1600 km. of track and more than 200 jobs. The first railway to rapidly expand in this area, Central Western Railway, has been thriving. RailTex, Goderich-Exeter Railway (GER), Iron Road Railways (IRR) and the Cape Breton and Central Nova Scotia line (CB&CNS) are demonstrating small-scale but steady growth on routes under 320 km.

Railway lines with service between Canada and the US are: Burlington Northern Railroad; CN North America; CP Rail System; Conrail; CSX Corp.;

Norfolk Southern Corp.; Santa Fe Railway; Southern Pacific Lines; and Union Pacific Railroad.

Rail transport is changing, especially in light of new intermodal opportunities, but it will have to accelerate in Canada, the US and Mexico if today's railroad magnates seek to build a north-south system to rival the transcontinental marvel created by their 19th-century predecessors.

COMMUNICATIONS

Telecommunications

In 1962, a consortium of Canadian companies was formed to bring about a more competitive telecommunications industry to Canada. These companies formed what is now known as the Canadian Business Telecommunications Alliance (CTBA). The CTBA and other groups have lobbied over the past thirty years for more competition, and in 1992, the Canadian Radiotelevision and Telecommunications Commission announced changes in long-distance competition. Rates dropped almost immediately, and today, an average long distance call in Canada costs about 40 percent less than two years ago.

New products and services are also becoming available to the Canadian consumer. In 1993, the national Telecommunications Act replaced he telecommunications section of the old Railway Act, helping to reduce costs in most every province.

Competition is increasing in Canada, though further changes still need to be made. Saskatchewan's SaskTel is still owned by the provincial government, but for the most part, Canadian telecommunications is privatizing and gaining group. The federal government has now created an advisory council for the information superhighway, and equal access to long-distance services is available nationally.

Local, long distance and international service are generally reliable and available from several providers, although the nine largest phone companies account for 85 to 90 percent of the C$8 billion market total. Since long distance competition opened in 1992, between 160 and 270 alternative carriers have registered with the CRTC to offer a range of services. These companies lease telephone lines and switching equipment in bulk from the Bell networks and then resell chunks of that service to customers at discount rates. Canadian residential consumers have therefore been bombarded with print and television ads, and door-to-door sales pitches.

The trend toward deregulation attempts to keep pace with the rapid development of telephone hardware and software, including: technology "convergence" that will allow computer users to transmit voice, data and video over phone lines; and wireless communications that allow individuals to take their phones with them and number portability that permits the user to take the phone number with them as well.

The largest carriers—including the Stentor companies, Unitel Communications, and more recently, Sprint Canada, can tailor communications packages for all market sizes. Other carriers target the mid-sized or small clients' needs, offering connections within a defined radius from a major city. The carrier can offer a specifically-designed package linking a Canadian center and a single foreign city, such as connecting Canadians with an interest in doing business in Hong Kong. In the near future, a forestry company could tap into a "forestry industry line."

Availability of new services affects the shape of work. Currently, about three million Canadians work at home (compared to 41 million across North America), which creates savings in real estate, higher productivity and increased morale among employees. One study suggests professionals will account for 13 percent of the expected 15.4 million mobile workers in the US by the year 2000.

Telecommunications Equipment In response to the new mobility, growth in the information technology sector is soaring: In Canada, there are 1.4 million cellular telephone users (growing at an annual rate of 30 percent) and about 650,000 pagers users (growing at an annual rate of 15 to 20 percent). Technological devices such as microprocessors, keyboards and flat screens are moving toward miniaturization while personal computers, hard drives, modems and networks are moving toward portability. Many companies offer products which provide an impressive array of services:

- Ark Telecom has developed the Act-One Satellite Communications Terminal, which simultaneously supports telephony, data, fax, imaging, video and audio. The terminal operates in hubless, full mesh networks while providing leased, switched, and shared services.
- Cylink's Access Control System is a complete management control of asynchronous dial-in and dial-out access. It also manages groups of portable and home computers, remote offices, dial-in routers and bridges, and RS-232 devices.
- Exfor E. O. Engineering offers the industry's first touch-screen mini-OTDR, the Fiber Tool Box. Its features include complete OTDR functions, power meter, visual fault locator, and the DocuNet Trace Management System.
- Optimal Performance from Network General Canada is intelligent software for the optimization, capacity planning, and design of enterprise networks.

Electronic Information Services

Several types of electronic information services are available for voice and data in Canada, although the market is new and not available in all areas, especially outside major cities. These range from simple calls to a prerecorded message to interactive databases which allow an individual to access information or execute a transaction. Electronic mail, voice mail, and fax mailboxes are widespread transmission choices. The major phone companies are creating long-term strategies to broaden the technology base for developing new equipment, with the overall goal of transforming the telephone, cable, and computer networks into a fully integrated system. In April of 1994, a plan was announced to invest C$8.5 billion over ten years to bring fiber optic cable lines to 90 percent of Canadian homes. In Quebec, a conglomerate consisting of six Canadian companies and a US media company, known as Universal Bi-directional Interactive, is planning to deliver interactive services to 80 percent of Quebec households by 2002.

Convergence, one of the communication industry's favorite buzzwords, describes a time when telecommunications, cable and broadcasting, computers and software merge into a single technology. No such system currently exists, but a large part of this puzzle, called Computer Telephony Integration (CTI) is in place. Businesses who want their best customers to avoid the delays of voice mail flag relevant names; when a call comes in, the computer screen brings up the customer's file automatically. Any company using 800 telephone numbers can, with a CTI system, instantly recognize those calling from long distance and bump them to the front of the line. Several Canadian firms are offering the interface systems, and their use is spreading rapidly.

Audiotext Services Development here is contradictory. Bell Canada, the first provider for videotext in Canada, withdrew its Alex service from the market. According to the company, information service providers were reluctant to offer their services through Alex until it had established a large subscriber base, while subscribers were reluctant to use it until more service providers had signed up to offer their services. This situation should sort itself out in a couple of years, when demand increases.

Videoconferencing This concept remains embryonic, with interesting possibilities. BC Tel Advanced Communications has launched videoconferencing and local area network (LAN) interconnection services in one of the first commercial applications of asynchronous transfer mode (ATM) architecture. Other companies are attracted by the opportunity to utilize excess bandwidth on private networks, locate cost savings, and recognize the need for global groups to work together. There are no major problems with the technology, equipment costs are declining, and consultants and associations are beginning to support the technology. Calling time and rooms have to be booked in advance, but these scheduling problems may be solved by desktop videoconferencing.

The Internet Since 1990, Canada's partnerships in business, education, research, the arts and cultural communities, and government have focused on building an information highway second to none. Consumers have two options when entering this high-speed communications network. They can use television and risk becoming "video vegetables," or the more cerebral access through personal computers. The first offers a passive response; with the second, the consumer controls the direction of the superhighway.

The Canadian backbone network has ten regional Internets, one in each province. Canadians are entering the Information Superhighway in ways different than their southern neighbors. More than half prefer to receive education services, although the most popular features for 18 to 34-year-olds are home banking and movies on demand. Online banking is the next most popular general use, followed by electronic tax filing and news. The least desirable services are real estate listings, video games and home shopping.

Because the Internet is loosely built around a US government research network, it originates at research facilities and on university campuses; Canadian businesses are relative newcomers. Advertising and marketing on the Internet is a delicate matter, since it is strictly against "netiquette" to mass mail to Internet addresses. Even though the advertising cannot come to users, users can go to the ads. The challenge is in drawing users to the sites. One solution involves creating what amounts to on-line shopping malls.

Canadian businesses can enter the Internet through major commercial on-line services like America Online or Compuserve, but these companies offer only limited access to features like the World Wide Web (WWW), FTP, and Telnet. Other services primarily provide Internet access, but may

---

INFORMATION TECHNOLOGY REVENUE GROWTH - 1993

Data Communications	18.3%
Voice Equipment	17.4%
Software & Services	10.7%
Single-user systems	7.7%
Mainframes	-36.8%

Source: International Data Corporation (Canada) Inc.

also have other files, databases and services available. Because their main emphasis is on Internet connections, these may be the best choice for businesses looking for full access to the Internet. Delphi is the leading provider of this type. Other companies, like Netcom or Alternet, will provide a full connection, some technical support, and perhaps user software. These may be less expensive for heavy Internet users, but novices are probably better off beginning with the larger, user-friendly on-line service providers.

Important Addresses

CONTENTS

Introduction	279
Government	**280**
Government Agencies	280
Provincial Government Trade Offices	280
Embassies and Trade Offices	281
Foreign Embassies in Canada	286
Trade Organizations	**289**
General Business and Trade Organizations	289
Provincial Trade Organizations	289
Foreign Business Organizations in Canada	291
Industry-Specific Associations	291
Financial Institutions	**294**
Banks	294
Stocks and Commodities	296
Insurance	296
Services	**297**
Market Research Firms	297
Advertising	297
Legal Services	298

INTRODUCTION

The following addresses have been gathered from a wide range of sources. We have attempted to verify each address at press time; however, it is likely that some of the information has already changed. Inclusion of an organization, product, or service does not imply a recommendation or endorsement.

Unless otherwise noted, all addresses are in Canada; the international country code for calling Canada is [1] and is not shown in the Canadian address listings. Area codes are given in parentheses, while non-Canadian country codes are in square brackets. Refer to the chapter "Business Travel" for details on making telephone calls in Canada.

Canadian addresses normally follow a fairly standard format. Names of buildings may be used but are not common. The suite, office, or floor number (often called "Level") is given on the same line as the street address, either before or after the street address. The city is on the next line, followed by the state name or abbreviation, and the four-digit post code.

Some common elements and abbreviations in Canadian addresses follow:

States & Territories

AB	Alberta
BC	British Columbia
MB	Manitoba
NB	New Brunswick
NT	Northwest Territories
NS	Nova Scotia
ON	Ontario
PE	Prince Edward Island
PQ	Quebec
SK	Saskatchewan
YT	Yukon Territories

GOVERNMENT

GOVERNMENT AGENCIES

Canadian International Trade Tribunal
Standard Life Centre
333 Laurier Ave. West
Ottawa, ON K1A 0G7
Tel: (613) 993-4601 Fax: (613) 998-4783

Department of Agriculture and Agri-Food
Market & Industry Services Branch
Sir John Carling Bldg., 5th Fl.
930 Carling Ave.
Ottawa, ON K1A 0C5
Tel: (613) 759-1000, 995-9554, 995-8963 Fax: (613) 759-6643, 992-1559, 996-5911

Department of Fisheries and Oceans
200 Kent St.
Ottawa, ON K1A 0E6
Tel: (613) 993-0999 Fax: (613) 990-1866, 7292
Internet WWW site: http://192.139.141.30

Department of Foreign Affairs and International Trade
Lester B. Pearson Bldg.
125 Sussex Drive
Ottawa, ON K1A 0G2
Tel: (613) 944-4000, 995-1851, 996-9134 Fax: (613) 944-6500, 996-3443, 952-3904
Internet WWW site: http://www.dfait-maeci.gc.ca

Department of Health
Journal Tower South, Suite 1406
365 Laurier Ave. West
Ottawa, ON K1A 0K2
Tel: (613) 992-4581 Fax: (613) 996-0364

Department of Human Resources Development
140 promenade du Portage
Ottawa-Hull, ON K1A 0J9
Tel: (819) 994-6013 Fax: (819) 953-3981

Department of Indian Affairs and Northern Development
Les Terrasses de la Chaudière
10 Wellington St.
Ottawa, ON K1A 0H4
Tel: (613) 995-5586 Fax: (613) 997-1587

Department of Natural Resources
580 Booth St.
Ottawa, ON K1A 0E4
Tel: (613) 995-3065 Fax: (613) 996-9094

Department of Western Economic Diversification
Centennial Towers
200 Kent St., 8th Fl.
PO Box 2128, Stn D
Ottawa, ON K1P 5W3
Tel: (613) 952-9378 Fax: (613) 957-1155

Environment Canada
Terrasses de la Chaudiere
11 Wellington St., 28th Fl.
Hull, PQ K1A 0H3
Tel: (819) 997-2800, 1441 Fax: (819) 953-2225
Internet WWW site: http://www.doe.ca

Finance Canada
International Trade & Finance Branch
Esplanade Laurier
140 O'Connor St.
Ottawa, ON K1A 0G5
Tel: (613) 992-1573, 996-7861 Fax: (613) 996-8404, 995-5176
Internet WWW site: http://www.fin.gc.ca/fin-eng.html

Health Canada
Brooke Claxton Bldg.
Ottawa, ON K1A 0K9
Tel: (613) 957-2991 Fax: (613) 941-5366

Industry Canada
International Business
C. D. Howe Bldg.
235 Queen St.
Ottawa, ON K1A 0H5
Tel: (613) 954-3508, 2788 Fax: (613) 954-0540,1894,5716
Internet WWW site: http://info.ic.gc.ca/ic-data/

Public Works and Government Services Canada
Place du Portage, Phase III
11 Laurier St.
Hull, PQ K1A 0S5
Tel: (819) 956-2300, (613) 736-2400 Fax: (819) 994-8404, (613) 998-9603

Revenue Canada – Commercial Systems Operations and Taxation
Headquarters Bldg.
875 Heron Road
Ottawa, ON K1A 0L8
Tel: (613) 954-6844, 957-3503 Fax: (613) 957-7476

Revenue Canada – Customs and Excise
Connaught Bldg.
MacKenzie Ave.
Ottawa, ON K1A 0L5
Tel: (613) 995-2960, 957-9192 Fax: (613) 952-6608, 957-9039

Solicitor-General Canada
Sir Wilfrid Laurier Bldg.
340 Laurier Ave. West
Ottawa, ON K1A 0P8
Tel: (613) 991-2799 Fax: (613) 993-7062

Standards Council of Canada
45 O'Connor St., Suite 1200
Ottawa, ON K1P 6N7
Tel: (613) 238-3222 Fax: (613) 995-4564

Statistics Canada
Statistics Canada Regional Reference Centres
R. H. Coats Bldg.
Tunney's Pasture
120 Parkdale Ave.
Ottawa, ON K1A 0T6
Tel: (613) 951-8116 Fax: (613) 951-0581
Internet WWW site: http://www.statcan.ca

Transport Canada
Transport Canada Bldg.
Place de Ville
330 Sparks St.
Ottawa, ON K1A 0N5
Tel: (613) 990-2309 Fax: (613) 995-0351, 996-9622

PROVINCIAL GOVERNMENT TRADE OFFICES

Alberta
Alberta Economic Development & Tourism
Tourism, Trade & Investment
Commerce Place
10155 – 102 St.
Edmonton, AB T5J 4L6
Tel: (403) 427-2280 Fax: (403) 427-1700

British Columbia
Office of the Premier
British Columbia Trade Development Corporation
999 Canada Place, Suite 730
Vancouver, BC V6C 3E1
Tel: (604) 844-1900 Fax: (604) 660-2457

IMPORTANT ADDRESSES 281

Manitoba
Manitoba Trading Corporation
155 Carlton St., 4th Fl.
Winnipeg, MB R3C 3H8
Tel: (204) 945-2420

Manitoba Industry, Trade & Tourism
155 Carlton St., 6th Fl.
Winnipeg, MB R3C 3H8
Tel: (204) 945-2066 Fax: (204) 945-1354

New Brunswick
Department of Economic Development & Tourism
Centennial Bldg., 5th Fl.
670 King St.
PO Box 6000
Fredericton, NB E3B 5H1
Tel: (506) 453-2850 (Communications & Promotion)
Fax: (506) 444-4586

Northwest Territories
Corporate & Technical Services
Bldg. NUP-2
PO Box 1320
Yellowknife, NT X1A 2L9
Tel: (403) 873-7115 Fax: (403) 873-0101

Nova Scotia
Nova Scotia Economic Renewal Agency
Investment & Trade
1800 Argyle St.
PO Box 519
Halifax, NS B3J 2R7
Tel: (902) 424-8920 Fax: (902) 424-0582

Ontario
Ministry of Economic Development, Trade & Tourism
Trade Development Branch
Hearst Block
900 Bay St.
Toronto, ON M7A 2E1
Tel: (416) 325-6515 Fax: (416) 325-6509

Prince Edward Island
Department of Economic Development & Tourism &
Enterprise PEI
Enterprise PEI
Shaw Bldg., 4th FL.
95 Rochford St.
PO Box 2000
Charlottetown, PE C1A 7N8
Tel: (902) 368-5800 Fax: (902) 368-4224

Quebec
Ministère de L'Industrie, du commerce, de la Science et de la technologie
710 Place d'Youville, 9e étage
Quebec, PQ G1R 4Y4
Tel: (418) 691-5950 (Renseignements) Fax: (418) 644-0118

Ministère des Affaires Internationales, de l'Immigration et des Communautés culturelles
Édifice Hector-Fabre
525 boul Réne-Levesque est
Quebec, PQ G1R 5R9
Tel: (418) 649-2300 Fax: (418) 649-2656

Saskatchewan
Saskatchewan Economic Development
Trade Development and Trade Policy
1919 Saskatchewan Drive
Regina, SK S4P 3V7
Tel: (306) 787-2222 (Trade Development)
Tel: (306) 787-8910 (Trade Policy)

Yukon
Yukon Economic Development
Economic Programs Branch
211 Main St.
PO Box 2703
Whitehorse, YT Y1A 2C6
Tel: (403) 667-5466 Fax: (403) 668-8601

EMBASSIES AND TRADE OFFICES

Algeria
Canadian Embassy
PO Box 225
Alger-Gare
Algiers, Algeria
Tel: [213] (2) 69-16-11 Fax: [213] (2) 69-39-20

Argentina
Canadian Embassy
Casilla de Correo 1598
1000, Buenos Aires, Argentina
Tel: [54] (1) 805-3032 Fax: [54] (1) 806-1209

Australia
Canadian High Commission
Commonwealth Ave.
Canberra, ACT 2600, Australia
Tel: [61] (6) 273-3844 Fax: [61] (6) 270-4069

Austria
Canadian Embassy
Laurenzerberg 2,
A-1010 Vienna, Austria
Tel: [43] (1) 531-38-3000 Fax: [43] (1) 531-38-3906

Bangladesh
Canadian High Commission
GPO Box 569
Dhaka 1000, Bangladesh
Tel: [88] (2) 883639, 607071-77 Fax: [88] (2) 883043

Barbados
Canadian High Commission
PO Box 404
Bridgetown, Barbados
Tel: [809] 429-3550 Fax: [809] 437-8474

Belgium
Canadian Embassy
2 Tervuren Ave.
B-1040 Brussels, Belgium
Tel: [32] (2) 741-06-20 Fax: [32] (2) 741-06-06

Brazil
Canadian Embassy
Caixa Postal 00961
Brasilia - DF 70359-970, Brazil
Tel: [55] (61) 321-2171 Fax: [55] (61) 321-4529

Cameroon
Canadian Embassy
PO Box 572
Yaoundé, Cameroon
Tel: [237] 23-02-03, 22-16-90, 23-23-11 Fax: [237] 22-10-90
E-mail: yunde$$paris.03$gc+eaitc.aecec$$telecom.canada$ca

Chile
Canadian Embassy
Casilla 771
Santiago, Chile
Tel: [56] (2) 696-2256 Fax: [56] (2) 696-0738
E-mail: stago.td@stago01.x400.gc.ca

All addresses and telephone numbers are in Canada unless otherwise noted. The country code for Canada is [1].

China
Canadian Embassy
19 Dongzhimenwai Street
Chaoyang District
Beijing 100600, China
Tel: [86] (1) 532-3536 Fax: [86] (1) 532-4072
E-mail: td.bejing@bejing03.x400.gc.ca

Colombia
Canadian Embassy
Apartado Aereo 53531
Santafe de Bogota 2, Colombia
Tel: [57] (1) 313-1355 Fax: [57] (1) 313-3046
E-mail:
bgota$$bgota.01$gc+eaitc.aecec$$telecom.canada$ca

Costa Rica
Canadian Embassy
Apartado Postal 351-1077 Centro Colon
San José, Costa Rica
Tel: [506] 296-4149 Fax: [506] 296-4280

Côte d'Ivoire
Canadian Embassy
01 BP 4104
Abidjan 01, Côte d'Ivoire
Tel: [225] 21-20-09 Fax: [225] 22-05-30

Office of the Canadian Embassy
PO Box 362
Niamey, Niger
Tel: [227] 75-36-86 Fax: [227] 75-31-07

Croatia
Canadian Embassy
c/o Hotel Esplanade
Mihanoviceva 1
41000 Zagreb, Croatia
Tel: [385] (1) 477-884 Fax: [385] (1) 477-913
E-mail: dt+id/dv+zagreb.ste@gemdes.x400.gc.ca

Cuba
Canadian Embassy
Calle 30 No. 518
Miramar
Havana, Cuba
Tel: [53] (7) 33-2516 Fax: [53] (7) 33-2044, 33-1069

NOTE: Send all mail to:
Commercial Division
PO Box 500 (HVAN)
Ottawa, Ontario K1N 8T7

Czech Republic
Canadian Embassy
Commercial Division
Na Petynce 120
169 00 Prague 6, Czech Republic

As of November 30, 1995:
Mickiewiczova 6
125 33 Prague 6, Czech Republic
Tel: [42] (2) 357-685, 2431-1108/1109/1110/1111/1112
Fax: [42] (2) 35 09 25, 2431-0294

Denmark
Canadian Embassy
Kristen Bernikowsgade 1
DK=1105 Copenhagen K, Denmark
Tel: [45] (33) 12-22-99 Fax: [45] (33) 12-42-10
E-mail: copen.td@copen.01x400.gc.ca

Dominican Republic
Office of the Canadian Embassy
Apartado 2054
Santo Domingo, Dominican Republic
Tel: [809] 685-1136 Fax: (809) 682-2691

Ecuador
Canadian Embassy
Apartado 17-11
Quito, Ecuador
Tel: [593] (2) 506162/3 Fax: [593] (2) 503108

Egypt
Canadian Embassy
PO Box 1667 Kasr El Doubara
Cairo, Egypt
Tel: [20] (2) 354-3110 Fax: [20] (2) 354-7659

Ethiopia
Canadian Embassy
PO Box 1130
Addis Ababa, Ethiopia
Tel: [251] (1) 713022 Fax: [251] (1) 713033

European Union
Mission of Canada to the European Union
avenue de Tervuren, 2
1040 Brussels, Belgium
Tel: [32] (2) 741-0660 Fax: (011-32-2) 741-0629
E-mail: canada@mail.interpac.be

Finland
Canadian Embassy
PO Box 779
00101 Helsinki, Finland
Tel: [358] (0) 171-141 Fax: [358] (0) 601-060

France
Canadian Embassy (Paris)
35, avenue Montaigne
75008 Paris, France
Tel: [33] (1) 44-43-29-00 Fax: [33] (1) 44-43-29-98
(Economic/Commercial)
E-mail:
paris*td$$paris.02$gc+eaitc.aecec$$telecom.canada.ca

Gabon
Canadian Embassy
PO Box 4037
Libreville, Gabon
Tel: [241] 74-34-64/65 Fax: [241] 74-34-66

Germany
Canadian Embassy
Postfach 12 02 40
53044 Bonn, Germany
Tel: [49} (228) 968-0 Fax: [49] (228) 968-3900

Office of the Canadian Embassy
Internationales Handelszentrum
Friedrichstrasse 95, 23rd Fl.
10117 Berlin, Germany
Tel: [49] (30) 261-1161 Fax: [49] (30) 262-9206

Ghana
Canadian High Commission
PO Box 1639
Accra, Ghana
Tel: [233] (21) 228555, 228566, 773791 Fax: [233] (21) 773-792
E-mail: td.accra@accra01.x400.gc.ca

Greece
Canadian Embassy
4 Ioannou Ghennadiou St.
115 21 Athens, Greece
Tel: [30] (1) 725-4011 Fax: [30] (1) 725-3994

IMPORTANT ADDRESSES   283

Guatemala
Canadian Embassy
PO Box 400
Guatemala City, C.A., Guatemala
Tel: [502] (2) 33-6102/04, 63-4348 Fax: [502] (2) 33-6189

Guyana
Canadian High Commission
PO Box 10880
Georgetown, Guyana
Tel: [592] (2) 72081-5 Fax: [592] (2) 58380
E-mail:
grgtn$$extott.18$gc+eaitc.aecec$$telecom.canada$ca

Haiti
Canadian Embassy
PO Box 826
Port-au-Prince, Haiti
Tel: [509] 23-2358 Fax: [509] 23-8720

Hong Kong
Commission for Canada
 GPO 11142
Hong Kong, Hong Kong
Tel: [852] 2847-7414 Fax: [852] 2847-7441
E-mail: td.hkong@hkong02.x400.gc.ca

Hungary
Canadian Embassy
Kiralyhago Ter 8-9
H-1126 Budapest XII, Hungary
Tel: [36] (1) 156-1251 Fax: [36] (1) 155-8650

India
Canadian High Commission
PO Box 5208
New Delhi, India
Tel: [91] (11) 687-6500 Fax: [91] (11) 687-5387, 687-6579

Indonesia
Canadian Embassy
PO Box 8324/JKS.MP
Jakarta 12084, Indonesia
Tel: [62] (21) 525-0709 Fax: [62] (21) 571-2251, 570-1494

Iran
Canadian Embassy
PO Box 11365-4647
Tehran, Iran
 Tel: [98] (21) 873-2623/25 Fax: [98] (21) 873-3202

Ireland
Canadian Embassy
Canada House
65 St. Stephen's Green
Dublin 2, Ireland
Tel: [353] (1) 478 1988 Fax: [353] (1) 478 1285

Israel
Canadian Embassy
PO Box 6410
Tel Aviv 61063, Israel
Tel: [972] (3) 527-2929 Fax: [972] (3) 527-2231

Italy
Canadian Embassy
Via G.B. de Rossi 27
00161 Rome, Italy
Tel: [39] (6) 44598-1 Fax: [39] (6) 44598-754
E-mail: rome@rome01.x400.gc.ca

Jamaica
Canadian High Commission
PO Box 1500
Kingston 10, Jamaica
 Tel: (809) 926-1500 Fax: (809) 960-3861
E-mail:
kngtn$$kngtn.01$gc+eaitc.aecec$$telecom.canada$ca

Japan
Canadian Embassy (Tokyo)
7-3-38 Akasaka
Minato-ku
Tokyo 107, Japan
Tel: [81] (3) 3408-2101 Fax: (G3 System) [81] (3) 3470-7280, 3479-5320

Jordan
Canadian Embassy
PO Box 815403
Amman 11180, Jordan
Tel: [962] (6) 666-124 Fax: [962] (6) 689-227

Kazakhstan
Canadian Embassy
34 Vinogradova
480100 Almaty, Kazakhstan
Tel: [7} (3272) 50-93-81 Fax: [7] (3272) 50-93-80
E-mail: dt=id/dv=almaty.ste@gemdes.x400.gc.ca

Kenya
Canadian High Commission
PO Box 30481
Nairobi, Kenya
 Tel: [254] (2) 214-804 Fax: [254] (2) 226-987, 216-485

Korea
Canadian Embassy
CPO Box 6299
Seoul 100-662, Korea
Tel: [82] (2) 753-2605/8, 753-7290/3 Fax: [82] (2) 755-0686, 756-0869 (Qué), 773-8966 (AB)

Kuwait
Canadian Embassy
PO Box 25281 Safat
13113 Kuwait City, Kuwait
Tel: [965] 256-3025 Fax: [965] 256-4167

Latvia
Canadian Embassy
Doma Laukums 4
Riga LV-1977, Latvia
Tel: [371] (2) 783-0141 Fax: [371] (2) 783-0140

Lebanon
Canadian Embassy
PO Box 60163 Jal-El-Dib
Beirut, Lebanon
Tel: [961] (1) 521-163 Fax: [961] (1) 521-167

 Malaysia
Canadian High Commission
PO Box 10990
50732 Kuala Lumpur, Malaysia
Tel: [60] (3) 261-2000 Fax: [60] (3) 261-3428/261-1270
E-mail: tradcan@po.jaring.my

Mexico
Canadian Embassy
Apartado Postal 105-05
11560 Mexico City, DF, Mexico
Tel: [52] (5) 724-7900 Fax: [52] (5) 724-7982

Morocco
Canadian Embassy
CP 709
Rabat-Agdal, Morocco
Tel: [212] (7) 67-28-80 Fax: [212] (7) 67-21-87

Netherlands
Canadian Embassy
Commercial Division
PO Box 30820
2500 GV The Hague, Netherlands
Tel: [31] (70) 361-4111 Fax: [31] (70) 365-6283

All addresses and telephone numbers are in Canada unless otherwise noted. The country code for Canada is [1].

New Zealand
Canadian High Commission
PO Box 12-049
Thorndon, Wellington, New Zealand
Tel: [64] (4) 473-9577 Fax: [64] (4) 471-2082

Nigeria
Canadian High Commission
PO Box 54506
Ikoyi Station
Lagos, Nigeria
Tel: [234] (1) 262-2513/4/5/6 Fax: [234] (1) 262-2517
E-mail:
lagos*td$$paris.03$gc+eaitc.aecec$$telecom.canada$ca

North Atlantic Council
Léopold III Boulevard
1110 Brussels, Belgium
Tel: [32] (2) 726-4646 Fax: [32] (2) 728-7129

Norway
Canadian Embassy
Oscars Gate 20
0244 Oslo, Norway
Tel: [47] 22-46-69-55 Fax: [47] 22-69-34-67
E-mail: td.oslo@oslo01.x400.gc.ca

Pakistan
Canadian High Commission
GPO Box 1042
Islamabad, Pakistan
Tel: [92] (51) 211-101-4 Fax: [92] (51) 211-540

Canadian Trade Office
Beach Luxury Hotel, 1st Fl.
M.T. Khan Road
Karachi, Pakistan
Tel: [92] (21) 561-0672 Fax: [92] (21) 561-0684

Peru
Canadian Embassy
Casilla 18-1126
Correo Miraflores
Lima 18, Peru
Tel: [51] (14) 44-4015, (Night Line: 44-4688) Fax: [51] (14) 44-4347

Philippines
Canadian Embassy
PO Box 2168
Makati Central Post Office
1261 Makati City, Metro Manila, Philippines 1299
Tel: [63] (2) 810-8861 Fax: [63] (2) 810-1699, 810-8839

Poland
Canadian Embassy
Ulica Jana Matejki 1/5
00-481 Warsaw, Poland
Tel: [48] (22) 29-80-51 Fax: [48] (22) 29-64-57
E-mail: wsaw.td@wsa01.x400.gc.ca

Portugal
Canadian Embassy
Av. da Liberdade 144, 4th Fl.,
1250 Lisbon, Portugal
Tel: [351] (1) 347-4892, 347-4896 Fax: [351] (1) 342-5628

Romania
Canadian Embassy
PO Box 2966
Post Office No. 22
71118 Bucharest, Romania
Tel: [40] (1) 222-9845, 312-0365 Fax: [40] (1) 312-0366

Russia
Canadian Embassy
Starokonyushenny Pereulok 23
Moscow 12100, Russia
Tel: [7] (095) 956-6666 Fax: [7] (095) 241-9034

Saudi Arabia
Canadian Embassy
PO Box 94321
Riyadh 11693, Saudi Arabia
Tel: [966] (1) 488-2288 Fax: [966] (1) 488-0137

Canadian Trade Office
PO Box 8928
Jeddah 21492, Saudi Arabia
Tel: [966] (2) 665-1050 Fax: [966] (2) 669-0727

Senegal
Canadian Embassy
PO Box 3373
Dakar, Senegal
Tel: [221] 23-92-90 Fax: [221] 23-92-90

Singapore
Canadian High Commission
PO Box 845
Singapore 9016, Singapore
Tel: [65] 225-6363 Fax: [65] 225-2450, 226-1541 (Commercial)
E-mail: cdatanjs@singnet.com.sg

South Africa
Canadian Trade Office
PO Box 1394
Parklands 2121
Johannesburg, South Africa
Tel: [27] (11) 442-3130 Fax: [27] (11) 442-3325
E-mail: jburg@pret01.x400.gc.ca

Spain
Canadian Embassy
Apartado 587
28080 Madrid, Spain
Tel: [34] (1) 431-4300 Fax: [34] (1) 577-8911, 431-2367

Canadian Trade Office
Travessera de les Corts 265
08014 Barcelona, Spain
Tel: [34] (3) 410-6699 Fax: [34] (3) 410-7755

Sri Lanka
Canadian High Commission
PO Box 1006
Colombo, Sri Lanka
Tel: [94] (1) 69-58-41/42/43, 69-87-97 Fax: [94] (1) 68-70-49

Sweden
Canadian Embassy
PO Box 16129
S-103 23 Stockholm, Sweden
Tel: [46] (8) 453-3000 Fax: [46] (8) 24 24 91
E-mail: stklm@stklm01.x400.gc.ca

Switzerland
Canadian Embassy
PO Box 234, CH-3000
Berne 6, Switzerland
Tel: [41] (31) 352-63-81 Fax: [41] (31) 352-73-15
E-mail: bern.cda@ping.ch

Syria
Canadian Embassy
PO Box 3394
Damascus, Syria
Tel: [963] (11) 611-6692, 611-6851, 611-6870 Fax: [963] (11) 611-8034

Taiwan
Canadian Trade Office
365 Fu Hsing North Road, 13th Fl.
Taipei, 10483, Taiwan
Tel: [886] (2) 713-7268 Fax: (011-886-2) 712-7244

Tanzania
Canadian High Commission
PO Box 1022
Dar-es-Salaam, Tanzania
Tel: [255] (51) 46000/9 Fax: [255] (51) 46000/9 (Ask for fax)

Thailand
Canadian Embassy
PO Box 2090
Bangkok 10500, Thailand
Tel: [66] (2) 237-4126 Fax: [66] (2) 236-6463, 236-7119 (Commercial)
E-mail: bngkk*td$$bngkk.02$gc+eaitc.aecec$$telecom.canada$ca

Trinidad and Tobago
PO Box 1246
Port of Spain, Trinidad and Tobago
Tel: [809] 623-7254 Fax: [809] 624-6440, 624-4016
E-mail: AMMON*Gabriella*gma$$pspan.02$gc+eaitc.aecec$$telecom.canada$ca

Tunisia
Canadian Embassy
CP 31, Le Belvédère 1002
Tunis, Tunisia
Tel: [216] (1) 796-577 Fax: [216] (1) 792-371
E-mail: tunis*td$$paris.03$gc+EAITC.AECEC$$TELECOM.CANADA$CA

Turkey
Canadian Embassy
Nenehatun Caddesi 75,
Gaziosmanpasa, 06700 Ankara, Turkey
Tel: [90] (312) 436 12 75 Fax: [90] (312) 446 28 11, 446 44 37 (General)

Ukraine
Embassy of Canada
PO Box 205
Kiev 252001, Ukraine
Tel: [380] (44) 212-0212, 212-3550, 212-0312, 212-0412, 212-2864 Fax: [380] (44) 212-2339

United Arab Emirates
Canadian Consulate
PO Box 52472
Dubai, United Arab Emirates
Tel: [971] (4) 521717 Fax: [971] (4) 517722

United Kingdom of Great Britain
Canadian High Commission
Macdonald House
One Grosvenor Square
London W1X 0AB, England
Tel: [44] (171) 258-6600 Fax: [44] (171) 258-6384, 258-6322 (Tourism)

United States of America
Canadian Embassy
50l Pennsylvania Ave., NW,
Washington, D.C. 20001, USA
Tel: [1] (202) 682-1740 Fax: [1] (202) 682-7726

Canadian Consulate General
One CNN Center
South Tower, Suite 400
Atlanta, Georgia 30303-2705, USA
Tel: [1] (404) 577-6810, 577-1512 Fax: [1] (404) 524-5046

Canadian Consulate General
Three Copley Place, Suite 400
Boston, Massachusetts 02116, USA
Tel: [1] (617) 262-3760 Fax: [1] (617) 262-3415

Canadian Consulate General
One Marine Midland Center, Suite 3000
Buffalo, New York 14203-2884, USA
Tel: [1] (716) 858-9500 Fax: [1] (716) 852-4340

Canadian Government Trade Office
One Gateway Center, 9th Fl., South Wing
Pittsburgh, Pennsylvania 15222, USA
Tel: [1] (412) 392-2308 Fax: [1] (412) 392-2317

Canadian Consulate General
Two Prudential Plaza
180 North Stetson Ave., Suite 2400
Chicago, Illinois 60601, USA
Tel: [1] (312) 616-1860 Fax: [1] (312) 616-1877, 616-1878 (Trade)

Canadian Consulate General
St. Paul Place, Suite 1700
750 North St. Paul St.
Dallas, Texas 75201, USA
Tel: [1] (214) 922-9806 Fax: [1] (214) 922-9815

Canadian Consulate General
600 Renaissance Center, Suite 1100
Detroit, Michigan 48243-1798, USA
Tel: [1] (313) 567-2340 Fax: [1] (313) 567-2164
Internet WWW site: http://bizserve.com/canadian-detroit

Canadian Government Trade Office
250 East Fifth St., Suite 1120
Cincinnati, Ohio 45202
Tel: [1] (513) 762-7655 Fax: [1] (513) 762-7802

Canadian Government Trade Office
2100 Terminal Tower
50 Public Square
Cleveland, Ohio 44113-2204, USA
Tel: [1] (216) 771-0150 Fax: [1] (216) 771-1688

Canadian Consulate General
California Plaza, 10th Fl.
300 South Grand Ave.
Los Angeles, California 90071, USA
Tel: [1] (213) 346-2700 Fax: (213) 346-2767
E-mail: CONGEN@ix.netcom.com

Canadian Government Trade Office
4370 LaJolla Village Dr., Suite 620
San Diego, California 92122, USA
Tel: [1] (619) 597-7050 Fax: [1] (619) 457-2844

Canadian Government Trade Office
50 Fremont St., Suite 1825
San Francisco, California 94105, USA
Tel: [1] (415) 543-2550 Fax: [1] (415) 512-7671
E-mail: CdnTrade@ix.netcom.com

Canadian Government Trade Office
333 West San Carlos St., Suite 945
San Jose, California 95110, USA
Tel: [1] (408) 289-1157 Fax: [1] (408) 289-1168

Canadian Consulate General
701 Fourth Ave. South, Suite 900
Minneapolis, Minnesota 5415-1899, USA
Tel: [1] (612) 333-4641 Fax: [1] (612) 332-4061

All addresses and telephone numbers are in Canada unless otherwise noted. The country code for Canada is [1].

Canadian Consulate General
1251 Avenue of the Americas
New York, New York 10020-1175, USA
Tel: [1] (212) 596-1600 Fax: [1] (212) 596-1793
E-mail: cngny@cngny01.x400.gc.ca

Canadian Government Trade Office
90 Westcott Road
Princeton, New Jersey 08540, USA
Tel: [1] (609) 252-0777 Fax: [1] (609) 252-0792

Canadian Consulate General
412 Plaza 600, Sixth and Stewart Streets
Seattle, Washington 98101-1286, USA
Tel: [1] (206) 443-1777 Fax: [1] (206) 443-1782
E-mail: seatl.td@seatl01.x400.gc.ca

Venezuela
Canadian Embassy
Apartado Postal 62302
Caracas 1060-A, Venezuela
Tel: [58] (2) 951-6166/67/68, 951-4114, 951-6171/72/73, 951-6190, 951-6306/7/8 Fax: [58] (2) 951-4950

Vietnam
Canadian Embassy
31 Hung Vuong St.,
Hanoi, Vietnam
Tel: [8] (42) 235500 Fax: [84] (42) 235351

Yugoslavia
Canadian Embassy
Kneza Milosa 75
11000 Belgrade, Yugoslavia
Tel: [381] (11) 644-666 Fax: [381] (11) 641-480

Zambia
Canadian High Commission
PO Box 31313
Lusaka, Zambia
Tel: [260] (1) 250 833 Fax: [260] (1) 254 176

Zimbabwe
Canadian High Commission
PO Box 1430
Harare, Zimbabwe
Tel: [263] (4) 733-881 Fax: [263] (4) 732-917

FOREIGN EMBASSIES IN CANADA

Embassy of Algeria
435 Daly Ave.
Ottawa, ON K1N 6H3
Tel: (613) 232-9453 Fax: (613) 232-9099

Embassy of Argentina
90 Sparks St., Suite 620
Ottawa, ON K1P 5B4
Tel: (613) 236-2351 Fax: (613) 235-2659

High Commission of Australia
50 O'Connor St., Suite 710
Ottawa, ON K1P 6L2
Tel: (613) 236-0841 Fax: (613) 236-4376

Embassy of Austria
445 Wilbrod St.
Ottawa, ON K1N 6M7
Tel: (613) 789-1444 Fax: (613) 789-3431

High Commission of the Bahamas
360 Albert St., Suite 1020
Ottawa, ON K1R 7X7
Tel: (613) 232-1724 Fax: (613) 232-0097

High Commission of Bangladesh
85 Range Road, Suite 402
Ottawa, ON K1N 8J6
Tel: (613) 236-0138 Fax: (613) 567-3213

Embassy of Belgium
80 Elgin St., 4th Fl.
Ottawa, ON K1P 1B7
Tel: (613) 236-7267 Fax: (613) 236-7882

Chargé d'affaires of Bolivia
130 Albert St., Suite 504
Ottawa, ON K1P 5G4
Tel: (613) 236-5730

Embassy of Brazil
450 Wilbrod St.
Ottawa, ON K1P 6M8
Tel: (613) 237-1090 Fax: (613) 237-6144

Embassy of Bulgaria
325 Stewart St.
Ottawa, ON K1N 6K5
Tel: (613) 789-3215 Fax: (613) 789-3524

Chargé d'affaires of Chile
151 Slater St., Suite 605
Ottawa, ON K1P 5H3
Tel: (613) 235-4402 Fax: (613) 235-1176

Embassy of China
515 St. Patrick St.
Ottawa, ON K1N 5H3
Tel: (613) 789-3434 Fax: (613) 230-9794

Embassy of Colombia
360 Albert St., Suite 1002
Ottawa, ON K1R 7X7
Tel: (613) 230-3761 Fax: (613) 230-4416

Embassy of Costa Rica
135 York St., Suite 208
Ottawa, ON K1N 5T4
Tel: (613) 562-2855 Fax: (613) 562-2582

Embassy of Côte d'Ivoire
9 Marlborough Ave.
Ottawa, ON K1N 8E6
Tel: (613) 236-9919 Fax: (613) 563-8287

Embassy of Cuba
388 Main St.
Ottawa, ON K1S 1E3
Tel: (613) 563-0141 Fax: (613) 563-0068

Chargé d'affaires of the Czech Republic
50 Rideau Terrace
Ottawa, ON K1M 2A1
Tel: (613) 749-4442 Fax: (613) 749-4989

Embassy of Denmark
85 Range Road, Suite 702
Ottawa, ON K1N 8J6
Tel: (613) 234-0704 Fax: (613) 234-7368

High Commission of the Dominican Republic
Place de Ville, Tower B, Suite 1610
112 Kent St.
Ottawa, ON K1P 5P2
Tel: (613) 236-8952 Fax: (613) 236-3042

Embassy of Ecuador
50 O'Connor St., Suite 1311
Ottawa, ON K1N 6L2
Tel: (613) 563-8206 Fax: (613) 235-5776

Embassy of Egypt
454 Laurier Ave. East
Ottawa, ON K1N 6R3
Tel: (613) 234-4931 Fax: (613) 234-9347

Embassy of El Salvador
209 Kent St.
Ottawa, ON K2P 1Z8
Tel: (613) 238-2939 Fax: (613) 238-6940

Embassy of Finland
55 Metcalfe St., Suite 850
Ottawa, ON K1P 6L5
Tel: (613) 236-2389 Fax: (613) 238-1474

Embassy of France
42 Sussex Drive
Ottawa, ON K1M 2C9
Tel: (613) 232-1795 Fax: (613) 232-4302

Embassy of Gabon
4 Range Road
Ottawa, ON K1N 8J5
Tel: (613) 232-5301 Fax: (613) 232-6916

Embassy of Germany
275 Slater St., 14th Fl.
Ottawa, ON K1P 5H9
Tel: (613) 232-1101 Fax: (613) 594-9330

Embassy of Greece
76–80 MacLaren St.
Ottawa, ON K2P 0K6
Tel: (613) 238-6271 Fax: (613) 238-5676

Embassy of Guatemala
885 Meadowlands Drive, Suite 504
Ottawa, ON K2C 3N2
Tel: (613) 224-4322 Fax: (613) 224-4434

Embassy of Haiti
112 Kent St., Suite 212
Ottawa, ON K1P 5P2
Tel: (613) 238-1628 Fax: (613) 238-2986

Embassy of Honduras
151 Slater St., Suite 300A
Ottawa, ON K1P 5H3
Tel: (613) 233-8900 Fax: (613) 232-0193

Embassy of Hungary
299 Waverley St.
Ottawa, ON K2P 0V9
Tel: (613) 230-2717 Fax: (613) 230-7560

High Commission of India
10 Springfield Road
Ottawa, ON K1M 1C9
Tel: (613) 744-3751 Fax: (613) 744-0913

Embassy of Indonesia
287 MacLaren St.
Ottawa, ON K2P 0L9
Tel: (613) 236-7403 Fax: (613) 563-2858

Embassy of Iran
245 Metcalfe St.
Ottawa, ON K2P 2K2
Tel: (613) 235-4726 Fax: (613) 232-5712

Chargé d'affaires of Iraq
215 McLeod St.
Ottawa, ON K2P 0Z8
Tel: (613) 236-9177 Fax: (613) 567-1101

Embassy of Ireland
170 Metcalfe St.
Ottawa, ON K2P 1P3
Tel: (613) 233-6281 Fax: (613) 233-5835

Embassy of Israel
50 O'Connor St., Suite 1005
Ottawa, ON K1P 6L2
Tel: (613) 567-6450 Fax: (613) 237-8865

Embassy of Italy
275 Slater St., 21st Fl.
Ottawa, ON K1P 5H9
Tel: (613) 232-2401 Fax: (613) 233-1484

Embassy of Japan
255 Sussex Drive
Ottawa, ON K1N 9E6
Tel: (613) 236-8541 Fax: (613) 563-9047

High Commission of Kenya
415 Laurier Ave. East
Ottawa, ON K1N 6R4
Tel: (613) 563-1773 Fax: (613) 233-6599

Embassy of Korea
151 Slater St., 5th Fl.
Ottawa, ON K1P 5H3
Tel: (613) 232-1715 Fax: (613) 232-0928

Embassy of Lebanon
640 Lyon St.
Ottawa, ON K1S 3Z5
Tel: (613) 236-5825 Fax: (613) 232-1609

High Commission of Malaysia
60 Boteler St.
Ottawa, ON K1N 8Y7
Tel: (613) 237-5182 Fax: (613) 237-4852

Embassy of Mexico
45 O'Connor St., Suite 1500
Ottawa, ON K1P 1A4
Tel: (613) 233-8988 Fax: (613) 235-9123

Embassy of Morocco
38 Range Road
Ottawa, ON K1N 8J4
Tel: (613) 236-7391 Fax: (613) 236-6164

Embassy of the Netherlands
275 Slater St., 3rd Fl.
Ottawa, ON K1P 5H9
Tel: (613) 237-5030 Fax: (613) 237-6471

High Commission of New Zealand
Metropolitan House, Suite 727
99 Bank St.
Ottawa, ON K1P 6G3
Tel: (613) 238-5991 Fax: (613) 238-5707

Embassy of Nicaragua
130 Albert St., Suite 407
Ottawa, ON K1P 5G4
Tel: (613) 234-9361 Fax: (613) 238-7666

High Commission of Nigeria
295 Metcalfe St.,
Ottawa, ON K2P 1R9
Tel: (613) 236-0521 Fax: (613) 236-0529

Embassy of Norway
90 Sparks St., Suite 532
Ottawa, ON K1P 5B4
Tel: (613) 238-6571 Fax: (613) 238-2765

High Commission of Pakistan
151 Slater St., Suite 608
Ottawa, ON K1P 5H3
Tel: (613) 238-7881 Fax: (613) 238-7296

Chargé d'affaires of Paraguay
1300 Dowler Ave.
Ottawa, ON K1H 7S1
Tel: (613) 593-9306 Fax: (613) 593-1590

Embassy of Peru
170 Laurier Ave. West, Suite 1007
Ottawa, ON K1P 5V5
Tel: (613) 238-1777 Fax: (613) 232-3062

Embassy of the Philippines
130 Albert St., Suite 606
Ottawa, ON K1P 5G4
Tel: (613) 233-1121 Fax: (613) 233-4165

All addresses and telephone numbers are in Canada unless otherwise noted. The country code for Canada is [1].

Embassy of Poland
443 Daly Ave.
Ottawa, ON K1N 6H3
Tel: (613) 789-0468 Fax: (613) 789-1218

Embassy of Portugal
645 Island Park Drive
Ottawa, ON K1Y 0B8
Tel: (613) 729-0883 Fax: (613) 729-4236

Embassy of Romania
655 Rideau St.
Ottawa, ON K1N 6A3
Tel: (613) 789-3709 Fax: (613) 789-4365

Embassy of Russia
285 Charlotte St.
Ottawa, ON K1N 8L5
 Tel: (613) 235-4341 Fax: (613) 236-6342

Saudi Arabia
99 Bank St., Suite 901
Ottawa, ON K1P 6B9
Tel: (613) 237-4100 Fax: (613) 237-0567

Embassy of Slovakia
50 Rideau Terrace
Ottawa, ON K1M 2A1
Tel: (613) 749-4442 Fax: (613) 749-4989

High Commission of South Africa
15 Sussex Drive
Ottawa, ON K1M 1M8
Tel: (613) 744-0330 Fax: (613) 741-1639

Embassy of Spain
350 Sparks St., Suite 802
Ottawa, ON K1R 7S8
Tel: (613) 237-2193 Fax: (613) 236-9246

Embassy of Sweden
Mercury Court
377 Dalhousie St.
Ottawa, ON K1N 9N8
Tel: (613) 236-8553 Fax: (613) 236-5720

Embassy of Switzerland
 5 Marlborough Ave.
Ottawa, ON K1N 8E6
Tel: (613) 235-1837 Fax: (613) 563-1394

Embassy of Thailand
180 Island Park Drive
Ottawa, ON K1Y 0A2
Tel: (613) 722-4444 Fax: (613) 722-6624

Embassy of Tunisia
515 O'Connor St.
Ottawa, ON K1S 3P8
Tel: (613) 237-0330 Fax: (613) 237-7939

Embassy of Turkey
197 Wurtemburg St.
Ottawa, ON K1N 8L9
Tel: (613) 789-4044 Fax: (613) 789-3442

Embassy of the Ukraine
331 Metcalfe St.
Ottawa, ON K2P 1S3
Tel: (613) 230-2961 Fax: (613) 230-4765

High Commission of United Kingdom
80 Elgin St.
Ottawa, ON K1P 5K7
 Tel: (613) 237-1530 Fax: (613) 237-7980

Embassy of the United States of America
100 Wellington St.
PO Box 866, Stn B
Ottawa, ON K1P 5T1
Tel: (613) 238-4470 Fax: (613) 238-8750

Embassy of Uruguay
130 Albert St., Suite 1905
Ottawa, ON K1P 5G4
Tel: (613) 234-2727 Fax: (613) 233-4670

Embassy of Venezuela
32 Range Road
Ottawa, ON K1N 8J4
Tel: (613) 235-5151 Fax: (613) 235-3205

Embassy of Viet Nam
25B Davidson Drive
Gloucester, ON K1J 6L7
Tel: (613) 744-4963 Fax: (613) 744-1709

Chargé d'affaires of Yugoslavia
17 Blackburn Ave.
Ottawa, ON K1N 8A2
Tel: (613) 233-6289 Fax: (613) 233-7850

Embassy of Zaire
 18 Range Road
Ottawa, ON K1N 8J3
Tel: (613) 236-7103 Fax: (613) 567-1404

High Commission of Zimbabwe
332 Somerset St. West
Ottawa, ON K2P 0J9
Tel: (613) 237-4388 Fax: (613) 563-8269

TRADE ORGANIZATIONS

GENERAL BUSINESS AND TRADE ORGANIZATIONS

Action Canada Network
251 Laurier Ave. West, Suite 804
Ottawa, ON K1P 5J6
Tel: (613) 233-1764 Fax: (613) 233-1458
E-mail: actcan@web.apc.org

Business Council of British Columbia
1050 Pender St. West, Suite 810
Vancouver, BC V6E 3S7
Tel: (604) 684-3384 Fax: (604) 684-7957

Business Council on National Issues
Royal Bank Centre
90 Sparks St., Suite 806
Ottawa, ON K1P 5B4
Tel: (613) 238-3727 Fax: (613) 236-8679

Canadian Association of Regulated Importers
2525 St. Laurent Blvd., Suite 203
Ottawa, ON K1H 8P5
Tel: (613) 738-1729 Fax: (613) 733-9501

Canadian Association for Corporate Growth
c/o ABN AMRO Bank Canada
Aetna Tower, 15th Fl.
T-D Centre
PO Box 114
Toronto, ON M5K 1G8
Tel: (416) 365-2932 Fax: (416) 367-1485

Canadian Association of Family Enterprise
7100 Woodbine Ave., Suite 310
Markham, ON L3R 5J2
Tel: (905) 940-9646 Fax: (905) 940-8141

Canadian Chamber of Commerce
55 Metcalfe St., Suite 1160
Ottawa, ON K1P 6N4
Tel: (613) 238-4000 Fax: (613) 238-7643

Canadian Council of Better Business Bureaus
115 Apple Creek Blvd., Suite 209
Markham, ON L3R 6C9
Tel: (905) 415-1750 Fax: (905) 415-1752
E-mail: ccbbb@incoramp.net

Canadian Council for International Business
50 O'Connor St., Suite 1011
Ottawa, ON K1P 6L2
Tel: (613) 230-5462 Fax: (613) 230-7087

Canadian Council for Public-Private Partnerships
Toronto Domionion Bank Tower, Suite 4700
PO Box 48, Stn Toronto Dominion
Toronto, ON M5K 1E6
Tel: (416) 601-8333 Fax: (416) 868-0673

Canadian Exporters' Association
99 Bank St., Suite 250
Ottawa, ON K1P 6B9
Tel: (613) 238-8888 Fax: (613) 563-9218

Canadian Federation of Independent Business
4141 Yonge St., Suite 401
North York, ON M2P 2A6
Tel: (416) 222-8022 Fax: (416) 222-4337

Canadian Franchise Association
5045 Orbitor Drive, Bldg. 12, Suite 201
Mississauga, ON L4W 4Y4
Tel: (905) 625-2896 Fax: (905) 625-9076

Canadian Importers Association Inc.
210 Dundas St. West, Suite 700
Toronto, ON M5G 2E8
Tel: (416) 595-5333 Fax: (416) 595-8226

Canadian Institute of Chartered Business Valuators
277 Wellington St. West
Toronto, ON M5V 3H2
Tel: (416) 204-3396 Fax: (416) 977-8585

Canadian Institute of Customs Brokers
555 Burnhamthorpe Road, Suite 305
Etobicoke, ON M9C 2Y3
Tel: (416) 622-5807

Canadian International Institute of Applied Negotiation
50 O'Connor St., Suite 1422
Ottawa, ON K1P 6L2
Tel: (613) 237-9050 Fax: (613) 230-1651

Canadian International Trade Association
2 Carlton St., Suite 611
Toronto, ON M5B 1J3
Tel: (416) 351-9728 Fax: (416) 351-9911

Canadian Labour Market & Productivity Centre
55 Metcalfe St., 15th Fl.
Ottawa, ON K1P 6L5
Tel: (613) 234-0505 Fax: (613) 234-2482

Canadian Organization of Small Business Inc.
The Voice of Business
PO Box 11246, Stn Main
Edmonton, AB T5H 3J5
Tel: (403) 423-2672 Fax: (403) 423-2751

Canadian Quality Council
1229 Meadow Brook Drive
Airdrie, AB T4A 1W7
Tel: (403) 948-3959 Fax: (403) 948-3959

Foundation for the Advancement of Canadian Entrepreneurship
49 Wellington St. East
Toronto, ON M5E 1C9
Tel: (416) 363-9182

National Entrepreneurship Development Institute
(Institut national de développement d'entrepreneurship)
3601 rue Saint-Jacques, Suite 30
Montreal, PQ H4C 3N4
Tel: (514) 937-2228 Fax: (514) 937-6557

National Quality Institute
360 Albert St., Suite 1540
Ottawa, ON K1R 7X7
Tel: (613) 237-4111 Fax: (613) 237-7171

Parliamentary Centre for Foreign Affairs & Foreign Trade
275 Slater St.
Ottawa, ON K1P 5H9
Tel: (613) 237-0143 Fax: (613) 235-8237

PROVINCIAL TRADE ORGANIZATIONS

Alberta
Alberta Chamber of Commerce
Edmonton Centre
TD Tower, Suite 2105
Edmonton, AB T5J 2Z1
Tel: (403) 425-4180 Fax: (403) 429-1061

Better Business Bureau of Central & Northern Alberta
Capitol Place
9707 – 110 St., Suite 514
Edmonton, AB T5K 2L9
Tel: (403) 482-2341 Fax: (403) 482-1150

All addresses and telephone numbers are in Canada unless otherwise noted. The country code for Canada is [1].

Better Business Bureau of Southern Alberta
7330 Fisher St. SE, Suite 350
Calgary, AB T2H 2H8
Tel: (403) 531-8784

British Columbia
Better Business Bureau of Mainland BC
788 Beatty St., Suite 404
Vancouver, BC V6B 2M1
Tel: (604) 682-2711 Fax: (604) 681-1544

Better Business Bureau of Vancouver Island
1005 Langley St., Suite 201
Victoria, BC V8W 1V7
Tel: (604) 386-6348 Fax: (604) 386-2367

British Columbia Chamber of Commerce
700 West Pender St., Suite 1607
 Vancouver, BC V6C 1G8
 Tel: (604) 683-0700 Fax: (604) 683-0416

Manitoba
Better Business Bureau of Winnipeg & Manitoba
365 Hargrave St., Suite 301
Winnipeg, MB R3B 2K3
Tel: (204) 943-1486 Fax: (204) 943-1489

Manitoba Chamber of Commerce
167 Lombard Ave. East, Suite 167
Winnipeg, MB R3B OV6
Tel: (204) 942-2561 Fax: (204) 942-2227

New Brunswick
Atlantic Provinces Chamber of Commerce
236 George St., Suite 110
Moncton, NB E1C 1W1
Tel: (506) 857-3980 Fax: (506) 859-6131

Newfoundland
Better Business Bureau of Newfoundland
360 Topsail Road
PO Box 516
St. John's, NF A1E 2B6
Tel: (709) 364-2222 Fax: (709) 364-2255

Nova Scotia
 Better Business Bureau of Nova Scotia
1888 Brunswick St., Suite 601
Halifax, NS B3J 3J8
Tel: (902) 422-6581 Fax: (902) 429-6457

Offshore Trade Association of Nova Scotia
1800 Argyle St., Suite 813
Halifax, NS B3J 3N8
Tel: (902) 425-4774 Fax: (902) 422-2332

Ontario
Better Business Bureau of Metropolitan Toronto Inc.
One Saint Johns Road, Suite 403
Toronto, ON M6P 4C7
Tel: (416) 766-5744, (Info Line) 766-3222 Fax: (416) 766-1970

Better Business Bureau of Mid-Western Ontario
354 Charles St.
Kitchener, ON N2G 4L5
Tel: (519) 579-3080 Fax: (519) 570-0072

Better Business Bureau of Ottawa & Hull
130 Albert St., Suite 603
Ottawa, ON K1P 5G4
Tel: (613) 237-4856, 233-3562 Fax: (613) 237-4878

Better Business Bureau of South Central Ontario
 100 King St. East
Hamilton, ON L8N 1A8
Tel: (905) 526-1111 Fax: (905) 526-1225

Better Business Bureau of Western Ontario
200 Queens Ave., Suite 616
London, ON N6A 1J3
Tel: (519) 673-3222 Fax: (519) 673-5966

Better Business Bureau of Windsor & District
500 Riverside Drive West
Windsor, ON N9A 5K6
Tel: (519) 258-7222 Fax: (519) 258-1198

Canadian Chamber of Commerce – Toronto Regional Office
Heritage Bldg., BCE Place, Box 818
181 Bay St.
Toronto, ON M5J 2T3
Tel: (416) 868-6415 Fax: (416) 868-0189

Ontario Centre for International Business
c/o Laurier Trade Development Centre
Wilfred Laurier University
75 University Ave. West
Waterloo, ON N2L 3C5
Tel: (519) 884-1970 ext. 6909

Ontario Chamber of Commerce
2345 Yonge St., Suite 808
Toronto, ON M4P 2E5
Tel: (416) 482-5222 Fax: (416) 482-5879

Quebec
Bureau D'éthique Commerciale de Montreal Inc.
(Better Business Bureau of Montreal Inc.)
2055 rue Peel, Suite 460
Montreal, PQ H3A 1V4
Tel: (514) 286-9281 Fax: (514) 286-2658

Bureau D'éthique Commerciale de Quebec Inc.
(Better Business Bureau of Quebec Inc.)
485 rue Richelieu
Quebec, PQ G1R 1K2
Tel: (418) 523-2555 Fax: (418) 523-2444

Canadian Chamber of Commerce – Quebec Regional Office
1080 Côte du Beaver Hall, Suite 1430
Montreal, PQ H2Z 1T2
Tel: (514) 866-4334 Fax: (514) 866-7296

World Trade Centre - Inforum Montreal
380 rue Saint-Antoine ouest, Suite 2100
Montreal, PQ H2Y 3X7
 Tel: (514) 849-1999 Fax: (514) 847-8343
E-mail: wtc.mtl@lantemette.com

Chambre de Commerce du Quebec
500 place d'Armes, Suite 3030
Montreal, PQ H2Y 2W2
Tel: (514) 844-9571 Fax: (514) 844-0226

Saskatchewan
Better Business Bureau of Saskatchewan
2080 Broad St., Suite 302
Regina, SK S4P 1Y3
Tel: (306) 352-7601 Fax: (306) 565-6236

Saskatchewan Chamber of Commerce
Chateau Tower, Suite 1630
1920 Broad St.
Regina, SK S4P 3V2
Tel: (306) 352-2671 Fax: (306) 781-7084

Yukon
Yukon Chamber of Commerce
208 Main St., Suite 201
Whitehorse, YT Y1A 2A9
Tel: (403) 667-2000 Fax: (403) 667-4507

FOREIGN BUSINESS ORGANIZATIONS IN CANADA

Brazil-Canada Chamber of Commerce
Carleton Tower, Suite 720
2 Carleton St.
Toronto, ON M5B 1J3
Tel: (416) 596-0992 Fax: (416) 596-1257

British Canadian Chamber of Trade & Commerce
7100 Woodbine Ave., Suite 305
Markham, ON L3R 5J2
Tel: (905) 475-3896 Fax: (905) 475-0311

Canada-Arab Business Council
55 Metcalfe St., Suite 1160
Ottawa, ON K1P 6N4
Tel: (613) 238-4000 Fax: (613) 238-7643

Canada China Business Council
110 Yonge St., Suite 802
Toronto, ON M5C 1T4
Tel: (416) 954-3800 Fax: (416) 954-3806

Canada Czech Republic Chamber of Commerce
Exchange Tower, 14th Fl.
2 First Canadian Place
PO Box 198
Toronto, ON M5X 1A6
Tel: (416) 367-3432 Fax: (416) 367-3492

Canada-Finland Chamber of Commerce
1200 Bay St., Suite 604
Toronto, ON M5R 2A5
Tel: (416) 964-7400 Fax: (416) 964-1524

Canada-India Business Council
Canadian Chamber of Commerce
55 Metcalfe St., Suite 1160
Ottawa, ON K1P 6N4
Tel: (613) 238-4000 Fax: (613) 238-7643

Canada-Indonesia Business Council
260 Adelaide St. East, Box 110
Toronto, ON M5A 1N1
Tel: (416) 366-8490 Fax: (416) 947-1534

Canada-Israel Chamber of Commerce
48 St. Clair Ave. West, Suite 1100
Toronto, ON M4V 2Z2
Tel: (416) 961-7302

Canada-Japan Trade Council
75 Albert St., Suite 903
Ottawa, ON K1P 5E7
Tel: (613) 233-4047 Fax: (613) 233-2256
E-mail: cjtc@magi.com

Canada-Netherlands Chamber of Commerce
34 King St. East, Suite 1100
Toronto, ON M5C 2X8
Tel: (416) 368-0350 Fax: (416) 368-7231

Canada-Pakistan Business Council
4329 ave King Edward
Montreal, PQ H4B 2H4
Tel: (514) 488-3979 Fax: (514) 488-3070
E-mail: 75323.2252@compuserve.com

Canada-Russia Business Council
330 Bay St., Suite 812
Toronto, ON M5H 2S8
Tel: (416) 862-2821 Fax: (416) 862-2820

Canadian Council for the Americas
145 Richmond St. West, 3rd Fl.
Toronto, ON M5H 2L2
Tel: (416) 367-4313 Fax: (416) 367-5460

Canadian German Chamber of Industry & Commerce Inc.
480 University Ave., Suite 1410
Toronto, ON M5G 1V2
Tel: (416) 598-3355 Fax: (416) 598-1840

Chamber of Commerce for Belgium & Luxembourg in Canada
Tour de la Bourse
PO Box 528
Montreal, PQ H4Z 1J8
Tel: (514) 845-4650

Chambre de commerce française au Canada – Ontario
130 Bloor St. West
Toronto, ON M5S 1N5
Tel: (416) 921-2910

Chambre de commerce française du Canada
360 rue Saint-Francois-Xavier
Montreal PQ H2Y 2S8
Tel: (514) 281-1245 Fax: (514) 289-9594

Chambre de commerce sud-africaine à Montreal
770 rue Sherbrooke ouest, 13e étage
Montreal, PQ H3A 1G1

Danish Canadian Chamber of Commerce
15 Wertheim Court., Suite 403
Richmond Hill, ON L4B 3H7
Tel: (905) 882-9901 Fax: (905) 882-5472

Ireland-Canada Chamber of Commerce
2020 rue University, Suite 1600
Montreal, PQ H3A 2A5
Tel: (514) 288-5705 Fax: (514) 288-6629

Italian Chamber of Commerce of Toronto
901 Lawrence Ave. West, Suite 306
Toronto, ON M6A 1C3
Tel: (416) 789-7169 Fax: (416) 789-7160

Scandinavian Canadian Chamber of Commerce
602 Hastings St. West, Suite 822
Vancouver, BC V6B 1P2
Tel: (604) 669-4428

Swedish Chamber of Commerce
2 Bloor St. West, Suite 1504
Toronto, ON M4W 3E2
Tel: (416) 925-8661 Fax: (416) 929-8639

Swiss Canadian Chamber of Commerce (Ontario) Inc.
21 Iron St.
Etobicoke, ON M9W 5E3
Tel: (416) 243-1201 Fax: (416) 243-1808

INDUSTRY-SPECIFIC ASSOCIATIONS

Aerospace Industries Association of Canada
60 Queen St., Suite 1200
Ottawa, ON K1P 5Y7
Tel: (613) 232-4297 Fax: (613) 232-1142

Association des Fabricants d'Engrais du Quebec
(Quebec Fertilizer Manufacturers Association)
8075 rue Jobert
CP 218, Succ. Jean-Talon
Montreal, PQ H1S 2Z2
Tel: (514) 324-5081 Fax: (514) 324-6166

Automotive Industries Association of Canada
1272 Wellington St.
Ottawa, ON K1Y 3A7
Tel: (613) 728-5821 Fax: (613) 728-6021

Bakery Council of Canada
885 Don Mills Road, Suite 301
Don Mills, ON M3C 1V9
Tel: (416) 510-8041 Fax: (416) 510-8043

All addresses and telephone numbers are in Canada unless otherwise noted. The country code for Canada is [1].

Brewers Association of Canada
155 Queen St., Suite 1200
Ottawa, ON K1P 6L1
Tel: (613) 232-9601 Fax: (613) 232-2283

Canada Beef Export Federation
6715 - 8 St. NE, Suite 235
Calgary, AB T2E 7H7
Tel: (403) 274-0005 Fax: (403) 274-7275

Canada Grains Council
360 Main St., Suite 760
Winnipeg, MB R3C 3Z3
Tel: (204) 942-2254 Fax: (204) 947-0992

Canadian Advanced Technology Association
388 Albert St.
Ottawa, ON K1R 5B2
Tel: (613) 236-6550 Fax: (613) 236-8189

Canadian Apparel Federation
130 Slater St., Suite 605
Ottawa, ON K1P 6E2
Tel: (613) 565-3047 Fax: (613) 231-2305

Canadian Association of Agri-Retailers
1090 Waverley St., Suite 107
Winnipeg, MB R3T 0P4
Tel: (204) 989-9300 Fax: (204) 989-9306

Canadian Association of Chemical Distributors
700 Dorval Drive, Suite 505
Oakville, ON L6K 3V3
Tel: (905) 844-9140

Canadian Association of Fish Exporters
1770 Woodward Drive, Suite 212
Ottawa, ON K2C 0P8
Tel: (613) 228-9220 Fax: (613) 228-9223

Canadian Association of Petroleum Producers
350 7th Ave. SW, Suite 2100
Calgary, AB T2P 3N9
Tel: (403) 267-1100 Fax: (403) 261-4622

Canadian Chemical Producers' Association
350 Sparks St., Suite 805
Ottawa, ON K1R 7S8
Tel: (613) 237-6215 Fax: (613) 237-4061

Canadian Concrete Masonry Producers' Association
1013 Wilson Ave., Suite 101
Downsview, ON M3K 1G1
Tel: (905) 635-7179 Fax: (905) 630-1916

Canadian Construction Association
85 Albert St., 10th Fl.
Ottawa, ON K1P 6A4
Tel: (613) 236-9455 Fax: (613) 236-9526

Canadian Council of Grocery Distributors
CP 1082, place du Parc
Montreal, PQ H2W 2P4
Tel: (514) 982-0272 Fax: (514) 849-3021

Canadian Drug Manufacturers Association
4120 Yonge St., Suite 606
Toronto, ON M2P 2B8
Tel: (416) 223-2333 Fax: (416) 223-2425

Canadian Electrical Association
1 square Westmount, Bureau 1600
Montreal, PQ H3Z 2P9
Tel: (514) 937-6181 Fax: (514) 937-6498

Canadian Electrical Contractors' Association
23 Lesmill Road, Suite 207
Toronto, ON M3B 3P6
Tel: (416) 391-3226 Fax: (416) 391-3926

Canadian Exporters Association
99 Bank St., Suite 250
Ottawa, ON K1P 6B9
Tel: (613) 238-8888 Fax: (613) 563-9218

Canadian Federation of Agriculture
75 Albert St., Suite 1101
Ottawa, ON K1P 5E7
Tel: (613) 236-3633 Fax: (613) 236-5749

Canadian Food Brokers Association
70 Aitken Circle
Unionville, ON L3R 7L1
Tel: (905) 477-4644 Fax: (905) 477-9580

Canadian Gas Association
55 Scarsdale Road
Don Mills, ON M3B 2R3
Tel: (416) 447-6465 Fax: (416) 447-7067

Canadian Horticultural Council
1101 Prince of Wales Drive., Suite 310
Ottawa, ON K2C 3W7
Tel: (613) 226-4187 Fax: (613) 226-2984

Canadian Importers Association, Inc.
210 Dundas St. West, Suite 700
Toronto, ON M5G 2E8
Tel: (416) 595-5333 Fax: (416) 595-8226
Above serves as contact source for:
    Association of International Automobile
Manufacturers of Canada
    Canadian Association of Footwear Importers Inc.
    Canadian Meat Importers Committee
    Customs & Legislation Committee
    Electronics Import Committee
    International Cheese Council of Canada

Canadian Lumbermen's Association
27 Goulburn Ave.
Ottawa, ON K1N 8C7
Tel: (613) 233-6205 Fax: (613) 233-1929

Canadian Manufacturers' Association
75 International Blvd., 4th Fl.
Toronto, ON M9W 6L9
Tel: (416) 798-8000 Fax: (416) 798-8050

Canadian Manufacturers of Chemical Specialties Association
56 Sparks St., Suite 702
Ottawa, ON K1P 5A9
Tel: (613) 232-6616 Fax: (613) 233-6350

Canadian Maritime Industries Association
100 Sparks St., Suite 801
Ottawa, ON K1P 5B7
Tel: (613) 232-7127 Fax: (613) 232-2490

Canadian Meat Council
875 Carling Ave., Suite 410
Ottawa, ON K1S 5P1
Tel: (613) 729-3911 Fax: (613) 729-4997

Canadian National Millers' Association
90 Sparks St., Suite 514
Ottawa, ON K1P 5B4
Tel: (613) 238-2293 Fax: (613) 235-5866

Canadian Nursery Trades Association
7856 Fifth Lane South
RR 4, Stn Main
Milton, ON L9T 2X8
Tel: (905) 875-1399 Fax: (905) 875-1840

Canadian Paint and Coatings Association
9900 blvd Cavendish, Bureau 103
St-Laurent, PQ H4M 2V2
Tel: (514) 745-2611 Fax: (514) 745-2031

IMPORTANT ADDRESSES

Canadian Pork Council
75 Albert St., Suite 1101
Ottawa, ON K1P 5E7
Tel: (613) 236-9239 Fax: (613) 236-6658

Canadian Pulp and Paper Association
Sun Life Bldg., Bureau 1900
1155 rue Metcalfe
Montreal, PQ H3B 4T6
Tel: (514) 866-6621 Fax: (514) 866-3035

Canadian Professional Sales Association
145 Wellington St. West, Suite 310
Toronto, ON M5J 1HB
Tel: (416) 408-2685 Fax: (416) 408-2684

Canadian Restaurant and Foodservices Association
316 Bloor St. West
Toronto, ON M5S 1W5
Tel: (416) 923-8416 Fax: (416) 923-1450

Canadian Seed Growers' Association
PO Box 8455
Ottawa, ON K1G 3T1
Tel: (613) 236-0497 Fax: (613) 563-7855

Canadian Tobacco Manufacturers' Council
99 Bank St., Suite 701
Ottawa, ON K1P 6B9
Tel: (613) 238-2799 Fax: (613) 238-4463

Canadian Wood Council
1730 St-Laurent, Suite 350
Ottawa, ON K1G 5L1
Tel: (613) 247-7077 Fax: (613) 247-7856

Club export agro-alimentaire du Quebec
(Quebec Agri-Food Export Club)
Édifice de Bleury, Bureau 102
200 rue MacDonald
St-Jean-sur-Richelieu, PQ J3B 8J6
Tel: (514) 349-1521 Fax: (514) 349-6923

Confectionery Manufacturers Association of Canada
885 Don Mills Road, Suite 301
Don Mills, ON M3C 1V9
Tel: (416) 510-8034 Fax: (416) 510-8044

Council of Printing Industries of Canada
4 King St. West, Suite 1330
Toronto, ON M5H 1B6
Tel: (416) 867-1520 Fax: (416) 867-1168

Dairy Farmers of Canada
75 Albert St., Suite 1101
Ottawa, ON K1P 5E7
Tel: (613) 236-9997 Fax: (613) 236-0905

Electrical and Electronic Manufacturers Association of Canada
10 Carlson Court., Suite 500
Rexdale, ON M9W 6L2
Tel: (905) 674-7410 Fax: (905) 674-7412

Federation of Export Clubs Canada
67 Yonge St., Suite 1402
Toronto, ON M5E 1J8
Tel: (416) 364-4112 Fax (416) 364-4074

Fisheries Council of Canada
141 Laurier Ave. West, Suite 806
Ottawa, ON K1P 5J3
Tel: (613) 238-7751 Fax: (613) 238-3542

Grocery Products Manufacturers of Canada
885 Don Mills Road, Suite 301
Don Mills, ON M3C 1V9
Tel: (416) 510-8024 Fax: (416) 510-8043

Hotel Association of Canada Inc.
130 Albert St., Suite 1016
Ottawa, ON K1P 5G4
Tel: (613) 237-7149 Fax: (613) 238-3878

Men's Clothing Manufacturers Association
555 rue Chabanel ouest, Bureau 801
Montreal, PQ H2N 2H8
Tel: (514) 382-3846 Fax: (514) 383-1689

Mining Association of Canada
350 Sparks St., Suite 1105
Ottawa, ON K1R 7S8
Tel: (613) 233-9391 Fax: (613) 233-8897

Motor Vehicle Manufacturers' Association
25 Adelaide St. East, Suite 1602
Toronto, ON M5C 1Y7
Tel: (416) 364-9333 Fax: (416) 367-3221

National Dairy Council of Canada
221 Laurier Ave. East
Ottawa, ON K1N 6P1
Tel: (613) 238-4116 Fax: (613) 238-6247

Northwest Territories Chamber of Mines
PO Box 2818
Yellownife, NT X1A 2R1
Tel: (403) 873-5281 Fax: (403) 920-2145

Oil & Colour Chemists' Association
c/o Sun Chemical Ltd.
48 Regentview
Brampton, ON L6Z 3G5
Tel: (905) 749-8133

Ontario Forest Industries Association
130 Adelaide St. West, Suite 1700
Toronto, ON M5H 3P5
Tel: (416) 368-6188 Fax: (416) 368-5445

Ontario Mining Association
110 Younge St., Suite 1501
Toronto, ON M5C 1T4
Tel: (416) 364-9301 Fax: (416) 364-5986

Ontario Painting Contractors Association
211 Consumers Road, Suite 305
Willowdale, ON M2J 4G8
Tel: (416) 498-1897 Fax: (416) 498-6757

Packaging Association of Canada
2255 Sheppard Ave. East, Suite E-330
Willowdale, ON M2J 4Y1
Tel: (416) 490-7860 Fax: (416) 490-7844

Pharmaceutical Manufacturers Association of Canada
1111 Prince of Wales Drive., Suite 302
Ottawa, ON K2C 3T2
Tel: (613) 727-1380 Fax: (613) 727-1407

Retail Council of Canada
210 Dundas St. West, Suite 600
Toronto, ON M5G 2E8
Tel: (416) 598-4684 Fax: (416) 598-3707

Retail Merchants' Association of Canada Inc.
1780 Birchmount Road
Scarborough, ON M1P 2H8
Tel: (416) 291-7903 Fax: (416) 291-5635

Sealant & Waterproofing Association
70 Leek Crescent
Richmond Hill, ON L4B 1H1
Tel: (416) 499-4000 Fax: (416) 499-8752

Structural Board Association
45 Sheppard Ave. East, Suite 412
North York, ON M2N 5W9
Tel: (416) 730-9090 Fax: (416) 730-9013

All addresses and telephone numbers are in Canada unless otherwise noted. The country code for Canada is [1].

Terrazzo Tile & Marble Association of Canada
30 Capstan Gate, Suite 5
Concord, ON L4K 3E8
Tel: (905) 660-9640 Fax: (905) 660-5706

Yukon Chamber of Mines
PO Box 4427
Whitehorse, YT Y1A 3T5
Tel: (403) 667-2090 Fax: (403) 668-7127

FINANCIAL INSTITUTIONS

BANKS

Central Bank

Bank of Canada
234 Wellington St.
Ottawa, ON K1A 0G9
Tel: (613) 782-8111 Fax: (613) 782-8655

Schedule I Banks

Bank of Montreal (Banque de Montreal)
129 rue St-Jacques ouest
Montreal, PQ H2Y 1L6
Tel: (514) 877-7110 Fax: (613) 877-8189
E-mail: spiggott@bicmtl.bmo.com
Internet WWW site: http://www.bmo.com

Bank of Nova Scotia (Scotiabank)
Scotia Plaza
44 King St. West
Toronto, ON M5H 1H1
Tel: (416) 866-6161 Fax: (416) 866-3750, 4988

Canadian Imperial Bank of Commerce (CIBC)
Commerce Court
PO Box 1, Stn Commerce Court
Toronto, ON M5L 1A2
Tel: (416) 980-2211 Fax: (416) 368-8843

Canadian Western Bank
10303 Jasper Ave., Suite 2300
Edmonton, AB T5J 3X6
Tel: (403) 423-8888 Fax: (403) 423-8897

National Bank of Canada (Banque Nationale du Canada)
600 rue de la Gauchetière ouest
Montreal, PQ H3B 4L2
Tel: (514) 394-4000, 5000 Fax: (514) 394-8219, 8434

Royal Bank of Canada
1 place Ville Marie
CP 6001, Succ A
Montreal, PQ H3C 3A9
Tel: (514) 874-2110 Fax: (514) 874-6582
Internet WWW site: http://www.royalbank.com

Toronto-Dominion Bank (TD Bank)
Toronto-Dominion Centre
PO Box 1, Stn Toronto-Dominion
Toronto, ON M5K 1A2
Tel: (416) 982-8222 Fax: (416) 982-5671
Internet WWW site: http://www.tdbank.ca

Schedule II Banks

Laurentian Bank of Canada (Banque Laurentienne du Canada)
1981 ave Collège McGill, Suite 1585
Montreal PQ H3A 3K3
Tel: (514) 284-3931 Fax: (514) 284-7519

Manulife Bank of Canada
2 Mississaga St. East
PO Box 68
Orillia, ON L3V 6H9
Tel: (705) 325-2328

Development Bank

Federal Business Development Bank
800 square Victoria
CP 335
Montreal, PQ H4Z 1L4
Tel: (514) 283-5904 Fax: (514) 283-7838

Foreign Bank Subsidiaries

ABN AMRO Bank Canada
Aetna Tower, 15th Fl.
 Toronto-Dominion Centre
PO Box 114, Stn Toronto-Dominion
Toronto, ON M5K 1G8
Tel: (416) 367-0850 Fax: (416) 367-1485

Amex Bank of Canada
American Express Place
101 McNabb St.
Markham, ON L3R 4H8
Tel: (905) 474-8000 Fax: (905) 474-8363, 1515

Banca Commerciale Italiana of Canada
130 Adelaide St. West, #1800
PO Box 100
Toronto, ON M5H 3P5
Tel: (416) 366-8101 Fax: (416) 366-2577

Bank of America Canada
4 King St. West, 18th Fl.
Toronto, ON M5H 1B6
Tel: (416) 863-5400 Fax: (416) 863-2350

Bank of Boston Canada (Banque de Boston du Canada)
500 boul René-Lévesque ouest, Suite 920
Montreal, PQ H2Z 1W7
Tel: (514) 397-9330 Fax: (514) 397-1133

Bank of Tokyo Canada
 South Tower, Suite 2100
Royal Bank Plaza
PO Box 42, Stn Royal Bank
Toronto, ON M5J 2J1
Tel: (416) 865-0220 Fax: (416) 865-9511, 0196

Banque Nationale de Paris (Canada)
BNP Tower
1981 ave Collège McGill
Montreal, PQ H3A 2W8
Tel: (514) 285-6000 Fax: (514) 285-6015, 6278

Barclays Bank of Canada
304 Bay St., 5th Fl.
PO Box 1
Toronto, ON M5H 2P2
Tel: (416) 359-8000 Fax: (416) 359-8230

BT Bank of Canada
North Tower, Suite 1700
Royal Bank Plaza
PO Box 100, Stn Royal Bank
Toronto, ON M5J 2J2
Tel: (416) 865-0770 Fax: (416) 941-9587

 Chase Manhattan Bank of Canada
Sun Life Centre
150 King St. West, 16th Fl.
PO Box 68
Toronto, ON M5H 1J9
Tel: (416) 585-3300 Fax: (416) 594-3370

Chemical Bank of Canada
100 Younge St., Suite 900
Toronto, ON M5C 2W1
Tel: (416) 594-9800 Fax: (416) 594-2266

Citibank Canada
Citibank Place
123 Front St. West, Suite 1900
Toronto, ON M5J 2M3
Tel: (416) 947-5500 Fax: (416) 947-5628, 5813

Crédit Lyonnais Canada
Centre ManuVie
2000 rue Mansfield, 18e étage
Montreal, PQ H3A 3A6
Tel: (514) 288-4848 Fax: (514) 288-5679

Crédit Suisse Canada
525 University Ave., Suite 1300
 Toronto, ON M5G 2K6
Tel: (416) 351-3500 Fax: (416) 351-3630

Dai-Ichi Kangyo Bank (Canada)
Commerce Court West, Suite 5025
PO Box 295, Stn Commerce Court
Toronto, ON M5L 1H9
Tel: (416) 365-9666 Fax: (416) 365-7314

Deutsche Bank (Canada)
222 Bay St., Suite 1100
PO Box 64
Toronto, ON M5K 1E7
Tel: (416) 369-8800 Fax: (416) 367-3290

Dresdner Bank Canada
2 First Canadian Place., Suite 1700
PO Box 430, Stn 1st Can Place
Toronto, ON M5X 1E3
Tel: (416) 369-8300 Fax: (416) 369-8362

Fuji Bank Canada
Canada Trust Tower, Suite 2800
BCE Place
161 Bay St.
PO Box 609
Toronto, ON M5H 2S1
 Tel: (416) 865-1020 Fax: (416) 865-9618

Hongkong Bank of Canada
885 West Georgia St. West, Suite 900
Vancouver, BC V6C 3E9
Tel: (604) 685-1000 Fax: (604) 641-1849

Industrial Bank of Japan (Canada) (IBJ Canada)
100 Yonge St., Suite 1102
PO Box 29
Toronto, ON M5C 2W1
Tel: (416) 365-9550 Fax: (416) 367-3452

International Commercial Bank of Cathay (Canada)
150 York St., Suite 901
PO Box 4037
Toronto, ON M5H 3S5
Tel: (416) 947-2800 Fax: (416) 947-9964

Mellon Bank Canada
Royal Trust Tower, Suite 3200
Toronto Domion Centre
Toronto, ON M5K 1K2
Tel: (416) 860-0777

 Mitsubishi Bank of Canada
Canada Trust Tower, Suite 3800
BCE Place
Box 518
161 Bay St., #3800
Toronto, ON M5J 2S1
Tel: (416) 365-1940 Fax: (416) 367-3579

All addresses and telephone numbers are in Canada unless otherwise noted. The country code for Canada is [1].

National Westminster Bank of Canada
South Tower, Suite 2060
Royal Bank Plaza
PO Box 10, Stn Royal Bank
Toronto, ON M5J 2J1
Tel: (416) 865-0170 Fax: (416) 865-0934

Republic National Bank of New York (Canada)
1981 ave Collège McGill
Montreal, PQ H3A 3A9
Tel: (514) 288-5551 Fax: (514) 286-4577

Sakura Bank (Canada)
Commerce Court West, Suite 3601
PO Box 59, Stn Commerce Court
Toronto, ON M5L 1B9
Tel: (416) 369-8531 Fax: (416) 369-0268

Sanwa Bank Canada
 Canada Trust Tower, Suite 4400
BCE Place
Box 525
161 Bay St.
Toronto, ON M5J 2S1
Tel: (416) 366-2583 Fax: (416) 366-8599

Société Général (Canada)
1501 ave Collège McGill, Suite 1800
Montreal, PQ H3A 3M8
Tel: (514) 841-6000

Sumitomo Bank of Canada
Ernst & Young Tower, Suite 1400
Toronto-Dominion Centre
PO Box 172, Stn Toronto Dominion
Toronto, ON M5K 1H6
Tel: (416) 368-4766 Fax: (416) 367-3565

Swiss Bank Corporation (Canada)
207 Queen's Quay West, Suite 780
PO Box 103
Toronto, ON M5J 1A7
Tel: (416) 203-2180 Fax: (416) 203-4303

Union Bank of Switzerland (Canada)
 154 University Ave.
Toronto, ON M5H 3Z4
Tel: (416) 343-1800 Fax: (416) 343-1900

U.S. Bank (Canada)
1055 Dunsmuir St., Suite 2684
PO Box 49303, Stn Bentall Four
Vancouver, BC V7X 1L3
Tel: (604) 685-8286 Fax: (604) 682-0473

STOCKS AND COMMODITIES

Alberta Stock Exchange
300 Fifth Ave. SW, 21st Fl.
Calgary, AB T2P 3C4
Tel: (403) 262-7791 Fax: (403) 237-0450

Montreal Exchange (Bourse de Montreal)
Tour de la Bourse
800 square Victoria
CP 61
Montreal, PQ H4Z 1A9
Tel: (514) 871-2424 Fax: (514) 871-3553

Toronto Stock Exchange
The Exchange Tower
2 First Canadian Place
Toronto, ON M5X 1J2
Tel: (416) 947-4700 Fax: (416) 947-4585

Vancouver Stock Exchange
Stock Exchange Tower
609 Granville St.
PO Box 10333
 Vancouver, BC V7Y 1H1
Tel: (604) 689-3334 Fax: (604) 688-6051

Winnipeg Stock Exchange
One Lombard Place, Suite 2901
Winnipeg, MB R3B 0Y2
Tel: (204) 987-7070 Fax: (204) 987-7079

INSURANCE

Insurance Companies

Canadian General Insurance Co.
2206 Eglinton Ave. East
Scarborough, ON M1L 4S8
Tel: (416) 288-1800 Fax: (416) 288-9756

Canadian Surety Co./Canada West Insurance Co.
2200 Yong St., Suite 1200
Toronto, ON M4S 2C6
Tel: (416) 487-7195 Fax: (416) 482-6176
E-mail: baddie@interlog.com (Barb Addie)

Dominion of Canada General Insurance Co.
165 Univesity Ave.
Toronto, ON M5H 3B9
Tel: (416) 362-7231 Fax: (416) 362-9918

Federation Insurance Co. of Canada
1080 côte du Beaver Hall
20e étage
Montreal, PQ H2Z 1S8
Tel: (514) 875-5790 Fax: (514) 875-9769

 General Accident Assurance Co. of Canada
2 First Canadian Place, Suite 2600
PO Box 410
Toronto, ON M5X 1J1
Tel: (416) 368-4733 Fax: (416) 368-9039

Gerling Global General Insurance Co.
480 University Ave., Suite 1600
Toronto, ON M5G 1V6
Tel: (416) 598-4651 Fax: (416) 598-9507

Guardian Insurance Co. of Canada
181 University Ave.
Toronto, ON M5H 2M7
Tel: (416) 941-5050 Fax: (416) 941-9791

Laurentian General, Insurance Co. Inc.
1100 blvd René-Lévesque ouest, 25e étage
Montreal, PQ H3B 4P4
Tel: (514) 392-6000 Fax: (515) 392-6328

Mercantile and General Reinsurance Co. of Canada
161 Bay St., Suite 3000
Toronto, ON M5J 2T6
Tel: (416) 947-3800 Fax: (416) 947-1386

Royal Insurance Co. & Western Assurance Co.
10 Wellington St. East
 Toronto, ON M5E 1L5
Tel: (416) 366-7511 Fax: (416) 367-9869

Société Nationale D'Assurance Inc.
425 blvd de Maisonneuve ouest, Bureau 1500
Montreal, PQ H3A 3G5
Tel: (514) 288-8711 Fax: (514) 288-8269

Sun Alliance Insurance Co.
48 Yonge St.
Toronto, ON M5E 1G8
Tel: (416) 362-2000 Fax: (416) 362-6950

Insurance Organizations

Association of Canadian Insurers (ACI)
2 Sheppard Ave. East, Suite 800
Toronto, ON M2N 5Y7
Tel: (416) 733-8722 Fax: (416) 223-6577

Insurance Brokers Association of Canada
181 University Ave., Suite 322
Toronto, ON M5H 3M7
Tel: (416) 367-1831 Fax: (416) 367-3687

Insurance Bureau of Canada
181 University Ave., Suite 1300
Toronto, ON M5H 3M7
Tel: (416) 362-2031 Fax: (416) 361-5952

SERVICES

MARKET RESEARCH FIRMS

Angus Reid Group, Inc.
160 Bloor St. East, Suite 610
Toronto, ON M4W 1B9
Tel: (416) 324-2900 Fax: (416) 324-2865

The Coopers & Lybrand Consulting Group
145 King St. West, Suite 2300
Toronto, ON M5H 1V8
Tel: (416) 869-1130 Fax: (416) 863-0926

Decima Research
1 Eglinton Ave. East, 7th Fl.
Toronto, ON M4P 3A1
Tel: (416) 483-1724 Fax: (416) 483-4441

Deloitte & Touche – Consulting and Market Research
98 Macdonell St., Suite 400
Guelph, ON N1H 8L1
Tel: (519) 822-1090 Fax: (519) 822-0247

Dun & Bradstreet Canada
 Dun's Marketing Services
5770 Hurontario St.
Mississauga, ON L5R 3G5
Tel: (905) 568-6000 Fax: (905) 568-6197

Environics Research Group Limited
45 Charles St. East
Toronto, ON M4Y 1S2
Tel: (416) 964-1397 Fax: (416) 964-2486

Gallup Canada Inc.
180 Bloor St. West
Toronto, ON M5S 2V6
Tel: (416) 961-2811 Fax: (416) 961-3662

Goldfarb Consultants
4950 Yonge St., 17th Fl.
North York, ON M2N 6K1
Tel: (416) 221-9200 Fax: (416) 221-2214

Professional Marketing Research Society
2175 Sheppard Ave. East, Suite 110
Willowdale, ON M2J 1W8
Tel: (416) 493-4080 Fax: (416) 491-1670

Southam Marketing Research Services
1450 Don Mills Road
Don Mills, ON M3B 2X7
Tel: (416) 445-6641 Fax: (416) 442-2248

ADVERTISING

Anderson Advertising
330 Front St., Suite 430
Toronto, ON M5V 3B6
Tel: (416) 591-3830 Fax: (416) 591-5531

Bates Canada
2 St. Clair Ave. West
Toronto, ON M4V 1L5
Tel: (416) 925-8835 Fax: (416) 925-1206

BBDO Canada
2 Bloor St. West
Toronto, ON M4W 3R6
Tel: (416) 960-1722 Fax: (416) 972-5656

BCP
413 St. Jacques West, 9th Fl.
Montreal, PQ H2Y 1N9
Tel: (514) 285-1414 Fax: (514) 842-5907

Blouin Coulombe Dube Thompson, Inc.
2060 rue de la Montagne
Montreal, PQ H3G 1Z7
Tel: (514) 844-2092 Fax: (514) 844-5771

Burson-Marsteller
 80 Bloor St. West
Toronto, ON M5S 2V1
Tel: (416) 964-8300 Fax: (416) 964-1917

CALA Human Resources Communications
63 rue de Bresoles
Montreal, PQ H2Y 1V7
Tel: (514) 288-9004 Fax: (514) 288-8464

D'Arcy Masius Benton & Bowles Canada
2 Bloor St. West, Suite 1400
Toronto, ON M4W 3R3
Tel: (416) 922-2211 Fax: (416) 922-8590

DDB Needham Group
33 Bloor St. East, 12th Fl.
Toronto, ON M4W 3T4
Tel: (416) 925-9819 Fax: (416) 921-4180

FCB Canada Ltd.
245 Eglinton Ave. East, Suite 300
Toronto, ON M4P 3C2
Tel: (416) 483-3600 Fax: (416) 489-8782

Foster Mead Advertising Ltd.
698 Seymour St., Suite 200
Vancouver, BC V6B 3K6
 Tel: (604) 682-0655 Fax: (604) 682-5155

GCI Communications
1881 Yonge St.
Toronto, ON M4S 3C4
Tel: (416) 322-0152 Fax: (416) 486-9783

Grey Canada
1881 Yonge St.
Toronto, ON M4S 3C4
Tel: (416) 486-0700 Fax: (416) 486-7340

Hill and Knowlton (Canada) Limited
One Eglinton Ave. East, Suite 700
Toronto, ON M4P 3A1
Tel: (416) 483-1511 Fax: (416) 483-4441

Marketel
1981 McGill College, Suite 1400
Montreal, PQ H3A 2Y1
Tel: (514) 286-9445 Fax: (514) 288-2520

McCann-Erickson Advertising of Canada, Ltd.
10 Bay St.
Toronto, ON M5J 2S3
Tel: (416) 594-6000 Fax: (416) 594-6274

Media Buying Services Ltd
150 Bloor St. West, Suite 705
Toronto, ON M5S 2X9
Tel: (416) 961-1255 Fax: (416) 961-4441

Ogilvy & Mather - Toronto
33 Yonge St.
Toronto, ON M5E 1X6
Tel: (416) 367-3573 Fax: (416) 363-2088

Palmer Jarvis Communications
1188 West Georgia St., Suite 1600
Vancouver, BC V6E 4A2
Tel: (604) 687-7911 Fax: (604) 662-8610

Pinnacle
1470 Peel St., Suite 740
Montreal PQ H3A 1T1
Tel: (514) 843-3382 Fax: (514) 843-4323

Sudler & Hennessey/Gall Inc.
60 Bloor St. West
Toronto, ON M4W 1J2
Tel: (416) 961-7733 Fax: (416) 961-8973

Wunderman Worldwide
60 Bloor St. West, 15th Fl.
Toronto, ON M4W 3B8
Tel: (416) 921-9050 Fax: (416) 961-0971

Young & Rubicam Ltd.
60 Bloor St. West
Toronto, ON M4W 1J2
Tel: (416) 961-5111 Fax: (416) 961-7890

LEGAL SERVICES

Association of Canadian Courts Administrators
215 Water St.
PO Box 68
St. Johns, NF A1C 6C9
Tel: (709) 729-2081 Fax: (709) 729-2161

Barreau de Montreal
(Bar of Montreal)
Palais de Justice
1 rue Notre Dame est, Suite 980
Montreal, PQ H2Y 1B6
Tel: (514) 866-9392 Fax: (514) 866-1488

Barreau du Quebec
(Quebec Bar Association)
Maison du Barreau
 445 boul Saint-Laurent
Montreal, PQ H2Y 3T8
Tel: (514) 954-3400 Fax: (514) 954-3407

Canadian Association on Competition Law
55 rue Saint-Jacques
Montreal, PQ H2Y 3X2
Tel: (514) 987-6242 Fax: (514) 845-7874

Canadian Association of Legal Assistants
PO Box 967, Stn B
Montreal, PQ H3B 3K5

Canadian Association of Legal Support Staff
PO Box 3186
Winnipeg, MB R3C 4E7

Canadian Association of Legal Translators
PO Box 919, Stn B
Ottawa, ON K1P 5P9
Tel: (514) 283-7516 Fax: (514) 283-0331

Canadian Bar Association
50 O'Connor St., Suite 902
Ottawa, ON K1P 6L2
Tel: (613) 237-2925 Fax: (613) 237-0185
Internet WWW site: http://www.algonquinc.on.ca/
cba.engmenu.html

 Canadian Bar Insurance Association
3080 Yonge St., Suite 5070
Toronto, ON M4N 3R2
Tel: (416) 488-0702 Fax: (416) 488-2254

Index

A

Access North America 87
addresses and telephone numbers 279–??
advertising 177
    firms 179
advising banks 252
agriculture 27, 30, 97, 104
aircrafts 31
airlines 140, 267
airports 269
Alberta 3, 175
American Revolutionary War 8
antiavoidance legislation 259
apparel 30, 36
arbitration 218
Asia 154
    travel offices 138
Asia Pacific Economic Cooperation agreement (APEC) 51, 72
Atlantic Region 158
attire 140, 160
audiotext services 276
Automotive Trade Agreement 16

B

Bank of Canada (BOC) 225
banks 235
Berne Convention 209
billboard advertisements 179
bills of exchange (B/Es) 252
bills of lading 249
Bloc Quebecois 4
boating equipment 31
British Columbia 3, 159, 175
building products 31
business cards 161
business culture 153–162
    education's impact on 155
    gestures 160
    greetings 160
    language and 157
    large vs. small firms 162
    making conversation 160
    negotiations and 156
    overview 146
    provincial attitudes concerning 158
    religion's impact on 155
    social values, beliefs, and behavior 154
    weather's impact on 155
business entities 183–194
business hours 148, 156
business registration 189, 218
    application procedures for 189
business travel 137–152

C

Cairns Group Agreement 71
Canada Act 8
Canada and EC Framework Agreement 70
Canada Business Corporations Act (CBCA) 209
Canada–Australia Trade Agreement (CANATA) 70
Canada-US Free Trade Agreement (CFTA) 214, 223
CanadExport 87
Canadian Banker's Association (CBA) 225
Canadian Cooperative Associations Act 75
Canadian Department of Commerce 169
Canadian Facts 169
Canadian Labour Congress (CLC) 15
capital gains and losses 256, 264
cash in advance terms 239
certificate of manufacture 249
certificate of origin 249
change of control considerations 259
changing money 235
Charlottestown Agreement 21
chemicals 28, 105
Chretien, Jean 4, 24
climate 2, 139
collecting bank 252
Commonwealth Conference 5
communications 149, 275
Competition Act 75, 221

computers 31, 38, 98
consular invoice 249
Consumer Packaging & Labeling Act 75
contracts 216, 218
Copyright Act 213, 220
corporate reorganizations 259
corporations 183–186, 218
    bylaws 186
    directors 185
    incorporating 184
    shareholders 185
    statutes 183
cost, insurance, and freight (CIF) value 250
cuisine 145–??, 145, ??–146
currency & foreign exchange 235–237
current issues 19–25
customs 138
    entry 140
Customs Cooperation Council (CCC) 71
customs entry 140

D

debt-to-equity rules 259
deductible expenses 262
demographics 163–168
Department of Foreign Affairs and International Trade (DFAIT) 44, 87, 184, 209
departure procedures 151
director's fees 263
discrepancy 252
dispute resolution 216
distribution channels 89
distributorships 188
documentary collections 239, 240–241, 252
documents against acceptance (D/As) 239, 240, 252
documents against payment (D/Ps) 239, 240, 252
Doing Business in Canada Association (DBIC) 44
double tax relief 266
double tax treaties 266
driving 148

E

economy 1, 7–18
    context 11
    gross domestic product (GDP) 9
    history 7
    size 9
    standard of living 10
    structure 12
    trade and investment 15
    trends 9
education 164, 199
Electricity and Gas Inspection Act 75
electronic information services 276
electronic products 28, 32
emergency information 151

energy 1, 14, 28, 168
environmental awareness 157
environmental protection industry 38
estate taxes 265
ethnicity 2, 157, 163
Europe
    travel offices 138
expatriates 197–199
Export and Import Permits Act 219
Export Development Corporation 87
exporting 30, 56, 180
    automobiles 58
    by region 58
    composition of 56
    export policies 85–95
    financing 92
    government agencies 85
    industrial and manufactured products 58
    lumber 56
    methods of 89
    minerals 57
    payments 92
    preparing products for 89
    regulations and licenses 88
    restrictions and prohibitions 88
    services 58
    tips 80
    wheat 57

F

FaxLink 87
Federal Business Development Bank (FBDB) 184
film and television 38
financial institutions 223–233
fishing 13, 97
Food and Drugs Act 75
foreign affiliates 259
foreign exchange 141, 236
Foreign Extraterritorial Measures Act (FEMA) 219
foreign investment 43–50, 52, 213
    incentives 49, 214
    Investment Canada Act of 1985 52
    limitations 53
    notification and review 213
    origin 44
    policy and changes 45
    regulatory agencies and investment assistance 50
    sectors 45
    size 44
Foreign Investment Review Act 219
Foreign Investment Review Act of 1973-74 45
foreign language media 149
foreign trade 51–61
    agreements 63–72
    balance of 54
    policies of 51
    sectors 54

significance of 51
size and balance of 53
trade zones 88
foreign-exchange controls 259
forestry 29, 99
franchising 39, 188
Free Trade Area of the Americas (FTAA) 72
free trade zones 37, 76
freight forwarders 92
French and Indian War, the 5
fur trade 13
furniture 32, 99

G

GDP 1
General Agreement on Tariffs and Trade (GATT) 27, 64, 173
    customs valuation 65
    definition 74
    provisions 64
    standards 65
Generalized System of Preferences (GSP) 65–67
gift giving 147
gift taxes 265
globalization 43
Goods and Services Tax (GST) 20, 259
gross domestic product (GDP) 1, 9

H

Halifax 271
Hamilton 272
harmonized system (HS) 74
Hazardous Products Act 75
health products 33, 100
holidays 151, 158
household appliances 34, 101
Hudson Bay Co. 13
Human Resources Development Canada 184

I

immigrants 138
immunization 139
import permits and licenses 249
importing 27–30, 58
    apparel 59
    automotive parts and service equipment 59
    by region 59
    composition of 59
    computer software 59
    distribution 78
    electronic components 59
    government regulation 73
    packing & labeling 79
    permits and licenses 74
    personal goods 141
    policies & procedures 73–84
    quality standards 76
    regulatory policies 75
    restrictions and prohibitions on imports 77
    services 59
    tariffs and import taxes 75
income tax
    employment 261
    minimum 262
income tax rates 261
Industrial Design Act 212, 220
industrial machinery 35
industrial minerals 105
Industry Canada 214
    Business Services 184
industry reviews 97–109
Inside Passage 13
Inter-American Development Bank (IDB) 71
interest rates 9
International Chamber of Commerce (ICC) 72, 240, 242, 253
international payments 239–254
    glossary 249, 252
    overview 239
    tips 241
Internet 276
Inuit tribe 20
investment activities 48
Investment Canada Act (ICA) 45–46, 49
Investment Development Program (IDP) 44
investment income 264
issuance 253

J

joint ventures 187

L

labor 15, 195–206
    employment termination 202
    hiring policies 202
    jury duty 201
    maternity leave 201
    minor employment 202
    relations with management 204
    safety 202
    statistics 165
    unemployment rate 15
    wages and benefits 203
    women and 200
    work force 196
land area distribution 3
language 2
    French vs. English in business 170
large corporations tax 259
law 207–222
    bankruptcy 218
    digest 218–222
    environmental 219

foreign investment 219
foreign trade 219
glossary 208
legal counsel 214
letters of credit (L/Cs) 239, 242–247, 253
    application 246, 246–247
    back-to-back 252
    common problems with 244
    confirmed 252
    deferred payment using 252
    irrevocable 253
    opening 246
    tips 248
    types of 245
    utilization of 244
Liberal Party 11
literacy rate 2
losses, relief for 264
lumber 13

M

magazines 178
Manitoba 3, 176
manufacturing 1, 39
marketing 169–182
    basics 169
    demographic trends and 172
    diversity and 171
    education and 172
    geography and climate 171
    government and 172
    keys to success 169
    regional differences 175
    religion 172
media 167
Meech Lake Accord 4, 21
minerals 29
mining 1
Miquelon 8
Montreal 139, 141, 156, 159, 171
    access to city from airport 141
    accommodations 142
    cuisine 145
    ports 271
Motor Vehicle Safety Act 75
motor vehicles 29
Mulroney, Brian 5, 12

N

National Trademark and True Labeling Act 75
national travel offices 137
natural gas 28
New Brunswick 158, 176
Newfoundland 3, 158, 176
newspapers 178
Nielsen Canada 169
Nonresident-Owned Investment Corporations (NROs) 260
North American Free Trade Agreement (NAFTA) 2, 4, 5, 27, 44, 46, 49, 51, 52, 55, 67, 156, 171, 173, 198, 209, 214, 217, 219, 223, 267, 273
    agricultural products and 69
    automobiles 69
    competition 68
    definition 74
    dispute resolution 68
    effect of 55
    energy 69
    environment 69
    financial services 69
    government procurement 68
    history 16
    intellectual property rights 68
    investment 68
    market access 68
    public procurement opportunities with 41
    rules of origin 68
    sanitary and phytosanitary measures 69
    services 68, 69
    supplemental agreements 70
    Tariff Elimination Schedule 260
    tariff elimination schedule 78
    tariffs 68
    technical standards 69
    telecommunications 70
    transportation 70
North American Treaty Organization (NATO) 5
Northwest Territories 3, 159, 177
notaries 216
Nova Scotia 158, 177

O

Office de la Langue Francaise 184
Office of the Superintendent of Financial Institutions (OSFI) 225
office supplies 33
oil 28
Ontario 3, 158, 176, 196
open account (O/A) payments 239
open account (O/A) terms 239, 253
opportunities 27–42
opportunities for growth 38–40
Oregon Treaty, the 5
Organization for Economic Cooperation and Development (OECD) 74
Ottawa 11, 139, 142
    access to city from airport 142
    accommodations 143
    cuisine 145
overland transport 272

P

Pacific Basin Economic Council (PBEC) 71
Pacific Coast, the 2

Pacific Economic Cooperation Conference (PECC) 71
packing & labeling 79, 90
    Consumer Packaging and Labeling Act 79
    customs clearance 81
    environmental 79
Paris Convention 71
Paris Union 209
Part IV Tax on Financial Institutions 259
partnerships 186–187
passive income of controlled foreign affiliates 259
Patent Act 220
payment arrangements 237
pension plans 259
Petro-Canada 11
plastics 35
pollution control equipment 35
population 163–164
population distribution 2
ports of entry 273
post office 149
Prairie Provinces 159
Precious Metals Marking Act 75
Prince Edward Island 158, 177
processed foods 97
promissory note 252
provincial payroll tax 259
provincial/territorial tax 259
public procurement 40–42
    current government projects 40
    financing 41
    procedures 41
public relations firms 180

Q

Quebec 3, 11, 19, 159, 177, 196, 221
    airport 269
    law 207
    ports 271
    secession 4
Quebec Act 8
Quebec City 8

R

radio 179
railroads 148, 274
real estate 47
Reform Party 4
religion 2
remitter 253
remitting bank 253
retirement 230

S

Saint John
    ports 271
Saskatchewan 3, 140, 176

selling 91
services 15
shipper's export declaration (SED) 249
social security taxes 265
sole proprietorships 188
Southeast Asia 2
sporting goods 37
St. Pierre 8
Standards Council of Canada Act 75

T

tax rates 255
    federal 261
    withholding 257
taxable income 258
taxation 255–266
    corporate 255
    nonresidents 265
    personal 261
taxi 148
telecommunications 29, 36, 39, 106, 275
telephones 149
television 179
Textile Labeling Act 75
textiles 30, 36
textiles & apparel 107
The Investment Canada Act (ICA) 209
Thunder Bay
    ports 272
time changes 140
timeliness 161
tipping 141
Toronto 140, 141, 154, 156, 158, 171
    access to city from airport 141
    accommodations 144
    airport 269
    cuisine 146
    ports 272
Toronto Stock Exchange 45
Toronto Stock Exchange (TSE) 230
toys 37, 107
trade commissioners 88
trade fairs 111–135
    exhibiting 112
    tips 114
    venues 113
Trade Marks Act 213
trade partners 61
trade secrets 220
Trademark Act 220
transfer pricing 259
Transport Canada 269
transportation 147, 166
transportation and communications 267–277
    glossary 268
travel information 152
    safety 150

travel times 139
travelers' checks 235
Treaty of Paris 8
trucking 273
Trudeau, Pierre 20
trusts 188

U

UN Convention on the International Sale of Goods (CISG) 71
unemployment 1, 197
Uniform Customs and Practices (UCP) 242
Uniform Rules for Collections (URC) 240
United Kingdom 5
United States
    Foreign Corrupt Practices Act (FCPA) 215
    reliance on 55
United States (US) 5
    travel offices 137
United States Canada Free Trade Agreement (FTA) 52, 55, 67
United States, the 2
US Foreign Corrupt Practices Act 215
US Relations 11
US-Canadian free trade agreement (CFTA) 20

V

validity 253
Vancouver 140, 142, 154, 159, 171
    access to city from airport 142
    accommodations 144
    airport 269
    cuisine 146
    ports 271
vehicles 37, 108
videoconferencing 276
visa and passport 138
    business visas 138
    requirements 138
    work permits 139

W

water transport 271
Windsor
    ports 272
Winnipeg 171
woman in business 146
women & business 157
work permits 139
World Trade Organization (WTO) 52, 65
World War I 8

Y

Yukon Territory 2, 3, 159, 177